U0165447

法與思系列
Law
Thinking

改良式的證據法則
與刑事訴訟

張明偉◆著

五南圖書出版公司 印行

推薦序

　　明偉君，勤奮精進，留學歸國沒幾年，就出版這一本超倫絕勝的論文集，我深以曾為他的碩士指導老師為榮。明偉君在出國攻讀博士前，曾任職書記官、公證人、總統府第一局，在公務繁忙之際，不曾或忘求學上進之心，考取競爭激烈的公費留學考試。在國外就讀期間，過著簞食瓢飲的生活，苦心勵志在短期內即取得法學博士資格，非一般人所能及。返國後，先回公務機關敘職，旋即受真理大學主動禮聘擔任教職，潛心論著，發表許多擲地有聲的重要文章，在新一代的年輕學者間逐漸嶄露頭角。刑事訴訟學界，多此一出類拔萃之稀有人才，深為臺灣慶幸。

　　明偉君的論文，思想宏偉，常有吞天吐地之磅礡大氣；邏輯嚴謹，令人折服其推理細膩之精妙。這本書收錄了他過去所著的中、英文論文，內容涵蓋了近幾年我國刑事司法改革的重大議題，常見其為辯證一議題，而追溯幾世紀之歷史沿革及思想源頭，旁徵博引世界各國之理論與實務差異。他的論文無疑填補了我國在倉促進行司法改革時所欠缺的理論基礎，也為未

來的刑事司法提出了更明確的方向與目標，也是因為這個原因，我認為他是最有潛力的年輕一代刑事訴訟法學者。

　　本書集結之論文包括當事人進行主義的引進、傳聞法則、證據排除法則、一事不再理、辯護制度、拒絕證言、不起訴處分之效力、軍事審判、非常上訴，都是近幾年刑事訴訟修法的重要議題。這些論文展現縝密的思想及敏銳的觀察，常於他人不疑處起疑，挖掘許多有趣的問題，再輔以其留學所得之精妙理論，提出許多卓越及宏偉的見解。例如，我國刑事訴訟法傳聞法則之規定為舉世所獨有，審判外之陳述是否有證據能力，完全依陳述對象之官位而定。如陳述之對象為法官，則無條件得為證據；如對象為檢察官，則原則上得為證據；如對象為警察，則原則上不得為證據。對此惡法，學者多僅撻伐痛斥，而未探究或闡釋其後之深層原因。明偉君另闢蹊徑，提出獨到之觀察，指出臺灣受歐陸法及日本法之影響，而早期歐陸法視檢察官為國王在訴訟上之代理人，戰前日本之裁判書係以天皇名義作成，致形成人民對司法官深信不疑（或不敢反對國王）之悠久傳統。再者，法官承受發現真實之沉重負擔，又將其他法官、檢察官視為同僚，自然會將他們面前所製作的筆錄，視作應信任之證據。每一篇論文，明偉君皆提出發人深省之獨到見解，不勝枚舉，令人一讀再讀不忍釋卷。

　　我們這一代研究刑事訴訟法的學者，應該是歷史上最幸運

的一群。傳統的訴訟制度,弊病百出,深為人民詬病。面對人民唾棄司法的狂浪,執政者驚惶下只知要改革司法,卻提不出一套完整能徹底解決問題的計畫;或者在提出部分計畫後,因為種種原因,卻不能貫徹執行。1999 年聲勢浩大的全國司法改革會議所作結論,有多少已經實施了?有許多決議,是司法院自己提出的議案,後來擱置不執行或反其道而行的,竟然也是司法院!大破之下,我們尚未大立,這一代的刑事訴訟法學者宛如遭逢百家爭鳴的春秋戰國時代,論述成理者,皆得自成一家之言。明偉君歸國僅僅幾年,就交出如此優秀的成績單,我深信他已是刑事訴訟學界的重要棟樑。

王兆鵬

97.4.21

自序

　　記憶中，只有在學位論文完成時有機會寫序，縱然也曾在一些期刊發表過十幾篇文章，這倒是第一次為了文章出版而序。雖不若當年完成學位論文之悸動，但第一次看到自己的作品集結成冊付梓，不禁感慨已隨此而逝的漫漫長夜；而能有一部作品問世，也算是對自己這些年的匆忙作了交代。

　　本書主要以制定於民國九十二年之刑事證據法則及其相關議題為論述中心，因司法院將之定位為改良式的當事人進行主義，故定名為「改良式的證據法則與刑事訴訟」。由於大陸法系的訴訟法制向來強調直接審理原則，因此我國學說與實務於二十一世紀以前，並不重視證據法則的發展。縱然筆者曾錄取教育部公費留學考試證據法組，但諷刺的是，在負笈美國之前，如同大部分法律人般，筆者並不大瞭解證據法則與訴訟法制之實質關連；而之所以會對證據法則產生興趣並在美國開始對證據法則的相關研究，一開始也只是蕭規曹隨務實地因應教育部規定而選修與證據法相關的課程。我國於民國九十二年通過並實施證據排除法則與傳聞法則，意外地使筆者在美國盲目

地探索一年後，對證據法則的研究有了確定的方向，並以之為論文主軸。

很幸運地，筆者對於證據排除法則與傳聞法則的彙整與比較法研究，能在論文口試前，通過澳洲墨爾本大學（MELBOURNE UNIVERSITY）、荷蘭提堡大學（TILBURG UNIVERSITY）與烏特勒支大學（UTRECHT UNIVERSITY）等世界著名大學法學院法學期刊的刊登審查（當然這項成果是當初說服指導教授讓我在第四學期結束前即完成博士學位的主要依據）；看到論文主要內容均已通過國際法學期刊審查並已獲刊登（並非只是在研討會發表之論文）的業績，過去那段平均一天有十五小時為論文奮鬥的焚膏繼晷、開完刀後旋即赴美日以繼夜地埋首寫作的瘋狂總算沒有白費；也足以證明自己辛苦完成的論文絕非如其他第三世界博士論文（The Third World Ph.D. Dissertation）般，毫無參考價值。希望這些不只是傳聞的論述，不致被學術界與實務界排除。而除了美式的證據排除法則與傳聞法則外，本書也介紹其他與證據法則發展相關的背景以及訴訟法上的制度，希望能一併充實對於證據法則的理解。

飲水自當思源，感謝所有在學習過程中曾給予指導的師長與前輩，特別是 GGU School of Law 的 Professor Dr. Sompong Sucharitkul 與 Professor Robert Calhoun 對於如何用英文完成學術論文的啟發與教導，以及 Professor Myron Moskovitz 對於如

何理解並詮釋美國證據法則的開示。而筆者也要特別感謝臺大法研所的王兆鵬教授，自筆者就讀臺大法研所碩士班以來，包括論文指導、出國進修、參與各種學術活動以及擔任教學工作等等，王老師不但一直給予指導與協助，更不吝提攜後進。雖然老師不斷勉勵後學迎頭趕上甚至超越，但是遇到一個比學生還用功、更加勤於著述的老師，能夠保持一定的距離就足以令人氣力放盡了。記得剛回國時曾在一次餐會中向某大法官提到我的指導教授是王兆鵬教授，這位大法官馬上就回應說：「你的老師很了不起，台灣的刑事訴訟法都被他改變了（我想以大法官的身分地位，應不須與我這後生小輩有所客套）。」，當下覺得有一個名聲好的老師，即使自己沒做什麼，也是一件令人感到光采的事。私下曾多次與同儕提及，老師就如同民法界的王澤鑑教授，一直在以著述立說的方式進行刑事訴訟法界的寧靜革命，相信在老師的繼續耕耘下，我國的刑事訴訟法制會更臻完善。

記得某部電影曾說過："It is hard to do the right thing, when you are not sure what it is. But when you know what the right thing is, it is hard not to do the right thing."、"This is something I just could not put behind me." 這應可為這本書的誕生，做一個暫時的註記。在此謹祝福各位老師身體健康，順利平安，好讓我有再次請益的機會。最後，感謝父母的養育與包

容，以及他們所賜予我剛毅的性格，希望他們對我的堅持與努力，會感到與有榮焉。

張明偉
97.4.15

目　錄

1 導　讀

　　證據裁判主義為當代各國刑事訴訟制度所採之基本原則，不論是職權主義的刑事訴訟制度或是當事人進行主義的刑事訴訟制度，均以證據為認定犯罪事實之基礎。根源於德國與日本之我國刑事法制，在過去帶有濃厚的職權主義色彩，因強調法院發現真實的義務，故要求法院依職權調查檢察官已指出的證據事實與未指出之證據事實，長此以往，漸漸形成院檢接力辦案的訴訟實務。由於此種實務現象常造成法院兼理調查與審判之職務，為避免審判及偵查分際之混淆，全國司法改革會議乃主張法院應居於客觀、中立、超然之立場，不宜接續檢察官主動蒐集犯罪證據之工作。為了落實民國 88 年 7 月所召開的全國司法改革會議所做成的前述決議，立法院陸續通過部分刑事訴訟法的修正案。自民國 91 年所通過的刑事訴訟法第 163 條第 2 項：「法院為發見真實，得依職權調查證據。但於公平正義之維護或對被告之利益有重大關係事項，法院應依職權調查之。」與民國 92 年所通過的規定（例如：證據排除法則、傳聞法則與詰問規則等源自英美法制等條文）來說，立法者似認在程序法上「限制法院職權調查義務的範圍」與「增定英美法制

的證據規則」即足以擺脫職權主義色彩，達成改良式當事人進行主義的修法目標。

　　遺憾的是，前述修法觀點似乎忽略了我國實務運作之所以帶有職權主義色彩的重要原因，那就是裁判上一罪的規定。本質上刑事訴訟程序係以實現國家刑罰權為主要目的，而國家刑罰權是否存在，原應依刑事實體法之規定為斷，由於我國刑法（曾）將想像競合犯、牽連犯與連續犯等複數構成要件該當的情形規定為科刑上一罪（裁判上一罪），因此關於檢察官所起訴的犯罪行為是否與其他未經起訴之犯罪行為構成科刑上一罪，即為法院在決定國家刑罰權實際內涵時，所不得不審查的對象。也就是說，在刑事判決既判力及於科刑上一罪所有犯罪事實的架構下，為避免被告因法院對所有犯罪事實評價不足而獲得輕判，在過去的刑事審判實務中，法院不得不依職權調查其他有可能與檢察官起訴書所指犯罪事實形成科刑上一罪關係之其他犯罪事實。鑑於刑事訴訟法歷次修正所持之理由均未論及刑事實體法規定對於刑事訴訟程序運作所造成的影響，本書第二章「從刑事訴訟法改良式當事人進行主義之修正談裁判上一罪規定修正」即以實體法與程序法的關連互動為前提，在裁判上一罪的規範基礎上，分析探討刑事實體法規定對刑事程序法運作所可能造成的影響，並指出刑事程序法的改革，不應忽略實體法規範本身所具之影響力，蓋以實現實體法為目的之程序法，本質上無法避免實體法規定所可能產生之影響。

　　我國刑事訴訟法制在民國 92 年出現了重大的變化，其中最

值得一提的，就是移植了源自英美法制的證據排除法則與傳聞法則。正因爲在歐陸法制的歷史中不存在證據排除法則與傳聞法則的證據法傳統，關於如何於具體個案中正確地解釋適用該等規定，難免使得習於職權主義之我國審判系統出現可以避免的誤解，例如在一則前立法委員疑似性侵害外傭的案件中，對於被告提出該名外傭之審判外脫罪陳述（陳述意旨約爲其於離開台灣前所做之筆錄內容不實），我國法院竟以傳聞法則爲由，排除了該審判外脫罪陳述之證據能力。若不自法制沿革的觀點對於「傳聞法則旨在排除審判外入罪陳述證據能力」有正確的認識，即不免出現如前述我國實務見解對於如何適用傳聞法則之誤解，而類此誤解所生排除審判外脫罪陳述之實務操作，恐將使英美等傳聞法則之發源國，產生啼笑皆非之驚嘆。爲能正確認識傳聞法則此一源自英美法系之制度，本書第三章「英美傳聞法則與對質條款的歷史考察」乃詳盡地介紹了英美傳聞法則之沿革與發展，特別就傳聞法則與美國憲法第六修正案中對質條款之關連，做出深度的歷史考察。

雖然美國聯邦最高法院關於對質條款已於 2004 年克勞佛案中揚棄了羅伯特斯案的見解，目前僅承認根深蒂固的傳聞例外；然而欠缺美國制憲背景的我國法制，是否亦需完全排除特別可信的傳聞例外，鑑於我國制憲者並未針對審判外陳述之容許性設定對質門檻，我國傳聞法則應否或於何程度內承認特別可信之傳聞例外，是否必然出現違憲之疑慮，並非不可討論，本書第四章「Adoption of the Common Law Hearsay Rule in a

Civil Law Jurisdiction: a Comparative Study of the Hearsay Rule in Taiwan and the United States（英美傳聞法則在大陸法域之移植：台灣與美國傳聞法則之比較研究）」即以職權主義的審理模式爲基礎，分析探討承認傳聞例外與否所涉及之爭議。我國刑事訴訟法之傳聞法則與美國聯邦證據法中之傳聞法則並不相同，其中又以刑事訴訟法第 159 條之 1 在法官或檢察官面前之陳述（原則上）具有證據能力之規定最爲特殊。此種以陳述者對象之身分決定陳述是否具證據能力的規定或許有些奇怪，但細究其原因，這或許是源自早期大陸法系的訴訟制度認爲檢察官是國王代理人、而且在封建制度下如日本戰前之裁判書係以天皇名義做成，類此信賴司法官員（或是不敢反對國王）的傳統下所形成之觀念。又因職權主義的刑事訴訟制度要求法院制作裁判書以交代裁判理由，法院在裁判書「自圓其說」之要求下，不得不自行探究未經檢察官提出之證據，以履行其發現實體眞實的義務，其中又以在法官或檢察官面前之陳述，爲最容易取得並得到法院信任之證據。因此，在檢察官舉證不足且法院有依職權調查證據以發現眞實的前提下，法院自行訊問有關人證並進而調查相關事證似爲法院爲完成判決義務所不得不採納的取證管道。易言之，前述法院發現眞實與調查證據之義務，似爲法院信任其親自或其他同僚聽取陳述的主要原因。

此外，另一個可能作爲刑事訴訟法第 159 條之 1 規定在法官或檢察官面前之陳述具有證據能力之原因，或許就是刑事實體法上裁判上一罪的規定對於刑事訴訟程序所可能造成的影

響。本質上英美法制證據能力之概念係以證據容許性（admissi-bility）為基礎，而所謂之證據容許性主要乃指陪審團能否接觸系爭證據。換言之，無證據能力乃指陪審團不得接觸該證據，該證據無法作為陪審團決定事實存否之判斷基礎。在英美法制下，只要檢察官與被告未提出之證據，因法院無依職權調查證據之義務，基本上是不會存在其他審判外陳述是否具證據能力之爭議。然而在大陸法系裁判上一罪的規定下，由於身兼事實認定者之職業法官必須調查其他檢察官未起訴之犯罪事實是否與已起訴之犯罪事實具有裁判上一罪之關係，在訴訟經濟之考量下，不免有必要透過向其他院檢調閱卷宗或是依職權補充訊問的方式進行審查。復由於在非陪審團審判架構下，證據容許性已不具有防止事實認定者（職業法官）接觸系爭證據之功能，因此在我國證據能力之概念應為容許系爭證據出現於裁判書而成為裁判理由之資格要件，而與英美法系之證據能力概念不同。或因我國在移植傳聞法則之過程中，未於法條或立法理由中明示傳聞法則旨在限制被告以外之人於審判外入罪陳述之證據能力，才會為了能在判決書中引用審判外非入罪陳述之目的下，出現「如刑事訴訟法第 159 條之 1 承認於其他法官或檢察官面前之陳述具有證據能力之條文」。換句話說，如果在立法過程中缺乏對英美傳聞法則功能意義完整與全面理解，或許就會出現類似「為避免法院依職權調查系爭案件事實是否為其他裁判上一罪之潛在犯罪事實時，因被告以外之人於其他法官或檢察官面前之審判外陳述會受到傳聞法則無證據能力之拘

束，而不能於裁判書中直接引用」之偏差思考，並認為在訴訟經濟之考量下，有必要制定刑事訴訟法第 159 條之 1 之規定。基本上，本章對於本條傳聞例外之解釋，乃延續著第二章程序法與實體法互動的觀點，並認為單從程序法本身並無法完整理解整體刑事司法體系的盲點。此外，本章亦針對其他傳聞例外之規定，進行與美國聯邦證據法的比較研究。整體而言，雖然我國刑事訴訟制度係以大陸法系制度為藍本，制定源自英美法制的傳聞法則仍為一值得肯定的立法。

　　除了傳聞法則外，我國刑事訴訟制度亦採取了美國式的證據排除法則。本書第五章「The Exclusionary Rule in Taiwan: Lessons from the United States（台灣的證據排除法則：以美國為鑑）」除了詳盡地介紹美國與我國關於證據排除之主要發展外，亦比較二者間之差異。首先，本章認為歐陸法系的憲法就人權保障的規定過於抽象，以致於需仰賴國會立法具體化相關人權保障事項。與此相對，美國憲法增修條文就隱私保障、不自證己罪、受律師協助、對質詰問以及一事不再理等事項，提供了較為明確的人權保障指標，以致於政府行為是否侵害了憲法保障的基本人權，有較為明確的判斷基準。在美國憲法人權保障的模式下，因較容易訴諸違憲審查，遂發展出排除違憲取證以為救濟之證據排除法則。此外，本章認為我國中央集權式的警察管理模式，為我國未能自行發展出證據排除法則的重要因素，蓋美國證據排除法則於一定程度上具有規範全國警察行為之功能，而此功能在我國卻不必仰賴司法機關以裁判之方式

予以實現。再者，由於我國刑事訴訟法制承認自訴制度，因此犯罪之被害人原有權決定是否自己追訴犯罪，而私自追訴係以私人取證為前提，縱使私人取證侵害了他人之人權，亦無涉於國家公權力之行使，因此以阻止警察不法為目的之美國證據排除制度，並不適用於自訴制度。雖我國實務曾有主張證據排除法則亦應適用於私人不法取證之場合，不過鑑於刑法已處罰某些私人不法取證之情形，且完全排除私人不法取證恐將導致被害人採取人權侵害更強烈的不法取證手段、甚至出現因被害人無法藉由合法管道伸張正義導致私刑相加之不當，因此本文主張證據排除法則僅應適用於國家不法取證的情形。最後，本文認為我國採取相對證據排除法則之立法並無不當，蓋美國之所以採行絕對證據排除法則乃因需排除者為違反憲法規定之違法取證，而反觀我國之證據排除法則僅以「違法」為前提，鑑於違法（例如僅違反技術性規定）未必導致違憲，且絕對證據排除法則亦容許例外不排除之情形存在，現行法未採取絕對排除之原則並不違人權保障之精神。

　　前述證據法則之制定原在保障刑事被告之基本人權，不過在最高法院 89 年台非字第 94 號判決：『中華民國憲法第 4 條明文：「中華民國領土，依其固有之疆域，非經國民大會之決議，不得變更之。」而國民大會亦未曾為變更領土之決議。又中華民國憲法增修條文第 11 條復規定：「自由地區與大陸地區間人民權利義務關係及其他事務之處理，得以法律為特別之規定。」且臺灣地區與大陸地區人民關係條例第 2 條第 2 款更指

明：「大陸地區：指台灣地區以外之中華民國領土。」揭示大陸地區仍屬我中華民國之領土；該條例第 75 條復規定：「在大陸地區或在大陸船艦、航空器內犯罪，雖在大陸地區曾受處罰，仍得依法處斷。但得免其刑之全部或一部之執行。」據此，大陸地區現在雖因事實上之障礙為我國主權所不及，但在大陸地區犯罪，仍應受我國法律之處罰，即明示大陸地區猶屬我國領域，並未對其放棄主權。本件被告○○○被訴於民國 82 年至 85 年間在大陸福州市犯有刑法第 339 條第 1 項之詐欺取財及第 215 條之業務登載不實文書罪嫌，即為在中華民國領域內犯罪，自應適用中華民國法律論處。』之規範下，我國法院乃有權處理台商（胞）在大陸發生的刑事糾紛。由於兩岸糾紛將隨著交流的增加而增加，如何處理隨之而來的訴訟問題，即有待兩岸政府共同處理，以避免有心人士利用傳聞法則之規定，在我方法院規避應有的處罰；而如何避免同一犯罪在兩岸同受刑事處罰，亦與人民權利保障息息相關。本書第六章「論兩岸民間交流糾紛之刑事訴訟障礙」在一事不再理原則之問題上，參考德國、美國等複數法域國家規定後主張：兩岸犯罪之處理應擱置國家主權問題並互相承認對方實際司法管轄範圍，在此基礎上再進一步具體協商和劃分何種犯罪類型應由那一方管轄，一經一方審理後他方即因一事不再理原則而不得行使管轄權；另在傳聞障礙議題上本文主張：於將來制定兩岸司法互助協定時，應針對某些特定型態的犯罪事件或規定在一定之條件下，約定由大陸政府將相關人證或物證送交台灣法庭地，以保

障在台被告之對質詰問權；或是在法庭便利的前提下，將某些
情形的被告引渡或遭送至犯罪發生地之管轄法院處理，以兼顧
被告與被害人雙方之權益，並實現個案中之司法正義。

　　在改良式當事人進行主義的刑事訴訟法修正採用了源自英
美法制的證據排除法則、交互詰問規則與傳聞法則後，法庭活
動於相當範圍內，即由法官主導轉為檢察官與辯護律師主導。
從英美法制的發展可知，證據法則原為控辯雙方如何進行與從
事法庭活動之準則，因此若欠缺足夠的法律知識，即難正確地
依循複雜的證據法則進行有效的法庭攻防。相較於檢察官所擁
有的豐富法律知識，被告往往因本身缺乏相關的法律素養而於
法庭活動中遭受到不利益，其間對於法律認知的差異，不但有
違武器平等的原則，亦與公平法院的概念背道而馳。因此被告
於審判中受律師協助的權利（律師權）並提出有利的辯護，即
成為得以有效對抗檢察官的重要機制。然若被告在非強制辯護
案件中未選任辯護人，也就是在被告為自己辯護的場合中，關
於被告有無足夠之專業能力為自己辯護、有無能力進行有效的
交互詰問、如何自我辯護始符合武器平等與公平法院之理念與
法院有無義務協助被告辯護等議題，均與如何落實憲法所保障
的辯護權息息相關。本書第七章「非強制辯護案件被告審判中
辯護權之保障」首先探討兩造對抗程序與受律師協助權利之起
源，在發現專業補竊制度（professional thief catchers）促進辯
護之需求後，肯認當事人進行主義之兩造對抗模式為律師制度
發展過程中的重要基石。另就美國律師權發展的經驗來看，貧

窮被告在重要的刑事訴訟程序（例如：起訴後出庭聲明程序、逮捕後警訊程序、指認程序、協商程序、預審程序、審判程序、量刑程序、上訴程序以及假釋程序）中，有免費受律師協助之權力。然而，有鑒於在美國複雜的證據法則與法庭程序規定下，聯邦最高法院亦承認被告有自我辯護之權利，本文遂主張將我國非強制辯護案件中未選任辯護人之被告視爲主張自我辯護之被告，並要求法院在自我辯護案件中履行一定的照護義務，以保障被告之辯護權並維公平法院之理念。

　　在保障被告辯護權並充實其法庭活動能力後，爲能完整地呈現法庭活動進行的全貌，避免事後當事人與上級審對於已進行的訴訟程序產生誤認，本書第八章「談刑事程序筆錄制作之實然與應然」遂將探討的觸角延伸到法庭活動的記錄上。雖然現行法規定書記官爲筆錄之制作者，然基於對實務操作之觀察，不難發現實務上普遍存在書記官完全依照訊問者（法官與檢察官）指示制作筆錄之現象。或有謂此乃訴訟指揮權行使下必然產生的結果，然而此種說法似乎不當地否認身爲國家公務員所具有的獨立性，蓋縱於行政機關文稿核判的過程中，承辦科員無權決定公文內容，但從公文稿記載本身而言，不難在事後判斷該公文之某部分是由科員擬稿、哪部分則是由科長或其他長官所增刪附記，此正爲公務員行使職務所具有獨立性之適例。本文除自美國法制發展肯認法庭記錄正確性將對上訴審查產生實質影響外，亦引用日本學者的觀點主張書記官在爲公益監督的基礎上，在依訊問者程序指揮權之指示記載後，有權依

自己實際聽聞附記與訊問者認知不同之陳述內容。

　　正因證據為事實認定之基礎，在發現真實的要求下，除被告得主張不自證己罪而不提供證據外，所有關於裁判的重要證據，均應提出於法院，證人因此即負有據實陳述之義務。然而要求所有的人均有義務據實陳述有時反而不利於社會的整體發展，例如在委託人諮詢律師的過程中，律師不免因此知悉一些委託人不希望外人知道的資訊、甚至於犯罪證據，若要求律師有義務提供所有因執行業務所知悉的相關的資訊，除將導致委託人因顧慮律師有可能洩漏隱私而無法充分與律師討論案情外，亦將造成由律師代替委託人自證己罪的特殊異象，並因此妨礙人民使用律師制度。又如醫師在診斷過程中常需仰賴病患提供有關的生活資訊以做出正確診斷，如要求醫師必須透露於診療過程中所獲悉之所有資訊以發現實體真實，求診之病患亦有可能擔心醫師出庭洩漏其個人隱私，不願意提供完整之資訊而耽誤了獲得有效醫療救助的機會，從而要求醫師有義務據實陳述其因執行業務所獲得的相關資訊，不但將破壞病患對醫師之信賴，此舉亦將有礙醫療功能的正常發展。換言之，為了維護更高的社會生活價值，促進相關的社會發展，有必要在一定範圍內，限縮據實陳述義務，承認拒絕證言之權利，發現真實不再被視為訴訟的唯一目的，畢竟要求被告敢作敢當地自證己罪以及要求子女大義滅親地出庭指證父母不法只能當作是一種道德訴求，違反社會大多數人的生活感情與利益，縱將強人所難的要求制定為法律，亦不免將因不受人民普遍支持而成為具

文。本書第九章「新聞記者拒絕證言之權能與界限」即以前述論述為基礎，分析探討新聞記者在現行法制架構下應否有權主張拒絕證言。本文主張不論是基於第四權理論所建構的公共監督角色，或是基於新聞生態上記者不願被視為抓耙子以免以後沒人願意接受其採訪的心態，要求記者據實陳述將是徒勞無功的一件事。既然已肯認新聞記者負有公共監督之權能，則於一定程度內承認記者有權拒絕證言，不強調發現真實，應無違當代訴訟法的主要思潮。

　　承接第六章所述，一事不再理向來被視為重要的憲法原則，避免人民因同一犯罪反覆受到調查審問而於程序上遭受到過度不利，我國刑事訴訟法第 260 條、第 302 條與第 303 條等相關規定，莫不以一事不再理為核心概念。然而何謂「一事」？何謂「再理」？一事需經調查到什麼程度才會產生阻斷再理之效力？諸如此類基本定義的提問，實務卻因刑事訴訟法第 260 條不起訴處分效力之規定混淆，而出現了與一事不再理規範法理相悖之觀點。舉例而言，喧騰一時的三一九槍擊案，不但在案發當時即對台灣社會造成巨大的衝擊，其後續的發展更意外地成為檢視藍綠政治立場的試劑；大凡支持泛綠陣營的人，傾向於支持維持該案的不起訴處分，而支持泛藍陣營的群眾，莫不認為該案有重新調查之必要（當然這樣的說法不代表所有認為有必要重新調查本案的人均為泛藍的支持者）。然若撇開政治的激情，由於台南地檢署已就三一九這個國人矚目的重大案件，綜合各種間接證據，本於推理作用，對業已死亡的

涉案人陳義雄做出不起訴處分，本案在法律程序上似應因此而
暫告一段落。然而法務部長與檢察高層曾在接受立法院詢問時
表示，在刑事訴訟法第 260 條的規範下，須有可供懷疑能撼動
案情的新事實或新證據，檢察官才能重啓偵查三一九槍擊案。
據其所述，三一九爭議已轉變成為一個法律爭議，而其爭議點
即在於：刑事訴訟法第 260 條關於不起訴處分效力之規定，是
否必然終結對三一九槍擊案件之續行調查？換言之，本案是否
須在發現「有可供懷疑能撼動案情的新事實或新證據」後，才
能重啓偵查？為釐清前述法律爭議，自應以一事不再理之規範
目的為探討之基礎。

在探討刑事訴訟法第 260 條不起訴處分效力規定之前，應
先說明的是，若以陳義雄是否涉案作為區分的標準，事實上與
邏輯上，三一九槍擊案僅存在下列三種可能：一、陳義雄未涉
案；二、陳義雄確涉案，惟另有其他共犯；三、陳義雄確涉
案，且該案僅陳義雄一人所為。在第三種情形中，由於本案被
告已死亡，無追訴之必要性，因此無論發現何種新事實或新證
據，均無從重新開啓該案之偵查程序，故得重啓偵查者，想必
係指涉類型一（陳義雄未涉案）或類型二（陳義雄確涉案惟另
有其他共犯）之可能性。果真如此，前述「在刑事訴訟法第 260
條的規範下，須有可供懷疑能撼動案情的新事實或新證據，檢
察官才能重啓偵查三一九槍擊案」之主張是否恆為真？即不禁
令人質疑。換言之，何以刑事訴訟法第 260 條竟對從未曾成為
偵查中心的其他涉案人，設下偵查程序上「須發現有可供懷疑

能撼動案情的新事實或新證據」如此高門檻的保護？賦予檢察官拒絕受理「對已偵結案件提出對其他涉案人告訴或告發」之權能，真的是刑事訴訟法第 260 條規定原所欲達成的規範目的嗎？即有釐清之必要。

由於刑事訴追不可避免地將對被追訴者產生某種程度以上的生活侵擾，故關於同一行為不受二次以上審問處罰的利益，不但早已存在羅馬法時代，美日德等國憲法均有雙重危險保障條款（Double Jeopardy Protection Clause）或一事不再理原則之規定。或因我國檢察官具有司法官屬性，因此遂有主張賦予不起訴處分具有類似確定判決阻斷續行偵審之效力，在法理上並不違背雙重危險保障條款之憲法精神。不過須特別指明的是，一事不再理原則的核心，乃在保障刑事被告於刑事訴訟程序上不受國家機關反覆訴追之憲法利益，縱然司法機關（在我國包含檢察機關）因此取得拒絕受理重複指控或訴追的地位，其亦不過僅係保障前述人民憲法上基本人權之反射而已。簡單來說，刑事訴訟法第 260 條之所以定有「須在發現有可供懷疑能撼動案情的新事實或新證據後，才能重啟偵查」之限制，其主要目的是在保障人民「同一行為不受二次以上審問處罰的憲法利益」。很明顯的，這樣的利益並不存在前述類型一或類型二之中，在欠缺前述保障憲法基本權利的要求下，國家機關也就無從取得拒絕受理同一被害事實的地位。也就是說，若本案另有陳義雄以外之涉案人，縱然是已存卷內之「舊事實或舊證據」亦足以作為所謂「重啟偵查」或「繼續調查」之基礎，蓋

此時憲法並無欲對陳義雄以外之人提供一事不再理之保障；反之，若本案並沒有陳義雄以外之涉案人，縱然果真發現「新事實或新證據」，在被告已死亡欠缺追訴必要性之現實下，其亦不足以作為「重啓偵查」之依據。因此對於三一九槍擊案應只有「是否有足夠證據指控其他被告」的問題，而無「法律上可否繼續調查本案，以發現其他被告」的問題。本諸前述說明，也只有在完全肯定僅陳義雄一人涉及本案的情形，才有本案已結案的說法；反之，可以肯定的是，如果假設尚有其他目前身分不明的被告涉案，則如同前桃園縣長劉邦友血案般，本案並未破案，只不過碰到了案件事實上無法突破的瓶頸，此時並不能說本案存在法律上無法進行的障礙，一但日後的調查另發現其他足資指控其他涉案人之證據，檢方的另行偵查並不需要新事實或新證據的支撐。如果到這裡的邏輯推論均無謬誤，則若能將「本案須在發現有可供懷疑能撼動案情的新事實或新證據後，才能重啓偵查」之說法，理解為「本案須在發現有其他足資指控其他涉案人之證據後，才能重啓偵查」，似乎也就未違刑事訴訟法第 260 條之規範目的。雖然本文認為三一九槍擊案將如同美國總統甘迺迪遇刺案般，其真正動機原因及真相將永遠無解，不過該案迄今所引發的法律爭議，本質上並不屬於一個得因政治立場不同而出現迥然不同結論的議題。希望在激情之餘，大家均能平心冷靜地看待這個不算太難的法律問題。就算本案最後的結果未如人願，也不應該是中性的法律問題使人義憤填膺。

　　本書第十章「不起訴處分與再議之檢討」以現行法有關不起訴與再議等規定為中心，除自相關實務爭議指出賦予不起訴處分具有如確定判決般之實質確定力有所不當外，亦自偵查程序之本質探討不起訴處分應有之效力。蓋在我國刑事訴訟程序朝向改良式當事人進行主義修正後，審判程序的內涵已迥異於偵查程序之本質。過去以檢察官與法官都屬司法官、審判程序與偵查程序內涵大同小異、甚至審判程序乃接續偵查程序調查事證的說法，主張賦予不起訴處分實質確定力之論述，應已失其所據。審判程序除須對人證進行交互詰問程序外，關於事實認定，尚有待三級三審的程序定讞後，始足生確定事實的效力。既然在兩造對抗模式的公開法庭中，已踐行較完善保障人權的訴訟程序，尚需經過三級三審程序始生確定案件事實的效力，何以在進行職權糾問、且由檢察官一造秘密主持所進行的偵查程序後所做成的不起訴處分，尚未經過任一審級公開法庭的審理，即有確定事實之效力？易言之，基於權力分立之觀點，本文主張應只有法院有權確認刑罰權基礎事實是否存在，檢察官相關的事實認定，充其量不過僅具有建議之性質，並不具有拘束法院之效力，故若以之作為不起訴處分實質確定力之判斷基礎，似有侵害法院事實認定權限之疑義。另基於導致有罪判決風險之實質確定力應來自於法院之公開審理程序，而非檢察官糾問式的偵查程序，為免實務繼續不當糾纏於不起訴處分實質確定力之範圍，本文亦主張應廢除刑事訴訟法第 260 條不起訴處分具實質確定力之規定。

　　雖然民國 92 年的刑事訴訟法修正未曾言及該次修法是否適用軍事審判程序，不過我國實務卻曾出現軍事審判機關認為「軍事審判法不受刑事訴訟法修正拘束」之見解，雖然在最高法院的堅持下，軍事審判機關多已踐行刑事訴訟法所採用之證據排除法則、傳聞法則以及交互詰問程序，不過在該次軍司法審判機關見解衝突的過程中，卻令人發現憲法第 9 條之規定迄今仍形同其文般地不受重視。蓋自憲法第 9 條：「人民除現役軍人外，不受軍事審判。」之字義而言，不難推論不具現役軍人身分之人民，不應接受軍事審判。不過實務上普遍存在的現象卻與此相違背，本書第十一章「軍人身分與刑事審判權劃分之探討」旨在檢討此一違背憲法明文規定之實務操作。除探討軍司法審判程序劃分之基礎外，本文更分析了現行軍事審判法與刑事訴訟法間之差異。在整理相關實務見解後，本文發現目前實務所採之審判恆定原則（司法院院字第 1078 號解釋），其實是以訓政時期約法為依據，只不過在行憲後長期戒嚴的背景下，憲法第 9 條一直不被重視，才會讓行憲前的實務見解有效適用於行憲後。在肯認司法院院字第 1078 號解釋已過時而不應再適用之後，本文主張軍司法審判僅應以憲法第 9 條之規定做為劃分之基礎。

　　除了前述與證據法修正相關聯的議題外，本書第十二章「非常上訴制度中『審判違背法令』意義之初探──兼論最高法院 79 年台非字第 246 號判決之商榷」將針對非常救濟程序進行研析。本文自一具體個案出發，檢討何以現行法制無法救濟

一明顯錯誤的裁判。按「調查之必要性」原為一不確定之法律概念，其實際內涵為何本有待具體個案予以充實。既然最高法院 76 年台非字第 128 號判例：「被告犯有應併合處罰之數罪，經法院分別判處有期徒刑確定，其中一罪之有期徒刑先執行期滿後，法院經檢察官之聲請，以裁定定其數罪之應執行刑確定後，其在未裁定前已先執行之有期徒刑之罪，因嗣後合併他罪定應執行刑之結果，檢察官所換發之執行指揮書，係執行應執行刑，其前已執行之有期徒刑部分，僅應予扣除，而不能認為已執行完畢。」與 86 年台非字第 78 號判決：「原確定判決認定之事實，係被告前因違反麻醉藥品管理條例案件，經法院判處有期徒刑七月，於民國 84 年 9 月 12 日執行完畢。詎被告又基於概括之犯意，自民國 85 年 4 月 19 日起，迄同年 9 月 15 日止，連續犯非法吸用化學合成麻醉藥品罪。依此事實，原判決適用刑法第 47 條之規定論以累犯，其適用法律即難謂有違背。至檢察官於前案執行完畢後，復依原法院另案以 85 年度聲字第 589 號合併定應執行刑之刑事裁定，重新簽發執行指揮書，再度發監執行應執行刑剩餘之刑期，並非原確定判決確認之事實，亦與原確定判決認定事實與卷內訴訟資料是否相符無關。自不得執以指摘其適用法律有所違誤。」實際上均於事後「後見之明」地要求下級審法院應正確做出後犯罪是否該當累犯的判斷，則於非常上訴調查必要性之判斷上，何以不能相同地以事後發現的情節，在個案正義的考量下，認為既然被冒用姓名者未於緩刑期內更受有期徒刑以上刑之宣告，而不符撤銷緩刑

之要件，原撤銷緩刑宣告之裁定（審判），即因調查不備而
「違背法令」。蓋國家機關若於訴訟程序上出現疏漏，本不應
歸責於被告，該等錯誤原應由職司審判之「司法部門」負起補
正之責任；倘若因此而使為被告之當事人受有若何之不利益，
甚或因此侵害人權，實不足以保障人民憲法上基本權益，亦不
足以贏得人民對於司法之信賴。

2 從刑事訴訟法改良式當事人進行主義之修正談裁判上一罪規定修正

壹、前　言

自從民國 88 年 7 月所召開的全國司法改革會議確定我國之刑事訴訟制度將朝「改良式當事人進行主義[1]」之方向修正

---

[1] 關於改良式當事人進行主義的內涵，可參考司法院以下之說明：所謂「改良式當事人進行主義」，其重點在於貫徹無罪推定原則，檢察官應就被告犯罪事實，負實質的舉證責任，法庭的證據調查活動，是由當事人來主導，法院只在事實真相有待澄清，或者是為了維護公平正義以及被告重大利益時，才發動職權調查證據。「改良式當事人進行主義」除了可以釐清法官與檢察官的權責分際、彰顯公平法院的理念外，更有助於「發見真實」。因為按照檢察制度的分工，檢察官可以聯合偵查犯罪，有權力指揮調度檢察事務官、司法警察（官）蒐集犯罪證據，所以檢察官應該最能夠掌握被告的犯罪事證，在制度設計上，自然應該讓檢察官負起實質的舉證責任。另外，被告是不是成立犯罪，關係到被告自己的生命、自由、財產及名譽，從何處蒐集有利的證據供法院調查，被告當然最為清楚，也最為積極。所以作為法院裁判基礎的證據，自然是由當事人提出最為適當，只有在當事人的舉證沒有能夠讓法院形成心證，或者是為了維護社會公義及被告重大利益時，法院才需要介入調查，以發見真實。而這樣的制度設計保留了職權主義的優點，與美國刑事審判使用陪審制或日本刑事訴訟法只規定「法院得依職權調查證據」的當事人進行主義有所差別，其出發點完全是考量我國的國情及歷史文化背景，符合我國憲法關於實質正當法律程序的要求，也因此我們稱它為「改良式當事人進行主義」。http://www.judicial.gov.tw

後，歷經幾次的翻修，現行之刑事訴訟制度已迥異於制定於民國 56 年、以職權主義爲基礎的舊刑事訴訟法制。而爲因應改良式當事人進行主義之變革，檢察系統也相應地在原本「偵查」與「執行」的功能分工上，增加了「公訴組」，以落實新法關於檢察官「實質蒞庭」的規定。參與過舊法時代刑事訴訟實務的法律工作者，應不難感受此一系列的修法對於法庭活動所產生的「革命性」改變；簡單來說，檢察官與辯護人不再只是消極的參與（或參觀）刑事審判活動，法院也不必越俎代庖地扮演著追訴者的角色[2]。取而代之的，檢察官與辯護人除必須積極地參予法庭活動外（如對質詰問之進行、傳聞排除之爭執等），本於當事人進行之理念，原則上檢察

---

[2]　參照刑事訴訟法第 163 條修正理由：一、爲貫徹無罪推定原則、維護被告訴訟權益、實現公平法院之理想，法院與檢察官之權責應重新界定。依照檢察制度之分工，檢察官得利用檢察一體原則，發揮上下一體、聯合偵查追訴犯罪之功能，而其亦爲偵查之主體，有權指揮調度檢察事務官、司法警察（官）等偵查輔助機關從事犯罪證據之蒐集與調查，故擁有龐大公權力、於第一線從事偵查職務之檢察官應最能掌握被告犯罪事證是否存在，使其負提出證據及說服責任，應爲制度設計所當然，且無實際之困難。又衡諸經驗事實，被告有罪與否，攸關其生命、自由、財產及名譽得失，從何蒐集有利證據以供法院調查，被告亦知之最詳，且最爲積極。故供爲裁判基礎之證據方法或證據資料確以當事人提出或聲請調查最爲適當。而爲避免審判及偵查分際之混淆，法院不宜接續檢察官主動蒐集犯罪證據之工作，實應居於客觀、中立、超然之立場，在當事人互爲攻擊、防禦之訴訟架構下，依據實質正當法律程序之原則進行審判，僅於當事人主導之證據調查後，仍無法發見真實時，始斟酌個案情形，無待當事人之聲請，主動依職權介入調查。

官與辯護人亦必須擔負確定審判活動範圍的責任[3]。然而，由於現行刑事訴訟法除於第 163 條第 1 項原則性規定：「當事人、代理人、辯護人或輔佐人得聲請調查證據，並得於調查證據時，詢問證人、鑑定人或被告。審判長除認為有不當者外，不得禁止之。」外，其於同條第 2 項亦規定：「法院為發見真實，得依職權調查證據。但於公平正義之維護或對被告之利益有重大關係事項，法院應依職權調查之。」此項規定但書之解釋，對於現行刑事訴訟法究竟在什麼程度內保留了職權主義的色彩，具有決定性的影響。由於此部分自修法

---

[3]　參照刑事訴訟法第 163 條修正理由：四、依當事人主義之對立辯證原則，法院為發見真實，而依職權調查證據，僅屬輔助性質，通常係在當事人聲請調查之證據全部或主要部分均已調查完畢後始補充進行。五、在強化當事人進行色彩後之刑事訴訟架構中，法院依職權調查證據變成僅具補充性、輔佐性，因此在例外地依職權進行調查證據之情況下，為確保超然、中立之立場，法院於調查證據前，應先給予當事人陳述意見之機會。爰參考日本刑事訴訟法第 299 條第 2 項之法例，增列本條第 3 項，規定法院於職權調查證據前，應給予當事人等陳述意見之機會。七、進一步言，刑事訴訟法所稱之「調查」，原有雙重之意義，一為「發見證據之調查」，一為「踐行證據調查程序之調查」。本條第 1 項修正後，係強調當事人有聲請調查證據之權利，凡當事人所聲請調查之證據足以影響判決之結果，且有調查之可能者，法院仍有加以發見及踐行調查程序之職責。其第 2 項前段則指法院於前項當事人所主導之證據調查完畢後，認為事實未臻明白仍有待澄清時，得斟酌具體個案之情形，無待當事人之聲請，主動依職權蒐集案卷外之證據並踐行證據調查程序。但書則要求法院就公平正義之維護或對被告利益有重大關係事項，一律負有調查義務。故本條之修正非謂法院得無視於當事人之聲請或棄公平正義及被告利益之維護於不顧，而完全免除其調查證據之職責，併予指明。

之初即已引起廣泛之討論，並已有相當之說明文獻[4]甚至是批評[5]可資參考；由於先前之文獻已提出不少具有說服力的觀點，本文無意亦無力犬尾續貂般地在實務就具體案件事實作出裁判並形成多數意見之前，抽象地另指出如何適用該項但書的

---

[4] 相關之文獻包括：尹章華，我國刑事法院職權調查之探討，法令月刊，第43卷，第8期，1992年8月；三井誠，起訴狀一本主義與訴因制度，收錄於「刑事訴訟起訴狀一本主義及配套制度」法條化研究報告（上），最高法院學術研究會，1999年4月；王兆鵬，刑事舉證責任理論，收錄於氏著刑事被告的憲法權利，翰蘆圖書，1999年8月；司法院，刑事訴訟法第161條、第163條條文修正草案補充說帖，法學講座，第2期，2002年2月；法務部，對刑事訴訟法第161及163條修正草案之意見，法學講座，第3期，2002年3月；何賴傑，「應」還是「得」？一字之差，差已矣！http://www.pra-tw.org/pra_4/pra_4_1_25.htm；何賴傑，刑事法院依職權調查證據之範圍與限制，收錄於林山田主持：刑事訴訟法改革對案，元照，2000年10月初版一刷；何賴傑，事實審法院蒐集證據之義務—評最高法院87年度台非字第1號判決，政大法學評論，第61期，1999年6月；何賴傑，法院依職權調查證據相關法條之對案，台灣本土法學，第16期，2000年11月；林山田，別迷失在主義的叢林中～為職權原則與調查原則申冤，收錄於刑法的革新，學林文化，2001年8月初版一刷；林永謀，關於刑事訴訟制度之改革與刑事訴訟法第163條之修正—兼及刑訴法第161條，法令月刊，第51卷，第10期，2000年10月；張哲倫，論審判中檢察官之舉證責任，國立中興大學法律碩士論文，1998年7月。

[5] 例如：苟法院有「闡明義務未盡」，致判決之訴訟關係有「不明」或「不當」之情事，仍可構成「應於審判期日調查之證據未予調查」之判決違法事由。至於此處所謂應依職權調查證據之「闡明義務之範圍」，係指法院本諸「公平法院」理念，而有「維持審判公平」之職務，是故一、進行審判前提之訴訟條件足備否？諸如時效是否消滅？是否既判力所及等？及二、在「訴因事實範圍內」，被告所犯是否為較輕罪刑之事實等（指重罪變輕罪之情況，不包括輕罪變重罪之情況），例如起訴重傷害致死，審理後法院認應是過失致死時，法院於檢察官不願就此部分舉證，或被告不知應作此部分防禦時，本渠維持審判公平之職責，即「應」依職權調查，此時法院即屬應依職權調查之範圍，在此範圍內，法院仍應依職權蒐集證據方法，及調查證據證明力。如法院在闡明義務範圍內，未依職權調查證據完備，致審判發生不當結果，

法則。

　　相對地，由於刑事訴訟程序之進行，除以程序法本身之適用爲核心外，更重要地，乃在具體確定國家刑罰權後（審判）並進一步地使之實現（執行），職故，具體規範國家刑罰權之刑事實體法本身，其規範之方式與形式亦將對於刑事訴訟程序的進行造成一定的影響；舉例而言，如果沒有刑法第 55 條想像競合犯與牽連犯之規定，學說上不致出現探討其裁判既判力之問題研究[6]；如果沒有刑法第 56 條連續犯的規定，實務上亦不至於出現司法院大法官釋字第 152 號解釋所處理之爭議。特別就法制沿革來說，由於我國刑法在制定的過程中，主要係以德國與日本爲繼受的對象，因此，源自於大陸法系的刑事實體法是否能夠藉由移植自美國法上的刑事訴訟制度予以完整實現，似乎有重新思考的空間。鑒於刑事訴訟法第 163 條之修正理由

仍可構成「應於審判期日調查之證據未予調查」之判決當然違背法令上訴理由。是故如謂在當事人主義下，只有「法院應依職權調查證據之範圍如何」之問題，凡屬法院應依職權調查證據範圍內之事項，法院即有「蒐集證據方法及調查證據證明力之義務」，蓋法院沒有蒐集證據，如何依職權調查證據證明力。故根本沒有所謂「法院只有調查證據證明力之義務，沒有蒐集證據方法之義務」之法說，亦沒有所謂「法院只有發現真實之權利，沒有發現真實之義務」之說法，凡此皆屬誤解法院在當事人主義本諸公平法院理念，應有之審判職責。參閱朱朝亮，法院職權調查之範圍，http://www.perl.idv.tw/pra_4/pra_4_1_28_2.htm

6　例如：陳樸生，刑事訴訟法爭議問題研究，第七章，「想像競合犯之既判力」，頁 121-153，五南圖書出版公司，1994 年 12 月 6 刷；林永謀，析述併合數罪與裁判上一罪所關之審判範圍，法令月刊，第 44 卷第 10 期，1993 年 10 月；莊松泉，審判不可分原則之理論與實際，政治大學法律研究所碩士論文，1993 年 6 月；李進誠，一事不再理原則之研究，文化大學法律研究所碩士論文，1985 年 6 月。

並未對此一問題有所說明，且此部分涉及事實審法院是否踐行
其職權調查「義務」，本文擬自實體刑法上裁判上一罪的觀點
切入，探討現行改良式當事人進行主義架構下的刑事訴訟制
度，究竟與根源於職權主義之裁判上一罪之實體法規定間，是
否存在齟齬或矛盾而導致新的刑事訴訟制度於運作上出現危
機？此外，關於源自不同法系之實體法與程序法間，是否有可
能予以調和，本文亦將提出進一步的說明。

貳、職權主義與裁判上一罪之審理

　　雖然歐陸各國在法國大革命後已漸漸揚棄實行於中世紀的
糾問制度，而朝向控訴主義的方向前進[7]，在此一趨勢下，關於
當代的刑事訴訟法制，向來仍存在有職權主義與當事人進行主
義之分別。由於我國在法制繼受的沿革上，係以歐陸法為師，
因此制定於民國 24 年與民國 56 年的刑事訴訟法，均帶有濃厚
的職權主義色彩。所謂職權主義的刑事訴訟程序[8]，並不承認當

---

[7]　參閱王兆鵬，當事人進行主義爭議之評議，刑事法雜誌第 43 卷第 4 期，頁 36。
[8]　在此一制度下，法官負擔蒐集證據，調查證據之主要義務。法官負責主導審
　　判，為審判中的靈魂，積極地指揮訴訟程序的進行。證人之訊問由法官負最
　　主要的責任。證人首先由法官對其訊問，證人就所知事實提供一口語化的陳
　　述。除非為幫助證人完整清楚地陳述事實外，法官原則上對證人的陳述不能
　　打斷。當證人陳述所之事實完畢後，法官才可以進一步地詰問證人其他問題，
　　或證人的信用能力。當法官結束全部訊問後，當事人雙方才被允許對證人發
　　問。參閱王兆鵬，當事人進行主義爭議之評議，刑事法雜誌第 43 卷第 4 期，
　　頁 36-37。

事人對於訴訟標的與訴訟進行享有處分的權利[9]，且認法院應本其職權發現眞實[10]。

　　除了上述法官積極就檢察官起訴之犯罪事實探究實體眞實的特色外，關於職權主義下法官負擔蒐集證據、調查證據義務之範圍，除了檢察官起訴所指出的犯罪及其事實外，是否尚及於其他部分的犯罪事實？鑒於國家刑罰權之單複，係以刑事實體法之規定爲依據，因此，其他未被起訴之犯罪事實與已被起訴之犯罪事實是否再實體法上僅屬一罪，而爲同一刑罰權所涵蓋，並無從單自刑事訴訟法的規定尋得解答。簡單來說，由於刑法分則之條文所規定的犯罪構成要件，通常是預先設定爲一人以既遂的型態實行一罪[11]，本質上乃針對「行爲人單次實現犯罪構成要件」爲法律效果之規定[12]；因此，當「行爲人多次實現犯罪構成要件（亦即實現複數犯罪構成要件）」時，便無法自刑法分則之規定得出應有的法律效果，而需求

---

[9]　參閱俞叔平，刑事訴訟法學，頁 5，中國法學編譯社印行，1956 年 10 月修正版。

[10]　參閱陳樸生，刑事訴訟法爭議問題研究，頁 30，五南圖書出版公司，1994 年 12 月 6 刷。

[11]　此即「一人一罪原則」；參閱（日）野村稔著，全理其、何力譯，刑法總論，頁 445，法律出版社，2001 年 3 月。

[12]　即便刑法分則上之結合犯，係結合二以上之犯罪構成要件所組成，其於評價上仍屬單一構成要件之實現。

諸刑法總則之規定[13]，始有可能於行為人多次實現犯罪構成要件時，做出該「複數構成要件實現是否為同一刑罰權所涵蓋」的正確評價[14]。亦即，在正統職權主義下，法院本渠最後正義決定者之定位，而有最終真實發現者之職務，是故為發現最終真實之必要，當然有調查證據主導權（包括裁判上一罪之關係是否存在），自應依職權調查證據（包括證據方法之蒐集

---

[13] 值得注意的是，數罪併罰所要討論的並不單只是罪數的問題，而是在處理行為人犯數罪時，應如何處罰的問題。此等以處理「行為人多次實現犯罪構成要件之法律效果」為核心之問題，即稱為「競合問題」；而為處理競合問題所提出的理論，則稱為「競合論」。關於競合論的詳細說明，參閱張明偉，數罪併罰中有期徒刑之執行，頁 32 以下，國立台灣大學法律學研究所碩士論文，2002 年 6 月。

[14] 由於刑法評價的最終工作，並非僅在確認多少構成要件被實現；而是藉由被實現之構成要件，以確認行為人之可罰性為何；對於單一構成要件實現的情況，其行為可罰性之認定，可以藉由反應行為不法內涵的法律效果規定，加以確認；惟如有多數構成要件被實現時，在個別構成要件中，雖有專屬之法律效果，但卻欠缺整體評價的法律效果，因此，刑法對於多數規範被實現的情況，其法律效果的判斷，必須在個別構成要件規定以外，另外再行規範之。然而，何種情況會發生多數構成要件被實現的情況？由於事實情狀萬端，其可能為一行為所實現，亦有可能被數行為所侵害，然而，不論係一行為或數行為所實現之數構成要件，在法律效果的決定上，均不能從個別構成要件中求得，蓋此種情況並不同於單一構成要件實現情況。因此，刑法評價所涵蓋之範圍，應同時包含單一規範實現，以及複數規範實現之事實情狀，而二者間最大之差異，係可罰性認定問題，對於單一構成要件實現的情況，其可罰性的認定，僅需從該規定之法律效果確認即可，惟複數構成要件實現的情況，則需另創可罰性認定之基礎，亦即法律效果決定之標準。基本上，刑法根本的評價關係，係從一行為人之一行為，侵害一客體，造成一規範（構成要件）之實現，以確認一可罰性存在，作為評價的基礎。在一行為實現一構成要件的結構中，可罰性乃源自於該構成要件禁誡規範的非價判斷，而不法內涵則反映在法律效果的規定中參閱柯耀程，競合論之回顧與前瞻，刑法七十年之回顧與展望紀念論文集（一），頁 323-324，元照出版公司，2001 年 1 月。

及證據證明力之調查），並得依調查證據所得心證，變更檢察官請求審判之對象及範圍，至於當事人之舉證活動，只不過居於協助法院發現最終真實之目的而為。是故最終真實發現不當，致刑事司法正義無從實現之責任，自然即在法院，不在檢察官[15]。

　　關於複數犯罪構成要件實現之處罰，與裁判上一罪規定相關且值得注意的是，在職權主義刑事訴訟制度發展的歷史上，曾經針對複數犯罪構成要件實現創設單一刑罰原則此種涵蓋範圍最廣，類似於裁判上一罪的實體法規定。所謂單一刑罰原則係指：「雖然行為人觸犯數罪，但是判決時並不就數罪分別宣告其刑罰，而是直接就所犯數罪，包括的確定一個刑罰[16]。」

---

[15]　參閱朱朝亮，法院職權調查之範圍，http://www.perl.idv.tw/pra_4/pra_4_1_28_2.htm

[16]　參閱黃榮堅，犯罪的結合與競合，刑法問題與利益思考，頁450，月旦出版社股份有限公司，1995年6月。立法例上就犯罪競合採單一刑罰原則者，計有：1974年的奧地利刑法第28條第1項：「行為人單一行為或獨立之多數行為，違犯數個同種或異種之可罰行為，而同時接受裁判時，如其所競合之法律，僅規定自由刑或罰金刑者，僅處以一個為一之自由刑或罰金刑。此一刑罰依科以嚴重刑罰之法律定之。除有特別減輕其刑之規定外，其處罰不得低於各競合法律所規定最低刑罰之最高度。」、1937年的瑞士刑法第68條第1項：「行為人之一行為或數行為觸科處自由刑之罪，處以罪重犯罪行為之刑罰，並為相當之加重。但最重不得超過法定刑的二分之一，並受最重法定本刑之限制。」與一九五八年的法國刑法第5條第1項：「數重罪或輕罪競合者，僅依最重之刑處斷之。」參閱林山田，競合論概說與行為單數，政大法學評論第39期，頁34。

根本上單一刑罰原則，並不考量各種競合型態，而僅對犯罪競合問題作單一法律效果之處理[17]。自其較不考慮競合型態而著重國家刑罰權實現便利的特質，似不難發覺此種將複數構成要件實現評價為具有單一可罰性的實體法規定本身，帶有濃厚的職權主義色彩；而自其著重於行為人整體可罰性卻忽卻略個別行為可罰性之特質而言，亦難解免於行為人刑法之批評。自法制沿革之觀點而論，裁判上一罪之規定實係近代行為刑法與行為人刑法二者論戰妥協下之產物，其存在本身並非法理上之必然。

如果刑法總則的規定就「行為人多次實現犯罪構成要件」的特定類型（如我國舊刑法中關於想像競合犯、牽連犯與連續

---

[17] 雖單一刑制度，並不對個別之罪刑予以個別宣告，而僅宣告單一之執行，但刑的形成過程，則具有相當大的彈性，實不應將單一刑制度內在實質意義誤解為僅得以一刑為限。又於單一刑制度上，雖對個別罪之各刑不予宣告，但其卻為刑罰裁量上之重要判斷基礎，並非全無作用。此外，亦有以單一刑制度而爭論「行為刑法」及「行為人刑法」者，實為誤解（至少認識有偏差）單一刑制度之角色，蓋雖採單一刑制度可想像對刑罰裁量份量之加重，但採單一刑制度並非表示於刑罰裁量上，只注重行為人，進而認定係「行為人刑法」，此種推論方式本身於命題上，即不成立。參閱柯耀程，競合論之回顧與前瞻，註 58 之說明，刑法七十年之回顧與展望紀念論文集（一），頁 359，元照出版公司，2001 年 1 月。不過，由於在此立法原則下，實務上容許法官依「從一重處罰」的法則，不必分別考慮各種法規評價上的困難，而為「統一刑」的宣告，對於刑罰目的之實現，可謂較為便捷。但是，此說在有些情況，難免有籠統論罪之嫌，不如分離處罰主義的立法，對個別犯罪行為的評價，較能實現「罪有應得」之公平處罰的理念。故德國刑法改革法案的研究，經過討論的結果，除於德國少年刑法第 31 條第 1 項之立法，採統一處罰的立法原則以外，仍保留分離之競合犯理論。參閱蘇俊雄，競合理論之探討，法令月刊第 49 卷第 2 期，頁 5。

犯之裁判上一罪規定）作出「單一可罰性」的「一罪」評價，則爲探求具體個案刑罰權所包含的範圍，在職權主義的架構下，法院此時即應依職權主動調查是否仍存在與檢察官起訴之犯罪事實具有裁判上一罪關係之其他犯罪事實，否則，若法院僅單純審理檢察官所起訴的犯罪事實，而漏爲審酌與該被訴事實具有裁判上一罪關係之其他犯罪事實，此時法院所爲之犯罪評價（現實實現之刑罰權），即不免異於刑法規定之可罰性內涵（抽象規定之刑罰權）。因此，在實體法規定刑罰權單一的前提中，關於裁判上一罪之審理，學說上遂有提出「公訴不可分」與「上訴不可分」之觀念[18]，作爲法院依職權調查審理與檢察官起訴之犯罪事實具有裁判上一罪關係之其他犯罪事實之理論依據[19]。而刑事訴訟法第 267 條：「檢察官就犯罪事實一部起訴者，其效力及於全部。」與同法第 348 條第 2 項：「對於判決之一部上訴者，其有關係之部分，視爲亦已上訴。」中

---

[18] 參閱陳樸生，刑事訴訟法實務，頁 347 以下與頁 493，作者自刊，1984 年 4 月修訂 4 版；陳運財，刑事訴訟之舉證責任與推定，收錄於：刑事證據法則之新發展——黃東雄教授七秩祝壽論文集，頁 471，學林，2003 年 6 月。

[19] 按刑事訴訟法第 302 條第 1 款規定，案件曾經判決確定者，應為免訴之判決，係以同一案件，已經法院為實體上之確定判決，該被告應否受刑事制裁，既因前次判決而確定，不能更為其他有罪或無罪之實體上裁判，此項原則，關於實質上一罪或裁判上一罪，其一部事實已經判決確定者，對於構成一罪之其他部分，固亦均應適用，但此種事實係因審判不可分之關係，在審理事實之法院，就全部犯罪事實，依刑事訴訟法第 267 條規定，本應予以審判，故其確定判決之既判力自應及於全部之犯罪事實，惟若在最後審理事實法院宣示判決後始行發生之事實，既非該法院所得審判，即為該案判決之既判力所不能及，是既判力對於時間效力之範圍應以最後審理事實法院之宣示判決日為判斷之標準，最高法院 88 年度臺上字第 2576 號判決可資參照。

關於「一部」與「全部」之規定，正可作為在職權主義之刑事訴訟架構下，法院職權調查義務受到實體法規定影響之例證。

　　鑒於法院於真實發現的要求下具有依職權調查、探知檢察官未於起訴書中載明但與所起訴犯罪事實具有裁判上一罪關係之其他犯罪事實的義務，或許在法制的沿革發展上，可以大膽的推論歐陸法系所發展的職權主義，某種程度上與其實體法上所存在的裁判上一罪規定間，具有相互依存的關係。換句話說，為了避免抽象規定的刑罰權與具體實現的刑罰權在實質內涵上有所出入，在禁止雙重處罰的誡命要求下，課予法院積極調查義務的職權主義刑事訴訟制度，或許是因應大陸法系刑事實體法有關裁判上一罪規定所不得不然的選擇。就此而言，我國實務上關於裁判上一罪既判力所採之見解：「刑事訴訟法第 302 條第 1 款規定，案件曾經判決確定者，應諭知免訴之判決，此項訴訟法上所謂一事不再理之原則，關於實質上一罪或裁判上一罪，均有其適用，牽連犯係裁判上一罪，如其方法或結果之犯罪行為，業經判決確定，其效力當然及於全部，倘檢察官復就牽連犯中之方法或結果行為，重行起訴，即應諭知免訴之判決，不得再予論科[20]。」與「案件曾經判決確定者，應為免訴之判決，此項原則關於實質上一罪或裁判上一罪，均有

---

[20]　參閱最高法院 60 年台非字第 77 號判例。該件之案例事實為：「本件被告陳○○以簽發彰化商業銀行東港分行 58 年 10 月 28 日期（非常上訴理由誤為 59 年 10 月 24 日期）支票號碼一為 389206 號（非常上訴理由誤為 38920 號），一為 389207 號，票面金額一為新台幣八千一百四十元，一為一萬五千三百元

其適用。連續犯係裁判上之一罪，其一部分犯罪事實曾經判決確定者，其效力當然及於全部，故檢察官復將其他部分重行起訴，亦應諭知免訴之判決[21]。」於相當程度上，應可視為此一職權主義背景的反映。當然，各國刑事實體法間關於如何構成

　　空頭支票兩張，連同其他空頭支票一百餘張，向人詐騙現款之所為，業經屏東地方法院檢察官認為被告觸犯違反票據法及詐欺二罪，其間有方法結果之牽連關係，應從一重之詐欺罪處斷，於58年12月16日提起公訴，並經台灣高等法院台南分院於59年7月6日判決，維持第一審判決，論處被告詐欺罪有期徒刑三年六月，確定在案，乃屏東地方法院檢察官於案經判決確定後，於59年11月25日又將前案已經判決及之被告簽發彰化商業銀行東港分行第389206號，第389207號票面金額新台幣八千一百四十元，一萬五千三百元兩張空頭支票再行提出，重行提起公訴，屏東地方法院不諭知免訴之判決，竟於59年12月11日從實體上判處被告罰金拘役，一罪兩判，顯屬於法不合，且於被告不利，上訴人於判決確定後，認為違法，提起非常上訴，洵有理由。」本件案例事實適足以作為裁判上一罪之牽連犯所有犯罪事實難於一次審理程序中完全發覺之例證。

21　參閱最高法院49年台非字第20號判例。該件之案例事實為：「本件被告楊朝於民國45年4月29日向景美鎮萬盛里陳細悌騙取毛豬五隻之所為，業經台北地方法院認為與其同年5月2日持鄭阿招空頭支票二紙向高銘濤騙購毛豬十一隻之犯行，係基於一概括之犯意，於民國47年11月29日依連續詐欺罪判處罰金一千元確定在案，該判決雖未涉及被告於45年5月4日向台北市東園街念燕鑾、陳蕭娥騙購毛豬四隻之事實，但原法院既認與被告騙購陳細悌毛豬五隻之犯行，係基於概括犯意，應以連續犯論，自屬裁判上之一罪，而為原法院47年11月29日確定判決效力之所及，乃原法院檢察官於47年12月19日復就被告於45年4、5月間先後詐取陳細悌毛豬五隻，念燕鑾、陳蕭娥毛豬四隻之事實，以連續詐欺重行提起公訴，原法院於前案判決確定後，不依首開說明對後提之公訴，為被告免訴之判決，竟就實體上審查，於48年1月19日又以連續詐欺論再度判處罰金三百元，顯有違誤，且不利於被告，上訴人於判決確定後，認為違法提起非常上訴，洵有理由，自應由本院將原判決撤銷另行判決，以資糾正。」本件案例事實適足以作為裁判上一罪之連續犯所有犯罪事實難於一次審理程序中完全發覺之例證。

單一可罰性的評價，仍有不同的規定，其訴訟實務也有不同的相應發展。

參、朝向改良式當事人進行主義之刑事訴訟法修正與裁判上一罪所造成的影響

一般來說，採行職權主義的刑事訴訟制度具有三大缺點：一、在審判前法官已受到卷宗的影響，並過早形成心證；二、法官一人兼任審判者、追訴者與辯護者三重角色，導致法官的中立性受到質疑；三、由於法官富有積極調查之義務，造成當事人對於案件的審判不夠投入[22]。又由於在當事人進行主義制度下，當事人兩造對其所主張的事實，各自負擔證據的蒐集及調查義務，審判者處於被動聽審的角色。當事人雙各自傳喚對自己有利的證人，當一方對自己的證人訊問完畢後，由對造接手對證人訊問。通常對造會攻擊他方證人的信用能力，或設法自他方證人問得有利的證詞。在兩造對證人訊問完畢後，即令審判者對事實仍有不明瞭之處，原則上亦不可對證人直接發問問題。裁判者在審判前對事實豪不知情，在當事人雙方互提供證據的過程中，事實的真相才逐漸地被批露，被展開，被發

---

22 參閱王兆鵬，當事人進行主義爭議之評議，刑事法雜誌第 43 卷第 4 期，頁 38。

現，及被證實 ²³。換句話說，在純正當事人主義下，法院僅為公平審判機關，為當事人兩造爭瑞的仲裁者，不是最後正義決定者，當然即無最終真實發現之職務可言。故審判之目的僅在解決雙方當事人間之「訴訟爭點」，非在實現法院主觀的最終正義 ²⁴。因此，於我國向來即有著眼於當事人進行主義之優點 ²⁵，倡議我國應採行美國式當事人進行主義與日本式起訴狀

23　參閱王兆鵬，當事人進行主義爭議之評議，刑事法雜誌第 43 卷第 4 期，頁 37。

24　從而審判之對象及範圍，即應由當事人自行決定，並應由雙方當事人就審判對象及範圍，自行建立訴訟爭點、自行決定調查證據之順序、方法及範圍，故調查證據之主導權即在當事人，至於法院則退居公平法院之立場，本諸訴訟關係之「闡明義務」，在當事人所設定之審判對象及範圍內，於當事人主導調查證據後，倘訴訟關係尚有不明或不當之處，始進行「補充的」、「補正的」調查證據，故法院在「闡明義務之範圍」內，法院仍有「應依職權調查證據」之問題。在當事人進行主義下，法院並非全然只是「消極聽訟」，法院仍有其「維持公平審判」無可迴避之職務。惟此職務，僅屬「訴訟關係闡明義務」，不再是「最終真實發現義務」，是故縱即法院於審判中發現訴因外之新真實，亦只能曉諭檢察官依法定程序請求變更「訴因」，除非檢察官已依法院之曉諭變更訴因，否則法院對「訴因以外之新事實」，亦不得逕行判決，否則即構成「未受請求事項予以裁判」之判決違法事由。至於最後正義無從實現之責任，由於法院已盡其應盡之闡明權，以審判對象及範圍決定權（包括訴因之變更、撤回、追加權等）及調查證據之主導權皆檢察官，故最終真實發現不當，及最後正義無從實現之責任，自然即在檢察官，不在法院，蓋法院只是公平審判機關，只負「維持公平審判」之義務，不是最後正義決定機關，故無最終真實發現義務。參閱朱朝亮，法院職權調查之範圍，http://www.perl.idv.tw/pra_4/pra_4_1_28_2.htm

25　通常來說，該制度主要有四優點：一、使當事人感受較受尊嚴較被重視；二、使當事人較能接受訴訟的結果；三、較易產生正確的判決；四、使法官的地位較超然中立。參閱王兆鵬，當事人進行主義爭議之評議，刑事法雜誌第 43 卷第 4 期，頁 39。

一本主義的刑事訴訟制度[26]，以爲職權主義缺點的救濟。

　　爲了落實民國 88 年 7 月所召開的全國司法改革會議的決議，立法院乃陸續通過刑事訴訟法的修正案。其中又以民國 91 年及民國 92 年間所通過的法案，對於過去刑事訴訟制度產生的影響最爲重大。雖然民國 92 年所通過的法案中，包含諸如：證據排除法則、傳聞法則與詰問規則等使得法庭活動具有當事人進行主義外觀等條文，不過，於民國 91 年所通過的刑事訴訟法第 163 條第 2 項：「法院爲發見眞實，得依職權調查證據。但於公平正義之維護或對被告之利益有重大關係事項，法院應依職權調查之。」關於法院職權調查義務範圍的規定，卻是我國的刑事訴訟制度是否眞正擺脫職權主義色彩的關鍵[27]。如前所述，如果當事人對於訴訟的標的、程序進行所爲的意思表示原則上不能產生拘束法院調查權限行使的效力，那麼在法院仍然保有訴訟程序進行之主導權之情形中，法院仍得一如往常般地在刑事訴訟法第 163 條第 2 項但書之規範下依職權調查證據（只要法院說明於具體個案中存在於公平正義之維護或對被告

---

[26] 參閱顧立雄，挽救刑事審判，取得人民信賴唯一的出路——採行「起訴狀一本主義」之刑事訴訟制度，律師雜誌第 232 期 1 月號，頁 2。

[27] 蓋「訴訟制度究應採當事人主義或職權主義？不過是審判中誰該被定位為：最後正義實現者、最終真實發現者之選擇問題，事實上也僅有此二種選擇。若有修正亦不過是職權主義之修正或當事人主義之修正，但不管如何修正，絕對不可以發生理念相互矛盾之情事，否則即會發生權責不清，倒致訴訟制度崩潰之情事。」參閱朱朝亮，法院職權調查之範圍，http://www.perl.idv.tw/pra_4/pra_4_1_28_2.htm

之利益有重大關係事項）[28]；果如此，所實施之訴訟制度究竟
爲何？似乎完全取決於審判者的裁量。不過，若實務在實際運
作上採酌限縮刑事訴訟法第 163 條第 2 項但書適用之見解[29]，
並承認原則上當事人兩造才是事實的決定者，或許仍可形成與
修法目的相符之具改良式當事人進行主義色彩之訴訟實務。當
然即使存在類此之「主義」與「路線」之爭，此次的修法至少
足以評價爲關於當事人程序參與權保障（對被告而言）與強制
（對檢察官而言）的修正，而朝此方向的修正，相較於我國過
去的刑事訴訟實務過度職權化所造成人權保障不周的現象，亦
屬有意義且值得肯定的修正。

　　然而，若將此一刑事訴訟法第 163 條第 2 項但書應如何適
用的問題與裁判上一罪的規定相結合，其所衍生的問題即非單
純地如前述僅需討論「如何限縮刑事訴訟法第 163 條第 2 項但
書適用」此一問題即可。依現行刑事訴訟法第 161 條第 1 項：

---

[28]　觀之修法後迄今之現行實務運作，似乎早已爲學者所預言：法官得依一己之
喜惡，自行決定是否依職權調查證據。法官若爲「職權主義派系者」，主動
依職權調查一切證據，以取代檢察官或律師的角色，依修正草案意見，判決
爲合法，當事人不得請求救濟，上級法院不得糾正。反之，若法官爲「當事
人進行主義派系者」，從不主動調查證據，僅依據檢察官或律師所提證據裁
判，「棄真實發現於不顧」，依修正草案意見，判決亦爲合法，當事人亦不
得請求救濟，上級法院亦不得糾正。參閱王兆鵬，當事人進行主義爭議之評
議，刑事法雜誌第 43 卷第 4 期，頁 51-52。

[29]　參閱劉秉鈞，法院職權調查之範圍，收錄於：刑事證據法則之新發展——黃
東雄教授七秩祝壽論文集，頁 363，學林，2003 年 6 月；何賴傑，新法之刑
事法院職權調查證據，收錄於：刑事證據法則之新發展——黃東雄教授七秩
祝壽論文集，頁 415，學林，2003 年 6 月。

「檢察官就被告犯罪事實,應負舉證責任,並指出證明之方法。」第 161 條之 2 第 1 項:「當事人、代理人、辯護人或輔佐人應就調查證據之範圍、次序及方法提出意見。」以及第 166 條以下關於詰問規則等規定,在行為人實現「單數」犯罪構成要件的前提下,原則上刑事訴訟之進行係以檢察官與被告所提出的犯罪事實與證據為審判之中心,此時只要原則限縮刑事訴訟法第 163 條第 2 項但書的適用,刑事訴訟程序的進行,幾乎可完全呈現出當事人進行主義的訴訟構造,並符合此次修法的精神。不過在行為人實現「複數」犯罪構成要件的情形中,在此次之修法理念下,原則上檢察官應就所有形成裁判上一罪的犯罪事實提起公訴,法院才有可能逐一針對支持各該犯罪事實之證據進行修法後的審理程序,並就是否有傳聞法則的適用、是否應證據排除與控辯雙方進行探討。不過,若出現檢察官僅就裁判上一罪的部分犯罪事實提起公訴,並僅就起訴的事實部分與被告進行攻防,則法院是否具有依職權調查、探知檢察官未於起訴書中載明但與所起訴犯罪事實具有裁判上一罪關係之其他犯罪事實的義務?在舊刑法第 55 條、第 56 條、刑事訴訟法第 267 條、第 348 條第 2 項的規範架構下,答案似乎是肯定的。學者間亦有提出:「因現行法第 267 條仍維持公訴不可分,且第 300 條容許法院依職權變更檢察官起訴引應適用之法條,故當事人調查證據結束,法院發覺有其他裁判上一罪關係之案件,或在同一案件之範圍內,檢察官所主張之事項與法院心證形成之事實不一致者,就擴張之部分或變更之罪名,應認

於公平正義之維護有重大關係事項[30]。」相類似的觀點。也就是說，在刑事訴訟法第 163 條第 2 項但書的規範下，縱然出現檢察官僅就裁判上一罪的部分犯罪事實提起公訴，法院仍應本於職權主義的精神，依職權探知是否存在其他檢察官未於起訴書中載明但與所起訴犯罪事實具有裁判上一罪關係之犯罪事實。如此一來，在裁判上一罪的審理過程中，就檢察官未於起訴書中載明但與所起訴犯罪事實具有裁判上一罪關係之其他犯罪事實而言，法院便無法僅站在一個具有聽訟角色的中立裁判者之地位，進行案件之審理；其必須因裁判上一罪之規定而留意、調查客觀上是否存在其他檢察官未於起訴書中載明但與所起訴犯罪事實具有裁判上一罪關係之犯罪事實之角色，將使得刑事訴訟法第 163 條之立法目的：「在強化當事人進行色彩後之刑事訴訟架構中，法院依職權調查證據變成僅具補充性、輔佐性」的原則規定，在遭遇裁判上一罪的案件時，反而成為一項可能造成修法精神變調的原則。而如此般因是否有裁判上一罪規定之適用而區分法院是否為中立審判者的論點，亦將造成現行刑事訴訟程序是否具有當事人進行主義的色彩，出現「一國兩制」的莫名現象。諷刺的是，雖然於修法過程中，曾經出現「法務部堅持法院不應放棄發現真實的義務，而應採兼顧檢察官舉證責任與法院職權調查義務折衷式刑事訴訟制度。不

---

[30]　參閱陳運財，刑事訴訟之舉證責任與推定，收錄於：刑事證據法則之新發展——黃東雄教授七秩祝壽論文集，頁 471，學林，2003 年 6 月。

過，原則上可以接受司法院研議的改良式當事人進行主義，不
再堅持原所提的改良式職權進行主義[31]。」之妥協過程，不過
就修法就裁判上一罪規定之適用結果來說，與其稱此次之修法
為「改良式之當事人進行主義」，不如又回到法務部原本之主
張，仍然名之為「改良式職權進行主義」更為貼切[32]。

　　更有甚者，裁判上一罪範圍的不明確，亦將導致改良式當
事人進行主義的實際運作，偏向原本所採行的職權主義。蓋於
上述最高法院 60 年台非字第 77 號判例之拘束下，某犯罪事實
與前已判決確定的他犯罪事實是否具有（存在）裁判上一罪之
關係，實務上往往成為辯方在其他後發生之案件進行中，爭執
是否為前裁判既判力所及之爭點。因此，關於裁判上一罪之單
一刑罰權的實際內涵與範圍，特別是牽連犯與連續犯等不以單
一行為為審理對象之情形，在被告通常本身不主動聲明並缺少
被害人報案的情況下，是不容易發覺的。舉例來說，在行為人
以偽造文書之方法進行詐欺行為的例子中[33]，由於涉案的被害

---

[31]　參閱馬淑華，法部：不堅持改良式職權新制，中央日報，http://www.cdn.com.
tw/daily/1999/07/06/text/880706ag.htm.

[32]　與此見解相似者，有主張：由於上述改良式當事人主義訴訟制度對法院之定
位，本質上係採後者，即法院始為最後正義決定者，及最終真實發現者，雖修
法強調檢察官之蒞庭舉證義務，惟對審判中法院之職能，仍不脫上述定位，故
本質上，與其說是「修正式當事人主義」，毋寧說是「修正式職權主義」。參
閱朱朝亮，法院職權調查之範圍，http://www.perl.idv.tw/pra_4/pra_4_1_28_2.
htm.

[33]　相關之實務見解，請參閱最高法院 26 年渝上字第 1435 號判例：「犯一罪而
其方法或結果之行為犯他罪者，刑法第 55 條既規定從一重處斷，則牽連犯之
一罪，如經判決確定其牽連之他罪，即使未曾審判，因原係裁判上之一罪，
即屬同一案件，亦不能另行追訴。」

人的不同，在欠缺詐欺罪被害人報案的情形中，並不容易發覺該偽造文書行為產生了詐欺的結果。此時，若於偽造文書判決確定後始發覺詐欺罪，不論詐欺罪之被害人有多少，只要後發覺的詐欺與偽造文書行為符合刑法第 55 條後段牽連犯的規定，該詐欺罪將獲判免訴[34]。此一案例，適足以說明我國刑事實體法所規定裁判上一罪之實際刑罰權（可罰性）內涵與範圍不易確定之特徵。依此所述，在我國之現行制度中，既然已確定之判決將可能因裁判上一罪之規定而出現既判力擴張之現象，在避免具體實現之刑罰權範圍與抽象規定之刑罰權內含有所出入，法院即有義務調查是否存在其他符合裁判上一罪規定之犯罪事實；如此一來，裁判上一罪之規定實成為我國刑事訴訟制度仍然保留相當程度的職權主義色彩之關鍵。既然我國法上之裁判上一罪客觀上具有不易確定具體刑罰權範圍之特質，則於訴訟程序上，要求檢察官、自訴人與法院必須巨細靡遺地依職權調查所有包含於裁判上一罪之所有犯罪事實，在實際操作上似乎難以完全實現並違訴訟經濟的原則。此外，考之刑事訴訟法第 163 條第 2 項之修正理由，並未慮及裁判上一罪規定將對修法目標產生何等程度之衝擊，自可推論於立法之初立法者並不欲法院的職權調查義務乃繫之於被訴案件是否屬裁判上一罪

---

[34]　不過，依現行刑事訴訟法第 422 條之規定，此時或可藉由「為受判決人之不利益聲請再審」之程序，由檢察官向該關法院提出再審之申請，作為此種情形的救濟途徑。

此一不確定事實。從而，在上述裁判上一罪規定確會衝擊新法修正目的的認知下，關於二者間之衝突，究應如何調和，似乎已成為亟待解決之重要課題。

　　基於以上的說明，在我國刑事訴訟制度改採改良式當事人進行主義的變革中，裁判上一罪的規定與其內涵，或許已成為此次修法目的能否實現的關鍵。由於立法例上，我國並非第一個改採當事人進行主義訴訟制度的國家，因此比較法的借鏡，或許可以成為我國法制修正發展的參考。

肆、比較法的觀察

　　由於我國刑事法源自於德國與日本，因此德日二國的刑事訴訟發展，或可為我國之參考。不過，德國法並未揚棄其傳統職權主義的刑事訴訟制度，在德國刑事訴訟法第 244 條第 2 項之規範下，原則上法院為查明事實真相，應依職權主動就對判決有重要性之事實與證據加以調查[35]，故雖德國刑法較之戰前已明顯限縮裁判上一罪的範圍（例如刪除牽連犯與連續犯之規定），但由於該國刑法係以行為之單複作為區分觀念的競合與實在的競合的依據[36]，從而德國刑事訴訟制度運作關於裁判上

---

[35]　參閱 Claus Roxin 著，吳麗琪譯，德國刑事訴訟法，頁 475，三民書局，1998 年 11 月初版。

[36]　參閱陳樸生，刑事訴訟法爭議問題研究，頁 125，五南圖書出版公司，1994 年 12 月 6 刷。

一罪係以一行爲爲適用前提，此部分基於一行爲一處罰原則所形成的規定，較之我國裁判上一罪之規定，乃顯得單純、容易而不至產生歧異。因其仍採職權主義之刑事訴訟制度，故與我國目前法制現狀不符。

　　日本雖於明治維新時師法大陸法系而制定刑事訴訟制度，不過在其戰敗受美軍託管並代爲擬定非戰憲法的背景下[37]，日本的刑事訴訟制度於戰後受到美國法的影響極大。值得注意的是，雖然連續犯之規定已於昭和二十二年被刪除[38]，在大陸法系的傳統下，日本刑法第 54 條第 1 項仍保有想像競合犯與牽連犯之規定，就仍然保存牽連犯規定與同受美國刑事訴訟制度影響而言，日本的刑事訴訟概況，應較接近於我國，而值得進一步的探討。

　　依照日本的學說與實務之說明，將牽連犯視爲裁判上一罪並只爲單一刑罰權的評價的理由在於：「實行某個犯罪之際，通常預想到把在客觀類型上歸屬於其他犯罪的行爲作爲手段，或者作爲所伴隨的結果來加以實施，並且行爲者也認識到這點；從刑法的規範角度來看，與其說對於各個獨立的犯罪加以獨立的非難，不如說對於整體進行評價，對其加以最重的規範

[37] 參閱（日）蘆部信喜著，李鴻禧譯，憲法，頁 47 以下，月旦出版社，1995 年 1 月初版。

[38] 參閱（日）野村稔著，全理其、何力譯，「刑法總論」，頁 456，法律出版社，2001 年 3 月。

的非難更為合理[39]。」不過這種欲將整體牽連犯所包含的全部犯罪事實作單一刑罰權評價的意見，在日本採訴因制度與起訴狀一本主義的架構下，是否可能全面實現，仍有待詳明。

由於現行日本刑事訴訟法採用訴因制度，其結果是裁判的意思表示內容不能涉及訴因以外的要素。然而，即便在這樣的理論架構下，關於裁判的效力是否及於裁判上一罪中未被檢察官指出的犯罪事實部分？仍然不明確。通說基於「審判範圍及於公訴事實同一性的其他事實」以及「被告在公訴事實的同一性範圍內處於危險的地位」二項觀點認為，由於在公訴事實同一性的範圍內，只承認一個刑罰權，加上檢察官負有追訴義務，而告訴人也是追訴的一方，故一事不再理之效力應及於公訴事實的同一性範圍；即使不可能同時追訴或不能變更訴因，一但對某種訴因作出判決，就不允許在訴因與公訴事實的範圍內再次起訴[40]。換言之，如果檢察官漏未指出裁判上一罪中的部分犯罪事實與罪名，在法院已就一個刑罰權作成評價且該案件已告確定的情形中，基於一事不再理之原則，檢察官與法院即不能再對同一刑罰權範圍內的其他事實予以追訴處罰。

上述日本通說的見解與我國實務向例所採，並無太大的出入。只不過在這樣的論理結構中，似乎認為檢察官就裁判上一

---

[39] 最大判昭和 24 年 12 月 21 日刑集 3 卷 12 號 2048 頁；參閱（日）野村稔著，全理其、何力譯，「刑法總論」，頁 459，法律出版社，2001 年 3 月。

[40] 參閱（日）田口守一著，劉迪、張凌、穆津等譯，刑事訴訟法，頁 307，法律出版社，2000 年 1 月。

罪的部分犯罪事實具有實質處分的權限，蓋若檢察官未將裁判
上一罪的其他犯罪納入訴因之中，當事人間即無機會就該部分
之事實與證據進行攻防，此時在裁判既判力的拘束下，其他
犯罪的被害人便失去就其被害部分請求國家進行刑事訴追的
機會[41]；此種情形於其他犯罪屬告訴乃論之罪，而被害人不及
提出告訴導致訴訟條件欠缺時尤為明顯。而雖然日本刑事訴訟
法第 298 條第 2 項：「法院在認為必要時，得依職權調查證
據。」與我國刑事訴訟法第 163 條第 2 項但書之規定相類似，
日本的實務卻認為：本條項之規定「只是為了協調職權主義與
當事人主義之間的關係。被告人、辯護人提出的證據不充分
時，從當事人對等原則出發，法院有義務依職權調查證據。相
反，檢察官一方提出證據不充分時，如果法院依照職權調查證
據，那就是過分的職權主義。但是，檢察官提出證據的行為明
顯存在漏洞，法院有義務督促檢察官[42]。」也就是說，法院的
職權調查義務只有在辯方提出證據不充分時才有適用；如果檢
察官漏未指出裁判上一罪所包含的部分罪名與犯罪事實，為了
避免審判實務太過偏向職權主義，在採訴因制度而不採公訴不
可分原則的立法架構下，法院並無義務依職權調查是否存在此
種情形。由此可知，日本法之發展亦無法於論理上完整說明何
以在當事人進行主義之架構下，既判力及於裁判上一罪之全部

---

[41]　按日本刑事訴訟法並無為受判決人不利益申請再審之規定，此點與我國不同。

[42]　最判昭和 33 年 2 月 13 日刑及第 12 卷第 2 號；參閱（日）田口守一著，劉
　　迪、張凌、穆津等譯，刑事訴訟法，頁 307，法律出版社，2000 年 1 月。

犯罪事實。

　　與我國類似,義大利也是一個具有職權主義傳統卻改採當事人進行主義訴訟制度的國家。雖然義大利的刑事訴訟制度於1988年後改採美國式的當事人進行主義[43],不過由於該國之刑事實體法,並未有裁判上一罪之規定[44],因此該國刑事審理實務尚不致出現類似於我國或日本關於裁判上一罪既判力範圍的問題。而美國的刑事訴訟制度為當事人進行主義的代表性國家,縱然美國的刑事司法制度針對數罪(Multiple Offenses)訂有合併(Combined)的量刑程序[45],不過究其實質,此種規定迥異於我國與日本的裁判上一罪規定,該程序應不致於導致其法院必須於審理過程中有義務依職權調查是否存在其他犯罪。縱上所述,從比較法的觀點來說,大概只有日本法遭遇類似於我國因改採改良式當事人進行主義所面臨的難題。不過,前述各國的法制發展經驗,特別是日本,並無法就我國所面臨裁判上一罪規定與刑事訴訟法改良式當事人進行主義的修正出現交集時所產生的問題,提供進一步明確又完整的解答。究應如何處理?似乎有待我國法界前輩們自行找尋本土化的出路。

---

[43] See Ennio Amodio and Eugenio Selvaggi, An accusatorial system in a civil law country: the 1988 Italian Code of Criminal Procedure, 62 Temple Law Review 1211, 1211 (1989).

[44] 參閱陳忠林,義大利刑法綱要,中國人民大學出版社,1999年10月。

[45] See United States Sentencing Commission, Federal Sentencing Guidelines Manual, 288-300, West Group, 2000.

伍、實體法與程序法間之平衡：爲實體法規定而「改良」？

　　其實不論是我國法或是日本法，在處理類似因裁判上一罪規定所衍生的程序法問題時，所需面對的主要挑戰，就是裁判既判力與一事不再理原則究應如何解釋適用，方不致與當事人進行主義的訴訟制度，相互衝突。不過，由於在刑事訴訟制度採行當事人進行主義的刑事實體法，並未見有類似於裁判上一罪的規定；而於刑事實體法中採行裁判上一罪制度的法域，亦未曾自發性地發展出類似當事人進行主義的訴訟制度；因此，如我國與日本般欲將非同根生的程序法移植到不同的實體法架構中，似乎不可避免地會出現源於法制移植過程所產生猶如制度間「水土不服」的現象。換句話說，若實體法之相關規定未相應於程序法之變革作同步或相容的修正調整，就我國的現況而言，所謂的「改良式」當事人進行主義，恐將因堅持實體法的規定，而朝向「改良式」的職權進行主義發展；另就日本的情形來說，似亦將因避免訴訟制度過度朝向職權主義靠攏的觀點，導致實體法上裁判上一罪的規定必須容許實體刑罰權內涵與抽象刑罰權範圍不一致的「變調式」裁判上一罪的現象繼續存在。

　　藉由以上的探討，應該不難發現現行刑事訴訟法第 163 條第 2 項但書規定在適用上存在無法僅自程序法本身之觀點獲得完整說明的盲點。從而，回頭檢視刑事實體法的規定是否洽

當，或許是一條值得嘗試的途逕。然而，在處理此類程序法議
題與檢視刑事實體法中裁判上一罪的相關規定前，似應先了
解，雖然從沿革上來說，我國與日本的刑事法制，乃奠基在十
九世紀末的德國法；不過現行各國法制關於裁判上一罪所涵蓋
的範圍，卻存在廣狹的差異。先就德國法的規定來說，為了避
免一罪數罰，德國刑法界遂認為：應先探討形式上的數罪（複
數構成要件該當），於實質上是否僅為一罪。德國刑法實務在
罪數之判斷上，係運用刑法學理論提出之「行為單數」與「行
為複數」之法概念，針對具體行為事實，首先判斷究屬行為單
數、抑屬行為複數。若屬行為單數，則續行判斷法律競合現
象，除外其餘者即屬想像競合；若認定屬於行為複數，則應進
而判斷是否為「與罰之前行為」或「不罰之後行為」，其餘即
屬犯罪複數之「實質競合」。立法上既無牽連犯與連續犯，理
論上亦無吸收犯[46]。現行的德國刑法已揚棄過去有關連續犯與
連犯的規定，因此關於複數構成要件實現之裁判上一罪，僅包

---

[46] 按德國刑法規定之犯罪單數，僅規定想像競合，犯罪競合僅規定實質競合，
至於牽連犯與連續犯，則均未規定於刑法之中。相關說明，另可參閱林山田，
「刑法通論下冊」，頁572，1998年2月增訂6版。另參閱陳樸生，刑事訴
訟法爭議問題研究，頁125，五南圖書出版公司，1994年12月6刷。

含想像競合一種[47]。日本之刑法雖已刪除連續犯的規定，不過其裁判上一罪的範圍除想像競合犯外，尚及於牽連犯之規定。而因我國刑法仍保有連續犯之規定，故我國裁判上一罪規定之範圍顯較德日之規定更為廣泛。

　　既然職權主義的殘留某種程度上繫之於裁判上一罪的規定，是否必須完全廢除裁判上一罪的規定才可能使得改良式當事人進行主義的目標落實在實務的運作上？其實這個問題還是

---

[47]　在德國刑法中所謂想像競合是指：同一行為觸犯數項犯罪構成要件或發生多數的同樣罪名的法益侵害，例如行為人開一槍而同時間構成二人以上的傷亡情形，應如何科刑處斷的問題。以上兩種競合的型態，其作用乃在於決定如何處斷行為人同時該當數項犯罪構成要件之行為，亦即應以「數罪」或「一罪」論處之問題有關，故亦被稱之為「純正的競合」。至於所謂「法規競合」以及「不罰的後行為」的競合，在「表象概念上」雖有多數構成要件並存的情形，但是實際上其所牽涉的問題，乃一行為所該當的犯罪構成要件；因為法規競合是一行為而有多種評價規範並存的情形，所以在「雙重評價禁止原則」之下，要求法官對行為做處斷時，只能適用其中一個法條，而排除其他法條的適用。所以在法理上，法規之競合，實乃屬應優先適用何項法規的問題，並非實質上去判斷應以一罪或數罪論處的問題。就此，學術上亦稱之為「假象的競合」，而與純正的競合在概念上應予區分。實質競合係指同一行為人，出自多次犯意，分別實行多數獨立的犯罪構成事實，而在同一刑事訴訟程序中，接受裁判罪予以「數罪併罰」的犯罪競合。不過，以上配合刑法論罪法則規定的相關競合概念，主要涉及想像競合情形中的處斷上「犯罪單一」以及在實質競合場合中之「犯罪多數」的概念；其與犯罪理論上的「行為單一」與「行為複數」的概念，雖然有關聯性，但是犯罪理論體系與論罪理論體系的概念，並非完全一致。蓋行為單數與複數的概念，僅是形成犯罪單數或複數的條件之一，而做為論斷的一項癥結點而已。論罪的競合理論，尚有犯罪單元概念以外之刑罰衡平的考量問題。故刑法理論上的行為單數或複數的概念，並不完全等於法典上論罪規定中的「一行為」或「數行為」的概念；從而，自不宜將行為之單數的法律概念，直接視同刑法就想像競合犯所規定的「一行為」。參閱蘇俊雄，競合理論之探討，法令月刊第49卷第2期，頁4。

必須從裁判既判力與一事不再理二者互為表裡的觀點來尋求解答。由於裁判上一罪的規定將複數構成要件實現的客觀狀態整體評價為單一可罰性,因此國家對之只有一個刑罰權。如果已經行使過刑罰權,自不許國家再次針對同一刑罰權客觀事實重複行使,否則即會對行為人造成雙重處罰的不利益。然而,主張這樣說法的人往往忽略裁判上一罪規定本身範圍是否合理的問題。也就是說,雙重危險的禁止,必須建立在同一犯罪的基礎上,如果對於同一犯罪的概念過度擴張其範圍,即使在採職權主義訴訟構造的制度下,本質上似乎不可避免法院在具體實現刑罰權時,會無意間遺漏同一犯罪概念內之部分犯罪事實。如果單一刑罰權所涵蓋的範圍過於廣泛,不可避免的也將造成裁判既判力與一事不再理的範圍於事後過度擴張。因此,如何將複數構成要件實現合理地評價為單一可罰性,方不致於造成訴訟進行中「事實決定者(職權主義的法院;當事人進行主義的檢辯雙方)」於事實認定時的過度負擔,應為處理前開我國改採改良式當事人進行主義訴訟制度所面臨的難題時,所應一併思考解決的議題。不過,本文並不認為必須完全廢除所有裁判上一罪的規定,才有可能落實此次修法的精神。

既然限制裁判上一罪成立的範圍,與限制法院職權調查具有一定程度的正向關係,只要能夠合理地避免單一刑罰權所涵蓋的範圍過於廣泛,法院亦不必於訴訟程序進行中,為避免實體刑罰權的實現與抽象刑罰權的規定不一致,而必須依職權調查是否存在與被訴事實具有裁判上一罪關係的其他犯罪事實。

由於審判的進行，不論在職權主義的國家與當事人進行主義的國家，均係以犯罪事實爲中心，而犯罪事實又以犯罪行爲爲核心，因此，將審判的重心置於犯罪行爲之上，並將既判力的範圍限縮在該犯罪行爲之上，並不會造成不合理之處。反之，由於牽連犯與連續犯之成立係以複數的犯罪「行爲」爲前提，在被告一般不會主動告知檢警與被訴犯罪事實有牽連或連續關係的其他犯罪事實、被告享有不自證己罪的權利、其他未被起訴犯罪事實的被害人並無於起訴前提出告訴的義務……等等現實下，訴訟審理的進行，並不易涵蓋至未被起訴的犯罪「行爲」部分；而進一步將裁判既判力與一事不再理的效力擴及法院未能審理的部分，非但抹煞被害人實現正義的機會，也變相鼓勵被告牽連犯罪與連續犯罪。從而，此種源自「近代」歐陸法系思潮的產物（將複數「行爲」所形成的複數犯罪構成要件實現評價爲單一可罰性），並不符合「當代」保護犯罪被害人、承認被告在訴訟程序上享有不自證己罪權、緘默權、對質詰問權並與無罪推定原則等刑事思潮相違背。

　　此外，較之我國刑法第 50 條：「裁判確定前犯數罪，併合處罰之。」之規定，僅以行爲人本身是否具有連續犯意或牽連意圖等主觀上因素，作爲區分複數行爲實現複數構成要件是否成立一罪或數罪的標準，似乎亦無法說明何以主觀上惡性較強（因其原本即打算侵害較多法益）或客觀上造成損害較大的被告，反而受到較輕微的制裁（因只被評價爲一罪，自較被評價爲多罪更加輕微）。且將單一刑罰權的範圍擴及連續犯與牽連

犯等由複數「行為」所形成的複數犯罪構成要件實現，似乎太
過注重行為人的因素而有太過偏向「行為人刑法[48]」的色彩並
違背「當代」「行為刑法」的思維。在此種認知下，本文建議
我國刑法裁判上一罪的修正，應著眼於是否得合理要求偵審機
關於調查審理過程中發覺所有犯罪事實的觀點，作為思考的起
點。本文參考德國刑法的規定，認為：除以「一行為」為核心
的想像競合犯應予保留外，應刪除以「複數」行為為核心的連
續犯與牽連犯規定。而對於「一行為」的概念內涵，亦應避免
過度擴張而涵蓋無法合理地於調查時發覺的客觀社會事實部
分。然而，修法畢竟是一個緩不濟急的程序，在實體法制尚未
修正前，現行的改良式當事人進行主義似乎不可避免地將因裁
判上一罪的現行規定而帶有某種程度的職權主義色彩。上述未
於修法理由中所慮及、源自實體法上裁判上一罪規定所衍生的
問題，或許正是此次修法所以必須名之為「改良式」當事人進
行主義的原因。不過由於「一行為」概念之實際內涵乃刑法解
釋的問題，本文宥於篇幅，不擬深論。

陸、結　論

經由以上的說明，本文認為在實體法尚未修正限縮裁判一

---

[48]　例如：德國少年刑法第31條第1項之立法，即係基於行為人刑法的理念而對
少年犯罪採統一處罰（單一刑罰原則）的立法原則。參閱蘇俊雄，競合理論
之探討，法令月刊第49卷第2期，頁5。

罪之規定前，我國的刑事訴訟實務，尚無法完全落實當事人進行主義的精神，而法院也因此必須負有發現真實之義務，成為最後的事實認定者[49]。雖然日本的實務在訴因制度下認為只有在辯方明顯與控方在證據調查尚處於不對等的地位時，法院才有依職權調查之義務；藉以維持當事人進行主義之訴訟架構。然而這樣的說明，仍然無法調和職權主義實體法與當事人進行主義程序法間所存在之矛盾（亦即：何以實體法的規定無法透過程序法的運作完全落實？）。因此，在肯認程序法上人權保障目的具有較高普世價值的二十一世紀，面對這樣源自於不同訴訟架構與不同刑事思潮時空背景之實體法與程序法所衍生的矛盾，本文不得不建議，應透過修改近代刑法上裁判上一罪的規定，以避免訴訟進行將因所審理之案件是否屬於裁判上一罪時，出現一國兩制的怪象，如此始有可能藉由落實控辯雙方「武器對等」原則的實現，達成改良式當事人進行主義修正中，所揭櫫之「為建構公平正義之訴訟制度，以完成改造跨世紀現代司法制度」之理想目標。（本文曾於 93.09 經評為首選刊載於司法院刑事訴訟新制實施週年專刊）

---

[49] 簡單來說，如果法院職權調查之義務僅及於檢察官所起訴之犯罪部分，而不及於與該被起訴犯罪具有裁判上一罪關係之其他犯罪，則刑事訴訟法第 163 條第 2 項但書之適用，尚可限縮於當事人進行主義的架構中；反之，倘若法院之職權調查義務除及於檢察官所起訴之犯罪部分外，尚及於與該被起訴犯罪具有裁判上一罪關係之其他犯罪時，在發覺該未被起訴犯罪的目的下，實際的訴訟審理進行，仍不免具有傳統的職權主義色彩。

3 英美傳聞法則與對質條款的歷史考察

壹、前　言

　　自從民國 88 年 7 月所召開的全國司法改革會議確定我國之
刑事訴訟制度將朝「改良式當事人進行主義」之方向修正後，
現行的刑事訴訟制度已大異於制定於民國 56 年、以職權主義為
基礎的舊刑事訴訟法制，值得一提的是現行刑事訴訟法已增定
職權主義所無之傳聞法則規定。雖然傳聞法則已成為現行刑事
訴訟程序之一大焦點，不過此一濫觴於英美法系之制度，其本
身之沿革歷程為何，在我國向來欠缺完整之介紹與說明。為避
免國人對傳聞法則產生誤認，並導致我國刑事訴訟實務對傳聞
議題出現偏離焦點之解釋與裁判，本文乃不湍簡陋，除企圖能
將英美法系近千年發展之傳聞法則，作一概要性的描述外，並
大致說明現行美國聯邦證據法關於傳聞法則之規定。由於本文
旨在介紹英美傳聞法則之發展，因此關於我國實務上傳聞法則
之爭議，並不在本文論述範圍之內，尚有待來日他文再為處
理。此外，雖然我國學說與實務關於傳聞法則之論述尚不致汗
牛充棟，不過在民國 92 年之刑事訴訟法修正後，學說上已出現

為數可觀之闡述；為免本文所述流於重複而無新義，因此，本文之相關論述主要係以英美法之第一手資料為主要的研究對象。

貳、傳聞法則的規範意義

　　為了保障群眾的生命與財產的安全，人類長久以來一直在尋找與建立一套能公平發現事實與解決紛爭的刑事訴訟程序[1]。不管在任何時代，只要人們間出現糾紛，「確認相關事實」與「運用法律原則」以解決當事人間之爭端向來即為審判工作的重要目的[2]。在此紛爭解決的過程中，雖然事實審判（認定）者必須決定所爭執之事實為何，然在英美法之規範上，不論是民事或刑事案件，卻必須由指控者擔負證明的責任[3]。

　　通常來說，正義的概念包含「公平、公正的訴訟程序」與「正確的訴訟結果」[4]。不過，若假定「發現實體真實」為刑事訴訟的首要目標，在充斥著「訴訟律師對具高度關聯性之證據

---

[1] See John C. Klotter, Criminal Evidence, 1-2 (Ohio Anderson Publishing, 1992).

[2] See Penny Darbyshire, Eddey on the English Legal System, 107 (London Sweet & Maxwell, 1992).

[3] 此部分與大陸法系之刑事訴訟操作傳統，有極大之不同。參閱吳巡龍，對質詰問權的保障與限制－釋字第 582 號解釋評析，月旦法學雜誌，第 115 期，頁 97，2004 年 12 月。

[4] See Roger C. Park, et al., Evidence Law: A Student's Guide to the Law of Evidence as Applied in American Trials, 1 (West, 1998).

提出異議」與「法院經常排除具高度證據價值之證據」的美國刑事訴訟實務下，即便身為一個法律人也難免對於美國的刑事審判程序之目的感到困惑[5]。由於在程序上，事實認定必然先於法律適用，從而，前述美國法制排除證據之現象似乎隱含著：法律爭議之解決在美國審判上往往是最不重要的議題[6]。雖然法律系統本身的主要任務乃在於「決定何者為已發生的事實」[7]與「達成正義」；不過，本諸「事後無法完整地發現與呈現所有已發生或存在的事實」之理念，在普通法下所發展出的兩造主義（或稱當事人進行主義）訴訟架構，即與前述正義概念有所出入[8]。換言之，實體真實並非英美刑事訴訟制度所追求的終極目標；取而代之者，乃是所謂程序真實的概念。

　　幾個世紀以來，非法律人慣用傳聞一詞，指稱二手資訊或泛指不可靠的資訊[9]；不過，普通法法院卻將傳聞一詞，作為一個新興的法律概念[10]加以操作。基本上，人們普遍具有輕信傳言與風聞言事的特質[11]；此外，在未接觸特定案件卷證與知悉

---

[5]　See John C. Klotter, supra note 1, 1.

[6]　See William Burnham, Introduction to the Law and Legal System of the United States, 77 (West Group, 1999).

[7]　See John H. Langbein, Historical Foundations of the Law of Evidence, 96 Colum. L. Rev. 1168, 1168 (1996).

[8]　See Roger C. Park, supra note 4, 2.

[9]　See Steven I. Friedland, et al., Evidence Law and Practice, 308 (LexisNexis, 2000).

[10]　See G. Michael Fenner, The Hearsay Rule, 8 (Carolina Academic Press, 2003).

[11]　See Lon Fuller, The Forms and Limits of Adjudication, 92 Harv. L. Rev. 353, 382 (1978).

相關案情之前，調查者通常不易決定應詢問何種問題與應如何
調查事實[12]。在這樣的認知下，兩造主義的制度設計者便強
調：將調查事實的責任自事實認定者抽離是避免審判者形成偏
見的唯一途徑[13]。一但確定了「事實認定者不負調查事實之責
任」此一命題，在制度設計上，便另外需求一套足以公平規範
證據提出的程序（證據）法則；某種程度來說，英美法乃藉由
「建立一套如何提出事證於法院的證據法則」來達成「事實認
定者不負調查事實責任」之目標[14]。而此種以當事人兩造負責
蒐集與提出證據、並由被動的事實認定者負責審判的美國刑事
審判制度本身，可謂集兩造主義理論之大成[15]。在比較法上，
一般認為當代大陸法系與英美法系間最大的差異即在於事實之
調查與認定部分；一套獨立於民、刑事訴訟法的證據法系統，
已成為普通法發展上的一大特徵[16]。誠如 James Bradley Thayer
教授於 1898 年所述，「若從普通法證據規則之角度而言，美國
的證據法則在排除具高度證明價值證據之規範上是相當獨特
的；本質上，類似英語系國家於訴訟法外獨立發展出一套高度

---

[12] 如學者所述，"You cannot decide which facts matter unless you have already selected, at least tentatively, applicable decisional standards." See Mirjan Damaska, Presentation of Evidence and Factfinding Precision, 123 U. Pa. L. Rev. 1083, 1087 (1975).

[13] See William Burnham, supra note 6, 78.

[14] See Penny Darbyshire, supra note 2, 107.

[15] See Roger C. Park, supra note 4, 1.

[16] See John H. Langbein, supra note 7, 1168-9.

精密且複雜證據法則的現象，於非英語系國家的法制中並未曾見[17]。」。持平而論，Thayer 教授對美國證據法的描述直到今日仍具有一定的價值，在相當之程度上，美國的證據法學迄今仍致力於「非證據（non-evidence）」與「不可容許之證據（inadmissible evidence）」間之區分[18]。

在眾多獨立制定一套證據法則的理由中，最重要的原因，其實乃在於對平民陪審團（lay jury）的不信任；舉例而言，傳聞法則的制定主要是因為未受過法學訓練的陪審員（lay jurors）無法適當的評價審判外陳述之證據價值；而對於使用品格證據（character evidence）的限制則是因為陪審團通常賦予其過高的證明力，或陪審團易於據與本案無關的（irrelevant）非行紀錄，形成對被告不適當、不利益的偏見[19]。在一則西元 1816 年著名的 Berkeley Peerage 案例中，英國最高民事訴訟法庭（the Court of Common Pleas）即曾針對傳聞法則提出說明，其謂：「在大陸法系的國家，法官決定事實與法律爭議。由於法官們信賴自己在做出裁判時不會受到傳聞證據的影響，也不會賦予傳聞證據過度的價值，因此他們並不認為接觸傳聞證據會

---

[17] See James Bradley Thayer, A Preliminary Treatise on Evidence at the Common Law, 1-2 (Boston Little Brown, 1898).

[18] 然而大陸法系的法律學者，向來難以理解英美法上獨立發展、制定證據規則的意義與價值。See Thomas P. Gallanis, The Rise of Modern Evidence Law, 84 Iowa L. Rev. 499, 500 (1999).

[19] See Christopher B. Mueller, et al., Evidence Under the Rules, 1 (New York Aspen Law & Business, 2000).

有何種危險。但是在英國,由於僅有陪審團是事實的裁判者,且因爲沒有人知道究竟傳聞法則會對普通陪審員產生何種影響,故將傳聞證據排除便是一種適當的做法[20]。」。

與美國憲法第 6 增修條文中的其他權利不同,對質條款(the Confrontation Clause)的增訂理由是不清楚的[21]。一般來說,對質條款賦予被告於證人作證時「在場(to be present)」與「詰問(to cross-examine)」之權利[22]。不過,就其文義而言,該增修條文並未明確地說明對質條款與傳聞法則間存在何種關聯[23]。此外,早期的立憲文件除未說明何以被告有權與證人對質外,更未說明對質一詞語出何處[24]。鑒於立憲者只花了五分鐘在形式上討論美國憲法第六增修條文中的對質條款,事實上並不可能自法律史之角度對此條款從事立法意旨的探尋[25]。不過,傳誦超過幾個世紀的瓦特瑞雷(Sir Walter Raleigh)乙案[26],或可作爲何以美國的權利法案會條列對質條款於其中,

[20] See John H. Langbein, supra note 7, 1169-70.
[21] See Randolph N. Jonakait, The Origins of the Confrontation Clause: An Alternative History, 27 Rutgers L. J. 77, 77 (1995).
[22] See Christopher B. Mueller, supra note 19, 423.
[23] See Roger C. Park, supra note 4, 368.
[24] See Murl A. Larkin, The Right of Confrontation: What Next? 1 Tex. Tech. L. Rev. 67, 67 (1969).
[25] See Howard W. Gutman, Academic Determinism: The Division of the Bill of Rights, 54 S. Cal. L. Rev. 295, 332 (1981).
[26] See 399 U.S. 149, 156-7, n. 10 (1970).

並限制傳聞證據適用之說明[27]。

　　曾任美國聯邦最高法院首席大法官之馬歇爾，曾於西元1913 年的米馬訴黑本（Mima Queen and Child v. Hepburn）乙案中，針對傳聞法則提出以下的說明：「所有關於證據法的問題對人民的生命、自由與財產而言，是非常重要的。證據法是祖先們智慧的累積；其中傳聞證據本質上不具證據能力，便是前述證據法長期發展下的一個例證。縱然傳聞證據概念本身即假定有較其更佳的非傳聞證言存在，不過該假定本身並非傳聞證據應予排除的主要原因。相對地，傳聞證據本身的缺陷、其無法使人確信所指述之事實為真之本質與其所具掩飾虛偽陳述之可能性等，聯合起來才是傳聞證言不具證據能力之原因[28]。」。在西克力訴美國（Hickory v. United States）乙案中，美國聯邦最高法院亦承認：「傳聞證言是指非陳述者於審判中以口頭或書面提出，以證實所述事項為真正為目的之審判外陳述[29]。」。結果，事實認定者於審判中並不會接觸到被歸類為傳聞證言之審判外陳述[30]。在 20 世紀初期，美國

---

[27]　See Kenneth J. Graham, The Right to Confrontation and the Hearsay Rule: Sir Walter Raleigh Loses Another One, 8 Crim. L. Bull. 99, 100 (1972); see also Graham C. Lilly, Notes on the Confrontation Clause and Ohio v. Roberts, 36 U. Fla. L. Rev. 207, 209 (1984).關於本案之中文文獻，參閱王兆鵬，對質詰問權與強制取證權，收錄於氏著，刑事被告的憲法權利，頁146，翰蘆圖書出版有限公司，1999 年 3 月。

[28]　See 11 U.S. 290, 295-6 (1813).

[29]　See 151 U.S. 303, 309 (1894).

[30]　See Michael H. Graham, "Stickperson Hearsay": A Simplified Approach to Understanding the Rule Against Hearsay, 1982 U. of Ill. L. Rev. 887, 888 (1982).

聯邦最高法院曾在馬踏斯訴美國（Mattox v. United States）乙案中，首次將對質條款適用於聯邦與州的刑事案件中[31]。而美國聯邦最高法院除在加州訴格林（California v. Green）乙案中，承認：「對質條款與傳聞法則二者均在保護類似的價值[32]。」外，更在達騰訴伊凡斯（Dutton v. Evans）乙案中，宣示：「對質條款與傳聞法則二者乃出於同源。」[33]。通常來說，每當美國聯邦最高法院對對質條款改採不同的解釋途徑時，傳聞證據的證據容許性便會改變。如同寇伊訴愛荷華（Coy v. Iowa）所述：「跟隨褪色的羊皮卷來到我們社會的對質權，其存在可追溯至西方文明的濫觴初始[34]。」。本質上，對質權的中心價值乃在要求指控犯罪的證人必須出庭與被告面對面接觸[35]。自從對質條款賦予刑事被告憲法上與指控證人對質之權利後，學者間莫不爭相分析最高法院就對質條款所闡述之法理[36]。同時，傳聞例外在說理上亦須與對質條款不相牴觸才被承認。客觀地說，若欲對於傳聞例外的法理有所理解，則必須對於英美證據法則的發展歷史有詳細的認識[37]。

---

[31]　See 156 U.S. 237 (1895). 此外，科比訴美國（Kirby v. United States）乙案亦同。 See 174 U.S. 47 (1899).

[32]　See 399 U.S. 149, 155 (1970).

[33]　See 400 U.S. 74, 86 (1970).

[34]　See 487 U.S. 1012, 1015 (1988).

[35]　See Frank R. Herrmann, et al., Facing the Accuser: Ancient and Medieval Precursors of the Confrontation Clause, 34 Va. J. Int' l L. 481, 543 (1994).

[36]　See Roger C. Park, supra note 4, 368.

[37]　See John C. Klotter, supra note 1, 1.

參、中世紀之發展

一、帶有控訴主義色彩的羅馬法

　　縱然在羅馬法時代，刑求被告與證人是一個普遍的現象，不過其時所採的刑事訴訟程序，本質上是建立在控訴模式之上的[38]。與伊利諾訴愛倫（Illinois v. Allen）乙案[39]相類似，在當時，被告已有權利於不利他的程序中在場。從西賽羅（Cicero）的佛林演說（Verrine Orations）中亦可知，羅馬法已要求控訴者到場提出其對被告的控訴與相關的證據，藉以保障被告與指控者接觸之機會。當代對質權的二大要素：被告於審判中到庭與被告與指控者接觸，似已在羅馬時代的刑事訴訟程序中佔有一席之地[40]。

　　隨著羅馬法的發展，同時肩負著事實發現與法律適用職責的法官，建立了一套蒐集證據與判斷證據容許性之規則[41]。制定於西元 534 年的查士丁尼法典（the Emperor Justinian's Code）除集過去的羅馬法於大全外，更將之實證法化[42]。從早期開始，教會一直擔負著處理信徒間之糾紛與懲戒神職人員之

---

[38]　關於羅馬法時代證據規則之說明，see C. A. Morrison, Some Features of the Roman and the English Law of Evidence, 33 Tul. L. Rev. 577, 579-81 (1959).

[39]　See 397 U.S. 337, 338 (1970).

[40]　See Frank R. Herrmann, supra note 35, 485-90.

[41]　See John C. Klotter, supra note 1, 6.

[42]　See Frank R. Herrmann, supra note 35, 493.

責任[43]。而早在基督教成爲羅馬帝國之國教前，教會即已承認將指控者與被指控者雙方，於審判程序中集合在一起是世俗法院（the secular courts）達成正義的必要條件。當盛行於世俗法院的控訴程序，於第 4 世紀開始以法律的形式支配教會的懲戒程序，向教會對神職人員提出的刑事不法指控與其隨之而來的審判程序也開始以前述之控訴程序爲範本。當其後所發展出包含查士丁尼敕令九十（Justinian's Novel 90）在內的寺院法亦肯認「未到庭者不遭不利認定」之原則，教宗貴格一世（Pope Gregory I）更要求所屬之神職人員必須賦予被告在法庭上享有與指控者接觸的機會，否則任何有罪判決均可能因違反此項準則而被認定爲無效；從而，被告得主張與反對證人接觸的權利亦獲確保。雖然關於控訴程序之形成是否完全建立在教宗貴格一世的前述準則之上存有爭執，不過，在法庭上賦予被告有與指控者接觸的機會乙事，卻因此被視爲被告本身的基本權利[44]。

隨著羅馬帝國的衰亡，世俗法中已不存在類似舊羅馬法審判程序的法律規範，來處理社會中的刑事控訴；日耳曼式的考驗判罪法（ordeal）、宣誓（oath）與爭鬥（battle）反而逐漸成爲歐洲大陸處理刑事控訴的正常機制。隨著時間的經過，以控訴模式爲內涵的羅馬法刑事訴訟程序早已被人所淡忘，不過，

---

43 See Stephen W. Findlay, Canonical Norms Governing the Deposition and Degradation of Clerics, 5 (Catholic University of America Canon Law Studies No. 130, 1941).

44 See Frank R. Herrmann, supra note 35, 496-500.

教會卻因仍沿襲羅馬法的訴訟傳統（如要求證人到庭作證），而成為保存傳統羅馬刑事程序於後世的唯一機構。在第 9 世紀中葉，（經查證被偽造的）伊瑟多教令（the pseudoisidorean forgeries）即主張：「要求控訴證人到庭指控」乙事，乃是被告防禦的基石。不過，由於羅馬帝國滅亡後並無實證法對此作相關規範，前述對被指控者之程序保障一開始只適用於神職人員的懲戒程序[45]。

　　為了建立一套可以同時適用於教會與世俗的刑事程序規則，格拉第教令（the Decretum of Gratian）調和了教會法與羅馬法的刑事訴訟程序[46]。隨著時代之推移，最後世俗法院的刑事訴訟程序也轉變如格拉第教令所指示般，與教會法及羅馬法極為類似；舉例而言，在一本關於中世紀羅馬程序法早期發展的論文集「書馬歐林（the Summa Olim）（1177/90）」中，作者即因被告有權要求控訴證人到場宣誓其所言為真，而禁止傳聞證言於刑事法庭之適用。不過，前述兩造主義與控訴模式的刑事程序，在 13 世紀卻因糾問制度與秘密詢問證人等審理方法的採用，而告終止。基本上，誠如「面對控訴者：對質條款於中世紀前之預兆（"Facing the Accuser: Ancient and Medieval Precursors of the Confrontation Clause"）」一書所述，對質條

---

[45]　Id., at 500-9.

[46]　See Charles Donahue, Jr., Ius Commune, Canon Law, and Common Law in England, 66 Tul. L. Rev. 1745, 1746-9 (1992).

款實際上乃源自於羅馬法的刑事訴訟程序[47]。

二、羅馬法之背離

雖然羅馬法早已保障刑事被告有要求指控者到庭與被告接觸的權利，令人不解的是，何以在 12 世紀末期，世俗法院與教會法院最終均允許法官在被告不在場的情況中秘密詢問證人[48]。為了取代上述羅馬法的控訴原則，歐洲大陸的國家如法國、義大利與德國，紛紛採行一套允許法官在不受任何限制的前提下，單獨接觸與評價證據的訴訟法則[49]。在此種新構思的程序下，兩造當事人只能以口頭或書面向法官提出問題，並請求法官詢問證人；不過，值得注意的是，法官的發問權並不受當事人請求之限制，法官仍可自行依職權提出任何問題以探尋實體真實。雖然此種糾問程序明顯地與前述查士丁尼敕令九十相互牴觸，中世紀的法學家卻主張，前述查士丁尼敕令九十只要求當事人有機會在不利其陳述於法庭作成時在場。某種程度來說，與反方（控訴）證人接觸並親見其宣誓，對被告確認該證人是否適格而言，具有重要的意義；因為，此一對質權之行使是被告唯一有機會防止審判者僅基於偏見或不實證言做出

---

[47] See Frank R. Herrmann, supra note 35, 514-5.

[48] Id., at 517-8.

[49] See John C. Klotter, supra note 1, 6.

裁判的程序階段[50]。

　　由於格拉第教令所規範之控訴模式刑事訴訟程序在操作上太過於麻煩，太過保護被告的權利，並太過於仰賴個別控訴者發起以處罰被告為目的的刑事訴訟程序，教宗英諾森三世（Pope Innocent III）遂倡導一種與之迥異、並賦予法官主動調查所有犯罪相關證據權限的刑事程序，亦即糾問模式的刑事訴訟程序[51]。基本上，本諸羅馬法與教會法的兩造控訴程序已不合時宜的認知，不論是國家或教會，在 13 世紀均主張以糾問式的程序進行犯罪偵防[52]；只不過這樣的說法似乎忽略了程序法本身亦應包含公共利益的考量在內[53]。

　　伴隨糾問程序的實施與普遍，許多刑求的方法也逐漸被採用。自從中世紀起，因歐陸法系逐漸視被告自白本身在刑事程序中為「證據女王」，允許國家以刑求的方式取供即不難想見[54]。不過，在巴特勒斯主張：「使用未經被告對質而取得之證言有損被告利益」後，合法之刑求必先滿足「已提出一

---

[50]　See Frank R. Herrmann, supra note 35, 516-21. For example, Novel 90's chapter 9 provided: "all parties have a right to be present when a witness gives testimony against them."

[51]　本質上，'inquisitio' 這個拉丁文即含有審判者得依職權調查蒐集犯罪證據與發現犯罪者的意義在內。 Id., at 523.

[52]　See Richard M. Fraher, The Theoretical Justification for the New Criminal Law of the High Middle Ages: Rei Publicae Interest, Ne Crimina Remaneant Impunita, 1984 U. Ill. L. Rev. 577, 581 (1984).

[53]　See 309 U.S. 227, 237-8 (1940).

[54]　See Frank R. Herrmann, supra note 35, 530.

定數量顯示被告有罪的證據」此一要件[55]；例如：已提出之有罪證據包含證人的陳述，則該證人必須接受第二次傳喚，且於被告面前宣誓後陳述對被告的指控[56]。雖然在特別的宗教異議糾問程序中，證人必須在被告面前指控犯罪此一概念已被普遍接受[57]，不過在 13 世紀中，卻因宗教異議案件普遍被認為是十分嚴重的犯罪，為避免被告知悉證人的身分以保護證人的安全，該原則卻出現例外，並且，此一例外迅速地蠶食了前述證人必須在被告面前指控犯罪的原則規定。結果，為取得被告的自白，原用以處理宗教異議案件的糾問程序，不但導致被告必須在不知指控者為何人的情形中，接受冗長的秘密訊問程序；而此種剝奪被告與證人對質機會的做法，也漸成為糾問模式下的常態[58]。

三、兩造主義與控訴模式之再現

上述以糾問模式為核心之刑事訴訟程序，一直普遍被採用。直到 16 世紀中葉，除了宗教異議案件外，歐洲大陸的刑事

---

[55] See Walter Ullmann, Reflections on Medieval Torture, 56 Jurid. Rev. 123, 125-8 (1944). For an excellent short summary of the law of torture, see John H. Langbein, Torture and the Law of Proof: Europe and England in the Ancien Regime, 12-6 (Uni. of Chicago Press, 1977).

[56] See Frank R. Herrmann, supra note 35, 534.

[57] See Henry C. Lea, A History of the Inquisition of the Middle Ages, 437 (New York, Harper & Bros, 1888).

[58] See Frank R. Herrmann, supra note 35, 535-7.

訴訟程序已普遍接受被告有權與反對證人在法庭上面對面接觸；不過，當時被告並無權對證人交互詰問，亦無權主張親自在場聽取證人之陳述。或許如已故的約翰亨力韋格摩教授（Professor John Henry Wigmore）所述：交互詰問是發現真實最有效的工具；不過，因 16 世紀之前所肯認「被告與反對證人在法庭上面對面接觸之權利所具之識別作用」並非不可取代[59]，如不從人類易於他人背後說壞話的人性的角度出發，似無法詮釋何以必須要求證人必須現實地出現在被告之面前[60]。持平而論，前述要求證人必須現實地出現在被告之面前之原則，可謂根源於羅馬法與教會法之規定，並已有超過千年之歷史[61]。

　　與上述歐陸發展相對，在英國的法制史上，約有三、四百年的期間，陪審團扮演著與現在的陪審團完全不同的功能。一開始，擔任陪審員係以「對於該地區之犯罪與有可能是犯人之居民已有認識」為其要件；事實上，在 16 世紀以前，當陪審團係由已對該案件有私知之人所組成，且陪審員仍有權私下主動諮詢將不出庭指控之證人時，英國的審判制度並不需要傳聞法則來規範控辯雙方之法庭活動[62]。到了 17 世紀末，雖然證人到庭陳述之機制已漸普遍使用，因當時之刑事審判程序僅僅具有

---

[59]　Id., at 543.
[60]　See Coy v. Iowa, 487 U.S 1012, 1020 (1988).
[61]　See P.R. Glazebrook, The Reign of Mary Tudor, 1977 Crim. L. Rev. 582, 585 (1977).
[62]　See John C. Klotter, supra note 1, 280.

簡單之形式，陪審團也只能被動地接觸在法庭上所提出之證據；陪審團通常會在被告同意交付審判後立即對該案件進行審判[63]。然而，隨著陪審制度之發展[64]，一系列規範證據容許性的複雜法則逐漸形成[65]。不過，在都繹王朝時代（the Tudor times），只有少數的證據規則限制證據提出[66]。一但證人於公開法庭作證已成慣例，過去只有陪審員獨占對犯罪事實與對被告人格認識的法理基礎，即被打破；而一但法官有機會與陪審員接觸相同的證據，法官自亦可對證據（包含物證與證人之證言）做出評價，並進一步就如何適用法律對陪審團提出建議。從而，關於法官如何在審判中規範證人證言，即成為一重要之議題；證據法本身，亦因此成為英美法制中重要的課題[67]。隨著陪審團的發展與英國法人權保障傳統之形成，為避免陪審團受到虛偽陳述與無關聯性證據的誤導，一套能指引法官與陪審員的證據法則，遂逐漸形成[68]。

　　由於審判只能基於經驗論而非認識論做出裁決，因此各個

---

[63]　See Stephan Landsman, The Rise of the Contentious Spirit: Adversary Procedure in Eighteenth Century England, 75 Cornell L. Rev. 497, 505 (1990).關於陪審團功能變遷之中文資料，參閱王兆鵬，美國刑事訴訟法，頁 370，元照出版公司，2004 年 9 月。

[64]　See John H. Langbein, supra note 7, 1171.

[65]　See John C. Klotter, supra note 1, 13.

[66]　See Stephan Landsman, supra note 63, 506.

[67]　See John H. Langbein, supra note 7, 1171.

[68]　See John C. Klotter, supra note 1, 7.

社會的文化，亦成為影響如何妥適做出裁決的重要因素[69]。鑒於決定證據容許性之標準一直隨著兩造訴訟模式在英國法制的演變而調整，過去都鐸王朝與史都華王朝在審判上用以決定與證明事實所採用的規則即易因新規則的形成而改變[70]。從歷史的角度來說，因擔心陪審員無法妥適正確評價「未親自於法庭作成之證言」，而選擇排除可能具有高度證明價值證言的傳聞法則，是英國法制對於當代證據法則最重要的貢獻[71]。

肆、對質條款與傳聞法則在近代之發展

一、序論

　　雖然早在西元 1603 年瓦特瑞雷即曾對傳聞證據提出質疑，直到該案發生十多年後，排除傳聞證據才逐漸在英國生根[72]。在 18 世紀間，證據規則的改變更加速了刑事訴訟程序朝兩造模

---

[69] See Charles R. Nesson, et al., Constitutional Hearsay: Requiring Foundamental Testing and Corroboration Under the Confrontation Clause, 81 Va. L. Rev. 149, 151-52 (1995).

[70] See John C. Klotter, supra note 1, 13; John H. Langbein, supra note 7, 1172 and Stephan Landsman, supra note 63, 513.

[71] See John H. Langbein, supra note 7, 1172.

[72] See Jon R. Waltz, et al., Evidence: Cases and Materials, 89 (Foundation Press, 1999).

式之發展[73]。同時，長期累積的司法案例也孕育了證據排除規則，並導致陪審員只能接觸「由法官決定，具有關聯性與真實性」之證據[74]。證據排除規則除了具有「防止陪審團接觸不可靠之證據並受其誤導」[75]外，摩根教授（Professor Edmund M. Morgan）亦曾主張，普通法所採的證據排除途徑，如傳聞法則，係源自於兩造主義訴訟模式強調由當事人雙方提出證據的本質限制[76]。這樣的說法正好說明了被動的事實認定者（陪審團）在傳聞法則的形成過程中，扮演了十分重要的角色；相對地，在此思考下，何以歐陸法系的刑事訴訟程序無法自發地發展出如傳聞法則般複雜的證據規則，也就不難理解了。到了 19 世紀初期，因法官在刑事審判中已對爭議事項無所知悉，控辯雙方遂擔負起詰問證人的主要責任，證人有不自證己罪的特權亦開始被人們所接受[77]。

　　現任教於美國耶魯大學法學院（Yale Law School）的約翰藍濱教授（Professor John H. Langbein）曾指出，現代證據法形成之關鍵，乃在於持續至 18 世紀末期兩造模式刑事訴訟程序的

---

[73] See Stephan Landsman, supra note 63, 513-72. 在我國，亦有基於兩造模式之觀點，理解傳聞法則之論述，參閱林永謀，傳聞證據（上），司法周刊，第1162期，第二版，2004 年 12 月 3 日。

[74] See John C. Klotter, supra note 1, 7.

[75] The dominant view, advanced by Professors Thayer, Wigmore, and Holdsworth, focused on the jury itself. See Thomas P. Gallanis, supra note 18, 501.

[76] See Edmund M. Morgan, Basic Problems of Evidence, 243 (1963).

[77] See John H. Langbein, supra note 7, 1199.

迅速發展[78]。惟在證據法則（特別是傳聞法則）蓬勃發展的 18
世紀中葉，美國憲法增修條文第 6 條尚未制定。究竟制定美國
憲法增修條文第 6 條中對質條款對傳聞法則發展有何影響，自
西元 1791 年開始，向來即為學界爭論不休之重要議題[79]。基本
上，在決定傳聞證言是否具證據容許性前，必須先考慮於審判
中容許該傳聞證言是否會違反對質條款之規定。沿革上，至少
有五種理論，如：抽象理論（the minimalist theory）、產品理
論（the production theory）、可信度理論（the reliability the-
ory）、中心理論（the centrality theory）與程序理論（the procedural theory），可作為說明傳聞證言是否具證據容許性之操
作基礎[80]。從而，在刑事訴訟程序中，即便審判外之陳述已符
合傳聞例外之規定，刑事被告仍可執對質條款挑戰容許該傳聞
證言之合憲性[81]。儘管如此，在採兩造模式與控訴原則的刑事
訴訟程序中，誠如美國聯邦最高法院於方克訴美國（Funk v.
United States）乙案中所述，所有證據規則係以其能否成功地導
出本案真實為基礎，當過去被視為必要的舊證據規則已被證明
存有明顯的謬誤時，新證據規則即應取而代之[82]。因此，證據
規則迄今仍不斷在演變中。

---

[78]　Id., at 1172.

[79]　See Roger C. Park, supra note 4, 368.

[80]　關於各該理論之內涵，see Christopher B. Mueller, supra note 20, 428-9. 中文部
　　　分，參閱王兆鵬，美國刑事訴訟法，頁 380，元照出版公司，2004 年 9 月。

[81]　See Roger C. Park, supra note 4, 367.

[82]　See 290 U.S. 371, 381 (1933).

　　雖然現代證據法之中心目標是在規範陪審程序中真實發現的程序[83]，美國聯邦最高法院卻遲至西元 1895 年才在馬踏斯訴美國乙案中，開始闡述傳聞法則與對質條款之關聯。此外，自西元 1965 年的波伊特訴德州（Pointer v. Texas） 案開始，藉由美國聯邦憲法第 14 增修條文的正當程序條款之解釋，各州亦必須提供刑事被告憲法上對質條款之保障[84]。

二、18 世紀與 19 世紀之傳聞法則

　　一般說來，在 17 世紀與 18 世紀前期，類似目前大陸法系的刑事訴訟程序，審判法官擔負著詢問證人與被告的職責[85]，並支配整個訴訟程序的進行[86]。如基爾福瑞吉爾伯特（Geoffrey Gilbert） 在其名著「證據法（The Law of Evidence）[87]」中所述，一直到 17 世紀末，律師在刑事訴訟程序與法庭活動中幾乎是無足輕重，整個刑事訴訟程序亦非奠基於兩造模式之上[88]。此外，由於交互詰問於當時並非普遍接受的程序，審判活動幾

[83]　See John H. Langbein, supra note 7, 1174.
[84]　See 380 U.S. 400 (1965).
[85]　See Randolph N. Jonakait, supra note 21, 82.
[86]　See John H. Langbein, The Criminal Trial Before the Lawyers, 45 U. Chi. L. Rev. 263, 315 (1978).
[87]　See Thomas P. Gallanis, supra note 18, 505. 基本上，該書本質上是當時實務運作準則之彙編。 See John H. Langbein, supra note 7, 1173.
[88]　See Randolph N. Jonakait, supra note 21, 83.

乎全繫於書面資料之審理上[89]。或許「欠缺其他可靠的資訊來源」或是「原始證人無法到庭作證」等因素，可以作爲法院一直到 18 世紀初期，均普遍允許傳聞證言作爲審判基礎的原因[90]。而律師甚少出現於偵查或審判等刑事程序之現實狀況[91]，亦成爲規範法庭活動之證據法則無法健全發展的重要因素[92]。縱然到了 18 世紀中葉，已初步發展的傳聞排除法則，也因審判法官享有廣泛裁量權而迭遭忽略[93]。在這樣的環境中，法院適用傳聞法則甚爲寬鬆，且關於應如何適用亦不一致，不論是言詞或是書面證據，適用上均少有限制[94]。儘管如此，17 世紀末與 18 世紀初之法學家，似乎已意識到，若不對傳聞證據加以限制，並不洽當[95]。由於允許傳聞證據事實上等同於要求事實認定者相信其陳述之內容爲眞實，受該傳聞不利影響之一方不但無機會詰問該證人，亦無法挑戰該法庭外陳述之可信性[96]。

　　爲了排除未親自到庭作證的供述並要求當事人證明供述的

---

[89]　See Stephan Landsman, supra note 63, 592, 595; see also Thomas P. Gallanis, supra note 18, 505; Geoffrey Gilbert, The Law of Evidence, 112 (Facsimile of the 1754 edition, Garland Publishing Inc., 1979).

[90]　See Thomas P. Gallanis, supra note 18, 514.

[91]　See Randolph N. Jonakait, supra note 21, 94.

[92]　See Stephan Landsman, supra note 63, 533.

[93]　See Thomas P. Gallanis, supra note 18, 503.

[94]　See Stephan Landsman, supra note 63, 565. In other words, the courts treated the whole matter inconsistently, and in most cases permissively. See Thomas P. Gallanis, supra note 18, 514.

[95]　See John H. Langbein, supra note 7, 1187.

[96]　See Stephan Landsman, supra note 63, 566.

可信性，在偶然的機會中，法院自發地（非為回應當事人之異議）發展出傳聞法則[97]。在法院主導發展的傳聞規則下，審判上開始逐漸形成交互詰問規則以供律師詰問到場之證人。隨著交互詰問規則與律師在法庭上提出異議的成長，司法對於審判程序之控制開始減退[98]，一套以當事人雙方進行詢問與詰問為制度核心的新刑事訴訟程序規則乃開始發展。從 18 世紀中葉開始，證據法開始禁止法官引導證人陳述，亦禁止法官告誡證人僅能基於自己本身的知識（非傳聞）陳述，否則律師針對傳聞提出異議的法庭攻防活動即無由出現；傳聞法則在此階段的複雜化亦經常造成律師與法院間，就如何適用傳聞法則出現爭執[99]。此部分的爭執實質上促進了現代證據法的發展。由於禁止傳聞證據之原則乃奠基於兩造模式的訴訟構造[100]，欲踐行愈嚴格的傳聞排除法則，也就只能在愈傾向於兩造模式的訴訟構造中落實了。此外，亦因 18 世紀的法官漸漸體認到使用傳聞證據的風險；一套更加嚴格、以到庭陳述為原則的傳聞法則遂隨

---

[97] Id., at 567.

[98] See Randolph N. Jonakait, supra note 21, 89.

[99] This approach shifted responsibility for the development of the case from the court to the litigants. Over the years, courts gradually grew more circumspect about hearsay. As courts and counsel moved with increasing frequency to bar witnesses from reciting hearsay material, judges and lawyers alike were getting more and more adept at identifying hearsay and keeping it away from the jury. See Stephan Landsman, supra note 63, 534.

[100] See Eleanor Swift, A Foundation Fact Approach to Hearsay, 75 Calif. L. Rev. 1339, 1375-6 (1987).

之漸漸發展，兩造間相互爭論與詰問對方證人的現象，也漸成常態；在刑事訴訟上，法官與律師間越來越嚴格地依傳聞法則進行訴訟程序[101]。結果，禁止傳聞證據便成為 19 世紀以來，現代證據法的主要指標[102]。

　　此外，如約翰比第（John M. Beattie）所述，為避免控方證人為獲取利益而到庭指控[103]，辯方律師在 18 世紀的 80 年代，針對可能心存不良而另有目的的證人，發展出一套嚴格而有效的詰問規則[104]。由於當時著名的學者如湯瑪斯匹柯（Thomas Peake）、威廉大衛依凡斯（William David Evans）與飛利浦（S. M. Phillips）均在其學術論著中對證言多所著墨，口頭證據規則即成為當時最蓬勃發展的證據法領域；18 世紀末與 19 世紀初期即因前述證據規則的蓬勃發展，而被稱為證據法體系發展的「春潮（spring-tide）」；而藉由肯認證據排除係奠基於證據本身之適切性，並區分證據的證明力與可容許性，證據議

---

[101] See Stephan Landsman, supra note 63, 565.

[102] In summary, during the eighteenth century, the growth of the hearsay rule came in three stages: "In the earliest years of the century there was little concern about the use of out-of-court words. By the 1730s, the rudiments of the hearsay rule were established and at least sporadically applied. By the closing decades of the century a more sophisticated rule had been developed and was being applied in a constantly broadening range of cases." See Thomas P. Gallanis, supra note 18, 503.

[103] See John M. Beattie, Scales of Justice: Defense Counsel and the English Criminal Trial in the Eighteenth and Nineteenth Centuries, 9 Law & Hist. Rev. 221, 231, 245 (1991).

[104] See John H. Langbein, supra note 7, 1198.

題在法庭上越來越重要，而刑事訴訟程序也因此變得更傾向於
兩造模式，並高度依賴兩造的舉證與詰問[105]。雖然基爾福瑞吉
爾伯特認為宣誓本身是供述是否具證據力的首要條件，不過，
湯瑪斯匹柯等學者卻不認為證人法庭上之宣誓是審判中供述證
據的核心議題[106]。

　　例如湯瑪斯匹柯於其名著「證據法概要（A Compendium
of the Law of Evidence）」中即曾指出，「證據法未曾因陳
述者階級身分之不同而賦予不同階級者陳述不同證據價值，
證據法只要求證人親自到庭陳述，並接受對造的詢問與交互
詰問」；因此，交互詰問才是供述證據是否具證據能力的前
提[107]。此外，威廉大衛依凡斯亦曾對兩造模式的形式審判程
序，轉變為要求法官只能在審判中被動地接收兩造提出證據乙
事，作出說明[108]。他強調，律師高度的法庭技巧是交互詰問的
核心，而此種兩造模式的審判構造，實係源於羅馬法賦予被告
有權本於己方之認知對控方證人親自詢問的傳統；而飛利浦嗣
後更論證舉凡不自證己罪之特權、禁止檢方誘導訊問與嚴厲對
待敵方證人的傳統，均係建立在嚴格的交互詰問規則之上[109]。

---

[105] See Stephan Landsman, supra note 63, 597.

[106] See Thomas P. Gallanis, supra note 18, 509 and Stephan Landsman, supra note 63, 598.

[107] See Thomas Peake, A Compendium of the Law of Evidence, 7-8 (Facsimile of the 1801 edition, Garland Publishing Inc., 1979).

[108] See John H. Langbein, supra note 7, 1200.

[109] See Stephan Landsman, supra note 63, 599.

早在 19 世紀初期，當學者間已開始主張「刑事審判程序在本質上是一場兩造間嚴厲的爭鬥過程」時，交互詰問規則便漸被視爲英美刑事審判程序的核心。直到 19 世紀初期，法官原擁有的廣泛裁量權已大部分被嚴格的證據排除規則所取代；這些經歷重大改變的發展，使得 19 世紀初期的證據規則，已具現代證據規則的雛形[110]。總體說來，當中立而被動的事實認定者被視爲自由權利的最後防線，證據法則的發展變成爲限制司法官僚控制兩造模式刑事訴訟程序的重要手段；交互詰問制度最終取代了糾問模式的審理結構[111]。

上述重視口頭證據的發展，亦可於湯瑪斯史泰機教授（Professor Thomas Starkie）的大著「證據法實務選集（A Practical Treatise of the Law of Evidence）」得到印證；據約翰亨力韋格摩教授所述，由於基爾福瑞吉爾伯特的著作自 18 世紀末起已漸失影響力，到了 1824 年，證據法的體系已漸完備，言詞證據法則也已發展達到與書面證據法則相當的水準。由於史泰機認爲口頭證據比書面證據更爲可靠，他不僅致力於傳聞法則的推廣，也補述了許多基爾福瑞吉爾伯特未予說明的議題[112]。證人有自證己罪之疑慮時，得免除作證義務的原則也在此時建立[113]。

---

[110] See Thomas P. Gallanis, supra note 18, 503.

[111] In fact, the too active judge, like Buller in Rex v. Shipley, 21 St. Tr. 847 (1783-4), was subjected to the sharpest criticism. See Stephan Landsman, supra note 63, 604.

[112] See Thomas P. Gallanis, supra note 18, 516, 523.

[113] See Bent v. Baker, 3 T.R. 27, 100 Eng. Rep. 437 (K.B. 1789).

審判法官亦開始被要求於特定個案中，決定證人是否將因到庭陳述而於事後遭到訴追[114]。縱然書面證據本身與證人適格仍然是重要的議題，從 19 世紀的 20 年代開始，口頭證據的證據容許性亦開始成為法庭活動中的重要議題[115]；此部分也可以從 1755 年至 1824 年間的法庭紀錄得到印證[116]。

　　隨著傳聞禁止原則的發展，證人陳述須受到越來越多的限制；如果證人欲提出傳聞陳述，該傳聞必須符合傳聞例外之規定才具證據適格；傳聞陳述的證據適格性也因此成為法庭爭議的重心[117]。誠如約翰藍賓教授所述：「以證人審判中口頭陳述為核心議題的現代證據法，已取代了盛行於 18、19 世紀之交的舊法。現代證據法已放棄將書面證據視為最佳證據的想法，交互詰問除已取代宣誓而成為接受口頭證據的最主要真實性擔保機制，亦已取代其他標準而成為是否允許傳聞例外的思考基礎。從中世紀開始，將英美法制活潑化的證據法則主要建立在避免陪審審判的缺陷之上。由於法律允許未接受過法律訓練的普通陪審員不附理由與不負任何後續責任地作出裁決，本質上陪審員之裁決無從事後審查，且充滿無法避免的誤判風險。從中世紀開始，雖然證據法本身即隨著陪審模式的演變而轉變，不過，證據法肩負矯正陪審制度本質上缺陷此一主要任務，卻

---

[114] See Evans v. Yeatherd, 2 Bing. 133, 130 Eng. Rep. 256 (K.B. 1824).

[115] See Thomas P. Gallanis, supra note 18, 524.

[116] See John H. Langbein, supra note 7, 1188.

[117] See Thomas P. Gallanis, supra note 18, 529.

是古今一貫地未曾改變[118]。」。

三、美國憲法第六修正案在馬踏斯案作成前之實踐

　　由於 19 世紀前的英國普通法並不保障所有的刑事被告均有接受律師協助之權利，賦予被告接受律師協助權利的美國憲法第六修正案，即非將當時英國法制入憲的一個規定[119]。姑不論接受律師協助權的起源為何，如阿希爾瑞德阿瑪教授（Professor Akhil Reed Amar）所述，權利法案「並非創造了新權利，事實上它係確認了自然法上已存在的權利。」[120]。因此，制憲者對聯邦法官所設的憲法上制約[121]，某種程度上源自將殖民時期的刑事訴訟程序合憲化的企圖。結果，不但對質程序成為被告挑戰其指控者的程序擔保，辯方主導的交互詰問亦成為被告挑戰前述指控的主要程序；對質權也成為擔保被告在新形成的兩造模式中，有機會對證人交互詰問的依據[122]。

　　如前所述，在 19 世紀末前，美國聯邦司法實務上並沒有一個以對質條款為主要論述核心的判決。不過，自西元 1791 年權

---

[118] See John H. Langbein, supra note 7, 1194.

[119] See Randolph N. Jonakait, supra note 21, 109.

[120] See Akhil Reed Amar, The Bill of Rights and the Fourteenth Amendment, 101 YALE L. J. 1193, 1206 (1992).

[121] See Akhil Reed Amar, Fourth Amendment Principles, 107 HARV. L. REV. 757, 773 (1994).

[122] See Randolph N. Jonakait, supra note 21, 113.

利法案通過開始，亦有少數判決針對對質條款作出間接的說明。舉例而言，在西元 1807 年，首席大法官馬歇爾（Chief Justice Marshall）在美國訴布爾（United States v. Burr）乙案中即曾主張，對質條款主要在限制傳聞證言的適用[123]；不過該判決卻未說明何以須在審判中限制傳聞證言。然而在立國初期，部分州最高法院的判決已指出，對質條款係以保障被告在審判中有機會交互詰問證人為其法理基礎，蓋交互詰問本身即是對質條款的核心價值[124]。在州訴韋伯（State v. Webb）乙案中，北卡羅來納州最高法院即主張：「沒有人應受到其無機會進行交互詰問之證言之不利影響，是一項自普通法時代已存在，本諸自然正義的法則。」[125]；在州訴阿特基斯（State v. Atkins）乙案中，田納西州的最高法院亦主張：「允許傳聞證據將會危害自由[126]。」縱使北卡羅來納州與田納西州的對質條款在文字上有所出入，依照其法院之判決[127]，二者對於對質條款的理解卻相同[128]。此外，在州訴坎陪爾（State v. Campbell）乙案中，南卡羅來納法院在公平法院的考量下，排除了已逝證人在被告未到場時，驗屍官詢問下之證言，該判決指出：「證人須於裁判前接受被告的對質與詰問是一則不可省略的正當法律程

---

[123] See 25 F. Cas. 187, 193 (1807).

[124] See Randolph N. Jonakait, supra note 21, 122.

[125] See 2 N. C. (1 Hayw.) 77, 77 (1794).

[126] See 1 Tenn. (1 Overt.) 229, 229 (1807).

[127] See 10 Tenn. (2 Yer.) 58, 59-60 (1821).

[128] See Randolph N. Jonakait, supra note 21, 123.

序。只有交互詰問程序才能揪出騙子、暴露錯誤並避免錯誤不當的聯想[129]。」。簡言之，在馬踏斯案作成前，美國對質條款的發展幾乎只停留在州的層次，並以交互詰問為其核心。如藍道夫強納凱教授（Professor Randolph N. Jonakait）之說明：「對質條款與其他第六修正案的規定，實質上係將已在各州行之有年的程序入憲化。這些程序有效地保障了被告的利益。辯方的交互詰問便是核心。為了確定聯邦法院的審判程序落實前述對被告的保障，美國憲法第六修正案之對質條款，實已將辯方的交互詰問權包含在內[130]。」。

四、在對質條款下所發展之傳聞法則

在美國聯邦最高法院開始審查對質條款之後，傳聞證言的證據容許性，便成為爭議的焦點。某種程度來說，對質權[131]與傳聞法則[132]二者均以事實認定為核心。在西元 1965 年之前，由於最高法院在庫勒維其訴美國（Krulewitch v. United States）乙案中認為，該院對於下級聯邦法院的監督權，允許該院決定傳聞證據之證據能力；對質權與傳聞法則間的區分並不引人注

---

[129] See 30 S.C.L. (1 Rich 124, 125) 51-2 (1844).

[130] See Randolph N. Jonakait, supra note 21, 124.

[131] In Ohio v. Roberts, the Court held that the purpose of the Confrontation Clause is to augment accuracy in the fact-finding process. See 448 U.S. 56, 65 (1980).

[132] See G. Michael Fenner, supra note 10, 4.

意 [133]。此外，以對質條款為基礎，該院在模特斯訴美國（Motes v. United States）乙案中，主張：如可歸責於控方之原因，導致證人無法於審判中出庭作證，則在預審程序（preliminary hearing）所取得的證述，因不屬傳聞法則的例外，故不具證據能力 [134]。美國聯邦最高法院除在馬踏斯訴美國案中，已肯認他案審判中之證述，於證人已死亡時具證據能力 [135] 外，亦在科比訴美國案中，肯認瀕死陳述（dying declarations）之證據能力 [136]。雖然美國聯邦最高法院似乎已將對質條款與傳聞法則等價齊觀 [137]，不過，實質上二者之本質並非相同。

美國聯邦最高法院曾在巴伯訴佩基（Barber v. Page）乙案中指出，包含對重要證人交互詰問之對質權是一項審判上之權利，只允許辯方在預審階段對重要證人交互詰問將違反對質條

---

[133] See 366 U.S. 440 (1949); see also FindLaw, Confrontation, available at http://caselaw.lp.findlaw.com/data/constitution/amendment06/08.html (last visited, Oct. 20, 2004). In addition, the Court in Delaney v. United States concluded that the co-conspirator exception to the hearsay rule was consistent with the Confrontation Clause. See 263 U.S. 586, 590 (1924).

[134] See 178 U.S. 458 (1900). However, if a witness' absence had been procured by the defendant, testimony given at a previous trial on a different indictment could be used at the subsequent trial. See Reynolds v. United States, 98 U.S. 145 (1879).

[135] See 156 U.S. 237, 240 (1895).

[136] The prosecution was not permitted to use a judgment of conviction against other defendants on charges of theft in order to prove that the property found in the possession of defendant now on trial was stolen. See 174 U.S. 47, 61 (1899).

[137] See FindLaw, Confrontation, available at http://caselaw.lp.findlaw.com/data/constitution/amendment06/08.html (last visited, Oct. 20, 2004).

款[138]。因此，對質權對被告所提供的保障較之傳聞法則為廣。除了發現真實之外，提供被告挑戰不利證據機會之對質權，更包含程序正義的要素在內[139]。舉例而言，美國聯邦最高法院在加州訴格林（California v. Green）乙案中即指出：「雖然對質條款與傳聞法則一般被視為以保護相似的價值為目的，但若主張二者之內涵完全重疊，且對質條款只不過是將普通法上傳聞法則之發展條文化的規定，即不甚洽當。非但本院未曾作出類此之見解，相對地，本院反而曾認為將符合傳聞例外之審判外陳述作為裁判之基礎，仍有可能違反對質條款之規定。在肯認對質條款與傳聞法則二者所保護者為相似的價值的前提下，如州證據法創造了其他的傳聞例外，該規定本身往往將引發是否違反對質條款之爭議[140]。」因此，只要是證人可能到庭作證，不論其先前陳述已具高度之可信性，該證人都必須到庭接受被告方的交互詰問。

　　然而，在斯耐得訴麻州（Snyder v. Massachusetts）[141]乙案承認被告有權在公平審判中為自己辯護的判決基礎上，美國聯邦最高法院在達騰訴美國[142]乙案中，似乎放棄了前述加州訴格林的嚴格標準；該判決指出：「對質條款之主要任務，乃在促

---

[138] See 390 U.S. 719, 725-26 (1968).

[139] See Note, Confrontation, Cross-Examination, and the Right to Prepare a Defense, 56 Geo. L. J. 939, 940 (1968).

[140] See 399 U.S. 149, 155-6 (1970).

[141] See 291 U.S. 97, 121-2 (1934).

[142] See 400 U.S. 74, 76 (1970).

進刑事訴訟實務上之真實發現，以擔保事實認定者有充分堅實的基礎，評估審判外陳述之真實性[143]。」。換言之，只要具備「證人宣誓後在陪審團前作證」與「被告有機會交互詰問」等對質條款之二大要素，因事實認定者此時可藉由交互詰問等機制評估傳聞證言的真實性，該審判外陳述即具有證據能力[144]。

在達騰訴美國案作成十年後，美國聯邦最高法院在俄亥俄訴羅伯特斯（Ohio v. Roberts）乙案中，建立了一套用來決定採用審判外陳述是否違反對質條款的雙階測驗（two-pronged test），該判決指出：「對質條款在兩個層次限制了傳聞證言之證據能力。首先，為符合立憲者傾向於採用面對面之指控模式，憲法第六修正案建立了必要性原則。即便在交互詰問已於審判前實施的情形中，控訴方仍必須證明證人無法到庭。其次，在證人無法到庭的情形中，為求發現真實並給予被告抗辯之機會，對質條款只允許具有值得信賴標誌的傳聞證言。簡單來說，當證人無法出庭作證時，對質條款要求確認證人是否真無法出庭。即便該證人確實無法出庭，傳聞證言亦只在具備真實性指標的前提下，才具有證據能力。一般來說，只要符合證據法中根深蒂固的傳聞例外，即可認為已具真實性指標。而若所舉之傳聞非屬證據法中根深蒂固的傳聞例外，如不具其他真

---

[143] See 400 U.S. 74, 89 (1970).

[144] See FindLaw, Confrontation, available at http://caselaw.lp.findlaw.com/data/constitution/amendment06/08.html (last visited, Aug. 20, 2005).

實性擔保，即應予已排除[145]。」。簡言之，在羅伯特斯案的說明下，對質條款並不必然排除證人審判外陳述之證據能力；在符合證據法中根深蒂固的傳聞例外或具有其他特別的可信性擔保之前提下，證人審判外陳述即具證據能力。

　　然而在聯邦證據法第 803 條傳聞例外的規定中，並未要求所有之傳聞例外均需符合證人無法到庭作證的要求，因此羅伯特斯案所建立之第一要件（證人無法到庭）是否與聯邦證據法第 803 條傳聞例外的規定相互衝突，即可能出現爭議。事實上，聯邦最高法院在羅伯特斯案之注釋中，即曾引用達騰案，對此一爭議提出說明，其認為被告不能到庭之事由，並非絕對不能免除之要件；只要交互詰問不具實際的功效，被告是否到庭作證即非關鍵[146]。既然檢方不必在所有的案件中提出證人不能到庭的說明，羅伯特案中所建立的雙階測驗，或許只能被稱為單階測驗；只要符合可信性要件，證人審判外陳述即具備證據能力。

　　由於在證人有可能出庭作證的情形中，前述羅伯特斯案仍留下了「在什麼情況下，檢方應證明證人無法到庭作證」之疑問，因此美國聯邦最高法院在美國訴依納迪（United States v. Inadi）乙案中，即針對此一疑問作出說明。雖然依納迪案肯定了羅伯特案關於對質條款並不要求所有的證人均必須到庭陳述

---

[145] See 448 U.S. 56, 65-6 (1980).

[146] Id., at 65, note 7.

的主張[147]，由於該案中共犯審判外之陳述是焦點，因此美國聯邦最高法院遂主張，只有審判外之陳述是在先前之司法程序中作成，該審判外之陳述才符合必要性要件[148]；也就是說，不符合聯邦證據法第803條傳聞例外且非在先前之司法程序中作成之審判外陳述，並不須討論其是否符合可信性要件，該審判外陳述不具有證據能力；此判決強調「共犯之證言在前司法程序中作成」，是欲免除證人到庭陳述（羅伯特案中必要性原則）而使審判外陳述具證據能力的前提。其後，審判外陳述「在前司法程序中作成」即成為免除證人到庭陳述之要件，依納迪案事實上即限縮了羅伯特案之適用。

在羅伯特案之基礎上，美國聯邦最高法院在寇依訴愛荷華（Coy v. Iowa）乙案中指出，係爭制定於西元1985年，允許未成年被害人在審判中單向指控被告之愛荷華州法律，並不能被視為根深蒂固的傳聞例外，並宣告該法律違憲[149]。不過二年後，在馬里蘭訴客來格（Maryland v. Craig）乙案中，同院卻認為該州一項允許性侵害未成年被害人利用電視單向指控性侵害被告，以避免該被害人在審判中與被告面對面接觸的法律合憲[150]。雖然寇伊案對於對質條款之解釋係建立在「保護被告在

---

[147] See 475 U.S. 387, 394-6 (1985).

[148] See FindLaw, Confrontation, available at http://caselaw.lp.findlaw.com/data/constitution/amendment06/08.html (last visited, Oct. 20, 2004).

[149] See 487 U.S. 1012, 1021 (1988).

[150] See 497 U.S. 836 (1990).

審判中與其指控者（證人）對質」的基礎上[151]，客來格案卻認
為審判外之證言可在未賦予被告與證人面對面機會的情形中，
具證據能力[152]。從而，縱然判決先例已表示出：制憲者較支持
證人得與被告面對面對質之審判模式[153]，制憲者此部分之傾向
有時亦須在公共政策與必要性的考量下讓步[154]。如美國聯邦最
高法院在寇依案中所言：「被告與控訴證人面對面對質之權
利，只有在促進重要的公共政策或具其他真實性擔保的前提
下，才可以被省略[155]。」易言之，憲法第六修正案中之對質
（confronted）並不單純僅指面對面之對質，否則對質條款將禁
止所有審判外之陳述[156]。

　　在寇伊案作成十多年後，美國聯邦最高法院在克勞佛訴華
盛頓（Crawford v. Washington）乙案中，再次針對對質條款注
入活血[157]。該案被美國實務界與學界視為對質條款發展過程
中，一則具革命性意義與震撼效果的判決[158]。如前所述，雖然
羅伯特斯案與依納迪案已建立起一套判斷審判外陳述是否違反

---

[151] See 487 U.S. 1012, 1021 (1988).

[152] See 497 U.S. 836, 849 (1990).

[153] See Ohio v. Roberts, 448 U.S. 56, 63 (1980).

[154] See Mattox v. United States, 156 U.S. 237, 243 (1895).

[155] See 497 U.S. 836, 850 (1990).

[156] Id., at 849.

[157] See 124 S. Ct. 1354 (2004).

[158] See People v. Cage, 15 Cal. Rptr. 3d 846, 851 (Cal. Ct. App. 2004); United
States v. Manfre, 368 F. 3d 832, 833 (8th Cir. 2004); Also see Neil P. Cohen, et
al., Crawford v. Washington: Confrontation Revolution, 40 Tenn. B. J. 22 (2004).

對質條款之雙階標準；不過，在理解對質條款「並不要求所有的證據均為可信的，卻強調可信性須經由交互詰問此一特定的方式或得確認[159]。」後，克勞佛案廢棄了羅伯特斯案與依納迪案所建立之判斷標準，並重新打造了傳聞證據的容許性標準。依據克勞佛案所新建立之容許性標準，傳聞證據可區分為二大類型：證明性（testimonial）傳聞與非證明性（non-testimonial）傳聞；在非證明性傳聞之類型中，制憲者原即提供各州較為彈性之證據法發展空間，就如同羅伯特斯案亦肯認「未基於對質條款賦予被告對審判外陳述者進行交互詰問之證言」具證據能力；而在證明性傳聞的類型中，如同普通法之傳統，憲法第六修正案亦要求證人無法到庭陳述與交互詰問之機會為傳聞證據具證據能力之前提要件[160]。換言之，在證明性傳聞之類型中，克勞佛已取代羅伯特斯，成為判斷該傳聞是否具備證據能力之標準。

此外，克勞佛案亦補充了依納迪案之觀點，其認為：縱然審判外之陳述是在先前之司法程序中作成，如果被告在該司法程序中無「機會」對證人進行交互詰問，該審判外陳述亦無證據能力。從而，如果在先前司法程序中所作成之陳述，未經被

---

[159] See 124 S Ct., at 1370.

[160] Id. 亦有將 testimonial statement 譯為口供式供述證據，而將 non-testimonial statement 譯為非口供式供述證據，參閱吳巡龍，對質詰問權合憲限制與違憲限制的分際－評最高法院94年台上字第812號判決，月旦法學，第71期，頁257，2005年6月。不過本文卻基於 testimonial statement 係以「所主張之事項為真實」為提出目的，故認「證明性」一詞較能充分表達該判決之意涵。

告交互詰問或是被告根本無機會交互詰問，羅伯特斯案與依納迪案即不再適用。然而，當法院遲遲未對何謂克勞佛案所指之證明性傳聞作出定義前，關於「證明性傳聞」之內涵為何，仍將爭議不休。儘管如此，基於上述美國立法上或司法上關於證據法的規定與解釋，美國法制中關於取得證據與評價證據的實務，顯較英國之相關法制嚴格[161]。

伍、現代傳聞法則

一、序論

依現行美國聯邦證據法第 802 條即規定：「除非本法另有規定，或依聯邦最高法院在國會法授權下所制定之規則另有規定，否則傳聞證言不具證據能力[162]。」，本質上傳聞法則可視為白話文中「直接告訴法官或陪審團[163]」之法律上同義詞外。值得注意的是，如亞瑟貝斯特教授（Professor Arthur Best）所述，「傳聞法則的迷思在於沒有一個人真正地了解它，不論是法學院的學生或是執業律師，均常在傳聞議題上犯錯。有

---

[161] See John C. Klotter, supra note 1, 8.

[162] It provides: "Hearsay is not admissible except as provided by these rules or by other rules prescribed by the Supreme Court pursuant to statutory authority or by Act of Congress."

[163] See Steven I. Friedland, supra note 9, 312.

時候一群了解傳聞法則的人，看起來就像一個秘密組織的成員[164]。」此外，傳聞法則亦為決定「證人在審判中所提出法庭外陳述」是否具證據能力之法庭規則[165]；傳聞法則本身並非一個簡單的議題。

　　一般說來，適用審判外之陳述存在四大風險：觀察錯誤、記憶錯誤、陳述錯誤與扭曲事實[166]。美國聯邦證據法第 102 條規定亦在說明該法係以尋求正義、減少不必要的成本與耽誤、促進證據法的發展與確保在法庭上呈現事實為目的[167]。除了第 501 條特權規定與真實無關外，證據法在追求真實的目的下，只承認具有關聯性之證據具有證據能力，並排除審判外陳述之證據能力[168]。如克勞佛案所述，排除傳聞證據之最主要原因，乃在於審判外之陳述者尚未接受被告的交互詰問，此因素除將賦予審判外陳述過高的價值外，亦將在事實認定之過程中，創造無法接受之危險[169]。換言之，審判外陳述之可信性問題，是自普通法時代以來，一直被視為排除傳聞證言之重要基礎，而

---

[164] See Authur Best, Evidence, 61 (New York Aspen Law & Business, 2001).

[165] See G. Michael Fenner, supra note 10, 5.

[166] See Christopher B. Mueller, supra note 20, 125. 關於中文文獻可參閱王兆鵬，美國刑事訴訟法，頁 380，元照出版公司，2004 年 9 月。

[167] It provides: "These rules shall be construed to secure fairness in administration, elimination of unjustifiable expense and delay, and promotion of growth and development of the law of evidence to the end that the truth may be ascertained and proceedings justly determined."

[168] See G. Michael Fenner, supra note 10, 4 and John C. Klotter, supra note 1, 275.

[169] See Steven I. Friedland, supra note 9, 312 and Roger C. Park, supra note 4, 241.

排除傳聞證言也被視為公平審判之一大要素。當然，在當事人一方有權提出任何證據證明其主張之前提下，關聯性要件與傳聞法則二者似乎旨在限制其提出證明的方式[170]。

顯而易見地，並非所有的傳聞均不具可信性，某些傳聞較之其他傳聞具有較高度的可信性；而有時似乎值得冒著事實認定錯誤之風險而承認部分的傳聞具有證據能力[171]。在篩選並決定何者為較為可信傳聞的歷程中，自普通法時代開始，法院逐漸創造出一些承認傳聞具有證據能力之例外規則[172]。某種程度來說，承認傳聞法則之例外係建立在人類某些直覺性與心理性，關於何種人與人之溝通內容為真之假設之上[173]。無論採認何種傳聞例外，公平性與司法效率向來均為主要之考量[174]。同時，必須加以強調的是，傳聞法則的目的，乃在於協助事實認定者在尋找事實真相的過程中，不受低可信性證據的影響[175]。

二、美國法上之傳聞定義及其疑義

美國聯邦證據法第 801 條（c）將傳聞定義為：以證明所指

---

[170] See Authur Best, supra note 164, 65.

[171] See G. Michael Fenner, supra note 10, 9.

[172] See John C. Klotter, supra note 1, 276.

[173] See Authur Best, supra note 164, 61.

[174] 舉例來說，一份西元 1971 年針對美國刑事法院所作的調查指出，公平性與效率是承認傳聞例外時，所必須考慮的因素。See Advisory Committee on Rules of Evidence, Revised Draft, 51 F.R.D. 315 (1971).

[175] See G. Michael Fenner, supra note 10, 8.

述者係眞實爲目的，而有別於審判中由到庭證人所作成之他人陳述[176]。在此規定下，傳聞證言除包含所有的口頭與書面陳述外，亦包含與陳述具有相同意義之目的性舉動[177]。不過前述傳聞定義卻因其以複雜而不精確的文字表達敍述一個簡單的概念而迭受批評[178]。簡單來說，傳聞證言爲一種以主張其所指述爲眞實爲目的，陳述者於審判外所作之陳述[179]。雖然這個白話文式的定義不大複雜，不過，此定義並未說明「何者係審判外之陳述」以及如何該當「以證明所指述爲眞正爲目的」[180]。

在美國聯邦證據法第 801 條（d）定義下，「證人先前之陳述（prior statement by witness）」與「對方之陳述（admission by party-opponent）」二者並非傳聞陳述。與同法第 803 條及第 804 條相對，第 801 條（d）(2) 經常不被視爲傳聞陳述之一類。由於對方之陳述符合同法第 801 條（c）之定義，第 801 條（d）(2) 之規定似乎與傳聞定義相衝突，故第 801 條（d）(2) 究竟是否可歸類爲傳聞陳述，即令人十分困擾。事實上，與現

---

[176] Rule 801(c) of Federal Rules of Evidence provides: '"Hearsay" is a statement, other than one made by the declarant while testifying at the trial or hearing, offered in evidence to prove the truth of the matter asserted.'

[177] 此部分可參照聯邦證據規則第 801(a) 之規定："A statement is (1) an oral or written assertion, or (2) nonverbal conduct of a person, if it is intended by the person as an assertion."

[178] See James W. McElhaney, The Heart of the Matter, 89 ABA J. 50, 52 (2003).

[179] See Christopher B. Mueller, supra note 19, 123.

[180] See James W. McElhaney, supra note 178, 52.

行證據法將對方之陳述（含共犯陳述）定義爲非傳聞不同[181]，傳統以來，普通法即將現行第 801 條（d）(2) 定義爲傳聞例外，且目前許多州證據法仍採此種定義[182]。某種程度來說，此種將第 801 條（d）(2) 定義爲非傳聞的規範模式，背後之理由是深奧難解甚或是過度操作的[183]。或許如已故的約翰亨力韋格摩教授所述，將對方之陳述定義爲非傳聞是實務上較容易處理證據之規範模式；而聯邦證據法的起草者似乎也採納了約翰亨力韋格摩教授所建議，將對方之陳述定義爲非傳聞[184]。如聯邦證據法諮詢委員會所述，將對方之陳述定義爲非傳聞僅簡單因公平概念要求，在兩造模式的訴訟架構下，當事人一方須受其本身之陳述所拘束[185]。從而，不論將對方之陳述定義爲傳聞或非傳聞，亦不論原陳述者在審判中作相同之陳述，美國聯邦證據法第 801 條（d）(2) 所指述之審判外陳述均具證據能力[186]。不過，在克勞佛案作成後，是否會出現被告主張美國聯邦證據法第 801 條（d）(2) (E) 關於共犯犯意聯絡之陳述具證據能力

---

[181] See Roger C. Park, supra note 4, 267.

[182] See James W. McElhaney, supra note 178, 54.

[183] See Roger C. Park, supra note 4, 254.

[184] See James W. McElhaney, supra note 178, 54.

[185] See FRE 801 (d) (2) advisory committee's note, cited in Roger C. Park, supra note 4, 254 n 58 (West, 1998).

[186] See James W. McElhaney, supra note 178, 56.

之規定[187]違反對質條款之爭議,尚有待觀察;惟至少目前在州層次的刑事案件中,已可見類此「州證據法中關於共犯犯意聯絡之陳述具證據能力之規定,是否違反州憲法對質條款」之爭執[188]。

依羅結派克教授(Professor Roger C. Park)所述,傳聞本身存在二種類型之定義:以所主張之事項為中心或以陳述者為中心;依前者定義,審判外之陳述只有在證明所指述者為真實時才屬於傳聞;依後者定義,審判外陳述只有在陳述之價值繫於陳述者之信用時才屬於傳聞[189]。不過在克勞佛案作成後,傳聞之定義應兼採二者,不但以尋求真實為目的,亦以藉由交互詰問確認證人本身之信用為內涵[190]。因此,為更了解傳聞之定

---

[187] The statements have to be made in furtherance of the conspiracy and during the course of the conspiracy. See United States v. Tombrello, 666 F. 2d 485, 490 (11th Cir.), cert. denied, 456 U.S. 994 (1982). However, mere conversations between conspirators, merely narrative declarations, and causal admissions of culpability are not statements in furtherance of the conspiracy. See United States v. Tille, 729 F. 2d 615 (9th Cir. 1984). There must be independent evidence of the conspiracy. See United States v. Jannotti, 729 F. 2d 213 (3rd Cir. 1984). Also see Patrick J. Sullivan, Bootstrapping of Hearsay under Federal Rule of Evidence 801 (d) (2) (E): Further Erosion of the Coconspirator Exemption, 74 Iowa L. Rev. 467 (1989).

[188] See Arnold v. State, 751 P. 2d 494, 504-05 (Alaska App. 1988); Nunez v. People, 737 P. 2d 422, 424-26 (Colo. 1987); cited in Roger C. Park, supra note 4, 266, n 106.

[189] See Roger C. Park, "I Didn't Tell Them Anything About You": Implied Assertions as Hearsay Under the Federal Rules of Evidence, 74 Minn. L. Rev. 783, 783 (1990).

[190] See Christopher B. Mueller, supra note 19, 126.

義，如果到庭之證人非被告欲交互詰問者，其非眞正之證人，且其所提出之陳述即爲審判外之陳述[191]。若提出審判外陳述之目的並非在證明其所指述之內容爲眞實，則傳聞法則於此時並不適用，該非以證明其所指述內容爲眞實之審判外陳述，即應具證據能力[192]；蓋在事實認定者並不須判斷該審判外陳述所指述者是否爲眞實的前提下，並無必要對陳述者進行交互詰[193]。舉例而言，當證人陳述其曾聽到有人說「小心！」，如同該證人陳述其曾看見有人穿藍毛衣或其曾見有人跑過馬路般，因該陳述之目的並非在證明「須小心何事」，故其非傳聞[194]。

　　一般而言，由於「被告欲交互詰問之對象」係指「主張該審判外陳述之內容爲眞實」之人，故如該陳述者是否到庭作證與所陳述之內容是否爲眞實無涉時，該陳述即非傳聞；反之，如對審判外陳述之眞實性有疑義，且到庭作證之證人非眞正的證人時，該審判外之陳述即爲傳聞[195]。顯而易見地，傳聞法則旨在要求眞正的證人到庭陳述並回答對造之詢問；當提出審判外陳述之目的，僅在證明有人說過什麼，而非證明其所說過的都是眞實的，此時傳聞法則並不適用[196]。在前述分析下，只有

---

[191] See James W. McElhaney, supra note 178, 52.

[192] See Authur Best, supra note 164, 65.

[193] See Roger C. Park, supra note 4, 241.

[194] See Authur Best, supra note 164, 68.

[195] See James W. McElhaney, supra note 178, 53.

[196] See Authur Best, supra note 164, 68.

[197] See James W. McElhaney, supra note 178, 54.

少數審判外之陳述將該當傳聞證言[197]。

三、傳聞例外之確認

　　當陪審員對系爭案件不具私知逐漸成為擔任陪審員之實質要件時，傳聞法則才開始發展[198]；不過普通法與聯邦證據規則[199]卻承認，在被告有機會對該陳述者進行交互詰問[200]或該審判外之陳述符合可信性擔保[201]之前提下，該審判外之陳述乃例外地具有證據能力；實際上，雖然排除傳聞之主張具有堅強之政策基礎，並如前首席大法官馬歇爾所述，排除傳聞是基於傳聞本質上之缺陷[202]，不過，當某些傳聞本身所隱含之誤判風險較其他類型之傳聞為低時，普通法與聯邦證據規則均承認其為傳聞之例外，而賦予該審判外陳述具證據能力[203]。因許多審判外之陳述均符合傳聞例外而具有證據能力，該排除傳聞之原則似乎已成為例外[204]。基本上，如果在個案中，如所欲引用之審判外陳述不存在虛偽之風險，而承認該審判外之陳述亦不違司法公正時，將該審判外之陳述歸類為傳聞例外而具證據能

---

[198] See John C. Klotter, supra note 1, 280.

[199] See Authur Best, supra note 164, 89.

[200] See Steven I. Friedland, supra note 9, 312.

[201] See Roger C. Park, supra note 4, 254.

[202] See John C. Klotter, supra note 1, 280.

[203] See Authur Best, supra note 164, 65, 102.

[204] See Roger C. Park, supra note 4, 266.

[205] See John C. Klotter, supra note 1, 281.

力，並無不當[205]。

　　原則上，聯邦證據規則所列之二十八種例外，可分爲二大類；第一類係指聯邦證據法第 804 條證人不能到庭陳述之情形，而第二類則指虛僞風險較小之傳聞[206]，此種聯邦證據法第 803 條所規定之傳聞例外並不考慮證人是否能到庭作證[207]，且該條所包含之傳聞例外數量最多；本質上，該條所規定之傳聞例外（超過二十個）均不要求審判外之陳述者到庭作證[208]。依聯邦證據法第 805 條之規定，只要雙重傳聞中之個別傳聞均符合傳聞例外之規定，亦不適用傳聞排除之原則。此外，尚有前二類型所未涵蓋[209]之概括性傳聞例外（catch-all exception）[210]。簡言

---

[206] See Authur Best, supra note 164, 102.

[207] See Daniel Stewart, Jr., Perception, Memory, and Hearsay: A Criticism of Present Law and the Proposed Federal Rules of Evidence, 1 Utah L. Rev. 1 (1970).

[208] See Roger C. Park, supra note 4, 268.

[209] See Authur Best, supra note 164, 102.

[210] FRE 807 provides: "A statement no specifically covered by Rule 803 or 804, but having equivalent circumstantial guarantees of trustworthiness, is not excluded by the hearsay rule if the court determines that (A) the statement is offered as evidence of a material fact; (B) the statement is more probative on the point for which it is offered than any other evidence which the proponent can procure through reasonable efforts; and (C) the general purposes of these rules and the interests of justice will best be served by admission of the statement into evidence. However, a statement may not be admitted under this exception unless the proponent of it makes known to the adverse party sufficiently in advance of the trial or hearing to provide the adverse party with a fair opportunity to prepare to meet it, the proponent's intention to offer the statement and the particulars of it, including the name and address of the declarant."

之，雖然自 18 世紀起，傳聞法則便己開始在審判中禁止使用傳聞陳述，幾世紀以來，傳聞例外卻在緩和傳聞法則的嚴厲性要求下，逐漸累積與發展[211]。一般說來，只要允許某類型傳聞例外之法理係基於使用審判外陳述之必要性，而非基於審判外陳述者之可信性，因此時證人是否能到庭作證，涉及是否有必要使用該審判外陳述，只有在證人不能到庭作證得到證明時，該審判外之陳述始具證據能力[212]。

陸、結　論

由於在採行美國式的傳聞法則前，我國並未從比較法的觀點，深入地探討我國的法制結構應如何與該制度協調，因此源自法制移植之齟齬，難免時有所聞。本文嘗試介紹美國刑事訴訟程序發展過程中，關於對質條款與傳聞法則的重要發展歷程；除了希望讀者能充分了解美國傳聞法則與大陸法系證據法，在沿革上有何重大差異外，同時亦祈本文之說明，能作為我國實務在操作傳聞法則時，得以先對傳聞法則本身制度目的與相關之發展，有基本的認知與理解之媒介。否則僅僅採用某個制度之規定本身，而忽略了對其相關發展與沿革歷程的認識，難免因各地風俗文化民情之不同，而出現橘逾淮為枳之意

---

[211] See John C. Klotter, supra note 1, 280.
[212] See Authur Best, supra note 164, 102.

外。舉例而言，由於在我國的訴訟結構中，職業法官仍然擔任事實認定的工作，因此在移植以陪審審判為思考核心之傳聞法則時，似乎不得不相應地作些調整。如果欠缺了這一層的認識，而認為必須移植美國整套的證據法制，難免流於矯枉過正。至於該如何在個別的傳聞議題上，承認美國傳聞法則的適用，因此部分已逾對美國傳聞法制發展考察之範圍，尚待他日深論。（本文前身「A Historical Study on Evidential Hearsay and the Confrontation Clause of the United States」曾發表於 Tilburg Foreign Law Review (13 Tilburg Foreign Law Review 43), 2006.01；後經翻譯改寫後發表於 95.04 月旦法學雜誌）

4 英美傳聞法則在大陸法域之移植：台灣與美國傳聞法則之比較研究

Adoption of the Common Law Hearsay Rule in a Civil Law Jurisdiction: a Comparative Study of the Hearsay Rule in Taiwan and the United States[1]

1. Introduction（導論）

Over the past decades, the criminal justice system of the Republic of China on Taiwan (ROC) has long been criticized for its insufficient human rights protection, especially for the alleged criminal offenders. From 1947 to 1987, Taiwan enforced martial law and was in a state of siege. In this era of martial law rule,

---

[1] By Ming-woei Chang, Assistant Professor of Law, Aletheia University Department of Financial Economic of Law, Tamsui, Taipei, Taiwan, ROC; Areas of Specialization: Criminal Law, Criminal Procedure, Evidence Law, and Latin-Notary Law. S.J.D., Golden Gate University School of Law, San Francisco, CA, USA; LL.M. (I.P.), Franklin Pierce Law Center, Concord, NH, USA; LL.M. & LL.B., National Taiwan University College of Law, Taipei, Taiwan, ROC. Email: mwconqueror@yahoo.com.tw.

ordinary citizens in Taiwan lived for four decades with little anticipation of any recognition of their inherent human rights, not to mention the rights of the accused; to some extent, it was considered a privilege for an ordinary Taiwanese citizen to claim any right to an impartial trial. The guarantee of due process in the criminal justice system—which is today widely perceived as essential to civil rights in any modern democracy—was virtually non-existent in ordinary criminal proceedings in Taiwan.

Following Taiwan's development of democratic institutions, which began in 1987, with numerous interpretative pronouncements of the Grand Justice Council[2] as well as extensive knowledge accumulated from the introduction and comparison of various modern foreign criminal justice systems (such as the United States, Japan and Germany), the people of Taiwan started to review their legal system. They gave particular focus to its criminal justice system as well as to the police power that influenced the daily life of people most. They gradually reached the conclusion that the ROC CPC (CPC), based mainly on the continental Ger-

---

[2]　Within the framework of the Constitution of the Republic of China, the Grand Justices en masse ensure the Constitution's effectiveness by actively guarding it from violations, and resolving disputes rising from its application. See the ROC Judicial Yuan and its Grand Justice Council, at http://www.judicial.gov.tw (last visited Sep. 18, 2004).

man system and enacted in 1967,[3] was clearly out of date.

To prevent miscarriage of justice, the design of criminal procedures must be focused on the protection of the rights of the alleged offenders. In fact, the degree to which the rights of the alleged offenders are protected during criminal proceedings has

---

[3] As reported, "In the late Qing dynasty there was a concerted effort to establish legal codes based on European models. Because of the German victory in the Franco-Prussian War and because Japan was used as the model for political and legal reform, the law codes which were adopted were modeled closely after that of Germany. The existing German-based legal codes were then adopted by the new Republic of China government, but they were not immediately put into practice - following the overthrow of the Qing dynasty in 1911, China came under the control of rival warlords and had no government strong enough to establish a legal code to replace the Qing code. Finally, in 1927, Chiang Kai-shek's Kuomintang forces were able to suppress the warlords and gain control of most of the country. Established in Nanjing, the KMT government attempted to develop Western-style legal and penal systems. Few of the KMT codes, however, were implemented nationwide. Although government leaders were striving for a Western-inspired system of codified law, the traditional Chinese preference for collective social sanctions over impersonal legalism hindered constitutional and legal development. The spirit of the new laws never penetrated to the grass-roots level or provided hoped-for stability. Ideally, individuals were to be equal before the law, but this premise proved to be more rhetorical than substantive. In the end, most of the new laws were discarded as the Kuomintang became preoccupied with fighting the Chinese Communists and the invading Japanese. Law in the Republic of China on Taiwan is based on the German-based legal system which carried to Taiwan by the Kuomintang. In the area of constitutional law, the Republic of China uses the 1947 Constitution which was promulgated for both Mainland China and Taiwan although numerous changes have been made to take into account the fact that the Republic of China only controls Taiwan and two counties of Fujian." See Wikipedia, Chinese Law, at http://en.wikipedia.org/wiki/Chinese_law (last modified, Dec. 6, 2004).

been regarded as one of the indexes of a nation's civil develop-ments. In order to improve human rights protection both of the citizens and alleged offenders in Taiwan, the Taiwanese govern-ment decided to amend its Criminal Procedure Code (CPC). Critical drafts of the CPC were passed by Taiwan's Legislative Yuan[4] in 1990, 1993, 1995, 1997, 1998, 1999, 2000, 2001, 2002, and 2003, corresponding to the demand for human rights protec-tion.

From the viewpoint of comparative legal study, the recent legislation of Taiwan which might reshape the ROC criminal pro-cedure has given rise to a controversy regarding whether Taiwan's criminal justice system retains its inquisitorial tradition or has be-come pro-accusatorial since the former CPC was based upon con-tinental inquisitorial models and those current effective amend-ments are derived mainly from the American accusatorial model. However, this comparative study does not intend to solve the problem whether the new Taiwanese criminal justice system re-mains inquisitorial, but focuses merely on the newly enacted

---

[4] According to the ideas of Dr. Sun Yet-sen, who framed the Five-Power Constitution, enacted and promulgated in 1947, the Legislative Yuan shall be the supreme legislative organization of the State, to be constituted of members elected by the people, and it shall exercise legislative power on behalf of the people. In terms of its competence, power, and function, Taiwan's Legislative Yuan is equivalent to a parliament in other western democracies (such as the Congress in U.S.). See Introduction to the ROC Legislative Yuan, at http://www. ly.gov.tw (last visited Sep. 18, 2004).

hearsay rule in the ROC CPC and its counterpart in the United States. After offering a brief overview of the developments of the hearsay rule in Taiwan and its counterpart in the States, this study compares and analyzes why the developments of the hearsay rule in Taiwan differs from those in the United States.

2. Adoption of the Hearsay Rule in Taiwan （傳聞法則在台灣）

Before examining this topic, it is desirable to introduce the historical background of Taiwan, especially for those not familiar with this jurisdiction.

2.1　An Overview（概説）

Taiwan had been a neglected island before the 17th century. Before 1662, Taiwan was partly colonized by the Dutch (the Dutch East India Company from 1624) and by Spain (from 1628 to 1642, ousted by the Dutch). After Jheng Cheng-gong defeated the Dutch in 1662 and set up the Ming Dynasty Government, Taiwan was governed by the Chinese for the first time, and there were about 40,000 Chinese people living in Taiwan then.

Twenty-one years later, the then ruler, Jheng's grandson, surrendered control of the island to the Ching Dynasty, and the Ching Dynasty ruled Taiwan for the next 212 years until 1895. After Japan won the Sino-Japanese war, Taiwan was ceded to Japan in 1895 pursuant to the Treaty of Shimonoseki. From 1895 to 1945, Taiwan was controlled by the Japanese Government.

Following Japan's defeat and surrender in August 1945 at the end of World War II, Taiwan was retroceded to the Chinese people (then the Republic of China) on October 25th and again placed under Chinese governance.[5]

Before resuming sovereignty over Taiwan in 1945, the ROC government, under the administration of the Chinese Nationalist Party (i.e., the Koumintang, KMT), established its legal system following the example of Japan by enacting Western style, especially German-style, codes from the late 1920s to mid-1930s. In 1935, the ROC government enacted its first Chinese Criminal Procedure Code. Although the ROC legal system was based mostly on the German civil law system and was as such influenced by and modeled on the old Japanese and German codes, those individualist and liberal legal norms had not been practically enforced in China due to the chaos caused by continuous hostilities during the period after their promulgation. As an independent jurisdiction, Taiwan started its legal development under both Chinese and Japanese legal legacies, at that time principally civil law, even after the establishment of the People's Republic of China (PRC) on October 1st, 1949, but especially so after the KMT-led ROC central government retreated to Taiwan in December of 1949.

Generally speaking, the Republic of China on Taiwan has a

---

5   See Taiwan Yearbook 2003, at http://www.gio.gov.tw/taiwan-website/5-gp/yearbook/chpt03.htm (last visited Apr. 8, 2004).

codified system of law, of which the contents are mainly trans-
planted from abroad, and borrowed heavily from the laws of
other countries with similar codified systems[6] as well as traditional Chinese laws. The ROC Court system follows the continental civil law model. Procedures are inquisitorial rather than
accusatorial, and judges are active trial participants. The supreme
law of Taiwan is the ROC Constitution. The judicial system is
composed of three tiers: the Supreme Court, the High Court, and
the District Court. Professional judges decide all cases, including
facts and legal issues. Appeals to the High Court are as a matter
of right in Taiwan.[7] Appeals to the Supreme Court are limited
and specified by statute, but are generally available for all except
the smallest or most localized of cases.[8] Since the Supreme Court
reviews only issues of law, an appeal may be made to the Supreme Court only on the ground that the original judgment is in
violation of a law or an order.[9] While the Supreme Court does
not determine issues of fact, documentary proceedings are the
rule while oral proceedings are the exception.[10] As the legal system in the ROC is based on the civil law and code-based legal
traditions, legal matters are decided by reference to the Codes

---

6　See Kenneth Robert Redden, ed., *Modern Legal Systems Cyclopedia*, Volume
　2A, 40.12 (1984).
7　See Article 344 of the ROC CPC.
8　See Articles 376 to 382 of the ROC CPC.
9　See Article 377 of the ROC CPC.
10　See Article 372 of the ROC CPC.

and to the writings of scholars and judges who interpret the Codes. There is comparatively little judge-made law in Taiwan. Similar to the German criminal justice system, the main source of Taiwan's criminal procedure law is its CPC.[11] While some of the individual's rights guaranteed by the ROC Constitution have special relevance in the context of the criminal process, the jurisprudence of the Grand Justice Council has great relevance for the interpretation of criminal procedure law, although the interpretation of the CPC is the task of ordinary courts.[12]

As in Germany, there was no general statutory exclusionary rule that would make illegally obtained evidence inadmissible under the 1935 Chinese Criminal Procedure Code or the 1967 re-enacted ROC CPC. Only Paragraph 1 of Article 156 of the former ROC CPC did provide for inadmissibility of statements elicited by certain forbidden means, including violence, threat, inducement, fraud, unlawful detention, and other improper devices. Despite this provision, since the ROC Supreme Court did not care about how evidence was obtained, any evidence related to proving the truth of the matter at issue was admissible in the past.[13] In other words, the exclusionary approach of evidentiary

---

[11] Different from the highly constitutionalized criminal justice system in the USA, in Taiwan most issues of criminal procedure in the continental tradition are governed by detailed provisions of the CPC.

[12] See Thomas Weigend, Chapter 6, "Germany", in Craig M. Bradley, ed., *Criminal Procedure: A Worldwide Study*, 187 (1999).

[13] See 72 Tai Sun 1332 (1983). It should be noted that Taiwan's legal professionals do not cite a case using the parties' names. Instead, they cite case numbers.

hearsay rule did not exist in the ROC jurisdiction until 2003.

2.2 Pre-2003 Practice without Hearsay: Continental Direct Inquisition（民國 92 年以前之實務：直接審理）

In the continental inquisitorial tradition, virtually no scholars and judges recognized there was an American-style hearsay rule in Taiwan.[14] Since former Article 159 of the ROC CPC provided that "statements made by a witness outside the court shall be inadmissible unless otherwise provided by law," which looked like the definition of hearsay in the United States Federal Rules of Evidence (FRE),[15] and Articles 157, 158, and 206 of the ROC CPC[16] might be treated as exceptions to hearsay, it was questionable whether the 1967 ROC CPC adopted the American style hearsay rule while the minority opinion claimed those provisions

---

[14] It is noteworthy that the late Professor Pu-Shen Chen, a former Grand Justice and leading Professor of Law at National Taiwan University and National Chen Chi University, asserted that there was no hearsay rule in the ROC CPC. And statements made by a witness outside the court shall be admitted in evidence according to Article 165 and 166. See Pu-Shen Chen, *Criminal Evidence Rule*, 413 (Taipei, 1995) (in Chinese).

[15] Rule 801 (c) of the Federal Rule of Evidence provides: "Hearsay is a statement, other than one made by the declarant while testifying at the trial of hearing, offered in evidence to prove the truth of the matter asserted."

[16] Article 157 of the ROC CPC provides: "No evidence need be adduced to prove facts commonly known to the public." Article 158 provides: "No evidence need be adduced to prove such facts as are obvious to the court or have become known to it in performing its function." And Paragraph 1 of Article 206 provides: "An expert shall be ordered to make a report of his or her findings and results verbally or in writing."

constituted hearsay rule.[17]

In practice, based on the 1967 Advisory Committee Note, Article 159 of the ROC CPC had long been considered as deriving from the continental principles of "Direct Inquisition" and "Verbal Inquisition" instead of the common law hearsay rule. Hence, courts in Taiwan were bound by very few legal restrictions on the nature of evidence they received as explained by the ROC Supreme Court.[18] Generally speaking, any out-of-court verbal statement made by a witness other than an accused is inadmissible.[19] An out-of-court document made by a witness is inadmissible.[20] Interestingly, even though an out-of-court verbal statements should be inadmissible under former Article 159 of the ROC CPC, if it was "made by a co-defendant or a victim" and "recorded by law-enforcement-officers" and the court performed its duty to read related notes and other documents in the dossier which might be used as evidence against an accused at trial under former Paragraph 1 of Article 165 of the ROC CPC, without

---

[17] Only Professor Tung-Sheung Huang, Professor of Law and a former President of National Chun-Shin University, asserted the hearsay rule had existed in the ROC CPC before. See Tung-Sheung Huang, "Discussing the Hearsay Rule", *Military Law Journal*, Vol. 35-1, 16 (Taipei, 1989)(in Chinese).

[18] See the following ROC Supreme Court decisions: 70 Tai Sun 3864 (1981), 72 Tai Sun 1203 (1983), 77 Tai Sun 848 (1988), 79 Tai Sun 5140 (1990), 81 Tai Sun 4352 (1992), 82 Tai Sun 622 (1993), 83 Tai Sun 2785 (1994), 84 Tai Sun 2819 (1995), and 91 Tai Sun 2363 (2002).

[19] See 79 Tai Sun 5140 (1990).

[20] See 77 Tai Sun 848 (1988).

directly questioning the declarant, any out-of-court verbal statement made by a co-defendant or a victim during interrogation
by law-enforcement-officers was not only admissible but also
sufficient to secure conviction.[21] For example, in 72 Tai Sun
1203 (1983), the ROC Supreme Court held that

> [u]nder the 'Doctrine of Discretional Evaluation of Evi-
> dence', there is no limitation regarding the admissibility
> of the stereotype of evidence in the ROC criminal justice
> system. Victim's deposition made during police inter-
> rogation is not prohibited from being in evidence by Ar-
> ticle 159 of the ROC CPC. The court has the discretio-
> nary power to decide whether the 'victim's deposition'
> would prove guilt or innocence of the accused.

In other words, according to this decision, the victim's deposition
was not excluded by former Article 159 of the ROC CPC. While
this article mentioned "witness statements" only, it did not apply
to out-of-court statements made by co-defendants or victims since
they were not considered witnesses.

Even though former Article 159 of the ROC CPC excluded

---

[21] See the following ROC Supreme Court decisions: 71 Tai Sun 5946 (1982), 72
Tai Sun 1203 (1983), 77 Tai Sun 4249 (1988), 86 Tai Sun 4242 (1997), and 90
Tai Sun 6517 (2001).

an out-of-court verbal statement made by a witness, in 91 Tai Sun 2363 (2002), the Supreme Court ruled that "the statement recorded in private-made tape or video should be admissible if the defendant merely intended to prove what the witness had told before the court or a public prosecutor previously was not true." As a result, an out-of-court verbal statement was admissible for the purpose of impeaching the witness. In general, out-of-court verbal statements made by non-victim and non-co-defendant witnesses were inadmissible in the pre-2003 practice. Nonetheless, if an out-of-court verbal statement was made by a victim or a co-defendant and recorded by a government officer, only when the court fulfilled its obligation to investigate these statements under former Paragraph 1 of Article 165 of the ROC CPC would they be admissible as evidence. Under this practice, an out-of-court statement made by a co-defendant or a victim before any government officer sufficed to secure conviction. This practice resulted in unfairness especially when a defendant had no opportunity to respond to an out-of-court statement fully prepared, because he would only be confronted with this kind of information at the trial. While commentators began to sense that this kind of injustice was mainly caused by the absence of a hearsay rule, of meaningful protection of the right to confrontation, and of other procedural protection in Taiwan, claims to reform Taiwan's criminal justice system emerged, which eventually resulted in the adoption of the American-style hearsay rule.

2.3　The 2003 Hearsay Rule（民國 92 年之傳聞法則）

2.3.1　Definition（定義）

In 2003, in order to better the defendant's protection at trial, after years of debate on the adoption of the hearsay rule, the ROC Legislative Yuan finally revised its CPC by adding the hearsay rule. Unlike former Article 159 of the ROC CPC, the current Paragraph 1 of Article 159, providing that "[u]nless otherwise provided by law, any out-of-court verbal statement derivative from anyone other than the defendant himself shall be inadmissible," clearly delimits inadmissible hearsay in principle. Under this new provision, out-of-court statements made by co-defendants or victims are inadmissible hearsay. Only out-of-court statements made by the defendant himself are not hearsay. In addition, compared to former Article 159 of the ROC CPC which did not provide any hearsay exception, not all out-of-court statements made by witnesses are absolutely inadmissible because some hearsay exceptions were enacted in 2003. In short, as a civil law jurisdiction, Taiwan is currently using the common law hearsay rule.

2.3.2　Exceptions to Hearsay（傳聞例外）

In addition to the adoption of the hearsay rule, exceptions to Paragraph 1 of Article 159 of the ROC CPC have also been adopted. For instance, if an out-of-court verbal statement derived from anyone other than the defendant is made before a judge, it is admissible because of its reliable voluntariness.[22] If they do not contain obviously implausible circumstances, out-of-court verbal statements derived from anyone other than the defendant made before a public prosecutor are also admissible.[23] In addition, while an out-of-court verbal statement derived from anyone other than the defendant made before any law-enforcement-officer is inconsistent with the same declarant's statement at trial, the former statement is admissible if the court finds the previous statement is more reliable and deems it necessary to use the previous statement to prove the truth of the asserted matters.[24] If the declarant is unavailable to stand trial in that he is dead, has a mental disorder, has lost his memory, is incapable of talking, is living abroad, lost, or refuses to make a statement without justification, the former out-of-court verbal statement derived from anyone other than the defendant made before any law-enforcement-officer is admissible too when the court finds the out-of-court statement is more reliable and deems it necessary to use the out-of-court statement to prove the truth of the asserted matters.[25]

Besides the out-of-court verbal statements, public records and reports, and business records of regular activities are admissible in

---

[22] See Paragraph 1 of Article 159-1 of the ROC CPC and the Advisory Committee Note.

[23] See Paragraph 2 of Article 159-1 of the ROC CPC.

[24] See Article 159-2 of the ROC CPC.

[25] See Article 159-3 of the ROC CPC.

evidence unless obviously implausible circumstances exist.[26] Accordingly, a residual clause admitting any other document made in reliable circumstances is also adopted.[27] Within the scope of inadmissible hearsay, while both parties accept out-of-court statement in evidence at trial, hearsay is admissible only if the court finds it proper after considering the given context of the hearsay evidence.[28] In other words, the newly passed Article 159-5 of the ROC CPC allows both parties to dispose hearsay statements. Whether to object to the opponent's hearsay evidence depends on the party's own discretion. Nonetheless, the court remains entitled to make a final decision about the admissibility of hearsay evidence accepted by the parties. As a consequence, some pre-2003 admissible out-of-court statements[29] become inadmissible hearsay evidence because of Paragraph 1 of Article 159 and Article 159-2 of the current ROC CPC; some pre-2003 inadmissible out-of-court statements[30] today are admissible at trial according to Articles 159-3, 159-4 and 159-5 of the ROC CPC.

---

[26]　See Subparagraphs 1 and 2 of Article 159-4 of the ROC CPC.

[27]　See Subparagraph 3 of Article 159-4 of the ROC CPC.

[28]　See Paragraph 1 of Article 159-5 of the ROC CPC.

[29]　Such as: out-of-court statements were made by co-defendants or victims before government officers.

[30]　Such as: the out-of-court declarant (witness) is dead, has a mental disorder, has lost his memory, is incapable of talking, is living abroad, lost, or refuses to make a statement without justification.

2.4 Problems Caused by the 2003 Legislation （民國 92 年 立法之題義）

Although the American-style hearsay rule was initially adopted to improve human rights protection, the 2003 legislation also caused legal problems. For example, while there are more than twenty exceptions to hearsay in the United States Federal Rules of Evidence, only five articles in the 2003 legislation provide exceptions to hearsay in the ROC CPC. Why the ROC CPC merely provides five hearsay exceptions and whether these provisions provide enough hearsay exceptions have become important issues. Do Articles 159-1 to 159-5 of the ROC CPC cover all hearsay exceptions under the Federal Rules of Evidence of the United States? If not, why not? In addition, without any limitation, Article 159-1 of the ROC CPC admits out-of-court statements made before a judge or a public prosecutor. What is the rationale behind this article? Since the current hearsay rule excludes some previously admissible out-of-court statements, why does it accordingly admit some formerly inadmissible out-of-court statements made by private persons at trial? Compared to Articles 159-2, 159-3, and 159-4 of the ROC CPC requiring the court to find previous out-of-court statements reliable and necessary in order to admit them as evidence, it is unclear and even questionable why merely "stating" instead of "testifying" before a judge or a public prosecutor without requiring necessity and reliability would itself result in admissibility. While the Advisory

Committee Note in 2003 declared that the purpose of adopting the American-style hearsay rule was to protect the defendant's right to confront witnesses, it is unclear whether Article 159-1 of the ROC CPC admitting out-of-court statements violates this right. What the standard for deciding the admissibility of out-of-court statements should be thus emerges as a core legal problem regarding the hearsay rule in Taiwan.

Moreover, since 91 Tai Sun 2363 admitted an out-of-court statement for the purpose of impeaching the witness, it is unclear whether the 2003 legislation recognized this practice. It is also ambiguous about the scope of exclusionary hearsay adopted in Taiwan. Before looking at United States legislation for potential solutions to these problems, the development of exclusionary hearsay in the United States will be briefly described.

3. Exclusionary Hearsay and the Confrontation Clause in the United States
（對質條款與傳聞法則與美黃的發展）

3.1 The Pre-Mattox Practice of the Sixth Amendment in the United States（第六條正案在馬踏斯案前之實踐）

While, before the nineteenth century, English common law did not guarantee the assistance of counsel in all prosecutions, the Sixth Amendment, in granting a full right to counsel in all cases, did not constitutionalize English law.[31] Regardless of its origins, as noted by Professor Akhil Reed Amar, the Bill of Rights "was not simply an enactment of We the People as the Sovereign Legislature bringing new rights into existence, but a declaratory judgment by We the People as the Sovereign High Court that certain natural or fundamental rights already existed."[32] Thus, the Framers' concerns about federal encroachment and their desire to provide a check on federal judges[33] resulted in an attempt to constitutionalize the criminal procedure that had been developed in the colonies and the states.[34] As a result, since confrontation came to be the guarantee to allow an accused to challenge the information against him, and defense cross-examination had become the chief procedure for challenging such evidence, the right to confrontation guaranteed an accused the right to cross-examine witnesses as part of the newly emerging adversary system.[35]

As already mentioned, there was no federal case law totally focusing on the confrontation issue before the end of the ninete-

---

[31] See Randolph N. Jonakait, "The Origins of the Confrontation Clause: An Alternative History", 27 Rutgers Law Journal 77, 109 (1995).

[32] See Akhil Reed Amar, "The Bill of Rights and the Fourteenth Amendment", 101 *Yale Law Journal*. J. 1193, 1206 (1992).

[33] See Akhil Reed Amar, "Fourth Amendment Principles", 107 Harvard Law Review 757, 773 (1994).

[34] See Randolph N. Jonakait, supra note 31, 113.

[35] Id., at 115.

hall, in United States v. Burr, reasoned that the Confrontation Clause was adopted to restrict the admission of hearsay.[36] Since Justice Marshall did not explain why hearsay should be restricted, some constitutional-era opinions interpreting state provisions indicated that the purpose of confrontation was to guarantee the accused the opportunity to cross-examine witnesses at trial.[37] These opinions held cross-examination to be at the core of the right to confrontation.[38] In State v. Webb, a North Carolina case, the court rejected a South Carolinian's deposition that the absent accused had sold him the stolen horse by reasoning that "it is a rule of common law, founded on natural justice, that no man shall be prejudiced by evidence which he had not had the liberty to cross examine..."[39] In State v. Atkins, a Tennessee case, the court also rejected the former testimony as evidence, holding that

> frequent deaths may take place between the trial there and here, and it seems to us, that it would be dangerous to liberty to admit such evidence. It would go a great length in overthrowing this wise provision of the constitution. An inconvenience which could not exist in England, where there is no appeal as to matter of fact,

---

[36] See 25 F. Cas. 187, 193 (1807).
[37] See Randolph N. Jonakait, supra note 31, 122.
[38] Id.
[39] See 2 N. C. (1 Hayw.) 77, 77 (1794).

as here. The evidence cannot be received.[40]

Even though North Carolina's confrontation guarantee was word-
ed differently from Tennessee's, each, according to the Tennessee
court,[41] signified the same.[42] Moreover, in State v. Campbell, a
South Carolina case, for the purpose of pursuing a fair trial, the
court rejected the testimony of a then-dead witness, who had testified at a coroner's inquest in the absence of the accused.[43] The
court stated:

> [O]ne of the indispensable conditions of such due cour-
> se of law is, that prosecutions be carried on to the con-
> viction of the accused, by witnesses confronted by him,
> and subjected to his personal examination···. it is only
> in the examination and cross-examination, that the
> knave can be detected, errors of fact exposed, or false
> imaginations expunged...[44]

In short, the Pre-Mattox development of the Confrontation Clause
in the United States appeared mainly on the state level, with a fo-

---

[40] See 1 Tenn. (1 Overt.) 229, 229 (1807).

[41] See 10 Tenn. (2 Yer.) 58, 59-60 (1821).

[42] See Randolph N. Jonakait, supra note 31, 123.

[43] See 30 S.C.L. (1 Rich 124, 125) 51 (1844).

[44] Id., at 51-2.

cus on cross-examination. As proposed by Professor Randolph N. Jonakait,

> the Confrontation Clause, and other Sixth Amendment provisions, constitutionalized procedures already used in the states. These procedures allowed effective advocacy on behalf of the accused. Defense cross-examination was central to this. In trying to make sure that federal trials would use the procedures already developed by the Americans, the Sixth Amendment sought to guarantee defense cross-examination in the Confrontation Clause.[45]

3.2 Under the Confrontation Clause: the Post-Mattox Practice（馬踏斯案後的實踐）

When the Supreme Court started to review the Confrontation Clause, it focused on the admissibility of hearsay. To some extent, both the right to confrontation46 and the rule against hearsay[47] are directed at accurate fact finding. It was not necessary to clarify the relationship between the right of confrontation and the

---

[45] See Randolph N. Jonakait, supra note 123, 124.

[46] In Ohio v. Roberts, the Court held that the purpose of the Confrontation Clause is to augment accuracy in the fact-finding process. See 448 U.S. 56, 65 (1980).

[47] See G. Michael Fenner, *The Hearsay Rule*, 4 (Carolina Academic Press, 2003).

hearsay rule before 1965 in that the Court in Krulewitch v. United States reasoned its supervisory power over the inferior federal courts permitted it to control the admission of hearsay.[48] Moreover, on the basis of the Confrontation Clause, the Court in Motes v. United States had concluded that evidence given at a preliminary hearing could not be used as a hearsay exception at the trial if the absence of the witness was attributable to the negligence of the prosecution.[49] In addition to recognizing the admissibility of "testimony given at a former trial by a witness since deceased" in Mattox v. United States,[50] the Court also permitted "dying declarations" in Kirby v. United States.[51] The Court even seemed to equate the Confrontation Clause with the hearsay rule.[52]

Nonetheless, even though these two issues might look similar, they are not identical. The Court in Barber v. Page held the

---

[48] See 366 U.S. 440 (1949); see also FindLaw, Confrontation, available at http://caselaw.lp.findlaw.com/data/constitution/amendment06/08.html (last visited, Oct. 20, 2004). In addition, the Court in Delaney v. United States concluded that the co-conspirator exception to the hearsay rule was consistent with the Confrontation Clause. See 263 U.S. 586, 590 (1924).

[49] See 178 U.S. 458 (1900). However, if a witness's absence had been procured by the defendant, testimony given at a previous trial on a different indictment could be used at the subsequent trial. See Reynolds v. United States, 98 U.S. 145 (1879).

[50] See 156 U.S. 237, 240 (1895).

[51] The prosecution was not permitted to use a judgment of conviction against other defendants on charges of theft in order to prove that the property found in the possession of defendant now on trial was stolen. See 174 U.S. 47, 61 (1899).

[52] See FindLaw, Confrontation, available at http://caselaw.lp.findlaw.com/data/constitution/amendment06/08.html (last visited, Oct. 20, 2004).

right to confrontation should be a trial right which allows the accused to cross-examine an important witness at trial, and, unless the witness is unavailable, only granting the defendant the opportunity to cross-examine a crucial witness at a preliminary hearing would violate the Confrontation Clause.[53] Hence, the protection provided by the Confrontation Clause is broader than that provided by the hearsay rule. Besides seeking the truth, the right to confrontation should incorporate an element of fairness, of affording the defendant an opportunity to test the evidence against him, no matter how reliable that evidence may seem.[54]

According to these decisions, a rooted hearsay exception might be considered a violation of the Confrontation Clause. Thus,

---

[53] See 390 U.S. 719, 725-26 (1968).

[54] See "Note, Confrontation, Cross-Examination, and the Right to Prepare a Defense", 56 *Georgetown Law Journal* 939, 940 (1968). For instance, in California v. Green, the Court noted: "While it may readily be conceded that hearsay rules and the Confrontation Clause are generally designed to protect similar values, it is quite a different thing to suggest that the overlap is complete and that the Confrontation Clause is nothing more or less than a codification of the rules of hearsay and their exceptions as they existed historically at common law. Our decisions have never established such congruence; indeed, we have more than once found a violation of confrontation values even though the statements in issue were admitted under an arguably recognized hearsay exception… Given the similarity of the values protected, however, the modification of a State's hearsay rules to create new exceptions for the admission of evidence against a defendant, will often raise questions of compatibility with the defendant's constitutional right to confrontation. Such questions require attention to the reasons for, and the basic scope of, the protections offered by the Confrontation Clause." See 399 U.S. 149, 155-56 (1970).

whenever a witness is available, he is required by the Confrontation Clause to be subjected to cross-examination by the defense at trial even though his prior testimony did bear indicia of reliability. In other words, to comport with the defendant's right to confrontation, the unavailability of the witness must be shown if his prior out-of-court statement is to be introduced as non-hearsay at trial.

However, in Dutton v. Evans,55 under Snyder v. Massachusetts,[56] the Court seemed to abandon this strict requirement.[57] Therefore, presentation of a statement by a witness who was under oath, in the presence of the jury, and subject to cross-examination by the defendant was considered the only way of complying with the Confrontation Clause.[58] Ten years later, the

---

[55] See 400 U.S. 74, 76 (1970).

[56] See 291 U.S. 97, 122 (1934).

[57] The Court noted: "The decisions of this Court make it clear that the mission of the Confrontation Clause is to advance a practical concern for the accuracy of the truth-determining process in criminal trials by assuring that 'the trier of fact [has] a satisfactory basis for evaluating the truth of the prior statement.' Evans exercised, and exercised effectively, his right to confrontation on the factual question whether Shaw had actually heard Williams make the statement Shaw related. And the possibility that cross-examination of Williams could conceivably have shown the jury that the statement, though made, might have been unreliable was wholly unreal." See 400 U.S. 74, 89 (1970).

[58] "At least in the absence of prosecutorial misconduct or negligence and where the evidence is not crucial or devastating, the Confrontation Clause is satisfied if the circumstances of presentation of out-of-court statements are such that the trier of fact has a satisfactory basis for evaluating the truth of the hearsay statement, and this is to be ascertained in each case by focusing on the reliability of the

Court in Ohio v. Roberts[59] established a two-pronged test for deciding whether the Confrontation Clause was violated. Roberts held that

> [i]n sum, when a hearsay declarant is not present for cross-examination at trial, the Confrontation Clause normally requires a showing that he is unavailable. Even then, his statement is admissible only if it bears adequate 'indicia of reliability.' Reliability can be inferred without more in a case where the evidence falls within a firmly rooted hearsay exception. In other cases, the evidence must be excluded, at least absent a showing of particularized guarantees of trustworthiness.[60]

---

proffered hearsay statement, that is, by an inquiry into the likelihood that cross-examination of the declarant at trial could successfully call into question the declaration's apparent meaning or the declarant's sincerity, perception, or memory." See FindLaw, Confrontation, available at http://caselaw.lp.findlaw.com/data/constitution/amendment06/08.html (last visited, Oct. 20, 2004).

[59] See 448 U.S. 56 (1980).

[60] The Court ruled: "The Confrontation Clause operates in two separate ways to restrict the range of admissible hearsay. First, in conformance with the Framers' preference for face-to-face accusation, the Sixth Amendment establishes a rule of necessity. In the usual case (including cases where prior cross-examination has occurred), the prosecution must either produce, or demonstrate the unavailability of, the declarant whose statement it wishes to use against the defendant. The second aspect operates once a witness is shown to be unavailable. Reflecting its underlying purpose to augment accuracy in the fact-finding process by ensuring the defendant an effective means to test adverse evidence, the Clause countenances only hearsay marked with such trustworthiness that 'there is no material departure from the reason of the general rule.'" Id., at 65-6.

In summary, the Confrontation Clause did not exclude out-of-court statements of an unavailable declarant if they bore sufficient indicia of reliability. Moreover, evidence should be considered reliable if it fell within a firmly rooted hearsay exception or if it showed particularized guarantees of trustworthiness. While many hearsay exceptions provided in Federal Rules of Evidence 803 do not require a showing of unavailability, the question arose whether this requirement could be waived after Roberts. By citing Dutton v. Evans, the Court in a footnote to Ohio v. Roberts noted that a demonstration of unavailability was not always required, especially when the utility of trial confrontation seemed so remote.[61] As a result, since the prosecution was not always required to produce a seemingly available witness,[62] only the reliability prong should be met in any given case. Hence, Roberts did not establish a real two-pronged test.

Nonetheless, the Court later, in United States v. Inadi,[63] addressed the question left by Roberts: when should the prosecutor show the unavailability of the witness? Although the Court in Inadi affirmed Roberts by ruling that the Confrontation Clause did not require showing the unavailability of the declarant,[64] since the

---

[61]　Id., at 65 note 7.

[62]　Id.

[63]　See 475 U.S. 387 (1985).

[64]　Id., 394-6.

better evidence referred to the conspirator's out-of-court testimony made during conspiracy in this case, Inadi in fact narrowed Roberts by holding that "the rule of 'necessity' is confined to use of testimony from a prior judicial proceeding, and is inapplicable to co-conspirators' out- of-court statements."[65] Subsequently, in addition to co-conspiratorial out-of-court statements made during conspiracy, under Inadi, only in the case of out-of-court statements made during prior judicial proceedings could the prosecutor waive the requirement of producing or demonstrating the unavailability of the declarant.

On the basis of Roberts, the Court in Coy v. Iowa outlawed an Iowa statute that authorized placing a one-way screen between a child victim and a defendant at trial, because "the exception created by the Iowa statute, which was passed in 1985, could hardly be viewed as firmly rooted."[66] However, two years later, the Court in Maryland v. Craig upheld Maryland's law allowing the use of a one-way and closed circuit television to prevent a child victim in a sex crime from "facing" the defendant at trial.[67] While Coy's interpretation of the Confrontation Clause focused mainly on protecting the defendant's trial right to confront his accuser,[68] Craig adopted a different view, since "hearsay statements

---

[65] See FindLaw, Confrontation, available at http://caselaw.lp.findlaw.com/data/constitution/amendment06/08.html (last visited, Oct. 20, 2004).

[66] See 487 U.S. 1012, 1021 (1988).

[67] See 497 U.S. 836 (1990).

[68] See 487 U.S. 1012, 1021 (1988).

of nontestifying co-conspirators may be admitted against a defendant despite the lack of any face-to-face encounter with the accused."69 Thus, as evidenced by hearsay exceptions, even though the precedents have established that the Confrontation Clause reflects a preference for face-to-face confrontation at trial,[70] this preference must occasionally give way to considerations of public policy and the necessities of the case.[71] As suggested in Coy, precedents confirming "a defendant's right to confront accusatory witnesses may be satisfied absent a physical, face-to-face confrontation at trial only where denial of such confrontation is necessary to further an important public policy and only where the reliability of the testimony is otherwise assured."[72] The word "confronted" provided in the Sixth Amendment does not "simply mean face-to-face confrontation, for the Clause would then, contrary to our cases, prohibit the admission of any accusatory hearsay statement made by an absent declarant --- a declarant who is undoubtedly as much a 'witness against' a defendant as one who actually testifies at trial."[73]

In 2004, in Crawford v. Washington, the Supreme Court again injected new vitality into the Confrontation Clause,[74] which

---

[69] See 497 U.S. 836, 849 (1990).

[70] See Ohio v. Roberts, 448 U.S. 56, 63 (1980).

[71] See Mattox v. United States, 156 U.S. 237, 243 (1895).

[72] See 497 U.S. 836, 850 (1990).

[73] See Coy v. Iowa, 497 U.S. 836, 849 (1990).

[74] See 124 S. Ct. 1354 (2004).

had already been described as a revolutionary bombshell and an important paradigm shift in confrontation clause analysis.[75] Roberts and Inadi established the two-pronged test for determining whether admitting an out-of-court statement would violate the Confrontation Clause. The Crawford Court, however, realizing that the Confrontation Clause "commands not that the evidence be reliable, but that reliability be assessed in a particular manner by testing in the crucible of cross-examination,"[76] discarded this test and reshaped the legal framework for the admission of testimonial hearsay. Under Crawford, there are two types of hearsay evidence: testimonial and non-testimonial. As a result,

> [w]here nontestimonial hearsay is at issue, it is wholly consistent with the Framers' design to afford the States flexibility in their development of hearsay law --- as does Roberts, and as would an approach that exempted such statements from Confrontation Clause scrutiny altogether. Where testimonial evidence is at issue, however, the Sixth Amendment demands what the common

---

[75] See People v. Cage, 15 Cal. Rptr. 3d 846, 851 (Cal. Ct. App. 2004); United States v. Manfre, 368 F. 3d 832, 833 (8th Cir. 2004); Also see Neil P. Cohen, et al., "Crawford v. Washington: Confrontation Revolution", 40 *Tennessee Bar Journal* 22 (2004).

[76] See 124 S Ct. 1354, 1370 (2004).

law required: unavailability and a prior opportunity for cross-examination.[77]

In other words, if the statement is testimonial hearsay, Crawford supplements Roberts by subjecting the prior out-of-court statement made during judicial process to previous cross-examination, which also extends the requirement of demonstrating the unavailability of the witness to those beyond the limitation of Inadi. Hence, Roberts and Inadi will no longer apply if the prior out-of-court statement made during judicial process was not previously subjected to cross-examination. Nevertheless, while the Court intentionally declined to define the precise parameters of a testimonial statement in Crawford, it leaves an open question as to what statements are testimonial. Due to legislation of federal or state rules of evidence and court decisions, some of which interpret constitutional provisions, the rules for obtaining and weighing evidence are now more restrictive in the United States than in England.[78]

---

[77] Id.

[78] See John C. Klotter, supra note 1, 8.

3.3 Modern Evidential Hearsay: Definition and Exceptions（現代傳聞：定義與例外）

3.3.1 An Overview（概說）

Non-lawyers have for centuries used the term hearsay to signify that information is second-hand and therefore possibly unreliable.[79] However, as a legal concept, the common law courts created the term hearsay.[80] In fact, there was no need for a hearsay rule before the sixteenth century when juries were permitted to obtain evidence by consulting non-witness persons, and where jurors were chosen because they knew something about the case.[81] Chief Justice Marshall in 1813 justified the hearsay rule by stating that

> [a]ll questions upon the rules of evidence are of vast importance to all orders and degrees of men: our lives, our liberty, and our property are all concerned in the support of these rules, which have been matured by the wisdom of ages, and are now reversed from their antiquity and the good sense in which they are founded. One of these rules is, that hearsay evidence is in its

---

[79] See Steven I. Friedland, et al., *Evidence Law and Practice*, 308 (LexisNexis, 2000).

[80] See G. Michael Fenner, supra note 222, 8.

[81] See John C. Klotter, supra note 1, 280.

own nature inadmissible. That this species of testimony supposes some better testimony that might be adduced in the particular case, is not the sole ground of its exclusion. Its intrinsic weakness, its incompetency to satisfy the mind of the existence of the fact, and the frauds which might be practiced under its cover, combine to support the rule that hearsay evidence is totally inadmissible.[82]

Therefore, the Court in Hickory v. United States recognized that "[h]earsay is the prior out-of-court statements of a person, offered affirmatively for the truth of the matters asserted, presented at trial either orally by another person or in written form."[83] Consequently, when the statement is hearsay, the trier of fact is not in a position to assess the proper weight to be accorded the out-of-court statement.[84] Currently, Rule 802 of the Federal Rules of Evidence (FRE 802) states that "[h]earsay is not admissible except as provided by these rules or by other rules prescribed by the Supreme Court pursuant to statutory authority or by Act of

---

[82] See Mima Queen and Child v. Hepburn, 11 U.S. 290, 295-6 (1813).
[83] See 151 U.S. 303, 309 (1894).
[84] See Michael H. Graham, "*Stickperson Hearsay*: A Simplified Approach to Understanding the Rule Against Hearsay", 1982 *University of Illinois Law Review* 887, 888 (1982).

Congress." Hearsay is the legal equivalent of the common expression "tell it to the judge or jury."[85] The hearsay rule is a general rule of inadmissibility that must be considered whenever a witness testifies to a statement made outside of the courtroom.[86] Notwithstanding, hearsay itself is not an easy issue, as described by Professor Arthur Best: "The myth of hearsay is that no one understands it, and students and practicing lawyers always make mistakes about it. It does seem sometimes that the people who understand the hearsay doctrines are a kind of secret society."[87]

Generally speaking, four main risks are associated with out-of-court statements that would be substantially reduced by the safeguards of the trial process: the risk of misperception; the risk of faulty memory; the risk of misstatement; and the risk of distortion.[88] The provisions of FRE 102[89] explain that the purpose be construed to secure fairness in administration and elimination of unjustifiable construction of the Federal Rules of Evidence. Except for the privilege rules, the rules of evidence aim at the

---

[85]　See Steven I. Friedland, supra note 255, 312.

[86]　See G. Michael Fenner, supra note 222, 5.

[87]　See Arthur Best, Evidence, 61 (New York Aspen Law & Business, 2001).

[88]　See Christopher B. Mueller, supra note 29, 125.

[89]　It provides: "These rules shall be construed to secure fairness in administration, elimination of unjustifiable expense and delay, and promotion of growth and development of the law of evidence to the end that the truth may be ascertained and proceedings justly determined."

truth so that only relevant evidence is admissible.[90] There are many concerns about why hearsay statements should be excluded.[91] As shown in Crawford, most importantly, hearsay is excluded because the out-of-court declarant has not been cross-examined meaningfully by the adverse party,[92] which creates an unacceptable danger that the trier of fact will give too much value to the declarant's statement.[93] In other words, the reliability problems of out-of-court statements are thought to be so great that common law decisions and the Federal Rules of Evidence take the position that a rule of exclusion will produce the fairest results overall.[94] However, while a party could usually try to prove its case with any kind of evidence it can find, subject only to the requirement that the material be relevant, the hearsay rule contradicts the general freedom that evidence law gives parties to select their own kinds of proof.[95]

Of course, it is obvious that some hearsay evidence is more reliable than others, or that there is some particular need which is worth risking unreliable evidence in order to allow hearsay into court.[96] In seeking to allow as much evidence into court as poss-

---

[90] See supra note 222, 4.

[91] See John C. Klotter, supra note 1, 275.

[92] See Steven I. Friedland, supra note 255, 312.

[93] See Roger C. Park, supra note 4, 241.

[94] See Arthur Best, supra note 263, 65.

[95] Id.

[96] See G. Michael Fenner, supra note 222, 9.

ible while sifting out unreliable evidence, including a degree of justification to assure trustworthiness of the hearsay evidence, the courts have developed many exceptions to the hearsay rule.[97] In a sense, the hearsay rules are based on some intuitive assumptions about what kinds of communications are likely to be the most accurate.[98] No matter what exceptions to the hearsay rule are adopted, fairness and judicial effectiveness are major concerns. For instance, as stated in the Commission Report, "[a]n inquiry into the performance of America's criminal courts, therefore, must of necessity examine both their effectiveness and their fairness, and proposals for improving their operations must aim at maintaining or redressing the essential equilibrium between these two qualities."[99] Accordingly, it should be emphasized that the goal of the hearsay rule is to assist the trier of fact in the search for the truth by keeping the unreliable evidence away from the trier of fact.[100]

3.3.2　The Definition of Hearsay（傳聞定義）

FRE 801(c) defines hearsay as a "statement,[101] other than

---

[97] See John C. Klotter, supra note 1, 276.

[98] See Arthur Best, supra note 263, 61.

[99] See Advisory Committee Report on Rules of Evidence, Revised Draft, 51 F.R.D. 315 (1971).

[100] See G. Michael Fenner, supra note 222, 8.

[101] Rule 801(a) of Federal Rules of Evidence provides: "A 'statement' is (1) an oral or written assertion or (2) nonverbal conduct of a person, if it is intended by the person as an assertion."

one made by the declarant[102] while testifying at a trial or hearing, offered in evidence to prove the truth of the matter asserted." Under this provision, the term hearsay is a statement, oral, written, or nonverbal conduct of a person intended as a statement by that person, and not the witness, who has not seen, heard, or known of the fact by himself, but who has heard that statement and later testified what he has heard to the court.[103] Although hearsay is itself defined in this article, the language employed here is criticized as having turned a basically simple idea into a tangle of language and ideas so obscure that it becomes truly difficult to think or talk about that idea with clarity and simplicity.[104] To put it as simply as possible, hearsay is an out-of-court statement offered to prove the truth of the matter asserted.[105] While this plain definition is much easier to follow, it still does not explain "what an out-of-court statement is" or "whether the statement is offered to prove the truth."[106]

Nonetheless, under FRE 801(d), both "prior statement by

---

[102] Rule 801(b) of Federal Rules of Evidence provides: "A 'declarant' is a person who makes a statement."

[103] See Watchara Neitivanich, "Securing Online Commercial Transactions by Digital Signatures: A Comparative Analysis of the U.S. E-Sign Act and Thai E-Transactions Act", 224 (an unpublished S.J.D. Dissertation of the Golden Gate University School of Law, 2003, 12).

[104] See James W. McElhaney, "The Heart of the Matter", 89 *American Bar Association Journal* 50, 52 (2003).

[105] See Christopher B. Mueller, supra note 29, 123.

[106] See James W. McElhaney, supra note 280, 52.

witness" and "admission by party-opponent" are defined as non-hearsay.[107] Opposing exceptions in FRE 803 and FRE 804, FRE 801(d)(2) have often been referred to as exemptions or exclusions from the hearsay rule. It seems conflicting since admission by party-opponent, nonhearsay, under FRE 801(d)(2) fits the definition of FRE 801(c) that defines hearsay as an out-of-court statement offered for its truth. Whether Rule 801(d)(2) is hearsay or not becomes confusing and troubling at this point. In fact, instead of treating admissions and statements of co-conspirators as non-hearsay,[108] the traditional common law treated what has now been adopted in Rule 801(d)(2) as admissible exceptions to hearsay, which is followed by a number of state versions of evidence rules.[109] To some extent, the theory behind saying that admissions are not hearsay at all, as opposed to saying that they are hearsay falling within an exception, is rather abstruse and perhaps over-refined.[110] Probably because Dean John Henry Wigmore suggested it would be easier to deal with admissions if they could no more be treated as hearsay, the drafters of the federal rules then adopted Wigmore's suggestion and called admissions nonhearsay.[111] The advisory committee eventually adopted admission by

---

[107] It provides: "A statement is not hearsay if — (1) Prior statement by witness. (2) Admission by party-opponent."

[108] See Roger C. Park, supra note 4, 267.

[109] See James W. McElhaney, supra note 280, 54.

[110] See Roger C. Park, supra note 4, 254.

[111] See James W. McElhaney, supra note 280, 54.

a party-opponent as nonhearsay in that simple notions of fairness require a party to be stuck with his or her own statement, by noting that "[a]dmission[s] by a party-opponent are excluded from the category of hearsay on the theory that their admissibility in evidence is the result of the adversary system rather than satisfaction of the conditions of the hearsay rule."[112] As a result, no matter what it is called, the nonhearsay admission under FRE 801(d)(2), which refers to anything said or done by a party-opponent that is inconsistent with the position now taken at trial, should be admissible to prove its truth.[113] Moreover, after Crawford, if a statement fits the co-conspirator rule under FRE 801(d)(2)(E),[114] whether the defendant may claim that his constitutional right to confrontation was violated in federal courts becomes unclear; however, this argument should still be available at least under the

---

[112] See FRE 801 (d) (2) Advisory Committee's note, cited in Roger C. Park, et al., *Evidence Law: A Student's Guide to the Law of Evidence as Applied in American Trials*, 254 n 58 (West, 1998).

[113] See James W. McElhaney, supra note 280, 56.

[114] The statements have to be made in furtherance of the conspiracy and during the course of the conspiracy. See United States v. Tombrello, 666 F. 2d 485, 490 (11th Cir.), cert. denied, 456 U.S. 994 (1982). However, mere conversations between conspirators, merely narrative declarations, and causal admissions of culpability are not statements in furtherance of the conspiracy. See United States v. Tille, 729 F. 2d 615 (9th Cir. 1984). There must be independent evidence of the conspiracy. See United States v. Jannotti, 729 F. 2d 213 (3rd Cir. 1984). Also, see Patrick J. Sullivan, "Bootstrapping of Hearsay under Federal Rule of Evidence 801(d)(2)(E): Further Erosion of the Coconspirator Exemption", 74 *Iowa Law Review* 467 (1989).

confrontation clause of state constitutions.[115]

There are two types of definitions of hearsay according to Professor Roger C. Park's description:

Definitions of hearsay are usually either assertion-centered or declarant-centered. Under an assertion-centered definition, an out-of-court statement is hearsay when it is offered in evidence to prove the truth of the matter asserted. Under a declarant-centered definition, an out-of-court statement is hearsay when it depends for value upon the credibility of the declarant.[116]

The core idea against hearsay complies with the Confrontation Clause; however, after Crawford, the definition of hearsay should be both assertion-centered, seeking the truth, and declarant-centered, providing the defendant with an opportunity to challenge the declarant's testimonial qualities of sincerity, narrative ability, memory, and perception.[117] Hence, to better understand the definition of hearsay, if the testifying witness is not the same person the defendant wants to cross-examine, the testifying witness is not the real witness and the statement at issue is an out-of-court statement.[118] When an out-of-court statement is rel-

---

[115] See Arnold v. State, 751 P. 2d 494, 504-05 (Alaska App. 1988); Nunez v. People, 737 P. 2d 422, 424-26 (Colo. 1987); cited in Roger C. Park, supra note 4, 266 n 106.

[116] See Roger C. Park, "*I Didn't Tell Them Anything About You*: Implied Assertions as Hearsay Under the Federal Rules of Evidence", 74 *Minnesota Law Review* 783, 783 (1990).

[117] See Christopher B. Mueller, supra note 29, 126.

[118] See James W. McElhaney, supra note 280, 52.

evant without regard to whether it conveys accurate information, then the hearsay prohibition does not operate, and testimony about the statement is allowed.[119] Basically, there is no need to cross-examine the out-of-court declarant especially when the trier of fact can use the declarant's out-of-court statement in deciding issues other than the truth of the declarant's out-of-court statement.[120] While testimony that a witness heard a person say, "Look out!" is just like testimony that a witness saw a person wearing a blue sweater or running across a street, non-hearsay statements are not offered to prove the truth of what they assert.[121]

In general, the answer to "who the defendant wants to cross-examine to test what is being said or observed" depends on "whether the truth of the out-of-court statement matters."[122] Therefore, on the one hand, if the truth of the out-of-court statement does not make any difference and the declarant, the actual witness, is on the stand, the statement is not hearsay;[123] on the other hand, if the truth of the out-of-court statement matters and the testifying witness is not the real witness, the statement is hearsay. Obviously, the preference implied by the hearsay rule for having the actual speaker present in court and available to answer

---

[119] See Arthur Best, supra note 263, 65.

[120] See Roger C. Park, supra note 4, 241.

[121] See Arthur Best, supra note 263, 68.

[122] See James W. McElhaney, supra note 280, 53.

[123] Id.

clarifying questions has no application where the proponent's effort is to prove that words were said rather than prove that words were true.[124] Under this analysis, only a few out-of-court statements might constitute hearsay, for example: verbal acts, when something is done with words; verbal parts of acts, when an act and its accompanying words constitute a whole; and knowledge whether someone knows something.[125]

3.3.3 Exceptions to Hearsay（傳聞例外）

As jurors began to be chosen only if they had no knowledge of the case that would influence their decision, the hearsay rule began its development.[126] While the hearsay rule's primary purpose is to exclude testimony about out-of-court statements unless the adverse party has the opportunity for meaningful cross-examination,[127] the supreme irony of the hearsay doctrine is that a vast amount of hearsay is admissible at common law[128] and under the Federal Rules of Evidence.[129] Despite the strong policy grounds for excluding hearsay, and despite the fact that Justice Marshall argued that hearsay evidence should not be admitted because of

---

[124] See Arthur Best, supra note 263, 68.

[125] See James W. McElhaney, supra note 280, 54.

[126] See John C. Klotter, supra note 1, 280.

[127] See Steven I. Friedland, supra note 255, 312.

[128] See Roger C. Park, supra note 4, 266.

[129] See Arthur Best, supra note 263, 89.

its intrinsic weakness and incompetency,[130] and where the risks inherent in admitting some types of hearsay are less than those connected with others, the Federal Rules of Evidence and common law allow hearsay to be admitted in many circumstances covered by exceptions to the general principle of exclusion.[131] In general, the exceptions to the hearsay rule apply when surrounding circumstances provide guarantees of reliability.[132] Thus, if the purpose of the hearsay rule is not present in a specific case and if the interests of justice will be best served by admission of the statement into evidence, then the evidence should be admitted as an exception to the hearsay rule.[133]

The Federal Rules of Evidence divide their 28 exceptions to the hearsay rule into two categories. In the first are those that apply only when the declarant is unavailable under FRE 804.[134] The second category includes those where the risks inherent in admitting some types of hearsay are minimal;[135] the exceptions of the second set apply whether or not the declarant is available under FRE 803[136] and by far includes the larger number of exceptions.[137]

---

[130] See John C. Klotter, supra note 1, 280.
[131] See Arthur Best, supra note 263, 65, 102.
[132] See Roger C. Park, supra note 4, 254.
[133] See John C. Klotter, supra note 1, 281.
[134] It provides: "(a) Definition of unavailability. (b) Hearsay exceptions."
[135] See Arthur Best, supra note 263, 102.
[136] Sub-Provisions omitted.
[137] See Roger C. Park, supra note 4, 268.

According to FRE 805, hearsay included within hearsay is not excluded under the hearsay rule if each part of the combined statements conforms with an exception to the hearsay rule provided in these rules. Additionally, there is a catch-all exception[138] that allows admission of hearsay in circumstances that are not covered in any of the other twenty-eight exceptions.[139] Although one might expect a more widespread use of the idea that the declarant should be called if available,[140] more than twenty exceptions in FRE 803 do not have this requirement.[141] The only exceptions requiring unavailability in FRE 804 are those for dying declarations, for statements against interest, for former testimony, and for statements of personal and family history.[142] In summary,

---

[138] FRE 807 provides: "A statement not specifically covered by Rule 803 or 804, but having equivalent circumstantial guarantees of trustworthiness, is not excluded by the hearsay rule if the court determines that (A) the statement is offered as evidence of a material fact; (B) the statement is more probative on the point for which it is offered than any other evidence which the proponent can procure through reasonable efforts; and (C) the general purposes of these rules and the interests of justice will best be served by admission of the statement into evidence. However, a statement may not be admitted under this exception unless the proponent of it makes known to the adverse party sufficiently in advance of the trial or hearing to provide the adverse party with a fair opportunity to prepare to meet it, the proponent's intention to offer the statement and the particulars of it, including the name and address of the declarant."

[139] See Arthur Best, supra note 263, 102.

[140] See Daniel Stewart, Jr., "Perception, Memory, and Hearsay: A Criticism of Present Law and the Proposed Federal Rules of Evidence", 1 *Utah Law Review* 1 (1970).

[141] See Roger C. Park, supra note 4, 268.

[142] Id.

even though the rule prohibiting the admission of hearsay statements was formulated in criminal cases by AD 1700, exceptions
to the hearsay rule have developed through centuries because of
the strict exclusionary nature of the rule.[143] Nonetheless, where
the arguments supporting the exceptions are based on the necessity to use the out-of-court statements rather than on the likely truthfulness of the out-of-court declarant, the exception is allowed
only if there is proof that the declarant is unavailable.[144]

4. Comparative Analysis of the Hearsay Rule in Taiwan and the United States

（台灣與美國傳聞法則之比較研究）

In this section, this study intends to make a comparative
analysis of the legal foundations discussed above. While adopting
accusatorial elements in a civil-law-based jurisdiction may unavoidably result in unpredictable problems, tentative resolutions
to these problems will be submitted by this study if possible. In
principle, this study tries to provide resolutions to problems arising from the 2003 enactments of the hearsay rule in the ROC
CPC. Before comparing between Taiwan and the United States, it
is worth mentioning that in Taiwan the defendant is not considered a witness if he testifies. In other words, the defendant does
not testify under oath. This practice is much different from that
in the United States.

---

[143] See John C. Klotter, supra note 1, 280.
[144] See Arthur Best, supra note 263, 102.

4.1 Hearsay Definition

While Paragraph 1 of Article 159 of the ROC CPC simply defines inadmissible hearsay, the Federal Rules of Evidence of the United States provides a much more complicated definition of it. In a fashion similar to Paragraph 1 of Article 159 of the ROC CPC, FRE 802 provides: "Hearsay is not admissible except as provided by these rules or by other rules prescribed by the Supreme Court pursuant to statutory authority or by Act of Congress." Even though there is no provision in the ROC CPC providing the definitions similar to FRE 801 (a) and (b), such as the definitions applied in FRE 801 (a) and (b), a "statement" referred to in the ROC CPC should include (1) an oral or written assertion, or (2) nonverbal conduct of a person, if it is intended by the person as an assertion; and the term "anyone other than the defendant" means a person who makes a statement. Nevertheless, while FRE 801(c) provides that "'[h]earsay' is a statement, other than one made by the declarant while testifying at a trial or hearing, offered in evidence to prove the truth of the matter asserted," which focuses mainly on "if it is an out-of-court statement" and "if it is offered to prove the truth of the matter asserted," inadmissible hearsay under Paragraph 1 of Article 159 of the ROC CPC merely refers to an out-of-court statement "made by anyone other than the defendant." In other words, according to the hearsay definition provided by Paragraph 1 of Article 159 of the ROC CPC, an out-of-court statement made by a defendant is not hearsay whether or not he testifies at trial in Taiwan. Similarly, whether or not the defendant testifies at trial, although what he previously stated constitutes inadmissible hearsay under FRE 801 (c) and FRE 802, according to FRE 801 (d) (2)[145] excluding admissions from being hearsay, the defendant's prior out-of-court statement is not hearsay even if it is offered against the defendant. While common law defined these admissions as exceptions to inadmissible hearsay,[146] the Federal Rules of Evidence patently do not follow the common law approach.

Notwithstanding, while FRE 801 (d) (1)[147] provides that a

---

[145] It provides: "A statement is not hearsay if the statement is offered against a party and is (A) the party's own statement in either an individual or a representative capacity or (B) a statement of which the party has manifested an adoption or belief in its truth, or (C) a statement by a person authorized by the party to make a statement concerning the subject, of (D) a statement by the party's agent or servant concerning a matter within the scope of the agency or employment, made during the existence of the relationship, or (E) a statement by a coconspirator of a party during the course and in furtherance of the conspiracy. The contents of the statement shall be considered but are not alone sufficient to establish the declarant's authority under subdivision (C), the agency or employment relationship and scope thereof under subdivision (D), or the existence of the conspiracy and the participation therein of the declarant and the party against whom the statement is offered under subdivision (E)."

[146] See Arthur Best, supra note, 90.

[147] It provides: "A statement is not hearsay if the declarant testifies at the trial or hearing and is subject to cross-examination concerning the statement, and the statement is (A) inconsistent with the declarant's testimony, and was given under oath subject to the penalty of perjury at a trial, hearing, or other proceedings, or in a deposition, or (B) consistent with the declarant's testimony and is offered to rebut an express or implied charge against the declarant of recent fabrication or improper influence or motive, or (C) one of identification of a person made after perceiving the person."

"prior statement by witness" is not hearsay, according to Paragraph 1 of Article 159 of the ROC CPC, this out-of-court statement is hearsay because the declarant is not the defendant. Thus, although a prior statement by a witness is admissible at trial in the United States,[148] whether it is admissible at trial in Taiwan depends on its compliance with any hearsay exception provided in Articles 159-1 to 159-5 of the ROC CPC. In addition, since hearsay in the United States means a statement offered to prove the truth of the matter asserted under FRE 801 (c), if the statement is not offered to prove the truth, it is not hearsay.[149] In other words, the out-of-court verbal statement is admissible in evidence for another purpose than that of proving the truth in the United States. For example, if the out-of-court statement "I want to kill John" is offered to prove "the declarant did intend to kill John," then it is inadmissible hearsay, because the fact finder has to rely on the credibility of the declarant to decide if he really intended to kill John. But if it is offered merely to prove the declarant was alive at the time of making this statement, since nothing will be lost by the fact that the out-of-court declarant was not subject to cross-examination, it is not necessary to exclude it as

---

[148] In fact, FRE 801 (d) (1) treats selected types of statements by witnesses as falling outside the hearsay definition, under particular circumstances. Not all prior statements are defined as non-hearsay by FRE 801 (d) (1). See Arthur Best, supra note, 93.

[149] See Roger C. Park, et al., *Evidence Law: A Student's Guide to the Law of Evidence as Applied in American Trials*, 241 (West, 1998).

hearsay.[150] Moreover, FRE 806 admits any inconsistent evidence of a statement or conduct made by the declarant of a hearsay exception to attack the credibility of the declarant.[151] On the contrary, while Paragraph 1 of Article 159-1 of the ROC CPC does not provide the purpose of the out-of-court statement for defining inadmissible hearsay, therefore, even if it is not offered to prove the truth of the matter asserted, it seems to fall within the scope of inadmissible hearsay provided by Paragraph 1 of Article 159-1 of the ROC CPC. Under this viewpoint, the pre-2003 ROC Supreme Court decision 91 Tai Sun 2363 admitting an out-of-court statement for the purpose of impeaching the witness should be reversed. However, this 2003 legislation differs much from the hearsay practice in the United States. It is questionable whether Paragraph 1 of Article 159-1 of the ROC CPC should exclude an out-of-court statement provided mainly for impeachment purposes from inadmissible hearsay.

---

[150] Id.

[151] It provides: "When a hearsay statement, or a statement defined in rule 801(d)(2), (C), (D), or (E), has been admitted in evidence, the credibility of the declarant may be attacked, and if attacked may be supported, by any evidence which would be admissible for those purposes if declarant had testified as a witness. Evidence of a statement or conduct by the declarant at any time, inconsistent with the declarant's hearsay statement, is not subject to any requirement that the declarant may have been afforded an opportunity to deny or explain. If the party against whom a hearsay statement has been admitted calls the declarant as a witness, the party is entitled to examine the declarant on the statement as if under cross-examination."

As mentioned in the Advisory Committee Note, hearsay was adopted to protect the accused's right to confront witnesses. This is identical to its counterpart in the United States. In general, hearsay is excluded mainly because the out-of-court declarant has not been subject to the test of cross-examination, which creates an unacceptable danger that the fact finder will put too much weight on the non-testifying declarant's statement.[152] When there is no need to cross-examine the out-of-court declarant because the fact finder can use the out-of-court statement without relying on the credibility of the declarant, the out-of-court statement should not be excluded from evidence.[153] In other words, admitting an out-of-court statement in evidence for another purpose than that of proving the truth of the matter asserted will not infringe the accused's rights. Accepting it in evidence will not result in any violation of constitutionally protected rights. Thus, even though the 2003 legislation does not recognize the ROC Supreme Court decision 91 Tai Sun 2363, affirming this decision afterwards will not conflict with the legislative purpose of adopting the hearsay rule. Since any relevant and probative evidence is important to finding the fact, if an out-of-court statement is not used to prove the truth of the matter asserted, it should not be ex-

---

[152] See Roger C. Park, et al., Evidence Law: A Student's Guide to the Law of Evidence as Applied in American Trials, 241 (West, 1998).

[153] That is without relying on the sincerity, perception, memory, or narrative ability of the declarant. Id.

cluded from evidence merely because it happens to fall within the scope of the definition of inadmissible hearsay. Courts in Taiwan should feel free to follow 91 Tai Sun 2363 in admitting out-of-court statements as evidence. Moreover, this study suggests the ROC Legislative Yuan delimits the applicability of inadmissible hearsay by adding "an out-of-court statement is not hearsay if the purpose for offering it is other than proving the truth of the matter asserted" to Paragraph 1 of Article 159-1 of the ROC CPC.

4.2 Hearsay Exceptions（傳聞例外）

The issue of hearsay exceptions is both questionable and interesting because the 2003 legislation only has five provisions that include eleven types of hearsay exceptions,[154] whereas FRE 803, 804 and 807 provide a total of twenty-nine types of hearsay exceptions.[155] As a result, some hearsay exceptions provided in FRE are not adopted by the 2003 ROC legislation; some ROC hearsay exceptions are not found in the Federal Rules of Evidence. This study will compare those hearsay exceptions in this

---

[154] Those are: (1) Paragraph 1 of Article 159-1; (2) Paragraph 2 of Article 159-1; (3) Article 159-2; (4) Subparagraph 1 of Article 159-3; (5) Subparagraph 2 of Article 159-3; (6) Subparagraph 3 of Article 159-3; (7) Subparagraph 4 of Article 159-3; (8) Subparagraph 1 of Article 159-4; (9) Subparagraph 2 of Article 159-4; (10) Subparagraph 3 of Article 159-4; and (11) Article 159-5.

[155] FRE 803 provides 23 exceptions, FRE 804 provides 5 exceptions, and FRE 807 provides 1 residual exception.

section and discuss whether the 2003 ROC legislation provides enough hearsay exceptions. The following comparative analyses are based on the classifications of the ROC hearsay exceptions.

4.2.1 Out-of-Court Statements Made before a Judge or a Public Prosecutor（在法官與檢察官面前之陳述）

Article 159-1 of the ROC CPC deals with out-of-court statements made before a judge or a public prosecutor. According to the Advisory Committee Note, this kind of out-of-court statement is admissible in that neither a judge nor a public prosecutor will coerce a witness to make a statement. Under this provision, any out-of-court statement made before a judge or a public prosecutor, whether in criminal or civil proceedings, and whether or not the declarant was under oath, is admissible because a witness is free to make a statement or to testify. For example, if witness X testified in civil proceedings that Y was hit by Z, in criminal proceedings charging Z with injuring Y, the civil testimony of X would be admissible at the criminal trial whether or not X is available as a witness. Moreover, if judge or public prosecutor K heard L say he saw M kill N in person, even if L never testified in any criminal proceedings, what L said is admissible in M's trial according to this article.

This legislation admitting any out-of-court statement made before a judge or a public prosecutor is quite particular. No similar hearsay exception will be found in the Federal Rules of Evidence. It is unclear where this article originated. The rationale behind this provision is merely based on the voluntariness of the witness's statement of testimony, which might result from the continental tradition of trusting judges and public prosecutors. It is quite controversial, however, because these two hearsay exceptions do not protect the defendant's right to confront the witness. While this article provides no protection of the right to confrontation, the core value of the ROC hearsay rule is obscure even though the Advisory Committee Note clearly stated that the ROC hearsay rule had been adopted to protect the right to confrontation. Is it possible for the ROC criminal justice system to develop a unique hearsay system based on other than American sources? Since it is impossible to answer this question on the basis of the United States hearsay practice, this problem will be discussed in the next section.

4.2.2 Prior Inconsistent Out-of-Court Statements Made before Law-Enforcement-Officers under More Reliable Circumstances（先前不一致之陳述）

As mentioned above, under FRE 801 (c), a witness's own out-of-court words are hearsay even if they are quoted at trial by the same witness while their relevance depends on the truth of the matter asserted.[156] Since the fact finder can observe the declarant's in-court behavior and hear responses to cross-examination regarding the out-of-court statement, and the lack of these oppor-

---

[156] See Arthur Best, supra note, 93.

tunities to observe and to hear is the basis for excluding hearsay, it is not necessary to exclude an out-of-court statement made by a declarant who also testifies at trial.[157] This is why FRE 801 (d) (1) excludes prior statements by witnesses from inadmissible hearsay.

Contrary to this approach of the United States, under Paragraph 1 of Article 159-2 of the ROC CPC, even if the witness testifies at trial, his prior out-of-court statement still falls within the scope of inadmissible hearsay. Without any provision similar to FRE 801 (d) (1) excluding prior statements by witnesses from hearsay, it is necessary for the ROC CPC to create a hearsay exception to admit prior witness statements because there is no need to exclude this kind of out-of-court statement in general. Thus, Article 159-2 of the ROC CPC was adopted to provide grounds for admitting the same declarant's prior inconsistent out-of-court statement. Although it does not exclude the prior witness statement from the definition of hearsay, it still admits a prior inconsistent out-of-court witness statement in evidence at trial.

In addition, Article 159-2 of the ROC CPC only admits the prior inconsistent out-of-court witness statement when he testifies at trial and when the court finds the prior out-of-court statement more reliable and also necessary to prove the truth of the alleged offense. This means not every prior inconsistent out-of-court wit-

---

[157] Id.

ness statement is admissible. It is arguable, however, under what circumstances the court should find the prior out-of-court statement more reliable and also necessary to prove the truth of the alleged offense. FRE 801 (d) (1) (A) excludes prior inconsistent statement made by witness from hearsay only when "the declarant testifies at the trial or hearing and is subject to cross-examination concerning the statement," and "inconsistent with the declarant's testimony, and was given under oath subject to the penalty of perjury at a trial, hearing, or other proceedings, or in a deposition." These requirements result from the following concerns. While some scholars claimed the hearsay rule should be completely withdrawn from past statements of a person who is currently a witness at trial, others believed that the hearsay exclusion might be applied to out-of-court statements by someone who is presently a witness at trial.[158] To some extent, cross-examination at trial may be less effective than it would have been at the time the speaker made the statement.[159] To prevent well-organized parties from developing a practice of making records of interviews with prospective witness, which may result in no cross-examination at the time obtaining these statements, as well as subsequent introduction of these prior statements at a later trial,[160] the Federal Rules of Evidence thus require these prior statement to be "given under oath

[158] Id.
[159] Id.
[160] Id.

subject to the penalty of perjury" in addition to asking the declarant to be available for cross-examination. In other words, according to FRE 801 (d) (1) (A), if the prior inconsistent testimony was not under oath and not subject to the penalty of perjury, it is still hearsay. Even though Article 159-2 of the ROC CPC requires the prior inconsistent out-of-court statement to be made before law-enforcement-officers, it does not clearly set out similar requirements under which a prior inconsistent out-of-court statement can become admissible in evidence at trial. While judges are fact finders in Taiwan, whether it is necessary to exclude a prior inconsistent out-of-court statement without being under oath subject to the penalty of perjury from admissible hearsay in the ROC criminal justice system remains unclear. Thus, unless the ROC court adopts a viewpoint referring to FRE 801 (d) (1) (A) to interpret "when the court finds the prior out-of-court statement more reliable which is necessary to prove the truth of the alleged offense asserted," the scope of the admissibility of a prior inconsistent out-of-court statement looks broader than that in the United States.

4.2.3　Out-of-Court Statements Made before Law-Enforcement-Officers by Currently Unavailable Declarants as Trial Witnesses（未到庭者在執法人員前之陳述）

While Article 159-2 of the ROC CPC requires the declarant of the prior out-of-court statement to testify at trial, Article 159-3 of the ROC CPC then creates a hearsay exception without this requirement. As a result, when the declarant is not available as a witness at trial, whether his prior out-of-court statement is admissible falls within the scope of Article 159-3 of the ROC CPC. Similar to Article 159-2, Article 159-3 of the ROC CPC admits prior out-of-court witness statement only "when the court finds the prior out-of-court statement more reliable which is necessary to prove the truth of the alleged offense asserted." According to this provision, a prior out-of-court witness statement should be made before law-enforcement-officers. It then creates four circumstances either of which would result in admissible hearsay. In general, a prior out-of-court witness statement made before law-enforcement-officers is admissible when the declarant is unable to make a statement at trial because of death,[161] loss of memory, or physical or mental illness or infirmity at the time of the trial,[162] when the declarant's attendance at trial cannot be produced by judicial process or other reasonable means,[163] and when the declarant refuses to testify at trial without reasonable justification.[164] These hearsay exceptions have very identical counterparts in the Federal Rules of Evidence.

First of all, FRE 804 (a) defines "Unavailability as a witness." In a sense, "imposing the requirement of unavailability in

---

[161] See Subparagraph 1 of Article 159-3 of the ROC CPC.

[162] See Subparagraph 2 of Article 159-3 of the ROC CPC.

[163] See Subparagraph 3 of Article 159-3 of the ROC CPC.

[164] See Subparagraph 4 of Article 159-3 of the ROC CPC.

connection with certain hearsay exceptions is partly a result of tradition."[165] Generally speaking, this rule applies only when the in-court testimony of the out-of-court declarant is unavailable: "testimony unavailable."[166] If the declarant's in-court testimony of the out-of-court statement is available, then the hearsay exceptions in FRE 804 do not apply.[167] It is fair to say that FRE 804 (a) (2) is identical to Subparagraph 4 of Article 159-3 of the ROC CPC; FRE 804 (a) (3) and (4) are identical to Subparagraphs 1 and 2 of Article 159-3 of the ROC CPC; and FRE 804 (a) (5) is identical to Subparagraph 3 of Article 159-3 of the ROC CPC.[168] Sec-

---

[165] See Arthur Best, supra note, 122.

[166] See G. Michael Fenner, *The Hearsay Rule*, 282 (Carolina Press, 2002).

[167] Id.

[168] FRE 804 (a) provides: "'Unavailability as a witness' includes situations in which the declarant—

(1) is exempted by ruling of the court on the ground of privilege from testifying concerning the subject matter of the declarant's statement; or

(2) persists in refusing to testify concerning the subject matter of the declarant's statement despite an order of the court to do so; or

(3) testifies to a lack of memory of the subject matter of the declarant's statement; or

(4) is unable to be present or to testify at the hearing because of death or then existing physical or mental illness or infirmity; or

(5) is absent from the hearing and the proponent of a statement has been unable to procure the declarant's attendance (or in the case of a hearsay exception under subdivision b(2), (3), or (4), the declarant's attendance or testimony) by process or other reasonable means.

A declarant is not unavailable as a witness if exemption, refusal, claim of lack of memory, inability, or absence is due to the procurement or wrongdoing of the proponent of a statement for the purpose of preventing the witness from attending or testifying."

ondly, as a hearsay exception, while "former testimony" in FRE 804 (b) (1) should be made before a government officer in charge of legal proceedings,[169] it is similar to Article 159-3 of the ROC CPC which also requires the prior out-of-court statement to be made before law-enforcement-officers.

Nevertheless, on the issue of unavailability, Taiwan and the United States show different characteristics. FRE 804 (b) (1) provides that the witness making a prior out-of-court statement should have "an opportunity and similar motive to develop the testimony by direct, cross, or redirect examination." Article 159-3 of the ROC CPC, on the other hand, does not mention the same requirement. In other words, a prior out-of-court statement not subject to cross-examination might be admissible at trial in the ROC jurisdiction. Moreover, while FRE 804 (b) (1) also requires a prior out-of-court statement to be given under oath, Article 159-3 of the ROC CPC does not have this prerequisite. Any prior out-of-court statement not made under oath thus might be admissible according to this provision. While Article 159-3 of the ROC CPC requires the declarant to be unavailable at trial, it does suggest that these exceptions in this provision are less reliable

---

[169] It provides: "Testimony given as a witness at another hearing of the same or a different proceeding, or in a deposition taken in compliance with law in the course of the same of another proceeding, if the party against whom the testimony is now offered, or, in a civil action or proceeding, a predecessor in interest, had an opportunity and similar motive to develop the testimony by direct, cross, or redirect examination."

than those in Article 159-4 of the ROC CPC where there is no such requirement. These less reliable prior out-of-court statements are tolerated as evidence "because they involve situations where the out-of-court statements have some claim to reliability and there is a strong need for the information they contain."[170] Of course, if courts in Taiwan adopted a viewpoint referring to FRE 804 (b) (1) requiring a prior out-of-court statement to be given under oath and subject to cross-examination[171] to interpret "when the court finds the prior out-of-court statement more reliable which is necessary to prove the truth of the alleged offense asserted," the scope of the admissibility of a prior out-of-court statement when the declarant is unavailable as a witness at trial might look similar to that in the United States.

4.2.4 Admissible Out-of-court Statements in Writing
（可信文書）

In addition to Articles 159-1 to 159-3 of the ROC CPC, Article 159-4 of the ROC CPC also provides hearsay exceptions focusing on out-of-court statements made in writing. It is worth mentioning that this article imposes the requirement of "in writing" in connection with certain hearsay exceptions. As a result, if out-of-court statements are not in writing, they will not be admissible at trial under this provision. Unlike Article 159-3, Ar-

---

[170] See Arthur Best, supra note, 122.
[171] Id., at 123.

ticle 159-4 of the ROC CPC does not require the unavailability
of the declarant as a witness at trial. While the drafters of the
Federal Rules of Evidence believed the risk inherent in admitting
hearsay exceptions in FRE 803 is less than those in FRE 804,[172]
it is fair to say situations provided in Article 159-4 of the ROC
CPC are more reliable than those in Article 159-3 of the ROC
CPC. In general, hearsay exceptions in Article 159-4 of the ROC
CPC are based on the likely truthfulness of statements; when the
arguments supporting the exceptions are based on the necessity to
use the out-of-court statements, hearsay exceptions are allowed
only if the declarant is unavailable,[173] as is the case with the exceptions in Article 159-3 of the ROC CPC.

Article 159-4 of the ROC CPC creates three types of hearsay exceptions. Usually, documents made by government officers
other than law-enforcement-officers are admissible unless they
were made under unreliable circumstances.[174] And a document, if
kept in the course of a regularly conducted business activity, and
if it was the regular practice of that business activity to make the
document, of regular activity made by someone in charge of
making this document is admissible unless it was made under unreliable circumstances, too.[175] In addition to these two types,

---

[172] Id., at 102.
[173] Id.
[174] See Subparagraph 1 of Article 159-4 of the ROC CPC.
[175] See Subparagraph 2 of Article 159-4 of the ROC CPC.

there is a residual provision admitting other documents made under reliable circumstances in evidence at trial.[176] While the 2003
Advisory Committee Note on the ROC CPC clearly refers to
FRE 803 which also provides hearsay exceptions not imposing
the requirement of availability of the declarant as a witness at trial, it is desirable to understand the rationales behind those hearsay exceptions in FRE 803.

　　FRE 803 (4) excludes statements for purposes of medical diagnosis or treatment from inadmissible hearsay.[177] This exception
consists of two foundational elements: (1) "the declarant believed
that the out-of-court statement would result in medical diagnosis
or treatment," and (2) "a doctor would reasonably rely upon the
out-of-court statement in diagnosing or treating a patient."[178] Since it is reasonable to believe the declarant to tell the truth when
he is seeking medical diagnosis or treatment, this highly likely
truthfulness results in statements for purposes of medical diagnosis or treatment being admissible hearsay. In Taiwan, under
this rationale, statements for purposes of medical diagnosis or
treatment are excluded from inadmissible hearsay according to

---

[176] See Subparagraph 3 of Article 159-4 of the ROC CPC.

[177] It provides: "(4) Statements for purposes of medical diagnosis or treatment.
Statements made for purposes of medical diagnosis or treatment and describing
medical history, or past or present symptoms, pain, or sensations, or the
inception or general character of the cause or external source thereof insofar as
reasonably pertinent to diagnosis or treatment."

[178] See G. Michael Fenner, *The Hearsay Rule*, 194 (Carolina Press, 2002).

Article 159-4 of the ROC CPC. It is clear they are admissible under Subparagraph 2 of this article if medical doctors work in private hospitals. It is questionable, however, under which subparagraph they are admissible when medical doctors are considered non-law-enforcement-government-officers; if they work for public hospitals, this might invoke Subparagraph 1 of this article. However, this question has no bearing on the issue whether "statements for purposes of medical diagnosis or treatment" are admissible hearsay.

FRE 803 (5) excludes recorded recollection from inadmissible hearsay.[179] There are six foundational elements: (1) "the out-of-court statement must be recorded somewhere, in some way;" (2) "the out-of-court statement must have been made or adopted by the testifying witness;" (3) "at the time the testifying witness made or adopted the statement, she must have had knowledge of the matter recorded and that knowledge must have been fresh in her memory;" (4) "at the time of the trial, the testifying witness must no longer have no sufficient memory of the matter recorded to allow her to testify fully or accurately;" (5) "at trial, the wit-

---

[179] It provides: "(5) Recorded recollection. A memorandum or record concerning a matter about which a witness once had knowledge but now has insufficient recollection to enable the witness to testify fully and accurately, shown to have been made or adopted by the witness when the matter was fresh in the witness' memory and to reflect that knowledge correctly. If admitted, the memorandum or record may be read into evidence but may not itself be received as an exhibit unless offered by an adverse party."

ness must remember that record is accurate;" and (6) it "may be read into evidence but may not itself be received as an exhibit unless offered by an adverse party."[180] In a sense, this exception results from the fact that "the witness has forgotten something relevant."[181] Meanwhile, this exception is accepted because of its highly likely truthfulness, too. While FRE 803 (5) admits recorded recollection in evidence only when the testifying witness was the recorder of the out-of-court statement,[182] Subparagraph 2 of Article 159-4 of the ROC CPC does not impose a similar requi-

---

[180] See G. Michael Fenner, *The Hearsay Rule*, 211 (Carolina Press, 2002).

[181] Id., at 213.

[182] It should be noted that FRE 612 provides additional safeguards against the misleading use of the refreshed recollection procedure which is different from FRE 803 (5). See Arthur Best, supra note, 108. FRE 612 provides: "Except as otherwise provided in criminal proceedings by section 3500 of title 18, United States Code, if a witness uses a writing to refresh memory for the purpose of testifying, either— (1) while testifying, or (2) before testifying, if the court in its discretion determines it is necessary in the interests of justice, an adverse party is entitled to have the writing produced at the hearing, to inspect it, to cross-examine the witness thereon, and to introduce in evidence those portions which relate to the testimony of the witness. If it is claimed that the writing contains matters not related to the subject matter of the testimony the court shall examine the writing in camera, excise any portions not so related, and order delivery of the remainder to the party entitled thereto. Any portion withheld over objections shall be preserved and made available to the appellate court in the event of an appeal. If a writing is not produced or delivered pursuant to order under this rule, the court shall make any order justice requires, except that in criminal cases when the prosecution elects not to comply, the order shall be one striking the testimony or, if the court in its discretion determines that the interests of justice so require, declaring a mistrial."

rement. Unlike FRE 803 (5), even if no witness testifying at trial adopts this kind of out-of-court statement, it is admissible in evidence in Taiwan if it is already in the dossier.[183] Furthermore, while FRE 803 (5) ends with the following: "the memorandum or record may be read into evidence but may not itself be received as an exhibit unless offered by an adverse party," it seems unnecessary to impose a similar requirement on Subparagraph 2 of Article 159-4 of the ROC CPC because there is no jury trial, and the fact finders, the judges, already have full access to each of those documents in Taiwan.[184] Thus, it is fair to say Subparagraph 2 of Article 159-4 of the ROC CPC does not conflict with FRE 803 (5) in nature.

FRE 803 (6) and (7) deal with records as well as absence of

---

[183] Of course, the court has to inform the accused of this kind of record under Paragraph 1 of Article 165 of the ROC CPC.

[184] There are two reasons why FRE 803 (5) ends in this way, as explained by Professor G. Michael Fenner: "First, viva voce evidence is not physically in the jury room. It is not transcribed and sent into the jury room. Exhibits are physically presented in the jury room. If the record of the witness's recollection received into evidence, then it would go into the jury room, and would be a physical presence there the whole time the jurors were deliberating. Its presence in the room would give the recorded recollection more significance than it deserves. It would make the evidence easier to remember, and perhaps more prominent than it would otherwise be. Second, if there is a tendency to believe more readily things we read than things we hear, then giving the jury the statement in writing makes it more likely the jury will find it credible." See G. Michael Fenner, *The Hearsay Rule*, 212 (Carolina Press, 2002).

records of a regularly conducted activity as hearsay exceptions.[185]
There are four fundamental elements: (1) "the out-of-court statement must be a record (or an absence of an entry in a record)
that was made in the course of a regularly conducted business activity;" (2) "the record must have been made at or near the time
of the event recorded;" (3) "the record must be made by someone
who either: (a) had personal knowledge of what is recorded; or
(b) based the record on information provided by someone who
both had personal knowledge and provided the information in the
regular course of the particular activity involved;" and (4) "a trustworthiness clause [⋯] allows the judge to keep the evidence

---

[185] FRE 803 (6) provides: "A memorandum, report, record, or data compilation in
any form, of acts, events, conditions, opinions, or diagnoses, made at or near the
time by, or from information transmitted by, a person with knowledge, if kept in
the course of regularly conducted business activity, and if it was the regular
practice of that business activity to make the memorandum, report, record, or
data compilation, all as shown by the testimony of the custodian or other
qualified witness, or by certification that complies with Rule 902(11), Rule 902
(12), or a statute permitting certification, unless the source of information or the
method or circumstances of preparation indicate lack of trustworthiness. The
term 'business' as used in this paragraph includes business, institution,
association, profession, occupation, and calling of every kind, whether or not
conducted for profit." And FRE 803 (7) provides: "Evidence that a matter is not
included in the memoranda, reports, records, or data compilations, in any form,
kept in accordance with the provisions of paragraph (6), to prove the
nonoccurrence or nonexistence of the matter, if the matter was of a kind of
which a memorandum, report, record, or data compilation was regularly made
and preserved, unless the sources of information or other circumstances indicate
lack of trustworthiness."

out, even if the foundational elements are satisfied, if the judge is suspicious of the evidence."[186]

These two exceptions come from the fact that no one will have a current memory of the details recorded in the documents covered by FRE 803 (6) and (7).[187] Since business records are mainly "made for the purpose of running an enterprise rather than for some purpose in litigation,"[188] excluding them from inadmissible hearsay is persuasive. As explained in United States v. Baker, "business records have a high degree of accuracy because the nation's business demands it, because the records are customarily checked for correctness, and because recordkeepers are trained in habits of precision."[189] In short, these records in FRE 803 (6) and (7) are considered reliable not only because they are important to the business, but also because "they are kept with regularity and someone's job depends on keeping them and keeping them accurately."[190] Although these records are generally considered reliable, in order to bar unreliable records when there is a problem with the particular record, the final clause in FRE 803 (7) allows the trial judge to deny this hearsay exception.[191] Generally speaking, these two exceptions come from the reliabi-

---

[186] See G. Michael Fenner, *The Hearsay Rule*, 225-6 (Carolina Press, 2002).

[187] Id., at 226.

[188] See Arthur Best, supra note, 109.

[189] See 693 F. 2d 183, 188 (D.C. Cir., 1982).

[190] See G. Michael Fenner, *The Hearsay Rule*, 227 (Carolina Press, 2002).

[191] Id.

lity of these business records. Since Subparagraph 2 of Article 159-4 of the ROC CPC does not mention 'absence of entry in records kept in accordance with records of regularly conducted activity' at all, and there is already a similar trustworthiness clause in it, whether it is admissible is entirely up to the court. It is not necessary to have a provision focusing especially on 'absence of entry in records kept in accordance with records of regularly conducted activity.'

FRE 803 (8) excludes public records and reports from inadmissible hearsay.[192] This exception has three foundational elements: (1) "the out-of-court statement must be a public record or report;" (2) "it must set forth one of the following three kinds of things: (a) the activities of the office or agency that prepared the report; (b) matters the agency had a legal duty to observe and a legal duty to report upon; (c) factual findings resulting from an investigation made pursuant to authority granted by law;" and (3) "once the foundation for the exception is established the court can still decide that the evidence does not seem trustworthy and

---

[192] It provides: "(8) Public records and reports. Records, reports, statements, or data compilations, in any form, of public offices or agencies, setting forth (A) the activities of the office or agency, or (B) matters observed pursuant to duty imposed by law as to which matters there was a duty to report, excluding, however, in criminal cases matters observed by police officers and other law enforcement personnel, or (C) in civil actions and proceedings and against the Government in criminal cases, factual findings resulting from an investigation made pursuant to authority granted by law, unless the sources of information or other circumstances indicate lack of trustworthiness."

sustain the hearsay objection."[193] While it is almost impossible for the declarant who prepared public records and reports to remember the information recorded, and this kind of information might not be available elsewhere, any out-of-court statement in public records or reports will not be admissible at trial without this exception.[194] In addition, public records and reports are more reliable than live testimony because public officers are assumed to "perform their jobs properly and, therefore, that public records can be trusted."[195] Nonetheless, there is also a trustworthiness clause authorizing the trial court to deny the reliability of evidence admitted under this exception.[196] According to Subparagraph 1 of Article 159-4 of the ROC CPC, documents made by government officers other than law-enforcement-officers are admissible unless they were made under unreliable circumstances. This provision is quite identical to FRE 803 (8); they both admit almost all public records and reports but those made by law-enforcement-officers. Besides, the reliability clause of Subparagraph1 of Article 159-4 of the ROC CPC, "unless they were made under unreliable circumstances," is similar to the trustworthiness clause in FRE 803 (8). Similarly, FRE 803 (9) and (14) admit "records of vital statistics" and "records of documents

---

[193] See G. Michael Fenner, *The Hearsay Rule*, 239-40 (Carolina Press, 2002).

[194] Usually, the declarant is unlikely to have firsthand knowledge of the information recorded in the report. Id., at 241.

[195] Id.

[196] Id., at 242.

affecting an interest in property" in evidence.[197] Since both these records required to be made under law will be considered public records or reports in Taiwan, FRE 803 (9) and (14) are also covered by Subparagraph1 of Article 159-4 of the ROC CPC. Moreover, under this analysis, out-of-court statements adopted in previous judgments concerning previous conviction and personal, family, or general history, or boundaries, such as those in FRE 803 (22) and (23),[198] are admissible under Subparagraph1 of Article 159-4 of the ROC CPC.

As does FRE 803(7), FRE 803 (10) excludes absence of

---

[197] FRE 803 (9) provides: "Records of vital statistics. Records or data compilations, in any form, of births, fetal deaths, deaths, or marriages, if the report thereof was made to a public office pursuant to requirements of law." FRE 803 (14) provides: "(14) Records of documents affecting an interest in property. The record of a document purporting to establish or affect an interest in property, as proof of the content of the original recorded document and its execution and delivery by each person by whom it purports to have been executed, if the record is a record of a public office and an applicable statute authorizes the recording of documents of that kind in that office."

[198] FRE 803 (22) provides: "(22) Judgment of previous conviction. Evidence of a final judgment, entered after a trial or upon a plea of guilty (but not upon a plea of nolo contendere), adjudging a person guilty of a crime punishable by death or imprisonment in excess of one year, to prove any fact essential to sustain the judgment, but not including, when offered by the Government in a criminal prosecution for purposes other than impeachment, judgments against persons other than the accused. The pendency of an appeal may be shown but does not affect admissibility." FRE 803 (23) provides: "(23) Judgment as to personal, family, or general history, or boundaries. Judgments as proof of matters of personal, family or general history, or boundaries, essential to the judgment, if the same would be provable by evidence at trial."

public record or entry.[199] There are two fundamental elements of this exception: (1) "there must be evidence that the public official or agency in question regularly made and preserved such records or entries," and (2) "there must be either testimony or a Rule 902 (4) certification that a diligent search failed to uncover such a record or such an entry."[200] The need to admit this evidence is brought about by the fact that no public officer will remember what he did not make a particular entry about.[201] Since having a public officer testify what he did not make a particular entry about at trial is usually less reliable, admitting the absence of public record or entry in evidence is thus acceptable. Nonetheless, while Subparagraph 1 of Article 159-4 of the ROC CPC does not mention 'absence of public record or entry,' and contains a similar trustworthiness clause, whether this evidence is admissible is entirely up to the court. It is not necessary to have a provision focusing especially on 'absence of public record or entry.'

Similar to FRE 803 (6), FRE 803 (11) excludes records of re-

---

[199] It provides: "(10) Absence of public record or entry. To prove the absence of a record, report, statement, or data compilation, in any form, or the nonoccurrence or nonexistence of a matter of which a record, report, statement, or data compilation, in any form, was regularly made and preserved by a public office or agency, evidence in the form of a certification in accordance with rule 902, or testimony, that diligent search failed to disclose the record, report, statement, or data compilation, or entry."

[200] See G. Michael Fenner, *The Hearsay Rule*, 253 (Carolina Press, 2002).

[201] Id.

ligious organizations from inadmissible hearsay.[202] Although there is no equivalent article in Taiwan, FRE 803 (11) is covered by Subparagraph 2 of Article 159-4 of the ROC CPC, because religious records are usually made in regularly conducted activities. While FRE 803 (12) admits marriage, baptismal, and similar certificates in evidence at trial,[203] its counterpart is unseen in Taiwan. These marriage, baptismal, and similar certificates, however, can be admissible in evidence at trial through Subparagraphs 1 or 2 of Article 159-4 of the ROC CPC, depending on whether the recorder is authorized by public branches. If a certificate is made by a public officer or the recorder is authorized by law, then Subparagraph 1 of Article 159-4 of the ROC CPC applies. Otherwise Subparagraph 2 of Article 159-4 of the ROC CPC is applicable.

Unlike FRE 803 (13), which clearly admits family records in evidence,[204] there is no provision excluding these records from

---

[202] It provides: "(11) Records of religious organizations. Statements of births, marriages, divorces, deaths, legitimacy, ancestry, relationship by blood or marriage, or other similar facts of personal or family history, contained in a regularly kept record of a religious organization."

[203] It provides: "(12) Marriage, baptismal, and similar certificates. Statements of fact contained in a certificate that the maker performed a marriage or other ceremony or administered a sacrament, made by a clergyman, public official, or other person authorized by the rules or practices of a religious organization or by law to perform the act certified, and purporting to have been issued at the time of the act or within a reasonable time thereafter."

[204] It provides: "(13) Family records. Statements of act concerning personal or family history contained in family Bibles, genealogies, charts, engravings on rings, inscriptions on family portraits, engravings on urns, crypts, or tombstones or the like."

inadmissible hearsay in the ROC CPC. Nevertheless, there is a residual subparagraph, Subparagraph 3 of Article 159-4, allowing the court to admit other kinds of reliable out-of-court statements in writing at trial. Although the 2003 Advisory Committee Note on the ROC CPC does not clearly indicate what this subparagraph includes, based on the highly likely truthfulness, while "records of family history kept in family Bibles have by long tradition been received in evidence,"[205] family records in FRE 803 (13) may be admissible in evidence under Subparagraph 3 of Article 159-4 of the ROC CPC. Moreover, under this analysis, the other out-of-court statements similar to those in FRE 803 (15), (16), (17), or (18) may also be admissible in evidence at trial in Taiwan.[206] In short, while there is no category that needs to have

---

[205] In addition, "opinions in the area also include inscriptions on tombstones, publicly displayed pedigrees, and engravings on rings." See Advisory Committee Note to Original Rule 803, Exception (13), in Steven I. Friedland, et al., *Evidence Law and Practice*, 2001 Supplement, Appendices: Federal Rules of Evidence, 109 (LexisNexis, 2001).

[206] FRE 803 (15), (16), (17), and (18) provide: "(15) Statements in documents affecting an interest in property. A statement contained in a document purporting to establish or affect an interest in property if the matter stated was relevant to the purpose of the document, unless dealings with the property since the document was made have been inconsistent with the truth or the statement or the purport of the document. (16) Statements in ancient documents. Statements in a document in existence twenty years or more the authenticity of which is established. (17) Market reports, commercial publications. Market quotations, tabulations, lists, directories, or other published compilations, generally used and relied upon by the public or by persons in particular occupations. (18) Learned treatises. To the extent called to the attention of an expert witness upon cross-examination or relied upon

by the expert witness in direct examination, statements contained in published treatises, periodicals, or pamphlets on a subject of history, medicine, or other science or art, established as a reliable authority by the testimony or admission of the witness or by other expert testimony or by judicial notice. If admitted, the statements may be read into evidence but may not be received as exhibits." Moreover, Advisory Committee Note to Original Rule 803 provides the rationales behind these exceptions: "Exception (15). Dispositive documents often contain recitals of fact. Thus a deed purporting to have been executed by an attorney in fact may recite the existence of the power of attorney, or a deed may recite that the grantors are all the heirs of the last record owner. Under the rule, these recitals are exempted from the hearsay rule. The circumstances under which dispositive documents are executed and the requirement that the recital be germane to the purpose of the document are believed to be adequate guarantees of trustworthiness, particularly in view of the non-applicability of the rule if dealings with the property have been inconsistent with the documents. The age of the document is of no significance, though in practical application the document will most often be an ancient one;" "Exception (16). Authenticating a document as ancient, essentially in the pattern of the common law, as provided in Rule 901(b)(8), leaves open as a separate question the admissibility of assertive statements contained therein as against a hearsay objection. Wigmore further states that the ancient document technique of authentication is universally conceded to apply to all sorts of documents, including letters, records, contracts, maps, and certificates, in addition to title documents, citing numerous decisions. Since most of these items are significant evidentially only insofar as they are assertive, their admission in evidence must be as a hearsay exception;" "Exception (17). Ample authority at common law supported the admission in evidence of items falling in this category. While Wigmore's text is narrowly oriented to lists, etc., prepared for the use a trade or profession, authorities are cited which include other kinds of publications, for example, newspaper market reports, telephone directories, and city directories. The basis of trustworthiness is general reliance by the public or by a particular segment of it, and the motivation of the compiler to foster reliance by being accurate;" and "Exception (18). The writers have generally favored the admissibility of learned treatises, [⋯] but the great weight of authority has been that learned treatises are not as many exceptions as FRE 803 does,[207] Subparagraph 3 of Article 159-4 of the ROC CPC might be considered useful legislation.

Similar to Subparagraph 3 of Article 159-4 of the ROC CPC, FRE 807 also provides a residual exception to inadmissible hearsay.[208] In order to be admissible under this rule, FRE 807 re-

---

admissible as substantive evidence though usable in the cross-examination of experts. The foundation of the minority view is that the hearsay objection must be regarded as unimpressive when directed against treatises since a high standard of accuracy is engendered by various factors: the treatise is written primarily and impartially for professionals, subject to scrutiny and exposure for inaccuracy, with the reputation of the writer at stake. Sound as this position may be with respect to trustworthiness, there is, nevertheless, an additional difficulty in the likelihood that the treatise will be misunderstood and misapplied without expert assistance and supervision. This difficulty is recognized in the cases demonstrating unwillingness to sustain findings relative to disability on the basis of judicially noticed medical texts. The rule avoids the danger of misunderstanding and misapplication by limiting the use of treatises as substantive evidence to situations in which an expert is on the stand and available to explain and assist in the application of the treatise if desired. The limitation upon receiving the publication itself physically in evidence, contained in the last sentence, is designed to further this policy." Citations omitted. See Advisory Committee Note to Original Rule 803, Exception (15), (16), (17), and (18), in Steven I. Friedland, et al., Evidence Law and Practice, 2001 Supplement, Appendices: Federal Rules of Evidence, 110-1 (LexisNexis, 2001).

[207] See G. Michael Fenner, *The Hearsay Rule*, 256 (Carolina Press, 2002).

[208] FRE 807 provides: "A statement not specifically covered by Rule 803 or 804, but having equivalent circumstantial guarantees of trustworthiness, is not excluded by the hearsay rule if the court determines that (A) the statement is offered as evidence of a material fact; (B) the statement is more probative on the point for which it is offered than any other evidence which the proponent can procure through reasonable efforts; and (C) the general purposes of these rules

quires the statement to be "more probative on the point for which it is offered than any other evidence which the proponent can procure through reasonable effects,"[209] "no other evidence is reasonably available and is as probative as that offered under this exception."[210] In a sense, this exception meets the need for flexibility in the hearsay rules since common law rules allow judges to create hearsay exceptions when necessary.[211] If an offering party does not give notice of his intention to offer the evidence in question to the opposing party, this exception will not apply.[212] This exception has five foundational elements: (1) "trustworthiness;" (2) "relevance;" (3) "relative probative value;" (4) "application of the exception will serve the general purposes of these rules and the interests of justice;" and (5) "proponent's advance notice of his or her intention to use the rule."[213] While Subparagraph 3 of Article 159-4 of the ROC CPC does not mention the requirement to invoke the residual exception, referring to FRE

---

and the interests of justice will best be served by admission of the statement into evidence. However, a statement may not be admitted under this exception unless the proponent of it makes known to the adverse party sufficiently in advance of the trial or hearing to provide the adverse party with a fair opportunity to prepare to meet it, the proponent's intention to offer the statement and the particulars of it, including the name and address of the declarant."

[209] Id.

[210] See G. Michael Fenner, *The Hearsay Rule*, 347 (Carolina Press, 2002).

[211] Id.

[212] Id., at 345.

[213] Id., at 346.

807 might be a proper approach when deciding whether Subparagraph 3 of Article 159-4 of the ROC CPC applies.

4.2.5　Admissible Under Parties Agreement（當事人同意）

Although Articles 159-1 to 159-4 of the ROC CPC create many hearsay exceptions, parties are not allowed to invoke any of them because these exceptions only authorize courts to decide the admissibility of out-of-court statements. In fact, while parties agree to accept an out-of-court statement, admitting it in evidence at trial should not invade the right to confrontation because the accused gives it up. As a result, Article 159-5 of the ROC CPC creates another hearsay exception allowing parties to admit an out-of-court statement not included in Articles 159-1 to 159-4 of the ROC CPC. If allowing an out-of-court statement agreed on by parties results in an unfair trial, however, the court can deny admissibility. This fair trial clause is meaningful, especially so in a private prosecution where there is no government participation and parties might agree to accept an obviously false out-of-court statement for an unjust reason; for example, to impute the criminal or civil blame to another. In other words, under this fair trial clause, not all out-of-court statements agreed on by parties are admissible. The court can also deny the admissibility of this evidence even if the opposing party does not object to the out-of-court statement proffered.

There is no rule similar to Article 159-5 of the ROC CPC in the Federal Rules of Evidence. The practice in the United States

adversarial criminal justice system, however, might be similar because the trial judge will not exclude inadmissible hearsay from
evidence either if the opponent accepts it or does not object to it
in time. As a public prosecutor is assumed to play his role without prejudice, a fair trial issue will not result from an exclusively
adversarial trial system where there is no private prosecution. In
other words, it is not necessary to provide a similar fair trial
clause in the Federal Rules of Evidence while a district attorney
should not make an agreement with the defense party admitting
obviously false out-of-court statements in evidence at trial. A
legal basis allowing the ROC courts to deny the admissibility of
out-of-court statements agreed on by parties, however, might be
necessary under the civil law tradition requiring the courts to apply enacted law, especially so when the ROC CPC admits the
out-of-court statements agreed on by parties in evidence. Without
this fair trial clause, courts in Taiwan have to admit obviously
false out-of-court statements accepted by parties in evidence.
This practice is improper, all the more so when these out-of-court
statements are admitted by parties to impute the criminal or civil
blame to another.

4.2.6　Other FRE Admissible Hearsay Exceptions Not Found in the 2003 Legislation
（其他民國 92 年立法未明文之傳聞例外）

　　Although many hearsay exceptions provided in the Federal
Rules of Evidence can be available in Taiwan through directly in-

terpreting Articles 159-1 to 159-4 of the ROC CPC, there are still many FRE hearsay exceptions unavailable because none of the Articles 159-1 to 159-5 of the ROC CPC will cover them through direct interpretation, and courts in Taiwan are not allowed to admit them in evidence without reasonable justifications under the civil law tradition. Nonetheless, it is questionable whether some FRE hearsay exceptions not mentioned above might be implied in the ROC hearsay exceptions. In this subsection, this study will explore how many of hearsay exceptions in the Federal Rules of Evidence are not available in the ROC CPC.

First of all, hearsay exceptions similar to FRE 803 (1), (2), (3), (19), (20), and (21) are not provided in the ROC CPC. Although Articles 159-1 to 159-3 of the ROC CPC admit out-of-court statements in evidence at trial, these articles apply only when these out-of-court statements are made before a judge, a public prosecutor, or another law-enforcement-officer. Nevertheless, these FRE 803 hearsay exceptions do not require these statements to be made before government officers. For example, when an out-of-court statement similar to FRE 803 (1) is made before a judge, a public prosecutor, or another law-enforcement-officer, it might be admissible according to Articles 159-1 to 159-3 of the ROC CPC. Otherwise, its admissibility depends on whether Articles 159-4 to 159-5 of the ROC CPC apply. In fact, Article 159-5 of the ROC CPC usually does not apply to public prosecution. As a consequence, if the declarant of a FRE 803 (1), (2), (3), (19), (20) or (21) out-of-court statement does not make the statement before a judge, a public prosecutor, or another law-enforcement-officer, the admissibility of each of these statements at trial under Article 159-4 of the ROC CPC is questionable since this ROC law requires all admissible out-of-court statements to be in writing.

FRE 803 (1) excludes present sense impression from inadmissible hearsay.[214] This exception consists of two foundational elements: (1) "the out-of-court statement must have been made while the declarant was perceiving an event or a condition, or immediately thereafter," and (2) "the out-of-court statement must describe or explain the thing being perceived."[215] In fact, there is no categorical need for this exception.[216] While spontaneity may replace cross-examination which provides a way to probe for testimonial infirmities, including faulty perception, bad memory, lack of sincerity, dishonesty, and ambiguity, reliability is the only rationale behind this exception in that spontaneity is reflexive.[217] In other words, present sense impression is admissible because of its reliability. Based on this reliability test, it is reasonable to admit a FRE 803 (1) out-of-court statement not in writing, even if the declarant is not available as a witness at trial. While Article

---

[214] It provides: "(1) Present sense impression. A statement describing or explaining an event or condition made while the declarant was perceiving the event or condition, or immediately thereafter;"

[215] See G. Michael Fenner, *The Hearsay Rule*, 142 (Carolina Press, 2002).

[216] Id.

[217] Id., at 143.

159-4 of the ROC CPC only admits out-of-courts statements in writing in evidence at trial, the admissibility in evidence of an out-of-court statement similar to FRE 803 (1) under this legislation is problematic. It is also questionable how an out-of-court statement similar to FRE 803 (2), (3), (19), (20) or (21)[218] can be admissible in evidence at trial according to Article 159-4 of the ROC CPC.

Secondly, when the declarant is unavailable, FRE 804 (b) creates some hearsay exceptions. In order to apply these exceptions, FRE 804 (a) defines the unavailability for these hearsay ex-

---

[218] These FRE 803 exceptions provide: "(2) Excited utterance. A statement relating to a startling event or condition made while the declarant was under the stress of excitement caused by the event or condition;" "(3) Then existing mental, emotional, or physical condition. A statement of the declarant's then existing state of mind, emotion, sensation, or physical condition (such as intent, plan, motive, design, mental feeling, pain, and bodily health), but not including a statement of memory or belief to prove the fact remembered or believed unless it relates to the execution, revocation, identification, or terms of declarant's will;" "(19) Reputation concerning personal or family history. Reputation among members of a person's family by blood, adoption, or marriage, or among a person's associates, or in the community, concerning a person's birth, adoption, marriage, divorce, death, legitimacy, relationship by blood, adoption, or marriage, ancestry, or other similar fact of personal or family history;" "(20) Reputation concerning boundaries or general history. Reputation is a community, arising before the controversy, as to boundaries of or customs affecting lands in the community, and reputation as to events of general history important to the community or State or nation in which located;" and "(21) Reputation as to character. Reputation of a person's character among associates or in the community."

ceptions.[219] It is accepted that FRE 804 (a) (1) includes "any of the evidentiary privileges[220] and the constitutional privilege against self-incrimination."[221] Although Article 159-3 of the ROC CPC also admits some out-of-court statements made before law-enforcement-officers in evidence when the declarant is unavailable to testify as a witness at trial, it does not provide a defini-

---

[219] FRE 804 (a) provides: "'Unavailability as a witness' includes situations in which the declarant—(1) is exempted by ruling of the court on the ground of privilege from testifying concerning the subject matter of the declarant's statement; or (2) persists in refusing to testify concerning the subject matter of the declarant's statement despite an order of the court to do so; or (3) testifies to a lack of memory of the subject matter of the declarant's statement; or (4) is unable to be present or to testify at the hearing because of death or then existing physical or mental illness or infirmity; or (5) is absent from the hearing and the proponent of a statement has been unable to procure the declarant's attendance (or in the case of a hearsay exception under subdivision b(2), (3), or (4), the declarant's attendance or testimony) by process or other reasonable means. A declarant is not unavailable as a witness if exemption, refusal, claim of lack of memory, inability, or absence is due to the procurement or wrongdoing of the proponent of a statement for the purpose of preventing the witness from attending or testifying."

[220] See FRE 501. It provides: "Except as otherwise required by the Constitution of the United States or provided by Act of Congress or in rules prescribed by the Supreme Court pursuant to statutory authority, the privilege of a witness, person, government, State, or political subdivision thereof shall be governed by the principles of the common law as they may be interpreted by the courts of the United States in the light of reason and experience. However, in civil actions and proceedings, with respect to an element of a claim or defense as to which State law supplies the rule of decision, the privilege of a witness, person, government, State, or political subdivision thereof shall e determined in accordance with State law."

[221] See G. Michael Fenner, *The Hearsay Rule*, 283 (Carolina Press, 2002).

tion of the unavailability similar to FRE 804 (a) (1). As a result, even if the out-of-court declarant "is exempted by ruling of the court on the ground of privilege"[222] from testifying at trial, his prior out-of-court statement should be inadmissible since Article 159-3 of the ROC CPC does not create a hearsay exception similar to FRE 804 (a) (1). The ROC Supreme Court decision admitting an out-of-court statement after the declarant invoked his privilege at trial, 90 Sun Zon Gum One 17, where the witness made a statement against the defendant during police interrogation but refused to testify at trial by invoking his privilege,[223] thus will be reversed under this legislation. Nonetheless, it is unclear why the 2003 legislation does not incorporate an FRE 804 (a) (1)-style exception into Article 159-3 of the ROC CPC. Generally speaking, FRE 804 (a) (1) upholds the unavailability of the declarant who invoked the privilege to refuse to testify and admits the prior out-of-court statement in evidence because of its reliability and a strong need for this kind of information.[224] Based on the highly likely truthfulness of the statement, pre-2003 ROC Supreme Court decision 90 Sun Zon Gum One 17 should be affirmed. Hence, the admissibility in evidence of an out-of-court statement similar to FRE 804 (a) (1) under the 2003 legislation demands

---

[222] See FRE 804 (a) (1).

[223] In this pre-2003 legislation murder case, the out-of-court statement against the defendant is similar to that provided in FRE 804 (b) (1).

[224] See Arthur Best, supra note, 123.

further discussion.

Besides FRE 804 (b) (1), hearsay exceptions similar to FRE 804 (2), (3), (4), and (6)[225] are not provided in the ROC CPC. As discussed above, if these out-of-court statements are made before a judge, a public prosecutor, or another law-enforcement-officer, they might be admissible in evidence at trial through Articles 159-1 to 159-3 of the ROC CPC. If they are in writing, they might also be admissible under Article 159-4 of the ROC CPC. The

---

[225] These FRE 804 (b) exceptions include: "(2) Statement under belief of impending death. In a prosecution for homicide or in a civil action or proceeding, a statement made by a declarant while believing that the declarant's death was imminent, concerning the cause or circumstances of what the declarant believed to be impending death. (3) Statement against interest. A statement which was at the time of its making so far contrary to the declarant's pecuniary or proprietary interest, or so far tended to subject the declarant to civil or criminal liability, or to render invalid a claim by the declarant against another, that a reasonable person in the declarant's position would not have made the statement unless believing it to be true. A statement tending to expose the declarant to criminal liability and offered to exculpate the accused is not admissible unless corroborating circumstances clearly indicate the trustworthiness of the statement. (4) Statement of personal or family history. (A) A statement concerning the declarant's own birth, adoption, marriage, divorce, legitimacy, relationship by blood, adoption, or marriage, ancestry, or other similar fact of personal or family history, even though declarant had no means of acquiring personal knowledge of the matter stated; or (B) a statement concerning the foregoing matters, and death also, of another person, if the declarant was related to the other by blood, adoption, or marriage or was so intimately associated with the other's family as to be likely to have accurate information concerning the matter declared. (6) Forfeiture by wrongdoing. A statement offered against a party that has engaged or acquiesced in wrongdoing that was intended to, and did, procure the unavailability of the declarant as a witness."

admissibility of these out-of-court statements is problematic when they are neither in writing nor made in front of law-enforcement-officers. While these hearsay exceptions similar to FRE 804 (b) are also based on the reliability of these out-of-court statements,[226] courts in Taiwan face a real problem if they need to admit these out-of-court statements in evidence without a statutory basis.

After examining the hearsay rule in both the Federal Rules of Evidence and the ROC CPC, it is obvious that the ROC CPC omits some important reliability-based hearsay exceptions as provided in FRE 803 and 804. While courts in Taiwan have to apply an enacted statute, they are not allowed to create hearsay exceptions other than those provided in Articles 159-1 to 159-5 under civil law traditions. It is difficult and unreasonable for the Taiwanese courts to admit an out-of-court statement in violation of an enacted law. When these out-of-court statements are neither in writing nor made in front of law-enforcement-officers, the question of the admissibility of these out-of-court statements is particularly salient in Taiwan as these statements are considered extremely reliable. Since the hearsay rule of the ROC CPC itself does not provide enough exceptions to admit almost all kinds of reliable and trustworthy out-of-court statements contained in the Federal Rules of Evidence, which are considered necessary to find the truth, "how to admit these out-of-court statements not

---

[226] For the rationales behind FRE 804 (b), see Arthur Best, supra note, 123-7.

provided as hearsay exceptions in the ROC CPC" depends on "whether they could be admitted in evidence by other non-hearsay provisions in the ROC CPC." An analysis of the latter question will be necessary and meaningful in a civil-law-based criminal justice system where the court is still entitled to collect and investigate evidence without any party participation.

4.3　The Trial Court（審判法院）

The most striking difference between adjudication proceedings in Taiwan and the United States is jury trial. As mentioned before, historically, evidence law became necessary only when a passive and neutral fact finder was needed. This development resulted in Anglo-American law being devoted to determining which facts constitute evidence and which evidence is admissible.[227] In continental criminal justice systems where the judge decides both the law and the facts, "strict enforcement of hearsay [···] is less practicable."[228] While there is no jury trial in Taiwan, and the judge decides both the law and the facts, it seems reasonable that there was no hearsay rule in the ROC CPC. Nonetheless, while the 2003 Advisory Committee Note clearly stated that the 2003 hearsay rule legislation derives mainly from the Federal Rules of Evidence of the United States, it is interesting why the drafters of the 2003 hearsay rule did not adopt all or most of the FRE hear-

---

[227] See Thomas P. Gallanis, "The Rise of Modern Evidence Law", 84 *Iowa Law Review* 499, 500 (1999).

say rules. On the contrary, for example, the 2003 ROC legislation omits some hearsay exceptions provided in FRE 803 and 804, but creates Article 159-1 of the ROC CPC unseen in the Federal Rules of Evidence. It is also interesting whether the Taiwanese drafters were aware of these differences and what they might result in. If they created these differences intentionally, why so? If not, how can the unprovided hearsay exceptions be admitted in evidence under the current framework of the ROC CPC? Since the hearsay doctrine exists largely because a lay jury cannot properly evaluate statements made outside of its presence, and the rules governing character evidence assume that lay juries usually place too much weight on such proof or often employ it improperly for punitive purposes,[229] mistrust of lay juries is the single overriding reason for the law of evidence.[230] Thus, it is obvious common law hearsay rule will not play the same role in a non-jury trial system. It is then interesting what the common law hearsay rule means in a non-jury trial jurisdiction. In this subsection, this study will explain why it was almost impossible for continental criminal justice systems to develop a common law tri-

---

[228] See Gordon Van Kessel, "A Summary of Mirjan R. Damaska's Evidence Law Adrift", 49 *Hastings Law Journal* 359, 359 (1998).

[229] See Christopher B. Mueller, et al., *Evidence Under the Rules*, 1 (New York Aspen Law & Business, 2000).

[230] See Stephan Landsman, "The Rise of the Contentious Spirit: Adversary Procedure in Eighteenth Century England", 75 *Cornell Law Review* 497, 565 (1990).

al system which supports common law rules of evidence.[231]

Also, this study will explore the institutional limitations of the hearsay rule in a civil-law-based legal framework and suggest potential resolutions to hearsay-related problems arising from the 2003 hearsay legislation in Taiwan.

4.3.1　Trial Court Obligations in Fact-Finding（審判法院發現眞實之義務）

The United States Supreme Court in Faretta v. California found the Sixth Amendment to

> guarantee that a criminal charge may be answered in a manner now considered fundamental to the fair administration of American justice --- through the calling and interrogation of favorable witnesses, the cross-examination of adverse witnesses, and the orderly introduction of evidence. In short, the Amendment constitutionalizes the right in an adversarial criminal trial to make a defense.[232]

As Professor Stephan Landsman pointed out, there are three essential elements in an adversarial criminal trial: "utilization of a neutral and passive fact finder, reliance on party presentation of

---

[231] Id.

[232] See 422 U.S. 806, 818 (1975).

evidence, and use of a highly structured forensic procedure."[233] Under this approach, the trial court reviews evidence for the fact finder, the jury. Nonetheless, the trial court is not responsible for collecting evidence for the jury. In a criminal case, the prosecutor has to present evidence in order to see the defendant convicted. Similarly, the defendant also has to produce evidence when necessary. In other words, both fact investigation and presentation of evidence are controlled by parties.[234] The trial court merely decides whether the presented evidence is admissible so that the fact finder can consider it. As described in Daubert v. Merrel Dow Pharmaceuticals Inc., the trial court just plays the role of "gate keeper" because it merely determines which evidence should be admitted.[235]

The situation in a civil law country is quite different. First of all, there is no common law jury trial. The trial court itself is fact finder. Instead of having parties produce satisfying evidence to the trial court, the court has to study all circumstances of the case so that it pronounce judgment on the basis of all necessary

---

[233] Stephan Landsman, *Adversarial Justice: The American Approach to Adjudication*, 2 (West, 1988).

[234] See Renee Lettow Lerner, "The Intersection of Two Systems: An American on Trial for An American Murder in the French Cour d'Assises", 2001 *University of Illinois Law Review* 791, 797 (2001).

[235] See 509 U.S. 579 (1993).

information.[236] While the parties and their attorneys are not in charge of gathering and presenting evidence,[237] and the court has to make a written judgment explaining the conviction or acquittal, continental criminal justice systems usually allow the judge to collect and investigate evidence in addition to that presented by the trial parties.[238] This procedural aspect concerning the court as fact finder distinguishes an inquisitorial adjudication process from an accusatorial (or adversarial) one. Nevertheless, it itself is not enough to justify why there could not emerge a common-law-like practice of parties-controlled fact investigation and presentation of evidence in the developments of continental criminal justice systems.

In addition to this procedural viewpoint, there is another important factor why continental criminal justice systems would not develop common law rules of evidence. This factor concerns substantive criminal law. For instance, in Taiwan, Article 55 of the ROC Criminal Law, which is derived from a civil law tradition, provides; "If one act constitutes several unlike offenses or the

---

[236] See Renee Lettow Lerner, "The Intersection of Two Systems: An American on Trial for An American Murder in the French Cour d'Assises", 2001 *University of Illinois Law Review* 791, 797 (2001).

[237] See Gordon Van Kessel, "A Summary of Mirjan R. Damaska's Evidence Law Adrift", 49 *Hastings Law Journal* 359, 360 (1998).

[238] For example, former Paragraph 1 of Article 163 of the ROC CPC provided: "The court shall, for the sake of discovering the truth, ex officio investigate evidence."

means employed or the results of the commission of one offense constitute another unlike offense, only the most severe of the prescribed punishments shall be imposed." This means that the court is required to investigate and consider the other offense not charged by the public or private prosecutor because otherwise the uncharged offense could not be punished or indicted anymore. Moreover, while Article 56 of the ROC Criminal Law provides: "If several successive acts constitute like offenses, such successive acts may be considered to be one offense, but the punishment prescribed for such offense may be increased up to one half," and treats several successive offenses as a single one, the court is also required to discover "how many like offenses in the world" the defendant has committed lest the defendant should benefit from an incomplete investigation.[239] In a sense, the defendant is subject to only one criminal punishment if all of his misconducts fall within the scope of Articles 55 and 56 of the ROC Criminal Law. These articles are all the more decisive when the defendant continues to make related or successive offenses after having been in-

---

[239] In fact, Articles 55 and 56 of the ROC Ciminal Law stem from the 1871 German Criminal Law. Although the current German Criminal Law does not have provisions similar to the second half of Articles 55 and 56 of the ROC Criminal Code, while the German Criminal Procedure Code has not adopted common law evidence rules at all, the abolition of these provisions after World War II was not preceded by considerations as to whether these provisions would result in a common law style criminal trial.

dicted.[240] Under these continental criminal law provisions, it is understandable why common law rules of evidence focusing mainly on the presentation of evidence by the parties would not emerge: the court is expected to investigate all related crimes in addition to those the defendant is charged with.[241] In other words, allowing parties to control the collection and presentation of evidence would inevitably discard these criminal law provisions, which might eventually impair the fact-finding function of the trial court that is required to convict the defendant of all of his punishable misconducts.

These criminal law provisions not only make the past ROC criminal justice practice merely nominally adversarial, but also make the current pro-accusatorial reforms of the ROC CPC appear more pro-inquisitorial.[242] The court is still required and entitled to

---

[240] In these circumstances, it is impossible for the prosecutor (public or private) to indict all misconducts subject to one punishable power of the defendant.

[241] Once the 2005 legislation will have entered into effect on July 1st 2006, only the following paragraph of the current Article 55 of the ROC Criminal Law will survive: "If one act constitutes several unlike offenses, only the most severe of the prescribed punishments shall be imposed." In other words, the court is still required to investigate if other offenses fall within the scope of the newly enacted provision. Of course, the scope requiring the court to investigate ex officio will be much smaller than it was in the past.

[242] As mentioned before, a fundamental difference between the inquisitorial system and the accusatorial system concerns the investigation and presentation of evidence: party control versus judicial control. See Renee Lettow Lerner, The Intersection of Two Systems: An American on Trial for An American Murder in the French Cour d'Assises, 2001 U. Ill. L. Rev. 791, 797 (2001).

investigate whether the scope of the prosecution completely covers all misconducts under one category of punishable acts.[243] In short, whenever the court has a duty to look into all of the defendant's punishable misconducts rather than to focus merely on the original charges, criminal practice in Taiwan or any other civil-law-based jurisdictions with similar criminal law provisions would still be similar to the traditional inquisitorial model since the court still has to play an active role in fact investigation at trial. Professor Mirjan R. Damaska clearly notices there are three important pillars supporting common law rules of evidence[244] and justifying the Anglo-American fact-finding process: "the peculiar organization of the trial court; the temporal concentration of proceedings; and the prominent roles of the parties and their counsel in legal proceedings."[245] The above-mentioned viewpoint derived from continental substantive criminal law mentioned might supplement his claims by explaining why continental criminal justice systems did not evolve the common law evidence rules in the late eighteenth and the nineteenth centuries.[246]

Although the 2003 Advisory Committee Note on the ROC CPC did not unambiguously address this issue as to why to adopt

---

[243] See Article 267 of the ROC CPC. See also 88 Tai Sun 2576 (1999)and 26 U Sun 1435 (1937).

[244] See Gordon Van Kessel, "A Summary of Mirjan R. Damaska's Evidence Law Adrift", 49 Hastings Law. Journal 359, 359 (1998).

[245] See Mirjan R. Damaska, Evidence Law Adrift, 4 (Yale University Press, 1997).

[246] Id.

Article 159-1 of the ROC CPC admitting the out-of-court statement made in front of a judge or a public prosecutor in evidence at trial, the fact that the court still plays a role as fact finder and the need to discover all material evidence to prove all offenses falling within the scope of Articles 55 and 56 of the ROC Criminal Law might partly justify it. In other words, Paragraph 2 of Article 163 of the ROC CPC still allows the court to investigate evidence ex officio, and especially so when it is necessary to discover the truth and conduct a fair trial. An inquisitorial approach to the fact-finding process emphasizing "official inquiry"[247] has survived the 2003 pro-accusatorial reforms of the ROC CPC. It seems fair to say that the adoption of Article 159-1 of the ROC CPC signifies that the 2003 legislation with regard to the hearsay rule tolerates non-adversarial fact-finding proceedings, which are very different from their counterpart in the United States. While the hearsay rule was initially adopted to prevent lay jurors from hearing unreliable hearsay,[248] deriving from the bifurcated trial structure, it is not designed for a civil-law-based inquisitorial criminal justice system. In a sense, adoption of the common-law-based hearsay rule conflicts with the civil-law-bas-

---

[247] See Renee Lettow Lerner, "The Intersection of Two Systems: An American on Trial for An American Murder in the French Cour d'Assises", 2001 *University of Illinois Law Review* 791, 797 (2001).

[248] See Christopher B. Mueller, et al., *Evidence Under the Rules*, 1 (New York Aspen Law & Business, 2000).

ed fact-finding process. Nonetheless, since the ROC lawmakers intended to build a more continentally-based accusatorial trial system, it was considered necessary to introduce some accusatorial elements, including the hearsay rule, in the ROC CPC. To prevent the court from playing its past active role at trial, the 2003 hearsay rule provides the defendant with a procedural right to challenge the admissibility of the out-of-court statements and requires the prosecutor to respond to this challenge. The 2003 legislation has indeed resulted in a criminal process that is less inquisitorial. Consequently, there is room for the adoption of the hearsay rule, which is not at odds with the current ROC trial system. While the trial process in Taiwan is not strictly accusatorial, some inquisitorial characteristics remain. As a result, there are two types of hearsay exceptions in the ROC CPC: one is based on the inquisitorial tradition,[249] the other on the adversarial or accusatorial tradition.[250]

Even though some hearsay exceptions provided in the Federal Rules of Evidence are not found in the ROC CPC, they might be admissible under an inquisitorial hearsay exception according to Article 159-1 of the ROC CPC, and especially so when an adversarial and accusatorial approach of fact-finding is unavailable and impossible. For example, if the prosecutor seeks to admit an out-of-court statement similar to FRE 803 (2), he may ask the

---

[249] See Article 159-1 of the ROC CPC.
[250] See Articles 159-2 to 159-4 of the ROC CPC.

court to apply an inquisitorial hearsay exception according to Article 159-1 of the ROC CPC. Furthermore, the court can invoke its inquisitorial powers to investigate evidence ex officio according to Paragraph 2 of Article 163, even if the parties do not require the court to do so. When the court collects evidence ex officio, no hearsay rule applies, not only because it is not designed for an inquisitorial process but also because hearsay evidence is admissible under the inquisitorial evidential tradition.[251] Hearsay evidence is considered by the fact finder in continental criminal justice systems mainly because "there is enough time to seek out the declarant when available or to collect information regarding the declarant's credibility when unavailable."[252] Thus, if a judge or a public prosecutor interrogated the witness who heard the excited utterance during a pretrial stage or investigation, it may be admissible. In addition, if the court tends to admit this out-of-court statement, it can then borrow the dossier of another case, in which an out-of-court statement was made before a judge or a public prosecutor. It is clear that Article 159-1 of the ROC CPC was not designed to protect the defendant's right to confront the witness. In fact, it is basically an enactment stemming from the

---

[251] See Renee Lettow Lerner, "The Intersection of Two Systems: An American on Trial for An American Murder in the French Cour d'Assises", 2001 *University of Illinois Law Review* 791, 831 (2001).

[252] See Gordon Van Kessel, "A Summary of Mirjan R. Damaska's Evidence Law Adrift", 49 *Hastings Law Journal* 359, 359 (1998).

inquisitorial evidential legacy even though no jurisdiction has adopted an article similar to Article 159-1 of the ROC CPC.

Even though the 2003 legislation adopts two types of hearsay exceptions, it is not clear if the framers intentionally created this entirely new style of distinguishing hearsay exceptions and there is no clue of this intention in the 2003 Advisory Committee Note. Nonetheless, Article 159-1 and Paragraph 2 of Article 163 of the ROC CPC really provide inquisitorial fact-finding proceedings to assist the court in determining the truth when these 2003 adversarial and accusatorial hearsay exceptions are not available for fact-finding. This might be why the 2003 reforms of the ROC CPC is merely entitled pro-accusatorial instead of accusatorial and no one really thinks it proper and necessary to establish a strictly accusatorial and adversarial trial system in Taiwan.

If the purpose of the 2003 reforms of the ROC CPC includes establishing a more accusatorial model of its criminal justice system as well as responding to demands of human rights protection, it is necessary to consider abandoning, or at least revising, Articles 55 and 56 of the ROC Criminal Law in order to release the court of its duty to investigate whether any other offenses fall within the scope of Articles 55 and 56 of the ROC Criminal Law, which might make the court less active and more neutral at trial.[253] It is interesting that scholars or experts in the field of comparative criminal procedure rarely mention the reason why merely revising the civil-law-based criminal procedure code is not enough to establish an accusatorial model of criminal trial

from the viewpoint of substantive criminal law. Even those scholars from civil-law-based jurisdictions that have already adopted
some accusatorial elements into their criminal justice systems[254]
do not address this issue. Nevertheless, the accusatorial nature of
the ROC criminal justice system depends partly on the extent to
which the court is required to investigate and collect evidence ex
officio under Articles 55 and 56 of the ROC Criminal Law.[255]
The less the court is required to investigate ex officio, the more
accusatorial the ROC trial process will be. Of course, even without these criminal law problems, if the court still plays its role of
fact finder, it is questionable to what extent the ROC criminal
justice system should become accusatorial and adversarial.

4.3.2　Correlations of Jury Trial and Evidence Law（陪審團審判與證據法之關聯）

　　While some scholars and judges describe evidence law as

---

[253] The author of this study is glad to note that partly based on the author's
suggestions to abolish or revise Articles 55 and 56 of the ROC Criminal Law,
the ROC Legislative Yuan in January 2005 revised the ROC Criminal Law,
including the abolition of the second half of Articles 55 and 56 of the ROC
Criminal Law. See Ming-woei Chang, "Articles 55 and 56 of the ROC Criminal
Law and the Pro-Accusatorial Reforms of the *ROC Criminal Procedure Code*",
*in the ROC Judicial Yuan Anniversary Review of the Pro-Accusatorial Reforms
of the ROC Criminal Procedure Code*, 39-63 (Taipei, Sep. 2004) (in Chinese).

[254] These jurisdictions include Japan and Italy.

[255] Only Article 55 of the ROC Criminal Law will govern this issue after July 1st
2006.

the "child of the jury system,"[256] exclusionary hearsay rules are necessary "to protect the jury against cognitive shortcomings."[257] As a result, the jury, the fact finder, can only consider admissible evidence.[258] The admissibility of evidence refers to the jury's contact with evidence. In general, the jury will not be in contact with inadmissible evidence, so that the fact finder is not in danger of deciding a case on the basis of unreliable hearsay. While the parties are responsible for the investigation of facts and the presentation of evidence, the adversarial and accusatorial evidence law including the hearsay rule focuses on this fact investigation process controlled by parties. In other words, the common law hearsay rule is applicable to evidence presented by the parties.

In the ROC criminal justice system, however, the court, instead of the jury, is the fact finder. In addition to evidence presented by the parties, the court also collects evidence for fact investigation through official inquiry and other methods of evidence gathering. As a consequence, there are two categories of evidence: one is presented by the parties and the other is collected by the court. While the court still plays a role as fact finder,

---

[256] See Charles T. McCormick, "Law and the Future: Evidence", 51 *Northwestern University Law Review* 218, 225 (1956).

[257] See Roger C. Park, "An Outsider's View of Common Law Evidence", 96 *Michigan Law Review* 1486, 1486 (1998).

[258] Usually the fact finder knows nothing about inadmissible evidence because the court has already excluded it.

it seems less meaningful to discuss the admissibility of evidence because the fact finder will inevitably be in contact with all kinds of evidence. In other words, the fact finder in a continental criminal justice system will be confronted with the out-of-court statement regardless of its admissibility. The rationale behind the common law hearsay rule preventing lay jurors from being presented with unreliable and untrustworthy out-of-court statements is thus not available and persuasive in continental bench trials. Since continental criminal justice systems put a greater reliance on judicial authority, it is fair to say that the exclusionary hearsay rule is not really necessary in an inquisitorial criminal justice system because professional judges are assumed and believed to be capable of finding the material truth. In addition, since jury verdicts are inscrutable in a common law jury trial system, a strict hearsay rule excluding the danger of putting too much weight on unreliable information and avoiding "unfair surprise in light of lack of ability to continuously check foundational factors"[259] becomes necessary as "a good prophylactic measure to counteract the defects of derivative informational sources"[260]. Hence, without the adversarial fact-finding proceedings distrustful of all kinds of government power and the jury trial, there is no need to adopt the whole set of common law hearsay rules in Taiwan. As the

---

[259] See Gordon Van Kessel, "A Summary of Mirjan R. Damaska's Evidence Law Adrift", 49 *Hastings Law Journal* 359, 359 (1998).

[260] See Mirjan R. Damaska, *Evidence Law Adrift*, 65 (Yale University Press, 1997).

court in Taiwan has to decide both legal and factual issues by providing a scrutable reasoning in written, and the fact finder will unavoidably be in contact with hearsay evidence, strict enforcement of the common law hearsay rule distinguishing admissible and inadmissible out-of-court statements is less practicable.[261]

As discussed above, while the court as fact finder still has the power to gather material evidence, this study suggests there are two types of hearsay exceptions in the ROC CPC. The adversarial and accusatorial hearsay exceptions, as do those in Articles 159-2 to 159-4 of the ROC CPC, apply only when the parties present the out-of-court statement. When an out-of-court statement is collected by the court's inquisitorial powers of fact investigation, only Article 159-1 of the ROC CPC will apply. In general, when the court finds the parties not presenting sufficient evidence to decide the case because of the adversarial and accusatorial hearsay rule, it may admit any reliable out-of-court statement in evidence ex officio by invoking an inquisitorial hearsay exception. Moreover, while there is no need to prevent lay jurors from hearing hearsay evidence, the meaning of the hearsay rule in the ROC CPC is different from its counterpart in a jury trial jurisdiction. Although the 2003 Advisory Committee Note on the ROC CPC recognizes the purpose of adopting the hearsay rule is to protect the defendant's right to confrontation, the right to con-

---

[261] See Gordon Van Kessel, "A Summary of Mirjan R. Damaska's Evidence Law Adrift", 49 *Hastings Law Journal* 359, 359 (1998).

front the witness under the Sixth Amendment to the United States Constitution should not be identical to that in the ROC CPC.

4.4　Exclusionary Approach to the Hearsay Rule（傳聞排除法則）

As suggested by this study, there are two categories of hearsay exceptions in the ROC CPC. While Articles 159-2 to 159-4 of the ROC CPC stem from common law hearsay exceptions, which protect the defendant's right to confront witnesses,[262] it is expedient to understand what the right of confrontation means in the United States. In other words, recent developments regarding the Confrontation Clause in the Sixth Amendment to the United States Constitution might provide legal professionals in Taiwan with many important clues when determining what the confrontation right means and what rights are protected by the hearsay exceptions in Articles 159-2 to 159-4 of the ROC CPC.

4.4.1　Roberts（羅伯特斯案）

Although many hearsay exceptions are provided in the Federal Rules of Evidence, the United States Supreme Court in California v. Green recognized that allowing a hearsay exception in a criminal case might constitute a violation of the Confrontation

---

[262] See the 2003 Advisory Committee Note on the ROC CPC.

Clause in the Sixth Amendment.[263] In other words, even an out-of-court statement falling within the scope of the hearsay exceptions might be excluded from evidence at trial, in particular when its admission would violate the defendant's right to confront the witness. As a consequence, the kind of out-of-court statement falling within the scope of the hearsay exceptions that could be admissible without violating the Confrontation Clause in the Sixth Amendment becomes a significant issue.

In Ohio v. Roberts, the United States Supreme Court was asked to consider "the relationship between the Confrontation Clause and the hearsay rule with its many exceptions."[264] Recognizing that a literal reading of the Sixth Amendment, as was done

---

[263] The Court ruled: "The issue before us is the considerably narrower one of whether a defendant's constitutional right 'to be confronted with the witnesses against him' is necessarily inconsistent with a State's decision to change its hearsay rules to reflect the minority view described above. While it may readily be conceded that hearsay rules and the Confrontation Clause are generally designed to protect similar values, it is quite a different thing to suggest that the overlap is complete and that the Confrontation Clause is nothing more or less than a codification of the rules of hearsay and their exceptions as they existed historically at common law. Our decisions have never established such a congruence; indeed, we have more than once found a violation of confrontation values even though the statements in issue were admitted under an arguably recognized hearsay exception. The converse is equally true: merely because evidence is admitted in violation of a long-established hearsay rule does not lead to the automatic conclusion that confrontation rights have been denied." See 399 U.S. 149, 155-6 (1970).

[264] See 448 U.S. 56, 62 (1980).

in Mattox v. United States,[265] would inevitably result in abrogating every hearsay exception that was long rejected as unintended and too extreme, Roberts refused to apply the Sixth Amendment in this way.[266] Moreover, without seeking an underlying theory of the Confrontation Clause in deciding the validity of all hearsay exceptions,[267] Roberts announced that the Confrontation Clause restricted the range of admissible hearsay in two ways.[268] The first was to establish a rule of necessity which required the prosecutors to produce or demonstrate the unavailability of the declarant.[269] After establishing the unavailability of a witness, Roberts also required the prior testimony to bear adequate indicia of reliability[270], because hearsay rules and the Confrontation Clause stemmed from the same roots.[271] Generally speaking, according to Roberts, an out-of-court statement would be "admissible only if it bears adequate 'indicia of reliability,'" which might "be inferred without more in a case where the evidence falls within a firmly rooted hearsay exception."[272] In other words, even though

---

[265] It ruled that there "could be nothing more directly contrary to the letter of the provision in question than the admission of dying declarations." See 156 U.S. 237, 243 (1895), quoted in Roberts, See 448 U.S., at 63.

[266] Id.

[267] See 399 U.S., at 162.

[268] See 448 U.S., at 65.

[269] Id.

[270] Id.

[271] See Dutton v. Evans, 400 U.S. 74, 86 (1970).

[272] It also held: "In other cases, the evidence must be excluded, at least absent a showing of particularized guarantees of trustworthiness." See 448 U.S., at 66.

trial by jury the court is not a fact finder, it was entitled to decide whether an out-of-court statement should bear adequate indicia of reliability if the evidence was not within a firmly rooted hearsay exception. The trial court would find and assess evidential reliability at its discretion. The discretionary power of the trial court played a main role in excluding an out-of-court statement not falling within a firmly rooted hearsay exception. Under the Roberts approach, a defendant would have no right to confront the witness if the trial court found the hearsay evidence reliable. The Confrontation Clause in the Sixth Amendment would not apply. In sum, whether the jurors would consider the hearsay evidence was up to the trial court.

4.4.2 Crawford (克勞佛案)

As a latter-day representative of the Framers, Justice Antonin Scalia, writing for seven members of the United States Supreme Court in Crawford v. Washington, overrules Ohio v. Roberts and its progeny.[273] In determining whether the Washington State Code at issue violates the Sixth Amendment, Crawford turns to the historical background of the Confrontation Clause that does not in itself provide sufficient information to resolve this case.[274] While Roberts allowed the reliability test to govern the admissibility of an out-of-court statement, it also deprived the ac-

---

[273] See 541 U.S. 36; 124 S. Ct. 1354 (2004).
[274] See 124 S. Ct., at 1359.

cused of the right to confront the witness, in particular when the trial court found that the out-of-court statement showed specific guarantees of trustworthiness.[275] Nonetheless, unlike the civil law tradition which "condones examination in private by judicial offi-cers,"[276] Crawford identifies that "the common-law tradition is one of live testimony in court subject to adversarial testing",[277] even though "England at times adopted elements of the civil-law practice."[278] In defending violations of the Stamp Act in inquisi-torial admiralty courts, which allowed the judicial officials to examine witnesses by ex parte interrogation before trial, John Adams once pointed out: "Examinations of witnesses upon Inter-rogatories, are only by the Civil Law. Interrogatories are un-known at common Law, and Englishmen and common Lawyers

---

[275] See 448 U.S., at 66.

[276] See 124 S. Ct., at 1359.

[277] Id.

[278] As Crawford noted: "Justices of the peace or other officials examined suspects and witnesses before trial. These examinations were sometimes read in court in lieu of live testimony, a practice that 'occasioned frequent demands by the prisoner to have his accusers, *i.e.* the witnesses against him, brought before him face to face.' Pretrial examinations became routine under two statutes passed during the reign of Queen Mary in the 16th century. These Marian bail and committal statutes required justices of the peace to examine suspects and witnesses in felony cases and to certify the results to the court. It is doubtful that the original purpose of the examinations was to produce evidence admissible at trial. Whatever the original purpose, however, they came to be used as evidence in some cases, resulting in an adoption of continental procedure." Id., at 1359-60.

have an aversion to them if not an Abhorrence of them."[279] Justice Scalia cites the most notorious instance of civil-law examination in the seventeenth century, the 1603 trial of Sir Walter Raleigh for treason, and some important English judicial reforms to justify his ruling.[280] After a thorough study of the history of the Confrontation Clause, the Court in Crawford finds that the admissibility of an out-of-court hearsay statement depends on "a prior opportunity for cross-examination."[281] Based on this historical finding, two inferences about the meaning of the Confrontation Clause can be drawn.[282]

As asserted by Justice Scalia, "the principal evil at which the Confrontation Clause was directed was the civil-law mode of criminal procedure, and particularly its use of ex parte examinations as evidence against the accused."[283] Moreover, "[...]the Fra-

---

[279] See John Adams, "Draft of Argument in Sewall v Hancock (1768-1769)", in *The Legal Papers of John Adams 194*, 207 (K. Wroth & H. Zobel eds. 1965), quoted in Crawford, Id., at 1362.

[280] Id., at 1360. ("Through a series of statutory and judicial reforms, English law developed a right of confrontation that limited these abuses. For example, treason statutes required witnesses to confront the accused 'face to face' at his arraignment. Courts, meanwhile, developed relatively strict rules of unavailability, admitting examinations only if the witness was demonstrably unable to testify in person. Several authorities also stated that a suspect's confession could be admitted only against himself, and not against others he implicated.")

[281] Id., at 1363.

[282] Id.

[283] Id.

mers would not have allowed admission of testimonial statements of a witness who did not appear at trial unless he was unavailable to testify, and the defendant had had a prior opportunity for cross-examination."[284] It was meaningless for Raleigh to confront those who read Cobham's confession in court.[285] Hence, Roberts subjecting "out-of-court statements to the law of evidence would render the Confrontation Clause powerless to prevent even the most flagrant inquisitorial practices."[286] To avoid the civil-law abuses of ex parte examinations that "might sometimes be admissible under modern hearsay rules,"[287] Crawford mainly applies the Confrontation Clause to "witnesses against the accused" for distinguishing the out-of-court testimonial statement from other

---

[284] As to this second aspect, the Court also notes: "The text of the Sixth Amendment does not suggest any open-ended exceptions from the confrontation requirement to be developed by the courts. Rather, the 'right...to be confronted with the witnesses against him,' is most naturally read as a reference to the right of confrontation at common law, admitting only those exceptions established at the time of the founding. As the English authorities above reveal, the common law in 1791 conditioned admissibility of an absent witness's examination on unavailability and a prior opportunity to cross-examine. The Sixth Amendment therefore incorporates those limitations. The numerous early state decisions applying the same test confirm that these principles were received as part of the common law in this country." Id., at 1365-6.

[285] Id., at 1364.

[286] Id.

[287] Id.

styles of hearsay[288] without providing a clear definition of "testimonial statements."[289]

As to exceptions to the Confrontation Clause, Crawford only admits those exceptions already established at the time of adoption of the Sixth Amendment in that

> the common law in 1791 conditioned admissibility of an absent witness's examination on unavailability and a prior opportunity to cross-examine. The Sixth Amendment therefore incorporates those limitations. The numerous early state decisions applying the same test

---

[288] As the Court mentioned: "'Testimony,' in turn, is typically '[a] solemn declaration or affirmation made for the purpose of establishing or proving some fact.' An accuser who makes a formal statement to government officers bears testimony in a sense that a person who makes a casual remark to an acquaintance does not. The constitutional text, like the history underlying the common-law right of confrontation, thus reflects an especially acute concern with a specific type of out-of-court statement." Id.

[289] However, the Court illustrates what might be considered testimonial: "Various formulations of this core class of 'testimonial' statements exist: 'ex parte in-court testimony or its functional equivalent --- that is, material such as affidavits, custodial examinations, prior testimony that the defendant was unable to cross-examine, or similar pretrial statements that declarants would reasonably expect to be used prosecutorially;' 'extrajudicial statements . . . contained in formalized testimonial materials, such as affidavits, depositions, prior testimony, or confessions;' 'statements that were made under circumstances which would lead an objective witness reasonably to believe that the statement would be available for use at a later trial,' These formulations all share a common nucleus and then define the Clause's coverage at various levels of abstraction around it. Regardless of the precise articulation, some statements qualify under any definition--for example, ex parte testimony at a preliminary hearing." Id.

confirm that these principles were received as part of the common law in this country.[290]

Consequently, since the Framers expressively refused to adopt a civil law system admitting pre-trial ex parte examinations of witnesses in evidence at trial, establishing the unavailability of the declaring witness and a prior opportunity to cross-examine should be necessary conditions for the admissibility of testimonial statements.[291] In other words, Crawford affirms a 1794 North Carolina ruling, State v. Webb, which held: "[I]t is a rule of the common law, founded on natural justice, that no man shall be prejudiced by evidence which he had not the liberty to cross examine."[292]

---

[290] Id., at 1366.

[291] Id., at 1367. The Court later clearly announces: "Our cases have thus remained faithful to the Framers' understanding: Testimonial statements of witnesses absent from trial have been admitted only where the declarant is unavailable, and only where the defendant has had a prior opportunity to cross-examine." Id., at 1369.

[292] See 2 N. C. 103, 104 (1794). Moreover, Crawford also notes: "Similarly, in State v. Campbell, South Carolina's highest law court excluded a deposition taken by a coroner in the absence of the accused. It held: '[I]f we are to decide the question by the established rules of the common law, there could not be a dissenting voice. For, notwithstanding the death of the witness, and whatever the respectability of the court taking the depositions, the solemnity of the occasion and the weight of the testimony, such depositions are ex parte, and, therefore, utterly incompetent.' The court said that one of the 'indispensable conditions' implicitly guaranteed by the State Constitution was that 'prosecutions be carried on to the conviction of the accused, by witnesses confronted by him, and subjected to his personal examination.'" Id., at 1362.

According to this historical analysis of the Confrontation Clause, from which Crawford finds the Roberts test obviously departs, a particular manner of assessing the reliability of a testimonial out-of-court hearsay statement is mandatory.[293] While admitting testimonial statements "deemed reliable by a judge is fundamentally at odds with the right of confrontation,"[294] the Confrontation Clause strictly requires cross-examination in determining reliability.[295] As a result, Crawford concludes, "[d]ispensing with confrontation because testimony is obviously reliable is akin to dispensing with jury trial because a defendant is obviously guilty. This is not what the Sixth Amendment prescribes."[296] The testimonial out-of-court statement without an opportunity for cross-examination will not be considered by the fact finder. A mere judicial determination of reliability cannot replace "the constitutionally prescribed method of assessing reliability"[297] even though the trial court acts in utmost good faith to find reliability.[298] Otherwise the fact-finding process in the United States will look much more inquisitorial in that the "Raleigh trial itself involved the very sorts of reliability determinations" which Roberts authorized.[299] Since the

---

[293] Id., at 1370.
[294] Id.
[295] Id.
[296] Id., at 1371.
[297] Id., at 1370.
[298] Id., at 1373.
[299] Id., at 1370.

Roberts test "fails to protect against paradigmatic confrontation violations,"[300] the trial judge's discretionary power to decide the reliability of the testimonial out-of-court statement is no longer decisive to a jury's consideration of hearsay evidence.

4.4.3　The Proper Exclusionary Approach to the ROC Hearsay Rule（我國傳聞法則應採之排除基礎）

As discussed earlier, Articles 159-2 to 159-4 of the ROC CPC derive from the common law hearsay rule. While they were also designed to protect the defendant's right to confrontation, it is meaningful to refer to the American experiences with the Confrontation Clause. To date, the United States Supreme Court has tried two different approaches dealing with this issue, as held in Roberts and Crawford. According to Roberts, the admissibility of an out-of-court statement depends on whether it falls within firmly rooted hearsay exceptions or bears particularized guarantees of trustworthiness.[301] Nevertheless, Crawford emphasizes the method of assessing the reliability of the testimonial statement, which requires the trial court to assess the reliability through cross-examination.[302] Even though Crawford now governs how to assess the reliability of testimonial hearsay, it does not necessarily follow that Taiwan has to adopt this exclusionary approach. On the con-

---

[300] Id., at 1369.

[301] See 448 U.S., at 66.

[302] See 124 S. Ct., at 1370.

trary, Crawford probably just illustrates what a civil-law-based criminal justice system should not adopt.

The Sixth Amendment to the United States Constitution clearly provides: "In all criminal prosecutions, the accused shall enjoy the right to [⋯] be confronted with the witnesses against him." Consequently, almost all criminal cases have focused on the right to confrontation when admissible hearsay was at issue. Contrary to this American practice, under the civil law tradition focusing heavily on "direct inquisition," courts in Taiwan rarely addressed the right to confrontation because there is no clear expression of this right in the ROC Constitution. In 1995, Interpretation No. 384 of the Grand Justice Council recognized the defendant's right to be confronted with the witnesses against him as being constitutional. Nonetheless, compared to the Confrontation Clause in the Sixth Amendment, it is less clear as to what the origins of the right to confrontation in Taiwan are. Moreover, the legislators in Taiwan can still impose restrictions on this constitutional right, not only because Article 23 of the ROC Constitution allows them to do so, but also because the history of the right to confrontation in the ROC does not require judicial officials to assess the reliability of an out-of-court testimonial statement through cross-examination. These legal characteristics of the ROC criminal justice system may justify why Article 159-1 of the ROC CPC, an unknown to the common law hearsay rule, was adopted. Obviously, from a historical viewpoint, the adversarial rationale behind Crawford requiring cross-examination to be the only method (with few exceptions recognized by 1791) of assessing the reliability is not applicable in Taiwan. While Justice Scalia heavily depends on the history of the Confrontation Clause to draw his conclusion, it is not necessary for Taiwan to draw on this historical authority and require the court to assess the reliability of an out-of-court testimonial statement only through cross-examination.

If in Taiwan cross-examination is not the only way to evaluate the reliability of an out-of-court testimonial statement, then Roberts might provide a good approach for deciding the admissibility of testimonial hearsay. In addition to cross-examination, Roberts allows the court to assess the reliability through two more methods. The first method is whether the hearsay statement falls within firmly rooted hearsay exceptions. Even though the civil law tradition does not really address this issue, this method is still applicable in Taiwan. The firmly rooted hearsay exceptions evolved in common law can properly illustrate what kinds of out-of-court statements are considered reliable. They are important clues for the ROC criminal justice system to determine the reliability of the out-of-court statements in any given case. If a hearsay exception provided in the Federal Rules of Evidence might be covered by the residual clause of the ROC CPC,[303] it is probably correct to admit it in evidence at trial in that it is considered reliable in common law. Even in the case of a hearsay

---

[303] See Subparagraph 3 of Article 159-4 of the ROC CPC.

exception such as FRE 804 (a) (1) that cannot be covered by the ROC CPC it would be proper to admit an out-of-court statement by exercising an inquisitorial power under Article 159-1 of the ROC CPC because of its highly likely reliability.

The second method allowed by Roberts is whether the out-of-court testimonial statement bears particularized guarantees of trustworthiness. As criticized in Crawford, the reliability test in Roberts is too "amorphous" to provide clear protection from even core confrontation violations.[304] It is true that Roberts will inevitably result in the fact-finding process depending heavily on the trial judge's discretionary power; for instance, what is decisive is "which factors the judge considers and how much weight he ac-

---

[304] Crawford reasoned: "Reliability is an amorphous, if not entirely subjective, concept. There are countless factors bearing on whether a statement is reliable; the nine-factor balancing test applied by the Court of Appeals below is representative. Whether a statement is deemed reliable depends heavily on which factors the judge considers and how much weight he accords each of them. Some courts wind up attaching the same significance to opposite facts. For example, the Colorado Supreme Court held a statement more reliable because its inculpation of the defendant was 'detailed,' while the Fourth Circuit found a statement more reliable because the portion implicating another was 'fleeting.' The Virginia Court of Appeals found a statement more reliable because the witness was in custody and charged with a crime (thus making the statement more obviously against her penal interest), while the Wisconsin Court of Appeals found a statement more reliable because the witness was not in custody and not a suspect. Finally, the Colorado Supreme Court in one case found a statement more reliable because it was given 'immediately after' the events at issue, while that same court, in another case, found a statement more reliable because two years had elapsed." Id., at 1371.

cords each of them."[305] It also seems fair to say that Crawford expressively prevents the trial court from exercising this discretionary power in the fact-finding process. Nonetheless, although admitting core testimonial statements under Roberts is considered to be the unpardonable vice which the Confrontation Clause intends to exclude,[306] this rationale is not necessarily true in Taiwan while the civil law tradition has never tried to avoid an inquisitorial fact-finding process such as the Raleigh trial. Besides, it is questionable whether it would be useful to follow Crawford in a civil-law-based criminal justice system.

It is worth mentioning that the fact-finding process is itself discretionary in nature. While evidence X conflicts with evidence Y in determining a factual issue, for example, it is up to the fact finder's discretionary power to decide which evidence is more reliable. Although Crawford prevents the trial court from assessing the reliability of an out-of-court testimonial statement at its discretion, it allows the fact finder, usually the jury, to employ almost absolute discretionary powers to decide the factual issues with little scrutiny while the jury is not required to justify its decision in writing. Probably, the traditional distrust of judicial officials in common law requires the trial process to be bifurcated in which only the fact finder is allowed to exercise this discretionary power. As a result, the fact finder hears testimonial evidence

---

[305] Id.

[306] Id.

only when it is made under cross-examination under Crawford. Besides, in a sense it is up to the legislature to admit an out-of-court statement in evidence at trial as a hearsay exception since not all hearsay exceptions evolved in common law have been adopted in the Federal Rules of Evidence.[307] Under Crawford, however, even the discretionary power exercised by the state or federal legislators to evaluate the reliability of the out-of-court testimonial statements is not allowed by the Confrontation Clause in the Sixth Amendment.[308] The Framers of the Confrontation

---

[307] As explained in the Advisory Committee's Introductory Note: "The approach to hearsay in these rules is that of the common law, i.e., a general rule excluding hearsay, with exceptions under which evidence is not required to be excluded even though hearsay. The traditional hearsay exceptions are drawn upon for the exceptions, collected under two rules, one dealing with situations where availability of the declarant is regarded as immaterial and the other with those where unavailability is made a condition to the admission of the hearsay statement. Each of the two rules concludes with a provision for hearsay statements not within one of the specified exceptions 'but having comparable [equivalent] circumstantial guarantees of trustworthiness.' Rules 803(24) and 804 (b)(6)[5]. This plan is submitted as calculated to encourage growth and development in this area of the law, while conserving the values and experience of the past as a guide to the future." See Steven I. Friedland, et al., eds., *Evidence Law and Practice*, 2001 Supplement, Appendices: Federal Rules of Evidence, 87 (LexisNexis, 2001).

[308] As noted in California v. Green: "While it may readily be conceded that hearsay rules and the Confrontation Clause are generally designed to protect similar values, it is quite a different thing to suggest that the overlap is complete and that the Confrontation Clause is nothing more or less than a codification of the rules of hearsay and their exceptions as they existed historically at common law. Our decisions have never established such a congruence; indeed, we have more than once found a violation of confrontation values even though the statements

Clause seemed to declare that only the fact finders, usually lay jurors, should be entitled to exercise discretionary powers in assessing reliability. The United States Supreme Court in Crawford once again clearly recognizes the common-law distrust of government officials by 1791 and continues to insist on this common law tradition in the twenty-first century. It is fair to say that the original intent of the Confrontation Clause—preventing the judicial and legislative powers from assessing the reliability of testimonial hearsay at its discretion—was built on the bifurcated trial structure. Only when the defendant waives his right to a jury trial will the trial court in the United States be allowed to exercise its discretionary powers to evaluate the credibility of evidence and decide the case.

If, on the other hand, the trial structure is not bifurcated and the court also plays the role of fact finder, it is questionable whether Crawford can stop the trial court from exercising discretionary powers. According to Paragraph 2 of Article 163 of the ROC CPC, the court is allowed to exercise its inquisitorial powers to find the material truth in order to decide a case. It is clear that the fact finder in Taiwan will eventually hear evidence whether or not it is admissible under the hearsay rule. In fact,

---

in issue were admitted under an arguably recognized hearsay exception. The converse is equally true: merely because evidence is admitted in violation of a long-established hearsay rule does not lead to the automatic conclusion that confrontation rights have been denied." See 399 U.S. 149, 155-6 (1970).

even following Crawford will not prevent the fact finder in Taiwan from hearing an out-of-court testimonial statement that is not made under cross-examination. When the court in Taiwan is presented with information not allowed by Crawford, either from the dossier or from the victim or the prosecution, it is natural for the court—as a fact finder it is required to explain its decision in writing—to assess if the testimonial hearsay is helpful to the truth-finding process. In a sense, the decision to investigate the fact ex officio under Article 159-1 of the ROC CPC depends on this process of assessing trustworthiness. In reality, evaluating the reliability and credibility of testimonial hearsay depends heavily on the judicial officials' experience. It is impossible for the court to decide if the hearsay information is probative and reliable without exercising discretionary powers. This practice is neither adversarial nor accusatorial while the defense party plays no part in the court's decision-making process. Since the court in Taiwan is assumed to employ its discretionary powers to decide what evidence is more reliable and credible and what additional facts require investigation, the purpose of Crawford to prevent the court from assessing the reliability of the out-of-court testimonial statements at its discretion will not be served in the ROC criminal justice system. Hence, whether or not the out-of-court testimonial statement bears particularized guarantees of trustworthiness, the second method of deciding the admissibility of hearsay evidence provided by Roberts, is a proper standard for determining the admissibility of out-of-court statements in the ROC criminal justice system. It is suitable to follow Roberts instead of Crawford while interpreting Subparagraph 3 of Article 159-4 of the ROC CPC.

Moreover, Crawford seems to prevent the fact finder from hearing inadmissible hearsay. It is less useful to follow Crawford in order to distinguish admissible hearsay from inadmissible hearsay evidence because the fact finder in Taiwan will hear both kinds. While there is an inquisitorial hearsay exception focusing merely on the voluntariness of the declarant's statement,[309] the court is not required to assess the reliability of an out-of-court statement through cross-examination. The court is allowed to evaluate the reliability of the hearsay evidence through any inquisitorial method. If trustworthiness and reliability can be established, regardless of the discretionary powers used to do so, cross-examination is no longer necessary. In other words, the right to confrontation in the ROC criminal justice system is not a constitutional mandate. The significance of the right to confrontation is very different from its counterpart in the United States, as held in Crawford. As a result, the adoption of the hearsay rule referring to the Federal Rules of Evidence would merely results in the ROC trial process becoming less inquisitorial since the court only has to follow the adversarial trial model when Articles 159-2 to 159-4 of the ROC CPC apply. Perhaps this is what the 2003 pro-accusatorial reforms really mean.

---

[309] See Article 159-1 of the ROC CPC.

4.5　Significance of the Adoption of the Hearsay Rule in the ROC Criminal Justice System（我國採行傳聞法則之重要意義）

While the ROC hearsay rule does not follow Crawford in excluding testimonial hearsay not made under cross-examination from admissible evidence, it is interesting to establish what the significance of the 2003 legislation is for the ROC criminal justice system. In general, there were two main weaknesses regarding out-of-court statements before 2003. First of all, the prosecutor had no part in the fact-finding process. In the past, after prosecution, the court was obliged to investigate all the material factual issues. The prosecutor's involvement in the trial process was limited to reading the indictment in the final stages of the trial. Sometimes the prosecutor filed an indictment just because the defendant was considered highly suspect, without sufficient evidence. While the prosecutors were absent during the fact-finding process, the defendant had to argue with the court. Usually, the court went through all related evidence whether or not it was presented by the prosecutor. This trial practice looked like a battle between the court and the defendant, which inevitably made the role of the court less neutral.

The second defect resulted from that the fact-finding process depended too much on out-of-court statements, such as police interrogation records. The ROC Supreme Court admitted almost all evidence relating to proving the truth of the matter at issue in the past.[310] In reality, out-of-court statements played an important part in prosecution. Sometimes the public prosecutor did not interrogate the witness who made a statement during police interrogation before indictment. While the court was only required to read the verbatim transcript made by law-enforcement-officers before pronouncing judgment, the court could summon the declaring witness at its discretion. The defendant had no legal right to present evidence or to ask the declaring witness to be present at trial. Nor did he have the right to be confronted with the witnesses against him. This practice would result in serious injustice, and especially so when the court, without further investigation ex officio, at its discretion and arbitrarily chose to believe an out-of-court declarant who intended to incriminate the defendant by merely making a statement during police interrogation. Besides, when the law-enforcement-officers might benefit from solving a serious criminal case or be pressured to do so, they had a tendency to find a culprit. This police malpractice made their reports less reliable. Ironically, the defendant had no equal status to argue with the party presenting incriminating evidence, not only because the prosecutors were always absent at the trial but also because doing so would make a bad impression on the fact finder.[311]

---

[310] See 72 Tai Sun 1332 (1983).

[311] This happened when the court collected evidence ex officio.

Although the adoption of the hearsay rule does not necessarily make the ROC criminal justice system non-inquisitorial, the 2003 legislation has resulted in a reduced inquisitorial practice. The ROC hearsay rule has put an end to the pre-2003 weaknesses. With the 2003 hearsay rule, the defendant has acquired the procedural right to argue the admissibility of incriminating out-of-court statements presented at trial. To prevent the defendant from arguing this issue with the court, which makes its role less neutral, the prosecutors are required to be present at trial.[312] The 2003 legislation requires the prosecutor to participate in the trial process more actively. Since Paragraph 1 of Article 159 of the ROC CPC excludes hearsay information in general, arguing with the prosecutor about the admissibility of out-of-court statement is becoming a regular trail feature. This post-2003 practice makes it possible for the court to play a more neutral role than it did before; the prosecutor rather than the court is responsible for answering the defendant's objections to admitting hearsay evidence. Furthermore, the defendant has finally achieved equal status to argue with the opposing party—whether a public or a private prosecutor—instead of with the fact finder. In sum, without the 2003 hearsay rule, it would have been difficult for the ROC criminal justice system to create pro-accusatorial or mitigated inquisitorial trial proceedings because the prosecutor would have

---

[312] See Paragraph 2 of Article 159-5 and Paragraph 1 of Article 161 of the ROC CPC.

had nothing to do there. With regard to the issues provided in Articles 159-2 to 159-4 of the ROC CPC at least, the defendant can challenge the admissibility of out-of-court statements, and the prosecutor has to respond to this challenge by advocating the admissibility of the hearsay evidence.

While pre-2003 trial proceedings depended too much on verbatim transcripts made by law-enforcement-officers, they often neglected the risks of intentionally false accusations expressed by out-of-court witnesses and some law-enforcement-officers. In the past, when the defendant had been falsely incriminated especially, injustices such as the one in the Raleigh trial,[313] where the defendant was convicted following an ex parte official inquiry, might occur if the court was inclined to consider the initial out-of-court statements reliable and desisted from investigating related

---

[313] As the Court noted in Crawford: "The most notorious instances of civil-law examination occurred in the great political trials of the 16th and 17th centuries. One such was the 1603 trial of Sir Walter Raleigh for treason. Lord Cobham, Raleigh's alleged accomplice, had implicated him in an examination before the Privy Council and in a letter. At Raleigh's trial, these were read to the jury. Raleigh argued that Cobham had lied to save himself: 'Cobham is absolutely in the King's mercy; to excuse me cannot avail him; by accusing me he may hope for favour.' Suspecting that Cobham would recant, Raleigh demanded that the judges call him to appear, arguing that '[t]he Proof of the Common Law is by witness and jury: let Cobham be here, let him speak it. Call my accuser before my face . . . .,' and, despite Raleigh's protestations that he was being tried 'by the Spanish Inquisition,' the jury convicted, and Raleigh was sentenced to death. One of Raleigh's trial judges later lamented that 'the justice of England has never been so degraded and injured as by the condemnation of Sir Walter Raleigh.'" See 124 S. Ct., at 1360.

evidence ex officio. Following the introduction of the 2003 hearsay rule—with regard to the out-of-court statements provided in Articles 159-2 to 159-4 of the ROC CPC in particular—the court can no longer admit out-of-court statements in evidence at trial without providing the defendant with the opportunity to question its admissibility. The prosecutors thus first have to prove these out-of-court statements are reliable. The defendant then has the opportunity to discredit these out-of-court statements. As a result, the 2003 legislation prevents the court from overly relying on verbatim transcripts. In a sense it not only limits the court in the use of its inquisitorial powers f the court, it also provides a clear guide for dealing with some kinds of hearsay evidence in the ROC criminal justice system.

5. Conclusions（結論）

Referring to the purpose of a continental criminal justice system, Professor Mirjan Damaska once explained: "[T]he idea that criminal proceedings could justifiably be used for purposes other than those of establishing the truth and enforcing the substantive criminal law is simply not part of the continental legal tradition."[314] While finding the truth remains the most important

---

[314] See Mirjan Damaska, supra note 123. Moreover, "the trial in a civil law system usually begins with an examination of the defendant by the judge, exploring the defendant's background as well as his knowledge of, or participation in, the alleged crime. Questions are frequently directed to the defendant throughout the remainder of the trial. While the defendant has the right to refuse to answer any questions, such refusals are exceptional." See William T. Pizzi, supra note 172.

concern in the ROC criminal justice system, without a reasonably persuasive justification, it is not easy for the court to exclude reliable and trustworthy evidence even though human rights protection is also an important issue. It is questionable if people in Taiwan would accept a criminal justice system resulting in the acquittal of a defendant who had clearly committed the offense he was charged with (as in the Simpson case in the United States). Moreover, while the American Bill of Rights defines human rights in more detail, the continental constitutional approach to human rights protection does not clearly specify the scope of human rights. Without a solid historical basis and a clear provision in the ROC Constitution, it is more difficult for an ROC court to draw on the constitution itself to determine what is constitutionally protected. While the persuasive justification for excluding reliable and trustworthy evidence results largely from obvious violation of the constitution, it is also difficult for the court to justify its decision to exclude evidence, when the contents of the constitutional rights in a continental-style constitution are less clear especially. Thus, courts in Taiwan have to explain more about how they exercise the balancing test and why they exclude evidence than the American courts do, which merely have to apply a totality-of-the-circumstances test to explain whether or not the governmental activity is illegal.

This study has extensively discussed the related developments of the hearsay rule in Taiwan and the right to confrontation in the United States. An examination of the hearsay rule in

Taiwan and the United States has shown that different criminal justice approaches result in different developments of the exclusionary method. In an accusatorial system, such as in the United States, the criminal justice practice is much more party-influenced or party-oriented than the hierarchically controlled continental criminal justice system in Taiwan.[315] The parties are responsible for investigating the facts and producing evidence at trial.[316] In a sense, evidential law governs the trial procedure in the accusatorial and adversarial system. As it is impossible to admit only in-court statements in evidence at trial, the hearsay rule provides the parties with a clear guideline for admitting out-of-court statements in evidence at trial. It is fair to say that the hearsay rule protects the defendant's right to confrontation in the Sixth Amendment. Nonetheless, under Crawford, hearsay rule cannot replace cross-examination in assessing the reliability of out-of-court statements. Under this viewpoint, the prosecutor is responsible for any violation of the constitutional right to confrontation[317] and will lose

---

[315] In fact, this practice results in the following description: "Americans view the state with suspicion and the law as their shield against official transgressions, who expect 'total justice': compensation for every harm suffered, observance of due process when their rights are at stake." See Kuk Cho, supra note 4, 298.

[316] See Renee Lettow Lerner, "The Intersection of Two Systems: An American on Trial for An American Murder in the French Cour d'Assises", 2001 *University of Illinois Law Review* 791, 797 (2001).

[317] For example, Crawford only admits testimonial out-of-court statements under hearsay in evidence at trial. If the prosecutor or the law-enforcement-officers cannot present the out-of-court declarant to make a statement under cross-examination, and the declarant does not testify at trial, his testimonial out-of-court statement will be inadmissible.

his case if important evidence is excluded, and the victim of a violation of the Confrontation Clause will benefit from the exclusionary hearsay rule.

However, in a jurisdiction without the accusatorial tradition, such as Taiwan, the public prosecutor is not merely regarded as a party.[318] And the defendant as a victim of a violation of the constitutional right to confrontation will not automatically benefit from misconduct perpetrated by the opposing party. Although the 2003 hearsay rule refers to the Federal Rules of Evidence, perhaps the different style of hearsay legislation in the ROC CPC results from this pro-civil-law idea. Without the burden of a heavy distrust in the judicial officials instilled by the Raleigh trial[319] and the bifurcated trial structure, the ROC hearsay rule has created a pro-inquisitorial exception, Article 159-1 of the ROC CPC, based mainly on the court's discretionary powers. In addition, although Articles 159-2 to 159-4 of the ROC CPC provide the defendant with the procedural right to challenge the ad-

---

[318] See Renee Lettow Lerner, "The Intersection of Two Systems: An American on Trial for An American Murder in the French Cour d'Assises", 2001 *University of Illinois Law Review* 791, 797 (2001).

[319] As mentioned in Crawford: "We have no doubt that the courts below were acting in utmost good faith when they found reliability. The Framers, however, would not have been content to indulge this assumption. They knew that judges, like other government officers, could not always be trusted to safeguard the rights of the people; the likes of the dread Lord Jeffreys were not yet too distant a memory. They were loath to leave too much discretion in judicial hands." See 124 S. Ct., at 1373.

missibility of out-of-court statements, they also allow the court to exercise its discretionary powers in assessing the reliability and determining the admissibility of out-of-court statements. As Roberts suggested, cross-examination is merely a preferred method, not the only method, to assess the reliability of out-of-court statements.[320] As a result, in Taiwan, admitting an out-of-court testimonial statement in evidence at trial without cross-examination does not necessarily conflict with the fair trial principle of criminal justice proceedings.

This study concludes that the ROC hearsay rule includes both inquisitorial and adversarial exceptions. As the court is still acting as fact finder under Articles 55 and 56 of the ROC Criminal Law and Paragraph 2 of Article 163 of the ROC CPC, and is required to justify its findings in writing, the accusatorial model and its accompanying rules of evidence should not apply in Ta-

---

[320] The Court held: "The historical evidence leaves little doubt, however, that the Clause was intended to exclude some hearsay. Moreover, underlying policies support the same conclusion. The Court has emphasized that the Confrontation Clause reflects a preference for face-to-face confrontation at trial, and that 'a primary interest secured by [the provision] is the right of cross-examination.'··· The Court, however, has recognized that competing interests, if 'closely examined,' may warrant dispensing with confrontation at trial···. This Court, in a series of cases, has sought to accommodate these competing interests. True to the common-law tradition, the process has been gradual, building on past decisions, drawing on new experience, and responding to changing conditions. The Court has not sought to 'map out a theory of the Confrontation Clause that would determine the validity of all··· hearsay exceptions.' But a general approach to the problem is discernible." See 448 U.S., at 63-5.

iwan without harmonization. For example, although not all hearsay exceptions in the Federal Rules of Evidence have been incor-
porated into Articles 159-2 to 159-4 of the ROC CPC, which
originate with common law rules of evidence, Article 159-1 of he
ROC CPC gives the court the legal power to admit any out-of-
court statement presented by the parties in evidence. Moreover,
Paragraph 2 of Article 163 of the ROC CPC allows the court to
admit out-of-court statements presented by the parties beyond Articles 159-1 to 159-4 of the ROC CPC if the court finds the statements bear particularized guarantees of trustworthiness. While
the court collects and investigates evidence ex officio, no hearsay
rule applies because the court is using its inquisitorial powers to
find the truth.[321] These powers should not be subject to any accusatorial limitations. It is worth noting that under the accusatorial hearsay rule of Article 159-2 of the ROC CPC, the court
cannot admit verbatim transcripts made during police interrogation in evidence if the declarant is not present at trial.[322] Yet, the-
oretically, the court can employ its inquisitorial powers to find
the truth ex officio even when the specific truth-finding approach
is not allowed as an accusatorial hearsay exception. In other wor-

[321] In a sense, the ROC Supreme Court in 90 Sun Zon Gum One 17 already
admitted the out-of-court statement in evidence by investigating evidence ex
officio before the 2003 legislation came into effect.
[322] This is because the ROC legal system only allows the Grand Justice Council to
outlaw any effective positive law, and lower courts cannot ignore an enacted
provision by interpreting it in an opposing way.

ds, this study suggests that the court can admit out-of-court statements presented by the prosecutors but not on the basis of Articles 159-1 to 159-4 of the ROC CPC under its inquisitorial powers. A hearsay exception provided in FRE 803 or 804 but not in Articles 159-2 to 159-4 of the ROC CPC might be admissible under either Article 159-1 or Paragraph 2 of Article 163 of the ROC CPC. Interestingly, it is not clear how the court should exercise its inquisitorial power to find facts when neither of the parties presents any information regarding these facts. At the very least, while the fact finder will inevitably hear all kinds of evidence after indictment, which might provide the court with the information it needs to exercise its inquisitorial power to investigate evidence, the hearsay practice in Taiwan should be more flexible than its counterpart in the United States.

The hearsay practice in Taiwan is not identical to its counterpart in the United States. While the ROC hearsay rule provides the defendant with a procedural right to challenge the admissibility of out-of-court statements and requires the prosecutor to be present at trial to respond to this challenge, it would be inaccurate to say it is meaningless to adopt the common law hearsay rule in the ROC criminal justice system. In fact, it is less meaningful—rather than meaningless—for the ROC criminal justice system to adopt the common law hearsay rule as it is used in the United States, because the American trial structure is bifurcated, the parties are responsible for the presentation of the evidence, and the fact finder is not required to explain decisions in writing. If the ROC criminal justice system intends to build a more markedly accusatorial trial practice similar, but not identical, to its counterpart in the United States, it might be possible to restrict the court in the exercise of its inquisitorial powers for the purpose of investigating evidence so that the parties will be responsible for the presentation of the evidence in most cases. However, it is impossible to prevent the court in Taiwan from hearing inadmissible evidence that might influence its decision and provide sufficient and necessary information to exercise its inquisitorial power to investigate evidence ex officio. If the court holds the view that the inadmissible hearsay evidence might possibly reveal the material truth, it will be difficult for the court to stop investigating evidence ex officio when it has to justify its decision in writing which will be scrutinized in appeal. In all fairness, it must be noted that the narrower Paragraph 2 of Article 163 of the ROC CPC and Articles 55 and 56 of the ROC Criminal Law are interpreted,[323] the less inquisitorial and the more accusatorial trial proceedings in Taiwan will be. This study does not offer suggestions for restricting the inquisitorial powers of the court to investigate evidence ex officio. That will require further empirical analysis of judicial decisions under the newly enacted Article 55 of the ROC Criminal Law.

---

[323] Only the newly enacted Article 55 of the ROC Criminal Law will be applicable on July 1st 2006.

Cite as: Ming-woei Chang, Adoption of the Common Law Hearsay Rule in a Civil Law Jurisdiction: a Comparative Study of the Hearsay Rule in Taiwan and the United States, vol. 10.2 ELECTRONIC JOURNAL OF COMPARATIVE LAW, (October 2006), <http://www.ejcl.org/102/article102-1.pdf>.

5

台灣的證據排除法則：
以美國為鑑

The Exclusionary Rule in Taiwan: Lessons from the United States

Over the past decades, the criminal justice system of the Republic of China on Taiwan has long been criticised for insufficient human rights protection, especially for alleged criminal offenders. From 1947 to 1987, Taiwan enforced martial law and was in a state of siege. In this era of martial law rule, ordinary citizens in Taiwan lived for four decades with little hope of any recognition of their inherent human rights.

Following Taiwan's development of democratic institutions, from 1987, with numerous interpretative pronouncements of the ROC Grand Justice Council,[1] Taiwan started to review its legal system. Particular focus was directed at the criminal justice system, as well as the police powers that influenced daily life most. The conclusion was gradually reached that the ROC Criminal Procedure Code, based mainly on the continental German system

---

[1]   See the ROC Judicial Yuan and its Grand Justice Council, at http://www.judicial.gov.tw (last visited Apr. 18th, 2005).

and enacted in 1967,[2] was out of date.

To prevent miscarriage of justice, the design of criminal procedures must include protection of the rights of the alleged offenders. As mentioned, "the degree to which the rights of the alleged offenders are protected during criminal proceedings has been regarded as one of the indexes of a nation's civil developments.[3] In order to improve human rights protection — of both citizens and alleged offenders in Taiwan — the Taiwanese government decided to amend its Criminal Procedure Code. Several important drafts of the ROC Criminal Procedure Code were passed by the ROC Legislative Yuan (see 'Introduction to the ROC Legislative Yuan', 2005) from 1990, corresponding to the demand for human rights protection.

From the viewpoint of comparative legal study, the 2003 ROC legislation to reshape ROC criminal procedure has created controversy regarding whether Taiwan's 'new' criminal justice system retains its inquisitorial flavour or has become more 'Pro-Adversarial' since the former Criminal Procedure Code was bas-

---

[2] 'Law in the Republic of China on Taiwan is based on the German-based legal system which carried to Taiwan by the Kuomintang. In the area of constitutional law, the Republic of China uses the 1947 Constitution which was promulgated for both Mainland China and Taiwan although numerous changes have been made to take into account the fact that the Republic of China only controls Taiwan and two counties of Fujian' (Wikipedia, 2005).

[3] See the ROC Judicial Yuan, The Protection of Human Rights, at http://www.judicial.gov.tw/b4/e6-1-1-1.htm (last visited Oct. 3rd, 2005).

ed upon continental inquisitorial models and those current effective amendments are derived mainly from the American adversarial model. However, this comparative study does not intend to resolve this problem but focuses instead merely on the newly-enacted exclusionary rule in the ROC Criminal Procedure Code and its counterpart in the United States. Although the United States exclusionary rule is sometimes described as a mandatory rule,[4] in a sense this is inaccurate and overly simplistic. After offering a brief overview of the developments of the exclusionary rule in Taiwan and its counterpart in the States, this article considers why the development of the exclusionary rule in Taiwan differs from the United States' experience. Further, this paper argues that differences between these two exclusionary rules will eventually become smaller, since both seem to apply similar 'balancing tests' when excluding evidence.

1. Adoption and Developments of the Exclusionary Rule in Taiwan（證據排除法則在台灣之採行與發展）

Generally speaking, the Republic of China on Taiwan has a codified system of law which draws heavily from the laws of other countries with similar codified systems (Redden, 1984: vol 2A, 40.12), as well as traditional Chinese laws. The ROC Court system follows the continental civil law model. Procedures are

---

[4] As mentioned, 'The United States' mandatory exclusionary rules are often criticized as being "peculiar"' (Cho, 1999: 261).

inquisitorial rather than adversarial, and judges are active participants at trial. The supreme law of Taiwan is the ROC Constitution. The judicial system is composed of three tiers: the Supreme Court, High Court, and District Court. Professional judges decide all cases, including facts and legal issues. Appeals to the High Court are as a matter of right in Taiwan (ROC Criminal Procedure Code, art 344). Appeals to the Supreme Court are limited by statute, but are generally available for all except the smallest or most localised of cases (ROC Criminal Procedure Code, arts 376-382). Since the Supreme Court reviews only issues of law, an appeal may be made to the Supreme Court only on the ground that the original judgment is in violation of a law or an order (ROC Criminal Procedure Code, art 377). Documentary proceedings, rather than oral proceedings, are the norm (ROC Criminal Procedure Code, art 372). As the legal system in the ROC is based on the civil law and code-based legal traditions, legal matters are decided by reference to the Codes and the writings of scholars and judges who interpret the Codes. There is comparatively little judge-made law in Taiwan. Like the German criminal justice system, the main source of Taiwan's criminal procedure law is its Criminal Procedure Code.[5] While some of the individual rights guaranteed by the ROC Constitution have special relevance

---

[5] Different from the US style of highly constitutionalised criminal justice system, most issues of criminal procedure in the continental tradition are governed by detailed provisions of the Criminal Procedure Code in Taiwan.

in the context of the criminal process, the jurisprudence of the Grand Justice Council has great relevance for the interpretation of criminal procedure law, although the interpretation of the Criminal Procedure Code is the task of ordinary courts (Weigend, 1999: 187).

As in Germany, neither the 1935 Chinese Criminal Procedure Code nor the 1967 re-enacted ROC Criminal Procedure Code contained a general statutory exclusionary rule making illegally obtained evidence inadmissible. However, Paragraph 1 of Article 156 of the former ROC Criminal Procedure Code did provide for inadmissibility of statements elicited by certain forbidden means, including violence, threat, inducement, fraud, unlawful detention and other improper devices. Despite this provision, since the Taiwanese Supreme Court did not care about how evidence was obtained, any evidence related to proving the truth of the matter at issue was admissible (see 72 Tai Sun 1332 (1983)).[6] In short, the exclusionary approach of evidentiary rule did not exist in the ROC jurisdiction until 1998.

1.1　The Pre-2003 Developments of the Exclusionary Rule in Taiwan（民國 92 年以前之發展）

Under the continental inquisitorial tradition, virtually no scholars or judges recognised any limitation on the admissibility

---

[6]　Taiwan's legal professionals do not cite a case by the parties' names. Instead, they cite a case by its case number.

of evidence in the ROC criminal justice system.[7] Based upon the continental trial principles of 'Direct Inquisition' and 'Verbal Inquisition', the ROC Supreme Court held on numerous occasions that trial courts in Taiwan were bound by very few legal restrictions on the nature of evidence they received.[8] Paragraph 1 of Article 165 provides that '[n]otes and other documents in the record which might be used as evidence against the accused shall be read to an accused. As this was the only requirement, any illegally-obtained evidence was admissible as long as it was read to the accused. However, influenced by the United States, discussion of the exclusionary rule emerged in the Taiwanese criminal practice for the first time in 1998, where the Taipei High Court reversed a Shilin District Court verdict that excluded illegally-obtained evidence in a fornication case (87 Sun E 1318 (1998)). The Taipei High Court in this case reasoned that the illegally recorded conversation between the defendants was not 'fruit of the

---

[7] It is noteworthy that the late Professor Pu-Shen Chen, a former Grand Justice and leading Professor of Law at National Taiwan University and National Chen Chi University, asserted that there was no hearsay rule in the ROC Criminal Procedure Code. And statements made by a witness outside the court shall be admitted in evidence according to arts 165 and 166. See Chen, 1995: 413.

[8] Those Supreme Court decisions include: 70 Tai Sun 3864 (1981); 72 Tai Sun 1203 (1983); 74 Tai Sun 6888 (1985); 75 Tai Sun 933 (1986); 77 Tai Sun 848 (1988); 79 Tai Sun 5140 (1990); 81 Tai Sun 4352 (1992); 81 Tai Sun 6531 (1992); 82 Tai Sun 622 (1993); 82 Tai Sun 4199 (1993); 83 Tai Sun 2785 (1994); 84 Tai Sun 538 (1995); 84 Tai Sun 2819 (1995); 85 Tai Sun 4455 (1996); and 91 Tai Sun 2363 (2002).

poisonous tree', because there was no American-style exclusionary rule under Article 165 of the ROC Criminal Procedure Code. Soon after this decision, the ROC Supreme Court recognised for the first time that an exclusionary rule was applicable in Taiwan's criminal justice system, on the basis of judicial integrity and fairness.[9] Hence, any evidence obtained through illegal wiretaps could not be allowed in a criminal trial, although the question of what kind of evidence should be excluded, and under what circumstances, remained to be developed by trial courts.

In a fornication case (88 Sun E 1953 (1999)),[10] a victim wife hired a person to wiretap and record telephone conversations between her husband and his lover. After wiretapping their conversation regarding their sexual intercourse, the victim wife accused both of them and a public prosecution was later filed. While the district court convicted two of them, the Taipei High Court acquitted them by declaring that：

---

[9] See 87 Tai Sun 4025 (1998). It held that illegally wiretapped communication by police should be excluded or it would prejudice the judicial integrity and fairness according to arts 8 and 16 of the ROC Constitution and Interpretation No. 384, 396, and 418 of the Grand Justice Council. Therefore it is necessary for the court to investigate if there existed illegal wiretapping.

[10] Fornication is a criminal offense in Taiwan. Article 239 of the ROC Criminal Law provides: a married person who commits adultery with another shall be punished with imprisonment for not more than 1 year; the other party to the adultery shall be subject to the same punishment. While the ROC does not publish its judicial opinions in a way similar to that in U.S., it is unusual to quote a case with accurate reference to the page or paragraph number.

Since wiretapping other's telephone conversation is a criminal offense, it violates the defendants' privacy protection if the tape is admitted as evidence at trial. In addition, admitting the tape in evidence at trial would prejudice judicial integrity and fairness and encourage others to do the same. Therefore, the wiretapped tape is inadmissible. (88 Sun E 1953 (1999))

In short, any evidence secured in violation of the criminal law is not admissible — even if the evidence is obtained by ordinary people and not police officers. This is dramatically different from the United States exclusionary practice which provides no exclusion remedy for evidence obtained unlawfully by private persons (*Burdeau v McDowell*, 256 US 465 (1921)).

In a case involving investigation of corruption, the police wiretapped and recorded the telephone conversation of the suspect, who was bribed over the phone. Although the defendant was convicted by the district court, the Taipei High Court again acquitted the defendant by declaring that :

The court would become a conspirator to invade privacy, the right of correspondence guaranteed by Article 12 of Constitution, if it admitted the wiretapped tape in evidence at trial. In addition, in this case, wiretapping did not coincide with the requirements in the recently adopted 'Correspondence Protection Act,' which regulates wiretapping, even though it was conducted before its legislation. (90 Sun E 1085(2002))

This ruling suggests that a recording obtained in violation of any statutory privacy protection would be inadmissible.

While the cases mentioned above excluded evidence because of privacy invasion and concerns of judicial integrity, the Taipei High Court took a different view in a drug producing case. It held that:

> Wiretapping conducted before the enactment of the Correspondence Protection Act in July, 14, 1988 is admissible in that the requirement of wiretapping according to that Act could not be violated before its promulgation. Since laws in effect when police conducting wiretapping did not expressively prohibit wiretapping, it is not fair to say wiretapping is inadmissible under no law. (90 Sun Gum Two 1112 (2002))

In this ruling, the court did not consider whether privacy protection would be violated or whether admitting evidence derived from wiretapping would prejudice judicial integrity and fairness. It merely declared that as there was no law regulating wiretapping, no law was violated and so there was no 'fruit of the poisonous tree'.

The case-law developments of the exclusionary rule between 1998 and 2003 were not limited to situations involving wiretapping. In a fraud case (90 Sun E 2046 (2002)), the police interrogated the defendant in violation of a procedure rule which prohibits the police from interrogating at night. The Taipei High Court declared:

> Whether the resulting confession should be excluded depends on a balancing test requiring the court to weigh the seriousness of the violation against the public interest. Since this illegal interrogation stopped at nine o'clock p.m., which did not constitute a serious violation, and the police did not intend to coerce the defendant to confess by conducting fearful methods, confession resulting from a procedural violation should not be excluded in this case. (90 Sun E 2046 (2002))

In other words, exclusion depends on the seriousness of the violation, the relevance of the piece of evidence for the resolution of the case and the seriousness of the offence. Violation of a procedural rule does not necessarily lead to exclusion of evidence. Thus, the High Court in Taiwan, for the first time, indicated that application of Taiwan's exclusionary rule should be a discretionary matter, in which the court balanced the factors listed above.

This stands in contrast to the American exclusionary rule that rigidly excludes evidence if any police activity is found to be unlawful (*Mapp v Ohio*, 367 US 643 (1961)).

In a handgun possession case, police officers intentionally conducted a search knowing that the address to be searched was incorrectly recorded on the search warrant (which made the warrant invalid). Nevertheless, the Taipei High Court did not exclude evidence derived from the search, stating:

> Although the police would eventually secure another valid search warrant with a correctly written address in advance in this case, it is necessary and important to seize the handguns as soon as possible, lest the defendant should pass them to others who might break societal order, it is [therefore] improper to exclude the handguns as evidence, for the offense is serious. (90 Sun Su 2229 (2002)).

Again, the court applied a balancing test to decide whether to exclude evidence. This suggests that when the situation is serious (such as when the defendant possesses handguns or something that might seriously prejudice social peace and order) the balancing test should not result in suppression, even if the police conduct was unlawful. However, if the illegal search resulted in financial records or commercial statements that might not prejudice the social peace and order, the balancing test would appear to favor the defendant and therefore evidence derived from the illegal search is more likely to be excluded (see 91 Sun Gum One 197 (2003)).

1.2　Post-2003 Practice under the Newly Legislated Exclusionary Rule（民國 92 年立法後之證據排除法則）

Although the ROC Supreme Court recognised the exclusionary rule in 1998, the formulation was quite abstract. This meant that lower courts did not develop a predictable approach to excluding illegally-obtained evidence, and there emerged different positions among appellate courts concerning how the rule should be applied. In 2003 the Legislative Yuan stepped in, and promulgated an exclusionary rule. Article 158-4 of the ROC Criminal Procedure Code provides: Unless otherwise provided by law, whether evidence derived from violation of procedural rule conducted by law-enforcement government officers should be excluded in a criminal case depends on the result of balancing human rights protection of the defendant against the public interest. This law unequivocally provides the court with a discretionary power to exclude evidence in certain circumstances. The Advisory Committee of the ROC Criminal Procedure Code suggested seven standards to be considered in exercising the discretion to exclude evidence:

1.　the seriousness of the violation of procedural rules;

2. the subjective intent of the violation;

3. infringement of human rights protection;

4. the seriousness of the offense;

5. the potential deterrence to government officers;

6. the possibility of discovering the evidence without the violation; and

7. prejudice to the defense(Lin, 2003: 10).[11]

Generally speaking, these criteria are consistent with the previous case-law developments discussed above.

The Taipei High Court for the first time in 2003 applied this newly-declared exclusionary rule in Article 158-4 of the ROC Criminal Procedure Code to a case involving the leaking of national secrets. The defendant was accused of revealing national secrets by faxing a Mr. Wang in Shanghai, China. While the defendant asserted that the fax records were obtained without a search warrant and should be excluded, the court ruled that:

In that the fax record was not obtained by the government officer in charge of criminal investigation, allowing it as evidence at trial would not coincide with the principle behind Article 158-4 of the ROC Criminal Procedure Code, which is intended to

---

[11] The Advisory Committee of the ROC Criminal Procedure Code expressively suggested these seven standards for Taiwanese courts to follow in the Advisory Note to Article 158-4 of the ROC Criminal Procedure Code(Lin, 2003: 10).

deter government misconduct. Thus, judicial integrity would not be tainted even if this fax record is admitted. (92 Sun E 1812 (2003))

This High Court decision is very different to the earlier one made in the fornication case (88 Sun E 1953), which applied the exclusionary rule to private persons.[12] Under this ruling, the newly adopted exclusionary rule applies only to governmental misconduct on the part of law-enforcement officers in charge of criminal investigations.[13] For evidence resulting from governmental misconduct on the part of officers not in charge of criminal investigation, the exclusionary rule does not apply. No Supreme Court decisions have addressed this issue yet,[14] and it remains uncertain whether the ROC Supreme Court will uphold this new ruling.

In addition to evidence obtained by law-enforcement officers, it is still unclear whether privately-obtained evidence should be excluded, if it is illegally secured. Although Article 158-4 of

---

[12] It is worth mentioning that this new decision is also different from its American counterpart which applies the exclusionary rule to governmental misconduct by any officer of law.

[13] Generally speaking, the phrase 'law-enforcement officers' in Article 158-4 of the ROC Criminal Procedure Code include the criminal court judge, the prosecutor, the police officers, and the other government officers according to the law. See 92 Sun E 1812 (2003).

[14] According to Article 376 of the ROC Criminal Procedure Code, the Taipei High Court decision of 92 Sun E 1812 was final. This is why the ROC Supreme Court did not have the opportunity to rule on this case.

the ROC Criminal Procedure Code seems to apply merely to law-enforcement officers' misconduct, as held in the Taipei High Court case of 92 Sun E 1812, in the wiretap case (92 Sun E 2258), the Taipei High Court ruled that the illegal wiretap obtained by the victim should be excluded because allowing it as evidence against the accused would violate Article 12 of the ROC Constitution that protects privacy of correspondence.[15] This decision did not address why the requirement of 'law-enforcement officers' illegality' in Article 158-4 of the ROC Criminal Procedure Code should not apply in this case. It did not explain in detail how allowing this illegal wiretap as evidence would unconstitutionally infringe the right to privacy of correspondence, especially when the government did nothing wrong. In a sense, the ruling in this case copies 88 Sun E 1953.

Nonetheless, in decisions following 92 Sun E 1812, evidence illegally obtained by the victim or by a third party has been held admissible (see 93 Sun E 140(2004), 93 Sun E 934 (2004), and 93 Sun Su 835(2004)). However, if a private person is controlled, helped, or asked by a law-enforcement-officer, the ROC Supreme Court employs Article 158-4 of the ROC Criminal Procedure Code to exclude evidence obtained by his or her private illegal behaviour (see 93 Tai Sun 2949 (2004)). Although the question of whether a specific private misconduct would be

---

[15] Article 12 of the ROC Constitution provides: 'The people shall have freedom of privacy of correspondence.'

treated as being controlled, helped, or asked for by a law-enforcement officer, (that is, whether the private person was acting as the agent of the law-enforcement officer) may become a significant issue in the future, it is unlikely to cause the courts too much concern, because it is primarily a question of fact.

It is not difficult to identify the differences in the exclusionary rule before and after 2003. The developments prior to 2003 seemed to exercise an abstract constitutional power to exclude illegally-obtained evidence, regardless of the official position of the obtainers. Courts employed a balancing test that depended on the result of balancing the constitutional privacy protection for the defendant against judicial integrity and fairness. While Article 158-4 of the ROC Criminal Procedure Code provides the statutory authority to invoke the exclusionary rule, it also requires the illegal evidence obtainer to be a law-enforcement officer or his or her agent (see 92 Sun E 1812 (2003)). In general, under the civil law tradition, all 'ordinary courts'[16] are required to apply any statute which covers the matter at issue. However, without mentioning why Article 158-4 of the ROC Criminal Procedure Code

---

[16] While the Grand Justice Council as a constitutional court is designed to exclusively resolve constitutional disputes under the ROC Constitutional scheme, ordinary courts are required to apply the statute if the matter at issue is provided. Ordinary courts are merely allowed to pend a trial and file that case to the Grand Justice Council when they find that applying statutes might be unconstitutional. See the ROC Judicial Yuan and its Grand Justice Council, supra note 1.

does not cover the field, some courts still claim a broader power to exclude evidence illegally obtained by a private person, merely by directly applying a constitutional provision, such as privacy protection (92 Sun E 2258 (2003)). It is unclear why this approach (stemming mainly from the case of 88 Sun E 1953) could survive the enactment of Article 158-4 of the ROC Criminal Procedure Code. Consequently, whether evidence illegally obtained by a private person would invoke the exclusionary rule remains a practical problem.

The 2003 enactment does not seem to have significantly altered the way courts exercise the discretion to exclude evidence. Both before and after 2003, rarely have the ROC courts discussed the discretionary part of the exclusionary rule. The circumstances in which illegally-obtained evidence would pass the balancing test remain unknown, or, at least, unexplained. How to properly exercise this discretionary power thus deserves more attention. Given the limited experience of employing the exclusionary rule in Taiwan, it is meaningful and possible to draw from the ideas used in the criminal justice system of the United States as the exclusionary rule stemmed mainly from the United States. It is useful now to provide a brief account of the history and development of the exclusionary rule in the United States.

2. The Exclusionary Rule in the United States
（美國的證據排除法則）

The "Exclusionary Rule" presents a controversial issue in

the criminal justice system. Generally speaking, there are some who believe it is needed to deter police from violating a person's constitutional right and to maintain judicial integrity (*Mapp v Ohio*, 367 US 643, 659 (1961)). While others think there should be no exclusionary rule in that it allows the guilty to go free without carriage of justice.[17] In this section, this paper will review its development in the United States criminal justice system.

The Fourth Amendment to the United States Constitution provides that

> The right of the people to be secured in their persons, houses, papers, and effects, against unreasonable searches and seizures, shall not be violated, and no Warrants shall issue, but upon probable cause, supported by Oath or affirmation, and particularly describing the place to be searched, and the persons or things to be seized.

Over the years, the United States Supreme Court has struggled to decide whether, and where, limits should be imposed on the government's search and seizure power (Jochner, 1999 citing Bacig-

---

[17] For example, Justice (then Judge) Cardozo mentioned that: 'under our constitutional exclusionary doctrine "the criminal is to go free because the constable has blundered."' *Mapp v Ohio*, 367 US 643, 659 (1961).

al, 1979). In general, if a court finds that a search or a seizure took place, it must next determine whether it was 'reasonable' within the meaning of the Fourth Amendment (Burnham, 1999: 275). Thus, whether the Fourth Amendment applies depends upon whether the person who is subjected to being searched or seized has a reasonable expectation of privacy in a specific situation. If a reasonable expectation of privacy exists, then the government has to show probable cause or its conduct would be unreasonable, and therefore illegal (Grano, 1984: 465). Probable cause exists where 'the facts and circumstances within knowledge, and of which they had reasonable trustworthy information, sufficient in themselves to warrant a man of reasonable caution in the belief that an offense has been or is being committed' (*Brinegar v United States*, 338 US 160, 169 (1949)). To determine whether probable cause exists, the Supreme Court currently applies, instead of the old two-pronged standard in Aguilar v Texas 378 US 108, 114-5 (1964) and *Spinelli v United States* 393 US 410, 412 (1969), the 'commonsense' approach adopted in *Illinois v Gates* 462 US 213, 230-2 (1983). Under this approach, the Court balances the government's interest in investigating crime against the extent of the intrusion into someone's privacy.

The United States Constitution does not provide remedies for any violation of the Fourth Amendment's restrictions on unreasonable searches and seizures. The best remedy for a violation of the Fourth Amendment has long been debated (Burnham, 1999: 286-7), but

> the rule that reliable and probative physical evidence of guilt may not be introduced in the prosecution's case-in-chief if it was obtained in violation of the defendant's fourth amendment rights was unknown to the law in this country for almost 100 years after the fourth amendment was adopted. (Department of Justice, Office of Legal Policy, 1989: 591)

2.1 Origins and Development of the Exclusionary Rule
（證據排除法則的起源與發展）

Writs and warrants were originally used by the Tudor monarchy as means of restricting freedom of the press and suppressing dissenting publications (*Marcus v Search Warrants of Property*, 367 US 717, 724 (1961)). The Fourth Amendment was created to provide a general right against search and seizure and to provide a specific right against general warrants (Department of Justice, Office of Legal Policy, 1989: 592). While the framers were greatly concerned about wrongful searches, the exclusion of evidence was not used in practice as a remedy. In fact it does not appear that the framers or ratifiers of the Fourth Amendment contemplated suppression as a remedy for its violation (Department of Justice, Office of Legal Policy, 1989: 594).

In *Adams v New York*, 192 US 585 (1904), the Supreme Court, following common law traditions, held that the use of evidence obtained in violation of constitutional rights under the Fourth Amendment was constitutional.[18]

The case that expressly created the exclusionary rule for Fourth Amendment violations is *Weeks v United States*, 232 US 383 (1914).[19] Although the decision in *Weeks* was limited to the illegal search conducted by federal agents and did not extend significantly beyond *Boyd*, the true significance of *Weeks* lay in the Court's sole reliance on the Fourth Amendment. After *Weeks*, two 1921 decisions, *Gouled v United States*, 255 US 298 (1921), and Amos v United States, 255 US 313 (1921), firmly established the exclusionary rule in the federal courts (Department of Justice, Office of Legal Policy, 1989: 596). This was reaffirmed by *Wolf v Colorado*, 338 US 25 (1949) which, for the first time, established that the security of one's privacy against arbitrary intrusion by the police is embodied in the concept of due process con-

---

[18] Exclusion of evidence as a remedy for a constitutional violation was discussed in two earlier Supreme Court cases. In *Boyd v United States*, 116 US 616 (1886), which contains the first mention of an exclusionary remedy, the Supreme Court excluded private papers as evidence, because to allow them would require the owner to be a witness against himself, in violation of the Fifth Amendment. In addition, the Court held that it constituted an unreasonable search and seizure in violation of the Fourth Amendment.

[19] In Weeks the Court held that evidence derived from a warrantless seizure by United States Federal Marshals was inadmissible: 232 US 383, 393 (1914).

tained in the Fourteenth Amendment (see *Irvine v California*, 347 US 128, 132 (1954); Bradley, 1993: 14, 19).

The exclusionary rule as applied in the United States also includes the 'fruit of the poisonous tree' doctrine, first established in *Silverthorne Lumber Co v United States*, 251 US 385 (1920). There the Court held that not only is evidence that is illegally seized inadmissible, but also any evidence or testimony obtained later as a result of the illegally seized evidence is inadmissible. Under this doctrine, any facts or leads discovered because of an earlier, illegal seizure are inadmissible because "if the 'tree' is tainted, its 'fruits' are also tainted" (O'connor, 2004).

2.2 From Federal to State Level（從聯邦到州）

It was not until 1960 that the Supreme Court, through decisions that substantially expanded the scope of the exclusionary rule, made the rule applicable to the states. In *Elkins v United States*, 364 US 206 (1960), the Court overruled the 'silver platter doctrine' announced in *Weeks*, stating that the question of whether evidence obtained by state officers and used against a defendant in a federal trial was obtained by unreasonable search and seizure is to be judged as if the search and seizure had been made by federal officers. Federal courts, therefore, could not use evidence illegally seized by state officers. As Justice Stewart stated in Elkins, the exclusionary rule 'is calculated to prevent, not to repair. Its purpose is to deter — to compel respect for the constitutional guarantee in the only effectively available way — by removing the incentive to disregard it' (364 US, 217).

One year later, in *Mapp v Ohio*, 367 US 643 (1961), the Supreme Court eventually overruled Wolf v *Colorado*, by completely breaking from the common law tradition 'that relevant evidence was admissible regardless of how it had been obtained' (Bradley, 2001: 375). *Mapp* set forth two justifications for the exclusionary rule: to deter law enforcement officers from violating constitutional rights by removing their incentive to do so; and to preserve judicial integrity.[20] Thereafter, all evidence obtained in violation of the Fourth Amendment and any other Constitutional right has been inadmissible. Although Justice (then Judge) Cardozo complained in *People v Defore*, 242 N Y 13, 21 (1920) that 'under our constitutional exclusionary doctrine the criminal is to go free because the constable has blundered,' Justice Clark responded to this viewpoint in *Mapp* by stating that:

In some cases this will undoubtedly be the result. But, as was said in *Elkins*, there is another consideration — the imperative of judicial integrity. The criminal goes free, if he must, but it is the law that sets him free. Nothing can destroy a government more quickly than its failure to observe its own laws, or worse, its disregard of the charter of its own existence. (367 US, 659).

---

[20]　However, the second basis of *Mapp* has largely been forgotten. See Burnham, 1999: 286-7. It is interesting that *Mapp* was not originally thought to be a Fourth Amendment case. Since it was, in fact, a First Amendment case, the exclusionary rule was neither briefed nor argued. See 367 US, at 645. See also Department of Justice, Office of Legal Policy, 1989: 598.

2.3　Expansions and Limitations on Mapp（麥普案之擴張與限制）

After *Mapp*, the Supreme Court continued to extend the scope of the judge-made exclusionary rule. In *Wong Sun v United States*, 371 US 471, 485 (1963), the Court further applied the exclusionary rule to 'verbal statements' that were regarded as fruits of an unlawful search. In addition, in *One 1958 Plymouth Sedan v Pennsylvania*, 380 US 693 (1965), the Court also applied the exclusionary rule to civil forfeiture proceedings on the grounds that they should be classified as quasi-criminal proceedings.

However, after the 1965 case of *Linkletter v Walker*, 381 US 618 (1965) the Supreme Court started to narrow its application of the exclusionary rule 'by placing ever increasing emphasis on the rule's deterrent purpose as opposed to other justifications that had been offered for it, and by balancing its apparent costs against its presumed benefits' (Department of Justice, Office of Legal Policy, 1989: 599).[21] In *United States v Calandra*, 414 US 338 (1974), for example, the Supreme Court refused to exclude unlawfully obtained evidence from grand jury proceedings.[22] The Court balanced the potential injury to the function of the grand

---

[21]　The Supreme Court has made a series of decisions with regard to limitation on the application of the exclusionary rule. See Burnham, 1999: 287.

[22]　The Court held that the exclusionary rule derives not from a personal constitutional right but comes from a judicial remedy created principally to deter unlawful police conduct.

jury against the marginal deterrence to be gained by applying it to grand jury proceedings and found that exclusion should not apply (414 US 338, 454 (1974)). Using a similar balancing test, in United States v Havens, 446 US 620 (1980), the Court held it is lawful to use illegally-obtained evidence to impeach testimony by a criminal defendant on cross-examination. In Stone v Powell, 428 US 465 (1976), using the same balancing approach, the Court determined that 'the rule does not provide a basis for granting federal habeas corpus relief to a state prisoner who had ample opportunity to litigate his Fourth Amendment claim in the state courts' (Burnham, 1999: 287).

Another limitation on the sweep of the exclusionary rule was the Court's determination that the exclusionary rule does not apply to evidence obtained by private persons. In *Burdeau v McDowell*, 256 US 465 (1921), the Court, using a 'totality of the circumstances' test, decided evidence that a private person obtains without governmental supervision or encouragement is not subject to the exclusionary rule because 'the exclusionary rule was characterized as a restraint upon the activities of the sovereign authority and not a limitation upon other than governmental agencies' (Kamisar et al, 2002: 135).

2.4　The Good Faith Exception（善意例外）

Despite this long pattern of cases contracting the sweep of the exclusionary rule, it was still true that illegally-obtained evidence could not be introduced at trial as part of the prosecutor's case-in-chief against a victim of a Fourth Amendment violation. Then, in *United States v Leon*, 428 US 897, 918 (1984), the Burger Court adopted a completely different approach and created a good faith exception to the exclusionary rule. Since one of the main justifications for the exclusionary rule is to deter police misconduct, as explained in Leon, it is unnecessary to apply the exclusionary rule if it turns out to have no deterrent effect. Therefore, under the good faith exception, the exclusionary rule does not bar use in the government's direct case of evidence seized by law enforcement officers who are objectively acting in reasonable reliance on a search warrant, found to be unsupported by probable cause, but issued by a detached and neutral magistrate (Department of Justice, Office of Legal Policy, 1989: 600).

While the Court's holding in *Leon* was limited to searches conducted pursuant to warrants, whether the Leon decision strongly suggest that the Court may be inclined to extend the 'reasonable good faith' doctrine to warrantless searches as well is open to speculation. The good faith exception has been extended to good faith reliance on the constitutionality of a statute (see *Illinois v Krull*, 480 US 340 (1987)) and good faith reliance on court maintained computer records (see Arizona v Evans, 514 US 1 (1995)).

2.5　The Standing to Claim the Exclusionary Rule
（主張證據排除法則之地位）

Another important issue is who is able to move to suppress

allegedly illegal evidence. Long before the Supreme Court authoritatively resolved this issue, 'the lower courts had developed the doctrine that a defendant lacked standing to challenge evidence seized in violation of a third party's constitutional right' (Kamisar et al, 2002: 749): *Jones v United States*, 362 US 257, 261 (1960).

The modern approach to standing appears in two Supreme Court cases. First, in *Rakas v Illinois*, 439 US 128 (1978), the Court held that whether the challenged search or seizure violated the Fourth Amendment rights depends upon whether a party has 'standing' (Kamisar et al, 2002: 756) to object to a search or a seizure. Next, in *Rawlings v Kentucky* (see 448 US 98 (1980), the Court rejected the idea that a claim of ownership of property seized during a search confers upon the owner the automatic right to challenge the search. Therefore, whether the defendant has a legitimate expectation of privacy became the requirement to confer standing. It is no longer sufficient to rely on possession or ownership of seized goods to establish an interest that has been invaded, if a justifiable expectation of privacy of the defendant was not violated in the seizure (FindLaw, 2000).[23]

---

[23] As noted by Findlaw, 'The Congressional Research Service, Library of Congress prepared this document, The Constitution of the United States of America: Analyis and Interpretation. Johnny H. Killian and George A. Costello edited the 1992 Edition. Johnny H. Killian, George A. Costello and Kenneth R. Thomas edited the 1996 and 1998 Supplements. George A. Costello and Kenneth R. Thomas edited the 2000 Supplement.' At http://www.findlaw.com/casecode/constitution (last visited, Oct. 5th, 2005).

3. Comparative Analyses of the Exclusionary Rule between the ROC and the United States（台灣與美國證據排除法則之比較分析）

As mentioned earlier, there are three issues emerging from Article 158-4 of the ROC Criminal Procedure Code. The first is whether Article 158-4 of the ROC Criminal Procedure Code applies to non-law-enforcement officers. The second issue is whether the exclusionary rule applies to evidence illegally obtained by private persons. Finally, the factors that courts should consider when exercising the discretionary power to exclude evidence is also unclear. In this section, this article will consider these issues in the context of the United States experience.

3.1 Different Approaches of Constitutional Protections of Human Rights（不同方式的憲法人權保障）

The structure of human rights protection in the United States Constitution influences the application of the exclusionary rule. While the illegality of evidence seized by the police is itself a matter of constitutional law under the Fourth Amendment, whether or not to use it at trial is also regarded as a constitutional issue in the United States. The exclusionary rule provides a remedy for a defendant whose Constitutional rights have been violated by a government agent. Unlike the United States style of human rights protection, the ROC Constitution provides its people with a more abstract style of human rights protection. For instance, while the Fourth, Fifth, and Sixth Amendments to the United States Constitution clearly grant people rights against unreasonable searches and seizures, double jeopardy, and self-incrimination and rights of confrontation and to a speedy trial, the ROC Constitution merely says that all people shall be equal before the law (art 7);[24] and personal freedom shall be guaranteed to the people (art 8). Further, people shall have freedom of residence and of change of residence (art 10); freedom of speech, teaching, writing and publication (art 11); and freedom of privacy of correspondence (arts 12 and 13).[25] Because arts 22 and 23[26] of the ROC Constitution authorise the government to restrict those freedoms of rights in the name of social order and public interest, courts and scholars rarely treat human rights protection as a constitutional issue under positive laws unless otherwise provided by the ROC Grand Justice Council.

For example, the Statute for Prevention of Gangsters of

---

[24] Article 7 of the ROC Constitution which provides that: 'All citizens of the Republic of China, irrespective of sex, religion, race, class, or party affiliation, shall be equal before the law.'

[25] This list is not exhaustive of all freedoms guaranteed by the ROC Constitution: see arts 13 to 21.

[26] Article 22 provides: 'All other freedoms and rights of the people that are not detrimental to social order or public welfare shall be guaranteed under the Constitution.' Article 23 provides: 'All the freedoms and rights enumerated in the preceding Articles shall not be restricted by law except such as may be necessary to prevent infringement upon the freedoms of other persons, to avert an imminent crisis, to maintain social order or to advance public welfare.'

1985 was designed and drafted to incarcerate violent hoodlums. Under the statute, the police were authorized to arbitrarily classify a person as a 'gangster', to force him to appear before the police, or arrest him if he failed to appear.[27] The police were further allowed to adopt a secret witness system, and to impose a rehabilitative program upon him, meaning an accused person could be sent to a vagrant camp where he or she would be deprived of nearly all civil rights without any participation or supervision of the prosecutor.[28] With this uncontrolled power of arbitrarily classifying certain persons as gangsters or hoodlums, the police could easily detain suspects, effectively avoiding the pro-

---

[27] To some extent, the police play roles as the prosecutors do under this Statute. See the former arts 5, 6, 7, 12, and 21 of the Statute for Prevention of Gangster.

[28] It says: 'The secret witness provision of Article 12 of said Act deprives of the right of the accused to confront the witnesses, and hampers the court's truth-finding function. Article 21 of said Act, without considering the necessity of detention, allows the imposition of correction and training programs on a prisoner, even after he has served his criminal sentence, and, therefore, jeopardizes his liberty. All the above articles of said Act exceed the extent of necessity, lack substantive propriety, and are inconsistent with the essence of the above Article of the Constitution. Furthermore, Article 5 of said Act, regarding the police's decision to consider a person as a gangster and to issue him admonitions, contradicts Article 16 of the Constitution because he could only appeal the decision to the National Police Administration, Ministry of the Interior, but has no right to lodge administrative appeal and institute administrative litigation. All of the Act's above Articles shall become null and void no later than December 31, 1996 after the promulgation of this Interpretation.' See Interpretation No. 384 of the Grand Justice Council (1990), available at: http://www.judicial.gov.tw/constitutionalcourt/EN/p03_01.asp? expno=384 (last visited, Oct. 5th, 2005).

cedural requirements prescribed in the ROC Criminal Procedure Code.[29] Under this police administrative mechanism, many gangsters or hoodlums were in fact 'created' instead of being 'discovered'. The police then had full discretion to charge an individual as a hoodlum because the suspect was deprived of the right to cross-examine the witness under the secret witness system, which offered the police an opportunity to produce fake witnesses in order to detain or incarcerate a suspect. Before the ROC Grand Justice Council declared this practice unconstitutional in 1995, lawyers and judges rarely challenged such Gangster proceedings on United States-style constitutional confrontation right grounds, because neither the ROC Constitution nor the ROC Criminal Procedure Code clearly provided the defendant the right to confront an accusing witness. In other words, because all 'ordinary courts' are required to apply the statute if the matter at issue is enacted under the civil law tradition, in most given cases, any restriction on human rights protection would be held constitutional if promulgated in law.

Since courts and scholars in Taiwan usually deal with criminal procedure issues directly based on the ROC Criminal Procedure Code, rather than the ROC Constitution itself, what the rights granted in the Constitution meant has, in the past, been unclear. However, as the ROC Grand Justice Council now recog-

---

[29] Id.

nizes a new pattern of human rights protection — including the confrontation right — in its Interpretations of No. 384, and 396,[30] human rights protection may become more similar to United States practices. So, for example, in the 1998 ROC Supreme Court decision, 87 Tai Sun 4025, which was decided directly based on constitutional human rights protection, the court held that as any evidence obtained through illegal wiretaps prejudices judicial integrity and fairness it could not be allowed as evidence in a criminal trial. This means that if the court in Taiwan determines that the evidence in question was seized in violation of procedural law, it must then consider whether admitting the evidence would violate the constitutional principle of proportionality. In other words, the court has to balance 'the defendant's interests ···

---

[30] It says: 'Since the disciplinary measures affect the right to hold public office granted by the Constitution and the members of the disciplinary authority are judges as construed under the Constitution, according to Article 82 of the Constitution and the intent under this Yuan Interpretation No.162, the authority itself shall adopt the mechanism of a court and the determination of disciplinary cases shall comply with the principle of due process of law so as to provide sufficient procedural safeguards to the disciplined persons. For example, the systems of direct trial, oral arguments, cross-examination, and defense may be adopted to provide the disciplined persons with a last opportunity to expound, etc., so as to implement the intent under Article 16 of the Constitution in relation to the safeguarding of the people's right to litigation. Review and amendment should be made by the relevant authorities with respect to the organization, name, and disciplinary procedure of the public servants' disciplinary authority.' See Interpretation No. 396 of the Grand Justice Council (1990), available at: http://www.judicial.gov.tw/constitutionalcourt/EN/p03_01. asp? expno=396 (last visited, Oct. 5th, 2005).

against the importance of the evidence and seriousness of the offense charged' (Bradley, 1983: 1034). Thus, while privately obtained evidence might be subject to the exclusionary rule in Taiwan, it is not in the United States. Even if the court in Taiwan finds evidence has been obtained in violation of procedural law, there does not necessarily exist any violation of constitutional rights because procedural law sometimes relates to mere administrative process. Without any clear constitutional mandate like that in the Fourth Amendment to the United States Constitution, it seems necessary to employ a balancing test under the name of due process if the court intends to exclude evidence based on constitutional principles. In short, 87 Tai Sun 4025 represented a new direction for the court in looking to the ROC Constitution for human rights protections.

However, the newly enacted Article 158-4 of the ROC Criminal Procedure Code in 2003 sets up a new exclusionary approach that is based mainly on statute instead of the Constitution. As with pre-2003 exclusionary rule practice, this law also provides the court with discretionary power to exclude evidence. Under this new legislation, the court cannot exclude illegally obtained evidence at trial merely because the government may have violated the constitutionally protected human rights, without first applying a kind of balancing test. Furthermore, public prosecutors are also entitled to exercise this discretionary power to exclude evidence, and both the courts and public prosecutors have to give reasons as to why or why not they have excluded the alleged illegally-obtained evidence in written decisions. This differs greatly from the United States practices, where courts have to exclude illegally obtained evidence unless 'the deterrence rationale loses much of its force,' (see *Colorado Springs Amusements, LTD. v Rizzo*, 428 U.S. 913, 918(1976)) which results in the exclusionary practices of the United States being 'the most rigid system inasfar [sic] as unlawfully obtained evidence must be excluded, and the court does not have discretion whether to admit the evidence' (Bradley, 2001: 376, quoting Hans Lensing). As Damaska once emphasised, 'the idea that criminal proceedings could justifiably be used for purposes other than those of establishing the truth and enforcing the substantive criminal law is simply not part of the continental legal tradition' (Damaska, 1973: 586). These different approaches to the administrative process of police power between Taiwan and the United States might explain why the exclusionary rule in the United States is so much more rigid than that in the ROC jurisdiction.

3.2 Different Practices of Police Administration（不同的警察管理實務）

In the United States, the police are 'fragmented'.[31] The link-

---

[31] 'As the Royal Commission pointed out, the English criminal justice system retains features distinct from those of the United States. For example, "the police are less fragmented than in the United States; there is a common discipline code for all forces; there are national representative bodies and a single Minister with responsibilities for the police service at national level; and there is a central inspectorate."' (Cho, 1999: 299). See also Van Kessel, 1986: 130-1.

ed concepts of local control and decentralization are two of the most important characteristics of the English system as adopted by the United States (Adler, Mueller and Laufer, 1994: 135). Since the police in the United States derived their authority and obtained their jobs largely from local politicians (Miller, 1975), the police in a sense have historically had a vested interest in keeping in office the politicians to whom they owed their jobs from the outset (Adler, Mueller and Laufer, 1994: 138). Given this locally-controlled and decentralized police power, each county or state might adopt different policies regarding police activities. Without a nationwide police administration, it is difficult to require all police departments to abandon particular investigative misconduct, so that judicial control — which is, of course, nationwide at the appellate level — becomes a necessary method to regulate daily policing activities. The exclusionary rule has been considered a valuable way to deter illegal governmental activity, to prevent the phrase 'unreasonable searches and seizures' from becoming meaningless (see *Mapp v Ohio*, 367 US, 655), and to ensure that the police do not engage in conduct that deprives a defendant of constitutionally-protected rights (see *United States v Leon*, 428 US, 918).

By contrast, the ROC has had a national police force since the ROC Constitution became effective in 1947. Art. 108(I)(17) of the ROC Constitution, provides that Taiwan has a unified and centralized police system that is very different from that of the

United State's localized or decentralized police system.[32] In addition, under Subparagraph 10 of Paragraph 1 of Article 109 and Subparagraph 9 of Paragraph 1 of Article 110 of the ROC Constitution,[33] the police force can be subdivided into national and local levels. Both are under the national police administration power of the Ministry of Interior (the ROC MOI). The ROC MOI conducts nationwide programs for training and promoting all police officers in Taiwan (Kurtz, year?), and enacts police regulations to control and supervise the police power.

The police functions in Taiwan are clearly defined in the Police Act. These include maintaining public order, protecting social security, preventing all dangers, and promoting the welfare of all people (see Police Act, art 1). Generally speaking, there is a common discipline code for all police forces; and there is a single supervisor with responsibilities for the police service at the national level. Even without the exclusionary rule, it is also possible to prevent the police from conducting illegal activities by

---

[32] Paragraph 1 of art 108 of ROC Constitution provides: 'In the following matters, the Central Government shall have the power of legislation and administration, but the Central Government may delegate the power of Administration to the provincial and hsien governments⋯17. Police system⋯'

[33] Paragraph 1 of art 109 of ROC Constitution provides: 'In the following matters, the provinces shall have the power of legislation and administration, but the provinces may delegate the power of administration to the hsien⋯10. Provincial police administration⋯'. And paragraph 1 of art 110 of ROC Constitution provides: 'In the following matters, the hsien shall have the power of legislation and administration⋯9. Admistration of hsien police and defense⋯'

setting forth a standardized process requiring them to comply with criminal procedural rules. This might be a more effective way to protect constitutional human rights than applying the exclusionary rule (Kurtz, 1995).

Thus, the more rigid exclusionary rule created by judicial power in the United States would not, in Taiwan, be considered a necessary and important method by which to administer local police power. If certain police activities are considered improper, irrespective of the reason, either the ROC Legislative Yuan passes a new Law or the Ministry of Interior enacts a new administrative regulation to prohibit those improper activities. Any violation of law or regulation may result in the violator being demoted or punished. If the problem is merely of local concern, both national and local administrations can change it. Under this administrative process, it is reasonable that a rigid exclusionary rule, excluding almost all illegally obtained evidence as a remedy for violation of constitutional rights, did not evolve itself in Taiwan. Of course, from the perspective of human rights protection, however, it would be much better to have both the national level of police administration and the exclusionary rule, rather than only one of the two.

3.3　Application of the Exclusionary Rule to Law-enforcement Officers Only（僅適用於實施刑事訴訟程序公務員證據排除法則）

Since Article 158-4 of the ROC Criminal Procedure

Code provides:

Unless otherwise provided by law, whether evidence derived from violation of procedure rule conducted by law-enforcement-government-officers should be excluded in a criminal case depends on the result of balancing human right protection of the defendant against the public interest,

the ROC courts do not extend the exclusionary rule to evidence illegally-obtained by non-law-enforcement officers. For example, the post-2003 decisions focus mainly on the provisional term 'violation of procedure rule conducted by law-enforcement government officers.'[34] There are two major rationales behind the exclusionary rule. The first is to maintain the fairness of the proceedings and to safeguard the integrity of judicial process; the other is, as in the United States, is to deter police misconduct (Bradley, 2001: 376).[35] It is necessary to identify which of the two is the main concern behind Article 158-4 of the ROC Criminal Procedure Code. If these Articles are designed to deter police

---

[34] The pre-2003 exclusionary practices clearly focused on the first rationale since decisions as 87 Tai Sun 4025 and 88 Sun E 1953 mainly addressed on judicial integrity and fairness.

[35] As *Leon* declared, the American style exclusionary rule is based on the second reasoning. See 428 US 897, 918 (1984).

misconduct only, then decisions similar to 92 Sun E 1812 should be affirmed. Otherwise, the exclusionary rule applies to both the privately-obtained evidence and the evidence obtained by all government officers.

Under the civil law tradition, only the legislative branch may create Laws. Ordinary courts are not entitled to make Laws, but can only interpret them. If ordinary courts suspect a Law might be unconstitutional, they can file their opinions with the ROC Grand Justice Council (the only institution empowered to decide constitutional issues). Since Article 158-4 of the ROC Criminal Procedure Code requires illegal activity on the part of the law-enforcement government officer as prerequisite to exercise the exclusionary power, courts should comply with this statute. If courts can apply Article 158-4 of the ROC Criminal Procedure Code to exclude both privately obtained evidence and that gathered by the non-law-enforcement officers,[36] then the constitutional court will lose its function, because no ordinary court will seek constitutional review of the legislation. Further, these provisions will become meaningless, as the court can then exercise discretionary power beyond the legislation. In other words, without any contradictory legislative opinion, this legislation seems to focus solely on deterring illegal activity of the law-enforcement government officer. This is similar to the American approach. Accordingly,

---

[36] In fact, no supporting legislative intent or implication can be found in this way.

the Taipei High Court decision, 92 Sun E 2258, which ignored these provisions, and excluded the illegal wiretap obtained by the victim by a direct exercise of the constitutional power, should be reversed. On this view, Article 158-4 of the ROC Criminal Procedure Code supersedes the pre-2003 judicial power to exclude evidence illegally obtained by the non-law-enforcement officers and private persons.

As mentioned, even though the United States exclusionary rule is rigid, it does not apply to all unlawfully obtained evidence (Bradley, 2001: 376). In a sense, the United States Supreme Court has ruled the exclusionary rule inapplicable in proceedings where applying it will neither professionalise police investigation nor deter the police misconduct. For example, in *Arizona v Evans*, 514 US 1 (1995), evidence obtained from an illegal search relying on court clerk misconduct was ruled admissible because excluding it would not deter police misconduct. From this viewpoint, it is reasonable for Article 158-4 of the ROC Criminal Procedure Code to focus merely on evidence illegally obtained by law-enforcement officers since it is not necessary to exclude all evidence unlawfully obtained by any government officer.

As to the deterrent effect, although Article 158-4 of the ROC Criminal Procedure Code does not adopt a mandatory exclusionary rule, it does not necessarily result in a criminal investigatory process being dominated by intentionally illegal governmental activities. While Paragraph 3 of Article 156 of the ROC Criminal Procedure Code requires the court to first investigate whether the defendant's confession results from any illegal governmental activity, the law-enforcement officers should be careful about the legality of their investigation. If their investigation is found illegal by the court, not only will their investigation outcome be excluded as evidence at trial, but the enforcement will be liable to either disciplinary or criminal punishments. Since the court will determine whether the illegal governmental activity is intentional before deciding whether to apply the exclusionary rule in any given case, disciplinary and criminal sanctions will eventually deter the government officers from intentionally violating citizens' constitutional rights, not least because the judicial process regarding whether to exclude illegally obtained evidence is, itself, an extra burden for government officers above their ordinary work.

In short, the discretionary approach to applying the rule also has a deterrent effect on governmental activities, although it may not be the same as that of a mandatory exclusionary rule. Even a non-mandatory exclusionary rule does go some way to deterring the law-enforcement officers from infringing the defendant's constitutional rights.

3.4　Inferences from the Private Prosecution System（自訴制度之影響）

Unlike criminal justice in the United States, Taiwan has a private prosecution system which originated from German sources. Considerations derived from a private prosecution system do not exist in the exclusionary practices of the United States. In general, a private prosecution allows the victim of a crime to assume the responsibility of prosecuting a suspect, without the government interfering. In Taiwan, a victim of crime may believe that he or she can more effectively prosecute a defendant than can the public prosecutors. This is especially true when the victim has collected enough evidence to prosecute and wishes to avoid the risk of the defendant going free because the government has failed to put together a solid case against the accused (ROC Criminal Procedure Code, art 326, para 2). Before the establishment of 'asking for trial' in 2002, private prosecution was the only choice available in the face of unfavorable prosecutorial policy (ROC Criminal Procedure Code, art 321).[37] However, if a public prosecutor has already started to investigate a case, a private prosecution will not be allowed, unless the case is chargeable upon complaint (ROC Criminal Procedure Code, art 323, para 1).[38] Consequently, without delegating to a lawyer, the court will dismiss the private prosecution (ROC Criminal Procedure

---

[37] In a case chargeable only upon complaint or request, a private prosecution may not be initiated if such complaint or request is no longer permitted. See art 322 of the ROC Criminal Procedure Code.

[38] Before 2000, a private prosecution was allowed before a public prosecutor concludes his investigation in the same case. Besides, if a public prosecutor knows prior to the conclusion of his investigation that a private prosecution has been initiated, he shall immediately stop such investigation and refer the case to the court.

Code, art 319, para 2).[39]

With a private prosecution, as with a public one, the full name, sex, age, domicile or residence of the accused, and other special identifying features must be provided, as well as facts and evidence of the offense (see ROC Criminal Procedure Code, art 320, para 1 (private prosecution) and art 264, para 2 (public prosecution)). Since the private prosecuting attorney is assumed to play the public prosecutor's role, a private prosecutor may perform any procedural act performable by a public prosecutor (ROC Criminal Procedure Code, art 329, para 1). A private prosecutor also has to prove the offense beyond a reasonable doubt while the court is also entitled to investigate the evidence. Interestingly, however, the law treats private prosecutions differently from public prosecutions. The ROC Criminal Procedure Code does not, for example, provide the private prosecuting attorney with rules for interrogating the accused or the witness, or to request assistance from the police before the trial. In addition, the court will question the private prosecutor before examining the accused. This is to clarify and determine if it is a case for civil action or to ensure that the private prosecution procedure is not being used to pressure the accused (ROC Criminal Procedure

---

[39] Before 2000, the private prosecution did not require an attorney to be delegated by a private prosecutor.

Code, art 326, para 2).[40]

While Article 320 of the ROC Criminal Procedure Code only places limited demands on the private prosecutor, the private prosecutor usually investigates and collects evidence in order to provide the information required by the relevant statute. Despite this common situation, there are no procedural rules that directly regulate private investigation or evidence collection. The current law only provides procedural rules for filing applications to obtain evidence that might be destroyed, forged, or altered immediately (ROC Criminal Procedure Code, arts 219-1 to 219-8). If the public prosecutor or the court does not respond to an application to obtain evidence in time, it becomes necessary for the victim to obtain the evidence himself or herself, or risk losing the case because of insufficient evidence.[41] If evidence unlawfully obtained by private parties was excluded, the private prosecution system would rapidly become dysfunctional. Without procedural rules regulating the private evidence obtaining process, how the victim can 'legally' conduct investigation and evidence collection depends mainly upon the substantive criminal law rather than criminal procedural law.

---

[40] In practice, the court distrusts the private prosecution to some extent because there is much commercial consideration before an attorney accepts delegation to file a private prosecution while a public prosecutor decides a case mainly based on legal opinion.

[41] In reality, a criminal offender will rarely allow the victim to collect evidence against him.

In general, if the victim violates substantive law when obtaining evidence, he should be punished, and is also responsible for monetary compensation. However, is it fair to exclude evidence unlawfully obtained by private persons, if they are already subject to criminal punishment? From Taiwanese decisions like 87 Tai Sun 4025 and 88 Sun E 1953, the answer seems to be 'yes'. This article, however, takes the opposite view, for two reasons.

Firstly, article 8, paragraph 1, of the ROC Constitution provides that 'Personal freedom shall be guaranteed to the people. Except in case of *flagrante delicto*, as provided by law, no person shall be arrested or detained otherwise than by a judicial or a police organ in accordance with the procedure prescribed by law.' Paragraph 1 of Article 88 of the ROC Criminal Procedure Code provides 'A person in flagrante delicto may be arrested without a warrant by any person.'[42] While the arresting person may misunderstand the meaning and the requirement of the warrantless arrest, it is possible the court finally finds out the alleged warrantless arrest to be unlawful under Article 88 of the ROC Criminal

---

[42] As to flagrante delicto, ROC Criminal Procedure Code art 88, para 2 provides: 'A person in flagrante delicto is a person who is discovered in the act of committing an offense or immediately thereafter.' In addition, art 88, para 3 provides: 'A person is considered to be in flagrante delicto under one of the following circumstances: (1) He is pursued with cries that he is an offender; (2) He is found in possession of a weapon, stolen property, or other item sufficient to warrant a suspicion that he is an offender or his person, clothes and the like show traces of the commission of an offense sufficient to warrant such suspicion.'

Procedure Code.[43] Regardless of the arresting person's good faith, the ROC courts never hold that evidence derived from this kind of illegal warrantless arrest is inadmissible. If privately-obtained evidence derived from an illegal warrantless arrest is admissible, what is the supporting rationale to exclude privately-obtained evidence derived from illegal search or seizure, given that the interests of personal freedom are much higher than all others?[44] For example, in fornication cases in Taiwan, if the Taipei High Court decision of 88 Sun E 1953 is affirmed, illegal wiretaps should be excluded. The victim spouse will then have no choice but to follow the suspects or he or she will lose any opportunity make an Article 88 arrest. To some extent, this hypothesized practice seems to encourage the victim to adopt a more serious freedom-infringing approach to obtain incriminating evidence in order to convict the accused. If so, this practice would be against the continental constitutional proportional prin-

---

[43] Under this article, anyone discovered in the act of committing an offense, or immediately thereafter, and who is pursued with cries that he is an offender, or who is found in possession of a weapon, stolen property, or other item sufficient to warrant a suspicion that he is an offender or his person, clothes and the like show traces of the commission of an offense sufficient to warrant such suspicion is subject to warrantless arrest.

[44] For example, personal freedom is in a higher rank than freedom of residence and of change of residence, speech, teaching, writing and publication, privacy of correspondence, religious belief, and assembly and association.

ciple behind Article 23 of the ROC Constitution[45] because following the suspect is a more serious freedom-infringing method rather than illegal wiretapping would be.

Secondly, in addition to violating the constitutional proportionality principle, excluding evidence unlawfully obtained by private persons is also counter to the practicalities of a criminal justice system. For instance, if illegal wiretapping is finally found punishable according to Article 315-1 of the ROC Criminal Code, then punishing the offender is enough to do justice. In addition to punishing the criminal offender who intends to resolve criminal disputes through criminal law suits, it is a bad way to exclude evidence unlawfully obtained by private persons for protecting the victim. If the victim finally finds it impossible to believe the court will resolve criminal disputes, then private revenge might emerge as a remedy for legal incompetence, and that would, of course, be absolutely contrary to ideas of rule of law. Moreover, since it is impossible to exclude evidence unlawfully obtained by private parties without determining the legality of the conduct through which the evidence was obtained, another legal issue emerges. In an action for fornication, for example, should the court be required to decide the legality of wiretapping (when

---

[45] It provides: 'All the freedoms and rights enumerated in the preceding Articles shall not be restricted by law except such as may be necessary to prevent infringement upon the freedoms of other persons, to avert an imminent crisis, to maintain social order or to advance public welfare.'

this was not the focus of the court action, and no indictment or charge has been laid)?

Thus, Article 158-4 of the ROC Criminal Procedure Code should not apply to evidence unlawfully obtained by private parties. Judicial decisions such as 87 Tai Sun 4025, 88 Sun E 1953, and 92 Sun E 2258 should therefore be reversed. In other words, only illegal behavior on the part of law-enforcement officers should result in the application of the exclusionary rule in Taiwan.

3.5　Invoking the Exclusionary Rule（證據排除法則之發動）

In order to exclude evidence via the exclusionary rule in the United States, three conditions must be met. First, the evidence should be the result of an improper governmental activity. Second, in addition to an illegal governmental activity, there must be actual evidence secured. Third, there must be a causal connection between the illegal governmental activity and the evidence secured from that illegal activity (Evangelista, 2001). If those conditions are met, under *Rakas v Illinois*, 439 US 128 (1978), the defendant also needs standing to object to the admission of the evidence. By contrast, in Taiwan, the 'standing' requirement does not exist. Even if a person is not the victim of the alleged illegal governmental activity, he or she is allowed to seek the exclusion of the illegally obtained evidence.

In addition, under the adversarial tradition, parties have the right to invoke the exclusionary rule, traditionally by way of a motion to suppress. If there is no argument by a party as to whether to suppress alleged illegally-obtained evidence, the court may not exclude evidence on its own initiative. By contrast, the ROC court has the power to make a decision whether to exclude evidence, even without parties' participation.[46] While the newly promulgated Paragraph 1 of Article 273 of the ROC Criminal Procedure Code allows the defense to argue whether to exclude evidence at the pre-trial stage, unlike the practice before 2003, the defense now has the opportunity to assert the exclusionary rule in both pre-trial and trial stages. A public prosecutor thus must address the exclusionary issue, too.

Since the exclusionary rule in Taiwan is less rigid than that in the United States (in that nothing should be excluded before applying a balancing test), it seems unnecessary to require any standard to narrow the scope of the exclusionary rule. While the 1998 ROC Supreme Court ruling, 87 Tai Sun 4025, was established on the fairness and the integrity of judicial proceedings instead of on the single purpose to deter the governmental illegal activities, the Leon justification[47] and the Rakas requirement[48]

---

[46] This judicial power makes the new practice in Taiwan pro-inquisitorial while the court in an accusatorial system is not entitled to decide this issue on its own initiative.

[47] The only rationale behind the exclusionary rule is the deterrent effect of police misconducts. See 428 US 897 (1984).

[48] This standing requirement narrows the scope of the exclusionary rule. See 439 US 128(1978).

would not work for the pre-1988 ROC criminal justice system. The private party would not be allowed to employ all possible means to 'discover' the truth since sometimes-illegal methods of investigation and their result may prejudice the integrity of judicial proceedings. As the Taipei High Court held in 88 Sun E 1953 (1999):

> Since wiretapping other's telephone conversation is a criminal offense, it violates the defendants' privacy protection if the tape is admitted as evidence at trial. In addition, admitting the tape into evidence would prejudice judicial integrity and fairness and encourage others to do the same. Therefore, the wiretapped tape is inadmissible. (88 Sun E 1953 (1999))

While the 2003 legislation about the exclusionary rule clearly focuses on illegal governmental activities, it obviously departs from the 1998 ROC Supreme Court decision. Thus, the potential application of the exclusionary rule in Taiwan should be similar to that in the United States except for the discretionary part. Since Article 158-4 of the ROC Criminal Procedure Code does not adopt a mandatory approach to the exclusionary rule either, the Rakas standing requirement is not applicable.

3.6 Similarity between the ROC and the United States Exclusionary Rules

（台灣與美國證據排除法則之相似性）

Returning to the United States exclusionary rule, it is based on the Bill of Rights setting up standards with which the government has to comply. Because the evidence that is excluded by the rule may, in fact, establish the defendant's guilt, applying this rule so as to acquit the defendant might cause more criticism even though it is recognised that freedom from unwarranted police intrusions into individual privacy is a freedom worth the societal cost of allowing the guilty to sometimes go unpunished due to the exclusion of otherwise reliable evidence (*Adone v State*, 408 So 2d 567, 577 (Fla. 1981)). Although the ROC adopts a less rigid exclusionary rule that allows the court as well as the public prosecutor to exercise a discretionary power before excluding evidence, there are similarities between the ROC and the United States exclusionary rules.

The United States Supreme Court in *Illinois v Gates*, 462 US 213 (1983) held that a search warrant based on a corroborated informant's tip may be properly issued if, under the totality of the circumstances set forth in the warrant application, including the veracity and basis of knowledge of the informant and any corroboration of the informant's information, there is a fair probability that contraband or evidence will be found in the place to be searched. It is arguable that *Gates* relaxed probable cause requirements and made it easier for police to secure search war-rants. The court in this case uses the rather vague term 'reason-able' in the Fourth Amendment and subjects it to an even more vague definition. Prior to *Gates*, 'reasonableness' had been grounded in the two-pronged 'Aguilar-Spinelli' standard, which gave some guidance to judges in determining reasonableness (Kamisar, 1984: 556). By replacing this two-pronged standard with a 'common sense' test based on the 'totality of the circum-stances' standard in *Gates*, the court has opted for what many critics claim is no standard at all (Grano, 1984: 465). This com-mon sense approach now, in effect, requires the court to apply its 'discretionary power' on a case-by-case basis instead of setting forth a clear and determinative standard in determining the reas-onableness from which probable cause might result. While this discretionary power makes the practice of the strict exclusionary rule more flexible, it is conceivable that some kinds of 'improper police behavior', which might result in 'unreasonableness' under the two-pronged Aguilar-Spinelli test in the previous United Sta-tes practice, would not result in any exclusion of evidence. For example, if improper police behavior occurred in Taiwan, even though a court, employing the two-pronged Aguilar-Spinelli test might hold that there existed no probable cause which would re-sult in such search and seizure being illegal, any evidence illegal-ly obtained by law-enforcement officers might not be excluded if the court found that public interest outweighed private interest. By contrast, courts in the United States have to exclude evidence unlawfully obtained by police officers in general if applying the two-pronged Aguilar-Spinelli test would result in such search and seizure derived from improper police behaviors to be illegal. However, the same 'improperly-obtained' evidence could be held 'legal' under the so-called 'totality of the circumstances' standard. This approach is more elastic in deciding the legality of search and seizure if the court does not intend to exclude evidence derived from improper police conduct.

It is worth mentioning that the most significant distinguishing characteristic between these two discretionary processes is 'when' to exercise the discretionary power, employing the balancing test or the common sense test. For instance, while the Fourth Amendment applies to any search and seizure conducted under color of law, whether by federal, state or local authorities (Purdy and Herron, 2000), courts in the United States still have to decide whether there existed probable cause, even though the alleged government behavior was authorised by law or a warrant, like that in *Gates*. By contrast, while courts in Taiwan rarely challenge the constitutionality of a promulgated law, illegal government misconduct might be held reasonable and evidence derived from this illegal government misconduct might be admissible at trial. Since the abstract nature of an enacted statute might outlaw reasonable and constitutional government conduct in Taiwan, it appears necessary for the court to apply a balancing test in determining whether to exclude the alleged illegally-obtained evidence, lest evidence derivative from illegal but reasonable search be excluded merely because of the deficiency and improperness of any enactment. Thus, this study argues that whether to exclude evidence under this American commonsense approach in determining the reasonableness[49] is somehow similar to that of the Taiwanese approach in balancing human right protection against the public interest, although the former does not focus on application of the exclusionary rule itself. It seems fair to say that the American judiciary also employs a kind of discretionary balancing test under the 'common sense approach' to decide 'whether the police have probable cause' and 'whether the alleged police conducts are reasonable'. Since the United States Supreme Court has made certain exceptions to the exclusionary rule, such as impeachment of a defendant's trial testimony at the criminal trial, grand jury testimony, sentencing, parole hearings, juvenile hearings, and deportation proceedings, and applies the discretionary power to decide whether there exist unreasonable searches and seizures, the 'so-called mandatory exclusionary rule' looks less 'mandatory' than initially described. As mentioned, the scope of the exclusionary rule in both Taiwan and the United States may look almost the same although the discretionary powers are exercised in different phases when deciding different issues.[50]

---

[49] It seems to indicate that constitutional restraints do not handicap law enforcement but leads to improved police training. See Adler, Mueller and Laufer, 1994: 224.

[50] For instance, in the United States, the discretionary power is exercised to decide whether evidence derived from improper official misconducts would result in

3.7 Suggestions for Exercising the Discretionary Exclusionary Power in Taiwan（對台灣行使證據排除裁量權之建議）

While it is clear that admitting evidence derived from 'illegal search and seizure' is unconstitutional in the United States, it is not clear whether official behavior that violates procedural law will also result in unconstitutionality in Taiwan. The procedure issue is primarily administrative; therefore, violating it might not automatically result in unconstitutionality. If violating a procedural rule is not unconstitutional, it is not necessary to exclude evidence derived from the violation. In other words, in the United States, the constitutionality of government conduct is decided through determining whether there is unreasonable search and seizure. On the contrary, in Taiwan, the same issue is determined via the process of concluding whether admitting evidence derived from illegal law-enforcement-officers violates the constitutional proportional principle under Article 23 of the ROC Con-

---

search and seizure to be illegal under the *Gates* commonsense test. On the other hand, in Taiwan, the discretionary power is exercised to decide whether violation of promulgated laws of law-enforcement-officers is unconstitutional under a balancing test. Thus, the discretionary powers to exclude evidence in both Taiwan and the United States are almost the same regardless of its 'mandatory' or 'discretionary' characteristic. Moreover, the exclusionary rule in Taiwan is more flexible than that in the United States not only because there has been no binding Supreme Court decision after the 2003 legislation in Taiwan but also because the exclusionary rule itself is of statutory issue.

stitution. This difference explains why Article 158-4 of the ROC Criminal Procedure Code allows the court and the public prosecutor to exercise the discretionary power, even though the illegality of improper police behavior has been already decided. As already analyzed supra under the civil law interpretative tradition and the deterrent purpose in Leon, Article 158-4 of the ROC Criminal Procedure Code applies to law-enforcement-officers only. Since courts in Taiwan have the discretionary power to exclude illegal evidence, the Gates approach in determining whether the searched and seized person has a reasonable privacy expectation, which might result in improperly-obtained evidence being illegal, is similar to the ROC discretionary approach in deciding whether to exclude evidence. The flexible "totality-of-the-circumstances" standard, other than the two-pronged Aguilar-Spinelli test, would better serve as a guide for the ROC courts to determine whether to exclude evidence unlawfully obtained by law-enforcement-officers.

The Advisory Committee on the ROC Criminal Procedure Code in Taiwan has already suggested seven standards to be considered in deciding whether to exclude evidence.[51] These are con-

---

[51] Those are: 1) the seriousness of the violation of procedure rule; 2) the subjective intent of the violation; 3) the infringement of human right protection; 4) the seriousness of the offense; 5) the potential deterrence to government officers; 6) the possibility to discover the evidence without this violation; and 7) prejudice to defense.

sistent with former practical developments. Regardless of its direct authority, exercising the discretionary power, according to Article 158-4 of the ROC Criminal Procedure Code, is almost the same as its previous counterpart under the ROC Constitution. This seems to be unavoidable because the exclusionary rule itself is created as a remedy to prevent constitutional rights from being 'little more than an empty platitude' (Allen, Kuhns and Stuntz, 1995: 604). Though this new exclusionary approach is set out on a statutory level, the power to exclude is originally constitutional. Any invocation of the exclusionary rule, thus, should be directly based on Article 158-4 of the ROC Criminal Procedure Code. The constitution was enacted to protect anyone from unconstitutional governmental activities; it is therefore reasonable not to apply the exclusionary rule to private illegal search and seizure (*Burdeau v McDowell*, 256 US 465 (1921); see also Burkoff, 1987).

Since determining whether to exclude evidence unlawfully obtained by law-enforcement officers is itself a constitutional issue, determining if this illegal evidence will violate the defendant's constitutional rights becomes the issue to be decided in Taiwan. Because there is no judicial opinion of the ROC Supreme Court instructing how to employ the exclusionary rule after 2003, and given that the suggestions of the Advisory Committee of the ROC Criminal Procedure Code are too abstract, the totality of the circumstances standard in *Gates* as well as other United States Supreme Court decisions might be informative for the exclusionary practice in Taiwan.

Before referring to *Gates*, it is necessary to distinguish the factual circumstances as between *Gates* and the ROC exclusionary practices. Usually the exclusionary issue arises from a warrantless case in Taiwan. Since *Gates* is not a warrantless case, it seems inappropriate to draw upon it to deal with the exclusionary issues in Taiwan. Nevertheless, even though the United States Supreme Court reasoned 'it may not be easy to determine when an affidavit demonstrates the existence of probable cause, the resolution of doubtful or marginal cases in this area should be largely determined by the preference to be accorded to warrants' (see *United States v Ventresca*, 380 US 102, 109 (1965)). As held in *Gates*,

> this reflects both a desire to encourage use of the warrant process by police officers and a recognition that once a warrant has been obtained, intrusion upon interests protected by the Fourth Amendment is less severe than otherwise may be the case. (462 US, at 237)

Moreover, if the constitutionality of governmental activities is the main concern of the exclusionary rule in both Taiwan and the United States, citing *Gates* as a reference to decide the exclusionary issues in Taiwan is appropriate.

Thus, while deciding whether to exclude evidence according to Article 158-4 of the ROC Criminal Procedure Code, courts in

Taiwan should consider those standards suggested by the Advisory Committee of the ROC Criminal Procedure Code. Referring to the United States experience with the exclusionary rule may result in those standards becoming less abstract. For example, in issuing a warrant, a judge has to

> make a practical, common-sense decision whether, given all the circumstances set forth in the affidavit..., including the 'veracity' and 'basis of knowledge' of persons supplying hearsay information, there is a fair probability that contraband or evidence of a crime will be found in a particular place. (462 US, at 238)

Without finding any substantial malice of the police, the ROC courts should not exclude evidence from warrantless search and seizures if the pre-trial judge would have made a practical and common-sense decision that there was a fair probability that criminal evidence would be found, and thus would have issued a warrant. Regardless of whether the illegal governmental activity in issue constitutes a criminal offense, if the defendant has no reasonable privacy expectation, any warrantless search and seizure should not infringe privacy. Without deciding the existence of any reasonable privacy expectation, it is impossible to know if admitting illegally obtained evidence will result in the court becoming a conspirator to invade privacy.[52] In theory, it was unnecessary for the Taipei High Court to be afraid of becoming a conspirator in a privacy invasion because it was unclear if the defendant had reasonable privacy expectation in 90 Sun E 1085（2001）. This Taipei High Court decision should therefore have been reversed.

After the Taipei High Court in 90 Sun E 2046 (2001) declared what should be considered in excluding illegally obtained evidence,[53] it is clear why the court in 90 Sun Su 2229 (2001) did not do so given the exigency of the situation which might have seriously prejudiced the societal peaceful order even though the police had acted in bad faith. It is not beyond reason why the court in 91 Sun Gum One 197 (2002) excluded the illegally obtained financial records or commercial statements because excluding those documents as evidence might not prejudice the societal peaceful order. Those decisions as well as the 'totality of the circumstances' test will provide a less abstract overview of the exclusionary rule in Taiwan.

While trials are only about guilt in the United States (see Moskovitz, 1995: 1135), trials in Taiwan are 'unitary', in the

---

[52] In other words, if there had been no reasonable privacy expectation, there was no privacy invasion.

[53] Those are: the seriousness of the violation, the relevance of the piece of evidence for the resolution of the case, and the seriousness of the offense. Thus, violation of procedure rules does not necessarily lead to exclusion of evidence.

sense that both the accused's guilt and sentence are determined at a single process.[54] Hence, in Taiwan, it is impossible to apply the exclusionary rule only to the question of guilt. Unlike the United States, if evidence is excluded at trial, the same evidence will be applicable in the following sentencing process in Taiwan. Nonetheless, the exclusionary rule is held not applicable in the proceeding of impeachment of a defendant's trial testimony at the criminal trial in the United States (see Walder v United States, 347 US 62 (1954); Harris v New York, 401 US 222 (1971)). This practice might be referred to in Taiwan.

4. Conclusions（結論）

In contrast to the United States common law system, finding the truth remains, formally, the most important concern in the ROC civil law criminal justice system (ROC Criminal Procedure Code, art 163, para 2). Accordingly, unless there is a persuasive justification, it is not easy for a court to exclude reliable and trustworthy evidence. This is despite the fact that human rights protections are also an important consideration. It must therefore still be questionable whether the people of Taiwan would accept a purely adversarial criminal justice system. Moreover, unlike the

---

[54] Also note that: 'The presumption in civil law systems is that the defendant should cooperate with the trial judge and answer questions completely. The defendant's cooperation is also encouraged by the fact that his sentence, as well as his guilt, is determined at a single trial.' Pizzi and Marafioti, 1992: 8.

American Bill of Rights which defines human rights in more detail, the continental civil law constitutional approach adopted in Taiwan regarding human rights protection does not clearly provide what 'human rights' should include. It is more difficult to draw upon the ROC Constitution itself to determine what rights are specifically constitutionally protected. While an obvious constitutional violation would amount to a persuasive reason to exclude reliable and trustworthy evidence, it is more difficult for the court to justify any exclusion of evidence when the contents of the constitutional rights in a continental-style Constitution are less clear. Thus, courts in Taiwan have to explain more fully their application of the balancing test and why they are excluding evidence, than do courts in the United States. So long as courts in Taiwan are required to find the truth, it is very difficult to adopt an Anglo-American trial system as the fact-finding process. The unitary trial structure and its accompanying inquisitorial nature of sentencing also distinguish the ROC trial proceeding from its United States counterpart. Based upon these differences, any legal reform in the ROC criminal justice system is unlikely to result in a pure accusatorial and adversarial trial process. The 2003 reform of the ROC Criminal Procedure Code thus was properly labelled 'pro-adversarial' in that merely adopting the exclusionary rule would not completely change its inquisitorial characteristics.

While the 2003 legislation did not completely change the inquisitorial nature of the ROC criminal justice system, that legislation has had considerable significance for the ROC criminal justice system. With this new rule, the defense party is granted the legal status necessary to challenge the admissibility of evidence and to actively participate in the trial process. For the first time, the court now has to decide admissibility through the adversarial process, before the end of trial process. In a sense the exclusionary rule derived from the Anglo-American criminal justice system can be more effective in protecting the accused's rights at trial, than the traditional ROC inquisition. As a result, providing the defendant the rights to challenge the admissibility of the illegally-obtained evidence is itself the most significant achievement of the 2003 pro-accusatorial legislation.

After examining the exclusionary rule in both nations, it is apparent that the versions of the rule in Taiwan and the United States evolved from different legal cultures and historical experiences. American colonial history has contributed immensely to the United States' accusatorial and adversarial judicial system. The parties are responsible for investigating the facts and producing evidence at trial (Lerner, 2001: 797). Participation of citizens via services on juries in the judicial system is designed to be a meaningful check against governmental arbitrariness on the judiciary. This practice intentionally furthers the federal system, which focuses on decentralized democracy. While the colonial history of Taiwan did not result in the same sort of institutionalised distrust of government powers, the courts have not, in every case, been able to discover the truth more accurately than Anglo-American courts. No legislative draft in the ROC Legislative

Yuan really intends to replace professional judges with another fact-finder.

In the accusatorial system, like the United States, the criminal justice practice is much more party-influenced or party-oriented than the hierarchically-controlled continental criminal justice system in Taiwan. Arguably, 'Americans view the state with suspicion and the law as their shield against official transgressions. They expect "total justice": compensation for every harm suffered, observance of due process when their rights are at stake' (Cho, 1999: 299, quoting Inga Markovits). The prosecutor is therefore assumed to be responsible for any violation of constitutional human rights protection conducted by the police and will lose his case if important evidence is excluded. In a jurisdiction without this accusatorial and adversarial tradition, like Taiwan, the public prosecutor is, however, not merely regarded as a party (Lerner, 2001: 797). And the victim of any violation of the constitution will not automatically benefit from any misconduct of his 'opposing party' through the exclusionary rule. Thus, the exclusionary rule does not derive from the idea that the public prosecutor should be responsible for the police misconduct. In addition, the exclusionary rule is not designed to be a mechanism from which the victim is entitled to benefit. Admitting illegally-obtained evidence at trial does not necessarily prevent 'justice'.

There emerged three main legal problems from promulgating Article 158-4 of the ROC Criminal Procedure Code. The ROC legal system only allows the Grand Justice Council to outlaw any effective positive law. Ordinary courts thus cannot ignore an enacted provision. The Taipei High Court decision, 92 Sun E 1812, made after the new provision was introduced, makes it clear that the exclusionary rule will only exclude evidence illegally obtained by law-enforcement officers,[55] and it will not apply to evidence obtained by the illegal activities of private persons or non-law-enforcement officers. This is reasonable, not only because the exclusionary rule is designed to be a remedy for violation of human rights protection, but also because constitutional human rights are initially created to prevent illegal invasions by the government.

Because considerations behind the discretionary power to exclude evidence are similar in both Taiwan and the United States, the ROC courts will consider the totality of the circumstances test set out in Gates in deciding the constitutionality of illegal governmental activities. Applying Gates in Taiwan will make the country's exclusionary practice less abstract. Ultimately, it is likely that the differences in the outcomes of the exclusionary rule in Taiwan and the United States will become minimal. To some extent, Mapp applies to Taiwan via employing a kind of balancing test while the court is exercising the discretionary power of the

---

[55] Although whether the Taiwanese Supreme Court will uphold this new ruling remains to be seen, this legislative and judicial trend is obviously distinct from the Taiwan High Court's former ruling in the 1999 adultery case, 88 Sun E 1953.

exclusionary rule. Anyway, it remains a difficult task to decide which approach to exclude evidence is more predictable in terms of outcomes.（本文原發表於 2006.08　8 The Australian Journal of Asian Law 68）

Reference List

1. Adler, Freda, Gerhard Mueller and William Laufer (eds) (1994) *Criminal Justice*. New York: McGraw-Hill.

2. Allen, Ronald, Richard Kuhns and William Stuntz (1995) *Constitutional Criminal Procedure: An Examination of the Fourth, Fifth, and Sixth Amendments and Related Areas*. Boston : Little Brown.

3. Bacigal (1979) 'The Fourth Amendment in Flux: The Rise and Fall of Probable Cause' [1979] *University of Illinois Law Journal* 763.

4. Bradley, Craig (1983) 'The Exclusionary Rule in Germany' 96 *Harvard Law Review* 1032.

5. Bradley, Craig (1993) *The Failure of the Criminal Procedure Revolution*. Philadelphia: University of Pennsylvania Press.

6. Bradley, Craig (2001) 'Symposium on the Fortieth Anniversary of *Mapp v Ohio: Mapp* Goes Abroad' 52 *Case Western Reserve Law Review* 375.

7. Burkoff, John (1987) 'Not So Private Searches and the Con-

stitution' 66 *Cornell Law Review* 627.

8. Burnham, William (1999) *Introduction to the Law and Legal System of the United States*. St. Paul, Minn.: West Group.

9. Chen, Pu-Shen (1995) *Criminal Evidence Rule* (in Chinese). Taipei: Sun-Min Publishing Co.

10. Cho, Kuk (1999) 'Reconstruction of the English Criminal Justice System and its Reinvigorated Exclusionary Rules' 21 *Loyola of Los Angeles International and Comparative Law Journal* 259.

11. Damaska, Mirjan (1973) 'Evidentiary Barriers to Conviction and Two Models of Criminal Procedure' 121 *University of Pennsylvania Law Review* 506.

12. Damaska, Mirjan (1997) *Evidence Law Adrift*. New Haven: Yale University Press.

13. Department of Justice, Office of Legal Policy (1989) 'Report to the Attorney General on the Search and Seizure Exclusionary Rule' 22 University of Michigan Journal of Law Reform 573.

14. Evangelista, Peter (2001) 'The Exclusionary Rule: Why the Criminal Goes Free When the Constable Blunders', at <http://members.aol.com/rmhmcj123/myhomepage/>.

15. FindLaw (2000) 'Enforcing the Fourth Amendment: The Exclusionary Rule', at <http://caselaw.lp.findlaw.com/data/con-

stitution/amendment04/06html>.

16. Grano, Joseph (1984) 'Probable Cause and Common Sense: A Reply to the Critics of Illinois v Gates' 17 *University of Michigan Journal of Law Reform* 465.

17. 'Introduction to the ROC Legislative Yuan' (2005)(in Chinese) at <http://www.ly.gov.tw>.

18. Jochner, Michele M. (1999) 'Recent US Supreme Court Fourth Amendment Rulings Expand Police Discretion', at <http://www.isba.org/Member/oct00lj/p576.htm>.

19. Kamisar, Yale (1984) 'Gates, "Probable Cause," "Good Faith," and Beyond' 69 Iowa Law Review 551.

20. Yale Kamisar et al., ed., (2002) *Modern Criminal Procedure: cases-comments-questions.* West Group. (10th ed.)

21. Kurtz, Howard (1995) 'Criminal Justice Centralization Versus Decentralization in the Republic of China', at: <http://www.doc.state.ok.us/DOCS/OCJRC/OCJRC95/950725f.htm>.

22. Lerner, Renee (2001) 'The Intersection of Two Systems: An American on Trial for An American Murder in the French *Cour d'Assise*' [2001] *University of Illinois Law Review* 791.

23. Lin, Huei-Hwan（2003）*Exclusionary Rule — theory and practice* (in Chinese), Taipei, Angle Publishing Co., LTD.

24. Miller, Wilbur (1975) 'Police Authority in London and New York City' 8 *Journal of Social History* 81.

25. Moskovitz, Myron (1995) 'The OJ Inquisition: A United States Encounter with Continental Criminal Justice' 28 *Vanderbilt Journal of Transnational Law* 1121.

26. Redden, Kenneth (ed) (1984) *Modern Legal Systems Cyclopedia*. Buffalo, NY: WS Hein.

27. O'Connor, Tom (2004) 'Search and Seizure: A Guide to Rules, Requirements, Tests, Doctrines, and Exceptions', at <http://faculty.ncwc.edu/toconnor/405/405lect04.htm>.

28. Pizzi, William and Luca Marafioti (1992) 'The New Italian Code of Criminal Procedure: The Difficulties of An Adversarial Trial System on A Civil Law Foundation' 17 Yale Journal of International Law 1.

29. Purdy and Herron, (2000) 'Full Circle' 3(1) *News from the Front*, at <http://www.newsfromthefront.com/archives/vol3no1_circle.htm>.

30. Taipei Times (1999), '"Big Brother" Makes Way for Due Process of Law', 18 November, available at <http://th.gio.gov.tw/show.cfm? news_id=3358>.

31. Van Kessel, Gordon (1986) 'The Suspect as a Source of Testimonial Evidence: A Comparison of the English and American Approaches' 38 *Hastings Law Journal* 1.

32. Weigend, Thomas (1999) 'Germany', in Craig Bradley (ed) *Criminal Procedure: A Worldwide Study*. Durham, NC: Carol-

ina Academic Press.

33. Wikipedia (2005) 'Chinese Law' at <http://en.wikipedia.org/wiki/Chinese_law>.

Cases Taiwan

1. 70 Tai Sun 3864 (1981).

2. 72 Tai Sun 1203 (1983).

3. 72 Tai Sun 1332 (1983).

4. 74 Tai Sun 6888 (1985).

5. 75 Tai Sun 933 (1986).

6. 77 Tai Sun 848 (1988).

7. 79 Tai Sun 5140 (1990).

8. 81 Tai Sun 4352 (1992).

9. 81 Tai Sun 6531 (1992).

10. 82 Tai Sun 622 (1993).

11. 82 Tai Sun 4199 (1993).

12. 83 Tai Sun 2785 (1994).

13. 84 Tai Sun 538 (1995).

14. 84 Tai Sun 2819 (1995).

15. 85 Tai Sun 4455 (1996).

16. 87 Sun E 1318 (1998) (fornication case).

17. 87 Tai Sun 4025 (1998).

18. 88 Sun E 1953 (1999) (fornication case).

19. 90 Sun E 1085 (2002).

20. 90 Sun Gum Two 1112 (2002) (drug producing case).

21. 90 Sun E 2046 (2002) (fraud case).

22. 90 Sun Su 2229 (2002) (handgun possession case).

23. 91 Tai Sun 2363 (2002).

24. 91 Sun Gum One 197 (2003).

25. 92 Sun E 1812 (2003) (leaking of national secrets).

26. 92 Sun E 2258 (2003).

27. 93 Sun E 140 (2004).

28. 93 Sun Su 835(2004).

29. 93 Sun E 934 (2004).

30. 93 Tai Sun 2949 (2004).

United States

1. *Adams v New York*, 192 US 585 (1904).

2. *Adone v State*, 408 So 2d 567 (Fla. 1981).

3. *Aguilar v Texas*, 378 US 108 (1964).

4. *Amos v United States*, 255 US 313 (1921).

5. *Arizona v Evans*, 514 US 1 (1995).

6. *Boyd v United States*, 116 US 616 (1886).

7. *Brinegar v United States*, 338 US 160 (1949).

8. *Burdeau v McDowell*, 256 US 465 (1921).

9. *Chapman v United States*, 365 US 610 (1961).

10. *Colorado Springs Amusements, LTD. v Rizzo*, 428 US 913 (1976).

11. *Elkins v United States*, 364 US 206 (1960).

12. *Gouled v United States*, 255 US 298 (1921).

13. *Harris v New York*, 401 US 222 (1971).

14. *Illinois v Gates*, 462 US 213 (1983).

15. *Illinois v Krull*, 480 US 340 (1987).

16. *INS v Lopez-Mendoza*, 468 US 1032 (1984).

17. *Irvine v California*, 347 US 128 (1954).

18. *Jones v United States*, 362 US 257, 261 (1960).

19. *Linkletter v Walker*, 381 US 618 (1965).

20. *Mapp v Ohio*, 367 US 643 (1961).

21. *Marcus v Search Warrants of Property*, 367 US 717 (1961).

22. *One 1958 Plymouth Sedan v Pennsylvania*, 380 US 693 (1965).

23. *People v Defore*, 242 NY 13 (1920).

24. *Rakas v Illinois*, 439 US 128 (1978).

25. *Rawlings v Kentucky* (see 448 US 98 (1980)).

26. *Silverthorne Lumber Co v United States*, 251 US 385 (1920).

27. *Spinelli v United States* 393 US 410 (1969).

28. *Stone v Powell*, 428 US 465 (1976).

29. *United States v Calandra*, 414 US 338 (1974).

30. *United States v Havens*, 446 US 620 (1980).

31. *United States v Leon*, 428 US 897 (1984).

32. *United States v Ventresca*, 380 US 102 (1965).

33. *Walder v United States*, 347 US 62 (1954).

34. *Weeks v United States*, 232 US 383 (1914).

35. *Wolf v Colorado*, 338 US 25 (1949).

36. *Wong Sun v United States*, 371 US 471(1963).

Legislation

1. ROC Constitution.

2. ROC Criminal Procedure Code.

3. Statute for Prevention of Gangster.

4. Police Act.

6 論兩岸民間交流糾紛之刑事訴訟障礙

壹、前　言

　　從 1987 年我方政府開放人民赴大陸探親以來，兩岸關係出現了重大的變化，由早期的冰冷對峙局勢，逐漸趨於緩和，希望以交流促進瞭解，以溝通化解敵意。隨著兩岸開放程度的提升，兩岸人民往來也日漸頻繁，除了返鄉探親之外，透過旅遊參訪等活動，兩岸人民也增加了許多相互交流與認識的機會。

　　基本上，兩岸同文同種，民族習性、語言、風俗等人文淵源特色多屬相近，此種高同質性的文化背景除係近年來兩岸互動衍生許多治安問題（諸如：人員偷渡、軍火槍械和毒品走私問題、經濟犯罪、組織犯罪問題等 [1]。）的重要因子外，更是兩

---

[1] 若就綜合性安全及非傳統性安全的概念及現象而言，有關兩岸交流互動衍生的社會治安問題，主要包括：偷渡、走私槍械、毒品、海上搶劫，刑事嫌疑犯、通緝犯逃亡至對岸藏匿，兩岸三地組織犯罪等問題，可分為以下類型：（一）非法入境問題；（二）走私問題；（三）國人犯罪潛逃大陸問題；（四）兩岸三地組織犯罪問題；與（五）台灣人民在大陸所面臨的人身安全問題。相關說明請參閱朱蓓蕾，兩岸共同打擊犯罪之議題與建議，available at: http://www.npf.org.tw/PUBLICATION/IA/094/IA-R-094-002.htm (last visited, Nov. 20, 2007)。

岸人民相互間旅遊參訪活動、甚至跨海醫療日趨熱絡的最主要因素。雖然前述兩岸交流活動尚不致衍生出重大的政治或治安問題，然而源自於兩岸間交流活動的紛爭（包含民事糾紛與刑事糾紛），卻是一個必須加以重視的問題，蓋若無法妥善處理此類糾紛，除將加深紛爭當事人間的不諒解與不平外，也有害於兩岸人民間的實質交流，而放任類此源自兩岸交流之糾紛長期間存在，恐亦將導致彼此間不信任感無限蔓延，甚或成為另一個統獨消長的轉折點[2]。

---

[2] 曾有論者主張，中國大陸官方對於千島湖事件的處理方式，是影響兩岸關係的一大轉折。其謂：「90年代初期，幾名台灣觀光客在山西，相繼遭到扒竊集團「干洗」，當地政府竟將成員逮捕後，不分首從，一律槍斃。雖然法院這樣的量刑太重，連原本遭竊的台灣人都看不下去，後悔自己不該報案。當時兩岸之間關系的密切，確實是與時俱增；連堅持台獨的基本教義派，也都知道台獨只是一種立場的表達，但在台灣永遠是少數的。然而中國政府一切的善意，竟然就由一個原本單純的刑事案件，成為浙江省政府官員口中堅稱的意外，最後竟成了兩岸統獨消長的轉折點。千島湖事件（1994年3月31日）爆發前，2月底台灣民意測驗中，認為「自己是台灣人」29.1%；認為「自己是中國人」24.2%；認為「自己既是台灣人又是中國人」43.2%；其余是不知道或拒答。但在千島湖事件發生後不久的4月底，同樣的民意測驗，認為「自己是台灣人」增加為36.9%；認為「自己是中國人」減少為12.7%；認為「自己既是台灣人又是中國人」45.4%；其余是不知道或拒答。同樣的民意測驗里，千島湖事件爆發前的2月底，「支持獨立」12.3%；「支持統一」27.4%；「維持現狀」44.5%；其余是不知道或拒答。千島湖事件發生後不久的4月底，「支持獨立」增加為15.5%；「支持統一」減少為17.3%；「維持現狀」54.5%；其余是不知道或拒答。千島湖事件對台灣人的自我認知與統獨趨勢，影響之大實在是歷史之最。當年台灣赴大陸的人數，從1,541,628，遽降到1,152,084人次。後來幾年雖然人數又開始增加，但統消獨長的趨勢卻仍然難以逆轉了。…千島湖事件爆發至今已經十年，32位罹難者的屍骨已慘遭浙江省政府「依法火化」。世界各國偵辦刑案，對有他殺之嫌的，都是命令家屬「依法不得火化」，惟獨在中國浙江省有此「特色」。浙江省政府在破

　　大致上來說，兩岸參訪交流活動可能產生的糾紛，如依加害者與被害者身分之區別，可分為下列幾種侵害類型：（1）台灣地區人民（以下簡稱台胞）在大陸地區加害於大陸地區人民（以下簡稱陸胞）；（2）台胞在大陸地區受害於陸胞；（3）台胞在大陸地區加/受害於台胞；（4）陸胞在台灣地區加/受害於陸胞；（5）陸胞在台灣地區加害於台胞；與（6）陸胞在台灣地區受害於台胞等六大糾紛組合類型。而在這六種糾紛組合中，類似千島湖事件那樣震驚兩岸的重大刑事事件，事實上並不多見；反之，較為常見者，倒是那些源自於旅遊購物的糾紛，例如：食宿等級未依合約、小費收取雜亂無章、攜帶國寶誤觸法令、行程改變未先告知、強迫推銷購買特產、使用偽鈔購物、不肖領隊為彌補低額團費而詐騙旅客購買劣質商品以及謊報旅客脫逃等非重大刑事事件[3]。為免兩岸人民因為這些導源

案後，只是一味夸贊自己的破案功勞，卻至今未對強迫火化尸體一事，向罹難者家屬道歉。劉錫榮這位台灣同胞人人「化成灰都認識」的大官，非但沒有因千島湖事件造成的兩岸關系大倒退而受到懲戒，反而仕途亨通。在1997年中共十五大上，成為中紀委常委，2002年還被選為中紀委副書記。這樣的官員成了中國官員「紀律」的代表，難怪台灣為何有這麼高比例的人不願與中國統一？這不是李扁兩人可以單獨搞起來的。」，available at: http://web.wenxuecity.com/BBSView.php? SubID=taiwan_best&MsgID=418 (last visited, Nov. 20, 2006)。

[3] 有一則相關的報導如下：「有一個大陸來台旅行團，昨天竟然被導遊帶到中正機場航警局報案，導遊聲稱有人想脫團逃跑，但警方深入瞭解，發現是導遊安排太多購物行程，團員不想參加，跟導遊爭取要有自由活動，雙方吵了起來，導遊就把整團人帶到警察局。這12名大陸旅客，都來自瀋陽，無奈地蹲在路邊，表情透露著不滿。因為昨天下午六點，他們整車被帶往中正機場航警局。不是來觀光，而是導遊指稱有人要脫團。不過警方調查發現，其實是

於兩岸參訪旅遊的刑事糾紛而嫌隙日深，甚而互不信賴，如何妥善並有效處理這些刑事案件，以抒發兩岸人民因相互間旅遊參訪等活動所產生之不滿，實同為兩岸政府所應嚴肅面對之課題。本文之作，旨在探討我國現行法制中，存在哪些不利於前述兩岸交流參訪糾紛事件刑事訴追之制度上障礙，並試圖找出超越相關追訴障礙之可能方法。

導遊要帶團員參加購物行程，但這些大陸旅客不想再買東西，倒是跟導遊爭取自由行動，好多走走逛逛，真正的認識臺灣。事實上，這些大陸旅客出團前已經告知有購物行程。但是到了購物地點，他們並不想再花錢，臺灣導遊卻一直鼓吹他們買東西，一直要再安排購物行程，所以雙方才在遊覽車上吵了起來，最後吵進了航警局。看來大陸旅客來臺灣，還真是被當作冤大頭。從行程來看，大陸遊客根本享受不到去臺灣旅遊的樂趣。臺北進店3家：珊瑚、手錶、免稅店；花蓮地區大理石工廠、台東地區珊瑚、高雄賣鑽石、阿里山賣假茶葉、日月潭賣鹿茸、靈芝⋯⋯，機場旁買特產。而且行程是臺北進出，非常趕行程。一天要跑300、400公里，加上臺灣多山路，幾乎整天都在車上。由魯銓旅行社低價接待的中國來台觀光團，疑因無法以購物備金彌補團費，向航警局謊報旅客要脫逃。這起中國來台觀光團旅遊糾紛發生在八月一日，初步瞭解，這個觀光團團費過低，旅客又不購物，無法拿備金彌補團費，旅行社疑似因此將旅客帶到航警局，謊報旅客要脫逃。經機場旅客服務中心值班人員和員警處理後，發生糾紛的中國旅行團當晚回到住宿飯店，並依照行程已於昨天上午離台。業者指出：如果不能遏止劣質購物行程，大陸觀光客來台旅遊的品質就無法保障！據瞭解，部分旅行業者的抽傭比例高達五成以上，導致觀光客買到的特產或茶葉，只能以品質低劣的產品混充。大陸五一黃金周，湧進了五千多位大陸觀光客到臺灣旅遊，透過媒體的追蹤，大陸客在各地大肆購物，豪氣出手的形象一再出現。早年臺灣旅客到香港大陸被當成「呆胞」帶去「海削」，如今風水輪流轉，大陸旅客到臺灣旅遊，被安排購物行程，當肥羊猛宰的說法，時有所聞。據瞭解，商店業者提供旅行業者購物抽傭行之多年，不過，大陸客來台之後有變本加厲的現象，大陸客必買的臺灣特產：鳳梨酥，茶葉等等，抽傭比例甚至傳出超過五成到六成以上，商店還要提供遊覽車司機茶水費，七折八扣之後，大陸觀光客買到的東西，品質恐怕會有相當大的落差！長此以往，將會導致旅遊品質迅速惡化。」參閱「別再叫我買！看大陸遊客在臺灣的悲慘遭遇」，available at: http://www.haoo.cn/html/article/2006/08/10/2322161.html (last visited, Nov. 20, 2006)。

貳、中華民國刑法適用於兩岸刑事案件所衍生之疑義

　　雖然依照現行刑法第 3 條：「本法於在中華民國領域內犯罪者，適用之。在中華民國領域外之中華民國船艦或航空器內犯罪者，以在中華民國領域內犯罪論。」規定，除了特別明文之犯罪類型外，我國刑法規定原則上似應只在我國台澎金馬領域內發生效力[4]。惟因我方最高法院 89 年台非字第 94 號判決曾

---

[4]　關於域外犯罪之效力，刑法相關規定如下：
第 5 條　本法於凡在中華民國領域外犯下列各罪者，適用之：
一、內亂罪。
二、外患罪。
三、第 135 條、第 136 條及第 138 條之妨害公務罪。
四、第 185 條之 1 及第 185 條之 2 之公共危險罪。
五、偽造貨幣罪。
六、第 201 條至第 202 條之偽造有價證券罪。
七、第 211 條、第 214 條、第 218 條及第 216 條行使第 211 條、第 213 條、第 214 條文書之偽造文書罪。
八、毒品罪。但施用毒品及持有毒品、種子、施用毒品器具罪，不在此限。
九、第 296 條及第 296 條之 1 之妨害自由罪。
十、第 333 條及第 334 條之海盜罪。
第 6 條　本法於中華民國公務員在中華民國領域外犯左列各罪者，適用之：
一、第 121 條至第 123 條、第 125 條、第 126 條、第 129 條、第 131 條、第 132 條及第 134 條之瀆職罪。
二、第 163 條之脫逃罪。
三、第 213 條之偽造文書罪。
四、第 336 條第 1 項之侵占罪。
第 7 條　本法於中華民國人民在中華民國領域外犯前 2 條以外之罪，而其最輕本刑為三年以上有期徒刑者，適用之。但依犯罪地之法律不罰者，不在此限。
第 8 條　前條之規定，於在中華民國領域外對於中華民國人民犯罪之外國人，準用之。

指出：『中華民國憲法第 4 條明文：「中華民國領土，依其固有之疆域，非經國民大會之決議，不得變更之。」而國民大會亦未曾為變更領土之決議。又中華民國憲法增修條文第 11 條復規定：「自由地區與大陸地區間人民權利義務關係及其他事務之處理，得以法律為特別之規定。」且臺灣地區與大陸地區人民關係條例第 2 條第 2 款更指明：「大陸地區：指台灣地區以外之中華民國領土。」揭示大陸地區仍屬我中華民國之領土；該條例第 75 條復規定：「在大陸地區或在大陸船艦、航空器內犯罪，雖在大陸地區曾受處罰，仍得依法處斷。但得免其刑之全部或一部之執行。」據此，大陸地區現在雖因事實上之障礙為我國主權所不及，但在大陸地區犯罪，仍應受我國法律之處罰，即明示大陸地區猶屬我國領域，並未對其放棄主權。本件被告○○○被訴於民國 82 年至 85 年間在大陸福州市犯有刑法第 339 條第 1 項之詐欺取財及第 215 條之業務登載不實文書罪嫌，即為在中華民國領域內犯罪，自應適用中華民國法律論處。』[5]。因此，除了陸胞在台灣地區加（受）害於陸胞、陸胞

---

[5] 類似之見解如最高法院 90 年度台上字第 705 號判決：『（三）原判決謂麻醉藥品管理條例第 13 條之 1 第 2 項第 1 款所規定非法運輸化學合成麻醉藥品，係指國內輸出國外，或在國內運送者而言。本件上訴人自我國統治權所不及之廣東省深圳市南澳漁港，運送安非他命至菲律賓被查獲，與非法運輸化學合成麻醉藥品之構成要件有間（見原判決理由五之（三））。似指大陸地區非屬我國領域。然中華民國憲法第 4 條明文：「中華民國領土，依其固有之疆域，非經國民大會之決議，不得變更之。」而國民大會亦未曾為變更領土之決議。又中華民國憲法增修條文第 11 條復規定：「自由地區與大陸地區間人民權利義務關係及其他事務之處理，得以法律為特別之規定。」且臺灣地

在台灣地區加害於台胞與陸胞在台灣地區受害於台胞等三種糾紛組合類型因其發生地在台灣地區而有中華民國刑法規定之適用外，諸如台胞在大陸地區加害於陸胞、台胞在大陸地區受害於陸胞、與台胞在大陸地區加（受）害於台胞等糾紛案件類型，縱然其糾紛發生地在大陸地區，依前述最高法院判決意旨，除中華民國刑法有其適用外，原則上我國法院對該等發生於大陸地區的刑事糾紛亦享有刑事管轄權。

區與大陸地區人民關係條例第2條第2款更指明：「大陸地區：指台灣地區以外之中華民國領土。」揭示大陸地區仍屬我中華民國之領土；該條例第75條復規定：「在大陸地區或在大陸船艦、航空器內犯罪，雖在大陸地區曾受處罰，仍得依法處斷。但得免其刑之全部或一部之執行。」據此，大陸地區現在雖因事實上之障礙為我國主權所不及，但在大陸地區犯罪，仍應受我國法律之處罰，即明示大陸地區猶屬我國領域，並未對其放棄主權。又依刑法第4條之規定，犯罪之行為或結果，有一在中華民國領域內者，為在中華民國領域內犯罪。本件原判決既謂上訴人將安非他命，自大陸地區廣東省深圳市南澳漁港運送至菲律賓，何以不能認係在我國領域內犯罪，而論以非法運輸化學合成麻醉藥品罪？原判決未詳實說明其理由，即逕為前揭認定，亦有理由不備之違誤。』與最高法院90年度台上字第2282號判決：『（三）按中華民國憲法第4條明文：「中華民國領土，依其固有之疆域，非經國民大會之決議，不得變更之。」而國民大會亦未曾為變更領土之決議。又中華民國憲法增修條文第11條復規定：「自由地區與大陸地區間人民權利義務關係及其他事務之處理，得以法律為特別之規定。」且臺灣地區與大陸地區人民關係條例第2條第2款更指明：「大陸地區：指台灣地區以外之中華民國領土。」揭示大陸地區仍屬我中華民國之領土；該條例第75條復規定：「在大陸地區或在大陸船艦、航空器內犯罪，雖在大陸地區曾受處罰，仍得依法處斷。但得免其刑之全部或一部之執行。」據此，大陸地區現在雖因事實上之障礙為我國主權所不及，但在大陸地區犯罪，仍應受我國法律之處罰，即明示大陸地區猶屬我國領域，並未對其放棄主權。原判決理由謂本件「因其偽造之私文書係在大陸地區為之，依刑法總則規定（見第3條至第7條）我國法院無管轄權」云云，揆諸前揭說明，難認適法。』等，亦同此旨。

　　然而，縱然在前述實務見解下，我國法院在法理上有權處理源於兩岸交流所生之刑事糾紛，這樣的見解卻太過於抽象而不夠精確。簡單來說，雖然在前述實務見解下我國法院對於發生在大陸地區的刑事糾紛亦有審判權與管轄權，不過，如何使在大陸地區發生刑事糾紛的加害人與被害人能夠實際上在台灣地區接受刑事審判或進行刑事訴訟程序，除因兩岸政治分離而於本質上屬於一種不可能的任務外，特別當受害之一方係台灣地區人民而在回到台灣地區後始向我方之檢警單位提出刑事告訴時，如何要求仍滯留大陸地區之被告（不論係台胞或陸胞）抵台接受偵查與審判，徵諸現行相關法制之闕漏，更屬一大難題；再者，關於陸胞在台灣地區之犯罪，雖兩岸人民關係條例第 75 條之 1：「大陸地區人民於犯罪後出境，致不能到庭者，法院得於其能到庭以前停止審判。但顯有諭知無罪或免刑判決之情形者，得不待其到庭，逕行判決。」提供了我方法院處理相關案件被告不到庭時的處理基礎，惟究其實際，在無諭知無罪或免刑判決之情形中，該條規定並未於實質上提供如何解決陸胞出境後未能再度回到台灣地區時，究應如何終局處理該件在台灣地區提起之刑事案件之依據[6]。換言之，究應如何妥善處理此種兩岸人民交流所產生的刑事案件，現行法制並未提供明確的處理標準。

---

[6] 事實上，一但出現此種類型的刑事案件，實務上也只能透過通緝的方式，在一定時間經過後，形式上地終結該件案件。

　　除了前述源於法制闕漏所產生如何終局處理兩岸刑事案件的實際困難外，現行法制中已有明文規定之部分，似乎亦存在一些阻礙兩岸犯罪刑事訴追之要素。由於筆者學植未深，本文旨在探討存在於我方法制可能存在之刑事訴訟障礙，至於大陸地區刑事訴訟法制是否存在其他相近或相異之規定，並不在本文探討之範圍內，相關之可能疑義，尚待來日就教於熟悉對岸刑事訴訟法制之法學先進。

參、一事不再理原則（禁止雙重危險法則）之適用疑義

一、關於一事不再理原則之內涵與其適用於兩岸刑事案件之疑義

　　按同一犯罪行為，不受重覆處罰，為刑事基本權之重要內容。依照前大法官吳庚所見：『我國刑事訴訟制度中，不僅明文規定同一犯罪行為不受二次審問處罰（刑事訴訟法第 302 條第 1 款、第 303 條第 2 款及第 4 款等），抑且在特種刑事案件中，全盤接受美國禁止雙重危險之法則，凡適用美軍在華地位協定之被告，依該協定第 14 條第 9 項之有關照會，「如被告被判無罪，他造當事人不得提出上訴；被告對任何判決不提出上訴時，他造當事人亦不得提出上訴…。」故雙重危險保障原

則，已溶入我國實證法體系之中[7]。』，前最高法院院長林明德更曾建議將雙重危險之禁止條款定於憲法條文內[8]。從而，只要

---

[7] 其並謂：『先就不受二次審問處罰而言，此一原則在刑事訴訟程序通稱為一事不再理（ne bis in idem）。多數意見基於實體判決與程序判決有別之前提，以最高法院駁回上訴之程序判決，祇有形式上羈束力，不具有實質確定力，與一事不再理原則無關為立論基礎，固有其訴訟技術上之依據。惟是否構成同一行為不受二次以上審問處罰應從憲法保障人身自由之根本精神予以解答，不應限於訴訟技術之層次。蓋不受二次處罰之原則在羅馬法上已經存在，並表現於下列法諺：Nemo debit bis puniri pro uno delicto, 或者 Nemo debet bis vexari pro una et eadem causa（英譯：a man shall not be twice vexed for one and the same cause）。18 世紀英國法學家布來克史東（Sir William Blackstone）在其經典著作「英格蘭法律詮釋」（Commentaries on the Laws of England,1790,IV,335）中宣稱：不受一次以上之危險乃舉世普遍之法則（"the plea of autrefois acquit, for a formal acquital,isgrounded on the universal maxim ⋯⋯that no man is to be brought into jeopardy of his life more than once for the same offense"）。美國聯邦憲法制定時，將已見諸殖民地各州憲法之條款列入聯邦憲法修正案第 5 條，此乃眾所熟知之雙重危險保障條款（double jeopardy protection clause）。二次大戰之後，德國基本法第 103 條第 3 項、日本憲法第 39 條亦均有類似規定，其他大陸法系國家則多以一事不再理之方式，規定於刑事訴訟法。所謂雙重危險保障或不受二次處罰原則其內涵如何？固無各國一致之標準，在英美法系國家適用此一原則之結果，非但一罪不能兩罰，凡經陪審團認定無罪者，檢察官亦不得上訴，使被告免再受審問處罰之危險；在大陸法系國家雖未如此嚴格之限制，但至少一如前述日本憲法之規定：「任何人就其已認定無罪之行為，不被追問刑事上責任，同一犯罪亦不得使其再受追問刑事上責任」，殆無疑問。』參閱司法院大法官釋字第 271 號解釋中，吳庚前大法官所提之不同意見書，available at: http://www.judicial.gov.tw/constitutionalcourt/P03_01_detail.asp? expno=271&showtype=%B7N%A8%A3%AE%D1 (last visited, Nov. 20, 2006)。

[8] 其曾於其所草擬憲法草案中建議於憲法草案第 18 條增訂雙重危險之禁止條款：『同一行為，經追訴處罰者，不得再追究其刑事責任。』其於該草案理由中指出：「（一）同一犯罪行為，不受重覆處罰，為刑事基本權之重要內容。故於公民及政治權利國際公約第 14 條第 7 款、美國聯邦憲法增修條款第 5 條、德國聯邦共和國基本法第 103 條第 3 項，及日本憲法第 39 條均設有明

發生在中華民國領域內之犯罪，被告均應受到一事不再理原則（或稱為「禁止雙重危險法則」）之保障。不過依兩岸人民關係條例第 75 條：「在大陸地區或在大陸船艦、航空器內犯罪，雖在大陸地區曾受處罰，仍得依法處斷。但得免其刑之全部或一部之執行。」之規定與最高法院 89 年台非字第 94 號判決等見解，發生在大陸地區之犯罪縱然已依大陸地區之法律規定接受刑事處罰，嗣後該被告進入台灣地區時，台灣地區之司法機關仍得對該同一事實（亦即前述發生在大陸地區之犯罪）進行追訴處罰。易言之，依據兩岸人民關係條例第 75 條之規定與最高法院 89 年台非字第 94 號判決等見解，大陸地區各級法院所

文。惟英美法上就刑事程序不得使被告就同一犯罪受雙重處罰之危險，稱之為「雙重危險之禁止」；而大陸法系，對於判決確定之案件，不允許就同一案再度予以追訴處罰，則稱之為「一事不再理」。兩者就保障刑事被告之同一犯罪行為不受重覆處罰之目的及機能，固無不同，惟理念上，前者係立於被告立場，基於保護被告免除重受刑事程序追訴處罰之危險而立論，後者係立於法院立場，基於確保法院確定判決權威及既判力之範圍而立論，故於訴訟法制設計及運作上，就一行為不兩罰之具體範圍，仍有不同。例如：檢察官是否得為被告之不利益提起再審？同一犯罪行為經刑事判決有罪後，得否再重覆論處其流氓行為？反之，經論處其流氓行為後，得否再重受刑事處罰？同一行為，經檢察撤回公訴後，得否重行提起公訴？經法院判決無罪後，檢察官重組事證，重行追究新罪名等，皆會因「一事不兩罰」之法制理念，究採「雙重危險禁止」或「一事不再理」而有不同。（二）按就人權侵害言，國家追訴程序之發動，及長期、重覆之訟累，實無異於刑罰，故基於正當法律程序理念，人民之刑事程序基本權，應不止受「禁止雙重處罰」之保障，更應進而提昇至受「禁止雙重追訴危險」之保障，始符憲法保障民權之宗旨。爰增訂本條文，規定「同一行為，經追訴處罰者，不得再行追究其刑事責任。」以資保障人權。』參閱林明德，談建議刑事基本人權入憲之必要性，available at: http://www.president.gov.tw/1_structure/famous/column/7_lmd20040501.html (last visited, Nov. 20, 2006)。

做出的刑事裁判，對我方各級法院而言，並無裁判上的拘束力
（如刑事訴訟法第 302 條第 1 款、第 303 條第 2 款及第 4 款等
效力），充其量其只能當作一種「免其刑之全部或一部之執
行」之參考事項。然而此種某種程度源自「憲法一中[9]」之實務

---

[9] 根據中華民國憲法第 4 條規定：「中華民國領土，依其固有之疆域，非經國
民大會之決議，不得變更之。」與司法院大法官釋字第 328 號解釋：「中華
民國領土，憲法第 4 條不採列舉方式，而為「依其固有之疆域」之概括規定，
並設領土變更之程序，以為限制，有其政治上及歷史上之理由。其所稱固有
疆域範圍之界定，為重大之政治問題，不應由行使司法權之釋憲機關予以解
釋。」及其解釋理由書：「國家領土之範圍如何界定，純屬政治問題；其界
定之行為，學理上稱之為統治行為，依權力分立之憲政原則，不受司法審查。
我國憲法第 4 條規定，「中華民國領土，依其固有之疆域，非經國民大會之
決議，不得變更之」，對於領土之範圍，不採列舉方式而為概括規定，並設
領土變更之程序，以為限制，有其政治上及歷史上之理由。其所稱「固有之
疆域」究何所指，若予解釋，必涉及領土範圍之界定，為重大之政治問題。
本件聲請，揆諸上開說明，應不予解釋。」之說明，凡按照中華民憲法法條
規定（如領土.主權…等）來定義「一個中國」的本質，即屬此處所稱憲法一
中之概念。前行政院長謝長廷亦認為：「根據憲法回應一中就是憲法一中」，
其指出：『依據台灣實踐憲法的民主經驗，當然可闡述對「一個中國」意涵
的理念，他才會提出「根據憲法回應一中就是憲法一中」的主張，如此　法
論法中國既不能片面曲解一中定義，台灣也不會吃虧。謝長廷倡議憲法一中，
曾引發各界正反兩極評價，下午他參加中華民國哈佛校友會主辦的「哈佛公
益論壇」，再度闡述憲法一中的概念。他說，不論親民黨主席宋楚瑜提議的
「兩岸一中」，或是爭論多時的「一中各表、九二共識」，均容易被中國曲
解為北京觀點的一個中國原則。謝長廷表示，中國有憲法、台灣也有憲法，
就法論法，台灣當然可以依據五十多年來，憲法藉民主制度實踐的經驗，闡
述對於一個中國意涵的觀點。他說，自提出憲法一中主張後，中方始終沒有
正面回應，即可知北京瞭解憲法一中很厲害，不敢隨便接招，否則就形同北
京承認台灣也有一部憲法。謝長廷指出，很可惜認同自己這番理念的人不多，
即使在民進黨內也遭受嚴厲批判，但該面對的問題總要面對，不能一直僵持
無解。他說，也有人批評修憲難度高，需要四分之三以上立委同意，以致無
法降低罷免總統門檻，但就因修憲門檻高，迫使朝野政黨必須經協商達成共
識，才有助於政局穩定。』 available at: http://times.hinet.net/news/20060812/
polity/6892f7d6c91c.htm (last visited, Nov. 20, 2006)。

見解，不免令人質疑，在一國領域內得重複審問處罰同一犯罪事實的觀點，是否有違前述一事不再理之憲法原則？而其他類似兩岸在政治上分離的地區（如德國）或是其他複數法域之國家（如美國）又是如何處理類此之爭議呢？以下將分別探討之。

二、德國法制對此爭議之處理

　　類似兩岸分治之現況，德國也曾經歷過分裂國家之階段。在德國統一之前，東、西德犯罪之裁判是否在對方法域亦具有拘束力？關於此一問題之處理，或因其與兩岸關係具有高度之類似性，而可作為我方判斷大陸地區刑事裁判效力之標準。一般來說，依照前西德「刑事案件司法及行政互助法（RHilfeG）」第 3 條之規定，只要符合該條規定之前東德法院刑事判決，前西德司法機關即承認該前東德刑事判決在前西德亦有既判力與執行力，從而前西德司法單位即不必對同一發生於前東德之犯罪事實再行追訴處罰[10]。換言之，前西德刑事案件司法及行政互助法第 3 條防止了在前西德領域內，出現同一犯罪事實先後在前東德與前西德均受到追訴處罰之「在一個德國領域內一事兩罰」現象[11]。

---

[10]　參考朱石炎，兩岸人民關係條例刑事章釋義，註一，法令月刊，第 43 卷第 10 期，頁 18，民國 81 年 10 月。

[11]　而這樣的現象或可與政治上「一個德國」之訴求，互為表裡。

三、美國法制之沿革

另外一種複數法域之類型當屬美國之聯邦制度，按美國除有五十個州（法域）外，尚有一個哥倫比亞特區法域與聯邦法域，共計五十二個法域。從而在憲法禁止雙重危險法則（Double Jeopardy Clause）之拘束下，對於同一犯罪事實而言，是否該州與聯邦均有追訴處罰之權限？或者在跨州犯罪之情形中，是否各相關州均有追訴處罰之權限？

如美國聯邦最高法院在格林訴美國（Green v. United States）乙案所述，本質上，美國憲法第 5 增修條文所規定的禁止雙重危險法則，除在防止各州透過提起刑事控訴之方式，針對同一犯罪事實多次侵擾被告，造成其不必要的訴訟花費與產生額外的心理負擔外，更在降低無罪被告因多次受審而被判有罪的可能性 [12]。從而原則上同一犯罪事實僅應受到國家司法機關「一次」追訴處罰，在任何有罪判決、無罪判決或赦免後，復

---

[12] The Double Jeopardy Clause of the Fifth Amendment states, "nor shall any person be subject for the same offence to be twice put in jeopardy of life or limb..." The purpose of this Bill of Rights guarantee that no individual be twice put in jeopardy was described vividly by the Supreme Court in Green v. United States: "The underlying idea ... is that the State with all its resources and power should not be allowed to make repeated attempts to convict an individual for an alleged offense, thereby subjecting him to embarrassment, expense and ordeal and compelling him to live in a continuing state of anxiety and insecurity, as well as enhancing the possibility that even though innocent he may be found guilty." See 355 U.S. 184, 187-8 (1957).

對同一犯罪事實進行或發動第二次以上的追訴或處罰，都有可能被視爲禁止雙重危險法則之違反 [13]。

　　值得注意的是，即便禁止雙重危險法則旨在保障被告就同一犯罪事實，不受二次以上的追訴或處罰，基於美國聯邦制度的特殊歷史背景 [14]，美國聯邦最高法院卻在美國訴蘭薩（United

---

[13] According to the Supreme Court, double jeopardy was historically understood as embracing three common-law pleas － autrefois acquit, autrefois convict, and pardon － that barred any criminal prosecution for the same crime for which defendant had already been acquitted, convicted, or pardoned, respectively. See United States v. Scott, 437 U.S. 82, 87 (1978); United States v. Wilson, 420 U.S. 332, 340 (1975); see also 4 William Blackstone, Commentaries 31 (discussing these pleas, and the now moot plea, autrefois attaint); 2 William Hawkins, A Treatise of the Pleas of the Crown 368 99 (photo.reprint 1978)(1716 1721) (similar discussion of autrefois acquit, autrefois convict, and pardon). See Akhil Reed Amar and Jonathan L. Marcus, Double Jeopardy Law After Rodney King, FN3, 95 Colum. L. Rev. 1, 1 (1995).

[14] As held in Health v. Alabama, "It is axiomatic that "[i]n America, the powers of sovereignty are divided between the government of the Union, and those of the States. They are each sovereign, with respect to the objects committed to it, and neither sovereign with respect to the objects committed to the other." [474 U.S. 82, 93] McCulloch v. Maryland, 4 Wheat. 316, 410 (1819). It is as well established that the States, "as political communities, [are] distinct and sovereign, and consequently foreign to each other." Bank of United States v. Daniel, 12 Pet. 32, 54 (1838). See also Skiriotes v. Florida, 313 U.S., at 77 ; Coyle v. Oklahoma, 221 U.S., at 567 . The Constitution leaves in the possession of each State "certain exclusive and very important portions of sovereign power." The Federalist No. 9, p. 55 (J. Cooke ed. 1961). Foremost among the prerogatives of sovereignty is the power to create and enforce a criminal code. See, e. g., Alfred L. Snapp & Son, Inc. v. Puerto Rico ex rel. Barez, 458 U.S. 592, 601 (1982); McCulloch, supra, at 418. To deny a State its power to enforce its criminal laws because another State has won the race to the courthouse "would be a shocking and untoward deprivation of the historic right and obligation of the States to maintain peace and order within their confines." Bartkus, 359 U.S., at 137." See 474 U.S. 82, 92-3 (1985).

States v. Lanza）乙案中，開始以「複數主權法則（dual sover-eign doctrine）」此一概念，排除禁止雙重危險法則適用於不同法域之複數刑事訴追[15]。美國聯邦最高法院甚至在亞貝訴美國乙案中指出，聯邦行使刑事訴追程序之權限，不因州已對同一行為人的同一犯罪事實提出刑事訴追而受阻礙[16]。其後，複數主權法則更擴張成為排除印地安區原住民審判與聯邦審判間適用禁止雙重危險法則之依據[17]。簡言之，雖然憲法第5增修條文中的禁止雙重危險條款未明文限制其適用之前提為同一法域之雙重刑事訴追，然在美國聯邦最高法院複數主權法則的解釋下，該條款之內涵似已轉換為：「在同一法域中，同一犯罪行為不受二次審問處罰（no person shall be put twice in jeopardy by "the same sovereign."）」此一以「同一法域（the same sovereign）之刑事訴追」，作為禁止雙重危險法則適用之前提要件。

不過複數主權法則卻非一項毫無爭議之法則，許多法官與學者均曾對複數主權法則提出批判。如美國聯邦最高法院前大

15　See United States v. Lanza, 260 U.S. 377, 382 (1922).

16　It held: "a federal prosecution is not barred by a prior state prosecution of the same person for the same acts." See Abbate v. United States, 359 U.S. 187, 188-9 (1959)

17　In United States v. Wheeler, the Supreme Court reasoned that if the power to punish tribe members emanated from the tribe's inherent sovereignty, double jeopardy could not be implicated by a subsequent federal prosecution for the same conduct. See 435 U.S. 313, 322 (1978).

法官布來克即認為該法則有違西方文明中長久存在的正當法律程序原則，其指出：對同一犯罪事實雙重審判的恐懼是自希臘羅馬時期即已存在的想法，即使在黑暗時期，前述禁止雙重危險法則仍透過寺院法與基督教文明之發展延續至今[18]。直至今日，在美國仍有不少學者主張：同一國家中其他法域之刑事訴訟程序，亦應具有使同一犯罪行為不受二次審問處罰之效力，憲法第 5 增修條文中的禁止雙重危險條款，不應限制於同一法域之雙重刑事訴追時，始有適用。而這樣的觀點，洽與前述德國統一前的法制概況相符。

四、禁止雙重危險法則於我國法上適用之疑義

按一事不再理原則之適用，係基於一個主權國家僅存有一個管轄權之思考，也就是說，在同一主權範圍內不得重複進行刑事訴追程序，倘出現重複訴追之情形，法院不得對其實體審理[19]。跨及兩岸之犯罪（不論源自何種原因，旅遊、訪問、走

---

[18] Justice Black said: "Fear and abhorrence of governmental power to try people twice for the same conduct is one of the oldest ideas found in western civilization. Its roots run deep into Greek and Roman times. Even in the Dark Ages, when so many other principles of justice were lost, the idea that one trial and one punishment were enough remained alive through the canon law and the teachings of the early Christian writers." See United States v. Barkus, 359 U.S. 121, 155 (1959). According to Justice Black, successive prosecutions for the same offense were prohibited even by the Church canons, which contained the maxim, "[not] even God judges twice for the same act." Id.

[19] 參閱黃東熊、吳景芳，刑事訴訟法論，頁 475，三民書局，2002 年 8 月；張麗卿，刑事訴訟法理論與運用，頁 171-2，五南圖書出版社，2002 年 8 月。

私……）究竟屬於國內犯罪或國外犯罪，因兩岸各自主張為主權國家，不免成為一個問題。由於現行大陸刑法第 10 條與我國刑法第 9 條均明定外國判決不適用一事不再理原則[20]，而對於涉及兩岸犯罪行為，關於是否認可對方判決乙事，兩岸作法其實相當一致，兩岸法制均將發生在對方領域內之犯罪比照在領域外犯罪，並未排除對同一案件之管轄權[21]。而觀之兩岸人民關係條例第 75 條：「在大陸地區或在大陸船艦、航空器內犯罪，雖在大陸地區曾受處罰，仍得依法處斷。但得免其刑之全部或一部之執行。」之規定用語與刑法第 9 條又大致相同，故若謂該法視大陸地區之判決為外國判決，亦將之排除一事不再理原則之適用，似無不當。易言之，縱主張沿用德國統一前之模式，認為兩岸目前同屬一個分裂的中國，在欠缺類似前西德刑事案件司法及行政互助法第 3 條規定以及兩岸並未承認對方刑事司法判決效力的前提下，難免產生行為人已在一方（通常係犯罪行為發生地）受罰，返國後仍須面對其國內刑事司法機

---

[20] 即對於同一行為在領域外犯罪，經外國法院確定裁判，仍得依國內刑法追究犯罪人之刑責，但在外國已受刑之全部或一部執行者，得免除其刑之全部或一部之執行。

[21] 在不承認兩岸關係具有聯邦制度色彩的前提下，中共當局此種將發生在對方領域內之犯罪比照在領域外犯罪之立法，似乎在刑事審判領域內，「忘記了」一個中國的原則。觀諸近年來港、澳地區回歸大陸成為特別行政區後，大陸實施區際司法協助方法，以一個主權國家對其不同法域地區分開行使管轄權作為基礎，就文書之送達、證據之調查、罪犯之移交、訴訟之移轉、判決之承認與執行等等事項，互相提供資訊，合作打擊犯罪，成效顯著之現實，大陸對台灣在刑事法制上的差別待遇，似有未洽。

關訴追之雙重審判現象。除非我方制定類似前西德刑事案件司法及行政互助法第 3 條規定以承認大陸地區之刑事司法判決效力，前述德國法制之觀點並不適用於我方之法制現況。

　　而美國法制上的沿革是否可作為我方處理兩岸犯罪之依據？首先必須說明的是，由於美國採行聯邦制度，因此若主張採取美國「複數主權法則」見解，似乎必須在前提上先承認大陸與台灣相互間正處於聯邦或准聯邦之關係，否則目前兩岸法制均將發生在對方領域內之犯罪比照在領域外犯罪，並未排除對同一案件之管轄權之作法，只能說是一種「（特殊？）國際間」的處理模式，國際上並無將此種複數主權法則視為一國內的刑法適用準則之先例。不過此部分涉及過高的政治性，本文不欲在此申論。

　　基於我方國家統一委員會關於一個中國涵義之說明：「民國 38 年起，中國處於暫時分裂之狀態，由兩個政治實體，分治海峽兩岸，乃為客觀之事實，任何謀求統一之主張，不能忽略此一事實之存在。」朱石炎教授曾指出：「在一國處於暫時分裂之客觀事實狀態中，兩區分治而各自有其統治權所及之地域，雖與聯邦架構不盡相同，惟兩區各本統治權作用而就犯罪行為依循一定程序進行追訴處罰，應可解為並未違反一事不再理原則。[22]」依此論述，或可謂前述複數主權原則在將兩岸現

---

[22] 參考朱石炎，兩岸人民關係條例刑事章釋義，註一，法令月刊，第 43 卷第 10 期，頁 16，民國 81 年 10 月。

行架構理解為類似聯邦關係之後,有其適用。惟鑑於複數主權原則已漸受批判,故兩岸犯罪之處理似應朝向「尊重現實擱置國家主權問題,先由互相承認對方之實際司法管轄範圍,並以此作為基礎,再進一步具體協商和劃分涉及兩岸具體犯罪類型之管轄權案件應由那一方管轄後,即應排除地方之干涉,一經一方審理之案件,他方即不得行使管轄權,而有一事不再理原則適用。[23]」之方向發展較為妥適。不論如何,此一源自是否違反憲法層次一事不再理原則之爭論,尚未出現在實務個案中,只是既然相關問題在合憲性層次上具有高度的可爭議性,自有必要先予詳明,以作為將來兩岸刑事案件處理獲得進一步發展時,一項重要的前提基礎。

肆、傳聞障礙

　　除前述憲法層次之爭議外,於實際案例中,人證與物證之欠缺,往往成為阻礙兩岸犯罪案件審理之主要原因。而人證部分,卻又可能因兩岸旅遊犯罪涵蓋兩岸因素(例如:在他方領域內犯罪、證人與被告無法至我方法院出庭……等等),導致某人證在他方領域內之供述是否在我方審判程序中仍具有證據

---

[23] 參閱周成瑜,兩岸海上犯罪問題與對策,軍法專刊,第 51 卷第 3 期,民國 94 年 3 月,available at: http://www.mnd.gov.tw/publication/subject.aspx? TopicID=454 (last visited, Nov. 20, 2006)。

能力（是否符合我國刑事訴訟法中傳聞法則之規定），亦成為一項即待解決之問題。

一、傳聞法則在我國之沿革

刑事訴訟法，乃是確定並實現國家於具體刑事個案中對被告刑罰權的程序規範，實體刑法藉此而得以實現。刑事訴訟法第 154 條第 2 項規定：「犯罪事實應依證據認定之，無證據不得認定其犯罪事實」，即揭示了證據裁判之原則。雖然歐陸各國在法國大革命後已漸漸揚棄實行於中世紀的糾問制度，而朝向控訴主義的方向前進 [24]，在此一趨勢下，關於當代的刑事訴訟法制，向來仍存在有職權主義與當事人進行主義之分別。由於我國在法制繼受的沿革上，係以歐陸法為師，因此制定於民國 24 年與民國 56 年的刑事訴訟法，均帶有濃厚的職權主義色彩。所謂職權主義的刑事訴訟程序 [25]，並不承認當事人對於訴

---

[24] 參閱王兆鵬，當事人進行主義爭議之評議，刑事法雜誌第 43 卷第 4 期，頁 36。

[25] 在此一制度下，法官負擔蒐集證據，調查證據之主要義務。法官負責主導審判，為審判中的靈魂，積極地指揮訴訟程序的進行。證人之訊問由法官負最主要的責任。證人首先由法官對其訊問，證人就所知事實提供一口語化的陳述。除非為幫助證人完整清楚地陳述事實外，法官原則上對證人的陳述不能打斷。當證人陳述所之事實完畢後，法官才可以進一步地詰問證人其他問題，或證人的信用能力。當法官結束全部訊問後，當事人雙方才被允許對證人發問。參閱王兆鵬，當事人進行主義爭議之評議，刑事法雜誌第 43 卷第 4 期，頁 36-37。

訟標的與訴訟進行享有處分的權利[26]，且認法院應本其職權發現真實[27]。類似德國的刑事訴訟制度，制定於 1935 年與 1967年的中華民國刑事訴訟法並無證據排除之規定，不過，我國刑事訴訟法第 156 條第 1 項本即不允許源自暴力，威脅，誘導，欺詐，不合法滯留和其他不恰當作為的自白。儘管有這一條文，我國最高法院長期以來似不關心證據怎樣獲得，依過去實務見解，通常法院可以考慮任何與待證事項有關的證據[28]。自從民國 88 年 7 月所召開的全國司法改革會議確定我國之刑事訴訟制度將朝「改良式當事人進行主義[29]」之方向修正後，歷經

---

[26]　參閱俞叔平，刑事訴訟法學，頁 5，中國法學編譯社印行，1956 年 10 月修正版。

[27]　參閱陳樸生，刑事訴訟法爭議問題研究，頁 30，五南圖書出版公司，1994 年12 月 6 刷。

[28]　參閱最高法院 72 台上字第 1332 號判例。

[29]　關於改良式當事人進行主義的內涵，可參考司法院以下之說明：所謂「改良式當事人進行主義」，其重點在於貫徹無罪推定原則，檢察官應就被告犯罪事實，負實質的舉證責任，法庭的證據調查活動，是由當事人來主導，法院只在事實真相有待澄清，或者是為了維護公平正義以及被告重大利益時，才發動職權調查證據。「改良式當事人進行主義」除了可以釐清法官與檢察官的權責分際、彰顯公平法院的理念外，更有助於「發見真實」。因為按照檢察制度的分工，檢察官可以聯合偵查犯罪，有權力指揮調度檢察事務官、司法警察（官）蒐集犯罪證據，所以檢察官應該最能夠掌握被告的犯罪事證，在制度設計上，自然應該讓檢察官負起實質的舉證責任。另外，被告是不是成立犯罪，關係到被告自己的生命、自由、財產及名譽，從何處蒐集有利的證據供法院調查，被告當然最為清楚，也最為積極。所以作為法院裁判基礎的證據，自然是由當事人提出最為適當，只有在當事人的舉證沒有能夠讓法院形成心證，或者是為了維護社會公義及被告重大利益時，法院才要介入調查，以發見真實。而這樣的制度設計保留了職權主義的優點，與美國刑事審判使用陪審制或日本刑事訴訟法只規定「法院得依職權調查證據」的當事人進行主義有所差別，其出發點完全是考量我國的國情及歷史文化背景，符合我國憲法關於實質正當法律程序的要求，也因此我們稱它為「改良式當事人進行主義」。Available at: http://www.judicial.gov.tw (last visited, Nov. 20, 2006)。

幾次的翻修，現行之刑事訴訟制度已迥異於制定於民國 56 年、以職權主義為基礎的舊刑事訴訟法制。

依照 1967 年刑事訴訟法之立法說明，舊法第 159 條係源自於直接審理原則與言詞審理原則，而非來自傳聞法則。由於最高法院未針對該條作成太多判例，各級法院亦不因該條規定而受到太多的限制。一般說來，證人法庭外的陳述原則上是不能被允許的；法庭外證人做的文書亦不能被接受。有趣的是，即使一個法庭外的（文字）陳述在舊刑事訴訟法第 159 條規定下不能成為證據，依照該法第 165 條第 1 項規定，被害人或共同被告在警訊中所作成之筆錄卻有（高度的）證據能力；例如，在最高法院 72 年台上字第 1203 號判例中，最高法院即認為：在中華民國的刑事審判系統中，並不存在任何對證據能力的評估的限制；從而被害人在警察訊問期間做的筆錄並未明顯地被刑事訴訟法的第 159 條所禁止，法庭有決定是否接受被害人警訊中之陳述之裁量權利。換句話說，根據這個判例，受害者的警訊筆錄不被以前的刑事訴訟法的第 159 條所排除。由於舊刑事訴訟法的第 159 條只提及證人陳述，鑒於過去共同被告與被害人沒被認為是證人，該條規定遂沒適用於共同被告或者受害者發表的法庭外的陳述。

即使舊刑事訴訟法第 159 條排除證人在法庭外陳述之證據能力，惟在 91 台上字第 2363 號判決中，最高法院認為在彈劾證人的目的下，審判外秘密記錄的錄音帶或者錄像能是可以考慮的，因被告僅僅打算證明證人在法庭之前或者一名檢察官之

前的陳述是不眞實的。此外,在刑事訴訟法第 165 條規範下,如果一個法庭外的陳述由受害者或者共同被告作成並且已由一名政府官員記錄時,法庭在依刑事訴訟法的第 165 條第 1 項規定履行調查義務後,前述陳述即取得證據能力。易言之,共同被告或受害者之審判外陳述,只要由任何政府官員作成,其本身即被允許。由於被告沒有機會回應此一法庭外陳述,因此多數認爲此種做法並不洽當。當台灣的法學者開始意識到這種不公平主要是源自傳聞法則規章的缺乏、以及欠缺對於對質權之保護,改革台灣刑事審判系統之主張於是出現,而這種主張最終導致美式傳聞法則規章的採用。縱上所述,較無爭論的說法是,傳聞法則一直到 2003 年才正式地存在於我國的刑事訴訟程序中。

二、傳聞法則在美國法制上之主要發展與其內涵

由於 19 世紀前的英國法並未保障所有刑事被告均得主張接受律師協助之權利,美國憲法第六修正案本質上並不是一項將當時英國法制入憲的規定 [30]。在 19 世紀末前,美國聯邦司法實務上並未出現過以對質條款爲論述核心的判決。在美國建國之初,對質條款的發展幾乎只停留在州的層次,並以交互詰問爲其核心。Professor Randolph N. Jonakait 即曾指出:「對質條款

---

[30] See Randolph N. Jonakait, The Origins of the Confrontation Clause: An Alternative History, 27 Rutgers L. J. 77, 109 (1995).

與其他第六修正案的規定，實質上係將已在各州行之有年的程序入憲化。這些程序有效地保障了被告的利益。辯方的交互詰問便是核心。爲了確定聯邦法院的審判程序落實前述對被告的保障，美國憲法第六修正案之對質條款，實已將辯方的交互詰問權包含在內[31]。」。

　　在美國聯邦最高法院開始審查對質條款之後，關於傳聞證言的容許性，便成爲爭議的焦點。某種程度來說，「對質權[32]」與「傳聞法則[33]」二者均以事實認定爲核心，不過在西元 1965 年之前，對質權與傳聞法則間的區分並不引人注意[34]，美國聯邦最高法院除肯認他案審判中之證述，於證人已死亡時具證據能力[35] 外，亦肯認瀕死陳述（dying declarations）之證據能力[36]。雖然美國聯邦最高法院似乎已將對質條款與傳聞法則等價齊觀[37]，但實質上二者本質並非相同，而傳聞陳述是否具證據能力亦非固定不變。

---

[31] Id., at 124.

[32] In Ohio v. Roberts, the Court held that the purpose of the Confrontation Clause is to augment accuracy in the fact-finding process.　See 448 U.S. 56, 65 (1980).

[33] See G. Michael Fenner, The Hearsay Rule, 4 (Carolina Academic Press, 2003).

[34] See 366 U.S. 440 (1949).

[35] See 156 U.S. 237, 240 (1895).

[36] See 174 U.S. 47, 61 (1899).

[37] See FindLaw, Confrontation, available at http://caselaw.lp.findlaw.com/data/constitution/amendment06/08.html (last visited, Nov. 20, 2006).

三、傳聞例外之基礎：高度真實性

美國聯邦最高法院曾建立一套決定審判外陳述是否違反對質條款的雙階測驗（two-pronged test）：「對質條款在兩個層次限制了傳聞證言之證據能力。首先，為符合立憲者傾向於採用面對面之指控模式，憲法第六修正案建立了必要性原則。即便在交互詰問已於審判前實施的情形中，控訴方仍必須證明證人無法到庭。其次，在證人無法到庭的情形中，為求發現真實並給予被告抗辯之機會，對質條款只允許具有值得信賴標誌的傳聞證言。簡單來說，當證人無法出庭作證時，對質條款要求確認證人是否真無法出庭。即便該證人確實無法出庭，傳聞證言亦只在具備真實性指標的前提下，才具有證據能力。一般來說，只要符合證據法中根深蒂固的傳聞例外，即可認為已具真實性指標。而若所舉之傳聞非屬證據法中根深蒂固的傳聞例外，如不具其他真實性擔保，即應予已排除[38]。」。簡言之，對質條款並不必然排除證人審判外陳述之證據能力，而在符合證據法中根深蒂固的傳聞例外或具有其他特別的可信性擔保之前提下，證人審判外陳述即具證據能力。然因聯邦證據法第803條之傳聞例外並未要求所有之傳聞例外均需符合證人無法到庭作證的要求，因此聯邦最高法院逐認為被告不能到庭之事由，並非絕對不能免除之要件；只要交互詰問不具實際的功效，被

---

[38] See 448 U.S., 65-6.

告是否到庭作證即非關鍵 [39]。既然檢方不必在所有的案件中提
出證人不能到庭的說明，羅伯特案中所建立的雙階測驗，實際
上只能被稱為單階測驗；只要符合可信性要件（具特別可信性
之擔保），證人審判外陳述即具備證據能力。

四、傳聞例外之基礎：對質詰問程序之實踐

　　相對於前述的羅伯特斯案，克勞佛訴華盛頓案被美國實
務界與學界視為對質條款發展過程中，一則具革命性意義與
震撼效果的判決 [40]。在理解對質條款「並不要求所有的證據
均為可信的，卻強調可信性須經由交互詰問此一特定的方式
獲得確認 [41]。」後，克勞佛案廢棄了羅伯特斯案所建立之判斷
標準，並重新打造了傳聞證據的容許性標準。依據克勞佛案所
新建立之容許性標準，傳聞證據可區分為二大類型：證明性
（testimonial）傳聞與非證明性（non-testimonial）傳聞 [42]；在

[39] Id., at 65, note 7.
[40] See People v. Cage, 15 Cal. Rptr. 3d 846, 851 (Cal. Ct. App. 2004); United States v. Manfre, 368 F. 3d 832, 833 (8th Cir. 2004); Also see Neil P. Cohen, et al., Crawford v. Washington: Confrontation Revolution, 40 Tenn. B. J. 22(2004).
[41] See Crawford v. Washington, 124 S Ct. 1354, 1370 (2004). (the Confrontation Clause "commands not that the evidence be reliable, but that reliability be assessed in a particular manner by testing in the crucible of cross-examination")
[42] 在我國，亦有將 testimonial statement 譯為口供式供述證據，而將 non-testimonial statement 譯為非口供式供述證據，參閱吳巡龍，對質詰問權合憲限制與違憲限制的分際－評最高法院 94 年台上字第 812 號判決，月旦法學，第 71 期，頁 257，2005 年 6 月。不過本文卻基於 testimonial statement 係以「所主張之事項為真實」為提出目的，故認「證明性」一詞較能充分表達該判決之意涵。

非證明性傳聞之類型中，制憲者原即提供各州較為彈性之證據法發展空間，就如同羅伯特斯案亦肯認「未基於對質條款賦予被告對審判外陳述者進行交互詰問之證言」具證據能力；而在證明性傳聞的類型中，如同普通法之傳統，憲法第六修正案亦要求證人無法到庭陳述與交互詰問之機會為傳聞證據具證據能力之前提要件[43]，在證明性傳聞之類型中，克勞佛已成為判斷該傳聞是否具備證據能力之標準。此外，官署中立性並不足以作為審判外陳述是否可用於刑事程序中之判斷標準；縱然審判外之陳述是在先前之司法程序中作成，如果被告在該司法程序中無機會對證人進行交互詰問，該審判外陳述亦無證據能力[44]。如果在先前司法程序中所作成之陳述，未經被告交互詰問或是被告根本無機會交互詰問，羅伯特斯案即不再適用。

五、現行我國法制肯認傳聞例外之基礎

在發展的過程中，英美證據規則均承認傳聞例外存在。從羅伯特斯案之說明可知，適當的真實性指標（adequate indicia of reliability），是證人審判外陳述具證據能力之基礎；而適當的真實性指標包含二大類型：「根深蒂固之傳聞例外（firmly rooted hearsay exception）」與「具特別可信性之擔保（particularized guarantees of trustworthiness）」。惟交互詰問本身不

---

[43]　See 124 S Ct., 1370.

[44]　Id., at 1368.

必然具有發現眞實之實際功效，已經交互詰問之供述亦不必然會反映出過去發生的實體之眞實。但因在交互詰問之過程中，非但事實認定者能直接觀察供述者供述時之神情，他造當事人亦可藉由該程序質疑其供述之可信性[45]，從而交互詰問程序之踐行向來即被視爲審判外陳述是否具特別可信性擔保之一項判斷標準，以之作爲認定實體眞實之依據，一直被認爲具有保障被告與維持程序公正之功用。爲保障被告對質詰問權，克勞佛案卻部分推翻了羅伯特斯案之說理，而只承認根深蒂固之傳聞例外爲免除對質詰問程序的唯一基礎。

雖被告的對質詰問權，將因克勞佛案獲得更大的保障。不過，該案是否在我國的刑事訴訟實務亦有適用，並非毫無疑義。基本上，傳聞法則係移植於英美法系之法律制度，其本身並非源自於我國固有的法律傳統。如 James Bradley Thayer 教授於 1898 年所述，「若從普通法證據規則之角度而言，美國的證據法則在排除具高度證明價值證據之規範上是相當獨特的；本質上，類似英語系國家於訴訟法外獨立發展出一套高度精密且複雜證據法則的現象，於非英語系國家的法制中並未曾

---

[45]　參閱吳巡龍，對質詰問權的保障與限制－釋字第 582 號解釋評析，月旦法學雜誌，第 115 期，頁 99，2004 年 12 月。

見 [46]。」；舉例而言，傳聞法則的制定主要是因為未受過法學訓練的陪審員無法適當的評價審判外陳述之證據價值；而品格證據的限制則是因為陪審團通常賦予其過高的證明力，或陪審團易於據與本案無關的非行紀錄形成對被告不適當、不利益的偏見 [47]。縱然現行之美國聯邦證據規則係制定於西元 1975 年，惟在英美法上千前的發展下，關於何種審判外陳述該當根深蒂固之例外而應成為具證據能力之傳聞，自有長久之脈絡可循。但在我國法制下，如何判斷何種審判外之陳述該當根深蒂固之例外，並非易事。一般說來，由於審判只能基於經驗論而非認識論做出裁決，因此各個社會的文化，亦構成如何妥適做出裁決的重要因素 [48]。換言之，縱然某項審判外之陳述於英美等國可能被視為傳聞法則根深蒂固之例外，然而若將該相同的審判外陳述置於我國之社會中，在不同文化傳統與社會環境之衝擊

---

[46] See James Bradley Thayer, A Preliminary Treatise on Evidence at the Common Law, 1-2 (Boston Little Brown, 1898). ("When a man raises his eyes from the common-law system of evidence, he is struck with the fact that our system is radically peculiar. ...a great mass of evidential matter, logically important and probative, is shut out...by an imperative rule, while the same matter is not thus excluded anywhere else. English-speaking countries have what we call a 'Law of Evidence'; but no other country has it; we alone have generated and evolved this large, elaborate, and difficult doctrine.")

[47] See Christopher B. Mueller, et al., Evidence Under the Rules, 1 (New York Aspen Law & Business, 2000).

[48] See Charles R. Nesson, et al., Constitutional Hearsay: Requiring Fundamental Testing and Corroboration Under the Confrontation Clause, 81 Va. L. Rev. 149, 151-2 (1995).

下，其是否仍將被視爲傳聞法則根深蒂固之例外？恐眾說紛紜。

　　此外，雖然在大法官釋字第 384 號與釋字第 582 號等解釋作成後，我國之學說與實務均已肯認「對質詰問權」是被告基於憲法所得享有的基本權利。不過其內涵是否與美國刑事訴訟程序之要求：「證人審判外陳述之可信性須經由交互詰問此一特定的方式獲得確認」完全相同，其實並不明確。基本上，相較於可作爲美國的權利法案何以會條列對質條款於其中，並限制傳聞證據適用基礎[49]之瓦特瑞雷將軍（Sir Walter Raleigh）乙案[50]，從大法官釋字第 384 號解釋開始所承認之對質詰問權，實則在我國法制上並不具任何歷史之淵源。因此，倘欲如克勞佛案般，以立憲者之意圖，作爲我國憲法亦如美國憲法般，要求在我國刑事訴訟程序上，「證人審判外陳述之可信性須經由交互詰問此一特定的方式獲得確認」，非但有些牽強，亦與外國法制在繼受傳聞法則時，據以承認傳聞例外之基礎有異[51]。從而，即便在大法官釋字第 582 號解釋：「憲法第 16 條

---

[49] See Kenneth J. Graham, The Right to Confrontation and the Hearsay Rule: Sir Walter Raleigh Loses Another One, 8 Crim. L. Bull. 99, 100 (1972); see also Graham C. Lilly, Notes on the Confrontation Clause and Ohio v. Roberts, 36 U. Fla. L. Rev. 207, 209 (1984).關於本案之中文文獻，參閱王兆鵬，對質詰問權與強制取證權，收錄於氏著，刑事被告的憲法權利，頁 146，翰蘆圖書出版有限公司，1999 年 3 月。

[50] See 399 U.S. 149, 156-7, n. 10 (1970).

[51] 關於日本法承認傳聞例外之理由可參閱（日）三井誠著，陳運財譯，起訴狀一本主義與傳聞法則，律師雜誌第 232 期，頁 76。1999 年 1 月。

保障人民之訴訟權，就刑事被告而言，包含其在訴訟上應享有充分之防禦權。刑事被告詰問證人之權利，即屬該等權利之一，且屬憲法第 8 第 1 項規定『非由法院依法定程序不得審問處罰』之正當法律程序所保障之權利。爲確保被告對證人之詰問權，證人於審判中，應依法定程序，到場具結陳述，並接受被告之詰問，其陳述始得作爲認定被告犯罪事實之判斷依據。」之說明下，克勞佛案亦不當然成爲我國傳聞例外之基準。從比較法的觀點來說，縱然我國之傳聞法則不採美國克勞佛案之立場，而擴及承認根深蒂固例外以外之審判外陳述亦具有證據能力，尚不至於出現違反立憲者意圖之批評。而以具眞實性擔保，而非以符合根深蒂固例外，作爲審判外陳述具證據能力之要件之規定，如現行刑事訴訟法第 159 條之 2 至第 159 條之 4 等規定，亦不致直接有違憲法對質詰問權之保障。

事實上，由於我國現行之刑事訴訟架構係以「改良式當事人進行主義」爲主軸，而非如美國之刑事訴訟程序係以絕對的當事人進行主義爲核心，關於證據之推敲，原不以必經當事人主導或進行爲其前提要件。從而，如允許審判外之陳述具證據能力而致當事人之一方無從於審判中對之進行交互詰問，固然有違美國法上被告對質詰問權與當事人進行訴訟模式之疑慮，不過，在我國對質詰問權之內涵不完全等同於美國法「以進行交互詰問此一特定訴訟程序作爲審判外陳述取得證據能力的原則」之前提下，這樣的實務操作並不會違反我國所遵循之訴訟模式。當然，如林永謀大法官所言，若「在採證上，若漫無限

制之容許傳聞，實易使法官以毫無根據之資料作爲裁判之基礎，而流於率斷[52]」，即便在羅伯特斯案之基礎上，亦不代表法院得恣意地容許傳聞證據，若其基於適當的眞實性指標而容許傳聞證據時，應要求法官在判決書中說明該審判外之陳述如何具特別可信性之擔保。因此，本文認爲克勞佛案所建立關於判斷審判外陳述是否具證據能力之標準，於我國並不適用；相對地，羅伯特斯案所建立之眞實性標準，較符合我國所採之刑事訴訟模式與實際上之需要。

六、傳聞法則在兩岸刑事犯罪處理上可能引起之爭議即其解決之建議

由於現行大陸地區的刑事訴訟制度並未採用傳聞法則，因此關於傳聞法則在刑事訴追程序中所可能導致的追訴障礙，自應限於發生在台灣地區的刑事訴訟程序，也就是說，發生在大陸地區的審判程序，不在本文討論的範圍之內。不論在前述「（1）台胞在大陸地區加害於陸胞；（2）台胞在大陸地區受害於陸胞；（3）台胞在大陸地區加／受害於台胞；（4）陸胞在台灣地區加／受害於陸胞；（5）陸胞在台灣地區加害於台胞；與；（6）陸胞在台灣地區受害於台胞」中哪一種犯罪侵害之型態，也不論犯罪發生地在大陸地區或台灣地區，一旦被害人或

---

[52] 參閱林永謀，傳聞證據（上），司法周刊，第 1162 期，第二版，2004 年 12 月 3 日。

證人無法在台灣地區的法院出庭接受刑事訴追，其先前所為之陳述是否具有證據能力，即出現傳聞法則是否適用之問題。至於被告無法到庭應訊受審乙事，事涉該刑事案件究應如何繼續進行或是暫時停止刑事訴訟程序，雖被告未到庭而無從對質詰問證人所引發之問題近於傳聞法則之規範目的，惟鑒於傳聞法則旨在探討被告以外之人在審判外之陳述是否有證據能力，故關於被告未到庭應訊受審乙事，不在本文探討之列。

　　關於兩岸刑事案件所可能遭遇之傳聞疑義，不外可以分為以下幾種類型：（Ａ）台胞在大陸地區加害於陸胞而陸胞向大陸地區之公安單位提出告訴，此時陸胞在公安單位之指控是否在我方之審判程序中有證據能力？（Ｂ）台胞在大陸地區加/受害於台胞，若加害之台胞已返台而受害之台胞未返台，此時受害之台胞在公安單位之指控是否在我方之審判程序中有證據能力？（Ｃ）陸胞在台灣地區加/受害於陸胞，若受害之陸胞已返回大陸地區而加害之陸胞被扣留，此時受害之陸胞在我方檢警單位之指控是否在我方之審判程序中有證據能力？（Ｄ）陸胞在台灣地區受害於台胞，若受害之陸胞已返回大陸地區，此時受害之陸胞在我方檢警單位之指控是否在我方之審判程序中有證據能力？依現行刑事訴訟法第159條第1項之規定：「被告以外之人於審判外之言詞或書面陳述，除法律有規定者外，不得作為證據。」，原則上只有在符合同法第159條之1至之5的情況下，被告以外之人於審判外之言詞或書面陳述，才可作為證據。關於前述不能到庭之證人在台灣地區或大陸地區的刑事指控（筆

錄），是否具備證據能力之問題，依該法第 159 條之 1：「被告以外之人於審判外向法官所爲之陳述，得爲證據。（第 1 項）被告以外之人於偵查中向檢察官所爲之陳述，除顯有不可信之情況者外，得爲證據。（第 2 項）」之規定，只要係在法官或檢察官面前所爲之陳述，其審判外之指控原則上即具備證據能力[53]。不過，當審判外之陳述非於法官或檢察官面前作成，而該證人於陳述後卻無法出庭證述時，除非出現同法第 159 條之 2 所定嗣後另於審判中陳述[54]、同法第 159 條之 3 所定之情事[55]、

---

[53] 其修訂理由為：「…二、被告以外之人（含共同被告、共犯、被害人、證人等）於法官面前所爲之陳述（含書面及言詞），因其陳述係在法官面前爲之，故不問係其他刑事案件之準備程序、審判期日或民事事件或其他訴訟程序之陳述，均係在任意陳述之信用性已受確定保障之情況下所爲，因此該等陳述應得作爲證據。三、檢察官職司追訴犯罪，必須對於被告之犯罪事實負舉證之責。就審判程序之訴訟構造言，檢察官係屬與被告相對立之當事人一方（參照本法第 3 條），是故偵查中對被告以外之人所爲之偵查筆錄，或被告以外之人向檢察官所提之書面陳述，性質上均屬傳聞證據，且常爲認定被告有罪之證據，自理論上言，如未予被告反對詰問、適當辯解之機會，一律准其爲證據，似與當事人進行主義之精神不無扞格之處，對被告之防禦權亦有所妨礙；然而現階段刑事訴訟法規定檢察官代表國家偵查犯罪、實施公訴，依法其有訊問被告、證人及鑑定人之權，證人、鑑定人且須具結，而實務運作時，偵查中檢察官向被告以外之人所取得之陳述，原則上均能遵守法律規定，不致違法取供，其可信性極高，爲兼顧理論與實務，爰於第 2 項明定被告以外之人於偵查中向檢察官所爲陳述，除顯有不可信之情況者外，得爲證據。」。

[54] 刑事訴訟法第 159-2 條：「被告以外之人於檢察事務官、司法警察官或司法警察調查中所爲之陳述，與審判中不符時，其先前之陳述具有較可信之特別情況，且爲證明犯罪事實存否所必要者，得爲證據。」。

[55] 刑事訴訟法第 159-3 條：「被告以外之人於審判中有下列情形之一，其於檢察事務官、司法警察官或司法警察調查中所爲之陳述，經證明具有可信之特別情況，且爲證明犯罪事實之存否所必要者，得爲證據：一、死亡者。二、身心障礙致記憶喪失或無法陳述者。三、滯留國外或所在不明而無法傳喚或傳喚不到者。四、到庭後無正當理由拒絕陳述者。」。

或符合同法第 159 條之 4 規定之文書 [56]，原則上陸胞審判外證述並不具備證據能力。簡單來說，關於陸胞於審判外所爲之陳述（不論在台灣地區或大陸地區作成）是否具備證據能力乙事，將因陳述之場合與當事人間是否合意 [57] 而有不同之效果。

基本上，若該陸胞審判外之陳述係由我方司法單位作成，

---

[56] 刑事訴訟法第 159-4 條：「除前三條之情形外，下列文書亦得爲證據：一、除顯有不可信之情況外，公務員職務上製作之紀錄文書、證明文書。二、除顯有不可信之情況外，從事業務之人於業務上或通常業務過程所須製作之紀錄文書、證明文書。三、除前二款之情形外，其他於可信之特別情況下所製作之文書。」。

[57] 刑事訴訟法第 159-5 條：「被告以外之人於審判外之陳述，雖不符前四條之規定，而經當事人於審判程序同意作爲證據，法院審酌該言詞陳述或書面陳述作成時之情況，認爲適當者，亦得爲證據。（第 1 項）當事人、代理人或辯護人於法院調查證據時，知有第 159 條第 1 項不得爲證據之情形，而未於言詞辯論終結前聲明異議者，視爲有前項之同意。（第 2 項）」，其修訂理由爲：「…二、按傳聞法則的重要理論依據，在於傳聞證據未經當事人之反對詰問予以核實，乃予排斥。惟若當事人已放棄原供述人之反對詰問權，於審判程序表明同意該等傳聞證據可作爲證據，基於證據資料愈豐富，愈有助於真實發見之理念，此時，法院自可承認該傳聞證據之證據能力。三、由於此種同意制度係根據當事人的意思而使本來不得作爲證據之傳聞證據成爲證據之制度，乃確認當事人對傳聞證據有處分權之制度。爲貫徹本次修法加重當事人進行主義色彩之精神，固宜採納此一同意制度，作爲配套措施。然而吾國尚非採澈底之當事人進行主義，故而法院如認該傳聞證據欠缺適當性時（例如證明力明顯過低或該證據係違法取得），仍可予以斟酌而不採爲證據，爰參考日本刑事訴訟法第 326 條第 1 項之規定，增設本條第 1 項。四、至於當事人、代理人或辯護人於調查證據時，知有本法第 159 條第 1 項不得爲證據之情形，卻表示『對於證據調查無異議』、『沒有意見』等意思，而未於言詞辯論終結前聲明異議者（Without Objection），爲求與前開同意制度理論一貫，且強化言詞辯論主義，確保訴訟當事人到庭實行攻擊防禦，使訴訟程序進行、順暢，應視爲已有將該等傳聞證據採爲證據之同意，爰參考日本實務之見解，增訂本條第 2 項。」。

在如前述（C）（D）之情形中，依刑事訴訟法第 159 條之 3 第 3 款之規定，該陸胞於我方警訊中之陳述或可因「滯留國外或所在不明而無法傳喚或傳喚不到者」符合傳聞例外而取得證據能力。然而在前述（A）（B）之情形中，陸胞在大陸公安前所作之指控是否在我方之刑事訴追程序中，亦取得證據能力，即不若前述（C）（D）那樣明確地於法有據。

由於大陸地區的公安人員不具備我國刑事訴訟法第 159 條之 3 所規定之檢察事務官、司法警察官或司法警察等身分，因此除非兩岸間明文協議承認對方之司法警察人員在己方亦具有司法警察人員之身分，否則刑事訴訟法第 159 條之 3 所規定之傳聞例外，將不適用於在大陸公安前所作陳述之情形。從而，只有刑事訴訟法第 159 條之 4 之規定，有可能使得在大陸公安前所作陳述取得證據能力。基本上，刑事訴訟法第 159 條之 4 本身，乃針對審判外所作成之書面，所爲傳聞例外之規定。值得一提的是，本條係針對文書所做之規定，若審判外之陳述非以文書之形式作成，本條之規定即無適用。與我國刑事訴訟法第 159 條之 3 不同，我國刑事訴訟法第 159 條之 4 並不以證人能否到庭爲要件，鑑於聯邦證據規則於立法時認爲聯邦證據規則 803 所承認之傳聞例外，其可信度應較聯邦證據規則 804 所承認之傳聞例外爲高[58]，似可據此主張我國刑事訴訟法第 159

---

[58] See Authur Best, Evidence, 102 (New York Aspen Law & Business, 2001).

條之 4 所指之審判外陳述，較之我國刑事訴訟法第 159 條之 3 所指之審判外陳述，是較具有可信度的。一般而言，我國刑事訴訟法第 159 條之 4 所規定之傳聞例外係基於其內容之高度可信性；不過如我國刑事訴訟法第 159 條之 3 所示，當使用來自審判外陳述資訊之必要性成為承認傳聞例外之唯一基礎時，只有在該傳聞陳述之陳述者不能到庭時，該審判外陳述之證據能力才可被承認[59]。

　　我國刑事訴訟法第 159 條之 4 創造了三種類型的傳聞例外，通常而言，未負擔犯罪偵防任務之公務員依其職權所製作之文書，因與其責任、信譽攸關，若有錯誤、虛偽等情事，公務員可能因此負擔刑事及行政責任，從而該等文書被視為具備高度之正確性；且因該等文書經常處於可受公開檢查（Public Inspection）之狀態，縱有錯誤，亦因其甚易發現而易予及時糾正，是以，除顯有不可信之情況外，其內容真實性之保障極高。而從事業務之人在業務上或通常業務過程所製作之紀錄文書、證明文書，因係於通常業務過程不間斷、有規律而準確之記載，因有會計人員或記帳人員等經常校對其正確性，且大部分紀錄係完成於業務終了前後，無預見日後可能會被提供作為證據之偽造動機，其虛偽之可能性甚小，何況如讓製作者以口頭方式於法庭上再重現過去之事實或數據亦有事實上之困難，因此認為該類文書本身亦具有一定程度之不可代替性，除非該

---

[59]　Id.

等紀錄文書或證明文書有顯然不可信之情況，否則有承認其為
證據之必要。除前 2 款之情形外，我國刑事訴訟法第 159 條之
4 第 3 款亦制定了補遺條款（residual provision），依此規定，
與公務員職務上製作之文書及業務文件具有同等程度可信性之
文書，例如官方公報、統計表、體育紀錄、學術論文、家譜
等，基於前開相同之理由，亦應准其有證據能力。

　　類似於我國刑事訴訟法第 159 條之 4 第 3 款之規定，聯邦
證據規則 807 亦有所謂的補遺條款（a residual exception）作為
承認傳問例外之概括依據[60]。依此規定，聯邦證據規則 807 係
以該審判外之陳述就系爭爭議之釐清，具有較其他可能獲得之
證據，更具證明價值為要件，故只有在無法取得比此種審判外
之陳述更具證據價值之證據時，才有此種傳聞例外之適用[61]。
某種程度來說，承認此種傳聞例外系為了使傳聞法則更具彈

---

[60] FRE 807 provides: "A statement no specifically covered by Rule 803 or 804, but having equivalent circumstantial guarantees of trustworthiness, is not excluded by the hearsay rule if the court determines that (A) the statement is offered as evidence of a material fact; (B) the statement is more probative on the point for which it is offered than any other evidence which the proponent can procure through reasonable efforts; and (C) the general purposes of these rules and the interests of justice will best be served by admission of the statement into evidence. However, a statement may not be admitted under this exception unless the proponent of it makes known to the adverse party sufficiently in advance of the trial or hearing to provide the adverse party with a fair opportunity to prepare to meet it, the proponent's intention to offer the statement and the particulars of it, including the name and address of the declarant."

[61] See G. Michael Fenner, supra note 45, 347.

性，蓋普通法原即允許法官在必要時有權創造可資適用之傳聞例外[62]。惟若提出此種審判外陳述之一方未事先對他造表明其提出此種傳聞例外之意圖並事先通知，此種傳聞例外即不能適用[63]。基本上，適用此種傳聞例外有五個要件：一、該審判外之陳述具可信性；二、該審判外之陳述具關聯性；三、該審判外之陳述具較高之證明價值；四、使用該審判外之陳述較符合正義之要求與五、提出此種審判外陳述之一方未事先對他造表明其提出此種傳聞例外之意圖並事先通知[64]。雖我國刑事訴訟法第 159 條之 4 第 3 款並未明文類此之前提要件，惟其於適用上，似仍應以聯邦證據規則 807 之規定作為是否適用我國刑事訴訟法第 159 條之 4 第 3 款之前提要件，似較妥適。

　　由於沿革上刑事訴訟法第 159 條之 4 乃以未負擔犯罪偵防任務公務員所作之文書為適用之前提，縱然承認大陸地區的公安人員具有類似我方司法警察的身分，前述在大陸地區的公安人員面前所為之審判外陳述，亦將因公安人員負有犯罪偵防任務而無刑事訴訟法第 159 條之 4 之適用可能。從而除非此時要求法院必須依職權發現真實（即依職權調查在大陸地區的公安人員面前所為之審判外陳述是否為真實），或是當兩岸刑事糾紛發生時，發現大陸地區被害人（包含陸胞與台胞）在大陸地區所作的警訊筆錄或是陸胞在台灣地區所作的警訊筆錄具有特

---

[62] Id.
[63] Id., at 345.
[64] Id., at 346.

別的眞實性擔保，否則在傳聞法則之限制下，在大陸地區的公安人員面前所爲之審判外陳述，將因其無法符合我方傳聞例外之規定，而在我方刑事訴追程序上，不具證據能力。而這樣的論點，難免導致在我方法院進行的刑事訴訟程序[65]，不得不因在大陸地區的公安人員面前所爲之審判外陳述無證據能力而不採用該證詞之內容，而以無罪判決收場。此時對於身在大陸地區之被害人而言，我國法制即未提供妥適的保障；蓋於一事不再理之原則下，既然在大陸地區所提之告訴，該被告已受無罪判決，縱其後被害人或相關證人進入台灣地區，並得接受被告對質詰問，該已受無罪判決之被告亦無需再因同一事件而接受刑事調查審問，法院亦不得再對該案件進行實質審理。此種結果將對身處台灣地區之被告產生過度保護，因而產生對相關被害人（不論是陸胞或台胞）保護不周之結果，長久以往，此種實務之操作恐將造成兩岸民怨之累積；果如此，實有悖兩岸交流旨在促進兩岸人民溝通互動之初衷，而有加以改弦更張之必要。故除兩岸犯罪之處理果應朝向前述「具體協商和劃分涉及兩岸具體犯罪類型之管轄權案件應由那一方管轄後，即應排除地方之干涉，一經一方審理之案件，他方即不得行使管轄權，而有一事不再理原則適用。[66]」之方向發展外，並應本諸兩岸

---

[65]　此即前述（A）台胞在大陸地區加害於陸胞而陸胞向大陸地區之公安單位提出告訴與（B）台胞在大陸地區加/受害於台胞，若加害之台胞已返台而受害之台胞未返台，此時受害之台胞在公安單位指控加害者之情形。

[66]　參閱周成瑜，同註23。

刑事案件發生之機率明顯高於我國與其他國家間國際犯罪事件之現實，於將來制定兩岸司法互助協定之時，審慎考慮傳聞法則在兩岸刑事犯罪之處理程序中所可能產生之影響，並提出有效的對策。舉例來說，針對某些特定型態的犯罪事件，可約定由大陸政府將相關人證或物證送交台灣法庭地，以保障在台被告之對質詰問權；或是在法庭便利的前提下，將某些情形的被告引渡或遣送至犯罪發生地之管轄法院處理，都將有助於個案司法正義之實現。當然，採取前述做法前，必須先確定相關經費是否足夠因應因此所產生之費用，以及應由何方負擔此一費用，此外兩岸之司法審判水平是否已趨於接近之程度，也是另外一個重要的焦點。否則，縱冒然達成相關協議，一但兩岸人民相互間仍不信任對方法院所作的判決，形式上的協議也無助於兩岸犯罪應如何訴追此一問題之解決。

伍、結　論

隨著兩岸人民間的往來日趨密切，兩岸犯罪所引發的問題也不免將與日俱增。對於在大陸地區的犯罪，雖依兩岸人民關係條例第 75 條及前述最高法院 89 年台非字第 94 號判決等實務見解，我方法院享有審判權與管轄權，不過這樣的主張，在兩岸均採憲法一中的架構下，是否將牴觸一事不再理之原則，在法理上恐生疑義。本文分別自兩德統一前之法制概況與美國聯

邦制度發展之觀點出發，探討一事不再理原則（或謂雙重危險禁止法則）在兩岸刑事案件處理中，所可能導致的合憲性爭議，並基於比較法之觀點進一步指出，在現行憲法秩序的約制下，現行兩岸法制關於兩岸犯罪之相關處理規定（亦即兩岸法制均將發生在對方領域內之犯罪比照在領域外犯罪，並未排除對同一案件之管轄權），似乎必須在前提上承認兩岸相互間存在或是處於一種類似美國聯邦制度之關係，否則在欠缺國際上存在將領域內之犯罪比照在領域外犯罪處理之規範模式下，現行將發生在對方領域內之犯罪比照在領域外犯罪之規範模式，不啻暗示著兩岸間在政治上處於「（特殊的？）國與國間的關係」；惟若如此解釋，勢必將悖於兩岸現行一中憲法之精神而導致該類觀點違憲之爭議。從而，在一中憲法之架構下，本文建議：兩岸犯罪之處理理應朝向「尊重現實擱置國家主權問題，先由互相承認對方之實際司法管轄範圍，並以此作為基礎，再進一步具體協商和劃分涉及兩岸具體犯罪類型之管轄權案件應由那一方管轄後，即應排除地方之干涉，一經一方審理之案件，他方即不得行使管轄權，而有一事不再理原則適用。[67]」之方向發展較為妥適。

此外，由於我國現行刑事訴訟制度已採改良式當事人進行主義之架構，並引進美式傳聞法則，因此被告以外之人於審判外之陳述，除非符合傳聞例外之規定，否則原則上不具備證據

---

[67]　同前註。

能力。本文除介紹美國法制上相關的傳聞發展外，並認為我方
傳聞例外之肯認應以該審判外陳述具有特別真實性擔保為前提
要件。在此前提下，除非可認發生在大陸地區之兩岸刑事案
件，或是陸胞來台觀光旅遊發生刑事糾紛時，大陸地區被害人
（包含陸胞與台胞）在大陸地區所作的警訊筆錄或是陸胞在台
灣地區所作的警訊筆錄具有特別的真實性擔保，否則該等陳述
原則上將因傳聞法則之規定而不具證據能力；此時在台灣地區
之被告似將因傳聞法則之規定而不當地額外受惠（蓋台灣地區
之被告將因作成於大陸地區之供述證據不被採納而獲判無
罪），並在台灣地區受到一事不再理之保障。雖然傳聞法則之
立法目的旨在保障被告之對質詰問權，而逕予作成於大陸地區
之警訊筆錄具有證據能力將有害於台灣地區被告之對質詰問
權，然而鑑於兩岸地區人民往來之頻繁程度明顯高於我方人民
與外國人民間之往來交流，面對類此源自兩岸交通障礙（例如
大陸地區之被害人或證人不易或無資力來台作證並接受被告對
質詰問）所產生之傳聞障礙，在我方之刑事訴訟程序上理應提
出更為實際與有效的防治之道，以避免兩岸人民間之互信因頻
繁方生的兩岸犯罪事件而受到侵蝕。有鑑於此，本文主張：為
落實台灣地區被告之對質詰問權，我方與大陸方面於將來制定
兩岸司法互助協定時，應針對某些特定型態的犯罪事件或規定
在一定之條件下，約定由大陸政府將相關人證或物證送交台灣
法庭地，以保障在台被告之對質詰問權；或是在法庭便利的前
提下，將某些情形的被告引渡或遣送至犯罪發生地之管轄法院

處理，以兼顧被告與被害人雙方之權益，並實現個案中之司法正義。

　　以上所述，乃針對兩岸犯罪發生時，依據兩岸現行法制架構在我方所可能引發之刑事訴訟障礙所爲之討論，爲求兩岸間之交流實質且正向，相關議題尚有待兩岸有關單位審愼研擬評估，妥適處理。惟著者學殖未深，疏漏之處，所在難免，僅以一己之思，不湍淺陋，拋磚引玉，並祈有識之士，一同爲解決兩岸犯罪之相關刑事訴訟障礙而努力。（本文前身曾發表於95.12 眞理大學財經法律學系「兩岸旅遊法律與租稅」學術研討會，經修正後收錄於本書）

7 非強制辯護案件被告審判中辯護權之保障

壹、前　言

　　刑事訴訟法第 31 條第 1 項明文規定強制辯護的範圍，依其規定：「最輕本刑爲三年以上有期徒刑之案件」、「高等法院管轄第一審之案件」或「被告因智能障礙無法爲完全陳述之案件」，若未經被告於審判中選任辯護人者，審判長應指定公設辯護人或律師爲其辯護。蓋上述強制辯護案件，或因案情煩雜、或因智能障礙者未能在訴訟程序中完全陳述，如被告未能充分獲得專業律師的協助，則訴訟上武器平等與公平法院之目標，即難達成；而交互詰問等複雜的法庭活動，亦難期於未獲專業律師協助時得以落實[1]。而無資力或低收入戶被告，雖依同

---

[1]　考量到被告於訴訟地位上並不平等，需要強而有力之辯護人保障其權益，實現刑事訴訟之正當程序，參考日本刑事訴訟法「國選辯護人」制度精神及我國現行公設辯護人條例、律師法相關規定，採行強制辯護案件雙軌制，於原來之刑事訴訟法第 31 條第 1 項增加法院得指定律師為被告辯護，以及低收入戶被告亦得聲請法院指定公設辯護人或律師之規定。律師接受法院指定為辯護人，並非基於契約關係，而係基於律師社會責任與法律規定，此等辯護案件通常稱之為義務辯護案件。參考司法院，義務辯護專區，available at: http://www.judicial.gov.tw/work/work02/work02-30.asp (last visited, Feb. 19th, 2008).

條項後段、法律扶助法第 13 條與第 14 條等規定，於其未選任辯護人而聲請指定、或其他審判長認有必要時，審判長亦應選任辯護人為其辯護，以保障其受律師協助之權利[2]。然而不可諱言的，在前述規範下，的確存在某些審判長不須指定公設辯護人或律師為其辯護，亦可繼續進行審判程序之非強制辯護案件，蓋依刑事訴訟法第 31 條第 2 項：「前項案件選任辯護人於審判期日無正當理由而不到庭者，審判長得指定公設辯護人。」之規定，倘非強制辯護案件之選任辯護人於審判期日無正當理由而不到庭，縱審判長未指定公設辯護人為其辯護，該案件之審理程序亦得繼續進行；而被告縱未於該類案件中選任辯護人，所進行之審判程序亦未違背法令。鑒於辯護制度屬於憲法上訴訟權保障之重要內涵已為大法官釋字第 396 號解釋所肯認[3]，而其內涵除了「被告為自己辯護」之權利外，更包括

---

[2]　王兆鵬教授稱被告享有受律師協助的權利為「憲法上之律師權」，關於律師權之理論基礎（如當事人對等、程序公平性以及保護被告利益），參閱王兆鵬，美國刑事訴訟法，頁 424-6，元照出版公司，2007 年 9 月，二版 1 刷。

[3]　參照釋字第 396 號解釋：「憲法第 16 條規定人民有訴訟之權，惟保障訴訟權之審級制度，得由立法機關視各種訴訟案件之性質定之。公務員因公法上職務關係而有違法失職之行為，應受懲戒處分者，憲法明定為司法權之範圍；公務員懲戒委員會對懲戒案件之議決，公務員懲戒法雖規定為終局之決定，然尚不得因其未設通常上訴救濟制度，即謂與憲法第 16 條有所違背。懲戒處分影響憲法上人民服公職之權利，懲戒機關之成員既屬憲法上之法官，依憲法第 82 條及本院釋字第 162 號解釋意旨，則其機關應採法院之體制，且懲戒案件之審議，亦應本正當法律程序之原則，對被付懲戒人予以充分之程序保障，例如採取直接審理、言詞辯論、對審及辯護制度，並予以被付懲戒人最後陳述之機會等，以貫徹憲法第 16 條保障人民訴訟權之本旨。有關機關應就公務員懲戒機關之組織、名稱與懲戒程序，併予檢討修正。」。

「被告委任法律專家（辯護人）爲其辯護」之權利[4]，從而律師權應定位爲辯護權之下位階權利。倘若被告在非強制辯護案件中實際上未選任辯護人，則於其審判程序中能爲被告辯護者，恐怕就只有被告自己而已了。值得注意的，在被告爲自己辯護的場合中，究竟被告有無足夠之專業能力爲自己辯護？有無能力進行有效的交互詰問？被告如何自我防禦方能達成訴訟上武器平等與公平法院之目標？法院是否有義務協助被告充實防禦能力？若有，其義務範圍爲何？未委任專業辯護人或未提供專業的辯護協助是否違反憲法所保障的辯護制度（辯護權）？諸如此類問題，均將出現在非強制辯護案件且未委任辯護人之審判程序中。因此，關於辯護權（訴訟防禦權）究應如何行使或實現始滿足憲法保障辯護權之初衷，即爲十分重要之課題。

貳、兩造對抗程序與受律師協助防禦的起源

佐登凡凱索教授（Professor Gordon Van Kessel）曾針對歐

---

[4] 通常指律師，惟依依據刑事訴訟法第 29 條但書之規定，在審判中經審判長許可，得選任非律師爲辯護人。因此我國法制下的辯護制度，並未採取律師壟斷的立法例。明確規定犯罪嫌疑人、被告人只能由執業律師擔任辯護人的國家和地區主要有：英國、美國、中國香港、澳大利亞、新加坡、丹麥、義大利等。參閱青竹山人，刑事辯護權的歸屬與刑事司法公正，http://www.juree.net/ShowArticle.asp? ArticleID=105 (last visited, Feb. 19th, 2008).

美法律體系間之差異,提出以下的看法:「強調律師間競賽、
強調保護人民對抗刑事追訴程序之規則與強調廣泛地使用由平
民組成陪審團的美式兩造對抗結構,係根源於對社會與政治制
度具有強烈影響、且屬於美式性格中自然成分的個人主義、人
民主義與多元種族主義。根本上由於美國人民普遍反對威權,
並對政府權力存有恐懼與不信任的看法,個人主義的發展阻礙
了朝向非兩造對抗結構方向的改革。這些基本態度引領美國人
民建立起以強勢律師參與以及平民陪審制為內涵、並以保護人
民對抗政府部門權威為核心的制度[5]。」。從以上這樣的描述
中,不難發現兩造對抗程序(adversarial process)與律師辯護
制度在美國刑事訴訟制度的重要性。一般而言,美國的刑事訴
訟制度兼具兩造模式(adversarial)與控訴模式(accusatorial)
的特徵在內。控訴模式要求與被告對立之政府部門負擔舉證責
任[6],兩造模式要求控訴者與被告形成互相對立的當事人兩造,

---

[5]   See Gordon Van Kessel, Adversarial Excesses in the American Criminal Trial,
      67 Notre Dame L. Rev. 403, 505 (1992)("The American style adversarial
      system---with its emphasis on the contest between the lawyers for the individual
      and for the state, rules designed to shield the accused from the process, and
      extensive use of the lay jury---has its roots in the individualism, populism, and
      pluralism that are natural ingredients of our character and that strongly influence
      our view of the proper structure and role of social and political institutions. A
      fundamental aspect of our individualism that stands in the way of reforms
      embracing nonadversary approaches is our antipathy toward authority: in
      particular, our fear and distrust of governmental power. These attitudes lead us to
      establish mechanisms--such as strong lawyers and the lay jury--that shield the
      individual from the authority of state institutions.").

[6]   See Murphy v. Waterfront Commission, 378 U.S. 52, 55 (1964).

二者雖不相同，彼此間卻具有互補之功能[7]。

　　現今兼具兩造模式與控訴模式特徵之美國刑事訴訟制度，實則源自中世紀英國採行之訴訟程序[8]。從歷史發展的角度而言，兩造模式的審判構造是一直到陪審團從證人的角色轉變為中立裁判者後才開始逐漸成型的[9]，蓋因此時控辯當事人雙方始須受到以確保審判程序公正進行為目的之法庭規則拘束。而在審判中遵守法定訴訟程序便是兩造模式的主要標誌，也是兩造模式與糾問模式間的重要差別[10]。徵諸實際，一開始並沒有人試圖計劃去建立一套兼具兩造模式與控訴模式特徵的刑事訴訟制度。即便是 18 世紀的英國法律工作者，也未曾自覺他們正在創造一套歷史上所未曾出現過的審判機制[11]。從中世紀開始，英國的法官與陪審員均有權主動發問[12]，而這樣糾問式的訴訟

---

[7]　See William Burnham, Introduction to the Law and Legal System of the United States, 259 (West Group, 1999).

[8]　此處之英國法制不包含源自大陸法系之蘇格蘭法 (the Scottish legal system)，而主要係指英格蘭法與威爾斯之法律傳統 (the legal traditions and developments of England and Wales)。關於英格蘭法的沿革發展，參閱: http://www.scotcourt. gov.uk (last visited, Feb. 21st, 2008).

[9]　關於陪審團司法功能之發展，請參閱易延友，陪審團審判與對抗式訴訟，頁 59-64，三民書局，2004 年 11 月初版 1 刷。

[10]　In a sense "an inquisitorial style is less likely to serve as a check on government powers, the role American Courts play in our system of checks and balances." See TEACHERS' RESOURCE GUIDE for LAW & JUSTICE, available at: http://www.19thcircuitcourt.state.il.us/bkshelf/resource/origin.htm (last visited, Feb. 24th, 2008).

[11]　See Stephan Landsman, The Rise of the Contentious Spirit: Adversary Procedure in Eighteenth Century England, 75 Cornell L. Rev. 497, 502 (1990).

[12]　See G. W. Keeton, Lord Chancellor Jeffreys and the Stuart Cause, 21, 22 (1965).

模式也一直持續到 18 世紀中葉兩造對立的訴訟模式開始出現為
止。某種程度來說，兩造對立的訴訟模式可視為對 18 世紀初期
廣遭濫用的專業捕竊制度（professional thief catchers）的一種
反省。

　　在公元 1692 年的時候，英國國會制定了該國的第一部刑事
法。在該法規範下，凡逮捕特定類型重罪（如公路搶劫）的犯
罪人，逮捕者便可於被逮者定罪後得到約四十英鎊（在當時是
一筆很大的數目）的獎賞。這個法律最後也促成了專業捕竊制
度的建立[13]。由於專業捕竊者主要是為了獲得經濟上的利益而
逮捕並訴追被告[14]，為能依法從政府部門獲得實質的回饋，他
們便開始扮演著類似今日檢察官般的角色，以證明其所指控的
人是竊盜犯為主要職責。在此基礎上，這些專業的捕竊者也開
始初步地發展出兩造對抗程序的訴訟技巧，以積極地參與指控
程序[15]。而為了得到更多的回饋，有些不肖的專業捕竊者便開
始誣指無辜者為竊盜犯，久而久之，此種攀誣手段逐蔚為風
氣。為防止專業捕竊者濫用其指控權力誣陷無辜，改革的聲浪

---

[13]　在該法制定後約半世紀內，專業捕竊制度的適用範圍，乃擴張至夜間竊賊
　　（burglars）、竊馬賊（horse-thieves）與偽幣製造者（coiners）等犯罪。See
　　Stephan Landsman, supra note 11, 573.

[14]　See Gerald Howson, It takes a Thief: The Life and Times of Johnathan Wild,
　　3-7 (London The Cresset Library, 1987).

[15]　See Stephan Landsman, supra note 11, 573 ("What the OBSP demonstrates
　　about them is that they were wise not only in the ways of the street, but of the
　　courtroom as well.").

逐逐漸出現。所提出的改革主要係針對如何控制並預防專業捕竊者僅爲獲經濟上利益而對無辜者提出捏造的虛僞指控[16]。

　　前述以利益爲導向的專業捕竊實務在某種程度上導致當時的法官與陪審員開始意識到專業捕竊者爲獲不當利益而誣告的現象。爲防止如查爾斯派翠克（Charles Patrick）與威廉密得斯（William Meeds）等違反當時司法正義的案件再次發生，在十七世紀末期，爲防止專業捕竊者爲獲不當利益而誣告，法庭活動也有相應的調整。雖然公正無偏的司法程序是改革專業捕竊制度的主軸，被指控者卻仍被要求與專業捕竊者爭執系爭案件指控之動機是否正當；在無辜被控者越來越多且專業捕竊者訴訟技巧越來越高的情形下，法官甚至開始鼓勵被指控者採用更有力的抗辯，以反駁專業捕竊者的指控，而這也就形成了兩造對抗制度的雛形[17]。在專業捕竊者易於爲獲取高額回饋而濫行誣攀無辜者的實務概況下，改革者乃逐漸提出一連串保護被指控者權利的程序規定。這些程序規定旨在規避所有對專業捕竊制度及其相關法制的批評。透過允許被告挑戰指控者動機的兩

---

[16]　See John H. Langbein, Shaping the Eighteenth-Century Criminal Trial: A View from the Ryder Sources, 50 U. Chi. L. Rev. 1, 113（1983）.

[17]　查爾斯派翠克（Charles Patrick）與威廉密得斯（William Meeds）等被控公路搶劫，然而主要的證據卻只有匿名共犯的指控。由於專業捕竊者可在被指控者被定罪後獲巨額賞金，因此匿名證人往往會被懷疑是捏造出來的。See Stephan Landsman, supra note 10, 578. 此與我國舊檢肅流氓條例時代所常見的由警察扮演秘密證人出庭指控或作證之實務怪象，頗有異曲同工之妙。關於舊檢肅流氓條例所衍生的不公不義，可參閱大法官釋字第 384 號解釋之案例事實。

造對抗模式所構築成的事實認定程序，始足以對被指控者提供必要的程序保護。而這樣的程序也促進了兩造間相互詰問的法庭活動。換言之，專業捕竊制度除了導致兩造對抗模式的成形外，更因該改革需要擅長法庭活動的專業人士協助受指控者滌清罪嫌而加強了在兩造對抗模式的審判程序中使用律師的必要，並促成了律師制度的發展[18]。

雖然普遍認為律師制度開始發展前的糾問模式在犯罪訴追上較有效率[19]，不過受律師協助的權利，在今日早已普遍被接受為被告所得主張之基本人權之一。若自沿革來說，一直到公元 1695 年，英國才開始承認被告有權在叛國（treason）案件中僱用律師為其辯護[20]；而到了西元 1730 年左右，律師制度才真正開始在非政治案件中有了普遍性的發展[21]。律師制度之成形乃奠基於專業捕竊者專業訴訟技巧的累積[22]。惟因十八世紀的法律學者咸認辯護律師的存在有礙於真實發現，況且法官對相關問題的職權詢問已有助於犯罪要件之釐清，並能維持公平的審判程序，從而辯護律師的參與仍因不太需要而相當有限[23]。

---

[18] See Stephan Landsman, supra note 11, 602-3.

[19] See G. W. Keeton, supra note 12, 22.

[20] 參閱王兆鵬，註二書，頁 424。

[21] See John H. Langbein, The Criminal Trial Before the Lawyers, 45 U. Chi. L. Rev. 263, 314 (1978).

[22] See Stephan Landsman, supra note 11, 578.

[23] See Ellen Hochstedler Steury and Nancy Frank, Criminal Court Process, 81 (West, 1996).

儘管如此，所有關於在重罪案件被告（felon）聘用（選任）律師的限制，最終仍在西元 1836 年被取消[24]。雖然十八世紀末期的法院傾向允許被告聘請律師，不過當時受律師協助乙事，尚未被承認具有權利的位階，而且律師在實際上也被禁止參與特定類型的案件[25]。如美國聯邦檢察總長所表示：「在當事人進行主義的對抗制度下，兩造皆必須充分爭執，全力挑戰對方，律師成爲制度成功的關鍵。如被告無資力聘請律師，當事人進行主義制度的功能即不能發揮，此一制度亦將瓦解。要求被告去挑戰、對抗檢察官，但卻因爲被告貧窮而否定其挑戰與對抗的工具（即律師），侵犯公平性及平等性[26]。」可知，當事人進行主義的訴訟模式實爲律師制度發展的重要基石。

參、受律師協助權利在美國的發展

　　由於早在西元 1791 年美國憲法第六修正案即已規定了刑事被告享有受律師協助的權利（the right to counsel）[27]，或因早

---

[24] See Stephan Landsman, supra note 11, 579.

[25] See Ellen Hochstedler Steury et al., supra note 23, 81.

[26] 參閱王兆鵬，註二書，頁 431。

[27] The Sixth Amendment to the United States Constitution states: "In all criminal prosecutions, the accused shall enjoy the right... to have the Assistance of Counsel for his defence."

期聯邦刑事案件數量有限，此項權利在聯邦層次很早便受到立法保障[28]。而因兩造對抗模式的訴訟結構要求控辯雙方均具有高度的訴訟技巧，受律師協助的權利在州的層次在早期也已受到重視；例如在西元 1854 年的韋伯訴霸德（Webb v. Baird）乙案中，印第安納州最高法院便已提到：「在一個文明社會中，不應有任何被告因貧窮未能僱用律師並受律師協助而使得其生命或自由受到危害，任何法院均不應審理此類案件。法院有責任保護貧窮刑事被告受律師協助的基本權利[29]。」。而許多州也在其州憲法、州法律以及判例法中，陸續發展出「刑事被告不應因貧窮而被剝奪受律師協助權利」之法則[30]。因此，貧窮

---

[28] The Sixth Amendment to the United States Constitution states: "In all criminal prosecutions, the accused shall enjoy the right...to have the Assistance of Counsel for his defense." The right to counsel in federal proceedings was well-established by statute early in the country's history, and was reaffirmed by the U. S. Supreme Court in 1938 in Johnson v. Zerbst. Available at: http://www.cae-fpd. org/History.htm (last visited, Feb. 21st, 2008)。The Supreme Court held that the Sixth Amendment required a lawyer to be appointed in all federal criminal cases. See Johnson v. Zerbst, 304 U.S. 458 (1938).

[29] In 1854, the Supreme Court of Indiana in Webb v. Baird held: " It is not to be thought of, in a civilized community, for a moment, that any citizen put in jeopardy of life or liberty should be debarred of counsel because he was too poor to employ such aid. No Court could be respected, or respect itself, to sit and hear such a trial. The defence of the poor in such cases is a duty resting somewhere, which will be at once conceded as essential to the accused, to the Court, and to the public." See 6 Ind. 13, 18.

[30] See Betts v. Brady, 316 U.S. 455, 477 (1942).(And most of the other States have shown their agreement by constitutional provisions, statutes, or established practice judicially approved, which assure that no man shall be deprived of counsel merely because of his poverty.)

被告有權免費獲得律師協助之法則，似已在州的層次開始獲得肯認，雖在 20 世紀中葉前，該法則尚未被各州普遍接受，不過當時大多數州已仰賴律師自發性地爲貧窮的重罪被告提供公益性質的免費法律服務以保障被告受律師協助的權利[31]。這或許是爲何聯邦最高法院在 20 世紀中葉前未能進一步;強制所有的州均落實「對貧窮被告提供免費律師協助」此項憲法權利保障的主要原因。

　　到了西元 1932 年，聯邦最高法院基於正當程序的要求，開始要求在所有死刑案件的審判程序中，只要被告主張受律師協助的權利，州政府均需提供免費的律師協助以符合正當法律程序的要求[32]。雖然十年後聯邦最高法院拒絕全面地將免費受律師協助之權力擴張到所有的州重罪（felony）案件中[33]，然而到了西元 1963 年該見解卻在著名的基甸訴文萊特（Gideon v. Wainwright）乙案中被推翻。基甸案除了肯認貧窮被告在重罪審判程序中有權免費地受到律師的協助，更進一步確認了在所有的刑事案件中，受律師協助的權利對於公平審判與正當法律

---

[31] Well into the 20th century, most states relied on the volunteer pro bono efforts of lawyers to provide defense for poor people accused of even the most serious crimes. While some private programs, such as the New York Legal Aid Society, were active as early as 1896 in providing counsel to needy immigrants, and the first public defender office began operations in Los Angeles in 1914, such services were non-existent outside of the largest cities. Available at: http://www.cae-fpd.org/History.htm (last visited, Feb. 21st, 2008).

[32] See Powell v. Alabama, 287 U.S. 45 (1932).

[33] See Betts v. Brady, 316 U.S. 455 (1942).

程序而言是一個基本的前提；因此，被告一但被起訴，不論貧富、階級或教育，均不應在沒有受律師協助的環境中，被迫在法庭上面對其指控者[34]。其後聯邦最高法院除將免費受律師協助的權利擴張適用到少年事件程序外[35]，更將該權利擴及於所有人身自由受到影響的輕罪（misdemeanor）案件[36]。反面言之，貧窮被告如無律師協助，即不得被科處拘役刑以上之刑及緩刑[37]。

　　貧窮被告除了在審判程序中有免費受律師協助之權力外，聯邦最高法院更將此權利擴張適用到其他重要的刑事訴訟程序中，例如：起訴後出庭聲明程序[38]、逮捕後警訊程序[39]、指認程序[40]、協商程序[41]、預審程序[42]、量刑程序[43]、上訴程序[44]以及假釋程序[45]。而在所有的訴訟程序中，不論是自行僱用或是

---

[34]　See 372 U.S. 335 (1963).

[35]　See In re Gault,387 U.S. 1 (1967).

[36]　See Argersinger v. Hamlin,407 U.S. 25 (1972).

[37]　See Scott v. Illinois, 440 U.S. 367 (1979) and Alabama v Shelton, 535 U.S. 654 (2002). 然而有些州卻對被告設有更周密的保護，參閱王兆鵬，註二書，頁432。

[38]　See Hamilton v. Alabama, 368 U.S. 52 (1961).

[39]　See Miranda v. Arizona, 384 U.S. 436 (1966).

[40]　See United States v. Wade, 388 U.S. 218 (1967); see also Moore v. Illinois, 434 U.S. 220 (1977).

[41]　See McMann v. Richardson, 397 U.S. 759 (1970).

[42]　See Coleman v. Alabama, 399 U.S. 1 (1970).

[43]　See United States v. Tucker, 404 U.S. 443 (1972).

[44]　See Douglas v. California, 372 U.S. 353 (1963).

[45]　See Mempa v. Rhay, 389 U.S. 128 (1967).

政府指定，律師所提供的協助必須是合理有效的（reasonably effective）才符合憲法第六修正案的規定，若律師的行爲存在極可能導致審判出現不同結果的瑕疵時，即有違憲法第六修正案中受律師協助權利之意旨[46]。若政府違反律師權的規定，其所取得的自白或陳述將完全不具證據能力[47]。

　　雖然美國憲法第六修正案保障被告受律師協助的權利，然而被告在審判程序中卻無「義務」接受律師協助，從而在其自由意志下，被告在審判程序中得選擇由自己爲自己辯護（pro

---

[46] "An error by counsel, even if professionally unreasonable, does not warrant setting aside the judgment of a criminal proceeding if the error had no effect on the judgment. Cf. United States v. Morrison, 449 U.S. 361, 364 -365 (1981). The purpose of the Sixth Amendment guarantee of counsel is to ensure that a defendant has the assistance necessary to justify reliance on the outcome of the proceeding. Accordingly, any deficiencies in counsel's performance must be prejudicial to the defense in order to constitute ineffective assistance under the Constitution." See Strickland v. Washington, 466 U.S. 668, 691-2 (1984). Standards are frequently not implemented, contracts are often awarded to the lowest bidder without regard to the scope or quality of services, organizational structures are weak, workloads are high, and funding has not kept pace with other components of the criminal justice system. The effects can be severe, including legal representation of such low quality to amount to no representation at all, delays, overturned convictions, and convictions of the innocent. Ultimately, as Attorney General Janet Reno states, the lack of competent, vigorous legal representation for indigent defendants calls into question the legitimacy of criminal convictions and the integrity of the criminal justice system as a whole. Available at: http://www.nlada.org/About/About_HistoryDefender (last visited, Feb. 21st, 2008).

[47] See Massiah v. United States, 377 U.S. 201 (1964).

se）[48]，此時法院不應強迫被告接受法院所指定之辯護人為其辯護[49]。不過法院在保護被告辯護權的考量下，仍得在審判程序中指定律師待命候補（stand-by counsel），並適時提供自我辯護之被告必要的法律諮詢[50]。縱使該名備位律師在審判程序中主動地打斷了被告的辯護陳述、甚至提出被告所不許的辯護方法，只要未實質地有害辯方利益，都未侵害憲法保障被告自我辯護的權利[51]。但因指定辯護的落實有賴國家財政實質補助，

---

[48]　See Adams v. United States ex rel. McCann, 317 U.S. 269, 275 (1942)(The short of the matter is that an accused, in the exercise of a free and intelligent choice, and with the considered approval of the court, may waive trial by jury, and so likewise may he competently and intelligently waive his Constitutional right to assistance of counsel. There is nothing in the Constitution to prevent an accused from choosing to have his fate tried before a judge without a jury even though, in deciding what is best for himself, he follows the guidance of his own wisdom, and not that of a lawyer).

[49]　See Faretta v. California, 422 U.S. 806 (1975).

[50]　Id., at 834, n 46. (Of course, a State may - even over objection by the accused - appoint a "standby counsel" to aid the accused if and when the accused requests help, and to be available to represent the accused in the event that termination of the defendant's self-representation is necessary.)

[51]　See McKaskle v. Wiggins, 465 U.S. 168, 186-7 (1984)(By contrast, counsel's interruptions of Wiggins or witnesses being questioned by Wiggins in the presence of the jury were few and perfunctory. Most of counsel's uninvited comments were directed at the prosecutor. Such interruptions present little threat to a defendant's Faretta rights, at least when the defendant's view regarding those objections has not been clearly articulated. On the rare occasions that disagreements between counsel and Wiggins were aired in the presence of the jury, the trial judge consistently ruled in Wiggins' favor. This was a pattern more likely to reinforce than to detract from the appearance that Wiggins was controlling his own defense. The intrusions by counsel at Wiggins' trial were simply not substantial or frequent enough to have seriously undermined Wiggins' appearance before the jury in the status of one representing himself.)

因此普遍爲貧窮被告指定律師爲其辯護恐將因案件過多而造成政府財政上的過度負擔，在有限的預算規模下，該如何避免指定辯護流於形式而無實質功效，是目前美國刑事司法體系所面臨的一大難題[52]。

肆、辯護權之內涵

　　爲了避免審判由財富決定，縱然美國憲法第六修正案僅明文刑事被告在審判程序中有受律師協助之權利，美國聯邦最高法院透過擴充解釋的法學方法，在刑事被告無資力聘請律師爲自己辯護的場合中，承認國家有義務提供被告免費的辯護律師[53]，以落實憲法上律師權的保障。惟不論係選任辯護或是義務辯護[54]，只要刑事被告在兩造模式的司法程序中（ad-

---

[52]　See Right to Counsel & Legal Services for the Poor, available at: http://www.abanet.org/publiced/lawday/talking/rtcounsel.html (last visited, Feb. 21st, 2008).

[53]　基本上從犯罪嫌疑人或被告遭警方逮捕開始，在每個重要的程序階段（例如：警訊、首次出庭、認罪協商、審判與量刑），犯罪嫌疑人或被告在刑事程序中均享有受律師協助之權利。

[54]　Courts have interpreted the Sixth Amendment right to counsel as guaranteeing the "effective assistance of counsel" to criminal defendants. It doesn't matter whether the attorney is hired by the defendant or appointed by the government. However, questionable strategic choices made by an attorney (and even serious lawyer errors, in some instances) do not usually cause a conviction to be thrown out, unless it is clear that the attorney's incompetence affected the outcome of the case. See FindLaw, Right to Counsel, available at: http://criminal.findlaw.com/crimes/criminal_rights/criminal_rights_courtroom/right_to_counsel.html (last visited, Feb. 19th, 2008).

versary proceedings）有效並實際地受到律師協助（亦即個別律
師不適任並未實際影響審判之結果），即未違反美國憲法第六
修正案所保障的律師權[55]。

　　雖然辯護權之本質爲一具有憲法位階之權利，然關於其
基礎理論與規範目的向來卻存在多元的觀點[56]，不過就某種
程度來說，或可認刑事訴訟發展的歷史就是辯護制度發展的
歷史，蓋其核心在于保證被指控人平等、及時、有效地行使
辯護權[57]。因此，其多元面向之特徵並無害於其保障刑事被告
權利之功能。我國法制並未明文辯護權之整體內涵[58]，惟大體

---

[55] See Brewer v. Williams, 430 U.S. 387, 401 (1977). (Rather, the clear rule of Massiah is that once adversary proceedings have commenced against an individual, he has a right to legal representation when the government interrogates him.) Some states extend the right to counsel to all matters where a defendant's liberty interest is threatened. The New Jersey Supreme Court unanimously held that, regardless of whether the proceeding is labeled as civil, criminal, or administrative, if a defendant faces a loss of liberty, she or he is entitled to appointed counsel if indigent. See Anne Pasqua, et al v. Hon. Gerald J. Council, et al, 186 N.J. 127 (2006)(March 2006).

[56] 關於刑事辯護制度訴訟價值的理論學說計有：（一）真實發現理論（Truth-finding theory）；（二）公平裁判理論（Fair-decision theory）；（三）真實發現與公平裁判相結合的理論（Truth-finding and fair-decision theories joined）；（四）權利理論（the rights theory）；（五）交易刺激理論（The bargaining incentive theory）以及（六）標準理論（The norm theory）。參閱熊秋紅，刑事訴訟制度之訴訟價值分析，available at: http://www.jcrb.com/zyw/n25/ca137877.htm (last visited, Feb. 19th, 2008).

[57] 參閱有關專家談刑事訴訟法再修改，熊秋紅發言部分，available at: http://big5.xinhuanet.com/gate/big5/news.xinhuanet.com/legal/2007-04/06/content_5942280.htm (last visited, Feb. 19th, 2008).

[58] 刑事訴訟法就偵查階段辯護人權利之規定相關定大致如下：

（一）得選任辯護人時機

第 27 條：「（第 1 項）被告得隨時選任辯護人。犯罪嫌疑人受司法警察官或司法警察調查者，亦同。（第 2 項）被告或犯罪嫌疑人之法定代理人、配偶、直系或三親等內旁系血親或家長、家屬，得獨立為被告或犯罪嫌疑人選任辯護人。（第 3 項）被告或犯罪嫌疑人因智能障礙無法為完全之陳述者，應通知前項之人得為被告或犯罪嫌疑人選任辯護人。但不能通知者，不在此限。」

第 88-1 條第 4 項：「檢察官、司法警察官或司法警察，依第 1 項規定程序拘提之犯罪嫌疑人，應即告知本人及其家屬，得選任辯護人到場。」

（二）偵查中指定辯護

第 31 條第 4 項：「被告因智能障礙無法為完全之陳述，於偵查中未經選任辯護人者，檢察官應指定律師為其辯護。」

（三）辯護人資訊交流權

第 34 條：「辯護人得接見犯罪嫌疑人及羈押之被告，並互通書信。但有事實足認其有湮滅、偽造、變造證據或勾串共犯或證人之虞者，得限制之。」

（四）米蘭達原則

第 95 條第 3 款：訊問被告應先告知左列事項：三、得選任辯護人。

（五）羈押告示

第 101 條第 3 項：「第 1 項各款所依據之事實，應告知被告及其辯護人，並記載於筆錄。」

（六）偵查中被告辯護人之在場權

第 245 條：「（第 2 項）被告或犯罪嫌疑人之辯護人，得於檢察官、檢察事務官、司法警察官或司法警察訊問該被告或犯罪嫌疑人時在場，並得陳述意見。但有事實足認其在場有妨害國家機密或有湮滅、偽造、變造證據或勾串共犯或證人或妨害他人名譽之虞，或其行為不當足以影響偵查秩序者，得限制或禁止之。（第 3 項）檢察官、檢察事務官、司法警察官、司法警察、辯護人、告訴代理人或其他於偵查程序依法執行職務之人員，除依法令或為維護公共利益或保護合法權益有必要者外，不得公開揭露偵查中因執行職務知悉之事項。（第 4 項）偵查中訊問被告或犯罪嫌疑人時，應將訊問之日、時及處所通知辯護人。但情形急迫者，不在此限。」

此外，就偵查階段，法務部定有「檢察機關辦理刑事訴訟案件應行注意事項」，警政署亦有「警察偵查犯罪規範」，就辯護人在場權之行使有所規範。

（一）檢察機關辦理刑事訴訟案件應行注意事項

本注意事項係根據刑事訴訟法所為之細則型規範，各點最後均附有法條依據，就辯護人在場權之規定可謂詳細。相關規定如下：

說來，在武器平等與公平法院之思考下，刑事辯護的主要內涵包括：辯護人在場陪同被告並提供相關諮詢；辯護人提醒與維護被告得主張之合法權利；辯護人在各個程序階段向被告解釋與說明其程序意義以及該程序之利益與不利益；辯護人防止並排除刑事執法人員侵害被告基本人權；辯護人監督整個訴訟程

---

1. 第 18 點（檢察官親自實施逕行拘提）：依刑事訴訟法第 88-1 條第 1 項逕行拘提被告時，應告知得選任辯護人到場。

2. 第 23 點（訊問或詢問時對辯護人之通知）：訊問或詢問被告時應以電話或書面通知辯護人。

3. 第 25 五點（對辯護人調查證據或證據意見之尊重與徵詢）：檢察官對於辯護人聲請調查證據應予重視，如有必要亦應主動提示證物予辯護人。

4. 第 27 點（辯護人接見、通信及在場權之限制）：限制或禁止辯護人在場應審慎認定，並應記明卷內及通知辯護人。

5. 第 28 點（辯護人之在場權）：檢察官訊問被告時辯護人在場者，應記明筆錄；於不違反偵查不公開之原則下，辯護人得在場札記。訊問完畢後宜詢問辯護人有無意見並記明筆錄。

6. 第 30 點（辯護人經通知未到之處置）：辯護人經合法通知而未到場者，宜為適當之等候後再行訊問或詢問。

7. 第 31 點（訊、詢問筆錄內容之確認）：如被告無法閱覽或明瞭筆錄內容，應許在場之辯護人協助閱覽。辯護人請求變更筆錄內容時，應將辯護人陳述記明筆錄。

8. 第 33 點（告知義務之踐行）：「米蘭達原則」之告知。

（二）警察偵查犯罪規範

於警局訊詢問階段，僅於數條文中提及（犯罪嫌疑人或配偶、家長等）得選任辯護人（第 110 點、118 點及第 120 點），選任辯護人未到場仍得詢問（第 105 點）以及詢問（犯罪嫌疑人）是否選辯護人並記明筆錄（第 125 點）等規定，範圍不逾「得選任辯護人」而已，就辯護人在場時究能行使何種權利雙字未提；是辯護人於警局詢問階段之功能極難發揮。

參閱郭怡青，我國檢警第一次偵訊犯罪嫌疑人律師陪訊現況，法扶會訊第 19 期，available at: http://www.laf.org.tw/tw/public/index_detial.php? H_ID=159 (last visited, Feb. 19th, 2008).

序合法進行；辯護人為被告之利益進行協商程序；辯護人調查有利於被告之事實與證據；辯護人於審判程序中對相關證人進行交互詰問；辯護人對違背法令或不當之詰問聲明異議；辯護人提出辯護以及提起上訴等等。縱被告主張為自己辯護，其自我辯護之內涵亦無不同。

伍、自我辯護「權」的定位

從以上的分析可知，不論是美國或是我國，法制面都存在強制辯護以外的案件類型。我國刑事訴訟法並未採取律師強制辯護制度，雖未明文承認刑事被告有自我辯護之權利，然在非強制辯護案件被告實際上未延聘律師為其辯護的情形中，無異承認被告為自己辯護之現象存在。但被告若未具備法律專業知識，逕任檢察官與被告兩造在法庭上進行攻擊防禦，不免實力懸殊而有違武器平等原則，此一現象非但有剝奪人民訴訟權之嫌，亦不免造成國家佔人民便宜之印象，減損人民對司法之信賴[59]。雖自我辯護存在前述弊端，惟關於該如何在審判程序中

---

[59] 法律扶助案件，即為補充上開制度之缺陷，由財團法人法律扶助基金會（簡稱基金會），結合各地律師公會之力量，對於無資力之被告提供刑事訴訟之辯護。被告如果想要依法律扶助法向財團法人法律扶助基金會（或分會）提出申請，法院一定會提供必要的協助。參閱司法院，義務辯護，available at: http://www.judicial.gov.tw/work/work02/work02-30.asp (last visited, Feb. 19th, 2008).

保障「非因貧窮卻未自行聘僱律師的非強制辯護案件被告」之辯護權，以達公平法院之理想，似乎尚未在我國引起普遍之注意。

　　相較於其他美國憲法增修條文所保障的基本權利（如緘默權、隱私權、對質權與陪審權等），若將自我辯護視為一種權利，行使該權利未必對被告有利，蓋不具備法律專業之被告實際上對相關法律規定的認識極為有限。如果再將檢察官具有豐富的法律知識與經驗考慮在內，可想而知的是，無助的被告將在一連串的訴訟活動中，遭受到嚴厲的考驗，甚至一不小心就失去自由。在此前提下，布萊克門大法官（Justice Blackmun）在 Faretta 乙案的不同意見書中，即因質疑「在被告自我辯護的案件中，相較於其他有律師辯護之案件，法院應否有不同的對待標準？」而否認被告有權主張自我辯護[60]。由於歷年來實際

---

[60] See 422 U.S., at 852 (In conclusion, I note briefly the procedural problems that, I suspect, today's decision will visit upon trial courts in the future. Although the Court indicates that a pro se defendant necessarily waives any claim he might otherwise make of ineffective assistance of counsel, the opinion leaves open a host of other procedural questions. Must every defendant be advised of his right to proceed pro se? If so, when must that notice be given? Since the right to assistance of counsel and the right to self-representation are mutually exclusive, how is the waiver of each right to be measured? If a defendant has elected to exercise his right to proceed pro se, does he still have a constitutional right to assistance of standby counsel? How soon in the criminal proceeding must a defendant decide between proceeding by counsel or pro se? Must he be allowed to switch in mid-trial? May a violation of the right to self-representation ever be harmless error? Must the trial court treat the pro se defendant differently than it would professional counsel? I assume that many of these questions will be

上在審判中行使自我辯護權的被告均沒有太好的下場，更有論者提出「行使自我辯護權的被告是一群與真實世界脫節的笨蛋[61]」與「自我辯護就是自我毀滅（self-destruction）[62]」等等批評。然而，縱使各界對於被告自我辯護權的檢討聲浪不斷，甚至連聯邦最高法院也承認主張自我辯護權的歷史背景（殖民時期對英國來的律師不信任以及本地律師嚴重不足[63]）

---

answered with finality in due course. Many of them, however, such as the standards of waiver and the treatment of the pro se defendant, will haunt the trial of every defendant who elects to exercise his right to self-representation. The procedural problems spawned by an absolute right to self-representation will far outweigh whatever tactical advantage the defendant may feel he has gained by electing to represent himself. If there is any truth to the old proverb that "one who is his own lawyer has a fool for a client," the Court by its opinion today now bestows a constitutional right on one to make a fool of himself.).

[61] See John F. Decker, The Sixth Amendment Right to Shoot Oneself in the Foot: An Assessment of the Guarantee of Self-Representation Twenty Years After Faretta, 6 Seton Hall Const. L. J. 483, 487 (1996).

[62] See Robert E. Toone, The Incoherence of Defendant Autonomy, 83 N. C. L. Rev. 621, 628 (2005).

[63] See 422 U.S., at 826-7 ("The colonists brought with them an appreciation of the virtues of self-reliance and a traditional distrust of lawyers. When the Colonies were first settled, 'the lawyer was synonymous with the cringing Attorneys-General and Solicitors-General of the Crown and the arbitrary Justices of the King's Court, all bent on the conviction of those who opposed the King's prerogatives, and twisting the law to secure convictions.' This prejudice gained strength in the Colonies where 'distrust of lawyers became an institution.' Several Colonies prohibited pleading for hire in the 17th century. The prejudice persisted into the 18th century as 'the lower classes came to identify lawyers with the upper class.' The years of Revolution and Confederation saw an upsurge of antilawyer sentiment, a `sudden revival, after the War of the Revolution, of the old dislike and distrust of lawyers as a class.").

已不復存在 [64]，不過鑑於被告本身對訴訟成敗之利害關係最深，防禦權及其下位階的辯護權自應歸被告個人所有，而非律師所有 [65]，近來已有實證研究肯認被告自我辯護權，並提出（一）只有少部分選擇自我辯護的被告有心理方面的問題、（二）選擇自我辯護的重罪被告其審判結果未明顯地劣後於由律師辯護的重罪被告、（三）自我辯護較能保障被告的程序利益、（四）自我辯護之結果往往優於拙劣（不適任）的強制指定辯護、以及（五）只有自我辯護能在審判中保護某種意識形態得到公正的審判等論點 [66]。換言之，被告自我辯護權並非毫無用處之權利，畢竟在被告自願行使自我辯護權且未導致事實在審判程序中遭到扭曲的前提下，承認被告有權主張不排除違法取得的證據或有權陳述對自己不利的事實，縱使有違一般辯護實務，並不因此即違反公平的概念。

我國法制並未如美國法制般全面承認被告之自我辯護權，蓋於強制辯護案件類型中，非但被告於其不同意由該指定辯護人辯護或不滿意指定辯護人所為之辯護時，並無拒卻由其繼續

---

[64] See Martinez v. Court of Appeals, 528 U.S. 152, 158 (2000)(Therefore, while Faretta is correct in concluding that there is abundant support for the proposition that a right to self-representation has been recognized for centuries, the original reasons for protecting that right do not have the same force when the availability of competent counsel for every indigent defendant has displaced the need-- although not always the desire — for self-representation.).

[65] See 422 U.S., at 834.

[66] See Erica Hashimoto, Defending the Right to Self-Representation: An Empirical Look at the Pro Se Felony Defendant, 85 N.C. L. Rev. 423 (2007).

辯護之法源，且自刑事訴訟法第 379 條第 7 款將「依本法應用辯護人之案件或已經指定辯護人之案件，辯護人未經到庭辯護而逕行審判者。」列為判決當然違背法令之事由以觀，為免判決嗣後遭廢棄，被告於強制辯護案件類型中不得主張自我辯護權。反面而言，被告於非強制辯護案件中即得主張自我辯護權，只不過在非強制辯護案件類型中，如果被告未於審判中自費選任辯護人為其辯護，法院亦無提供備位律師（stand-by counsel）作為被告諮詢之義務。在前述現實面的基礎上，似可將（一）「非無資力[67]」、「又不屬強制辯護案件」、「未於審判中自費選任辯護人為其辯護」之被告、以及（二）經評定為「顯無理由[68]」但被告主觀以為非顯無理由之案件被告，均

---

[67] 參照法律扶助法第 1 條：「為保障人民權益，對於無資力，或因其他原因，無法受到法律適當保護者，提供必要之法律扶助，特制定本法。」、第 3 條：「本法所稱無資力者，係指符合社會救助法之低收入戶或其每月可處分之收入及可處分之資產低於一定標準者。前項所稱一定標準之認定辦法，由基金會定之。」與第 13 條：「無資力者，得申請法律扶助。」等規定，法律扶助主要係以無資力者為扶助之對象。

[68] 法律扶助法第 16 條第 1 項：「法律扶助之申請，如有下列情形之一者，不應准許：一、依申請人之陳述及所提資料，顯無理由者。」又財團法人法律扶助基金會曾針對「審查強制辯護案件是否顯無理由注意要點」於民國 93 年 12 月 13 日第六次法規委員會決議如下：
一、「顯無理由」之定義：
（一）依申請人陳述之事實，將受較起訴書或原判決相同或更不利之判決者。但如有其情可憫或減刑、免刑或緩刑等可從輕量刑之事由者，不在此限。
（二）申請人承認起訴書或判決書所載全部事實，且無其情可憫或減刑、免刑或緩刑等可從輕量刑之事由者。
（三）申請人陳述事實與起訴書或原判決不同，但依其陳述，將受較起訴書或原判決相同或更不利之判決者。但如有其情可憫或減刑、免刑或緩刑等可從輕量刑之事由者，不在此限。

視為主張自我辯護之被告，蓋在其有資力聘請辯護人而又不願意自費聘請辯護人的情形中，或許其仍願意接受（甚至等待）免費的指定辯護，鑑於司法資源有限，不應浪費，將其有資力卻不自費聘請辯護人之矛盾行徑解為「傾向於主張自我辯護權」，尚不致曲解律師權旨在保障貧窮被告之本意。

陸、法院在自我辯護案件中應扮演的角色

在米蘭達告示（Miranda Warnings，我國刑事訴訟法第95條）之規範下，訊問被告應先告其得選任辯護人之權利，蓋若法院未於審判程序開始前告知被告此項權利，無從判斷被告是否知悉其得主張辯護權，更遑論其是否志願並且理智地放棄（voluntary and intelligent waiver）受律師協助的權利而成為自我辯護之被告[69]。除了辯護權外，美國法制上尚存在其他必須由法官直接告知被告（不論有無律師為其辯護）、而且只有被告自己得志願並理智地放棄（縱其有辯護律師亦

二、下列案件不得以顯無理由駁回。

（一）死刑案件。

（二）行為人為精神障礙、智能不足者。

（三）行為人行為時未滿十八歲。

參閱財團法人法律扶助基金會，審查強制辯護案件是否顯無理由注意要點，available at: http://www.laf.org.tw/tw/announce/index_detail.php? Anno_ID=15 (last visited, Feb. 19th, 2008).

[69] See 422 U.S., at 835.

不得代其放棄）的權利，例如無罪答辯並要求審判之權（the right to plea not guilty and the right to trial）與接受陪審審判之權[70]（the right to jury trial）。這樣的規範似乎在一定範圍內認為法院有告知義務，以保障被告的利益。由於我國刑事訴訟法第 2 條第 1 項亦要求法院應於被告有利及不利之情形一律注意，參照前述美國法有關告知義務的規範架構，似可認前述米蘭達告示之要求為我國法院告示義務之規範基礎。不過在我國的自我辯護案件中，除了前述「米蘭達告示」與「是否為認罪之答辯（刑事訴訟法第 273 條第 1 項第 2 款）[71]」等告示外，是否仍存在其他在保護義務與告示義務拘束下，法院應告知被告之事項（亦即法院在何等範圍內有保障與補充被告防禦權與辯護權之告知義務）？即為探討辯護權保障時有必要進一步釐清的議題。

　　沒有爭議的是，法院的告知義務當然不應及於向被告建議「如何於實質上進行攻防的策略性問題」，此舉除將有害法官

---

[70] See Boykin v. Alabama, 395 U.S. 238, 243 (1969)(Several federal constitutional rights are involved in a waiver that takes place when a plea of guilty is entered in a state criminal trial. First is the privilege against compulsory self-incrimination guaranteed by the Fifth Amendment and applicable to the States by reason of the Fourteenth. Malloy v. Hogan, 378 U. S. 1. Second is the right to trial by jury. Duncan v. Louisiana, 391 U. S. 145. Third is the right to confront one's accusers. Pointer v. Texas, 380 U. S. 400. We cannot presume a waiver of these three important federal rights from a silent record.).

[71] 此項告示或可解為被告得主張進入通常訴訟程序或簡式（簡易）訴訟程序之告示，與前述美國法院告示被告得為無罪答辯並要求審判相類似。

中立聽訟的地位外，亦將反向地鼓勵被告主張自我辯護以尋求在訴訟程序中得到法官實質的協助，蓋於實際上沒有任何一個律師會比主持審判程序並撰寫判決書的法官更了解案件將往哪個方向進行，也沒有一個律師會比法官更了解該如何使判決朝無罪的方向發展。不過除了前述於訊問開始前須踐行刑事訴訟法第 95 條之告示義務外，法院是否有義務在審判程序（包含訊問及準備程序）的每個階段告一段落後、甚至在檢察官每次對被告提出質疑後，「重複」告知自我辯護被告行使關於保持緘默以及請求調查有利證據之權？又法院在必要關鍵時刻是否有義務告知被告其於此時不應行使緘默權？首先，由於自我辯護的被告大多不具有足以抗衡檢察官的法律專業能力，因此在欠缺律師保障其緘默權的前提下，即使要求法院在某些須要被告回應的場合（亦即在必要的訴訟階段），重複告知被告得保持緘默權，藉以稍微補強被告法律專業之不足，在訴訟經濟的考量下，不但未過度增加法院的負擔，在武器平等及公平法院的思考下，此類告知義務亦未違刑事訴訟法第 95 條於訊問被告「時」須告知米蘭達警告之規定。因此，法院應有義務在必要時重複告知自我辯護被告得行使緘默權。

在被告已選擇自我辯護的審判程序中，除非存在特別保護的必要事由，原則上法院並不須要就相關法律議題或證據法則提供被告任何協助或建議，否則不啻形成自我辯護即為法院代為辯護的亂象。然因在公平法院之思考下法院原有義務告知被告得請求調查有利證據，則於檢方提出對被告不利之事證後，

法院本應就此詢問被告有無有利證據待調查。由於被告在請求調查有利證據時[72]，不免出現「法院詢問該項證據與本案之關聯性」或者「被告主動對該項證據與本案之關聯性有所說明」之現象[73]，則法院告知被告得請求調查有利證據之義務，即等同於告知被告得積極陳述為自己辯護之義務；易言之，雖然「告知被告得積極陳述為自己辯護」於本質上迥異於「告知被告得消極地行使緘默權」，不過在公平法院與訴訟經濟的思考下，依刑事訴訟法第 95 條之規定，法院除有義務於必要時告知被告得消極地行使緘默權外，亦有義務於必要時告知被告得積極地行使辯護權。不過，雖然法院有義務告知被告得積極陳述為自己辯護，但此項告知義務，原則上應不及於「如何」積極為自己辯護，蓋相較於律師辯護的情形，關於如何辯護乙事，已因被告決定自我辯護，而欠缺由法律專家特別保護的必要。

　　我國證據法則採相對證據排除的法制架構，縱然證據係違法取得，並不當然因被告主張即遭排除（相對來說，亦不因被告未主張而必然不遭排除），既然用法的責任在法院，法院實無須詢問被告關於證據排除之意見。在改良式的當事人進行主義當中，交互詰問乃通常訴訟程序的核心所在，因此刑事訴訟

---

[72] 按依刑事訴訟法第 161 條之 1 之規定，被告原即有權在法院未詢問是否請求調查有利證據時，主動就被訴事實指出有利之證明方法。

[73] 否則法院得依刑事訴訟法第 163 條之 2：「（第 1 項）當事人、代理人、辯護人或輔佐人聲請調查之證據，法院認為不必要者，得以裁定駁回之。（第 2 項）下列情形，應認為不必要：一、不能調查者。二、與待證事實無重要關係者。三、待證事實已臻明瞭無再調查之必要者。四、同一證據再行聲請者。」之規定予以駁回被告調查證據之聲請。

法第 166 條第 1 項後段:「被告如無辯護人,而不欲行詰問時,審判長仍應予詢問證人、鑑定人之適當機會。」乃明文法院應於適當時告知被告得詢問證人與鑑定人。依此規定,雖可認自我辯護被告得自行詰問,然因交互詰問程序所涉技術面過高,為免於審判程序中出現法院教導被告行交互詰問之現象並造成訴訟程序出現不必要的延遲(訴訟不經濟),法理上應認法院於自我辯護案件中,當被告未主動自行詰問時,並無義務協助被告詰問證人或鑑定人,此時法院只要告知被告有權詰問即可,若被告不懂詰問之意義,法院亦無需自執教鞭,重新教育一個門外漢並使其成為交互詰問的專家。基本上,前述於必要時告知被告得積極地行使辯護權以及刑事訴訟法第 166 條第 1 項後段詢問證人與鑑定人等規定,已足以保障實際上未受律師協助之被告有適當與必要的陳述意見機會,畢竟法律不能保證由律師詰問一定比較好,而不進行詰問一定比較差,既已承認被告自白犯罪為進行簡式審判程序的前提,被告應有權決定是否詰問。如果承認被告得放棄詰問權,法院又何必一定要讓訴訟程序具有「交互」詰問的色彩?單方(檢察官或自訴人代理人)詰問難道一定侵害被告的辯護權嗎?因此,不應認為法院有協助被告以充實交互詰問程序的義務。

然而,縱可認法院無義務協助與告知自我辯護被告如何爭執審判中的陳述(即行交互詰問程序),法院在出現審判外的陳述時,是否有義務協助與告知被告依刑事訴訟法第 159 條之 5 第 2 項聲明異議呢?先就傳聞法則之爭執來說,由於事涉法

院如何適用傳聞法則以之認定事實，法院原有義務於判決書中交代其用法理由，被告如未適時就此聲明異議，雖不足以使得傳聞陳述頓時變質成非傳聞，不過卻有可能使得審判外的陳述成為刑事訴訟法第 159 條之 5 的傳聞例外。然而，依刑事訴訟法第 159 條之 5 第 1 項之規定，並非只要當事人雙方均同意傳聞陳述作為證據，該審判外陳述即必然具有證據能力，如果法院審酌該言詞陳述或書面陳述作成時之情況後，認為不適當者，該審判外陳述即不得作為證據。因此，如果課予法院於傳聞陳述提出時有詢問自我辯護被告是否同意該陳述作為證據之義務，若該陳述經法院審認不屬刑事訴訟法第 159 條之 1 至之 4 之傳聞例外，除將導致法院因實質上督促被告聲明異議而扮演被告實質辯護人的角色外，更將導致法庭成為法院與公訴人或自訴人的對抗之場合，而有失法院立場中立之疑慮。而依刑事訴訟法第 159 條之 5 第 2 項：「當事人、代理人或辯護人於法院調查證據時，知有第 159 條第 1 項不得為證據之情形，而未於言詞辯論終結前聲明異議者，視為有前項之同意。」以言詞辯論終結為詢問界線之規定，若認法院有義務於傳聞陳述提出時詢問自我辯護被告是否同意該陳述作為證據，則法院至少在言詞辯論終結時，亦有義務最後一次詢問被告是否欲追復尚未聲明之異議，如此恐亦造成訴訟不必要之拖延。由於法院於雙方當事人同意（含擬制同意）審判外陳述作為證據時，尚有「審酌該言詞陳述或書面陳述作成時之情況以決定審判外之陳述有無證據能力」之義務，鑑於該義務之履行尚足以防止被告

受到審判外陳述者任意攀陷，未違反公平法院的思考，縱然裁判時因而採用了某些原應排除的審判外陳述，而使裁判的結果不利於被告，亦不當然侵害了被告的防禦權與辯護權，蓋被告除有權辯護外，自亦應有權承認事實，絕不能因被告未聲明異議而發現（認定）不利的事實，即謂法院未協助與告知被告依刑事訴訟法第 159 條之 5 第 2 項聲明異議必然違反程序正義的概念。故而關於傳聞陳述應否排除之爭點，法院亦無告知之義務。此外，為了保障被告的資訊取得權，法院亦應主動告知被告關於刑事訴訟法第 33 條第 2 項：「無辯護人之被告於審判中得預納費用請求付與卷內筆錄之影本。」的權利，以免被告自行辯護時無案可本。

柒、結　論

本文旨在探討如何於審判程序中保障非強制辯護案件被告受律師協助之辯護權，自法制沿革的觀點來說，辯護權之需求源於兩造對抗模式訴訟程序（當事人進行主義）的發展，雖然說承認被告有權主張自我辯護的背景（對英國律師不信任以及美洲殖民地本土律師太少）已不復存在，由於自我辯護本身並非毫無是處，法制上仍應允許被告有權主張自我辯護，我國法雖未如美國法般全面承認被告有自我辯護權，惟於刑事訴訟法第 31 條第 1 項規定強制辯護範圍以外的案件類型中，一但被告未選任辯護人或法院未指定辯護人，實際上被告必須自己為自

己辯護，由於此時並不構成審判當然違背法令之事由，法理上應可將其視為被告行使自我辯護權。

　　不過由於被告所具備的法律知識在實質上無法與檢察官或自訴代理人相互抗衡，因此在武器平等的基礎上，似乎應該要求法院在必要時保障非強制辯護被告的辯護權，以免所進行的審判程序過於向控方傾斜而失其公平。不過若過度強調法院協助非強制辯護被告進行辯護的照護義務，又恐將導致審判程序出現審判者對抗控訴者的畸形發展。從而，該如何拿捏法院的照護義務即為法院在自我辯護案件中應扮演何種角色的核心。在訴訟經濟之考量以及刑事訴訟法第 95 條之規範下，本文認為：除了米蘭達告示外，法院有義務於訴訟程序開始時，告知被告有權不認罪並選擇進行通常訴訟程序；此外，法院尚有義務「重複」於必要時告知被告行使緘默權，亦應於個別證據調查程序完成前告知被告得就該調查之證據積極陳述為自己辯護（調查有利之證據）並得詰問及詢問證人（至於該如何詰問與詢問證人並不在法院照護義務之範圍內）。又因法院有認事用法之責，因此關於被告應否基於證據排除法則或傳聞法則針對特定證據聲明異議，法院並無告知被告之義務。最後，為了保障被告的資訊權，法院應告知被告得行使閱卷權。

　　若法院實際已踐行上述照護義務，縱非強制辯護案件被告於未受律師協助下接受審判，亦難謂所進行之審判程序有欠公平，蓋法律所保障者為公平審判之機會，辯護權保障亦僅及於訴訟攻防機會之平等，而不及於被告必獲無罪之判決。

8 談刑事程序筆錄制作之實然與應然

壹、前　言

　　喧騰一時的首長特別費案除了突顯以領據核銷的特別費究竟屬於公款或私款的爭議外，在馬英九特別費案的偵訊錄音曝光後，偵訊筆錄內容本身的眞實性，竟也成爲另一令人矚目的焦點。雖然檢辯雙方對於筆錄內容是否有違陳述者本意各執一辭[1]，不過依臺灣臺北地方法院 96 年度矚重訴字第 1 號判決所

---

[1] 參閱侯寬仁檢察官新聞稿：「今日（96.7.19）有媒體報導侯寬仁檢察官於偵辦馬英九特別費案時「筆錄不實」、「筆錄疑自問自答」，並引用律師所提供之所謂「證人吳麗洳於偵訊錄音譯文與偵查筆錄之對照表」，質疑檢察官有誘導訊問、制作不實筆錄等情事云云。依英美證法則，交互詰問程序中，禁止誘導訊問（Leading question），是審判中調查證據應遵守之原則，偵查中並沒有誘導訊問（Leading question）之問題；實務上，檢察官在訊問證人時，通常會提示各種文件資料讓受訊人回憶當時狀況，甚至以查證資料提示於證人，直接切入犯罪事實，訊問證人是否認知（記得）犯罪嫌疑人於行為時所爲之犯罪事實。本件實際上，證人吳麗洳爲出納人員，有無陷於錯誤本應是詐欺之法律構成要件，自然就應該以「如果你知道，你是否仍會同意核章…」等假設性用語之方式加以訊問。經向法院調閱當日偵訊錄音帶重聽多次，發現偵訊筆錄與錄音內容，雖未能作到隻字不漏，將詢答之全部詞句記下，然與受訊問人之真意尚無不合。而對照辯護人所提出之所謂錄音譯文則有遺漏，以致與錄音內容明顯不符，辯護人冒然提出並由媒體導，顯非允洽。

述[2]，偵訊筆錄之內容似與陳述者之實際陳述內容不盡相符。儘管各界對此種實務操作頗以爲然[3]，不過有趣的是，各方所指摘的對象都是該案的承辦檢察官，不明究理者，恐還以爲有爭議之偵訊筆錄乃承辦檢察官自行制作。又依照檢改會之聲明：

況且，在英美司法實務，偵訊譯文在辯護人尚未呈給審判長前便向媒體散播，則有藐視法庭之問題，我們應該相信司法，本件偵訊筆錄有無證據能力，尚留待審判調查，靜待審判結果，不要以誤導之方式傷害司法公信力。」，available at: http://www.pra-tw.org/view_topic.aspx? t=6645 (Mar. 1, 2008). 另可參閱檢改會 96.07.20 新聞稿，筆錄爭議應回歸法院調查：「7 月 18 日起，國內新聞媒體登載馬英九特別費律師認爲該案證人的筆錄，訊問檢察官侯寬仁在市政府祕書處出納吳麗洳時，筆錄記載與錄音內容有不符現象。經媒體大符報導後，引發特定陣營的強烈情緒。翌日承辦檢察官方面，則表示證人筆錄與錄音內容並無曲解證人意思，而是辯護律師在針對錄音譯文時故意隱匿受訊問人之關鍵回答，扭曲證人原意，並認爲辯護人於法庭審判將不完整的錄音譯文提供予媒體，有意圖影響審判之違法。」，available at: http://www.pra-tw.org/view_topic.aspx? t=6658 (Mar. 1, 2008).

2　該號判決理由陸甲四（八）：以上偵查筆錄之記載，或係檢察官以假設性用語「理論上」提問，筆錄中問題及應答卻略而未顯，或僅是證人以口頭語方式所爲「對」、「嗯」之言詞，而非針對問題回答，亦非爲筆錄所記載之肯定答覆，甚至在實務上整理證人回答以爲紀錄，亦未見如此差異，顯見該筆錄確有斷章取義之處，且有筆錄記載與實際問答不符之情，是筆錄記載與證人實際證述內容既有不符，彰顯前開偵查筆錄不具特信性，而有顯不可信情況，應依刑事訴訟法第 159 條之 1 第 2 項之反面解釋，上開部分之筆錄無證據能力，不能爲證據，應以本院勘驗筆錄代之。

3　據報導，「馬英九不滿檢察官僞造証人筆錄，決定控告檢察官侯寬仁，許文彬律師認爲，這對司法改革是個很好的機會，特別費案顯示了檢察官的權力傲慢，連政治人物都會覺得不公平，那一般尋常百姓不就更哭訴無門。許文彬律師表示，檢察官是否扭曲証人說法，要查清楚真相，慶幸法庭明察秋毫，算是已經還給當事人清白，對於檢察官的責任，過去有監察院，糾彈不法，而監察體系應該發揮，檢察系統本身，檢察長應該做好監督管理，自律委員會也應該發揮功能。」參閱中廣新聞網 (2008-01-04)，「馬英九告檢察官人權律師：司法改革好機會」，available at: http://news.sina.com.tw/politics/bcc/tw/2008-01-04/163114127681.shtml (Mar. 1, 2008).

「筆錄應據實記載，這是偵訊者的基本守則，若有違反，自當承擔法律責任。惟訊問筆錄畢竟與錄音之逐字譯文記錄不同，受訊問人因記憶模糊，或心理防衛，往往陳述會瑣碎、迴避、不統一，若一字一句記述，筆錄往往冗長、雜蕪，無法閱讀。為澄清受訊問人真實意思，反覆詰問後，確定其意思而為記錄，則有釐清事實的效果，此於偵查中，為深入真象，並從空白一片，累積證據，逐漸還原真實，尤有需求。即使在審判中，從已呈現之卷證開始進行調查以判明真實，仍有不得不整理筆錄的作法。若未能從整個偵訊過程審視，只擇取其中片段爭執筆錄之真實性，自難免發生無謂爭議[4]。」，不難了解我國司法實務並不要求筆錄須逐字記載[5]，從而一旦出現筆錄中所記載之陳述要旨與實際上之陳述錄音有所出入時，不論有利或不

---

[4] 參閱檢改會 96.07.20 新聞稿，筆錄爭議應回歸法院調查，available at: http://www.pra-tw.org/view_topic.aspx? t=6658 (Mar. 1, 2008).

[5] 除前述實務上之說明外，律師許文彬曾表示：「法律明文規定筆錄是記其要旨，並非逐字逐句記載，筆錄內容與應訊人原意有無出入，不在於一個字，而是視整體文字所表達意思是否違背應訊人原意。為確保筆錄內容不失真，刑事訴訟法規定訊問被告應全程錄音，如今雙方有爭議，就應以錄音內容為主。」。參閱中央社 (2007-07-19)，法界：若對筆錄內容有爭議應以錄音光碟為準，許文彬律師發言部分，available at: http://news.yam.com/cna/society/200707/20070719501010.html (Mar. 1, 2008). 此外，亦曾有立法委員提出筆錄僅須記載陳述要旨之修正草案，其草案規定為：「（第41條第1項）訊問被告、自訴人、證人、鑑定人及通譯，應當場錄音並應由書記官摘記要點獨立制作筆錄，記載左列事項：一、對於受詢問人之訊問及其陳述。二、證人、鑑定人或通譯如未具結者，其事由。三、訊問之年、月、日及處所。」。參閱咋觸集，刑事訴訟法第 34 條 41 條等條文修正草案，available at: http://fuldali.blogspot.com/2007/05/blog-post_07.html (Mar. 1, 2008).

利於被告，對於訴訟程序之公正性，在評價上均將產生一定程度之影響。針對上述源自筆錄記載所生之爭議，本文除將探討筆錄記載本身於訴訟程序中所具有的意義外，更將針對現行筆錄制作的實務，指出問題所在，並基於現行法關於筆錄制作規定，提出本文的看法。

貳、關於筆錄制作的規定與實務

筆錄者，乃指訴訟進行中記載事實經過之文書。蓋訴訟進行，必經若干階段，此種經過事實，均須逐一記錄，方足以資採證，並提供判斷之參考依據。在刑事訴訟法第 41 條第 1 項第 1 款：「訊問被告、自訴人、證人、鑑定人及通譯，應當場制作筆錄，記載左列事項：一、對於受訊問人之訊問及其陳述。」之規範下，筆錄不但應記載受訊問人之陳述，即對之所訊問之言詞亦應記載；如受訊問人連續陳述時，自應為連續之記載。受訊問人如為被告時，被告對於犯罪之嫌疑是否承認，所關至大，記載不容稍有曖昧不明。被告所陳述有利之事實與指定證明之方法尤須記載明確，為調查證據之準備。又陳述之態度，或侃侃而言，或惶悚不堪，均應記明，以供日後參證[6]。

6　參閱俞叔平，刑事訴訟法學，頁 76，中國法學編譯社印行，民國 45 年 10 月修正版。

又依刑事訴訟法第 43 條：「（訊問）筆錄應由在場之書記官制作之。其行訊問或搜索、扣押、勘驗之公務員應在筆錄內簽名；如無書記官在場，得由行訊問或搜索、扣押、勘驗之公務員親自或指定其他在場執行公務之人員制作筆錄。」之規定，原則上只要書記官在場，訊問者與筆錄之制作者即非同一人。查立法者所以要求由訊問以外之人制作筆錄[7]，除在保障筆錄記載之公正性與客觀性外，亦在保障訊問程序之受訊問者能以回答「問答題」而非「填空題」之方式陳述意見，避免訊問者與筆錄制作者為同一人時所可能出現忽略陳述者本意而由訊問者自問自答的弊端；蓋筆錄旨為記錄被告陳述而制作，因此筆錄上應記載被告自行陳述之內容，而非訊問者預期之內容[8]。

　　然而實務上關於筆錄制作的操作，卻與前述法文規定不盡相同。或因人力不足，通常警訊程序在刑事訴訟法第 43 條之 1 第 2 項的規定下，只要有全程錄音，訊問者與筆錄制作者常為同一人，而筆錄所呈現出來的，皆為筆錄制作者所認知的陳述要旨。而在偵查或審判程序中，因訊問者（檢察官或法官）與

---

[7] 刑事訴訟法第 43 條之 1 第 2 項：「前項犯罪嫌疑人詢問筆錄之制作，應由行詢問以外之人為之。但因情況急迫或事實上之原因不能為之，而有全程錄音或錄影者，不在此限。」之規定亦可資參照。

[8] 關於筆錄制作程序，「現行審判實務，檢察官多以偵訊筆錄做為證據認定被告犯罪，然偵訊筆錄之制作，多無標準程序，難以確保其正確性，故增定訊問時錄音及書記官制作筆錄之規定；偵訊之筆錄於實務上又多由實施訊問之人員，事先擬定問答之內容，若受訊問者之回答與擬定之答案不一時，方加以修改。」參閱咋觸集，刑事訴訟法第 34 條至 41 條等條文修正草案，available at: http://fuldali.blogspot.com/2007/05/blog-post_07.html (Mar. 1, 2008).

筆錄制作者（書記官）非同一人[9]，不免有時發生訊問者與筆錄制作者對受訊問者所爲陳述有不同認知的情形。雖然依現行法規定筆錄制作者爲書記官，惟訊問者卻對筆錄記載內容實際上有絕對的決定權，實務上常見訊問者要求書記官依照訊問者對受訊問者陳述之認知制作或修改筆錄[10]，而書記官通常也都配合訊問者之要求，而未堅持於筆錄呈現出其本身對受訊問者陳述之認知[11]。針對此一現象，中國人權協會甚至以「檢察署書

---

[9]　惟於少數案件中，存在檢察官自行制作筆錄之情形，比較有名者為發生於民國 78 年的吳蘇案，該案承辦檢察官高新武因上級壓力，自己制作吳蘇案之偵查筆錄。

[10]　據聯合報報導指出，法庭上播放錄音顯示，侯寬仁原本問吳麗泇，台北市政府 92 年發公函要「注意有無月初尚未發生即先支付情事」，是否表示市長有因公支出的事情發生，才來申領特別費？吳麗泇一再答稱「我都完全忘記了」，但侯寬仁未能將這個回答載明在筆錄中，反而自問自答說「因為那時候已經不是你做的」，甚至在他自己後來提出的譯文加記，吳麗泇說「對，對」。但事實上吳麗泇根本沒有這麼說，倒是侯寬仁轉對書記官說「是的，他（馬英九）應該是這樣」。還有，吳麗泇明明是回答「理論上，市長室的人如果有蓋出來，我們就蓋嘛」，但侯寬仁卻轉向對書記官說「如果市長蓋了領據，我們當然就相信市長」；證人說「市長室」，侯卻記為「市長」。參閱【聯合報／記者 蘇位榮】2007.07.24，冷眼集斷章取義 豈能輕輕放下，available at: http://www.news98.com.tw/dispbbs.asp? boardid=7&RootID=1454167&ID=1454167 (Mar. 1, 2008).

[11]　關於筆錄記載不實之指摘，有認為：「蘇建和等三人的辯護律師也有極為類似（偵訊筆錄記載不實）的主張，他們說蘇建和在承辦的崔紀鎮檢察官第一次訊問時曾否認犯罪，但檢方的筆錄卻避不記載，而檢察官訊問劉秉郎時則明顯引誘誤導，但筆錄中完全無法看到這樣的情節，直到辯方向法院調閱了偵訊的錄音帶，才真相大白，公共電視的「獨立特派員」節目還以這樣的內容制作一個專輯的報導。」參閱林峰正，馬英九與蘇建和，民間司改會電子報 2007 年 7 月 30 日第 382 期，available at: http://www.jrf.org.tw/newjrf/epaper/files/382-0730b.htm (Mar. 1, 2008).

記官制作偵訊筆錄時，均能按照被告所述內容詳細記載，而不缺漏或扭曲原意。」作為檢察官偵查階段司法人權評分標準之一[12]，適足以表徵筆錄制作內容正確性於人權保障之重要。縱此種實務運作之實然面足以說明：何以在首長特別費案中只有承辦檢察官而非依法應制作筆錄之書記官遭受批評，不過類此書記官僅依訊問者指示記錄之實務運作卻有違刑事訴訟法第43條之1第2項所揭示「訊問者與筆錄制作者非同一人以維筆錄記載客觀公正」之法理。雖然依刑事訴訟法第41條第2項：「前項筆錄應向受訊問人朗讀或令其閱覽，詢以記載有無錯誤。」與第3項：「受訊問人請求將記載增、刪、變更者，應將其陳述附記於筆錄。」等規定，受訊問人有權確認筆錄記載內容之真實性並請求更正筆錄，但事實上除了被告會因自己涉案而字斟句酌的仔細認真地審視筆錄記載之內容是否有違其陳述時本意外，非以被告身分出庭之受訊問人通常在訊問完畢後，並不會要求閱讀整份筆錄之內容即行簽名，此種現象通常導致筆錄記載是否有問題很難於第一時間即被發現[13]，蓋「證人歷

---

[12] 參閱陳運財，2002年台灣司法人權指標調查報告，中國人權協會出版，available at: http://www.cahr.org.tw/weball/HRindicator/judicial.htm (Mar. 1, 2008).

[13] 關於難以發現證人筆錄不實部分，律師賴素如指出：檢察官筆錄造成冤假錯案的傳言卻所在多有，如知名的蘇建和殺人案，很多說法都認為此案並沒有直接殺人的證據，但就以筆錄而定三人的死罪，絕對不公平。而吳麗洳的筆錄出現與本人陳述有重大不同，最初也沒有人知道此事，但卻因檢方傳吳麗洳為證人，認為吳麗洳的證詞可以對「馬英九定罪」有效果，才傳吳麗洳，要不是吳麗洳在法庭上表示「筆錄與所說的不合」，也不會發覺吳麗洳的筆錄有問題，可見筆錄是否有問題其實很難被發掘，這是一種「黑暗指數」極

經長時間訊問後，通常已疲累不堪，不會詳加檢視筆錄[14]」；
此時若筆錄記載與陳述內容有異，即易因受訊問人未確實審視
筆錄內容而未即時請求更正錯誤，並於其後產生筆錄內容眞實
與否之爭議[15]。對於前述筆錄制作者無權決定筆錄如何記載之

高的情況。參閱賴素如，「筆錄確實可被操控 人權難保」，available at: http://search.cdns.com.tw/loadfile.asp? sid=0&iid=0&did=45021&checksum=56647&query2=賴素如（Mar. 1, 2008）. 另可參閱 2007/09/27 聯合報社論，果若造假，必須查辦侯寬仁：「依通常實務經驗，被告在陳述完畢後，較會詳看筆錄內容（比率其實也不高），而證人在證述完畢後，會要求詳看筆錄者，則是少見。」。

14 關於證人通常不會仔細閱讀筆錄乙事，可參照下列說明：「莊秀銘指出，雖侯寬仁指稱吳麗洳事後看過筆錄，絕對沒有問題，但證人歷經長時間訊問後，通常已疲累不堪，不會詳加檢視筆錄，況且連律師都不敢以質疑態度看待筆錄，即使證人對筆錄簽名具結，也難保筆錄內容沒有失真。唯有勘驗錄音光碟，才能知道筆錄內容有無失真。」。參閱中央社（2007-07-19），法界：若對筆錄內容有爭議應以錄音光碟為準，莊秀銘律師發言部分，available at: http://news.yam.com/cna/society/200707/20070719501010.html（Mar. 1, 2008）. 而律師賴素如指出：一般人在應訊時期時心中都極為忐忑，就算是身為「證人」而不是被告，也對偵查庭上的肅穆氣氛極為恐懼，這點與過去帝王時期的「殺威棒喝」等形式上訊時的情形雖然已經不同，但心理反應卻還並無二致，所以當檢察官一問就是兩、三小時，又是特意的誘導、威嚇時，每個「證人」所期待的就是「趕快離開」，對於筆錄上到底記載些甚麼？根本不會細心的如馬英九一看就是二、三個小時才簽字，而是匆匆一撇或是根本沒看全部筆錄就在最後一行上簽字了事，這點在侯檢察官事件爆發後，有許多民眾都曾表達他們「只被允許看最後一頁筆錄」的說法，明確看出來「筆錄確實有可能被檢察官操控而任意記載的可能性」。參閱賴素如，「筆錄確實可被操控 人權難保」，available at: http://search.cdns.com.tw/loadfile.asp? sid=0&iid=0&did=45021&checksum=56647&query2=賴素如（Mar. 1, 2008）.

15 關於證人未確實閱覽筆錄，致不知筆錄實際記載內容為何，可參照最高法院85年台上字第 1 號判決之事實，依該判決說明：次按被告之自白，非出於強暴、脅迫、利誘、詐欺、違法押或其他不正方法，且與事實相符者，方得為證據，此觀刑事訴訟法第 156 條第 1 項之規定甚明。陳順隆在台北市調查處

實務現象，除將產生筆錄制作權歸屬之疑義外，當訊問者與筆錄記載者對於受訊問者陳述內容有不同認知時，究應如何制作筆錄以及訊問者應扮演何種角色等等，向來亦為我國司法實務所忽略之問題。從而，該如何調合上述筆錄制作法制與實務間之齟齬，以落實筆錄記載之公正性與客觀性，實有進一步予以詳明之必要。

參、筆錄記載正確性在刑事訴訟程序上之意義

我國訴訟實務向來僅要求書記官記載筆錄要旨即可，而於民國 92 年通過的刑事訴訟法第 44 條第 1 項第 7 款：「第 41

之片面供述，尚不能證明與事實相符，已如上述，且陳順隆在第一審及原審審理中，一再供稱：「黃運享交給我應是一百二十萬元才對」。「我自己要用」。「沒有交給甲」。「很冤枉，中午調查局人員把我送到調查局（台北市調查處），到第二天一直不讓我睡，也恐嚇我說：已偵辦六、七月無法交差，如不配合，要把達永案（陳順隆所涉之另一案件）拖下去」。又恐嚇我：要將我有女友事告訴我妻子，為求自保，我才承認（指依該調查處承辦人員之意思說：送一百萬元給上訴人），我認為法官能為他（指上訴人）洗清冤枉」。「筆錄作很多次，被訊二十多小時，他（指承辦人）不滿意就撕掉，寫很多次」。「在調查處我講我的，他寫他的（指筆錄記載不實）……」。「我很內疚，他（指台北市調查處承辦人員）一直要我這麼說（指說送錢給上訴人），我說我的，他寫他的……」。「在調查局（台北市調查處）從中午十二點開始訊問，有三、四組五、六個人問，一直不讓我睡覺，至隔天中午十二時止，共二十多小時等語」。依照前開說明，原審自有調查台北市調查處訊問陳順隆時，有無以脅迫、利誘或疲勞訊問等不正方法取供之必要。原審未予調查明白，率行判決，自有未盡職權調查之能事。

條第 1 項第 1 款及第 2 款所定之事項。但經審判長徵詢訴訟關
係人之意見後，認為適當者，得僅記載其要旨。」之規定，亦
首度將此種實務明文於審判筆錄規定中[16]。由於筆錄記載所呈
現出來之事實常成為檢察官據以起訴或是法院據以裁判之依
據，因此筆錄記載之正確性對於訴訟結果是否正確與公平而
言，有著相當重要的影響，也就是說，「如果最初的筆錄都出
現不實與扭曲的現象，而又沒有辦法加以更正與明辨，那就會
造成後來審判方向的錯誤，甚至會使得冤獄就此定案、而無從
補救[17]。」。我國最高法院就此除已承認：偵、審筆錄記載是
否錯誤於判決結果有實質影響應屬事實審法院於審判期日應
行調查之事項[18]外，更要求被告須於事實審審理時，提出筆

---

[16] 依其立法理由：「修正條文第 44 條之 1 第 1 項已規定審判期日應全程錄
音；必要時，並得全程錄影。故而，就審判期日之訴訟程序進行，均有錄音
或錄影資料為憑，為促進法庭紀錄之效率，對於第 41 條第 1 項第 1 款所定
受訊問人之訊問及陳述暨第 2 款所定證人、鑑定人或通譯未具結之事由等事
項，審判長得徵詢各該訴訟關係人之意見，於認為適當時，僅於審判筆錄內
記載其要旨，如法院或雙方當事人認為該記載事項有所疑義時，再就錄音或
錄影之內容予以核對即可，爰於本條第 1 項第 7 款增訂但書之規定，以應實
務運作之需要。」之說明，此款之修正係以審判筆錄有錄音或錄影可為稽核
為前提。此外，亦有立法委員提出之刑事訴訟法第 41 條修正草案，明文承
認訊問筆錄應由書記官摘記要點獨立制作筆錄。參閱咋觸集，刑事訴訟法第
34 條至 41 條等條文修正草案，available at: http://fuldali.blogspot.com/2007/05/
blog-post_07.html (Mar. 1, 2008).

[17] 參閱賴素如，「筆錄確實可被操控 人權難保」，available at: http://search.cdns.
com.tw/loadfile.asp? sid=0&iid=0&did=45021&checksum=56647&query2= 賴素
如（Mar. 1, 2008）.

[18] 參照最高法院 85 年台上字第 3391 號判決：「惟查（一）上訴人提出之開庭
錄音帶，係欲證明偵訊筆錄記載不實。則該錄音帶有無經剪輯失真，不難經

由鑑定查明，乃原審未送有關機關鑑定，即遽認該錄音帶真實性有疑問，無採證價值，難謂無應於審判期日調查之證據未予調查之違法。（二）刑法第213條公務員登載不實罪所稱之足生損害於公眾或他人，以有損害之虞為已足，不以實際發生損害為必要。原判決理由雖說明縱該錄音帶內容屬實，法院採信證人曾淑美、謝佳娟二人證詞，並不因上訴人對二證人所言答稱「無意見」或「他們要陷害我的」，而有不同之判決結果，亦難認有何損害於上訴人云云，然證人曾淑美、謝佳娟在前開上訴人對二證人所言答稱「無意見」或「他們要陷害我的」，而有不同之判決結果，亦難認有何損害於上訴人云云，然證人曾淑美、謝佳娟在前開上訴人妨害家庭等案偵查中，係證明上訴人有帶同一男一女至丙建築師事務所，由該男子勒住丙脖子，拉往會客室，令丙下跪，則上訴人指訴被告將檢察官訊其「對兩證人（指曾、謝二人）講的話有什麼意見？」所答「他們是要陷害我的」，載為「沒有」，如果屬實，無異上訴人已供認犯罪，自有影響法院判斷之虞，能否謂不足生損害於上訴人，殊堪研求。上訴意旨指摘原判決不當，非無理由，應認有發回更審之原因。」、86年台上字第1475號判決：「再查原審既已諭知被告無罪，則被告所提對其有利所謂82年3月26日申告時之錄音及譯文，即欠缺調查之必要性，原審不予調查，於判決並無影響。而上訴人於原審雖具狀請求傳訊制作偵查筆錄之書記官張明珠、林金淑、劉艾文，以查明該筆錄是否被變造，惟原審既未認定該筆錄被變造，亦未審酌被告所謂證明申告筆錄記載有誤之上開錄音帶，是上開證人亦無傳訊調查之必要。」、87年台上字第2474號判決：「原判決以證人劉蕙如於警局之證詞，據為被告丙、乙、戊、丁、庚、甲等六人共同殺人證據之一。然查被告等辯稱劉蕙如與丁之父林惠文談話時，陳明警訊筆錄記載不實云云，並提出錄音帶及其譯文為證。被告等上開辯解及所提談話錄音如何不足採，原判決未於理由內說明，即屬理由不備。」、93年台上字第1687號判決：「事實審法院如未於審判期日就上訴人否認犯罪所為有利之辯解事項及證據予以調查，亦不於判決理由內加以論列，率行判決，即有調查未盡及理由不備之違法。又筆錄內所載之被告陳述與錄音或錄影之內容不符者，除有急迫情況且經記明筆錄而未錄音、錄影之情形外，其不符之部分，不得作為證據，刑事訴訟法第100條之1第2項定有明文。故審理事實之法院，遇有被告抗辯其未有如訊問筆錄所載之陳述時，應先調取該訊問過程之錄音或錄影帶，加以勘驗，以判斷該筆錄所載被告之陳述得否作為證據。」與96年台上字第1442號判決：「原判決理由引用上訴人於94年12月19日警詢時自承伊騎機車前往高雄縣林園鄉○○○路十八號欲殺死乙等情，為認定上訴人有殺乙犯意之證據之一。惟上訴人於原審否認有殺乙之犯意，並辯稱：伊警詢時未供承有殺乙之犯意，警詢筆錄記載不實等語，並請求勘驗警詢錄音帶，原審就此未予調查，又未說明不予調查之理由，亦有可議。」

錄記載錯誤之抗辯，並應具體指出有何筆錄與錄音不符之情
事[19]，惟如被告僅泛言筆錄記載不實，或原審並未採信有爭議
之筆錄內容，縱有筆錄記載不實之情事，亦不該當判決違背法
令[20]。然而，筆錄記載有無錯誤（正確性）除將導致前述審判
程序是否違背法令出現爭議外，是否亦將構成其他法律爭議，
亦值得進一步觀察。

　　保障刑事被告不論貧富貴賤均能平等地享有公正審判的權
利，是一項從西元 1215 年的大憲章便已開始追求的目標[21]，蓋

---

[19] 參照最高法院 95 年台上字第 37 號判決：「又審判期日之訴訟程序，專以審
判筆錄為證，刑事訴訟法第 47 條定有明文，事實審審理時，上訴人始終未曾
抗辯偵、審筆錄與各該錄音內容有何不符之情形，事實審之審判筆錄在卷可
稽，上訴意旨（二）並未具體指出有何筆錄與錄音不符之情事，僅憑其主觀
之臆測，徒以事實審之偵、審筆錄可能與錄音內容不符，不能採筆錄記載之
內容為判決之基礎云云，指摘原判決違法，亦非依據卷內資料為原判決具體
違法指摘之上訴第三審適法理由。」。

[20] 參照最高法院 93 年台上字第 3572 號判決：「原判決並未採上訴人等於警訊中
之筆錄為斷罪之資料，另共同被告廖日明於警訊、偵查及第一審法院之供述，
原審法院已於審判期日提示並告以要旨後，訊問上訴人等有無意見，上訴人等
均答「沒有意見」，且於調查證據完畢前審判長仍訊問上訴人及其選任之辯護
人「尚有何證據請求調查？」均答「沒有」，並未聲請與廖日明對質，有審判
筆錄可稽。於法律審之本院始再爭執上訴人等之警訊筆錄記載不實，原審法院
未詳查，且未命上訴人等與廖日明對質，即採為證據，有應於審判期日調查之
證據未予調查之情形，顯非依據卷內資料執為指摘之合法上訴理由。」。

[21] See Griffin v. Illinois, 351 U.S. 12, 16-7 (1956)("Providing equal justice for poor
and rich, weak and powerful alike is an age-old problem. People have never
ceased to hope and strive to move closer to that goal. This hope, at least in part,
brought about in 1215 the royal concessions of Magna Charta: "To no one will we
sell, to no one will we refuse, or delay, right or justice...No free man shall be
taken or imprisoned, or disseised, or outlawed, or exiled, or anywise destroyed;
nor shall we go upon him nor send upon him, but by the lawful judgment of his
peers or by the law of the land."").

在刑事訴訟程序中，被告之膚色、資力或宗教等差異，不應作
爲被告於訴訟程序上受到差別待遇的基礎，畢竟前述因素與被
告是否有罪沒有必然的關聯，以之作爲剝奪被告接受公平審判
之理由，並不洽當[22]。雖然美國聯邦憲法並未要求各州有義務
提供有罪被告上訴救濟的絕對權利[23]，不過提起上訴爲被告不
服有罪判決時所應享有之基本人權[24]，已爲正當法律程序的重
要內涵。一但法律承認此項基本人權（上訴權），即不應以被
告貧窮否定其上訴權，否則有可能在上訴審翻案之有罪被告，
即可能因貧窮而喪失其生命、財產或自由[25]。而爲使被告能夠

---

[22] Id., at 17-8 ("In criminal trials a State can no more discriminate on account of poverty than on account of religion, race, or color. Plainly the ability to pay costs in advance bears no rational relationship to a defendant's guilt or innocence and could not be used as an excuse to deprive a defendant of a fair trial.").

[23] See Mckane v. Durston, 153 U.S. 684, 687 (1894)("An appeal from a judgment of conviction is not a matter of absolute right, independently of constitutional or statutory provisions allowing such appeal. A review by an appellate court of the final judgment in a criminal case, however grave the offense of which the accused is convicted, was not at common law, and is not now, a necessary element of due process of law. It is wholly within the discretion of the state to allow or not to allow such a review.").

[24] See People v. Montgomery, 24 N.Y. 2d 130, 132 (1969)("A defendant has a fundamental right to appellate review of a criminal conviction."); see also People v Harrison, , 85 N.Y. 2d 794, 796 (1995).

[25] See 351 U.S., at 18-9 ("There is no meaningful distinction between a rule which would deny the poor the right to defend themselves in a trial court and one which effectively denies the poor an adequate appellate review accorded to all who have money enough to pay the costs in advance⋯. But that is not to say that a State that does grant appellate review can do so in a way that discriminates against some convicted defendants on account of their poverty⋯. Thus to deny adequate review to the poor means that many of them may lose their life, liberty or property because of unjust convictions which appellate courts would set aside.").

充分地行使上訴的權利，下級審的審判記錄必須完整記載審判程序中所有發生的事件與所有進行的程序[26]，以使被告知悉提起上訴之具體理由為何。如果有罪被告因無資力支付下級審審判記錄之費用而失去上訴的權利（機會），因僅有資力之有罪被告得支付下級審審判記錄費用並獲得上訴救濟，那麼審判結果公正與否無異以被告之資力為前提，如此即有違公正審判之目標[27]。

　　綜上所述，提供筆錄記載內容旨在保障被告的上訴權，避免被告因缺乏對訴訟程序重要資訊（筆錄記載內容）的了解，於上訴程序中遭受不利益。然而，對被告而言，縱免費提供審判記錄，若筆錄內容存在實質錯誤，那麼不完整或錯誤的資訊提供，不僅有害於被告之資訊取得權，亦無助於被告上訴權的行使，因此，筆錄記載之正確性，對於被告上訴權之保障而

---

[26]　See People v. Harrison, 85 N.Y. 2d 794, 796 (1995)("To facilitate that right, section 295 of the Judiciary Law requires that full stenographic notes be taken of all trial proceedings and, on request of counsel during a jury trial, "each and every remark or comment by [the] judge...and every exception taken to any such ruling or decision" must be recorded. The People acknowledge that Judiciary Law § 295 applies to criminal proceedings and that the voir dire of prospective jurors is a part of the trial within the meaning of the statute.").

[27]　See 351 U.S., at 19 ("Such a denial is a misfit in a country dedicated to affording equal justice to all and special privileges to none in the administration of its criminal law. There can be no equal justice where the kind of trial a man gets depends on the amount of money he has. Destitute defendants must be afforded as adequate appellate review as defendants who have money enough to buy transcripts.").

言，即爲十分重要。只不過，欠缺完整或正確的審判記錄，並不必然導致原審判程序無效而須再審[28]，而只有在筆錄記載闕漏或筆錄記載錯誤等情事，必將導致上訴法院無法針對上訴部分審查下級法院所進行之審判程序是否違背法令時，才能撤銷原裁判並進行再審的程序[29]。換言之，除了原審存在明顯而有害的錯誤得經上訴審裁定再審外，只有在闕漏或誤植之筆錄內容成爲上訴審查之重要部分，而當事人雙方無法就闕漏或誤植之事實爭點達成合意時，因本次上訴已無審查對象，才有裁定再審之必要，惟通常基於重要證人再次出庭不易與訴訟經濟之考量，上訴審原則上應儘量避免裁定進行再審程序。

在刑事訴訟程序中，筆錄記載正確與否，除將成爲事實審

---

[28] See Herndon v. City of Massillon, 638 F. 2d 963, 965 (6th Cir. 1981)("A party may not seek a new trial simply because matters occurring in the court are not reflected in the transcript. Rather, that party must at least attempt to cure the defect by reconstructing the record as provided. "); see also Hyramotive Mfg. Corp. v. Securities and Exchange Com'n, 355 F. 2d 179, 180 (10th Cir. 1966) ("The inability to obtain a stenographic transcript of testimony is not enough alone to warrant a new trial.").

[29] See Bergerco, U.S.A. v. Shipping Corp. of India, Ltd., 896F. 2d 1210, 1217 (9th Cir. 1990)("The lack of a complete transcript does not automatically warrant reversal. However, in certain circumstances, the original transcript may be so essential to meaningful appellate review that a remand for a new trial is necessary to insure a fair appeal.... We conclude that an appellant seeking a new trial because of a missing or incomplete transcript must 1) make a specific allegation of error; 2) show that the defect in the record materially affects the ability of the appeals court to review the alleged error; and 3) show that a ... proceeding [authorized by the rule] has failed or would fail to produce an adequate substitute for the evidence.").

判決程序是否違背法令之判斷基礎外，更將對被告資訊取得權
與上訴權，產生重大的影響，蓋一但筆錄記載錯誤，即有如提
供被告錯誤的訴訟資訊；假若被告無法取得正確與完整的訴訟
資訊，即無法期待其能於訴訟程序進行中，甚至於是否提起上
訴程序的決定過程中，做出正確與公正的決定。而若記載不完
整與闕漏的筆錄無法完整地呈現下級審於訴訟結果有實質影響
之重要事項如何審審判之過程，亦將影響上訴審是否能正確審
查下級審所進行之審判程序並作出裁判。既然筆錄記載正確與
否將左右上下級法院是否能作出正確的裁判，並影響被告之資
訊取得權，基於公平法院之要求，避免被告在資訊錯誤的條件
下做出不正確的訴訟攻防，或方向錯誤的上訴主張，自應保障
被告有權取得內容記載正確與完整的筆錄，以充實被告防禦的
權能。既然筆錄記載正確與否對於訴訟結果是否公正具有重要
的意義，當被告或其他受訊問者，甚至訊問者本身都對於筆錄
的內容產生疑義時，究竟該有什麼機制保障筆錄記載的正確性
與客觀性，似為我國學說與實務論述向來所未觸及的議題。雖
有立法委員曾提出刑事訴訟法第 41 條第 3 項修正案：「被告得
依第 1 項當場之錄音制作逐字筆錄，經公證人公證後以書狀送
達法院為法院筆錄[30]。」嘗試賦予被告制作逐字筆錄（非筆錄
要旨）之權，惟此項草案亦僅授權「被告」於「事後」提出

---

[30] 參閱咋觸集，刑事訴訟法第 34 條至 41 條等條文修正草案，available at: http://
fuldali.blogspot.com/2007/05/blog-post_07.html (Mar. 1, 2008).

「經公證人公證」筆錄新版本之權利，至於訊問者與筆錄制作者對於陳述內容出現不同認知時，該如何決定筆錄內容並處理其間的爭議，並不在前述草案涵蓋範圍之內。是否在前述「事後模式」之外，仍存在其他由非被告在「事中」更正筆錄的模式，以保障記載內容與訴訟結果的公正與客觀，應為亟待處理之課題。

肆、落實由非訊問者制作筆錄之必要性

在我國刑事訴訟程序交互詰問法制正式上路之初，即曾有執業律師以「法院書記官的記錄能力無法配合冗長的法庭攻防發言」為由，質疑司法當局僅強化審檢法庭活動卻忽略書記官角色的改革作法，提出「只顧詰問者、被詰問者滔滔不絕的發言，而不顧正確與完整的記錄存卷，那麼，其陳述內容如何作為證據被正確地引用呢？」的質疑，並認為忽略書記官角色之實務運作，恐將導致交互詰問新制之美意落空[31]。雖其進一步

---

[31] 其說明如下：當「交互詰問」過程要作成書面記錄成為官方卷證，以作法官裁判依據，書記官筆錄（電腦打字）的速度跟不上，於是在法庭上發言者要等待書記官作筆錄，勢必打斷發言，拖延時間。如此一來，過程越拖越長，時間浪費越多。而且，等候記錄，既干擾發言者的思路，又難顯現即席機智問答的功效，失去新制所要達成的「發見實質的真實」之原意，新制的美意遂大打折扣。假如不等待書記官的記錄而逕自持續發言，則筆錄就可能發生掛一漏萬的瑕疵。儘管有同步錄音，仍因書面記錄未呈現完整的發言內容，閱覽卷宗時無法窺知交互詰問的原貌，無從引為攻防及裁判的依據。如此一

質疑「僅記載筆錄要旨（非逐字記載）」與「避免檢辯因對筆錄所載一兩個字或一小段話有意見而要求訂正或增補，造成詰問停頓，影響案件進行，且易給證人、被告思考的時間，無法即問即答，致不利於眞實之發見。」二者間之實質關聯[32]，惟其並未針對「檢辯對筆錄內容認知不同」與「訊問者與記錄者對筆錄內容認知不同」等爭議，提出解決的方法。由於該文具體強調書記官據實記錄於刑事訴訟程序中的重要性，該如何落實書記官據實記錄，實爲刑事訴訟程序所不應忽略的議題。

來，冗長的新制程序豈非白做工了嗎？至於說，可以事後播聽錄音帶以知悉全部發言內容，然則，「聽」過而無「寫」存紀錄，又將如何引用？如何徵信？何況，各審級的法官、檢察官、辯護人都須播聽，人力物力之浪費將可預料。所以，書記官的角色扮演，其實是這一刑訴新制成敗的重要關鍵。書記官的人力配置與打字能力，甚至於從「聽」到「寫」的語文素養之訓練，都是不可或缺的。試問司法行政當局考量到「書記官角色」這一重要環節了嗎？參閱許文彬，刑事訴訟新制應重視書記官角色，available at: http://www.president.gov.tw/1_structure/famous/column/7_xwb20040501.html (Mar. 1, 2008).

[32] 其說明如下：殊不知，那筆錄上的「一兩個字」或「一小段話」，往往正是案情的關鍵所在，才會引起兩造要求訂正或增補。如今，司法行政當局就為著怕詰問停頓、拖延時間，而不惜錯過把這關鍵筆錄記載內容弄個清楚的機制，豈非本末倒置乎？如此距離「發見真實」的目標豈非行愈行愈遠了嗎？司法行政當局又說，書記官的筆錄只要記載「要旨」就好了，所以不必把電腦螢幕開著供各方當場檢視。殊不知，要把發言者的整個發言內容，濃縮成「要旨」而記之，並不見得比隨聽隨寫而完整地記錄來得簡單輕鬆。因為，若要歸納發言者發言內容的準確意思，而記下全部發言內容所要表達的中心旨意，那麼，一方面，必須「從頭聽到尾」再回過頭來記，始能採擷其「要旨」而無誤，如此，豈會較諸邊聽邊寫而完整地記錄來得快呢？另一方面，若要完整無誤地歸納發言的「要旨」而記之，則非有高明的語文素養訓練者豈能勝任？不怕扭曲原意或掛一漏萬嗎？參閱許文彬，刑事訴訟新制應重視書記官角色，available at: http://www.president.gov.tw/1_structure/famous/column/7_xwb20040501.html (Mar. 1, 2008).

　　由於訊問者之記憶難免有錯，為使起訴者或審判者於制作
書類時有確實可信的參考依據，訴訟進行之過程遂有逐一記錄
之必要，而筆錄即為此處所指訴訟進行中記載事實經過之文
書。雖然刑事訴訟第 41 條與第 44 條已規定筆錄應記載之事
項，不過筆錄內容究應依訊問者或記錄者甚至被訊問者之認知
而制作，現行法卻未提供完整的解決之道。依刑事訴訟法第 41
條第 2 項：「前項筆錄應向受訊問人朗讀或令其閱覽，詢以記
載有無錯誤。」與第 3 項：「受訊問人請求將記載增、刪、變
更者，應將其陳述附記於筆錄。」等規定，受訊問人有確認筆
錄記載內容有無錯誤並請求更正筆錄之權，由於此時僅應將其
陳述附記於筆錄，因此受訊問者並無權請求刪除與其主觀認知
不同的筆錄記載。然若訊問者與記錄者對於陳述內容認知不同
時，因不存在類似「訊問人請求將記載增、刪、變更者，應將
其陳述附記於筆錄。」之規定，是否表示記錄者應依訊問者之
請求直接將原記載增、刪、變更，而不須就此情事附記於筆
錄？換言之，當原筆錄已作成甚至逐字記錄但訊問者要求依其
認知制作筆錄要旨時，筆錄之內容究應由誰決定？訊問者？或
是書記官？

　　由於檢察官與法官在偵查與審判程序中享有訴訟指揮權，
因此有認書記官在偵審程序中如何記錄乙事，應在訊問者指揮
權所涵蓋的範圍內；依其說明：「訊問之法官或檢察官所以應
簽名於非其制作之筆錄上，乃因法官與檢察官對此有指揮命令
之權，簽名除表示負監督責任之意，亦在確保該文書之證據

力。」、「另有使在場參與或蒞視制作文書之人簽名蓋章者，如訊問被告、證人、鑑定人及通譯筆錄，應由受訊問人緊接其記載之末行簽名、蓋章或按指印；搜索、扣押及勘驗筆錄，應令依法命其在場之人簽名、蓋章或按指印，要亦出以確保文書證據力之意；惟此類筆錄之制作，應屬書記官之職權，故雖未經上述之人簽名、蓋章或按指印，該文書（筆錄）仍非無效，至其可否採信，則應由法院依自由心證判斷之[33]。」，似認書記官制作筆錄之職權應完全受制於檢察官或法官之訴訟指揮權；又在未違訴訟指揮之前提下，縱受訊問人或其他依法命其在場之人（不同意筆錄記載內容）未簽名於筆錄上，亦不致生筆錄當然無效之結果；亦即，書記官依刑事訴訟法第 43 條制作筆錄之職權，並不完整。然而，縱可認這樣的觀點與大陸法系信賴司法官公正行使訴訟指揮權之傳統有關，其主張書記官僅應依訊問者指示記錄之說法，似已與前述「由訊問以外之人制作筆錄旨在保障筆錄記載之公正性與客觀性與避免訊問者自問自答」的規範目的有所違背。

隨著訴訟程序的推移，在補充訊問者記憶與提供檢察官與法官制作書類參考的目的下，遂有以審判筆錄、訊問筆錄、勘驗筆錄等多種文書保留程序進行準確記錄之必要。當記錄內容是否準確出現爭議，也就是訊問者與記錄者對於陳述內容認知

---

[33] 參閱林永謀，刑事訴訟法釋論（上），頁 219，作者自版，2006 年 10 月初版 1 刷。

不同時，是否存在有別於訴訟指揮觀點之解決模式？不同於前述由訊問者完全監督指揮之立場，有日本學者指出，雖然書記官應根據法官的命令（訴訟指揮權）進行法庭活動，但是本諸國家公務員的公益角色，書記官於另一方面亦應具有獨立擔當「公共證明」的任務。以此為前提，在書記官接受法官命令制作以及變更文書內容的時候，如果認為該命令的內容不正當，縱仍應依據該命令制作、變更文書，但同時書記官亦可以將自己的意見附加於後[34]，以反映真實的情況，並使上級法院有機會知悉此過程。換言之，此說承認在檢察官與法官訴訟指揮權監督下，書記官仍保有完整獨立的筆錄制作權，蓋書記官身為文官體系之一員，縱其在訴訟指揮下仍負有忠實記載「法官或檢察官對於陳述認知理解（陳述要旨）」之義務，尚不致因該義務之履行而於法理上必然喪失其公益之角色，故應認書記官有依自身對陳述認知理解記載筆錄之權責較為妥當。

　　毫無疑問的，依照法官指示一句書記官才記錄一句之記錄方式，特別當法官係依其個人對陳述整理後之要旨所指示者與原陳述次序或內容有出入時，不但不足以反映審判全貌，難免也使上級法院審閱卷宗時無法了解下級審之實際審理情形，甚至使狡猾之一方藉主張筆錄要旨與其陳述原意不符而脫罪、卸

---

[34]　為了實現正當、快速裁判的目的，日本學者亦有人主張法院書記官應與法官的密切協作，更加積極主動地參與訴訟運作，以發揮法庭管理人的作用。參閱（日）松尾浩也著，丁相順翻譯，金光旭校對，日本刑事訴訟法（上卷），頁236-7，中國人民大學出版社出版，2005年8月1版1刷。

責，或使法院花費許多時間重新調整，甚至誤判[35]。從而於法理上原應認由非訊問者制作筆錄，並賦予書記官獨立完整的筆錄制作權，始足以維筆錄記載之公正與客觀。縱然大陸法系之刑事訴訟制度，因於傳統上對司法官能公正行使訴訟指揮權有一定程度的信賴，然此傳統本身並未導致訴訟指揮權為一不受上級審監督之權力。而因筆錄本身適為上級審監督下級審訴訟程序是否依法進行或者違背法令之主要依據，如果書記官必須按照訊問者所整理之「陳述要旨」記錄，而無權另行記載「本身所認知與訊問者指示不同的內容」以及「訊問者要求如何記載或更改記載的過程」，上級審又將如何自筆錄記載探究該內容究為「訊問者認知的要旨」、「記錄者認知的要旨」甚至「庭訊過程的真實內容」？一但筆錄記載的內容無法真實地呈現出當初庭訊的過程，刑事訴訟法第 47 條：「審判期日之訴訟程序，專以審判筆錄為證。」之規定，若所證者為不真實的程序，又將具有什麼意義呢？因此，在現行檢察官與法官享有訴訟指揮權並主導程序進行的現實下，實務上慣見書記官僅依訊問者認知之要旨記載筆錄（亦即書記官僅扮演訊問者分身的角色）的方式，是有問題的。進一步言之，由於檢察官與法官在制作書類時，並無全盤照錄書記官筆錄記載全文之義務，因此檢察官與法官本即有將原陳述（或其筆錄記載）以要旨之方式

---

[35] 參閱蔡東賢，論法庭記錄電腦化──第一階段體檢司法改革藍圖，司改雜誌第 020 期（1999/4/15），available at: http://www.jrf.org.tw/mag/mag_02s.asp?SN=529 (Mar. 1, 2008).

表現於書類之權限，從而如其於訊問時「僅」要求書記官將其整理之要旨一併記載於筆錄中，以爲將來制作書類時參考，只要不禁止或阻止書記官依本身認知另行記載，尚可將之解爲制作書類草稿之過程，而認該訴訟指揮並無不當。蓋縱訊問者要求記載之要旨與原陳述次序或內容有異，由於以該要旨爲判斷基礎的起訴書或判決書，將於法院審判及審級救濟時，成爲司法審查的標的，要求依要旨記載本身尚不致使與本案判決有實質影響之訴訟指揮不受司法監督。若依現行實務而謂訊問者之訴訟指揮權得限制或禁止書記官依自身認知制作筆錄，除有無法完整呈現訴訟程序進行過程、致上級審無從審查之流弊外，亦否定具有國家公務員身分之書記官獨立行使職權以保全訴訟資料的公益地位。換言之，落實由非訊問者制作筆錄，維護書記官獨立制作筆錄之權限，實可視爲法院審判或審級監督所不可或缺之重要機制。

其實，實務上會存在或形成前述「依照法官指示一句書記官才記錄一句之記錄方式」之運作模式，並非沒有原因，蓋於過去相當長的一段歷史中，書記官之取才管道主要有二，一爲經由司法特考書記官考試或書記官普通考試所產生，另一爲經由書記官委任升等考試所產生。或因前者留任比例較低，在公務員任用法修正停止任用正式雇員之前 [36]，長期以來法院書記

---

[36] 依現行公務員任用法第 15 條第 1 款：「雇員升委任考試及格者，取得委任第一職等任用資格。」之規定，正式雇員通過委任升等考試，縱尚未派委任職，仍得於日後派任委任第一職等公務員之資格。

官以後者占多數，由於後者在擔任書記官前大多未接受過正式的法學教育，以致於其在擔任書記官職務之初，大部分缺乏足夠的法律學識以應付龐雜的法律業務，反應於記錄實務上，即出現仰賴檢察官與法官提供法律協助始能完成記錄工作的現象。既然大部分的書記官皆有賴檢察官與法官的協助以完成大部分的工作[37]，長此以往，檢察官與法官似亦自覺有協助書記官之義務，復透過職務監督的進行，不免壓縮了書記官獨立行使（記錄）職權的空間。然而，在公務員任用法禁止任用無考試資格者擔任正式雇員後，有資格參加委任升等考試者也已逐年減少，目前經由書記官特考擔任書記官職務者，大多為法律系畢業的科班生，反倒已成為書記官的主要構成分子。既然書記官的素質已大幅提昇，過去以書記官程度不足以獨立制作筆錄之主張，在特考書記官成為主流，在升等書記官逐漸退休淡出記錄之後，也漸漸不具有說服力，該是將獨立制作筆錄的權限回歸書記官以落實由非訊問者實質制作筆錄的時候了。

伍、筆錄記載之法制化－代結論

特別費案所引發筆錄內容記載不實的爭議，曾因被告身分

---

[37] 舉例而言，在偵查或審判程序中如有發文函查之必要，除非是例稿發文，否則大多由承辦檢察官或法官於案件進行單上草擬該公文，書記官多僅扮演打字的角色，此與一般行政機關的發文程序有很大的差異。

的敏感特殊而喧嘩一時，遺憾的是，該爭議焦點僅為承辦檢察官是否有意扭曲證人陳述，當鎂光燈不再，關於筆錄內容是否應完全依訊問者的指示或意思記載（僅記載訊問者認知的陳述要旨）之議題，卻未曾得到應有的關注。本文除自我國有關筆錄制作之法制與實務，肯認筆錄記載正確與否為事實審法院應於審判期日調查之事項外，更自美國司法實務的發展，肯認筆錄記載之正確性為審級救濟能否發揮功能所不可或缺的重要前提。雖然受訊問人有權閱覽筆錄並請求將筆錄記載增、刪、變更，但若筆錄完全依照訊問者之意思制作，當受訊問人（特別是證人）放棄筆錄閱覽權或放棄請求增、刪、變更筆錄記載權，筆錄記載的正確性，甚至訴訟程序是否違背法令，即有可能出現爭議。縱使被告事後得提出訊問程序錄音之譯文，以排除與錄音內容不同之筆錄記載[38]，但在正當程序的要求下，國家機關本應儘量維護筆錄記載之正確性，此際，落實由非訊問者實質制作筆錄，應為確保筆錄記載內容正確較符程序經濟的機制了。

---

[38] 參照刑事訴訟法第 44 條之 1 第 2 項：「當事人、代理人、辯護人或輔佐人如認為審判筆錄之記載有錯誤或遺漏者，得於次一期日前，其案件已辯論終結者，得於辯論終結後七日內，聲請法院定期播放審判期日錄音或錄影內容核對更正之。其經法院許可者，亦得於法院指定之期間內，依據審判期日之錄音或錄影內容，自行就有關被告、自訴人、證人、鑑定人或通譯之訊問及其陳述之事項轉譯為文書提出於法院。」與第 100 條之 1：「（第 1 項）訊問被告，應全程連續錄音；必要時，並應全程連續錄影。但有急迫情況且經記明筆錄者，不在此限。（第 2 項）筆錄內所載之被告陳述與錄音或錄影之內容不符者，除有前項但書情形外，其不符之部分，不得作為證據。」。

　　按刑事訴訟法第 41 條第 2 項：「前項筆錄應向受訊問人朗讀或令其閱覽，詢以記載有無錯誤。」第 3 項：「受訊問人請求將記載增、刪、變更者，應將其陳述附記於筆錄。」與第 44 條第 2 項：「受訊問人就前項筆錄中關於其陳述之部分，得請求朗讀或交其閱覽，如請求將記載增、刪、變更者，應附記其陳述。」等規定，已足以作為訊問者（含書記官）與受訊問者對筆錄記載內容有不同認知時之處理依據，若果有疑義，訊問者尚可實施勘驗，以杜爭端。不過，當訊問者與書記官對於陳述內容之認知有所差異時，而受訊問人未表示意見時，現行法卻未提供解決之道。基於書記官制作筆錄之規定，本文主張此時應由書記官先行記載其所認知之陳述內容，若訊問者有不同意見，書記官亦應記載訊問者所整理之訊問要旨，以為程序進行之記錄。訊問者亦可就其有疑問之記載，重行訊問原陳述者，若訊問者認為受訊問人前後陳述不一，或書記官原記載確有出入，為求筆錄記載客觀真實，亦可當庭諭命勘驗錄音，以明疑義。當然，若書記官之本職學能有所欠缺，致其無法跟上陳述而為確實之記載，前述主張將增加庭訊所需之時間，影響開庭之效率，惟因此乃技術層面之問題，尚不足以作為否定書記官獨立制作筆錄，扮演公益監督角色之理由。故而在書記官本職學能已強化之前提下，本文反對實務上書記官僅記載訊問者口述陳述要旨之作法，畢竟當訊問者所整理的陳述要旨與陳述者所為之實際陳述存在明顯差異的情形中，要求或容許書記官「充耳不聞」地忽略陳述者原意而僅記載訊問者要求之主

張，不但明顯有違公正程序的要求，更將使得閱卷權成為無意
義之資訊取得手段。

　　本文之作，旨在對現行記錄實務進行檢討，並釐清記錄工
作在刑事訴訟程序中具有的意義與應有的定位，並無欲對個案
有所評論。或因特別費案過度敏感，以致該案發生迄今尚未見
有關記錄權責歸屬之探討，祈本文能發揮拋磚引玉之效，吸引
更多對此問題之重視及討論。

9 新聞記者拒絕證言之權能與界限

壹、問題之提出

　　民國 88 年 7 月間，台北地檢署指揮調查局台北市調查處，針對前交通部長秘書駱志豪所涉洩密案展開調查，除駱志豪因涉案重大被收押禁見外，檢調雙方也針對中國時報、今周刊兩媒體的記者住處進行搜索，引發司法戕害新聞自由之輿論抨擊。另於民國 89 年 10 月間，為偵辦國安局上校組長劉冠軍貪污案所引發之洩密案外案，由台北地檢署主任檢察官所指揮搜索中時晚報報社及記者住處之舉動，又再度引起軒然大波，除了招致新聞界異口同聲之指摘外，台北地檢署檢察長也於同年月五日首次以發布新聞稿之方式，對外說明該次搜索確具急迫性與必要性，並無違法不當可言。

　　綜觀前指二次新聞媒體人員遭受搜索之事件，之所以出現前述爭議，似乎在於媒體所主張享有的新聞自由，與檢調單位所認知的新聞自由，在界限與範圍上出現齟齬所致，因此關於新聞自由此一概念，究應有何等之內涵，其概念範圍之合理射程為何，即有予以究明之必要。此外，在市場競爭之機制下，

爲了吸引讀者、增加銷售量，媒體難免會以聳動的話題、獨家報導的方式，獲取商業利益，當其報導之內容涉及犯罪或有犯罪嫌疑時，是否本於新聞自由的要求，即當然使得媒體從業人員享有拒絕證言之權限？亦值得進一步加以檢討。

貳、 新聞自由與新聞來源保密

一、 新聞記者之界定

長久以來，對於何爲新聞記者，一直未有明確的界線；加以媒體業管理規範之不足，不但八卦小報之設立如雨後春筍般之出現，甚至出現「大家都有記者證」的浮濫現象。對於記者之定位，首應根除此種亂象。

現行法對於「記者業」並未有明確的規範，然而制定於民國 32 年、卻於民國 34 年暫緩實施的新聞記者法，似可提供定位上的參考。該法第 1 條規定：「本法所稱新聞記者，謂在日報或通訊社擔任發行人、撰述、編輯、採訪或主辦發行及廣告之人」。而爲確保新聞記者具有足以勝任其職務的專業能力，該法第 3 條乃規定請領新聞記者證書之要件 [1]。揆諸目前新聞界

---

[1] 該條所規定之要件如下：一、在教育部認可之國內外大學或獨立學院之新聞系或新聞專科學校畢業，得有證書者。二、除前款外在教育部認可之國內外大學獨立學院或專科學校修習文學、教育、社會、政治、經濟或法律各學科畢業，得有證書者。三、曾在公立或經立案之私立大學專門學校就前二款各

之良莠不齊，不論自律或是他律，對於所謂的新聞記者，在專業性的要求下，實有加以管理之必要，至於究應如何界定新聞記者之範圍，有待對於「言論自由」與「新聞自由」之釐清[2]，本文不擬深論。

二、 新聞自由之定位

新聞自由是透過大眾媒介傳布資訊或概念（理念），而不受到政府限制（干預）的權利。新聞自由是近世才有的概念（約 16 世紀和 17 世紀初），是人類對抗極權統治而衍生出的利器。然而，時至今日，世界上仍有許多國家或地區無法享受此種權利。以美國爲例，自殖民時代即有此概念。並且在建國之後，受美國憲法第一修正案所保障：「國會不得制定任何法律……限制言論或新聞自由。」(Congress shall make no law abridging the freedom of speech or the press)。新聞自由是美國憲法中的人權法案所揭櫫的四大自由之一，是民主政治正常運作所不可或缺的基石。透過新聞媒體的報導，人民可以了解政府的各項活動，故而有學者認爲沒有新聞自由的憲法即不是憲

學科教授一年以上者。四、在教育部認可之高級中學或舊制中學畢業，並曾執行新聞記者職務二年以上，有證明文件者。五、曾執行新聞記者職務三年以上，有證明文件者。

2 亦即前者之重點爲評論，後者之重點爲事實報導；關於評論之部分如何始受新聞自由的保障，參閱黃國鐘：新聞倫理與言論自由，律師通訊 166 期，頁 22，民國 83 年 7 月。

政民主 [3]。

　　新聞自由為一種憲法所保障的基本權利，我國憲法雖然沒有明文規定，但解釋上，新聞自由應為憲法第 11 條所保障的出版自由所包含 [4]。至於何以新聞自由於民主政治下具有不可或缺的地位？甚至成為檢驗「民主政治」的判準？能否單純自言論自由之角度予以理解？

　　我們常聽說新聞媒體是第四權，是指新聞媒體為政府立法、行政、司法三權以外的第四權，這其中並含有監督制衡的意義。根據第四權理論，憲法之所以要保障新聞自由的目的，是在保障新聞媒體的獨立性及完整性，以維持新聞媒體的自主性，使其能提供未被政府控制或影響的資訊、意見及娛樂，以促使人們對政府及公共事務的關心，並進而引起公共討論，而能善盡監督政府的功能。因此，新聞自由就是要保障新聞媒體能充分發揮其監督政府功能的一種基本權利。基於第四權理論的新聞自由，是憲法為了保障新聞媒體作為現代民主社會一個重要的制度，而給與新聞媒體一種基本權利的保障，是一種「制度性基本權利」；也是一種為維護新聞媒體能達成監督政府功能的「工具性基本權利」；一種只有新聞媒體才能享有的基本權利。因此，基於第四權理論的新聞自由，不僅在權利的

---

[3]　參閱楊日旭：憲法上的新聞自由是不是絕對的權利？（一），國魂 557 期，頁 70，民國 81 年 4 月。

[4]　參閱林子儀：新聞自由的意義及其健全之道，律師通訊 166 期，頁 12、13，民國 83 年 7 月。

基礎理論，同時在權利的性質上，均與言論自由不同[5]。提出新聞自由第四權理論的美國 Potter Stewart 大法官亦曾指出：「憲法保障新聞自由的目的，並不在保障新聞媒體成為一個公眾討論的中立性論壇，一個言論思想的自由市場，也不是要將新聞媒體當成是政府與人民間一個中立的訊息溝通管道，而是為了保障新聞媒體的獨立性及完整性，以維持新聞媒體的自主性，使其提供未被政府控制或影響的資訊、意見及娛樂，以促使人民對於政府及公共事務的關心，並進而引起公眾討論，而能善盡監督政府的功能」。因此新聞自由之功能在於監督政府，若新聞媒體之報導目的不在於監督政府，即難以認符合憲法保障之新聞自由[6]。

三、 新聞自由與權利侵害

國內新聞事業發展，受了自由主義極度盛行的影響，而使新聞「公害」、文字「暴行」處處可見。一般而言，現今國內的媒體報導存在下述弊端：（一）渲染色情：為迎合大眾口味，競相以低級趣味和社會新聞為題材，不良廣告充斥版面，新聞媒介成為犯罪行為的間接幫凶，而日前發生的「老少配」風波，各報競以大篇幅、詳盡的報導，更置社會責任、新聞道

5　同前註。

6　參閱黃朝貴：談新聞自由－從檢察官搜索中時晚報談起（一），法務通訊第2040期，第三版。

德於不顧。（二）侵犯隱私：媒體記者常以「公眾知的權利」為由，刺探影歌星或政治人物之個人隱私，且任意以文字或圖像在媒體上發表。（三）報紙審判：根據「中華民國報業道德規範」第 3 項對「犯罪新聞」的規範，「犯罪案件法院未判決有罪前，應假定被告為無罪」；但與之相對的，每天「報紙審判」的情況比比皆是，如此不但妨礙法官有獨立審判，更使當事人權益受到嚴重損害。（四）誹謗名譽：未經確定、證實的傳聞、耳語在報上、雜誌登出，使當事人名譽受損；此外，謾罵、攻訐的情況亦十分普遍。這些不負責任的人身攻擊言論，已到了讓人怵目驚心的地步。

雖然新聞自由在民主政治發展過程中具有舉足輕重的地位，惟於人人以追求最大利潤為目標的資本社會中，卻經常會出現為謀取商業利潤，假新聞自由之名侵害他人的案例；倘若新聞界利用新聞自由批評時政、影響決策時，忽略職業道德、社會責任及輿論公正等原則，含沙射影、杜撰扯謊，亦將造成不可小覷的後遺症。故有將此種僭越膨脹的新聞自由霸道的第四權斥之為「報痞政治」或「報閥獨裁」[7]。而除前述誹謗、侵害隱私權、報紙審判等情事時常出現於現實生活中外，甚至有以虛偽捏造的手段，「創造」出具有商業價值的新聞。因此，當新聞自由與所謂的國家安全或是人民其他權利出現衝突時，究應如何加以釐清、調和，除使國家安全、個人名譽得與人民

---

7   同註 3。

知之權利間取得平衡外，並使新聞自由不被濫用、亦不受不當限制，仍有待努力。不過，由於以第四權理論爲基礎的新聞自由，屬於一種工具性的權利，因此在比較之下，如認爲對新聞媒體的新聞自由採取管制措施，將更能促進原先保障新聞自由所追求之利益時，政府採取適當的管制措施，並不當然構成違憲[8]。換言之，在民主法治國家，沒有任何權利可以無限擴張，尤其是與其他基本權利或公權力之行使衝突時，必須經過法益衡量，作適度讓步[9]。即便承認新聞自由是憲法第 11 條所保障之權利，但權利沒有絕對的，權利是可以限制的，而權利之限制必須符合一定的目的，否則有損及憲法保障權利之旨[10]，而誠如陳新民教授所言：「人權的可限制性及必要性限制和人權的肯定論自始至終是一起存在與發展，但限制人權之目的，乃在於保證人權不會被濫用，以及促進公共福祉，法治國家的憲法學要論究的是如何妥適地限制人權，而又不損及憲法保障人權的初衷[11]。」從而，釋字第 509 號解釋：「言論自由爲人民之基本權利，憲法第 11 條有明文保障，國家應給予最大限度之維護，俾其實現自我、溝通意見、追求眞理及監督各種政治或社會活動之功能得以發揮。惟爲兼顧對個人名譽、隱私及公共

8　同註 4，頁 13。

9　參閱黃朝貴：談新聞自由----從檢察官搜索中時晚報談起（二），法務通訊第 2041 期，第三版。

10　參閱黃朝貴：談新聞自由----從檢察官搜索中時晚報談起（三），法務通訊第 2043 期，第五版。

11　參閱陳新民：中華民國憲法釋論，頁 159；轉引自前註論文。

利益之保護，法律尚非不得對言論自由依其傳播方式為合理之限制。刑法第 310 條第 1 項及第 2 項誹謗罪即係保護個人法益而設，為防止妨礙他人之自由權利所必要，符合憲法第 23 條規定之意旨。至刑法同條第 3 項前段以對誹謗之事，能證明其為真實者不罰，係針對言論內容與事實相符者之保障，並藉以限定刑罰權之範圍，非謂指摘或傳述誹謗事項之行為人，必須自行證明其言論內容確屬真實，始能免於刑責。惟行為人雖不能證明言論內容為真實，但依其所提證據資料，認為行為人有相當理由確信其為真實者，即不能以誹謗罪之刑責相繩，亦不得以此項規定而免除檢察官或自訴人於訴訟程序中，依法應負行為人故意毀損他人名譽之舉證責任，或法院發現其為真實之義務。就此而言，刑法第 310 條第 3 項與憲法保障言論自由之旨趣並無牴觸。」[12] 之作成，適切反應出新聞媒體之新聞自由與

---

[12] 其解釋理由書亦指出：「憲法第 11 條規定，人民之言論自由應予保障，鑑於言論自由有實現自我、溝通意見、追求真理、滿足人民知的權利，形成公意，促進各種合理的政治及社會活動之功能，乃維持民主多元社會正常發展不可或缺之機制，國家應給予最大限度之保障。惟為保護個人名譽、隱私等法益及維護公共利益，國家對言論自由尚非不得依其傳播方式為適當限制。至於限制之手段究應採用民事賠償抑或兼採刑事處罰，則應就國民守法精神、對他人權利尊重之態度、現行民事賠償制度之功能、媒體工作者對本身職業規範遵守之程度及其違背時所受同業紀律制裁之效果等各項因素，綜合考量。以我國現況而言，基於上述各項因素，尚不能認為不實誹謗除罪化，即屬違憲。況一旦妨害他人名譽均得以金錢賠償而了卻責任，豈非享有財富者即得任意誹謗他人名譽，自非憲法保障人民權利之本意。刑法第 310 條第 1 項：「意圖散布於眾，而指摘或傳述足以毀損他人名譽之事者，為誹謗罪，處一年以下有期徒刑、拘役或五百元以下罰金」，第 2 項：「散布文字、圖畫犯前項之罪者，處二年以下有期徒刑、拘役或一千元以下罰金」係分別對以言

其他權益保護間存在一定程度之關係分際。也就是說，並不是一扣上新聞自由的大帽，就必然可解免於權利侵害之發生；在新聞自由的保障下，仍然承認權利侵害狀態之存在。

四、 新聞自由與新聞來源保密之關聯

　　除前述利用新聞自由侵害他人之情形外，若媒體未利用報導本身作為侵害他人之工具，卻於其報導過程中獲悉權利侵害情事，於刊載後常常導致政府機關（甚至該事件的被害人或其家屬）向其探尋事件內容（主要想知道新聞記者如何獲得採訪消息）。此時新聞記者是否應透露消息來源？或者枉顧個案正義的放任權利侵害之狀態持續存在？

詞或文字、圖畫而誹謗他人者，科予不同之刑罰，為防止妨礙他人自由權益所必要，與憲法第 23 條所定之比例原則尚無違背。
　　刑法第 310 條第 3 項前段規定：「對於所誹謗之事，能證明其為真實者，不罰」，係以指摘或傳述足以毀損他人名譽事項之行為人，其言論內容與事實相符者為不罰之條件，並非謂行為人必須自行證明其言論內容確屬真實，始能免於刑責。惟行為人雖不能證明言論內容為真實，但依其所提證據資料，認為行為人有相當理由確信其為真實者，即不能以誹謗罪之刑責相繩，亦不得以此項規定而免除檢察官或自訴人於訴訟程序中，依法應負行為人故意毀損他人名譽之舉證責任，或法院發現其為真實之義務。就此而言，刑法第 310 條第 3 項與憲法保障言論自由之旨趣並無牴觸。
　　刑法第 311 條規定：「以善意發表言論，而有左列情形之一者，不罰：一、因自衛、自辯或保護合法之利益者。二、公務員因職務而報告者。三、對於可受公評之事，而為適當之評論者。四、對於中央及地方之會議或法院或公眾集會之記事，而為適當之載述者。」係法律就誹謗罪特設之阻卻違法事由，目的即在維護善意發表意見之自由，不生牴觸憲法問題。至各該事由是否相當乃認事用法問題，為審理相關案件法院之職責，不屬本件解釋範圍。

　　美國新聞媒體隨社會多元化、國外局勢及國內政情之丕變，一直扮演著積極報導的角色，並極力爭取新聞自由權利之更大活動空間。歷年來，特別是在 20 世紀 50 年代至 70 年代，因為美國民權運動及韓戰、越戰之衝擊，新聞媒體在爭取新聞自由的同時，又擴張要求，堅決主張要求新聞自由之豁免特權，認為新聞自由之真正維護必須享有新聞免責權。進而，其認新聞自由如無法律特別豁免權，即無法使新聞自由獲得確切之保障，並因此主張新聞自由為絕對之權利，而其內涵應包括：一、免受法院傳喚；二、不受大陪審團調查；三、獲取政府資訊免受干涉；免負誹謗刑責；五、免受警察搜查；六、記者、編者及發行人亦免民刑責任[13]。

　　新聞的獲得主要來自新聞記者的採訪，從而接受採訪的消息來源，倘若不欲被知悉該新聞係自其流傳出去，自會在乎新聞記者是否會將其透露出去，因此，除非新聞來源本身自願公開身分、或同意新聞記者揭露其身分，否則，破壞記者與新聞來源之關係，記者將被認為不可信，而使消息枯竭；並將導致新聞記者減低為民眾廣泛蒐集新聞素材資料、報導事實之能力。而且，司法機關或政府部門強迫記者交出新聞來源，似乎有強迫記者成為政府部門調查人員之虞。如此一來，不但造成新聞記者採訪新聞來源之困難度，間接導致新聞來源枯竭，亦

---

[13] 參閱楊日旭：憲法上的新聞自由是不是絕對的權利？（三），國魂 559 期，頁 64，民國 81 年 6 月。

將使新聞記者背負極大的心理壓力，造成新聞記者或消息來源者，產生自我壓迫制約、寒蟬效應；果真如此，勢必出現消息來源不敢說、記者採訪不到、不敢報導（怕被傳喚）等嚴重影響新聞自由的現象。就此而言，新聞來源之保密可謂為保障新聞自由所必要之手段。

參、 發現真實與新聞自由之衝突

一、 發現真實之障礙－拒絕證言與搜索扣押

在證據裁判主義的要求下，作為判決基礎的事實有賴證據予以認定。因此司法活動本身即負有真實發現之義務。然而在人性尊嚴的思考下，真實發現的要求並未被定位為訴訟活動的最高指導原則，其中拒絕證言權之承認即為歷史發展過程之一例證。然而正義如非基於真實，即難乎其為正義。如許隱匿真實，拒絕提供於法院，其裁判自難免於違誤而發生不公平之結果。是則任何關於作證義務之例外，必須基於適當而有真實價值之政策，辨明其為正當而後可[14]。

依德國刑事訴訟法第 53 條第 1 項規定：「對於下列情形，證人亦有證言拒絕權…現或曾參與期刊或廣播電台職業之籌備、製作或散布而獲知之作者、投稿人、寄付或支持保證人之

---

[14] 參閱李學燈：證據法比較研究，頁 634。

個人事項與對其活動所獲得之消息以及在編輯上所獲得有關寄付、支持與消息之事項。」同法第 97 條第 5 項規定:「如涉及第 53 條第 1 項第 5 款所列人員之證言拒絕權,對於該些人員、編輯、出版、印刷或電台所持有之文件、錄音帶、圖畫、資料儲存體、影像與其他顯像物,不得予以扣押[15]。」由此可知依德國刑事訴訟法之規定,新聞媒體人員不但得行使拒絕證言權,其業務上持有之物件亦不得予以扣押。此外,美國國會於1980 年亦基於憲法上對於新聞自由之保障並防止濫權搜索,制訂隱私保護法(Privacy Protection Act),依該法規定除非有少數例外情形,否則不得任意對新聞媒體人員持有之文件資料加以搜索、扣押[16]。

自德美二國之立法而論,不難理解縱然真實發現係訴訟程序所追求的目標,惟一但肯認更值得保護之社會價值存在,真實發現之訴訟目的亦非絕對的價值信仰。因此,倘若承認較真實發現具有更高保護利益的價值存在,即便造成發現真實某種程度的障礙,亦應肯認其為理性思考各種生活利益衝突後,不得不容認的折衷現象。故而,新聞自由的承認在某程度來說必定阻礙了真實的發現。我國刑事訴訟法中雖無類似德國及美國關於新聞媒體人員之拒絕證言權或對於新聞媒體人員不得搜索、扣押之明文規定,然追本溯源,前揭德國及美國之立法規

---

[15] 參閱蔡墩銘譯:德、日刑事訴訟法,頁 16、28。
[16] 參閱王兆鵬:論搜索扣押之客體—搜索新聞媒體、律師事務所,月旦法學雜誌第 68 期,頁 158,民國 90 年 1 月。

定實皆根源於憲法上對於新聞言論自由之保障，徵諸我國憲法第 11 條亦明文保障人民新聞自由之規定，一但肯認新聞記者就特定事項得主張拒絕證言權，即不得就該相關事證搜索扣押新聞記者。

二、 新聞來源保密與拒絕證言

在訴訟程序上，考量社會上人際關係的和諧以及值得保護的信賴關係，各國法制莫不承認與被告具一定關係的證人享有拒絕證言之權利，以免訴訟之進行過度破壞社會的和諧關係。畢竟在發現真實的同時，仍有必要維繫一些具有人性價值的東西。這給我們一種啓示，並不是一講追究犯罪，其他的價值就要全部犧牲。

而新聞記者因爲採訪新聞，難免親自看到某件事情或聽到某種消息，此時就法院所進行之審判案件而言，新聞記者自係處於證人的地位。基於前述理解，是否可認：如對記者加以傳訊或強迫其說出職業上所知悉知他人秘密，勢必會破壞其間（記者與消息來源）的信賴關係，而有必要賦予新聞記者拒絕證言之權利？

美國證據法學者 John Henry Wigmore 認爲[17]：在司法程序上，所有人都有就所有事實作證之義務。例外時，如有拒絕作

---

[17] 本段可參閱尤英夫：論新聞來源保密權利，全國律師，民國 89 年 12 月，頁 8。

證之特權，至少應具有四種基本要件：一、這項消息一定是發
生在秘密情況中，是不可以洩漏的；二、這種保守職業秘密的
因素，一定是雙方保持良好關係所不可缺少的；三、這項關係
在整個社會觀點來看，一定是必須努力培養的；四、這個消息
如果透露出來，所引起的損害，一定要比由訴訟的正確處理所
能獲得的利益大得多。根據這四個要件，Wigmore 贊成律師與
當事者間、牧師與懺悔者間有此特權存在。但似乎不贊成新聞
記者享有職業保密的權利。

　　與 Wigmore 之見解相對，Dr. Frederick S. Siebert 卻認為新
聞記者根據這 4 項標準，應享有拒絕證言之權利。他分析說[18]：
以第 1 項條件來說，提供消息的人和記者之間關係是秘密的，
依賴護相信任，互相尊重，那是根本沒有問題的。以第 2 項條
件來說，新聞記者和消息來源之間之關係，一定也會符合此一
條件。以第 3 項條件來說，隨時可以證明，社會是依賴新聞記
者提供消息的，而消息一定要充實和完整。在若干情況下，充
實和完整的消息是不容易得到的；除非消息來源的秘密，可以
得到保證。至於第 4 項條件，其認「此一條件假定社會的主要
功能是訴訟，因而需要得到在法院中發生的全部有關消息。」
「假定訴訟的功能在我們社會中是一項重要的功用，那也不是
唯一的功用。法庭為了作判決，應該有來源可以找到所有的有
關消息。」「不過，假如要求記者在法庭上宣佈他的消息來

18　同前註。

源，會嚴重地干擾他獲取和發布消息的能力的話，那麼法庭上要求宣佈消息來源的權力，便應該加以詳細的研究了。」「記者所保守的秘密，並不是在醫師、律師或教士有權保守秘密的一樣資料。很明顯的，這三種人中的任何一種，都有法庭認為非常有價值的證據資料來源。記者所保守秘密的，並不是消息本身，而是消息的來源。那就是提供消息者的姓名⋯記者所要做的是：保障這些害怕別人報復的來源，使他的消息來源不會阻塞」。

　　事實上，倘若記者所報導的消息具有一定程度以上的新聞價值，該事件的主角一定急欲找出究竟是誰透露此「不欲人知的消息」，並冀望加以澄清甚或予以報復。為了避免消息透露者遭受此等不利益，新聞記者實不應「恩將仇報」的陷該給予新聞者於不利，此等要求也構成了記者的職業道德，故應肯認媒體人員與消息來源者間的信賴關係是值得保障的社會利益。但是，是否有必要因此進一步承認新聞記者負有對消息來源保密之義務，亦即媒體人員與消息來源者間的信賴關係應受何等強度的保障？似無法由此導出，仍有待檢討。

肆、 新聞來源保密必要性之檢討

一、新聞來源保密義務之核心領域－公共監督之擔保

　　新聞自由係指對藉由報紙、雜誌、電視以印刷、攝影或錄影方式，將不同意見或思想傳達於眾的自由，此是屬於憲法第11條所保障的「出版自由」；另著眼於新聞的公共監督功能，認為新聞自由是獨立於言論自由以外的「第四權」，是另一種基本權利。從而，不論基於表現自我意志的本質，或所扮演的監督角色，新聞自由並非以保障或促進新聞傳播媒體自身之利益為目的，而是在於保障「傳播媒體作為社會公器」的監督功能，至少在保障新聞媒體能充分監督政府的範圍內應保障並承認新聞自由，而且是屬於憲法層次的保障。

　　新聞記者就其所採訪之來源或內容，如被法院或有關機關詢問時，有些國家的法律明文規定，新聞記者有拒絕透露的權利；但是大多數的國家並未賦予新聞記者有上述權利。就新聞界之觀點而言，由於在一個民主社會中，媒體的存在負有提供人民想要知道消息的義務（尤其是政治新聞），當記者的消息，是向關係人物採訪而得時，為免消息來源的枯竭以確保新聞自由，記者都會認為：保護消息來源的秘密，是記者天賦的權利[19]。

---

[19]　同註17，頁10。

新聞自由並非單純保障新聞言論發表自由，亦發展出其他具體保障意涵。其中防禦性權利：如拒絕洩漏資訊來源或拒絕政府進入新聞媒體事業場所進行搜索或扣押的建構，目的在於保障並強化第四權的監督功能。因此，本文認為：凡是涉及監督公權層次的新聞報導（此可認屬新聞自由的核心領域），除非其報導本身違反新聞自由本質上之限制（例如：該當犯罪行為），否則在保障新聞自由的合憲要求下，均應承認新聞記者負有新聞來源保密之義務；亦即此時新聞記者拒絕證言之主張，在憲法制度性保障新聞自由的要求下，應具有憲法上權利之屬性（位階）[20]，縱立法者亦不得以制定法之方式予以限制，現行刑事訴訟法雖無明文新聞記者享有拒絕證言權之規定，解釋上亦應認屬應然；從而，真實發現之訴訟要求即因而退居次位。

二、非新聞自由核心領域中承認新聞來源保密義務之基礎

除了前述公共監督的領域外，是否尚可承認新聞來源保密義務存立於其他的報導領域？雖然前已說明為何於公共監督的領域內，承認新聞記者負有新聞來源保密之義務；然而美國聯邦最高法院於 Brauzbwg v. Hayls,1972、In re Pappas,1972 及 U.

---

[20] 縱認其為憲法位階之權利，亦非擔保其為、絕對不受限制、絕對不可侵犯之權利。例如在國家安全之領域內，新聞自由即受到某種程度的限制。

S. v. Caldwell,1972 三案中，卻一概地拒絕承認新聞記者的新聞自由權包括新聞來源保密權，並認為新聞來源保密權既非憲法所保障之權利，即不應享有豁免權，故其必須出席回答聯邦大陪審團之傳訊調查。聯邦法院以「三合一」的方式將此三案併案處理，由懷特大法官代表五位多數大法官主撰判決文，就新聞自由何以不包括記者對新聞來源的保密權進一步說明：「迄今為止……拒絕作證的特權係源自憲法第 5 條修正案所作之不得強迫嫌犯自證其罪之規定。但本案當事人之一方，現要求本院透過解釋第 1 條修正案再為記者專創一個其他人均享受不到的記者作證豁免權，這一點本院不能接受。本院並非質疑言論、新聞及集會等自由權利對國家福祉的重要性，亦非建議說新聞採訪自由不符合憲法第 1 條修正案保障的條件；如果採訪新聞沒有若干保障，新聞自由即可能遭受剝奪。但本案既未涉及言論或集會自由之權利，亦無事前檢查或限制報紙何者可以刊登；官方亦未以明示或暗示命令該報紙刊登所樂加保留者，再者，本案更未涉及對出版特權之需索或課稅問題，由未涉及對出版資訊之內容加以民事或刑事責任之懲罰。同時，新聞之運用秘密消息來源亦未遭受禁止或限制；新聞記者仍具有以合法方法自由向任何方面採訪新聞，無人企圖規定該報公佈其消息來源，或者依所請而將消息來源毫無選擇的予以透露。」懷特大法官特別指出，聯邦憲法第 1 條修正案的民權自由條款並未保障新聞界可以違背其他有效法律的權利。例如反拖拉斯法或勞工法，陪審團簽發傳票召約證人出席作證的權威係執行其法

定工作最重要的部分，他說：「政府的基本功能即在於對國民
個人之人身即財產安全提供公平而有效之執法機構，大陪審團
在執法的過程中扮演一個憲法所賦予的角色。從本院所現有的
本案資料記錄中，吾人認為沒有理由認為公眾在執行法律及保
證有效的陪審過程的利益尚不足以超越採訪新聞所面臨當然而
無定的負擔。這種負擔據說是由於一般人堅信新聞記者亦如其
他公民，應在大陪審團進行對刑事案件調查過程中回答相關問
題」[21]。

　　雖然聯邦最高法院未承認新聞記者享有拒絕公佈其消息來
源之權利，惟若「大陪審團之調查過程完全是為破壞記者與其
採訪來源間之關係為目的時，新聞記者反將因該不合理之目的

---

[21]　同註 13，頁 64、65；該三案例之事實如下：
　　Brauzbwg v. Hayls,1972：Brauzbwg 係 Louisville Courier Journal 之記者，根
　　據祕密訪問幾個毒犯時個人的觀察，連續發表數篇專文，當時 Brauzbwg 曾向
　　毒犯提出保證將嚴守祕密，絕不洩漏消息來源及被訪者身分，後因案發，聯
　　邦大陪審團發出傳票，要其出席作證，這位記者即以聯邦憲法第 1 條修正案
　　新聞自由為理由，認為保護消息來源及被訪者的身分係憲法權利，所以拒絕
　　出席作證。
　　In re Pappas,1972：Pappas 係一電視新聞記者，曾訪問美國黑人之暴力叛亂組
　　織黑豹黨（Black Panthers）領導人物。該檔唯一黑人反白人統治之恐怖組織，
　　經美國各州宣佈為非法之暴力團體，在六〇年代爭取民權自由之激烈鬥爭中，
　　黑報黨扮演以暴力推翻白人統治建立黑人治國之獨立國家之角色。當這位記
　　者受邀進行訪問後，曾答允不發表訪問經過。後來仍由聯邦大陪審發出傳
　　票召其作證。
　　U.S. v. Caldwell,1972：紐約時報記者 Caldwell 曾取得舊金山地區黑豹黨信任
　　而進行秘密訪問，事後發表專訪數篇，聯邦大陪審團遂傳其出席調查會作證。

取得拒絕公佈其消息來源之權利」[22]。該案之不同意見中,更有主張:「一個記者享有憲法上的權利保障他與新聞採訪來源者的關係,新聞採訪權必須包括新聞消息來源的隱密權。」「一個記者要求免於大陪審團傳喚作證的豁免權並非記者個人的免責權,而係社會大重要保持與公眾所關心的資訊的取得權。」的呼聲。值得注意的是,該判決不過僅推導出新聞記者無法據聯邦憲法第一修正案之規定取得拒絕證言之憲法上權利,而拒絕證言在新聞自由中所具之重要性經由反對意見之闡述、強調,惟經由類似案例之探討,反而促使多數州立法機關制定保障新聞記者不被傳喚的規定(又稱為盾牌法案)。加州最高法院曾於 1999 年 11 月 1 日在一項判決中指出:「已於 1980 年經選民投票通過增訂列入加州憲法之新聞保護法給予新聞記者絕對的豁免權,檢察官不可強迫新聞媒體交出刑事案件的採訪筆記或其他未發表之資訊[23]」,適可為例證。因此,因此,就美國法的發展而論,似可承認在非屬新聞自由的核心領域中,新聞記者之拒絕證言權縱非憲法上之權利,亦因其與新聞來源間之關係具有值得保護之重要價值,而得列為法律上的權利。

　　就非涉及監督公權的新聞報導而論,雖然難免商業色彩,亦不乏以揭露社會上犯罪手法為宗旨的報導(例如:社會秘密

22　同前註。

23　參閱民國 88 年 11 月 4 日聯合報,第十一版。

檔案），而這些報導主要的特徵即在於記者親自見證了犯罪的發生或是與尚未破案的案件當事人曾有面對面的接觸、採訪（亦即犯罪行為人曾於媒體採訪時「自白」其犯罪手段、過程等）。政府機關若要追究該犯罪，最簡便之方法就是直接從新聞記者處取得相關的事證。此外，復鑑於人民對於生活週遭的潛在危機，原應享有知的權利；而強迫新聞記者透露相關消息來源，雖有利於個案的偵查、追訴，檢警憲調等偵防機關亦易因此而怠惰於偵防技巧的精進，而且此舉亦將陷該新聞記者於報復性的殺機中。因此，強迫新聞記者透露相關消息來源，非但將造成人民知的權利受損（亦即新聞來源枯竭），亦將使新聞記者招致無法預測的危險，此舉無異殺雞取卵，實非可採。

那麼在未明文規範新聞記者享有拒絕證言權的法制下，記者究應如何面對其作證義務？或者是說，是否尚存在其他的法律理由得以解免記者所負之作證義務？關於非新聞自由核心領域之報導，由於刑事訴訟法並無明文新聞記者享有拒絕證言權之規定，究應如何將上述解釋上之應然，落實於現實之中？當然，最有實效也是最緩不濟急的方法就是在法律中明文承認新聞記者於新聞自由的範圍內享有拒絕證言權（如現行民事訴訟法第 307 條第 1 項第 4 款及行政訴訟法第 146 條第 1 項第 3 款，均肯認得因職業上秘密事項主張拒絕證言權），而此部分尚待立法委員所提之刑事訴訟法第 182 條修正案（該案已將新聞記者亦列為得主張拒絕證言之主體）之通過。惟於前述修正案尚未通過前，或許在現行法未承認蔑視法庭罪且刑事訴訟法

第 193 條關於拒絕具結或證言之處罰輕微的前提下，法院妥協性的接受新聞記者「不記得了」的答覆，是較爲折衷的方法[24]。事實上，如果承認在某範圍內新聞記者享有拒絕證言權，則可謂於該範圍內之新聞自由並未受到限制；反之，則新聞自由即受到規範上的限制。因此，關於新聞自由應受到何種程度的限制，即應予以探討。

三、 新聞自由的限制

　　不論是否屬於公共監督之報導，新聞自由本質上係建構於人民知的權利之上。「知的權利」(people's right to know)之興起，乃源於人民有言論自由的觀念，換言之，人民除了有表達的自由外，也要有知道的權利，故其涵義有二：1.公衆有權利知道事情眞象。2.爲保障人民知的權利，媒體有採訪、報導自由。但近年來，由於知的權利被媒介記者濫用，故開始省思，知的權利應不是媒介或記者要讓大衆知道的權利，而是讀者大衆原有的知道權益，這意謂讀者有權知道什麼；亦即新聞記者應採訪報導者爲何，決定權在讀者。因此，針對新聞媒體向來以社會公衆代理人而主張「新聞界知的權利係代表社會大衆行使公衆知的權利」，美國聯邦最高法院於一九七四年曾在 Miami Herald Publishing Co v. Tornilta 一案中，表示「新聞界如果

24　參閱尤英夫：談新聞來源之保密問題，報學，第 7 卷第 2 期，頁 48。

要代表公眾行使知的權利，則必須以代理人資格行使，但不能單獨自行解釋為全權代理人」；而在同年之 Pell v. Pracunier 一案中，更指出「憲法並未准許新聞媒體對社會公眾凡未能分享的資訊而有特別的獲知權」；換言之，「新聞自由條款並未賦予報界得強迫政府提供資料或獲得一般民眾無法取得知資料的權利」[25]。

　　此外，基於國家機密之考量（亦即為維護國家安全及利益），亦有必要規定限制一般人得以自由知悉之事項，然而何者關係國家安全及利益，實際上因其為一不確定之概念，故在認知上可能因人而異。人民「知的權利」及新聞自由之觀念，在現代民主國家廣受重視，人民透過大眾傳播媒體得以知悉政府機關之行政運作，從而可對之提出建議、批評與進行監督，而達成主權在民的基本理念。故就新聞自由之立場而言，無不希望政府將最大範圍的資訊披露在民眾之前[26]。惟國家機密既係為維護國家之安全及利益而設，則若國家安全或利益有遭受侵害之虞，自須對國家機密而加以保護，而限制一般人可以自由知悉之空間。從而國家機密之保護與人民「知的權利」及新聞自由之界限，往往因著重或觀察之角度不同而異其結論。惟由於新聞自由之保障具有憲法位階的意義，因此限制新聞自由

---

[25]　參閱楊日旭：憲法上的新聞自由是不是絕對的權利？（五），國魂 561 期，頁 42，民國 81 年 8 月。

[26]　就此而言，由於人民對於公共監督之內容享有絕對知的權利，此亦可為關於第四權理論所指涉的範圍，新聞自由不應受到任何的限制之論據。

的規定（依據），皆不應出於和社會秩序（具體且爲法令明定之價值秩序）及公共利益（非明文的社會價值，但爲社會一般所接受）相扞格的立場而訂，特別當被限制新聞自由之領域本身具有高度公共監督之必要時，更應要求該限制新聞自由之舉動、目的具有更高之利益保護價值。也就是說，不能任意排除媒體行使憲法賦予的責任。因此，縱認中華民國報業道德規範、中華民國新聞記者信條、檢察警察暨調查機關偵察刑事案件新聞處理注意要點、媒體對性侵害事件之報導保護被害人之處理原則係刑事訴訟法第 245 條第 1 項、檔案法、廣播電視法第 21 條、法院組織法第 86 條、公共電視法、刑法誹謗罪洩密罪之具體詳細規定，而得據以爲限制新聞自由之依據[27]，在實際個案上仍應再依循憲法第 23 條所揭櫫的比例原則予以檢驗，進一步權衡該案件因限制新聞自由所得之利益與未限制新聞自由所得之利益（公共監督利益），否則遽以之爲限制新聞自由論據，難免率斷，亦易生箝制新聞自由之流弊。

　　另就非新聞自由核心領域之報導而言，在肯認新聞自由係以人民知的權利爲前提、且新聞自由知的範圍亦未大過人民知的範圍之後，關於前述非以公共監督爲核心的社會報導，是否亦應享有新聞自由之問題，本於人民對於生活週遭的潛在危機，原應享有知的權利，而強迫新聞記者透露相關消息來源，將陷該新聞記者於報復性的殺機中，並進而導致人民知的權利

27　同註 10。

受損（亦即新聞來源枯竭）之種種考慮，應可予以肯定。

伍、 新聞來源保密之範圍－代結論

　　基於以上的說明，關於如何界定新聞來源保密的範圍，實即影響新聞記者拒絕證言行使之界限。新聞自由雖因負有公共監督的目的而爲憲法位階的絕對性權利，卻非一毫無限制絕對性的權利。況且，新聞界濫用新聞自由的事例層出不窮，在美國甚至曾出現過虛僞報導竟以假亂眞地獲頒普立茲獎的案例[28]。因此，如何在新聞自由的要求下防止其遭濫用，應值三思。

　　Dr. Frederick S. Siebert 曾列舉起草任何類型的適當保障新聞記者法律時，所宜考慮的問題有：一、哪些新聞機構，可由法律賦予拒絕透露消息來源的特權？二、哪些與新聞事業有關的人員有拒絕透露的特權？三、此特權是否對所有類型的公務處理都適用，亦或僅是用某特定案件？四、特權能否放棄？誰可放棄？對於上述問題，全部能獲回答殊屬不易。不過美國聯邦最高法院在 Branzburg v. Hayes 一案判決中指出：新聞記者不能援用憲法第一修正案享有不透露消息來源的權利；但在該判

---

[28] 曾以報導一名八歲兒童吸食海洛因的故事而獲頒 1981 年普立茲新聞獎的珍妮特庫克（Janet Cooke），即以防止該兒童被害爲名，與報社（華盛頓郵報）共同拒絕透露消息來源。後因庫克小姐被發現其向郵報應徵的資料有僞造，經追查後，始承認該故事係杜撰，華盛頓郵報並因而退回普立茲獎。參閱註17，頁 11。

決中，不同意見認為在某種情況下可賦予記者拒絕透露消息來源的權利。他認為憲法保障言論自由，如要免除言論自由的保障，政府應證明其有絕對正當之理由。他要證明 1.記者的作證內容與案件有密切關係；2.作證內容為公眾利益所必需；3.作證內容別無他途可以獲得。此一標準，在有關新聞來源保密權利之案件，常被引用討論，亦可在討論 Dr. Frederick S. Siebert 所提出之問題時予以參考[29]。

回顧本文一開始所提有關新聞記者界定的問題，不論是報紙業、雜誌社、通訊社、廣播或電視，鑑於新聞自由之保護核心為「報導」，因此凡致力於新聞的流通與確保消息的獲得，均得主張拒絕證言權。反之，新聞事業中的印刷、排版、運送等部門的工作人員，便無法作如上之主張。而雖然於所有案件中均可主張，但如新聞記者對案件之處理為唯一之線索時、尤其牽涉犯罪，亦曾有論者主張此時之特權應受限制[30]。惟本文認為：如果記者本身涉及犯罪（例如：非屬合理知的權利所能涵蓋範圍的報導），由於違反新聞自由本質功能上之限制，即不在奠基於合理知的權利之上的新聞自由保障之範圍內，自無從假新聞自由之名行侵害他人法益之實；因此探討限制拒絕證言特權與否，不應將記者立於被告之地位來思考；換言之，除非限制拒絕證言特權之目的與新聞自由所欲達成的功能間在比

---

[29] 同前註。

[30] 同註 17，頁 12。

例原則的檢驗下能取得平衡，否則任何限制拒絕證言特權的主張，均將牴觸新聞自由所賴以建立的憲法價值，尤其在公共監督的領域內。

最後，關於新聞記者之拒絕證言權在新聞自由之核心領域中定位爲絕對的權能此一問題所可能產生之疑慮提出本文之見解，本文認爲：固然在將保障新聞自由核心領域之拒絕證言權定位爲絕對的憲法權利後，在新聞自由合理的限制領域外，不免造成新聞界肆無忌憚的報導幾近八卦的消息層出不窮，並導致名譽、隱私等人格權遭受侵害；惟若自另一個角度反向思考，似乎就不會覺得這個問題有多麼嚴重。換言之，社會上本即經常出現國會議員（立法委員）利用召開記者會的方式散佈「內幕消息」的現象，因此一但新聞報導藉由遁入國會議員言論免責權的保護傘下，原本即可避免透露消息來源；而相對的，縱屬八卦新聞，在市場機制的運作下，本質上即具有被大量報導的商業誘因。也因此，只要話題夠聳動，能見度高，國會議員多半亦樂於擔任新聞界的「傳聲筒」。因此，倘若一味的強迫新聞記者透露消息來源，新聞記者亦非絕無迴避之門道。試想：倘若當初在總統大選時，宋楚瑜的興票案或是陳水扁的彩券案是由新聞媒體揭露而非由立法委員揭露，顯而易見的，新聞界亦恐將遭受司法無止境的「糾纏」；而新新聞案如果係藉由立法委員以召開記者會的方式公佈而非媒體獨家報

導，亦不致纏訟迄今[31]。從而，既然承認國會議員在公共監督領域享有絕對的言論免責權（甚至非公共監督領域亦擁有），在考量新聞自由與國會在公共監督領域負有相同的「耙糞」角色，且二者在制度功能上具有高度「競合」的可能性，本文所主張「在新聞自由之核心領域中新聞記者之拒絕證言權在新聞自由之核心領域中應定位為絕對的權能」之此一見解，尚不至於造成難以想像或是無法彌補的損害。反之，若認為在新聞自由之核心領域中新聞記者之拒絕證言權在新聞自由之核心領域中不應定位為絕對的權能，於實際運作中，亦恐因立委諸公之介入而出現「口惠而實不至」之弊。既然法律無法避免媒體與國會之結合，對於可藉由「媒體與國會結合」之方式所規避之制約，實無規制之必要，以維法之公信力。

　　至於是否應賦予新聞記者在非公共監督領域之報導亦享有拒絕證言權？雖然該部分如前所述因非為新聞自由核心領域所涵蓋，尚不足評價為憲法上之權利，故就形式而言，尚得以立法的方式予以更大範圍之限制。惟本文認為：鑑於在非公共監督之範圍內，亦存在本質上值得人民高度重視之社會現象（如：新興犯罪型態、手法…等），雖報導諸該事件無涉人民監督政府之公益目的，因此部分如同公共監督領域般，亦具有高度公益性，故可認人民對此部分知的權利具有高度的保障必

---

[31]　按立委秦慧珠曾公佈王文洋密使案，其消息來源迄今亦無人知悉；媒體人員若利用此管道行「報導」之實，亦將無法可管。

要性。爲了建立此部分之制度性保障，似應承認新聞記者就此仍得享有法律上拒絕證言之權利。至於其他不具高度公益性之報導，由於不具更高價值的保護利益，自應承認私權侵害事實之釐清（眞實發現）具有高於新聞自由之價值，因此新聞記者於該等報導領域中便無法主張拒絕證言權。惟不論如何，關於新聞記者在非公共監督領域之報導是否享有拒絕證言權此一問題，仍有待於個案中具體衡量公益之保護必要性是否恆大於私益之保護必要性而定。

　　行文至此，若採以上之見解，進一步要檢討的，即在於新聞人員的自律，以及如何在欠缺民意支持的基礎下，應由哪些人行使此「第四權」。惟此非本文探討之焦點，另待探討。（本文曾發表於 90.10 法學叢刊）

10 不起訴處分與再議之檢討

壹、前　言

　　刑事訴訟程序乃國家確定刑罰權有無及其範圍之公法程序，在不告不理原則之支配下，刑事審判程序之進行，必有賴當事人（檢察官或自訴人）提起訴訟始得為之。在現行刑事訴訟架構中，除依刑事訴訟法第 319 條之規定，犯罪之被害人在委任律師的前提下得提起自訴而開始刑事審判程序外，惟有透過檢察官與軍事檢察官提起公訴，始有確定國家刑罰權是否存在及其範圍之可能。依照釋字第 392 號解釋：「司法權之一之刑事訴訟、即刑事司法之裁判，係以實現國家刑罰權為目的之司法程序，其審判乃以追訴而開始，追訴必須實施偵查，迨判決確定，尚須執行始能實現裁判之內容。」之說明，檢察官擔負著偵查、訴追、審判、刑之執行等刑事司法責任，以達成刑事訴訟之任務；換言之，除少數刑事犯罪係透過自訴程序實踐國家刑罰權外，對大多數刑事犯罪國家刑罰權之實現而言，檢察官事實上扮演著控制審判入口之守門員（gate keeper）角色，在此基礎上，檢察官「主動追訴，開起審判之門」等職責，是

檢察官功能地位具司法性的核心，沒有檢察官之司法性，即無刑事司法，更無法院之審判獨立可言，蓋刑事司法制度上之審檢分立原則，原非單指行政、司法之分立，而是指在司法權下，刑事訴訟程序中不再由法官為唯一的單獨之司法機關，而須另加檢察官為共同的司法機關[1]，以實現刑事司法正義。然而，若有權提起訴訟者無意進行訴追或在訴追程序中故意網開一面，縱有再嚴重之犯罪發生，國家刑罰權實際上亦無實踐之機會，果如此，所謂社會公平正義，恐亦無從維持。

學說上關於檢察官是否就公訴權之行使與否具有裁量權乙事，向來有起訴法定主義與起訴便宜主義[2]之分。依據刑事訴訟法第 251 條，及修正前第 253 條規定，原則上可認在 91 年 1 月刑事訴訟法修正前，我國刑事訴訟制度似採起訴法定主義，否定檢察官對偵查案件有自由處分權[3]，但在修正後刑事訴訟法第 253 條之 1「緩起訴制度」之影響下，刑事訴訟似已改採起訴裁量主義；也就是說，在現行我刑事訴訟制度下，關於檢察官追訴權之行使，係以起訴裁量為主，並以起訴法定主義為輔[4]。

---

[1] 參照劉邦繡，論職權再議，臺灣本土法學雜誌，第 57 期，頁 26，2004 年 4 月。國內目前研究修正刑事訴訟法時，仍偏重以審判為核心，常以法官觀點作為刑事程序思考的主軸，而忽略檢察官才係刑事程序全程參與者，法官僅參與刑事程序中之審判程序而已，但檢察官卻是自偵查、審判以迄執行均全程參與。參閱陳志龍，法治國檢察官之偵查與檢察制度，台大法學論叢，第 27 卷第 3 期，頁 82，1998 年 3 月。

[2] 參閱田宮裕，刑事訴訟法，頁 171，（日本東京）有斐閣，1998 年。

[3] 參閱黃東熊，刑事訴訟法論，頁 239，三民書局，1991 年。

[4] 參閱陳運財，緩起訴制度之研究，台灣本土法學雜誌第 35 期，頁 81，2002 年 6 月。

針對檢察官扮演控制審判入口守門員之角色而言，依現行刑事訴訟法之規定，檢察官在偵查終結後對於具體個案可做出起訴、緩起訴或不起訴等司法性處分，不過，檢察官也是人，在肯認人都可能犯錯的前提下，對於檢察官所做的各種處分，自有在制度上予以救濟保障之必要。以民國 93 年各地方法院檢察署所收之偵查案件來說，在偵查終結（含舊受）近三十萬件（約三十七萬八千人）中，依通常程序提起公訴者約六萬三千人，占終結人數之 16.6%；聲請簡易判決處刑者約七萬七千人，占終結人數之 20.3%；作出緩起訴處分人數約二萬五千人占 6.7%；至於不起訴處分人數為十二萬九千人（含依職權一萬四千人），占終結人數之 34.1%（依職權占 3.7%）；簽結為八萬四千人（其中通緝報結二萬一千人，送法院併案審理報結約二萬四千人，移送他管轄約一萬四千人，移送調解七千人，移送戒治所三千多人，餘為其他原因簽結），占終結人數之 22.4%。依民國 93 年之法務部統計資料，提起公訴或聲請簡易判決處刑的人數，僅占該年度終結人數之 36.9%，但不起訴或緩起訴的人數，卻占該年度終結人數之 40.8%[5]。換句話說，在現行刑事訴訟制度下，若不服檢察官之決定或意思表示，是否應予救濟？值得討論之主要對象應係對檢察官偵查終結決定之不起訴處分、緩起訴處分、撤銷緩起訴處分而言，蓋除其所佔

---

[5]　資料來源：見法務部法務統計 (http://www.moj.gov.tw/public/Attachment/5121822495041.pdf)。

之比例大於提起公訴或聲請簡易判決處刑之部分外，若已提起公訴或聲請簡易判決處刑，原即應以司法審判為主要之救濟程序。從而，當檢察官所為之不起訴處分、緩起訴處分或撤銷緩起訴處分出現違誤時究應如何救濟？現行再議制度是否已提供妥當、充分的救濟管道？誠為我國刑事司法實務所應重視之議題。

貳、現行刑事再議制度之法律構造

　　基本上，刑事案件除由自訴人自任原告，逕行向法院提起自訴以外，都要由檢察官代表國家實施偵查犯罪。案件經過偵查程序，所掌握的證據都不足以認定被告有犯罪的事實，也就是犯罪嫌疑不足，依刑事訴訟法第 252 條第 10 款的規定，就要對被告作出不起訴的處分。不過檢察官有時難免思慮不周，使被告倖逃法網，如放任應負刑事責任的被告逍遙法外，也與公平正義有違。因此，刑事訴訟法規定案件的告訴人在不起訴處分以後，可以依據再議的救濟程序，請求上級法院檢察署檢察長介入審查，檢視原檢察官的不起訴程序是不是妥適，上級檢察長審核結果，認為告訴人的再議無理由，即應依刑事訴訟法第 258 條第 1 項上段的規定將再議駁回。原檢察官的偵查尚未完備，可以命令原檢察官續行偵查，偵查已經完備，也可以命令原檢察官提起公訴。由此可知，再議是讓本已由檢察官向外

界宣告偵查程序終結的案件，恢復重新偵查的機制。不過，誰才有權利啓動這項機制，讓已終結的案件重新進入偵查程序？依刑事訴訟法第 256 條 [6] 第 1 項的規定，再議的權利屬於告訴人，因爲這條文規定告訴人接受不起訴處分書後，「得於七日內以書狀敘述不服之理由，經原檢察官向直接上級法院檢察署檢察長或檢察總長聲請再議。」。至於什麼人才具備「告訴人」資格，刑事訴訟法第 232 條很明白的規定，必須是犯罪的直接被害人，才「得爲告訴」。具有告訴資格的人在法定的告訴期間內實際提出告訴者，才是合法的告訴人。只有合法的告訴人，才能行使告訴權。另外刑事訴訟法還有一種依職權再議的規定，那是針對沒有告訴人的被告，所犯的又爲死刑、無期徒刑或最輕本刑爲三年以上有期徒刑的重罪，經檢察官偵查終結，認爲犯罪嫌疑不足，予以不起訴處分以後，依第 256 條第 3 項的規定，要按再議的程序依職權送再議。避免應該有罪的被告卻因爲原檢察官一時疏忽或因爲不當的法律見解不予追

---

[6]　其規定爲：「告訴人接受不起訴或緩起訴處分書後，得於七日內以書狀敘述不服之理由，經原檢察官向直接上級法院檢察署檢察長或檢察總長聲請再議。但第 353 條、第 353 條之 1 之處分曾經告訴人同意者，不得聲請再議。（第 1 項）不起訴或緩起訴處分得聲請再議者，其再議期間及聲請再議之直接上級法院檢察署檢察長或檢察總長，應記載於送達告訴人處分書正本。（第 2 項）死刑、無期徒刑或最輕本刑三年以上有期徒刑之案件，因犯罪嫌疑不足，經檢察官爲不起訴之處分，或第 253 條之 1 之案件經檢察官爲緩起訴之處分者，如無得聲請再議之人時，原檢察官應依職權逕送直接上級法院檢察署檢察長或檢察總長再議，並通知告發人。（第 3 項）」。

訴，發生讓他逍遙法外的情事[7]。

依刑事訴訟法第256條之規定，再議為檢察官所為之不起訴處分、緩起訴處分或撤銷緩起訴處分出現違誤時主要的救濟管道，據此，對於檢察官偵查終結之不起訴及緩起訴處分，若告訴人不服，在現行法架構下可循下列途逕尋求救濟：（一）、告訴人對不起訴處分不服聲請再議（刑訴法第256條第1項前段）。（二）、告訴人對緩起訴處分不服之聲請再議（刑訟法第256條第1項前段）。（三）、告訴人對其聲請再議遭駁回後仍向管轄之法院聲請交付審判（刑訟法第258條之1）。而被告亦可對檢察官撤銷其緩起訴處分表示不服，聲請再議（修正後刑事訴訟法第256條之1）請求救濟；此外，對於檢察官之處分除不服之告訴人可聲請再議為救濟外，更有無人不服檢察官處分之「職權再議」制度（刑訟法第256第3項）[8]。

值得注意的是，在現行法的規範下，並非所有的不起訴處分均有救濟的管道，依司法院院字第2550號解釋：「檢察官之偵查程序，以就所偵查案件為起訴或不起訴處分而終結，刑事訴訟法第315條所謂之終結偵查，自係指該案件曾經檢察官為起訴或不起訴之處分者而言，不能僅以其在點名單內記載偵查

---

[7]　參閱葉雪鵬，交付審判，是不起訴處分的最後救濟，2007.03.15 (www.moj.gov.tw/public/Data/732017101689.doc)。

[8]　參閱劉邦繡，論職權再議，臺灣本土法學雜誌，第57期，頁28，2004年4月。

終結字樣，即認為終結偵查，但其所為之起訴或不起訴處分，祇須對外表示，即屬有效，該起訴書或不起訴處分書之制作與否，係屬程式問題，不影響終結偵查之效力。」之說明，在無告訴人而不起訴之案件、或非屬死刑、無期徒刑或最輕本刑三年以上有期徒刑而不起訴之案件，或前述死刑、無期徒刑或最輕本刑三年以上有期徒刑之案件非因犯罪嫌疑不足而不起訴之案件中，一但檢察官就該案已對外為不起訴處分之表示，因無聲請再議之人，一經不起訴處分隨即確定，縱使告發人聲請再議，因屬不合法之聲請再議，原不起訴處分也不因此而未確定[9]，該不起訴處分於公告後即對外生效，而在刑事訴訟第260條之拘束下，該不起訴處分具有實質確定力，除非（一）發現新事實或新證據者。（二）有第420條第1項第1款、第2款、第4款或第5款所定得為再審原因之情形者，否則對同一案件不得再行起訴。

---

[9] 參照最高法院27年上字第2045號判例：「因告發而開始進行偵查之刑事案件，並無得為聲請再議之人，一經檢察官為不起訴之處分後，其處分即屬確定，雖上級法院首席檢察官本於監督權之作用，仍得復令偵查，但非有刑事訴訟法第239條所定可以再起訴之新事實新證據或再審原因，不得對於同一案件再行起訴，此與上級法院首席檢察官因認再議之聲請為有理由，命令續行偵查之案件不受此項限制者有別，觀於同法於不起訴、再行起訴及聲請再議各規定，殊無疑義。」與58年台上字第2576號判例：「刑事訴訟法第232條關於被害人告訴之規定，不包含國家在內，鹽務機關緝獲私鹽犯，函送偵查，仍係告發，而非告訴，對於不起訴處分不得聲請再議，不得聲請再議之人，所為再議之聲請為不合法，原不起訴處分，並不因此而阻止其確定。」

參、再議制度之爭議

一、民國 91 年修法前

在民國 91 年 2 月 8 日刑事訴訟法修正前,依舊刑事訴訟法第 256 條:「告訴人接受不起訴處分書後,得於七日內以書狀敘述不服之理由,經原檢察官向直接上級法院首席檢察官或檢察長聲請再議。但有第 253 條第 2 項之情形者,不得聲請再議。不起訴處分得聲請再議者,其再議期間及聲請再議之直接上級法院首席檢察官或檢察長,應記載於送達告訴人處分書正本」之規定與司法院院字第 1576 號解釋:「對於不起訴處分之聲請再議,限於有告訴權人,且實行告訴者,方得為之。」之意旨,只有「已實行告訴權」之「告訴人」對檢察官「不起訴處分」「聲請再議」,為不服檢察官未於偵查終結提起公訴之唯一救濟途徑,蓋若檢察官偵查終結認為應對被告特定之犯罪事實予以「起訴」而提起公訴或聲請簡易判決處刑,該刑事爭議旋即成為法院審判權行使之對象,縱被告對此起訴決定有所不服,亦應在審判程序中向法院提出辯護以為救濟。換言之,91 年 2 月 8 日前之聲請再議,專指告訴人對不起訴處分不服而聲請再議;此時聲請再議主要是指告訴人不服不起訴處分,而向上級檢察機關檢察長請求變更原處分,回復偵查程序並提起

公訴之請求[10]；依修法前最高法院 89 年台非字第 128 號判決：
「聲請再議與聲明上訴，同為不服下級審之處分或裁判，向
上級審請求救濟之程序」之說明，可理解「聲請再議」之制
度，其主要目的及功能乃是對檢察官公訴權行使與否之救濟
制度。雖然關於再議制度之性質，在修法前學說上有認聲請
再議制度係一種救濟制度，亦有認為聲請再議制度是一種監
督機制[11]。然而在刑事司法制度下，因檢察事務之處理為各
個獨任之檢察官，為了監督檢察官行使檢察權，乃有檢察一
體原則[12]。檢察體系內部監督只能在檢察官尚未對外表示其

---

[10]　參閱黃東熊，刑事訴訟法論，1991 年，頁 243-244，三民書局；褚劍鴻，論不
　　　起訴處分之確定力與不當處分之救濟（上），法令月刊第 49 卷第 8 期，頁
　　　18，1998 年 8 月。

[11]　參閱鍾鳳玲，檢察官不起訴處分監督及審查制度之比較研究，法學叢刊第 185
　　　期，頁 1、18，2002 年 1 月。另依 32 年上字第 423 號判例：「因告發而進行
　　　偵查之刑事案件，並無得為聲請再議之人，一經檢察官為不起訴處分後即屬
　　　確定，雖上級法院首席檢察官，本於監督權之作用，仍得復令偵查，但非有
　　　刑事訴訟法第 239 條所定情形，不得對之再行起訴，此與上級法院首席檢察
　　　官，因認再議之聲請為有理由，命令續行偵查之案件不受此限制者有別。」
　　　之說明，似亦肯定上級法院檢察長在再議程序中得行使監督權。於 91 年 2 月
　　　修正刑事訴訟法前，台灣高檢署檢察長對於不得再議之案件，指定某類案件，
　　　（如貪瀆案件）一審檢察官為不起訴處分後將卷證送交二審檢察長審核，此
　　　乃檢察機關內部監督機制；見台灣高等法院檢察署加強二審檢察功能實施要
　　　點（民國 82 年 2 月 25 日修正）。但按無得再議之人一經不起訴處分，不起
　　　訴處分即確定，除非具有第 260 條之情形可再行偵查起訴，不能以第 258 條
　　　為由，命令原檢察官偵查或起訴；因為上級法院檢察署檢察長或檢察總長對
　　　於不起訴處分得依刑訴法第 258 條發回續查、或命令起訴，以有合法再議之
　　　聲請為前提。參閱陳樸生，刑事訴訟法實務，頁 348。

[12]　關於檢察一體原則，可述之如下：「檢察官對於法院，獨立行使其職權，惟
　　　所謂獨立行使職權者，乃指對外，亦即對其他機關而言。對內則有階級上下

之分命令服從之責，而檢察官追訴犯罪代表國家行使刑罰權，其所偵辦之案件繁雜，類型不一，非均能由單一之檢察官獨立承擔，因之，為集合全體檢察官之力量，積極發揮檢察官功能，全國各級檢察機關，自最高層級之檢察總長及各級檢察長，以至最基層之地方法院及其分院檢察署之檢察官，依上命下從之指揮系統，縱橫聯絡，猶如頭之使臂、臂之使指，構成一大金字塔型組織體系，以發揮整體功能，妥適行使檢察職權，此謂「檢察一體原則」。檢察制度雖屬一體，但檢察官既因審級而配置，其權限自屬各別，上級檢察官對於下級法院之判決，除有特別規定外，不得提起上訴。（28 年上字第 393 號判例）檢察官得於所配置之管轄區域以外執行職務，但配置各級法院之檢察官其執行職務或行使職權仍屬獨立並應讓法院之管轄定其分際。故下級法院檢察官對於上級法院之判決，或上級法院檢察官對於下級法院之判決，均不得上訴。同級法院之檢察官，對於非其所配置之法院之判決亦無聲明不服提起上訴之權。甲法院檢察官移轉乙法院檢察官偵查後逕向甲法院起訴之案件，甲法院審理時，例由配置同院之檢察官到庭執行職務，則第一審判決後，自應向同院到庭檢察官送達，如有不服亦應由同院檢察官提起上訴。（76 年台上字第 4079 號判例）。」參閱陳守煌，檢察一體新動力，參照 http://www.judicial.gov.tw/work/work07/work07-01.asp（最後造訪日：2007 年 4 月 8 日）。又臺灣花蓮地方法院 93 年度選訴字第 2 號刑事裁定：『我國刑事訴訟法上所規定之檢察職權，係以檢察官為行使主體為原則，例如刑事訴訟法第 264 條第 1 項規定：「提起公訴，應由檢察官向管轄法院提出起訴書為之」，又法院組織法第 61 條規定：「檢察官對於法院，獨立行使職權」，及刑事訴訟法第 344 條、第 347 條所定由檢察官提起上訴之上訴權等，堪認代表國家行使公訴權及上訴權者，皆係檢察官而非檢察長，僅例外於偵查中通緝之發佈、再議聲請之准駁、非常上訴之提起等權限交由檢察長或檢察總長為之。此亦可由起訴書以檢察署檢察官為文書全銜，並非由該署檢察長為全銜，起訴書並由個別承辦檢察官具名簽署，非由檢察長具名可窺知，堪認我國之檢察官具有職權行使之自主性及獨立性，其不同於一般行政官，反而享有類似法官對外獨立為意思表示之權限（甚至於刑事訴訟法第 260 條規定檢察官所為之不起訴處分已確定者或緩起訴處分期滿未經撤銷者，具有實質確定力，此即為類似司法權之權限）。由於每個檢察官即是一獨立之官署，所以當檢察官行使強制處分權、起訴裁量及上訴權時，為避免每個檢察官之追訴裁量或法律適用有不一致之處，造成犯罪追訴標準不一之情形，故在檢察體系內部建構一指揮體系，以便於讓檢察官之追訴意志予以統合，乃有「檢察一體」原理之產生，讓檢察總長、檢察長於發現各別檢察官有違法濫權、適用法令

不一致或追訴標準不一致或其他法定事由發生時，即得依法行使職務收取權及職務移轉權。由於檢察一體之主要目的僅在於統一檢察法令、追訴標準及協同檢察官之力量以發揮偵查之作用，故行政監督僅是附隨作用，堪認檢察長對檢察官動用指令權時，應有所節制，應係在檢察官具有裁量權限之便宜原則（指職權不起訴或緩起訴之案件）或署內各檢察官間、檢察官與檢察長間，就法律見解或訴追標準有截然不同之看法、意見紛歧時，或檢察官執行職務有違法或明顯不當者，為使檢察機關有一致的見解與起訴標準時，檢察長可以行使指令權。故檢察獨立性與檢察一體之目的均應在維護檢察權的公正行使，兩者關係應非彼此掣肘，而應相互配合。我國檢察一體之明文規範定大可從法院組織法第 63 條、第 64 條予以闡釋，按法院組織法第 63 條規定：「檢察總長依本法及其他法律之規定，指揮監督該署檢察官及高等法院以下各級法院及分院檢察署檢察官。檢察長依本法及其他法律之規定，指揮監督該署檢察官及其所屬檢察署檢察官。檢察官應服從前二項指揮監督長官之命令」。然上開規定並未明確規定檢察長之指揮監督權限何在，此應為立法之缺漏，尚未能因為該法無明文規定行使指揮監督權之範圍，即認為檢察長之指令權範圍漫無限制，否則刑事訴訟法第 264 條第 1 項、法院組織法第 61 條所示之檢察官獨立性原則，則形同具文。易言之，若檢察官對個案之起訴與否均應聽從於檢察長之指揮，則此時檢察官之身分宛如行政機關的承辦員，雖自己製作文書，然最終卻須聽命於上級命令為之，則將毫無獨立性可言，並與法院組織法第 61 條之規定或我國檢察官之定位相左。故檢察長之指揮監督應限於為統一檢察法令、追訴標準及協同檢察力量以發揮偵查作用之目的下而為之，為維護檢察權之公正行使，遂賦予檢察長行使職務移轉權及職務收取權。故法院組織法第 64 條規定：「檢察總長、檢察長得親自處理所指揮監督之檢察官之事務，並得將該事務移轉於其所指揮監督之其他檢察官處理之」。其行使上開二種指令權之標準，即應界定於檢察官有違法或明顯不當，或於有裁量權限之職權不起訴或緩起訴案件或檢察官與檢察長間就法律見解或訴追標準有截然不同之看法時，為使檢察機關有一致的見解與標準時而予行使。又因檢察署案件繁多，檢察官經分案偵查後至偵查終結前，檢察長於一般性案件大多無法知悉檢察官對個案之法律意見為何，而無法有效統一追訴之標準，故法務部依照法院組織法第 78 條之授權，訂定「地方法院及其分院檢察署處務規程」，該處務規程第 14 條規定：「下列事項由檢察長處理或核定之…二、主任檢察官、檢察官辦案書類之核定」，又於第 27 條第 1 項之規定：「檢察官執行職務撰擬之文件，應送請主任檢察官核轉檢察長核定」等，其用意應係僅為便於檢察長在案件終結對外發生效力前，透過送閱

偵查終結結果（起訴、不起訴、緩起訴）之前行使之；此也是檢察一體原則適用之基本原理。也就是說，檢察權行使之內部監督機制，原本應由上級檢察機關之檢察官或直屬檢察長或主任檢察官基於檢察一體原則在偵查終結前擔負與實現檢察體系內部監督之功能，而非於檢察權行使偵查終結之後另由上級檢察機關擔負檢察體系內部監督之任務。雖然聲請再議具有檢察體系上下級監督之附帶意義與功能，由於該案件已經偵查終結，聲請再議制度於設計上似不符檢察一體之精神與目的，因此不能將聲請再議，理解為單純檢察體系內部之監督機制[13]。

過程作為檢察長是否行使職務移轉權、職務收取權的最後機會，若檢察官確實將起訴書送閱，並讓檢察長有機會充分行使職務收取權或職務移轉權，則尚未能遽以該起訴書未經過檢察長核定，即認為該起訴不合法。故檢察官之書類有無經過送閱並非刑事訴訟法所定之法定要件，例如檢察官於夜間或假日所為之羈押聲請書、毒品案件之觀察、勒戒聲請書等，並未事先經過送閱程序，然上開二種書類亦屬前該處務規程所定應由檢察長核定之書類，惟為了符合檢察官聲請之時效性，全國之地檢署幾乎將羈押聲請書、毒品觀察勒戒聲請書一一套用檢察機關印信，此應為檢察長為符合偵查作為之必要，事前拋棄職務移轉或職務收取之行使權。』亦足供參照。

[13] 在法院組織法第 61 條至第 64 條之規範下，各級法院檢察署僅是管理檢察事務與檢察行政之處所而已，並非行使檢察權之單位，以國家名義行使檢察權者，為各個檢察官，因此檢察官乃獨任之機關，各自行使檢察權，也因檢察事務之處理為各個獨任之檢察官，為了監督檢察官行使檢察權，乃有檢察一體原則。檢察體系內部監督只能在檢察官尚未對外表示其偵查終結結果（起訴或不起訴、緩起訴）之前行使之；此也是檢察一體原則適用之基本原理。如我國檢察官之不起訴或緩起訴處分、起訴或聲請簡易判決處刑，在對外公告生效前，有所謂之送閱，即必須先將不起訴處分書送請主任檢察官、檢察長審閱，經核可後始對外公告，這就是檢察機關內部監督機制。檢察權行使之外部監督機制，則是由法院以訴訟監督來行使，例如刑訴法第 161 條第 2 項之起訴審查程序、第 258 條之 1 至第 258 之 4 條之交付審判強制起訴程序。參閱劉邦繡，論職權再議，臺灣本土法學雜誌，第 57 期，頁 31，2004 年 4 月。

　　前述再議之提起須以有告訴權人已向檢察官提出告訴為要件，然而這樣的觀點並非沒有爭議，蓋依刑事訴訟法第 232 條：「犯罪之被害人，得為告訴。」之規定，僅有犯罪被害人有資格提出告訴，因此關於某人是否為犯罪之被害人而得成為告訴權人，即有爭議。而若限縮被害人之範圍，得提出告訴或提起再議者，也就相應地受到限制。舉例而言，依司法院院字第 1016 號解釋：「聲請再議，依法既以告訴人為限，而偽證罪所侵害之法益係國家之審判權，故被偽證人向檢察官申告被偽證之事實，僅居告發人地位，對於不起訴處分，自不能聲請再議。」之說明，因偽證而受不利益之人，並非犯罪被害人，故不得提起告訴與聲請再議。然而院字第 1616 號解釋：「誣告罪以有使他人受刑事或懲戒處分之意圖為其構成要件，於侵害國家法益外，同時具有侵害個人法益之故意，被誣告人固可提起自訴，其向檢察官告訴，經檢察官不起訴處分者，亦得聲請再議。」卻認為因誣告而受不利益者符合刑事訴訟法第 232 條之規定而得提出告訴並聲請再議，其間之差異為何？何以意圖他人受刑事或懲戒處分，向該管公務員誣告者或意圖他人受刑事或懲戒處分，而偽造、變造證據，或使用偽造、變造之證據者[14]，該當為直接侵害個人法益之犯罪？而與誣告罪同樣足以動搖確定判決效力之偽證罪[15]，其受害人卻無從取得告訴

---

[14]　參照刑法第 169 條之規定。
[15]　刑事訴訟法第 420 條第 2、3 款規定：「二、原判決所憑之證言、鑑定或通譯已證明其為虛偽者。三、受有罪判決之人，已證明其係被誣告者。」。

人之地位（亦即何以偽證者未侵害被偽證者之個人法益）？何種侵害國家法益或社會法益之犯罪同時直接侵害個人法益 [16]？此等疑問並未見澄清 [17]。

---

[16] 參照司法院院解字第 3256 號解釋：「觸犯漢奸罪名同時直接侵害私人法益者，其被害之私人自得向檢察官告訴，並得對於不起訴之處分聲請再議，惟來文所舉懲治漢奸條例第 2 條第 1 項第 5 第 6 兩款供給敵人谷米金錢之例，係以供給行為為該罪之內容，而所供給之物資來源如何，在所不問，縱係由于勒徵勒派而來，究非該罪成立之要件，其被勒被派之人自仍不得謂為該罪之直接被害人。」之說明，若侵害國家法益或社會法益之犯罪同時直接侵害個人法益時，即得提出告訴。依最高法院 20 年上字第 55 號判例，犯罪被害人乃指因犯罪而直接受有損害之人，而不包括間接或附帶受害者。

[17] 雖最高法院 84 年 3060 號判決：「刑事訴訟法第 232 條規定，犯罪之被害人，得為告訴；所稱被害人云者，固指因犯罪行為其權益受直接之侵害者而言，不包括因此項犯罪而間接或附帶受害之人在內。然其權益之受害，究係直接受害，抑間接或附帶受害，則應依告訴意旨所指訴之事實，從形式上觀察其權益能否直接受有損害之虞，為判別之準據。至於確否因之而受害，則屬實體審認之範疇。就隱名合夥人之權益受害，能否對出名營業之行為人，提起告訴行使告訴權以言，依民法第 701 條所稱：隱名合夥，除該節另有規定者外，準用關於合夥之規定意旨，已徵不問出名營業人或隱名合夥人，對於合夥財產均有直接利害關係；如果合夥財產受有侵害，其各合夥成員之合法權益，亦直接受有侵害，自亦均為被害人，得向該管公務員提出告訴，請求訴追刑責之權。雖民法第 702 條規定，隱名合夥人之出資，其財產權移屬於出名營業人。乃係為使營業主體，對外之權利義務關係更臻明確單純，有益事業營運之便利，並維業務之信譽；但隱名合夥人與出名營業人間之內部關係，仍應受雙方原有契約所訂條款之拘束，而得行使對合夥帳簿之查閱，暨檢查合夥事務及財產狀況等之權利。因之，倘若出名營業人以就其執行之合夥事務，於業務上作成之文書，故為反於事實之不實登載者，勢必影響隱名合夥人分受營業所生之利益，及分擔其所生損失之有無或多寡；是以從形式上觀察，隱名合夥人告訴意旨之此項指訴，即不能認其權益，非直接受有損害，而不得對出名營業之行為人提起告訴。」認為：究係直接、間接或附帶受害，應依告訴意旨所指訴之事實，從形式上觀察其權益能否直接受有損害之虞，為判別之準據，至於確否因之而受害，則屬實體審認之範疇，不過如何「依告訴意旨所指訴之事實，從形式上觀察其權益能否直接受有損害之虞」

　　除前述究竟何種犯罪之「受害人（此處所指之受害人未必
該當刑事訴訟法第 232 條所指之被害人）」得提出告訴或聲請
再議之爭議外，再議制度雖已予犯罪被害人尋求上級檢察署檢
察長重新審查下級檢察官不起訴處分是否妥當之機會，不過對
於上級檢察長駁回再議之決定，被害人卻無法再尋求司法救
濟。此時若不起訴處分認定事實出現違誤不當之情形，在刑事
訴訟法第 260 條之拘束下，該經不起訴處分認定之事實即不當
地具有實質確定力，從而其後之刑事司法程序反到將受此種錯
誤事實之拘束[18]，此時對於犯罪被害人（告訴權人）之權益究
應如何保障，即有疑問[19]。此外，由於無告訴權人之案件經一

認定直接或間接受害，觀諸最高法院 93 年台抗字第 140 號裁定：「抗告意旨
略稱：抗告人自訴被告高智美涉犯刑法第 125 條第 1 項第 3 款之罪，該罪之
立法目的固在維護司法權之正當行使而設，但其所侵害之國家法益，同時亦
侵害抗告人之訴訟權，被告職司檢察業務，為參與偵查或起訴之檢察官，且
明知有罪之人，而無故不使其受追訴或處罰，及不將抗告人之再議案卷轉送
台灣高等法院檢察署，遽予報結，已另觸犯刑法第 211 條、第 213 條、第 216
條之偽造文書罪嫌，不能謂抗告人未受損害，抗告人既係直接被害人，自得
對其瀆職之行為提起自訴云云。查刑法第 125 條第 1 項第 3 款之罪係侵害國
家審判權之犯罪，不得提起自訴，原確定判決已詳敘其理由。縱其中涉有偽
造文書之罪，其法定刑與瀆職罪相同，但以情節比較，則以瀆職罪為重，依
刑事訴訟法第 319 條第 3 項但書規定，亦不得提起自訴，原確定判決維持第
一審所為諭知自訴不受理之判決，於法尚非有違。」之爭議，仍不明確。

[18] 參閱林鈺雄，刑事訴訟法下冊，第 596 至 601 頁，2001 年。

[19] 參照司法院 84.10.27 第 1035 次大法官會議不受理案件三：「本件聲請人以其
告訴被告吳春木等偽造文書案件，台灣新竹地方法院檢察署檢察官不採其提
出之證據，遽為不起訴處分，經聲請再議，復被台灣高等法院檢察署檢察官
為駁回之處分，適用法律顯有違憲疑義，聲請解釋憲法。查其聲請解釋之案
件，未經確定終局裁判，核與首開規定不合，依同條第 3 項規定，應不受
理。」以及同院 93.05.07 第 1243 次大法官會議不受理案件六：「本件聲請人

審檢察官為不起訴處分後該刑事爭議即告確定，若該檢察官之不起訴處分存在刑事訴訟法第 260 條所定得再行起訴之事實認定或法律見解之錯誤時 [20]，該如何救濟該不正確的不起訴處分，對於國家刑罰權能否正確、有效行使，即屬重要。若拋開現行刑事訴訟法條文之拘束，關於檢察官之不起訴處分是否宜賦予如確定判決般的效力，本身亦有很大的疑問，學者間如陳樸生教授與褚劍鴻教授等，均曾質疑刑事訴訟法第 260 條規定之妥當性 [21]，簡單來說，若依該條規定而認不起訴處分具有阻

因偽造文書案件，認臺灣臺北地方法院檢察署 90 年度偵字第 12905 號不起訴處分書及臺灣高等法院檢察署 90 年度議字第 3252 號再議駁回處分書，適用刑法第 210 條之構成要件與學說及最高法院相關判例要旨未盡明確一致，聲請解釋。查聲請人前曾以上開臺灣臺北地方法院檢察署之不起訴處分書及臺灣高等法院檢察署之再議駁回處分書適用刑法第 210 條有違憲疑義，聲請解釋，經本院認檢察署之處分書並非確定終局裁判，而以大法官第 1235 次會議議決不受理在案，茲復據以聲請解釋，核與司法院大法官審理案件法第五條第 1 項第 2 款之規定不合，依同條第 3 項規定，應不受理。」等決議之說明，犯罪被害人對於駁回再議之決定，已無再提救濟之機會，從而縱該不起訴處分之事實認定出現錯誤，在刑事訴訟法第 260 條之規定下，其後之刑事司法程序反到將受此錯誤事實之拘束，從被害人保護之角度而言，其不當之處不言可喻。

20 亦即：未發現新事實或新證據者；原判決所憑之證物未證明其為偽造或變造者；原判決所憑之證言、鑑定或通譯未證明其為虛偽者；原判決所憑之通常法院或特別法院之裁判未經確定裁判變更者；參與原判決或前審判決或判決前所行調查之法官，或參與偵查或起訴之檢察官，未因該案件犯職務上之罪已經證明者，或未因該案件違法失職已受懲戒處分，足以影響原判決者。

21 實務上認為不起訴處分具有實質確定力，此可參照最高法院 94 年台非字第 215 號刑事判決；但學說上有爭議，請參閱褚劍鴻，「論不起訴處分之確定力與不當處分之救濟（上）」，法令月刊第 19 卷第 8 期，頁 18-9，1998 年 8 月。另可參閱林永謀，刑事訴訟法釋論（中），頁 340，作者自版，2007 年 2 月。

斷當事人間就系爭刑事紛爭另行提告的效力（此即所謂一事不再理之效力），其規範基礎為何，即有詳加說明之必要，否則在無罪判決尚待三審定讞的法制架構下，何以檢察官在單獨進行偵查程序後所為之不起訴處分書能較法院所為之判決書更具有效力（特別在無告訴人的案件類型中，一審檢察官所為之不起訴處分書於對外公告表示時即生確定力，而一審之無罪判決尚待上訴程序終結或上訴期間經過後始生確定力）？又如認檢察官之起訴尚待法院判決確定始具確定犯罪事實與國家刑罰權存否之功能，何以在秘密偵查的結構[22]下，偵查結果為不起訴時，關於涉嫌犯罪之事實與國家刑罰權是否存在等爭議，即足以在未經公開審判之前提下確定犯罪事實為何？凡此種種，均為修法前不起訴處分所存在之疑義。

二、民國 91 年修法後

雖然聲請再議成功翻案的機率不高，不過據統計約有四成的告訴人不服原檢察官所做出的不起訴處分而聲請再議[23]，由

---

[22] 刑事訴訟法第 245 條第 1 項規定：「偵查，不公開之。」是所謂偵查不公開原則，或稱為「秘密偵查原則」、「偵查密行原則」。參閱林俊言，偵查不公開，http://www.tahr.org.tw/site/article/2001.03.08.htm（最後造訪日：2007 年 4 月 8 日）。

[23] 據統計，93 年各地方法院檢察署以不起訴處分或緩起訴處分或撤銷緩起訴處分之偵查案件中，得再議案件數分別為 5 萬 1 千件、1 萬 9 千件、1 千 9 百件；告訴人對於檢察官之不起訴處分或緩起訴處分或撤銷緩起訴處分表示不服，聲請再議案件則分別為 9 千 7 百件及 1 萬 9 千件、104 件，聲請再議案

此可知於現行刑事訴訟制度中,再議制度有其一定之重要性。於修法前,若案件業經檢察官為不起訴處分者,如告訴人聲請再議,本應尊重其意見而重行審核原不起訴處分是否洽當,惟如屬告發之案件,因無得聲請再議之人,為救濟修法前再議之提起須以有告訴權人已向檢察官提出告訴為要件,惟無告訴人之案件一經對外公告不起訴即告確定力所衍生之弊端,民國91年2月8日修正刑事訴訟法乃於第256條增訂第3項:「死刑、無期徒刑或最輕本刑三年以上有期徒刑之案件,因犯罪嫌疑不足,經檢察官為不起訴之處分,或第253條之1之案件經檢察官為緩起訴之處分者,如無得聲請再議之人時,原檢察官應依職權逕送直接上級法院檢察署檢察長或檢察總長再議,並通知告發人。」之職權再議規定。

　　觀諸職權再議之立法理由:「如屬告發之案件為免一經檢察官為不起訴或緩起訴處分,即告確定,自宜慎重」[24],該制度似以檢察機關內部監督機制之建立為規範目的。雖然職權再

件占不起訴及緩起訴處分及撤銷緩起訴處分得再議案件數之比率約為40.4%;聲請再議案件,絕大部分均由原檢察官送交上級法院檢察機關檢察長核辦,而由原檢察官駁回聲請或撤銷處分或由聲請人撤回聲請等情形,僅占0.6%。前項送交高等法院及分院檢察署之再議案件經辦理終結發回,八成四以不合法或無理由駁回聲請,命令續行偵查及命令起訴占9.7%,餘為其他原因。至於各地方法院檢察署辦理上級法院檢察機關發回命令續行偵查之再議案件,經統計93年全年重新偵查終結起訴者所占比率為15.6%,不起訴處分者比率為69.3%。資料來源:見法務部法務統計 (http://www.moj.gov.tw/public/Attachment/5121822495041.pdf)。

24　參閱立法院公報,第91卷第10期,頁954。

議制度著重於檢察機關內部監督之功能，也有助於不起訴處分本身妥當性之提升，不過該制度本身卻也衍生許多的疑義。按現行刑事訴訟法第 256 條第 2 項規定：「不起訴或緩起訴處分得聲請再議者，其再議期間及聲請再議之直接上級法院檢察署檢察長或檢察總長，應記載於送達告訴人處分書正本」，針對聲請再議程序已有明文，惟就無得聲請再議人之職權再議案件而言，原檢察官應依職權逕送直接上級法院檢察署檢察長或檢察總長再議之期間爲何？是否亦比照聲請再議期間之七日？就此現行刑事訴訟法並無規定，此種規範欠缺之法制現況，非但孳生原偵查結果已否確定之疑義，亦有害於被告權益之保障；蓋被告發之涉案人何時脫離被告身分，在原偵查程序已作出不起訴處分後，本應有一明確之判斷標準，畢竟偵查中被告之地位本身之失而復得，對任何人來說都是一種不利益。

　　除前述職權再議制度充實檢察機關內部監督之規範目的外，就再議制度內含救濟功能而言 [25]，職權再議制度本身亦有疑問。依最高法院 71 年台上字第 3409 號判例：「刑事訴訟法第 344 條第 4 項固規定宣告死刑或無期徒刑之案件，原審法院應不待上訴，依職權逕送該管上級法院審判並通知當事人，但同條第 5 項既規定前項情形，視爲被告已提起上訴，則上訴審之訴訟程序，仍應依法踐行。」之說明，職權上訴本質上仍屬

---

[25]　參照最高法院 89 年台非字第 128 號判決：「聲請再議與聲明上訴，同爲不服下級審之處分或裁判，向上級審請求救濟之程序。」

被告之上訴，爲被告不服法院判決之擬制，因而，此職權上訴之規定有阻斷判決確定之效果，具有訴訟法上之救濟途徑與意義[26]。不過，職權上訴與職權再議，卻存在不同的前提。按聲請再議原係告訴人請求檢察官回復偵查狀態並提起公訴，而上訴卻是被告請求法院回復審判程序並作出被告有罪之判決，若謂職權上訴係擬制被告提起上訴，則由於刑事訴訟法第256條係以無得聲請再議之人存在爲前提，職權再議又將擬制何人聲請再議、擬制何人請求救濟呢？如果無被救濟者存在，即不應認爲職權再議具有審級救濟之功能，從而，職權再議不能與職權上訴相提並論，並不能認爲具有訴訟上救濟途徑之意義[27]。

---

[26]　參閱劉邦繡，論職權再議，臺灣本土法學雜誌，第 57 期，頁 31，2004 年 4月。

[27]　又依刑事訴訟法第256條第3項，所謂無得聲請再議之人的緩起訴處分職權送再議案件，上級法院檢察署檢察長審查範圍為何？是緩起訴之適當與否嗎？上級檢察長能能撤銷該緩起訴處分嗎？然按緩起訴處分後，依刑事訴訟法第253條之3規定，被告於緩起訴處分期間內，檢察官得俟依職權或依告訴人之聲請撤銷緩起訴處分，繼續偵查或起訴，以有下列事由存在為條件：一是於緩起訴期間內故意更犯有期徒刑以上刑之罪，經檢察官提起公訴者，二是於緩起訴前，因故意犯他罪，而在緩起迄期間內受有期徒刑以上刑之宣告者，三是違背第253條之2第1項各款應遵守或履行事項者，為限。因此緩起訴處分職權再議，上級檢察長所可以審核之範圍也應只限於此（刑訴法第253條之3）；再者被告受緩起訴處分後，具有暫不受追訴上之訴訟法地位（參照刑訴法第256條之1，被告可以對撤銷緩起訴處分聲請再議），上級檢察長在緩起訴處分案件之職權送再議，審查中似乎不能以該緩起訴處分是否適當為由，予以撤銷該緩起訴處分，應以有否具有第253條之3事由為審查範圍。由上開說明職權再議審查範圍觀之，職權再議更能確認不是一種訴訟法上之救濟途徑，充其量只是檢察體系內部之監督機制而已。參閱劉邦繡，再議與交付審判之適用與疑義2，法務通訊第2100期，頁3-5，2002.09.05。

又依刑事訴訟法第 256 條第 3 項規定，職權再議係以下列檢察官處分爲對象：（一）以死刑、無期徒刑或最輕本刑三年以上有期徒刑之案件，因犯罪嫌疑不足，而不起訴處分；（二）被告所犯爲死刑、無期徒刑或最輕本刑三年以上有期徒刑以外之罪，檢察官參酌刑法第 57 條所列事項及公共利益之維護，而爲緩起訴處分。基本上類型（二）之緩起訴處分類型，係以被告所犯爲死刑、無期徒刑或最輕本刑三年以上有期徒刑以外之罪爲前提，故犯罪事實已可認定，亦足以確定被告所犯罪名，職權再議之對象及案件類型，應無可疑問。不過類型（一）之不起訴處分類型卻有疑義，蓋既認爲係因犯罪嫌疑不足，則何來認定死刑、無期徒刑或最輕本刑三年以上有期徒刑之案件；再者，檢察官認定犯罪事實適用刑罰法律，被告所爲犯罪之事實，是否屬於死刑、無期徒刑或最輕本刑三年以上有期徒刑罪名案件，必須以犯罪事實存在爲前提，否則無所謂重罪之案件存在。又檢察官在偵查進行中，對被告之犯罪嫌疑罪名，必須到偵查終結爲起訴或緩起訴決定時才會產生，不起訴並無所謂罪與刑；其次檢察官偵查犯罪也不受任何人所指法律之拘束，更不受告發人告發或移送報告之司法警察機關所指之罪、刑名之拘束，例如告發人指訴被告犯殺人未遂罪，其實只是傷害罪嫌，或警察機關移送被告犯擄人勒贖罪嫌，其實只是妨害自由罪嫌，經檢察官查無犯罪嫌疑，根本不存在所謂不起訴處分屬於死刑、無期徒刑或最輕本刑三年以上有期徒刑之案件，觀諸上述分析，可見此種類型之職權再議，根本不可能存

在，亦可見職權再議於立法上之不當[28]。

　　雖刑事訴訟法於民國 91 年 2 月增訂了職權再議制度，以救濟檢察官之不當不起訴處分或緩起訴處分，不過新制卻也同時衍生出前述立法過程中未曾想見之疑義。此外，關於不起訴處分是否宜維持其實質確定力，以及是否宜賦予不起訴處分具有確定系爭刑事爭議事實功能等問題，並未在歷次的刑事訴訟法修正過程中，得到充分討論並達成共識。鑒於不起訴處分之效力爲何將不可避免地影響如何救濟不起訴處分之制度設計，本文以下將自現行刑事訴訟法第 260 條規定出發，分析檢討該條規定之妥當性，以及再議制度存在之必要性。

肆、不起訴處分之確定力與一事不再理原則

一、不起訴處分效力之比較法觀察

　　依刑事訴訟法第 260 條：「不起訴處分已確定或緩起訴處

---

[28] 其更主張：在刑事訴訟法上訂立「職權再議」條款，應有可議之處，因為檢察體系之內部監督機制，應屬檢察體系組織法規範之範疇，且現行已有法院組織法第 63 條至 64 條之檢察一體原則之制度，至於現行檢察一體原則之明確法制化雖有闕漏處，則應於檢察體系組織法內檢討修正，殊無在刑事訴訟程序中再規範此檢察體系內部運作之監督機制，此立法上增列職權再議，應有未洽；參閱劉邦繡，論職權再議，臺灣本土法學雜誌，第 57 期，頁 32-3，2004 年 4 月。

分期滿未經撤銷者，非有左列情形之一，不得對於同一案件再行起訴：一、發現新事實或新證據者。二、有第 420 條第 1 項第 1 款、第 2 款、第 4 款或第 5 款所定得為再審原因之情形者。」之規定，原則上已確定之不起訴處分因不得對於同一案件[29]再行起訴而具有實質的確定力[30]。然而，關於不起訴處分是否具有實質確定力，該條規定並非舉世皆然，茲就美、日、

---

[29]　案件之構成，包括被告及所犯事實二種要素；參閱陳樸生，刑事訴訟法實務，頁 91，1994 年。

[30]　參照最高法院 94 年台非字第 215 號刑事判決：「刑事訴訟制度之建立，旨在經由訴訟程序之遵守，以擔保國家刑罰權之正確行使，而達到實現實體正義之目的，故刑事訴訟法第 379 條第 5 款規定法院不受理訴訟係不當者，其判決當然違背法令。又刑事訴訟法為配合由職權主義調整為改良式當事人進行主義，乃採行起訴猶豫制度，於同法增訂第 253 條之 1，許由檢察官對於死刑、無期徒刑或最輕本刑三年以上有期徒刑以外之罪之案件，得參酌刑法第 57 條所列事項及公共利益之維護，認為適當者，予以緩起訴處分，期間為一年以上三年以下，以觀察犯罪行為人有無施以刑法所定刑事處罰之必要，為介於起訴及微罪職權不起訴間之緩衝制度設計。其具體效力依同法第 260 條規定，於緩起訴處分期滿未經撤銷者，非有同條第 1 款或第 2 款情形之一，不得對於同一案件再行起訴，即學理上所稱之實質確定力。足見在緩起訴期間內，尚無實質確定力可言。且依上揭第 260 條第 1 款規定，於不起訴處分確定或緩起訴處分期滿未經撤銷者，仍得以發現新事實、新證據為由，對於同一案件再行起訴。此所謂新事實、新證據，即指在原處分確定前，未經發現，屬於原處分採證認事所憑證據及所認事實範圍以外之新事實、新證據而言。是本於同一法理，在緩起訴期間內，其效力未定，倘發現新事實、新證據，而認已不宜緩起訴，又無同法第 253 條之 3 第 1 項所列得撤銷緩起訴處分之事由者，自得就同一案件逕行起訴，原緩起訴處分並因此失其效力。復因與同法第 260 條所定應受實質確定力拘束情形不同，當無所謂起訴程序違背規定之可言，法院對此另行起訴之案件，自應予以受理、審判，並有同法第 267 條所定關於起訴不可分原則之適用，有本院 22 年上字第 1863 號、43 年台上字第 690 號判例可資參照。」。

德等國之法制說明於下。

由於美國聯邦最高法院認為檢察官起訴或不起訴之決定不適於司法審查[31]，因此美國檢察官對於起訴與否享有極大的裁量權[32]，即使證據確鑿，檢察官仍可在刑事政策或司法資源分配之考量下，做出不起訴之決定[33]。鑑於美國憲法增修條文第5條僅禁止政府部門對同一犯罪重複提起訴訟[34]，若不存在第

---

[31] See Wayte v. United States, 470 U.S. 598, 607-8 (1985). ("This broad discretion rests largely on the recognition that the decision to prosecute is particularly ill-suited to judicial review. Such factors as the strength of the case, the prosecution's general deterrence value, the Government's enforcement priorities, and the case's relationship to the Government's overall enforcement plan are not readily susceptible to the kind of analysis the courts are competent to undertake. Judicial supervision in this area, moreover, entails systemic costs of particular concern. Examining the basis of a prosecution delays the criminal proceeding, threatens to chill law enforcement by subjecting the prosecutor's motives and decision-making to outside inquiry, and may undermine prosecutorial effectiveness by revealing the Government's enforcement policy. All these are substantial concerns that make the courts properly hesitant to examine the decision whether to prosecute.")

[32] In the United States, the prosecutor is probably the most important decision-maker in the criminal process. The impetus to begin a criminal investigation usually emanates from a private complainant, and it is ordinarily the police who conduct the bulk of investigations; but the determinations whether to charge a suspect, what to charge him with, and what sanctions eventually to impose are made or substantially influenced by the prosecutor. Available at: http://law.jrank.org/pages/1857/Prosecution-Comparative-Aspects.html (last visited, Apr. 6th, 2007)。See also United States v. Goodwin, 457 U.S. 368, 380 (1982). A charging decision does not levy an improper "penalty" unless it results solely from the defendant's exercise of a protected legal right, rather than the prosecutor's normal assessment of the societal interest in prosecution. See Westen & Westin, A Constitutional Law of Remedies for Broken Plea Bargains, 66 Calif. L. Rev. 471, 486 (1978).

一次的處罰危險（first jeopardy），則重複處罰（double jeopardy）即無由出現。美國最高法院即認爲：除非在陪審審判中小陪審團已宣誓就職或在法官審判中第一個證人已具結宣誓，否則犯罪嫌疑人或被告受刑事處罰之危險即不發生[35]。既然美國檢察官不起訴決定並不發生第一次的處罰危險，從而不起訴決定後另爲起訴決定時，並不會造成第二次的處罰危險，也就是說，在美國的刑事訴訟程序中，對同一案件不起訴決定後另爲之起訴決定，並不違反美國憲法增修條文第 5 條之規定，從而不起訴決定並無拘束後訴能否提起之實質確定力。

　　日本刑事訴訟法對於在何種情形應不提起公訴，並無規定[36]；依日本刑事訴訟法第 259 條至第 261 條之規定，檢察官應將不起訴之意旨告知或通知犯罪嫌疑人、告訴人或告發人[37]。關於不起訴處分之效力，日本最高裁判所曾有明示：檢察官不

---

[33] 參閱鍾鳳玲，檢察官不起訴處分監督及審查制度之比較研究，法學叢刊第 185 期，頁 6，2002 年 1 月。

[34] The Fifth Amendment to the U.S. Constitution just says: "nor shall any person be subject for the same offense to be twice put in jeopardy of life or limb."

[35] The U. S. Supreme Court has held that jeopardy attaches during a jury trial when the jury is sworn. In criminal cases tried by a judge without a jury, also called a bench trial, jeopardy attaches when the first witness is sworn. Available at: http://law.enotes.com/everyday-law-encyclopedia/double-jeopardy (last visited, Apr. 6th, 2007)。

[36] 參閱褚劍鴻，「論不起訴處分之確定力與不當處分之救濟（上）」，法令月刊第 19 卷第 8 期，頁 21，1998 年 8 月。

[37] 參閱蔡墩銘，德日刑事訴訟法，日本刑事訴訟法，頁 65，五南圖書出版有限公司，1993 年 7 月。

起訴之犯罪，日後起訴，並不違反日本憲法第 39 條禁止雙重處罰之規定，蓋在日本僅刑事訴訟法第 340 條規定，檢察官撤回公訴，經裁判所為公訴不受理之裁定確定者，非就犯罪事實新發現重要證據者，不得就同一案件再行提起公訴[38]。簡單來說，日本法認為，不起訴處分僅係檢察官內部之意思決定，並無拘束力，仍得依其後之情況，就該案件再行起訴，與曾經判決確定之情形有別，自與二重訴追之禁止不生牴觸之問題，故此種不起訴處分，既不發生確定力，自得隨時繼續偵查[39]；正由於日本之刑事訴訟法並無類似我國刑事訴訟法第 260 條規定，因此在理論上，日本檢察官之不起訴處分並無實質確定力，檢察官為不起訴處分後，不論其不起訴之原因為何，日後如發現新事實新證據，自得再行調查起訴[40]。不過，相對於前述「不起訴處分不是法院的判決，不產生一事不再理效力。因此，即使作出不起訴處分，也可以再次起訴。」之觀點，學說上也有反對意見，蓋「人們難以理解，因為作為犯罪嫌疑人來說，儘管接受不起訴處分，但在時效期間內，因隨時可以再次起訴，嚴重威脅犯罪嫌疑人法律地位的穩定。」，因此，反對

---

[38]　參閱褚劍鴻，「論不起訴處分之確定力與不當處分之救濟（上）」，法令月刊第 19 卷第 8 期，頁 22，1998 年 8 月。

[39]　參閱陳樸生，刑事訴訟法實務，頁 329，1984 年。

[40]　參閱鍾鳳玲，檢察官不起訴處分監督及審查制度之比較研究，法學叢刊第 185 期，頁 2，2002 年 1 月。

意見「贊成不起訴處分時也可以適用第 340 條 [41] 的觀點。而且，如果沒有任何理由，隨意取消不起訴處分，可以認為是惡意追訴，應該追究濫用公訴權的問題。[42]」，此種以「不起訴處分後，關於犯罪事實重新發現重要證據為限，得就同一案件再提起公訴」之觀點，某種程度來說，反倒類似我國刑事訴訟法第 260 條第 1 款：「不起訴處分已確定或緩起訴處分期滿未經撤銷者，非有左列情形之一，不得對於同一案件再行起訴：一、發現新事實或新證據者。」之規定。

　　德國刑事訴訟法第 170 條第 2 項亦允許檢察官為不起訴處分（停止訴訟程序），依同法第 171 條：「檢察官對於請求提起公訴而未予受理或經偵查終結而停止刑事訴訟程序者，應將其理由通知告訴人。」之規定，檢察官應將不起訴之理由通知告訴人 [43]。不過關於裁量不起訴之效力，則應視該裁量不起訴是否已經被告同意或起訴後由法官徵求檢察官同意而為。如該不起訴處分係由檢察官個人決定，或經法官同意所為，則該不起訴處分並不具有實質確定力，不論有無發現新事實，檢察官

---

[41] 日本刑事訴訟法第 340 條規定：「因撤銷公訴所為之公訴不受理之裁定已經確定時，以在撤銷公訴後關於犯罪事實重新發現重要證據為限，得就同一案件再提起公訴。」參閱蔡墩銘，德日刑事訴訟法，日本刑事訴訟法，頁 84，五南圖書出版有限公司，1993 年 7 月。

[42] 參閱（日）田口守一著，劉迪、張凌、穆津等譯，刑事訴訟法，頁 108，法律出版社，2000 年 1 月。

[43] 參閱蔡墩銘，德日刑事訴訟法，德國刑事訴訟法，頁 83，五南圖書出版有限公司，1993 年 7 月。

均得重新開始追訴程序；惟若檢察官之裁量不起訴處分業經被告同意，則只有在發現新事實之前提下，檢察官才可以重行起訴[44]。

二、不起訴處分實質確定力之規範基礎

　　由前述比較法制之觀察可以發現，原則上外國刑事訴訟法制並未賦予不起訴處分具有阻斷再行起訴或另為判決之實質確定力，從而縱已為不起訴處分，檢察官仍有權決定是否再啟偵查並提起公訴，而法院亦得自實體上另為判決，此實與我國之現制大有不同。然而何以我國之不起訴處分具有實質確定力？依陳樸生教授所述：「我國現制，仍認檢察官與法院同其系統，其任務在實現國家刑罰權。因本法的安定性機能，其所為之不起訴處分，仍具有確定性，此觀之本法第 260 條之規定自明。[45]」，然而，「不起訴處分縱屬違法，但一經確定，非具有第 260 條所列情形，不得對於同一案件再行起訴，重在法的安定性。惟不起訴處分之性質，究與曾經判決確定者不同。如具有第 260 條所列情形，仍得對於同一案件再行起訴，因認其

44　參閱鍾鳳玲，檢察官不起訴處分監督及審查制度之比較研究，法學叢刊第 185 期，頁 11，2002 年 1 月。
45　參閱陳樸生，刑事訴訟法實務，頁 329，1984 年。

未具判決之既判力。[46]」，蓋「不起訴之案件，經過聲明再議，即為確定，自不得再行起訴。否則非特不起訴之效力，失之薄弱，而被告應否處罰，久懸不定，亦非善策，故不起訴之案件，以不得再行起訴為原則。惟不起訴處分，係決定訴訟進行之程序，犯罪之偵查權，並未因不起訴而歸消滅。[47]」；「國家既將公訴權委由檢察官行使，其不起訴、緩起訴若不賦予實體之確定力，則案件將懸而未定，有礙於法秩序之維持；況檢察官既將內部決定之不起訴或緩起訴表示於外，若謂仍可完全不顧而得隨時予以起訴，則被告將長期處於不安之狀態，其於國家、社會亦未必有利，因主張應賦予實體之確定力。[48]」。也就是說，賦與不起訴處分實質確定力之主要目的，在於保護被告於不起訴處分確定後不受處罰之法律地位[49]。而以類似提

---

[46] 也就是說，在刑事訴訟法第 260 條之拘束下，「具有實質確定力之不起訴處分經確定者，其公訴權既已喪失，自無從行使其實體的刑罰權。因之，刑事訴權之未行使，亦足為刑罰權消滅之一消極原因。」參閱陳樸生，刑事訴訟法實務，頁 332，1984 年。

[47] 參閱俞叔平，刑事訴訟法學，頁 207，中國法學編譯社印行，1956 年 10 月修正版。

[48] 參閱林永謀，刑事訴訟法釋論（中），頁 385，作者自版，2007 年 2 月。

[49] 按偵查中案件除起訴、緩起訴與不起訴外，尚有「簽結」之程序。基本上，若案件當事人經檢察官「簽結」，表示案件一開始檢方就認定當事人沒有具體犯罪的事實或不構成犯罪，因此以製作內部簽呈的方式結案，與不起訴處分意義不同。與此相對，「不起訴」是案件經檢方偵辦，並已將當事人列為被告後，偵查終結認為未涉案或罪嫌不足，不起訴確定後，除非日後有當事人涉案新事實新證據，否則不能重啟偵查。「簽結」則認為案子不需處理，不過，日後只要認為有必要處理，就能重啟偵查。因此，已將當事人列為被告後因認未涉案或罪嫌不足而為之不起訴處分確定，對被告而言，屬於值得保護之利益。

起再審之嚴格要件作為不起訴處分確定後,得否再行提起公訴之判斷標準,似亦賦予確定不起訴處分類似確定判決之效力,此即司法實務所指之一事不再理之效力[50]。

在保護被告不受處罰法律地位之要求下,不起訴處分確定後,除具有第 260 條之情形,依我國現制別無救濟之道。本質上,應否賦予檢察官所為之不起訴處分具有實質確定之一事不再理效力,本屬訴訟法上之一重要問題。關於其間利弊,難以一概而論,誠如陳樸生教授所析:「刑法,僅就抽象的刑罰權設其規定,欲對於具體案件確定其具體的刑罰權,在近代立法例採訴訟主義,此項審判權之行使,以訴之存在為前提,即所謂不告不理之原則。刑事訴權,我國現制雖採二元主義,其行使訴權之機關,分屬於檢察官與自訴人;然公訴權與自訴權不許其同時行使。故同一案件,經自訴人提起自訴者,固不許檢

50　參照最高法院 91 年台上字第 3454 號判決:「而本件自訴人等所敘及之刑法第 201 條之偽造有價證券罪、第 214 條使公務員登載不實罪、第 216 條行使偽造文書罪、第 304 條之強制罪、第 320 條第 1 項之竊盜罪等部分,均未為任何之偵查及處分,則本件是否與前揭台灣台南地方法院檢察署 84 年度偵字第 1076 號詐欺案屬同一案件,而有一事不再理之適用,自有研求之餘地。又本件自訴人等指上訴人等「以偽造之支票詐取運費及借款」、「以不實之財產讓渡而隱匿財產致自訴人等陷於錯誤而允為運送及借貸」為詐欺手段,而前揭不起訴處分書並未針對前開詐欺手段為評價判斷,則前後二案是否為同一案件,亦有斟酌之餘地。」與 92 年台上字第 7343 號判決:「又原判決於事實欄載稱胡惠琴於 86 年 10 月 23 日向台灣宜蘭地方法院檢察署提起毀損告訴云云,經查卷內並無該資料,其偵查結果如何?又 86 年度偵字第 4574 號(86 年 11 月 24 日提出告訴),經檢察官為游信雄不起訴處分,嗣告訴人胡惠琴聲請再議,結果如何?本件有無一事不再理之問題?應併予查明。」,均認為確定不起訴處分具有一事不再理之效力。

察官再行提起公訴；如經檢察官終結偵查[51]者，亦不許自訴人再行提起自訴。惟被害人果否行使其自訴權及何時行使，除受追訴權時效及告訴期間之限制外，並毋庸作何表示，亦毋庸為任何處分；檢察官之行使公訴權與否，則應為起訴或不起訴之處分。一經處分不起訴確定，即不得再行起訴，其限制較自訴為嚴；且經檢察官終結偵查者，又不得提起自訴。是自訴權因公訴權之不行使而受影響。從保護被告個人自由上言，固無可非議；從刑法以保護社會安全為其機能上言，則不無缺點。且訴權之行使，其目的在請求法院確定其刑罰權，其本身並無何種效能，更非行使司法權之可比。如認檢察官不行使訴權，具有行使司法權之同樣效果，則檢察官無異兼攝審判之權，一經確定，除具有第 260 條之情形外，又無救濟方法，其確定力較判決為強。總之，檢察官之不起訴處分究其性質言，不過訴權之未行使，即因案件未發現其具備可能條件或必要條件之故，既非訴權之捨棄，更非訴權消滅之原因。故案件雖經檢察官處分不起訴，乃檢察機關內部所為之決定，仍屬偵查階段，雖不宜有何拘束力，更不宜有何確定力，但本法仍沿舊制，其重視被告利益之保護，可以概見。[52]」；也就是說，雖然在法理上確定之不起訴處分不適宜具有實質確定力，現行刑事訴訟法第

51　作者註，現行法已將偵查終結改為開始偵查；現行刑事訴訟法第 323 條第 1
　　項規定：「同一案件經檢察官依第 228 條規定開始偵查者，不得再行自
　　訴。」。

52　參閱陳樸生，刑事訴訟法實務，頁 335，1984 年。

260 條卻僅本諸被告得主張不受重覆追訴利益之一事不再理觀點，賦予確定不起訴處分具有實質確定力。從而，關於被告得主張不受重覆追訴利益之一事不再理之內涵，實為判斷現行刑事訴訟法第 260 條規定當否之前提基礎。

三、一事不再理原則之意義

關於一事不再理原則之內涵，最高法院 55 年度台非字第 176 號判例已有闡述，其謂：「一事不再理為刑事訴訟法上一大原則，蓋對同一被告之一個犯罪事實，祇有一個刑罰權，不容重複裁判，故檢察官就同一事實無論其為先後兩次起訴或在一個起訴書重複追訴，法院均應依刑事訴訟法第 295 條（現行法第 303 條）第 2 款就重行起訴部分諭知不受理之判決。」刑事判決分為形式判決（無既判力的判決）和實體判決（有既判力的判決），前者如不受理判決，管轄錯誤判決；後者如有罪判決，無罪判決，免訴判決。所謂既判力，是指一個案子受到確定判決效力的保障，除非有特殊的情形可以提起再審和非常上訴之外，否則不能再以其他的訴訟程序來推翻一個確定判決的認定。由於不受理判決和管轄錯誤判決，並沒有實質上審理犯罪事實，因此沒有既判力；有罪判決，無罪判決已經實體的審理過犯罪事實，因此一旦確定，就以確定判決認定的事實為準，遮斷事後再就同一犯罪事實起訴審判的可能。至於免訴判決，因為是認定一個案子之前已經判決確定，或時效完成，

或曾經大赦，或犯罪後法律修正已經不罰，所以雖然沒有實質審理犯罪事實，仍然有既判力。既判力的效果，主要是在保障被告受確定判決保護的權利，以免被告因爲同一個事實一再被審判。當然，也避免了判決可能歧異的後果[53]。一事不再理原則也叫作禁止雙重審判（處罰）規則，是指一人不能因同一罪名兩次受審。英國適用該原則的最早時間要追溯到公元第 12 世紀，以後逐漸在判例法中確立了這一原則；幾百年來，禁止雙重審判規則被認爲是英國刑事司法制度的基石。美國憲法增修條文第 5 條「禁止政府部門對同一犯罪重複提起訴訟」之規定，即承繼了前述英國法治的傳統。時值今日，禁止雙重審判在憲法上具有三個層面的意義：一、禁止在同一犯罪無罪釋放後重新審判；二、禁止在同一犯罪已爲判決後重新審判；三、禁止因同一犯罪而受重覆處罰[54]。

原則上，美國憲法增修條文第 5 條「禁止政府部門對同一犯罪重複提起訴訟」之規定，非但在防止被告因同一犯罪事實而受二次以上的處罰，亦在防止被告遭受超過一次有罪裁判的

---

[53] 參照 http://blog.yam.com/ottohsu/article/5831142（最後造訪日：2007 年 4 月 8 日）。

[54] There are three essential protections included in double jeopardy: protection from being retried for the same crime after an acquittal; protection from retrial after a conviction; and protection from being punished multiple times for the same offense. Available at: http://www.bookrags.com/Double_jeopardy (last visited, Apr. 6th, 2007)。

風險[55]，蓋國家機關掌握所有資源，若允許其基於同一犯罪事實而多次對同一涉嫌者提起訴訟，不但將對被告產生不當的侵擾，亦有提高無辜被告終究受有罪裁判之風險[56]，對被告而言，極為不公。故在維護被告利益的考量下，賦予法院裁判具有最終性的效力，並禁止對同一犯罪重覆裁判[57]，或為維護社會公益所必要[58]；此一源自習慣法時代的法律原則，亦早於一百多年前已為美國聯邦最高法院所肯認[59]。

---

[55] See United States v. Ball, 163 U.S. 662, 669 (1896). ("The prohibition is not against being twice punished, but against being twice put in jeopardy; and the accused, whether convicted or acquitted, is equally put in jeopardy at the first trial.")

[56] See Green v. United States, 355 U.S. 184, 187-8 (1957). ("The underlying idea, one that is deeply ingrained in at least the Anglo-American system of jurisprudence, is that the State with all its resources and power should not be allowed to make repeated attempts to convict an individual for an alleged offense, thereby subjecting him to embarrassment, expense and ordeal and compelling him to live in a continuing state of anxiety and insecurity, as well as enhancing the possibility that even though innocent he may be found guilty.")

[57] See United States v. DiFrancesco, 449 U.S. 117, 130 (1980). ("This is justified on the ground that, however mistaken the acquittal may have been, there would be an unacceptably high risk that the Government, with its superior resources, would wear down a defendant, thereby 'enhancing the possibility that even though innocent he may be found guilty.' 'We necessarily afford absolute finality to a jury's verdict of acquittal - no matter how erroneous its decision.'")

[58] See Wayne R. LaFave et al., Criminal Procedure, 1176 (West, 2004).

[59] See Ex Parte Lange, 85 U.S. 163, 169 (1873). ("Blackstone in his Commentaries,7 cites the same maxim as the reason why, if a person has been found guilty of manslaughter on an indictment, and has had benefit of clergy, and suffered the judgment of the law, he cannot afterwards be appealed. Of course, if there had been no punishment the appeal would lie, and the party would be subject to the danger of another form of trial. But by reason of this universal principle, that no person shall be twice punished for the same offence, that ancient right of appeal

四、偵查程序與（雙重）刑事處罰危險

　　如前所述，一事不再理原則原在禁止法院對同一犯罪重覆裁判，蓋裁判程序本身對被告受有罪裁判來說，將造成極大的風險。不過，相同程度的風險，是否會來自於偵查程序？或有重新說明的必要。

　　細究刑事訴訟法第 260 條以類似提起再審之嚴格要件作為不起訴處分確定後，得否再行提起公訴之判斷標準，除在於保護被告於不起訴處分確定後不受處罰之法律地位外，亦賦予檢察官終結偵查程序之不起訴處分，具有類似法院判決之效力 [60]。

---

was gone when the punishment had once been suffered. The protection against the action of the same court in inflicting punishment twice must surely be as necessary, and as clearly within the maxim, as protection from chances or danger of a second punishment on a second trial. The common law not only prohibited a second punishment for the same offence, but it went further and forbid a second trial for the same offence, whether the accused had suffered punishment or not, and whether in the former trial he had been acquitted or convicted. Hence to every indictment or information charging a party with a known and defined crime or misdemeanor, whether at the common law or by statute, a plea of autrefois acquit or autrefois convict is a good defence.")

[60] 刑事訴訟法中規定的「新事實，新證據」是指全案不起訴處分前沒有被發現，到後來才發現者而言。而且如果認為被告有犯罪嫌疑的證據或事實，在不起訴處分前就已經提出，並經檢察官調查斟酌，就不是所謂「發現的新證據」。同時，如果檢方重新加以斟酌，因前後的觀點不同，導致事實的認定或證據的取捨有異，也不能作為新事實或新證據。參照最高法院 57 台上 1256 號判例：「刑事訴訟法第 260 條第 1 款所謂發見新事實或新證據者，係指於不起訴處分前未經發見至其後始行發見者而言，若不起訴處分前，已經提出之證據，經檢察官調查斟酌者，即非該條款所謂發見之新證據，不得據以再行起訴。」原則上，實務上認為刑事訴訟法第 260 條所謂「同一案件」，是指

不過這樣的觀點，本質上似乎有點矛盾，蓋檢察官的起訴處分尚待法院實質審理並判決確定後始生一事不再理效力，何以未經法院審理之檢察官不起訴處分，特別是無被害人或無告訴人不得再議（或不符職權再議規定）的案件，一經作成，在被告未具備受有罪判決風險的前提下，立即產生一事不再理之效力？又裁判程序過程中一事不再理效力發生前，尚有上訴程序或非常救濟程序以資緩衝救濟，何以前述不起訴處分本身即足生一事不再理效力？既然作成不起訴處分，即表示該案件並未進入審判程序，則此時被告並未因審判程序之發動，而遭受有罪判決的不利益可能，如此一來，該條規定所保護之對象為何？似不明確，難道刑事訴訟法第 260 條規定旨在保障國家機關不須對同一犯罪事實進行二次以上的調查？由此亦可知該條規定之爭議。

　　從另一個角度來說，如果沒有刑事訴訟法第 260 條之規定，或有主張此時犯罪嫌疑人即使已獲得檢察官不起訴處分，因在時效期間內隨時有可能再次被起訴，故其不受追訴之法律地位，恐將嚴重受到威脅。然而，如果一事不再理原則主要在「避免法院重覆審判所可能衍生的危險與不公平」，那麼即使承認前述被告在不起訴處分後不受追訴之法律地位亦值得保

「同一訴訟物體，即被告及犯罪事實均相同者而言，不以起訴或告訴時所引用之法條或罪名為區分標準」（52 年台上字第 1048 號判例參照）；所謂「新事實新證據」，祇須為不起訴處分以前未經發現，且足認被告有犯罪嫌疑者為已足，並不以確實證明犯罪為必要，既經檢察官就其發現者據以提起公訴，法院即應予以受理，為實體上之裁判（44 年台上字第 467 號判例參照）。

護，本諸秘密偵查程序與公開審判程序間之差異 [61]，也不應將確定不起訴處分視同確定判決而認其亦應具有一事不再理之效力，換言之，將訴權不行使（不起訴）視同為訴權與刑罰權不存在（無罪）而賦予相同的法律效果，本質上就是一種錯誤。至於究竟應該如何保護被告在不起訴處分後不受追訴之法律地位不任意受影響，乃另一問題，有待議者另為闡述，不應在此混淆。

伍、再議制度必要性之探討

一、檢察機關監督不起訴處分之再議制度

對於犯罪之追訴，除自訴程序外，原則上均由檢察官代表國家為之。不過檢察官之識見、判斷，未必均能正確無訛，是其所為之處分，自亦難免於過誤，而應有補救之道 [62]。當檢察官之起訴處分出現違誤時，其受不利益之被告尚得藉由審判程序尋求救濟，因此對被告而言，檢察官之起訴雖不當，惟仍有救濟之方法。然而，在刑事訴訟法第 260 條賦予不起訴處分或緩起訴處分實質確定力的前提下，當檢察官之不起訴處分（或

---

[61] 或謂在過去之刑事司法實務中，偵查與審判並無太大差異，然而在刑事訴訟程序已由職權主義改為改良式當事人進行主義之後，偵查與審判之意義已大不相同。

[62] 參閱林永謀，刑事訴訟法釋論（中），頁 368，作者自版，2007 年 2 月。

緩起訴處分）出現違誤時，如何對不當之「公訴權不行使」或
「公訴權緩行使」進行救濟，便成為一個問題。

　　關於防止不當之不起訴，大陸法系國家除基於檢察一體原則
由檢察機關自身內部上下監督外，另有賦予被害人「訴訟開始聲
請權」或賦予告訴人「異議權」等外部監督程序以為救濟[63]。就
再議制度旨在透過檢察機關內部自我審查之機會，以達檢察一
體之規範目的而言，於 91 年 2 月刑事訴訟法修正前，雖制度上
僅有告訴人聲請再議制度，惟依民國 82 年 2 月 25 日修正之台
灣高等法院檢察署加強二審檢察功能實施要點，台灣高檢署檢
察長對於不得再議之案件，得指定某類案件（如貪瀆案件）一
審檢察官為不起訴處分後，將卷證送交二審檢察長審核，亦足
徵檢察機關內部亦存在非法定之不起訴處分監督機制[64]。如前

---

[63]　參閱林永謀，刑事訴訟法釋論（中），頁 343，作者自版，2007 年 2 月。

[64]　但按無得再議之人一經不起訴處分，不起訴處分即確定，除非具有第 260 條之
　　　情形可再行偵查起訴，不能以第 258 條為由，命令原檢察官偵查或起訴；因為
　　　上級法院檢察署檢察長或檢察總長對於不起訴處分得依刑訴法第 258 條發回續
　　　查、或命令起訴，以有合法再議之聲請為前提，故於 2002 年修法前，此種類
　　　似職權再議之規定，並無法發揮多大的內部監督作用。然對於檢察官起訴裁量
　　　權之制衡，除內部監督外，似亦宜有檢察機關以外之監督機制。修法前如告訴
　　　人不服檢察官所為之不起訴處分，固得聲請再議，惟若經上級檢察機關檢察長
　　　駁回再議者，即乏進一步之救濟管道。2002 年之修法遂參考德國及日本之規
　　　定，增訂告訴人於不服上級檢察署之駁回處分者，得向法院聲請交付審判，由
　　　法院介入審查，以提供告訴人多一層救濟途徑。由於再議制度本身可歸類為檢
　　　察機關內部監督檢察一體原則之一部，因此本文不欲詳細處理不起訴處分外部
　　　監督程序之部分。最高法院 27 年上字第 2045 號判例指出，因告發而開始進行
　　　偵查之刑事案件，並無作為聲請再議之人，一經檢察官為不起訴處分後，其處
　　　分即屬確定。雖上級首席檢察官（即現制檢察長）本於監督權之作用，仍得復
　　　令偵查，但非有刑事訴訟法第 239 條（現行法為第 260 條）所定可以再起訴之
　　　新事實、新證據或再審原因，不得對於同一案件再行起訴。

所述，為救濟修法前再議之提起須以有告訴權人已向檢察官提
出告訴為要件，惟無告訴人之案件一經對外公告不起訴即告確
定力所衍生之弊端，並本諸：「如屬告發之案件為免一經檢察
官為不起訴或緩起訴處分，即告確定，自宜慎重」之規範目
的，民國 91 年 2 月 8 日修正刑事訴訟法乃於第 256 條增訂第 3
項：「死刑、無期徒刑或最輕本刑三年以上有期徒刑之案件，
因犯罪嫌疑不足，經檢察官為不起訴之處分，或第 253 條之 1
之案件經檢察官為緩起訴之處分者，如無得聲請再議之人時，
原檢察官應依職權逕送直接上級法院檢察署檢察長或檢察總長
再議，並通知告發人。」之職權再議規定。從而，依現行刑事
訴訟法制，對於不起訴處分內部監督之再議制度可分為聲請再
議與職權再議二種。然而不論何者，再議制度本欲藉著上級檢
察機關監督權之行使，以糾正下級檢察官違法或不當的不起訴
處分或緩起訴處分。

二、以再議制度監督不起訴處分之商榷

　　雖然不論是聲請再議或職權再議之目的，均在透過檢察機
關上下級監督之機制，以達救濟違法或不當不起訴處分之目
的。然而如本文前述再議制度之爭議所述，關於檢察一體原則
是否宜適用在再議制度乙事，原已非無爭議（如註十三前之說
明），又在無告訴人之不起訴處分案件中，既經檢察官查無犯
罪嫌疑，本質上根本不存在所謂不起訴處分屬於死刑、無期徒

刑或最輕本刑三年以上有期徒刑之案件（如註二十八前之說明），從而應如何判斷是否符合職權再議規定亦不明確之爭議下，以再議制度救濟不起訴處分，其妥當性並非無疑。

相對於前述聲請再議與職權再議之案件，在現行刑事訴訟法的架構下，尚有部分無告訴人聲請再議且亦不符合職權再議規定之偵查案件，此部分案件即停留在先前檢察官一作出不起訴處分該案件即為確定之情形。而由於聲請再議程序係由告訴人所發動，因此只要限縮犯罪被害人之範圍，一但無告訴人可聲請再議，在不符職權再議規定之情形中，恐亦將出現檢察官一作出不起訴處分該案件即為確定之情形。如果認為前述聲請再議與職權再議係透過再議制度監督不起訴處分，那又將如何解釋不符聲請再議與職權再議之案件無法透過再議制度監督不起訴處分之缺漏，難到在不符聲請再議與職權再議之案件中，其不起訴處分就必然正確無誤而不須監督嗎？又何以只有符合聲請再議與職權再議之案件才有監督不起訴之必要性呢？凡此疑義，均足以說明現行再議制度於不起訴處分監督上之不足與盲點。換言之，依現行再議制度之設計，再議制度並無法作為所有違法不當不起訴處分之監督機制。而縱經再議程序，案件已經上級檢察機關檢察長審核駁回，亦無法使得檢察機關之不起訴決定對被告產生受有罪判決之風險，蓋再議程序本質上迥異於審判程序，並無疑義。

其實，現今大部分國家的刑事訴訟法制均不太著重不起訴處分之監督，雖然日本法有檢察審查會之設，不過該機構之決

定並不具有拘束檢察官必須起訴之效力[65]。究其所以，實乃因各國之不起訴處分（決定）並不具有實質確定力所致；蓋其不起訴處分既不具備實質確定力，縱其有違法或不當之情事發生，亦只須由檢察官另對同一犯罪事實重行提起訴訟即足以救濟，根本無須討論應如何監督該不起訴處分之問題。從而，關於以再議制度監督不起訴處分所衍生之疑義，自亦又回到不起訴處分應否具實質確定力之問題上。換言之，再議制度是否必要存在，實乃繫於不起訴處分效力為何。

三、自法院認定事實之角度檢討不起訴處分實質確定力之妥當性

雖然學說上曾對不起訴處分具實質確定力提出質疑，並對不起訴處分較法院判決具較高效力乙事有所批評已如前述，不過，本文認為這些批評本身尚忽略了「偵查程序本身並不足以對被告產生有罪判決的風險，故不足以產生一事不再理之效力」此一前提。除此之外，如欲主張不起訴處分具有實質確定力，尚須釐清一個最基本的前提，那就是偵查程序是否有確認刑罰權基礎事實是否存在之權能。蓋如偵查程序本身即有權終局地確認刑罰權基礎事實不存在，則其所為之不起訴處分自應

---

[65] 關於日本檢察審查會之說明與介紹，參閱褚劍鴻，「論不起訴處分之確定力與不當處分之救濟（下）」，法令月刊第 19 卷第 9 期，頁 4-8，1998 年 9 月。

於確定後，發生阻斷後續可能與之相悖之偵查進行與公訴提起；反之，若偵查程序無法確認刑罰權基礎事實存在與否，則其所為之不起訴處分即不生拘束後訴訟程序得否就犯罪事實存否逕行認定之效果。

先就檢察官在偵查程序中是否有事實認定權而言，雖依刑事訴訟法第 264 條第 2 項第 2 款：「起訴書，應記載左列事項：二、犯罪事實及證據並所犯法條。」之規定，檢察官於起訴書中應記載犯罪事實，不過相較於刑事訴訟法第 308 條：「判決書應分別記載其裁判之主文與理由；有罪之判決書並應記載犯罪事實，且得與理由合併記載。」法院應於有罪判決書中記載犯罪事實之規定而言，檢察官於起訴書中所載之犯罪事實，僅應解為檢察官基於偵查結果所為之司法性建議，蓋檢察官依照糾問程序所得之證據與因之而推論出之犯罪事實，是否能通過改良式當事人進行主義審判程序的檢驗，尚未明瞭，從而檢察官所建議或推論之事實是否會被法院採納，於偵查終結（起訴）時即無從確定。故而在檢察官提起公訴的情形中，其於偵查終結時所為之事實認定，並無拘束法院之效力，其於偵查終結時所為刑罰權存在之判斷（建議），亦無終局確定之效力。

然而，依刑事訴訟法第 301 條第 1 項：「不能證明被告犯罪或其行為不罰者，應諭知無罪之判決。」之規定，當法院行使事實認定權後，認為不能證明被告犯罪事實存在或刑罰權不存在於所起訴之犯罪事實時，應為無罪之裁判；不過，依同法

第 352 條：「案件有左列情形之一者，應爲不起訴之處分：
一、曾經判決確定者。二、時效已完成者。三、曾經大赦者。
四、犯罪後之法律已廢止其刑罰者。五、告訴或請求乃論之
罪，其告訴或請求已經撤回或已逾告訴期間者。六、被告死亡
者。七、法院對於被告無審判權者。八、行爲不罰者。九、法
律應免除其刑者。十、犯罪嫌疑不足者。」之規定，當檢察官
不能證明被告犯罪或其行爲不罰時（例如第 8、第 9 與第 10
款），應爲不起訴之處分，此時檢察官之處分是否亦應類似刑
事訴訟法第 301 條第 1 項無罪判決般，對告訴人或告發人指摘
之事實，具有確認國家刑罰權不存在之效力？即值探討。

　　按「最高法院職掌民、刑事訴訟之終審裁判，當事人權益
之爭執，國家刑罰權之存否，至此定讞。[66]」，依照權力分立
之憲法精神，職司司法之法院始爲（最終）確認犯罪事實與國
家刑罰權存否之憲法機關，而法院以外之（非司法）機關，或
有依行政法規認定事實之權限，不過縱其於行政上具有認定事
實之權能，於涉案關係人間就事實存否有爭議時，依訴願法或
行政訴訟法等仍予其等提起訴願或行政訴訟之事實救濟機會。
換言之，關於國家機關事實認定權能之行使，不論行政機關或
司法機關，只要其所爲之事實認定具有終局確定之功能，制度
上均有給予相關當事人救濟之機會。就此種事實認定之救濟機

[66]　參照中華民國 85 年 6 月最高法院刑事庭法官研討會，對蘇建和等盜匪案件研討結論，http://www.tahr.org.tw/site/sue/menu3/result199606.txt（最後造訪日：2007 年 4 月 8 日）。

會來說，在不符聲請再議與職權再議之不起訴類型中，由於不起訴處分一作成時即告確定，此時如檢察官於事實認定過程中出現違誤，其所錯認之事實（含刑罰權不存在之誤判）不但無法救濟，而且在刑事訴訟法第 260 條賦予確定不起訴處分實質確定力之規定下，檢察官對同一案件縱事後認有必要將案件交由審判程序認定犯罪真相為何，反倒無法再行起訴。此種賦予單一國家機關終局認定事實權限並在出現錯誤時未予救濟機會之規範模式，本身即有可議之處；而進一步賦予此種未予救濟機會之不起訴處分實質確定力，自有未洽。

除前述不起訴處分於事實認定錯誤時未予救濟之不當外，通常來說，特別當國家刑罰權存否相關人間出現爭議時，按照權力分立之原理，司法機關本為確認犯罪事實與國家刑罰權存否之有權機關，本質上任何國家刑罰權存否所依據之事實，不能僅以檢察官單方作成之起訴書或不起訴處分書片面認定，而是必須經法院審理與辯論的正當法律程序，否則直接審理主義與言詞辯論主義等刑事訴訟基本原則都將被破壞無遺。如果說因為在過去的刑事訴訟實務中，法官與檢察官背景相同，且同依職權主義的糾問模式行使職權，而認為偵查與審判程序二者間差異不大，尚屬有據，蓋依舊刑事訴訟法第 163 條第 1 項：「法院應依職權調查證據」之要求下，過去法院經常接續著檢察官偵查的地位，主動蒐集犯罪證據之工作，而有違法院應保持中立、客觀及超然之立場。也就是說，在過去實務操作中，基於類似的偵查與審判程序，而賦予確定不起訴處分有如確定

判決之效力，思考邏輯上並無太大的不當。但是，自從刑事訴
訟程序朝向改良式當事人進行主義修正後，偵查與審判程序已
出現相當大的差異，基本上，目前的偵查程序仍為維持原來糾
問的精神，而審判程序卻已帶有部分當事人進行主義的色彩。
偵查程序中本諸糾問模式所獲之證據與事實認定，是否仍能見
容於改良式當事人進行主義，本身並非無疑問。鑑於不起訴處
分書所記載的犯罪事實，是一個沒有機會經過審判程序確認的
事實，在現行偵查與審判結構之差異上，偵查程序所確認之事
實既然在意義上迥異於審判程序所認定之事實，則賦予偵查結
果之不起訴處分具有類似確定判決般，在犯罪事實不存在與刑
罰權不存在部分具有實質確定力 [67]，即有不當。鑑於非屬審判
之偵查程序本身無法終局確定刑罰權基礎事實是否存在，再議
制度至多僅具有上級檢察長命令下級檢察官向法院提起公訴，
並由法院進一步確定刑罰權基礎事實是否存在之功能。既然有
效的再議亦僅具將案件送法院確認刑罰權基礎事實是否存在之
功能，則無效之再議自不應反致檢察機關成為有權認定刑罰權

---

[67] 參照最高法院 81 年台上字第 3183 號判決：「案件經檢察官偵查後，從實體
　　上認定被告之犯罪嫌疑不足，依刑事訴訟法第 252 條第 10 款規定為不起訴處
　　分確定者，其實質效果，就現行法而言，與受無罪之判決無異；故於該不起
　　訴處分書所敘之事實範圍內，發生實質上之確定力，非僅止於訴權之暫時
　　未行使而已。是以除合於刑事訴訟法第 260 條第 1、2 款所定原因，得再行起
　　訴外，別無救濟或變更方法。其於法院審判時，於事實同一範圍內，仍不得
　　作與之相反之認定，以維護法律效果之安定與被告自由人權之受適法保
　　障。」。

基礎事實存否之機關。

　　縱上所述，雖然職權再議與聲請再議制度均以監督檢察官不當或違法不起訴處分（含緩起訴處分）為目的，不過，鑑於現行再議制度無法涵蓋所有值得監督檢討的不起訴處分或緩起訴處分，再議制度本身並不是一個全面有效監督不起訴處分或緩起訴處分之機制；而鑑於偵查程序與審判程序本質上的差異，縱使經過再議制度，也未足使被告產生受有罪判決之風險，因此，不起訴處分本身，不論有無經過再議程序，均不致於產生一事不再理之效力。以此為基礎，刑事訴訟法第256條以再議制度救濟有問題之不起訴處分或緩起訴處分等，與同法第260條賦予確定不起訴處分類似確定判決實質確定力之規定，即有重新檢討之必要。也就是說，鑑於現行再議制度無法有效監督所有違誤之不起訴處分或緩起訴處分，除非規定所有不起訴或緩起訴處分之案件均須送交上級檢察機關檢察長核可，否則不應認為再議制度為監督違誤不起訴處分或緩起訴處分之唯一法定機制；而縱認為所有不起訴或緩起訴處分之案件均須送交上級檢察機關檢察長核可始生效力，也不必然表示經過檢察機關雙重確認之不起訴或緩起訴處分，具有與確定判決一樣的效力（一事不再理效力）。從而，廢除不起訴或緩起訴處分確定後再行起訴之限制，並將刑事訴訟法第303條第4款修正為：「曾為不起訴處分、撤回起訴或緩起訴期滿未經撤銷，其處分並無不當而再行起訴者。」，而由法院就重行起訴之案件審查原不起訴或緩起訴處分是否妥當無誤，並賦予經法

院審查過之刑罰權基礎事實具有一事不再理之效力，在學理上或是較爲洽當的方案：蓋於本質上，如果沒有了刑事訴訟法第260條之限制再行起訴規定，則在不起訴處分不具實質確定力之前提下，不起訴處分本身縱有錯誤，因不致無從救濟，再議制度本身究能發揮多少功能，對告訴人或告發人而言，也就不再那麼重要了。或許這是解決現行再議規定所衍生相關實務問題較簡單的處理方法。

陸、結　論

　　本文自再議制度監督不起訴處分之規範基礎出發，除探討再議制度所衍生之相關問題外，更自比較法的觀點，分析探討美日德等各國不起訴處分之效力與現行刑事訴訟法第260條如何導致我國實務過度重視不起訴處分之現象。爲了解詳明刑事訴訟法第260條規定之妥適性，本文自美國憲法人權法案中禁止雙重審判危險之觀點，探討所謂一事不再理原則之內涵，除釐清偵查程序與再議程序並不足致被告遭受有罪判決之風險外，並主張現行刑事訴訟法第260條賦予確定不起訴處分實質確定力之規定並不洽當。此外，本文基於權力分立之觀點，主張只有法院有權確認刑罰權基礎事實是否存在，檢察官相關的事實認定，充其量不過僅具有建議之性質，並不具有拘束法院之效力，故若以之作爲不起訴處分實質確定力之判斷基礎，似

有侵害法院事實認定權限之疑義。本諸糾問模式下偵查程序所確認之事實在意義上迥異於改良式當事人進行主義下審判程序所認定之事實，本文更肯定於制度上不應賦予偵查結果之不起訴處分具有類似確定判決般，在犯罪事實不存在與刑罰權不存在部分具有實質確定力。為免實務繼續不當糾纏於不起訴處分實質確定力之範圍，本文認為應廢除刑事訴訟法第 260 條不起訴處分具實質確定力之規定，畢竟導致有罪判決風險之實質確定力應來自於法院之公開審理程序，而非檢察官糾問式的偵查程序。（本文前身「再議制度之檢討」曾發表於 96.04 刑事法學會「起訴裁量制度之探討」學術研討會）

11 軍人身分與刑事審判權劃分之探討

壹、前　言

　　據報載最高法院和國防部高等軍事法院曾爲了軍事審判程序應否實行交互詰問程序乙事而「槓上了」[1]。由於軍事法院認爲，軍事審判法基本上還是由審判長主導證據調查的「職權進行」，和修正後由檢察官、被告主導證據調查程序的「當事人進行」刑事訴訟並不相同，因此無須「準用」交互詰問新制；不過，本諸「刑事訴訟新制改採交互詰問，軍事審判在不相牴觸的情形下，應該準用」之認知，最高法院以大法官釋字第 582 號及第 592 號解釋爲本，指出被告的詰問權是憲法上保障的權

---

[1]　按劉岳龍涉嫌於民國 89 年 6 月 29 日至 90 年 8 月 1 日任職海軍新江軍艦期間，受到父親劉禎國及母親陳金葉唆使，先後將職務上持有或偶然機會持有的「空援申請通信」等軍機資料交付劉禎國，供劉禎國攜赴大陸轉交中共官員獲取不法利益；關於海軍上士劉岳龍涉嫌洩漏軍機案經國防部高等軍事法院判處無期徒刑，但因是否應行交互詰問的程序爭議，最高法院以憲法保障被告詰問權爲由，二度發回軍高院更審。參閱王文玲，「上士洩密案 拒絕交互詰問 軍法司法槓上了」，2005/10/15 聯合報，available at: http://gb.udn.com/b5/www.udn.com/2005/10/15/NEWS/NATIONAL/NAT2/2953675.shtml (last visted, Sep. 29th, 2007)。

利，軍事法庭不能不附理由而置之不理，故以憲法保障被告詰問權為由，二度將該案發回國防部高等軍事法院更審[2]。表面上看來，本案似僅涉及軍事審判程序應否實行交互詰問此一爭點；然若進一步深究之，因本案被告已因羈押三個月依法喪失現役軍人身分，本案實際上不免涉及到軍司法審判權[3]之劃分

---

[2]　最高法院 94 年度台上字第 5672 號刑事判決指出：軍事審判法第 125 條規定：「刑事訴訟法關於證據之規定，與本章（第一編第十一章）不相牴觸者，準用之。」而刑事訴訟法第一編第十二章關於「證據」之規定，其中第 166 條、第 166 條之 1 至第 166 條之 7 等有關證人交互詰問之規定，業於 92 年 2 月 6 日經修正公布，並自同年 9 月 1 日施行。刑事訴訟法前開修正後之規定，其與軍事審判法第一編第十一章關於「證據」之規定，有何牴觸？何以不在準用之列？原審主要以：刑事訴訟法關於交互詰問之規定，其與軍事審判法第 151 條行合議審判案件，為準備審判起見，受命軍事審判官於審判期日前訊問被告及蒐集或調查證據之規定，及同法第 158 條、第 159 條規定：軍事檢察官陳述起訴要旨後，審判長應就被訴事實訊問被告；訊問被告後，審判長應調查證據，不同。以及軍事審判與刑事審判所適用之實體法受規範之對象有異等語為由，認無從準用刑事訴訟法上開修正後之規定，其理由說明仍難昭信服，而有未合。尤置司法院大法官釋字第 582 號、第 592 號解釋被告詰問權，係人民憲法上權益保障旨意於不問，殊嫌欠洽。

[3]　審判權係指法院審理司法案件之司法主權，我國憲法第 77 條即為司法主權之規定。凡國家在主權範圍內所得行使之司法權，均為審判權。參閱林鈺雄，刑事訴訟法上冊，頁 26，著者自印，2000 年初版。司法主權屬於國家，與其他國家之司法主權相對，本國之司法主權不受其他國家之干涉；另外，司法主權亦與國內其他權力相對，不受行政或立法之干涉。憲法第 77 條規定：「司法院為國家最高司法機關，掌理民事、刑事、行政訴訟之審判及公務員之懲戒」，即是此一司法主權之具體表現。質言之，審判權即為國家在主權所及範圍內所行使的司法權力。在各種審判權中，刑事審判權，是指對於刑事案件為審理裁判之權。我國憲法第八條明文規定：「人民身體之自由應予保障。除現行犯之逮捕由法律另定外，非經司法或警察機關依法定程序，不得逮捕拘禁。非由法院依法定程序，不得審問處罰。非依法定程序之逮捕、拘禁、審問、處罰，得拒絕之」。依此規定，國家的刑罰屬司法權，應由「法院」依嚴格的訴訟程序為之，始能保障法秩序，並維護個人權利。交由其他

在喪失現役軍人身分時，先前仍具現役軍人身分時所犯軍刑法之罪之刑事審判權究應如何歸屬之爭議[4]；蓋若在被告喪失現役軍人身分後即不適用軍事審判程序而應改用通常程序，普通法院自應依刑事訴訟法所定之證據調查方式實行交互詰問，從而前述軍事審判程序應否實行交互詰問之爭執亦不致於出現在本案之中。雖然此種說法並未終局地解決前述軍事審判程序應否實行交互詰問之爭議，不過若以本案之事實作為一個引子，或可終局地釐清在憲法第9條規定下，「被告喪失現役軍人身分時，刑事審判權究應如何歸屬」之疑義。

　　關於刑事審判權歸屬之劃分，長久以來即存在軍事審判程序與司法審判程序兩大類別；相較屬於普通審判權之司法審判，學說上也曾就軍事審判權的屬性與定位（司法權或統帥權）[5]，進行長期的爭辯[6]。惟不論其爭執為何，軍人既為穿著制

權力機關行使刑罰權，即使法有明文，亦屬違憲。參閱蔡新毅，由憲法觀點論軍事審判權之性質及其修正之相關問題（上）—兼評大法官會議釋字第四三六號解釋，司法周刊，第864期，第2版，1998年2月11；呂啟元，軍事審判權之研究，財團法人國家政策研究基金會論文，available at: http://www.npf.org.tw/PUBLICATION/CL/091/CL-R-091-039.htm (last visted, Sep. 29th, 2007)。

[4] 關於陸海空軍刑法修正對於刑事審判權之影響，參閱林俊益，修正軍刑法對審判權之影響，萬國法律，第120期，頁106-109，2001年12月；林俊益，新論現役軍人刑事審判權之歸屬，月旦法學雜誌，第79期，頁18-19，2001年12月。

[5] 按我國過去對於軍事審判權之性質，學說有三種見解：（一）統帥權說：主張軍事審判權是統帥權之運用，基於憲法第9條及第36條，軍事審判權屬於統帥所有，非屬司法院，不受其他外力之影響。因此，軍事的審級制度、核定覆判權等，均與一般司法有別，其主要目的在於貫徹統帥權之行使。（二）司法權限說：本說認為，憲法第9條，主要只在排除人民受軍事審判，並不

具有將軍事審判排除於司法之外之意旨。因此，軍事審判權仍為憲法第77條司法權之權限。尤其，憲法第9條置於「人民的權利義務」章中，足見其性質只在保障人民之權利，而非屬機關組織權限之規定，不能將之作為軍事審判權非屬司法權限的憲法根據。（三）折衷說：亦有學者認為，軍事審判權雖為刑事程序之一種，但現役軍人的身分特殊，為維護軍紀，兩者仍應有所區別，故軍事審判權應屬置於統帥權下的特殊司法作用。參閱章瑞卿，我國憲法審判權對軍事審判權之界限，律師雜誌，第250期，頁66-8，2000年7月。不過依陳樸生大法官：「軍事審判權本屬刑事程序之一種，不因審判機關之不同，而異其方式，亦應採訴訟主義，以訴訟之形式，並採司法權方式行之，惟現役軍人其身分特殊，職務亦異，具有特殊人格，其犯罪之影響與一般犯罪不同，是其處罰，重在維持軍紀之整飭，軍令之威信，藉以維護統帥權之作用。因此，軍事審判法，雖採訴訟制度，而軍事審判權之行使，仍置於統帥權之下」之觀點，事實上其亦認為軍事審判權屬於統帥權之性質，參閱陳樸生，軍事審判之共同性與特殊性，軍法專刊，第7卷第1期，頁12，1961年3月。

6　軍事審判法自民國45年7月7日公布實施後，對於維持軍紀雖頗有助益，但該法本於傳統「統帥權說」的見解，認為軍事審判權是統帥權之運用，並非司法權的一部分。基於此一理念，軍事審判屢屢違憲之質疑及適用上之困擾。國防部在釋字436號解釋作成前，曾一直憂慮大法官會宣告軍事審判制度違憲並將軍人之犯罪全歸司法審判，國防部似亦已知其中存在的違憲爭議。參閱李太正，釋字第436號試評及軍事審判制度改革芻議，月旦法學雜誌，第35期，頁32，2000年4月。關於軍事審判權之性質與其作用之說明，另請參閱黃東熊，刑事訴訟法論，頁82，1986年9月再版；陳新民，中華民國憲法釋論，頁590，2001年1月4版；陳運財，軍事審判之刑事訴訟法制化，月旦法學雜誌，第35期，頁40，2000年4月；劉錦安，論軍事審判之變遷，律師雜誌，第250期，頁30，2000年7月；李太正，軍事審判理論之檢討與展望（上），軍法專刊，第35卷第6期，頁32，1989年6月；李太正，軍事審判在憲法上之地位，軍法專刊，第34卷第10期，頁13，1988年10月；毛仁全，論我國實證法規範下之軍事審判制度，軍法專刊，第41卷第7期，頁13，頁29-32，1995年7月；呂啟元，軍事審判權之研究，財團法人國家政策研究基金會論文，available at: http://www.npf.org.tw/PUBLICATION/CL/091/CL-R-091-039.htm (last visted, Sep. 29th, 2007)。鑑於釋字第436號解釋對軍事審判制度就「軍事審判權之歸屬、定位」、「軍事審判制度之訴訟救濟方式」及「審判獨立之保障」等方面有所非難，於民國88年10月2日修正通過後之軍事審判法亦已就前述疑點做相當程度的修正，昔日關於軍事審判權是否屬司法權之爭議，可謂已因刑罰終審一元制之「司法上訴」規定而不復存在。

服之公民,除受法律限制外,其人身自由、生存權、工作權、財產權、訴願權、訴訟權、參政權等基本人權,理應與一般人民同受憲法之保障。縱軍人因負有保衛國家的神聖使命,軍隊以克敵致勝為首要目的,在軍人須服從軍令之前提上,軍事審判具有貫徹軍令、嚴肅軍紀之特殊目的,關於刑事犯罪之訴追與國家刑罰權之行使,軍事審判自應與司法審判有所差異[7],實際上,我國法制存在兩種類型之刑事審判程序,已屬不爭之事實。基本上,國家刑罰權除得由依刑事訴訟法設立普通法院行使外,尚可由本於特別審判權(軍事審判權)設立之特別法院(軍事法院)行使之;本諸特別審判權(軍事審判權)所制訂之程序規定,亦為實現國家刑罰權之「法定程序」。針對此一現象,學說上有認我國之刑事審判制度係採取普通法院與軍事法院分治主義[8],亦即現行憲法秩序關於刑事犯罪之追訴、審問及處罰,已容認「刑事司法二元化」現象存在[9]。縱然就刑事犯

---

[7] 參閱《法律案專輯第 276 輯-軍事審判法及軍事審判法施行法修正案》,頁 3,立法院公報處,2001 年 2 月,初版。

[8] 參閱葉雪鵬,刑事訴訟的審判權,法務通訊,第 2049 期,第 6 版,2001 年 9 月 6 日;亦有稱此為「軍、司法審判二元模式」,參閱趙磁生,從軍事審判法修正談變革,律師雜誌,第 250 期,頁 59,2000 年 7 月。

[9] 依司法院大法官解釋釋字第 436 號解釋:「憲法第 9 條規定:『人民除現役軍人外,不受軍事審判』,乃因現役軍人負有保衛國家之特別義務,基於國家安全與軍事需要,對其犯罪行為得設軍事審判之特別訴訟程序。查其規範意旨係在保障非現役軍人不受軍事審判,非謂軍事審判機關對於軍人之犯罪有專屬之審判權,而排除現役軍人接受普通法院之審判。至軍事審判之建制,憲法未設明文規定,雖得以法律定之,惟軍事審判機關所行使者,亦屬國家刑罰權之一種,具司法權之性質,其發動與運作,必須符合正當法律程序之最低要求,包括獨立、公正之審判機關與程序,並不得違背憲法第 77 條司法

罪之追訴、審問及處罰，憲法秩序容認不同刑事訴訟程序存
在，然因「國家之刑罰權只有一個，行使刑事審判權之機關，
雖有司法與軍法之分，但國家刑罰權僅對於每一被告之每一犯
罪而存在[10]」，從而對於人民犯罪之追訴、處罰而言，軍司法
訴訟程序相互間，應只存在排斥之關係；否則探討軍事審判程
序有無適用，將失去正面、積極的意義[11]。在承認軍事審判權

院為國家最高司法機關，掌理刑事訴訟審判，第 80 條法官依法律獨立審判，
不受任何干涉等有關司法權建制之憲政原理；規定軍事審判程序之法律涉及
軍人權利之限制者，亦應遵守憲法第 23 條之比例原則」，刑事司法二元化之
現象，已為我國法制所肯認。根據此項解釋文之觀點，可得知（一）軍事審
判機關對於現役軍人之犯罪，並非具有專屬審判權，亦即普通司法審判機關
亦應有審判權。（二）軍事審判係有別於普通訴訟程序的「特別訴訟程序」。
然則軍事審判之異於普通審判，究係由於審判權之不同，或僅為程序上之不
同，此一解釋文並未進一步闡明。參閱蔡墩銘，軍事審判與普通審判之關係，
月旦法學雜誌，第 35 期，頁 29-30，1998 年 4 月。

10　參閱陳樸生著，刑事訴訟法實務，頁 29，著者自印，民國 79 年 11 月重訂三
版。

11　依刑事訴訟法第 1 條第 2 項規定，現役軍人之犯罪，除犯軍法應受軍事審判
者外，仍應依本法規定追訴、處罰。軍事審判法第一條第一項則規定，現役
軍人犯陸海空軍刑法或其特別法之罪，依本法之規定追訴審判之，其在戰時
犯陸海軍刑法或其特別法以外之罪者，亦同。有鑑於刑事訴訟法與軍事審判
法之規定有異，二規範間之關係為合？有何矛盾？其矛盾究應如何解決？似
生疑義。理論上來說，軍事審判法為特別法，刑事訴訟法為普通法，若依特
別法優先適用於普通法之原則，似應優先適用軍事審判法。若另自該二法制
定時間之先後來說，刑事訴訟法制定公布施行於二十四年，軍事審判法則為
四十五年（其第 1 條第 1 項之規定，歷次修正均未變更），依後法優先適用
於前法之原則，似亦應優先適用軍事審判法之規定。關於軍事審判法前身之
陸海空軍審判法，因其規定軍人不論犯何罪，一律由軍法審判，較之刑事訴
訟法，係制定在先之前法，因此，陸海空軍審判法與刑事訴訟法之規範關係，
更形複雜，當時之國民政府，先後四次以命令之方式，規定應優先適用陸海
空軍審判法。詳可參考陳煥生，刑事審判權之競合，刑事法雜誌，第 41 卷第
2 期，頁 179-193，1997 年 4 月。

爲特別審判權之法制現狀下 [12]，本文不擬探討軍事審判程序存在之必要性或合理性此一暫有定論之議題 [13]，也無須深究軍事審判程序與刑事訴訟程序間，究屬審判權或是管轄權劃分之爭

---

[12]　參閱林鈺雄，刑事訴訟法上冊，頁 26，著者自印，2000 年初版。

[13]　參閱蔡墩銘，軍事審判與普通審判之關係，月旦法學雜誌，第 35 期，頁 28，1998 年 4 月；毛仁全，論我國實證法規範下之軍事審判制度，軍法專刊，第 41 卷第 7 期，頁 29，1995 年 7 月；蔡新毅，解構關於軍事審判之迷思，律師雜誌，第 250 期，頁 51，2000 年 7 月；謝添富、趙晞華，淺論軍事審判法修正後之若干法律問題及處理方式，律師雜誌，第 250 期，頁 33，2000 年 7 月；李太正，釋字第 436 號試評及軍事審判制度改革芻議，月旦法學雜誌，第 35 期，頁 32，1998 年 4 月。於司法院大法官釋字第 436 號解釋中，亦有大法官針對「何以現役軍人犯罪之追訴、處罰程序所以有不同於一般人民犯罪處理程序之必要」提出說明，如林大法官永謀於其所提之不同意見書中指出：「國家建軍，要在保國衛民，克敵制勝，若不奮迅振厲嚴肅而整齊之，何能達成。其張軍而不能戰，遇敵而不能攻者，建軍何為？是軍人或因身分、或因所犯係基於軍事特殊目的而定之罪，而依特別程序予以處罰」；而董大法官翔飛於其所提之協同意見書中議提及：「基於國家安全與軍事任務之特性，對軍人犯罪之追訴與處罰，應依特別立法，由軍事法院或軍事法庭行使軍事審判之特別訴訟程序」。基本上司法院大法官釋字第 436 號解釋認為，因現役軍人負有保衛國家之特別義務，基於國家安全與軍事需要，對其犯罪行為得設軍事審判之特別訴訟程序，不過此種說法非謂軍事審判機關對於軍人之犯罪有專屬之審判權。事實上關於何種犯罪應歸軍事審判機關審判，何種犯罪應歸普通審判機關審判，該號解釋文則未進一步闡明。實際上，立法院在審議軍事審判法時亦曾發現，各民主先進國家，除了美國外，都採取平時的軍事審判權回歸普通法院，只有戰時始承認軍事審判權的做法（例如，德、日），採取此一做法將可解決長久以來審判權爭議、不明的問題。然而，行政院、司法院均不支持這樣的想法，主要的理由在於：第一，效率：認為普通法院的效率不高，案件延滯的結果會給軍隊帶來不必要的困擾；第二，準備不及：認為戰時不可能立即成立能有效運作的軍事審判體系；第三，國情不同：我國因為有中共的威脅，所以不能廢除軍事審判制度。其後經過朝野協商後，軍事審判法並未廢止，仍維持多元制。參閱《法律案專輯第二百七十六輯－軍事審判法及軍事審判法施行法修正案》，頁 220-266，立法院公報處，2001 年 2 月，初版。

議[14]；然鑒於「軍司法審判權在軍事被告嗣後喪失現役軍人身分應該如何劃分」此一更為實用之議題迄今仍有未明之疑慮，且軍司法審判程序間實際上仍存在一定程度之差異，為究明前述最高法院和國防部高等軍事法院間之爭執是否果真無法避免，本文擬以軍事審判程序進行中「軍事被告喪失現役軍人身分」為中心，檢討我國實定法下刑事審判權歸屬之實然面，並進一步提出其劃分標準之應然面。以下，便先從軍司法審判程序間之差異談起。

貳、軍司法審判程序間之差異

一、軍司法審判程序劃分之基礎

憲法第9條：「人民除現役軍人外，不受軍事審判。」與國家安全法第8條第1項：「非現役軍人，不受軍事審判」等規定，揭示了「軍事審判例外」之憲法規範意旨。惟憲法雖於此明文承認軍事審判制度存在，但依該條之規定，並無從導出所有現役軍人之犯罪（特別是犯軍刑法之罪）均需接受軍事審

---

[14] 蓋縱認憲法第九條之規定並未承認軍事審判權為特別審判權，而認該條規定係將軍事審判程序與刑事訴訟程序當作管轄權劃分之依據，亦與本文所探討之核心部分不生齟齬，畢竟刑事訴訟法關於管轄之規定（刑事訴訟法第4條以下參照）與大法官針對違反管轄規定之效果所作之解釋（釋字第47號解釋與第168號解釋參照），於適用上均不應違反憲法第9條之明文規定。

判之必然性推論[15]；蓋既然憲法第 9 條之規定列於人民之權利義務章中，應只解為現役軍人權利義務之依據，該條規定「並未表示現役軍人即應受軍事審判，亦未表示現役軍人不得接受司法審判[16]」，則依該條之規定逕為現役軍人均應受軍事審判之推論，即有未洽[17]。依刑事訴訟法第 1 條第 2 項：「現役軍人之犯罪，除犯軍法應受軍事裁判者外，仍應依本法規定追訴、處罰。」與軍事審判法第 1 條：「現役軍人犯陸海空軍刑法或其特別法之罪，依本法之規定追訴審判之，其在戰時犯陸

---

[15] 蓋若以憲法第 9 條之規定為邏輯學上之涵蘊敘述（implication statement），則其同義之反對解釋，亦即與該涵蘊敘述有相同真質之間接推論，應為『若受軍事審判者，則為現役軍人』，至於是否現役軍人必受軍事審判，以及軍事審判之內涵如何，則無法由憲法第九條所規定之要件與效果間的邏輯關係，加以決定。易言之，本條之規定僅在排除非現役軍人受軍事審判之可能性，但不能由此導出現役軍人一律受軍事審判之結論。參閱蔡新毅，法治國家與軍事審判－詳析軍事審判，頁 291-292，永然文化出版股份有限公司，1994 年 6 月初版。

[16] 參閱陳志龍，人性尊嚴與刑法體系入門，頁 599，著者自印，1992 年初版。

[17] 雖然憲法第 9 條規定：「人民除現役軍人外，不受軍事審判」，往昔學者亦多以本條作為軍事審判權之憲法基礎，但揆諸其他憲法條文，則我國憲法是否承認「軍事審判權」，其實並無直接明文。此與日本憲法第 76 條明文禁止設立特別法院，不承認特別法院或特別審判權之存在，實有區別。不過，由於軍事審判法行之有年，且司法院亦未曾宣告其違憲，故我國研究刑事訴訟之學者，多承認軍事審判權，並認為軍事審判權為特別刑事審判權，應優先適用。惟軍法院是否對於現役軍人的所有犯罪均得審問處罰，則仍有爭論。雖然大部分學者均認為即使承認軍事審判權為特別審判權，其究非普通審判權，故對其行使應設有相當限制；但亦有學者認為，國家刑罰權只有一個，無論適用軍事審判法或刑事訴訟法，均屬國家行使刑罰權，並無限縮軍事審判權之必要。參閱呂啟元，軍事審判權之研究，財團法人國家政策研究基金會論文，available at: http://www.npf.org.tw/PUBLICATION/CL/091/CL-R-091-039.htm (last visted, Sep. 29th, 2007)。

海空軍刑法或其特別法以外之罪者，亦同。（第1項）非現役軍人不受軍事審判。但戒嚴法有特別規定者，從其規定。（第2項）」等規定，現役軍人於戰時[18]不論所犯何罪，均應依軍事審判法之規定追訴、審判；而於非戰時，現役軍人惟於犯「軍刑法之罪」時，始有軍事審判程序之適用。

由於憲法第9條在刑事審判權歸屬的議題上，實質地限縮了憲法第8條之適用，因此，建立在憲法第9條之上的軍事審判程序即可視為國家實行刑罰權之特別程序[19]，並得於規範目的內限制人民依憲法第8條所得主張之權利[20]。我國憲法僅規

---

18 依軍事審判法第7條之規定：「本法稱戰時者，謂抵禦侵略而由總統依憲法宣告作戰之期間。（第1項）戰時或叛亂發生而宣告戒嚴之期間，視同戰時。（第2項）」。

19 參閱林山田，刑事程序法，頁98，五南圖書，2001年增訂四版；林鈺雄，刑事訴訟法（上冊）－總論編，頁26，著者自印，2000年初版；黃東熊，刑事訴訟法論，頁32，三民書局，1999年增訂初版。

20 然而，縱已於制度上承認軍事審判權之存在，因其非屬普通審判權，而屬於普通審判權之例外，因此對於其所行使之權力自應予以相當之限制。如將其限於現役軍人犯軍法之罪，倘犯罪時間在平時，正常司法權可期待運作之情況，其似不必成為軍事審判權行使之對象，亦即現役軍人之犯罪仍應由普通司法權予以裁判。果如此，軍事審判權或軍事法院祇應存在於戰時，而不應存在於平時。假如軍事審判權祇有存在於戰時，則現役軍人在戰時所犯之罪，於戰時結束之後，軍事審判權應停止其運作，而軍事審判權在戰時結束之後既應停止運作，則在其停止運作之前軍事法院作成之判決未確定者，自應許其向普通法院上訴，以謀救濟。倘軍事審判權不僅存在於戰時，亦存在於平時，即戰時之終止，並無理由應認為戰時軍事法院作成之未確定判決，必須向普通法院上訴。究竟我國軍事審判權祇存在於戰時或亦存在於平時，無法從自憲法第9條之條文中予以解讀，亦無法從最近針對軍事審判權作成解釋之釋字第436號解釋文中予以窺見。不僅如此，前述解釋文亦無法完全釐清軍事審判權與普通審判權之關係。參閱蔡墩銘，軍事審判與普通審判之關係，月旦法學雜誌，第35期，頁29，1998年4月。

定非現役軍人不受軍事審判，而對現役軍人受軍事審判之範圍則無規定，則當然委由其他法律（程序法）定之[21]。簡單來說，由於現役軍人本即包括於憲法第 8 條所稱人民之內，原則上自應受該條之各種保障；只不過於其犯陸海空刑法或其特別刑法之罪時，得因憲法第 9 條規定，於審判程序上限縮憲法第 8 條規定之適用，而由非普通司法機關之軍事審判機關加以審訊與處罰[22]；「蓋人民如受軍事審判，則人身自由之保障，必不如受司法審判那樣周密[23]」。不過，究竟軍司法審判程序間存在何種差異？如原應適用普通審判程序卻改用或誤用軍事審判程序，又將對被告造成何種程度之不利益呢？軍司法審判程序間之差異（對人民於刑事審判上所造成之不利益）實為人民主張不受軍事審判之主要說理基礎。

二、行憲前之差異

　　在司法一元主義之架構下，只有普通法院才有審問與處罰犯罪之權限。然因軍法具有維持軍紀與保存部隊戰鬥力之效用，我國自古即有軍法之設，用以樹立領導威信，並貫徹軍令，維護軍紀；此觀之周禮有：「有合其卒伍，置其有司，以

---

[21] 參閱李維宗，軍、司法審判權在實務運作上的幾個爭議問題（下），軍法專刊，第 41 卷第 10 期，頁 19，1995 年 10 月。

[22] 參閱王致雲，人民除現役軍人外不受軍事審判之研究，憲政評論，第 13 卷第 5 期，頁 5。

[23] 參閱劉慶瑞，中華民國憲法要義，頁 61，1990 年 11 月版。

軍法治之」之記載，可得印證。清朝末年，因外患不斷，迭建
新軍，以禦外侮，惟此亦導致民國肇建以後，各地軍閥割據一
方，擁兵自重。民國四年北京政府所頒布之「陸軍審判條例」
與民國七年所公布之「海軍審判條例」，概列軍事法庭之訴訟
程序，實為民國之後，我國軍事審判制度之濫觴。其後國民政
府於民國 17 年所公布之「國民革命軍審判條例」、民國 19 年
之「陸海空軍審判法」、民國 26 年公布施行之「中華民國戰時
軍律」與民國 28 年之「軍事審判審限規則」等，均為我國行憲
前有關軍事審判之相關法規[24]。

　　大法官陳計男曾於釋字第 436 號解釋之協同意見書指出：
「蓋立憲之時，軍事審判制度早已存在，且隸屬軍事機關，然
其裁判品質，一般人民對之上有疑慮，故特赦明文保障人民不
受軍事審判」。依知名憲法學者劉慶瑞教授所見，行憲前之軍
事審判於下列各點，與普通司法審判不同：「（一）司法審判
以採三級三審制為原則，當事人對於法院判決，如有不服，得
行上訴，而軍事審判乃以一審終結為原則，被告無上訴之機
會，故審判疏誤之可能性較大；（二）司法審判採辯護制度，
而軍事審判原則上不許延請律師辯護，故審判的公平性較低；
（三）司法審判，法官依據法律獨立審判，不受任何干涉，而
軍事審判，軍法官須受其長官之命令，無獨立可言；（四）司

24　關於我國歷史上之軍法發展，參閱劉錦安，論軍事審判之變遷，律師雜誌，
　　第 250 期，頁 18-9，2000 年 7 月。

法審判乃以公開審判爲原則，而軍事審判，按照常例，軍於秘密之中行之，故較難期其公平 [25]」。由此段之說明，不難理解在行憲之前，軍司法審判程序存在巨大之差異，倘若原應適用普通審判程序卻改用或誤用軍事審判程序時，實將對被告造成即爲嚴重之程序不利益；此亦爲制憲者所欲保障一般人民不受軍事審判之目的所在。

三、1999 年軍事審判法修法前之差異

不過，前述行憲前之軍事審判程序於行憲後亦有變革。大體而言，制定於民國 45 年並於民國 56 年修定之軍事審判法，即曾針對上述弊端，有所改進；例如：（一）明定軍事審判庭公開行之，並獨立行使審判權，不受任何干涉；（二）軍事審判程序改採二審制，並有覆判、再審、非常審判等補救程序；（三）明文設立辯護人及輔佐人制度；（四）明定軍法官之任用資格並予以嚴明之身分保障 [26]。

然而，縱於行憲後軍事審判法已有上述之修正，細究其本身仍然存在以下之缺失：（一）審判獨立仍受質疑；（二）審檢分立流於形式；（三）誤解迅速裁判本旨；（四）未能落實

25　參閱劉慶瑞，中華民國憲法要義，頁 61，1990 年 11 月版。

26　參閱李鐘聲（法律學）校正，王雨聲發行，中華民國憲法精義，頁 41，憲政評論社出版，1997 年 10 月。

審判公開[27]。從而司法院大法官釋字第 436 號解釋遂指出：
「憲法第 9 條規定：『人民除現役軍人外，不受軍事審判』，
乃因現役軍人負有保衛國家之特別義務，基於國家安全與軍事
需要，對其犯罪行為得設軍事審判之特別訴訟程序，非謂軍事
審判機關對於軍人之犯罪有專屬之審判權。至軍事審判之建
制，憲法未設明文規定，雖得以法律定之，惟軍事審判機關所
行使者，亦屬國家刑罰權之一種，其發動與運作，必須符合正
當法律程序之最低要求，包括獨立、公正之審判機關與程序，
並不得違背憲法第 77 條、第 80 條等有關司法權建制之憲政原
理；規定軍事審判程序之法律涉及軍人權利之限制者，亦應遵
守憲法第 23 條之比例原則。本於憲法保障人身自由、人民訴訟
權利及第 77 條之意旨，在平時經終審軍事審判機關宣告有期徒
刑以上之案件，應許被告直接向普通法院以判決違背法令為理
由請求救濟。軍事審判法第 11 條，第 133 條第 1 項、第 3 項，
第 158 條及其他不許被告逕向普通法院以判決違背法令為理由
請求救濟部分，均與上開憲法意旨不符」。在此號解釋下，國
防部遂依貫徹審判獨立、落實人權保障與兼顧軍事需要等修法
精神[28]，擬定現行軍事審判法之條文。

27　參閱蔡新毅，修正軍事審判法前，應先正視軍事審判權之定位問題，軍法專
　　刊，第 41 卷第 1 期，頁 24-7，1995 年 1 月。
28　參閱國防部軍法局許可仁局長之說明，立法院公報，第 88 卷第 42 期，頁
　　36-38，1999 年 8 月。

四、現行軍事審判法與刑事訴訟法間之差異

1999 年 10 月所修正之軍事審判法施行前，關於現役軍人刑事審判權之歸屬，原有刑事訴訟法第 1 條第 2 項、修正前之軍事審判法第 1 條第 1 項及國家安全法第 8 條第 2 項之規定規範之。修正軍事審判法施行後，依該法第 237 條之規定，國家安全法第 8 條第 2 項，已自 90 年 10 月 2 日停止適用。是以，現行規範現役軍人刑事審判權歸屬之相關法律，僅有刑事訴訟法及軍事審判法二種。雖然軍事審判法已經歷前述修正，其所提供之人權保障亦較過去為優，然因刑事訴訟法自民國 88 年以後歷經幾次重大的修正，雖然軍事審判法曾於民國 91 年 1 月與 92 年 6 月間小幅修正[29]，解免部分軍事審判法與刑事訴訟法間之齟齬，且軍事審判法中訂有不少「如刑事訴訟法與軍事審判程序不相牴觸者得准用刑事訴訴法」之條文，惟在何種範圍內得准用修正後之刑事訴訟法，實際上存在不小的疑義。大體而言，現行軍事審判程序與刑事訴訟程序間，存在以下之差異：

（一）證據法則之適用

如前述劉岳龍洩密案之發回判決所示，目前軍司法審判程

---

[29] 民國 91 年 1 月之修正包含：第 111 條、第 111-1 條、第 112 條與第 215 條。而民國 91 年 1 月之修法計有修正：第 29 條、第 36 條、第 59 條、第 60 條、第 61 條、第 109 條、第 133 條、第 181 條、第 206 條與第 238 條；並增訂第 112-1 條、第 112-2 條與第 234-1 條。

序間之最大差異，乃在於軍事審判程序應否實行交互詰問之爭執。雖然在民國 88 年修定軍事審判法時，現行刑事訴訟法之證據章尚未修正，惟本諸證據法則於軍司法審判具共通性，有認民國 88 年之軍審法修法「已預慮該法有關證據之規定，即將參考英美法系證據法則之理論，檢討違反程序正義所取得證據之容許性亦即證據適格問題研擬採例示排除及概括補充體例（急流帶具體個案審酌人權保障及公共利益之均衡維護，而為取捨之相對排除法則）之修正趨向，特於軍審法第一編第十一章『證據』增訂第 125 條，明定『刑事訴訟法關於證據之規定，與本章不相牴觸者，準用之』，以因應未來實務運作之需要 [30]」。不過，觀之最高法院 94 年台上字第 2122 號判決理由之說明：『（二）、軍事審判法第 125 條規定：「刑事訴訟法關於證據之規定，與本章（第一編第十一章）不相牴觸者，準用之。」而刑事訴訟法第一編第十二章關於「證據」之規定，其中第 166 條、第 166 條之 1 至第 166 條之 7 等有關證人交互詰問之規定，業於 92 年 2 月 6 日經修正公布，並自同年 9 月 1 日施行。刑事訴訟法前開修正後之規定，其與軍事審判法第一編第十一章關於「證據」之規定，有何牴觸？何以不在準用之列？原審未深入研求詳予論述說明，逕以軍事審判法第 151 條

---

[30] 參閱謝添富、趙晞華，新修定刑事訴訟法搜索決定權回歸法院對軍事審判所生實務問題及處理方式，軍法專刊，第 47 卷第 9 期，頁 17-18，2001 年 9 月。

第 1 項、第 158 條、第 159 條、第 118 條第 1 項，分別有「行合議審判之案件，爲準備審判起見，得就庭員中指定軍事審判官一員爲受命審判官，於審判期日前訊問被告及蒐集或調查證據。」「軍事檢察官陳述起訴要旨後，審判長應就被訴事實訊問被告。」「訊問被告後，審判長應調查證據。」「卷宗內之筆錄及其他文書可爲證據者，應向被告宣讀或告以要旨，被告請求閱覽者，不得拒絕。」等規定，即認刑事訴訟法與軍事審判法在訴訟程序上有扞格，而謂無從準用刑事訴訟法上開修正後之規定，亦屬理由欠備。』，實務上似常出現軍事法院不依修正後之刑事訴訟證據法則認事用法之現象[31]。

值得說明的是，雖然軍事審判法第 125 條已明定「刑事訴訟法關於證據之規定，與本章不相牴觸者，準用之」，惟自美國之軍司法審判實務而論，由於軍事審判制度除於一般保障被告人權之刑事訴訟目的外，尚含有整飭軍紀、求取勝利等軍事作戰目的在內，軍事審判程序之證據法則與刑事訴訟程序之證

---

[31] 此外，最高法院 93 年度台上字第 5470 號刑事判決（中華民國 93 年 10 月 21 日）：『（二）軍事審判法第 125 條規定：「刑事訴訟法關於證據之規定，與本章（第一編第十一）不相牴觸者，準用之」。而刑事訴訟法第一編第十二章關於「證據」之規定，其中第 166 條、第 166 條之 1 至第 166 條之 7 等有關證人交互詰問之規定，業於 92 年 2 月 6 日經修正公布，並自同年 9 月 1 日起施行。該修正後之規定，與軍事審判法第一編第十一章關於「證據」之規定，有何牴觸？何以不在準用之列？原審未深入研求，即謂無庸準用該刑事訴訟法修正後之規定，要屬理由不備。』與最高法院 94 年度台上字第 5672 號等二則劉岳龍案之判決理由亦同此旨。

據規定二者間原本即存在相左之空間[32]。再者,前述最高法院之見解並未強求軍司法刑事審判程序均適用同一套證據規則,只不過在指摘軍事法院僅因實定規範之文字不同而草率認定「刑事訴訟法與軍事審判法在訴訟程序上有扞格」顯有不當,理由欠備;並進一步要求軍事法院說明其係基於何種理由,「未能準用」刑事訴訟法關於證據章之規定。然不論如何,人民將因軍事審判程序而很可能面對(接受)一套與刑事訴訟法規定相異、對人民基本人權保障較為薄弱的證據法則,已屬不爭之事實。至少現行軍事審判法第 118 條第 1 項:「卷宗內之筆錄及其他文書可為證據者,應向被告宣讀或告以要旨,被告請求閱覽者,不得拒絕。」之規定,係本諸我國舊刑事訴訟法第 165 條第 1 項純粹職權主義所為之規定,不論在軍事審判程序中應如何限縮該條文之適用,只要不廢止其規定、只要軍司法審判程序間在證據法則的採用上容有不同規範之空間,被告在刑事訴訟程序中所得享有並主張的對質詰問權,將受到很大的限制。此部分實為軍司法審判程序間之一大歧異。

(二)階級管轄制

在通常司法審判程序,存在事務管轄、土地管轄與指定管

---

[32] See Charles A. Shanor & L. Lynn Hogue, Military Law, 166 (West Publishing Co., St. Paul, Minn, 1996).

轄等劃分 [33]。與此不同者，在軍事審判程序，除土地管轄 [34] 外，尚存在因軍人階級而生之管轄區分（本文稱此爲「階級管轄 [35]」）。值得注意的是，依軍事審判法第 180 條第 6 項：「對於上訴軍事法院之判決，除依本法上訴最高法院或高等法院者外，不得再上訴。」之反面推論，現行之軍事審判制度已允許軍事被告，在符合一定之條件時，得對上訴軍事法院之判決，向最高法院或高等法院提起上訴。依該法第 181 條第 1 項但書之規定，第一審軍事法院所爲之「將官案件之判決」及「宣告死刑或無期徒刑之判決」，爲職權上訴案件。而依同條第 2 項之規定，第二審軍事法院所爲之「宣告死刑、無期徒刑之上訴判決」，爲職權上訴最高法院案件。而軍事被告對於最高軍事法院宣告有期徒刑以上，或高等軍事法院宣告死刑、無期徒刑之第二審判決者，得依同條第 4 項之規定，以判決違背法令爲理由，向最高法院提起第三審上訴。而對於高等軍事法院向尉官、士官、士兵及其同等軍人犯罪所宣告有期徒刑之第

---

[33] 參閱刑事訴訟法第 4 條、第 5 條與第 9 條。

[34] 參閱軍事審判法第 31 條第 1 項：現役軍人之犯罪案件，由犯罪地或被告之駐地或所在地之軍事法院管轄。

[35] 參閱軍事審判法第 27 條：地方軍事法院管轄尉官、士官、士兵及其同等軍人犯罪之初審案件。軍事審判法第 28 條：高等軍事法院管轄案件如下：一、將官、校官及其同等軍人犯罪之初審案件。二、不服地方軍事法院及其分院初審判決而上訴之案件。三、不服地方軍事法院及其分院裁定而抗告之案件。軍事審判法第 29 條：最高軍事法院管轄案件如下：一、不服高等軍事法院及其分院初審判決而上訴之案件。二、不服高等軍事法院及其分院初審裁定而抗告之案件。三、本法第 204 條之案件。

二審判決，得依同條第 5 項之規定，以判決違背法令爲理由，向高等法院提起第三審上訴，且依同條第 6 項之規定，對於前項高等法院之第三審判決，不得再上訴。又依該法第 199 條：「最高法院或高等法院對於上訴之案件，因原判決違背法令致影響事實之認定，或未諭知管轄錯誤係不當而撤銷者，應發回或發交原上訴或初審軍事法院。」之規定，由最高法院或高等法院管轄之第三審上訴，爲法律審。

　　雖然軍事審判程序亦採三級三審制，然經由以上之說明，可知軍事審判之審級管轄，將因被告之階級與其所受之刑期宣告，而有不同的管轄區分。對於軍事審判法第 27 條所規定之由地方軍事法院管轄案件第一審之尉官、士官與士兵而言，只要高等軍事法院所宣告之第二審判決非屬死刑或無期徒刑，該案件之第三審即由台灣高等法院管轄。如此，即異於一般（非軍法）案件之第三審（如果法律允許的話）係由最高法院管轄之常態。雖難謂由何者管轄第三審審判對人民基本權利保障較佳，惟不可否認的，這點的確是軍司法審判間之一大差異。

（三）非通常之偵查或審判程序

　　相較於軍事審判法僅有通常訴訟程序之規定，刑事訴訟法對於刑事案件之處理，則顯得較具彈性。舉例來說，雖然軍事

審判法關於被告之傳喚與拘提[36]、被告之訊問及羈押[37]、搜索扣押[38]、證據[39]、裁判[40]、偵查[41]、起訴[42]與審判[43]等，定有準用刑事訴訟法之規定，不過關於緩起訴[44]、聲請交付審判[45]、簡式審判程序[46]、簡易程序[47]與認罪協商程序[48]等非通常訴訟程序之規定，軍事審判法卻乏準用之明文。在現行之法制架構下，軍事被告在軍事審判程序中即無從主張因適用刑事訴訟法而可獲得之程序與實體利益。此種軍司法審判程序間之差異，亦致使軍司法審判程序劃分之探討，更具實益。

（四）刑事執行

　　除審判程序外，執行程序之發動與其指揮、監督機關之區分，亦為探討軍司法審判程序劃分之另一焦點。原則上，軍事法院檢察署之軍事檢察官指揮執行依軍事審判法進行刑事審判

---

[36]　參閱軍事審判法第 100 條。
[37]　參閱軍事審判法第 110 條。
[38]　參閱軍事審判法第 115 條。
[39]　參閱軍事審判法第 125 條。
[40]　參閱軍事審判法第 129 條。
[41]　參閱軍事審判法第 146 條。
[42]　參閱軍事審判法第 150 條。
[43]　參閱軍事審判法第 179 條。
[44]　參閱刑事訴訟法第 253-1 條至第 253-3 條。
[45]　參閱刑事訴訟法第 258-1 條至第 258-4 條。
[46]　參閱刑事訴訟法第 273-1 條至第 273-2 條。
[47]　參閱刑事訴訟法第 449 條至第 455-1 條。
[48]　參閱刑事訴訟法第 455-2 條至第 455-11 條。

程序所得之最終確定判決[49]；其中死刑判決須由國防部長發布執行命令[50]，並於軍事監獄內執行[51]；而處徒刑及拘役之人犯，則於軍事監獄內執行之[52]。雖刑事訴訟法關於執行之規定，在與軍法執行程序不相牴觸之範圍內得準用之[53]，惟因執行場所不同（軍法監獄與普通監獄）及其監督主管機關不同（國防部與法務部），似必導致軍司法執行處遇間存在一定程度之差別。要言之，軍事審判法與刑事訴訟法間所存在之上述諸差異，已足使軍司法審判程序應如何劃分之爭議，成為一值得重提並亟待釐清之課題。

參、喪失現役軍人身分後刑事審判權歸屬之實然

在確認軍事審判法與刑事訴訟法間，在適用上的確將對人民之基本權利造成差別待遇後，接下來本文將介紹現行實務關於犯罪與發覺均具現役軍人身分、惟於訴訟繫屬中喪失現役軍人身分時，該案件之刑事審判權究應如何歸屬之見解，為求理解之方便，此部分乃分就司法機關與軍法機關之見解，予以說明。

---

[49] 參閱軍事審判法第 229 條。

[50] 參閱軍事審判法第 231 條。

[51] 參閱軍事審判法第 232 條。

[52] 參閱軍事審判法第 234 條。

[53] 參閱軍事審判法第 236 條。

一、司法院解釋與最高法院刑事判決

目前實務關於軍司法審判權之劃分，可自下列實務見解中窺得其貌：

（一）司法院 23 年院字第 1078 號解釋

軍人犯罪，應以發覺在任官、任役中抑在免官、免役後而定其審判機關，陸海空軍審判法第 16 條規定甚明，如某甲犯罪發覺時確係現役軍人，縱令發覺後解除軍籍，亦不能變更審判管轄。

（二）最高法院 88 年度台上字第 5616 號刑事判決

按「現役軍人犯罪，由軍法機關追訴審判。但所犯為陸海空軍刑法及其特別法以外之罪，而屬刑法第 61 條所列各罪者，不在此限」，國家安全法第 8 條第 2 項定有明文。上開審判權歸屬之規範，乃對現役軍人之犯罪，因其身分之特殊而特別規定，重在犯罪時之身分，非以追訴審判時為基準，係軍事審判法第 1 條第 1 項前段及刑事訴訟法第 1 條第 2 項之特別規定，自應優先適用；至於犯罪在任職服役中、發覺在離職離役後之情形，因國家安全法未規定，應依軍事審判法第五條第二項規定，由法院審判。故現役軍人犯陸海空軍刑法及其特別法以外之罪，而非屬於刑法第 61 條所列各罪者，其犯罪及發覺均在任職服役中，縱令起訴及審判時已離職離役，仍應由軍法機關追

訴審判，尚無軍事審判法第 5 條第 2 項之適用。檢察官上訴意旨稱國家安全法第 8 條第 2 項所稱「現役軍人犯罪」，係指追訴審判時具有軍人身分者而言，尚非的論[54]。

（三）最高法院 94 年度台非字第 269 號刑事判決

　　本院按現役軍人犯陸海空軍刑法或其特別法之罪，依軍事審判法之規定追訴審判之。又犯罪在任職服役前，發覺在任職服役中者，依軍事審判法追訴審判；但案件在追訴審判中而離職離役者，初審案件應移送該管第一審之法院，上訴案件應移送該管第二審之法院審判。犯罪在任職服役中，發覺在離職離役後者，由法院審判。軍事審判法第 1 條第 1 項前段、第 5 條第 1、2 項分別定有明文。是現役軍人犯陸海空軍刑法或其特別法之罪，而其犯罪及發覺時均在任職服役中者，揆之前揭法條意旨，應由軍法機關審判，不因其在追訴審判中離職離役而異[55]。

二、國防部訓令

　　依國防部（七七）律御字第 1908 號令釋：按軍事審判法第 5 條第 1 項但書所謂「離職離役」一詞，前述本部（七六）律

---

[54]　最高法院 69 年台非字第 101 號判例亦同此旨，按此種觀點實係自軍事審判法第 5 條第 2 項規定反面推論所得。

[55]　事實上自軍事審判法修正後迄今，我國最高法院均採類此判決意旨之見解。

御字第 0747 號令釋以：「乃指因涉案以外之原因而合法離職離役而言，其因涉案而免職或停役者應不包括在內，以避免發生因案件正常進行而喪失審判權之情事，致使審判權陷於不確定之狀態。」此所謂之「涉案」，乃指所涉本案而言，倘係另涉他案而喪失軍人身分，則不為前開「因涉案而免職或停役」之情形，應屬軍事審判法第 5 條第 1 項但書移送法院審判之原因。另國防部 46 年 2 月 13 日（四六）準諮字第 16 號令及 46 年 9 月 12 日（四七）心昌字第 098 號令函釋亦主張：犯罪及發覺均在任職服役中之被告，無論追訴審判時是否離職，均應依軍事審判法追訴審判。

三、小結

　　由前述說明可知，現行實務關於軍司法審判權之劃分，係以「現役軍人犯軍刑法之罪且於發覺時仍具現役軍人身分」為標準，縱或於本案進行中喪失現役軍人身分，亦非移送普通法院審理之原因，被告仍應由軍法機關追訴審判。

肆、前述實務見解所引發之疑慮

　　雖於我國憲法第 9 條規定之反面解釋下，只有現役軍人犯罪始有受軍事審判之可能；惟於司法院大法官釋字第 272 號解釋：「人民除現役軍人外，不受軍事審判，憲法第 9 條定有明

文。戒嚴法第 8 條、第 9 條規定，非現役軍人得由軍事機關審判，則為憲法承認戒嚴制度而生之例外情形。」之意旨下 [56]，非現役軍人亦有可能受軍事審判，不過其範圍須限縮在戒嚴法第 8 條、第 9 條所規定之情形，蓋此時正當國家遭逢緊急變故之際，在軍事優先之考量下，原即不得不限制人民基本權利之行使。

然而，前述軍司法實務卻長久以來忽略了憲法第 9 條的規範精神，亦即：非現役軍人不受軍事審判。以前述劉岳龍洩密案而言，由於被告已於宣判前依法喪失現役軍人之身分，此時何以非現役軍人仍須接受軍事審判？查軍事審判法第五條：「犯罪在任職服役前，發覺在任職服役中者，依本法追訴審判。但案件在追訴審判中離職離役者，初審案件應移送該管第一審之法院，上訴案件應移送該管第二審之法院審判。（第 1 項）犯罪在任職服役中，發覺在離職離役後者，由法院審判。（第 2 項）前二項規定，按行為時之身分適用法律。（第 3 項）」本身，並未規定現役軍人犯軍刑法之罪後，於實際受審判、追訴時已不具備現役軍人之身分（如劉岳龍於審判程序中喪失現役軍人身分之情形），仍必須依軍事審判法之規定進行追訴、審判。就此法未明文之「法律漏洞」而言，此時是否可依「明示其一，排除其他」之法理，而認於軍事審判法第五條

---

[56] 由於大法官針對憲法所做之解釋與憲法有同等之效力，故此部分「非現役軍人得由軍事機關審判」規定或無違憲之疑慮。

無明文得依刑事訴訟法規定進行審判程序之情形下，反面推論此時仍應依軍事審判程序審理？如果答案是肯定的，則現役軍人所犯所有軍刑法之罪，除於離職離役後發覺者外，皆由軍法機關追訴、審判所造成非現役軍人接受軍事審判之現象，是否與憲法第 9 條「非現役軍人不受軍事審判」之立憲精神有所牴觸？雖然在司法實務運作上曾有檢察官主張應以被告實際上接受追訴審判時是否仍具現役軍人身分為現行憲法第 9 條之規範核心，故不應繼續援用前述國防部訓令之意旨[57]；且在軍事審判法之立法過程中曾有立法委員意識到此一憲法問題並對系爭「訴訟程序中喪失軍人身分者審判權歸屬」疑義指出：「因其人既已脫下軍服，不再具現役軍人身分，是否應移送法院審判，以符憲法第 9 條意旨[58]。」，遺憾的是，或因論證不構嚴謹、或因未能完整交代法制發展之沿革因而說服力不足，此種以憲法第 9 條重在接受追訴審判時是否具有現役軍人身分之觀點，於因循司法院 23 年院字第 1078 號解釋之實務操作下，未被最高法院接受；而前述立法委員之主張，亦在國防部官員似是而非之答詢後，未被採納[59]。

[57] 參閱最高法院 88 年度台上字第 5616 號刑事判決中檢察官上訴部分。
[58] 此為軍事審判法於審議時，立法委員邱太三所提之意見。參閱謝添富、趙晞華：淺論軍事審判法修正後之若干法律問題及處理方式，律師雜誌，民國 89 年 7 月號，第 250 期，頁 39。
[59] 查國防部認為犯罪及發覺均在任職服役中，而於追訴審判中離職離役仍應依軍事審判法追訴審判之理由如下：
（一）本條設計係基於公平及偵審上之方便考量；

　　值得注意的是，最高法院在另一則涉及因法規變更而喪失現役軍人身分之案件中（最高法院 92 年度台非字第 393 號刑事判決），卻一反前述軍司法實務之通說（司法院 23 年院字第 1078 號解釋），而主張普通法院於被告等因軍事審判法修正（限縮現役軍人範圍）後喪失現役軍人身分（因軍校生於民國 88 年之軍事審判法修正後已非現役軍人或視同現役軍人）之情

　　（二）依司法院院字第 1078 號解釋以下實務所揭示之一貫法理，本諸「審判恆定」原則，與憲法第九條之規定並無牴觸。

　　（三）犯罪及發覺時均具現役軍人身分，若因追訴審判中離職退伍，即將偵審中案件移交司法機關，對軍紀管理及戰力維持仍有相當程度之影響。且（1）被告如藉故辦理退伍而喪失其現役軍人身分，除可規避軍事審判外，若第 5 條第 3 項之實體準據法部分，亦改採刑法第 2 條第 1 項但書「從新從輕」原則，更可倖免對婦女強制性交等重罪之處罰。（2）被告為軍官或士官在押逾三月者，依軍官士官服役條例之規定，應予辦理停役，取消其現役軍人身分，遇重大案件無從於三月內完成偵查及審判，均將陷審判權於不安定之狀態。（3）士兵逃亡經通緝，及軍士官因案通緝，應依兵役法或前開法律辦理停役，取消其現役軍人身分，亦足使審判權於不安定狀態。

　　（四）依美國統一軍法典 1984 年增訂條款第 3 條，不僅亦有受軍事審判人員，不因其後之身分消滅，及軍隊逃亡人員，不因事後獲得退役資格，而免受軍事法庭之審判之規定，且更明定凡退役人員嗣後被控其退役係藉由詐欺者，由軍事法庭審判之，又倘上開控訴成立後，其在詐欺退役前所犯本法規定之各罪，亦均應由軍事法庭審判之。

　　（五）第 1 項但書之設計，乃因被告本非現役軍人，故在偵審中退伍者，移還司法機關；至於第二項係因既於被告退伍後才發覺其犯罪，強令被告返回部隊接受軍事審判，並非合理，於案件之偵審亦非便捷。若考量現役軍人因役期屆滿等合法離職離役事由，既已回復非現役軍人之身分，不應再受軍事審判之權利，本條例於再修正時，允宜參照前揭陸海空軍審判法第 16 條但書之立法例，增訂第 2 項為「犯罪及發覺在任職服役中，於追訴審判中依法離職離役者，依前項規定移送該管法院審判。但因本案而離職離役者，不在此限。」。

參閱謝添富、趙晞華，淺論軍事審判法修正後之若干法律問題及處理方式，律師雜誌，民國 89 年 7 月號，第 250 期，頁 41-2。

形中，即因被告等已失現役軍人身分而取得對該等被告軍法犯罪之刑事審判權[60]。雖然該案件之事實部分係因法令變更而喪失現役軍人身分，與前述軍司法實務係指因該案而喪失現役軍人身分之情形不同，並且於最高法院 92 年度台非字第 393 號刑事判決作成後，實務上之操作仍以前述之軍司法實務通說為

---

[60] 最高法院 92 年度台非字第 393 號刑事判決中指出：又現役軍人在任職服役前犯罪，發覺亦在任職服役前者，應由普通法院審判，此由軍事審判法第五條之規定即可證明；而 88 年 10 月 2 日修正前之軍事審判法第 3 條第 3 款規定陸、海、空軍所屬在校之學員、學生，係視同現役軍人，但該法條修正施行後，陸、海、空軍所屬在校之學員、學生，已非視同現役軍人，則如其涉嫌犯罪，且發覺時縱係軍事院校之學員、學生，自應由司法機關追訴處罰。此類原視同現役軍人身分，由軍事審判機關審判中尚未審結之案件，於軍事審判法前開條文修正施行後，應移送普通法院審判，此僅係審判機關之變更，法院應依刑事訴訟法之規定續行審判，此有司法院刑事廳 88 年 10 月 28 日電話傳真，檢察機關辦理軍事審判法修正施行後，軍事審判機關移送刑事案件應行注意事項可稽。本案被告翁志銘、張永佑二人於 85 年 9 月 20 日至同年月 24 日為陸軍軍官學校三年級學生，分別擔任該專指部入伍連第一排第三班及第一班教育班長時，涉嫌共同凌虐入伍生吳延鴻，致吳延鴻受傷，經陸軍第八軍團司令部軍事檢察官於 87 年 8 月 10 日依修正前陸海空軍刑法第 73 條濫用職權為凌虐罪及刑法第 277 條第 1 項傷害罪提起公訴。嗣國防部南部地方軍事法院，於審理中以被告等行為時均為陸軍軍官學校之學生，至 86 年 11 月 8 日始自軍校畢業分發部隊服役，而陸軍軍官學校於 86 年 8 月 5 日已將被告等函送陸軍第八軍團司令部偵辦，經該部軍事檢察官於同年 8 月 12 日收案辦理，足見被告等於犯罪被發覺時仍屬在校學生，但軍事審判法已於 88 年 10 月 3 日修正公布，被告等已非現行軍事審判法第 2 條、第 3 條規定之現役軍人或視同現役軍人，因而於 89 年 2 月 21 日以 89 法和字第 0577 號函將被告等移送有管轄權之司法機關，即台灣高雄地方法院審理。依前開說明，自應依法由司法機關續行審判，案經台灣高雄地方法院 89 年度易字第 962 號判決後，原審竟誤認被告等犯罪時及發覺時均係現役軍人，且軍事檢察官起訴時被告等已是少尉排長，為現役軍人為由，認普通法院就本案無審判權，乃撤銷第一審台灣高雄地方法院對被告等為科刑之判決，而為公訴不受理之諭知，揆諸前開說明，顯屬不受理訴訟之違法。

據，不過該案開創了喪失現役軍人身分後即移送普通法院審理之先例，卻值得予以注意。

　　根據司法院大法官第 436 號解釋，軍事審判只是基於國家安全與軍事需要，對軍人犯罪行為「得」設之特別訴訟程序；不過，軍事審判之所以為特別訴訟程序，究竟是以身分為區別標準，或者是以犯罪為區別標準？長久以來，即有爭議[61]。簡單來說，如果司法院 23 年院字第 1078 號解釋「於軍事審判程序繫屬中被告喪失現役軍人身分時，其審判權歸屬不須變動」之觀點應予維持，那麼最高法院 92 年度台非字第 393 號刑事判決「於軍事審判程序繫屬中被告喪失現役軍人身分時，其審判權歸屬必須變動」之觀點即應揚棄；反之，如果司法院 23 年院字第 1078 號解釋不應繼續援用，那麼我國軍司法審判實務關於刑事審判權歸屬之劃分標準，即應重行建構。有鑑於此，以下本文即就司法院院字第 1078 號解釋繼續作為軍司法審判之劃分標準，在現行法制秩序下之容許性為何，進行進一步的分析探討。

---

[61] 參閱呂啟元，軍事審判權之研究，財團法人國家政策研究基金會論文，available at: http://www.npf.org.tw/PUBLICATION/CL/091/CL-R-091-039.htm (last visted, Sep. 29th, 2007)。

伍、司法院院字第 1078 號解釋與軍司法審判之劃分

一、現役軍人身分與軍事審判

　　既然現行軍司法實務將導致其是否牴觸憲法第 9 條規定之疑義，則關於現役軍人犯罪在何種條件下接受軍事審判始爲憲法第 9 條所許，自屬前述違憲疑義之前提而爲一值得探究之焦點。在此認知下，關於現役軍人受軍事審判之法制沿革，或可爲詳明現行憲法第 9 條之規範本旨，提供一可循之脈絡。

　　關於軍事審判權之行使對象，向來存在以被告身分爲準（身分權說）或以所爲犯罪爲準（事物權說）、抑或二者兼而有之之區分。舉例而言，如以身分爲準，即祇要係現役軍人實施之犯罪，皆應成爲軍事審判權行使之對象；又如以犯罪爲準，即應以犯陸海空軍刑法規定之犯罪始屬軍事審判權行使之對象；如以身分與犯罪爲準，則必須現役軍人犯陸海空軍刑法規定之犯罪，始屬軍事審判權行使之對象 [62]。自比較法之角度而言，舉凡承認軍事審判法制之國家，關於軍事審判權之範圍，均有規定，而其究係採何種論點作爲依據，各國法制卻有

---

[62]　參閱蔡墩銘，軍事審判與普通審判之關係，月旦法學雜誌，第 35 期，頁 28，1998 年 4 月；如以被告犯罪時之身分爲準，又稱爲「身分權說」，如以被告所犯之罪爲準，又稱爲「事物權說」，參閱李太正，軍事審判在憲法上之地位，軍法專刊，第 34 卷第 10 期，頁 17，1988 年 10 月。

不同 [63]。若將我國刑事訴訟法第 1 條第 2 項：「現役軍人之犯罪，除犯軍法應受軍事裁判者外，仍應依本法規定追訴、處罰。」及軍事審判法第 1 條第 1 項：「現役軍人犯陸海空軍刑法或其特別法之罪，依本法之規定追訴審判之，其在戰時犯陸海空軍刑法或其特別法以外之罪者，亦同。」予以綜合解釋，似可認為：現役軍人惟於犯軍法之罪始受軍事裁判，現役軍人非犯軍法之罪，而係犯普通刑法之罪，即不受軍事裁判。就此而言，表面上或可認關於我國軍事審判之範圍，立法上係採事物權說；不過實際上，整體的法制狀況似非如此。

雖學說上有認：「自法制史觀之，軍事審判權與普通（刑事）審判權之區別標準，有由身分到犯罪的趨勢 [64]。」，惟若

---

[63] 關於各國軍事審判權之法制，可參閱參閱李維宗，軍、司法審判權在實務運作上的幾個爭議問題（下），軍法專刊，第 41 卷第 10 期，頁 19，1995 年 10 月；蔡新毅，解構關於軍事審判之迷思，律師雜誌，第 250 期，頁 52，2000 年 7 月；蔡新毅，由憲法觀點論軍事審判權之性質及其修正之相關問題（下），司法周刊第 866 期，第 2 版，1998 年 2 月 25 日；李太正，軍事審判理論之檢討與展望（上），軍法專刊，第 35 卷第 6 期，頁 33，1999 年 6 月；黃風譯，義大利軍事刑法典，頁 5，中國政法大學出版社，1998 年 5 月第 1 版。

[64] 此種觀點，似亦有其沿革上之依據；民國十九年時，依當時之陸海空軍審判法第一條第一項，陸海空軍軍人犯刑法所揭各罪者，依該法審判。此時，軍事審判權與普通（刑事）審判權截然二分，軍人犯罪一律受軍事審判，乃是以身分為區別標準。民國 24 年刑事訴訟法公布並正式施行，其第一條第二項規定：「軍人軍屬之犯罪，除犯軍法應受軍事審判者外，仍應依本法規定追訴、處罰」此一條文，正式引起軍事審判權與普通（刑事）審判權之歸屬爭議。由於陸海空軍審判法在性質上屬於特別法，依「特別法優於普通法」之原則，應優先適用而；但刑事訴訟法屬於後法，依「後法優於新法」，應優先適用！即使是判例，對此一問題，見解亦互有矛盾！有認為軍人犯軍法

自憲法第 9 條：「人民除現役軍人外，不受軍事審判。」、國家安全法第 8 條第 1 項：「非現役軍人，不受軍事審判。」及軍事審判法第 1 條第 2 項前段：「非現役軍人不受軍事審判。」等規定出發，我國軍事審判制度除以前述「事物權說」為依據外，尚以「審判時具現役軍人之身分」為軍事審判程序適用之前提。在此憲法秩序之要求下，對於刑事訴訟法第 1 條第 2 項及軍事審判法第 1 條第 1 項之理解，似必須同時兼顧被

以外之罪應依陸海空軍審判法追訴處罰的，也有認為應依刑事訴訟法追訴處罰的。惟無論如何，這些爭議實為軍事審判權「從身分到犯罪」之開端。軍事審判法制定後，於第 1 條明確規定，「對於現役軍人犯陸海空軍刑法或其特別法之罪，依本法追訴審判之，其在戰時犯陸海空軍刑法或其特別法以外之罪者，亦同」，此一規定，原則採「犯罪區別標準」，在戰時例外採「身分區別標準」。不過，由於台灣長期戒嚴，故本條形同具文，現役軍人犯罪仍依軍法審判。解嚴後，因為國家安全法第 8 條第 2 項規定：「現役軍人犯罪，由軍法機關追訴審判。但所犯為陸海空軍刑法及其特別法以外之罪，而屬刑法第 61 條所列各罪者，不在此限」，現役軍人犯罪仍只有少部分屬於刑法 61 條所列各罪者屬普通（刑事）審判，大部分仍依軍事審判；直到民國 88 年修正軍事審判法，增訂第 237 條，「國家安全法第 8 條第 2 項自中華民國 90 年 10 月 2 日停止適用」，始將軍事審判權之範圍回歸到軍事審判法第 1 條之明文。自此一法制史之發展，我們可以發現，基於法治國原則，軍事審判權之範圍，逐漸在擺脫「身分區別標準」，而邁向「犯罪區別標準」，在釋字 436 號解釋中，大法官明確指出「非謂軍事審判機關對於軍人之犯罪有專屬之審判權」，足見其亦傾向於揚棄「身分區別標準」。易言之，現役軍人只有觸犯特定犯罪，始依軍事審判法加以追訴、處罰；如果現役軍人所犯為一般犯罪，則仍應交由普通（刑事）法院依刑事訴訟法加以追訴、處罰。職是之故，則任何試圖將軍事審判權之範圍回歸到「身分區別標準」者，例如，主張「現役軍人犯罪，無論其犯罪類型之不同，均交由軍事法院審判」，明顯違背釋字第 436 號解釋及立法趨勢，有違憲之虞，實不可行。參閱呂啟元，軍事審判權之研究，財團法人國家政策研究基金會論文，available at: http://www.npf.org.tw/PUBLICATION/CL/091/CL-R-091-039.htm (last visted, Sep. 29th, 2007)。

告「偵審中身分」與「犯罪」二者，方為適當。換言之，關於審判權誰屬，除犯罪與身分外，尚應著重在追訴審判時被告是否具有軍人身分，此觀軍事審判法第五條：「犯罪在任職服役前，發覺在任職服役中者，依本法追訴審判。但案件在追訴審判中離職離役者，初審案件應移送該管第一審之法院，上訴案件應移送該管第二審之法院審判。（第 1 項）犯罪在任職服役中，發覺在離職離役後者，由法院審判。（第 2 項）」之規定與最高法院 87 年台上字第 1296 號判決：「應否由軍法機關追訴審判，係以行為人犯罪被發覺時及其接受追訴審判時是否具有現役軍人之身分為其認定之依據，而非以其犯罪時是否為現役軍人惟其認定之依據[65]」等，已將軍事被告之現役軍人身分

---

[65] 該判決理由為：惟按現役軍人犯罪，由軍法機關追訴審判。但所犯為陸海空軍刑法及其特別法以外之罪，而屬刑法第 61 條所列各罪者，不在此限。又現役軍人犯罪在任職服役前，發覺在任職服役中者，依軍事審判法追訴審判。國家安全法第 8 條第 2 項、軍事審判法第 5 條第 1 項前段分別著有明文。本件原判決以公訴意旨略以上訴人明知安非他命係禁藥，竟於 85 年 7 月中旬，○○○市○○區○○街八十號將安非他命免費供柯光俊吸用，涉有違反藥事法第 83 條第 1 項轉讓禁藥罪嫌等情。然原審依上訴人之供述及卷附之戶籍謄本、國防部人事次長室 86 年 7 月 14 日（八六）易昇字第 15276 號簡便行文表等相關證據，認定上訴人已於 85 年 8 月 5 日入伍服役，現仍在營服役中，為現役軍人，而公訴人起訴之上訴人犯罪時雖為 85 年 7 月中旬，但其查獲時間為同年 10 月 7 日，亦有警訊卷可按。是上訴人之犯罪時間為在任職服役前，發覺在任職服役中，依前開規定，應依軍事審判法追訴審判，法院無審判權，因而撤銷第一審關於上訴人科刑部分之判決，改判諭知公訴不受理，已詳予說明其所憑之證據及認定之理由。從形式上觀察，並無所謂違背法令之情形存在。復查國家安全法第 8 條第 2 項之規定，為刑事訴訟法第 1 條第 2 項之特別規定，應優先適用，而上訴人所涉犯之轉讓禁藥罪，其法定本刑為五年以下有期徒刑之罪，非屬刑法第 61 條所列之罪，自應依國家安全法第 8

列為判斷其是否接受軍事審判之標準，亦可得印證。從軍事審判法第五條與最高法院87年台上字第1296號判決已於某種程度範圍內排除以事務權說作為判斷軍事審判權範圍之標準，亦可推定早於民國45年首次制定軍事審判法時，立法者已有將「偵審中（發覺時）具現役軍人身分」作為判斷軍事審判權範圍之立憲精神，納入軍事審判法規定之考量。或許是在前述司法院院字第1078號解釋之影響下，才未通盤地將「被告偵審中是否具現役軍人身分」作為軍事被告應否接受軍事審判之判斷標準。惟沿用該號作成於民國23年之司法解釋似已忽略憲法第9條、國家安全法第8條第1項及軍事審判法第1條第2項前段所揭示「人民除現役軍人外，不受軍事審判」之規定，除於身分說與事物權說外，尚包含以「偵審中具現役軍人身分」作為限縮軍事審判權範圍之立憲精神。因此，關於司法院院字第1078號解釋之法理依據，即有進一步詳明之必要。

二、司法院院字第1078號解釋之合憲性基礎

自法制沿革的觀點來說，前述司法院院字第1078號解釋之

條第2項之規定，由軍法機關追訴審判。又是否為現役軍人，應否由軍法機關追訴審判，係以行為人犯罪被發覺時及其接受追訴審判時是否具有現役軍人之身分為其認定之依據，而非以其犯罪時是否為現役軍人為其認定之依據，此觀諸軍事審判法第五條之規定自明。上訴意旨對原判決所為不受理之判決，究竟有何不適用法則或適用不當，未依卷內訴訟資料具體指明，徒憑己意以上訴人犯罪時尚未入伍服役，非現役軍人，不應由軍法機關追訴審判，並援引刑事訴訟法第1條第2項之規定，泛指原判決違背法令云云，難謂係適法之上訴第三審理由。

作成，除係本於其軍閥割據、戰火綿迭之時代背景外，事實上尚有其法制上之依據（惟此點向來為法學家們論述時所忽略）。按依民國 19 年 3 月 24 日國民政府公布之陸海空軍審判法第一條第一項：「凡陸海空軍軍人，犯陸海空軍刑法或刑法所揭各罪，或違警罰法，或其他法律之定有刑名者，依本法之規定審判之。」與民國 26 年 6 月 1 日公布之「中華民國訓政時期約法」第 9 條：「人民除現役軍人外，非依法律，不受軍法審判」等規定，是否適於軍事審判僅屬「法律保留」之層次；且依其規定，軍事審判本質上並未如現行法般，兼含身分權說與事物權說二者之性質。因此，只要有實證法之依據，縱將軍事審判權擴及於因本案喪失現役軍人身分之刑事被告，並未違當時有效之憲法規範。以此為前提，司法院院字第 1078 號解釋自亦得評價為合憲之司法裁量，關於現役軍人之犯罪，「只要發覺在任職服役中，縱令起訴及審判時已離職離役，仍應由軍法機關追訴審判」之觀點，也就取得其合憲性之基礎[66]。而最

---

[66] 由於民國 24 年 1 月 1 日國民政府公布，同年 7 月 1 日施行之刑事訴訟法第 1 條第 2 項規定：「軍人、軍屬之犯罪，除犯軍法應受軍事裁判者外，仍應依本法之規定追訴處罰」與民國 19 年 3 月 24 日國民政府公布，民國 45 年 10 月 1 日廢止之陸海空軍審判法第 1 條規定：「凡陸海空軍軍人，犯陸海空軍刑法或刑法所揭各罪，或違警罰法，或其他法律之定有刑名者，依本法之規定審判之。非軍人而犯陸海空軍刑法第 2 條所揭之罪者，應由法院審理之。」規定異其旨趣。因而發生軍人犯軍法以外之罪，究竟應否歸軍法審判之問題。就理論言，陸海空軍審判法雖屬特別法，然公布施行在先，且刑事訴訟法既將軍人犯罪之管轄及追訴審判之程序明文予以變更，依後法優於前法之原則，則陸海空軍審判法與刑事訴訟法牴觸部分自應失效。惟事實並非如此，因其時軍人、軍屬犯軍法以外之罪，如歸由普通司法機關審判，窒礙實多。國民

高法院 30 年上字第 178 號判例:「軍人犯刑法所揭各罪,應依陸海空軍審判法審判之,為陸海空軍審判法第 1 條第 1 項所明定。雖刑事訴訟法第 1 條第 2 項規定,軍人軍屬之犯罪,除犯軍法應受軍事審判者外,仍應依本法規定追訴、處罰,但此項規定因與前開陸海空軍審判法有異,業經國民政府於民國 27 年 7 月渝字第 370 號訓令,凡抗戰期內軍人軍屬犯軍法以外之罪,暫照陸海空軍審判法辦理而停止其適用則抗戰期內之軍人,雖犯刑法上之罪,普通法院仍無受理之權。」與 42 年台非字第 19 號判例:「陸海空軍審判法第 1 條第 1 項,陸海空軍軍

政府乃於民國 25 年 2 月以第 185 號訓令規定:「在剿匪區域內,軍人、軍屬犯軍法以外之罪,暫照陸海空軍審判法辦理。」同年 9 月國民政府第 706 號訓令又將「剿匪區域內」之「區域」兩字改為「期」字。國民政府又於民國 27 年 7 月 11 日以渝字第 217 號訓令將前令「剿匪期內」改為「抗戰期內」,即「在抗戰期內,軍人、軍屬犯軍法以外之罪,暫照陸海空軍審判法辦理。」。抗戰勝利後,由於民國 33 年 1 月 12 日國民政府公布,同年 11 月 12 日施行之「特種刑事案件訴訟條例」第 1 條規定:「依法律規定適用特種刑事程序之案件及本條例施行前,依法令規定由軍事或軍法機關審理之案件,除軍人為被告外,均依本條例之規定審理之。本條例未規定者,仍適用刑事訴訟法及其他有關之法令。」因之,所有特種刑事案件,一概移歸司法機關審判,軍法審判範圍恢復常態。換言之,軍法與司法機關受理案件範圍,僅依被告有無軍人身分為劃分標準,而不以犯罪性質為斷。至於軍人犯軍法以外之罪者,國民政府於民國 35 年 2 月 12 日訓令將原令文字改為「軍人、軍屬犯軍法以外之罪,得暫照陸海空軍審判法辦理。」然查其間不論法規如何沿革,關於現役軍人之犯罪,只要發覺在任職服役中,縱令起訴及審判時已離職離役,仍應由軍法機關追訴審判。雖民國 45 年制定軍事審判法時,已將原陸海空軍審判法第 16 條後段但書規定刪除,惟就軍司法審判權歸屬之判定,仍係以前開司法院院字第 1078 號解釋為依據。參閱張明偉,軍事審判權之界限,法令月刊,第 45 卷第 4 期,頁 40-41,2003 年 4 月。

人犯刑法所揭各罪者，依該法審判之規定，於刑事訴訟法施行後，依後法優於前法之原則，已因刑事訴訟法第 1 條第 2 項所定軍人軍屬之犯罪，除犯軍法應受軍事裁判者外，仍應依本法規定追訴、處罰之明文，而停止其效用，是軍人軍屬犯軍法以外之罪者，除另有特別規定者外，自應依刑事訴訟法之規定追訴、處罰，至為明顯。國民政府於民國 35 年 2 月 12 日，雖有軍人軍屬犯軍法以外之罪，得暫照陸海空軍審判法辦理之訓令，但既定為得而不曰應，即非強制之規定，是此項命令，不過僅定為軍人軍屬犯軍法以外之罪，得暫照陸海空軍審判法辦理，並非排除刑事訴訟法第 1 條第 2 項之適用，因之軍屬犯軍法以外之罪時，軍事或軍法機關，固得予以審判，普通法院殊難謂無審判之權。」等相關實務見解，亦可謂係本諸前述中華民國訓政時期約法第 9 條而來。

三、憲法保留下之軍司法審判劃分

　　與中華民國訓政時期約法第 9 條之規定不同，民國 36 年 12 月 25 日施行之中華民國憲法第 9 條：「人民除現役軍人外，不受軍事審判」規定，實則已將「軍事審判權之行使不及於非現役軍人」之原則，提昇為「憲法保留」之層次。既然非現役軍人不受軍事審判已成為憲法明文列舉關於對人民基本權利之核心保障，從而前述源於「法律保留」層次之「司法院院字第 1078 號解釋」，在現行憲法第 9 條之規範下，原即應失其附麗。遺憾的是，自民國 36 年行憲以來，相關之軍司法實務運

作，似乎均無視於憲法第 9 條「憲法保留」規定之存在，導致應存在於刑事審判領域中所謂「層級化保留」之法治國憲政秩序，徒因司法院院字第 1078 號解釋之繼續運作而蕩然無存。軍司法實務此種長期忽略憲法第 9 條制憲精神，逕以民國 23 年作成之司法院院字第 1078 號解釋作爲「軍事審判程序中離職離役者仍應接受軍事審判」之論據，其不當之處實不言可諭。從而，針對我國軍事審判法制上之漏洞，應以合憲之解釋方法作爲爭端解決之依據，前述司法院院字第 1078 號解釋縱有沿革上之依據，在現行憲法規定已異於訓政時期約法之前提下，應認已成昨日黃花而不可採。自此以觀，現役軍人犯軍刑法之罪應否由軍法機關追訴審判，除以犯罪時與發覺時是否具有現役軍人之身分爲其認定之依據外，尙應以其「接受追訴審判時」是否亦具有現役軍人之身分爲判斷其應否受軍事審判之依據，而非僅以其犯罪時及發覺時是否爲現役軍人爲其認定之依據，如此方爲安適。

　　至於依憲法第 9 條規定將訴訟程序中喪失現役軍人身分之被告移送於普通法院之作法，並不會出現審判權陷於不安定之現象，蓋審判權安定與否，端視其歸屬是否明確而定，鑒於國家安全法第 8 條第 2 項之規定已停止適用，往昔實務上關於是否爲刑法第 61 條所列之犯罪所生之軍司法審判權爭議[67]已不復

---

[67] 參閱李維宗，軍、司法審判權在實務運作上的幾個爭議問題（上），軍法專刊，第 41 卷第 9 期，頁 28，1995 年 9 月。

存在。因此令人感到疑慮的，應僅爲審判權歸屬改變所造成之
訴訟不經濟與對軍事審判制度之衝擊。不論如何，這些顧慮均
不應成爲剝奪非現役軍人主張依刑事訴訟法之規定接受審判權
利之理由。

四、審判權歸屬變動無損於軍事審判制度目的

　　與修正前之規定相較，現行法制下軍事審判之範圍，已顯
得相當限縮[68]。或許有人會質疑在揚棄司法院院字第 1078 號解
釋後，軍事審判權之範圍將會不當地萎縮，並將對軍紀管理及
戰力維持造成負面影然[69]，例如國防部認爲：由於軍官或士官

---

[68] 於國家安全法第 8 條第 2 項：「現役軍人犯罪，由軍法機關追訴審判。但所
犯爲陸海空軍刑法及其特別法以外之罪，而屬刑法第 61 條所列各罪者，不在
此限。」停止適用後，在平時軍事審判之範圍已縮小至軍事審判法第 1 條第
1 項前段：「現役軍人犯陸海空軍刑法或其特別法之罪，依本法之規定追訴審
判之。」關於視同現役軍人之範圍，亦因軍事審判法第 3 條之修正僅餘：「依
法成立之武裝團隊、戰時納入戰鬥序列者」；另兵役法第 20 條修正前須無故
離營已逾一個月或羈押已逾三個月始停役之規定，亦因將通緝、羈押或觀察
勒戒列爲常備兵停役之原因而使現役軍人之範圍有所變動。

[69] 查反對廢除司法院院字第 1078 號解釋者，主要係針對軍事審判程序進行中，
被告喪失現役軍人之身分後，究應依軍事審判程序或司法審判程序進行之疑
義所提出；惟喪失現役軍人身分之原因，除有現役軍人本身可控制之事由
（如：失蹤、任軍職以外之公職、自招傷殘、服役期滿志願退伍、另犯他案
致遭通緝、羈押或觀察勒戒等）外，亦有現役軍人本身不可抗力之事由；不
論是否係人爲控制，合法原因之離職離役，有於原因發生即當然生效而不待
人事作業核定者，亦有須待人事作業核定始生效者。據此，被告在某種程
度上似乎具有決定是否繼續維持現役軍人身分之權能；關於是否接受軍事審
判，在不採司法院院字第 1078 號解釋的法秩序下，即不免出現繫於被告本身
主觀意願之不安定現象。

在押逾三月者，依軍官士官服役條例之規定，應予辦理停役；且士兵逃亡經通緝及軍士官因案通緝等，應依兵役法或前開法律辦理停役；因此，遇重大案件無從於三個月內完成偵查及審判等情形中，若不採司法院院字第 1078 號解釋，軍事審判程序之進行勢將因前開停役規定而終止[70]。惟本文認為，在憲法第 9 條之規範下，軍事審判制度本有其「嚴肅軍中紀律，鞏固領導統御，增強部隊戰力之原則」[71] 等「保證軍事利益和提高軍

---

[70] 參閱謝添富、趙晞華，淺論軍事審判法修正後之若干法律問題及處理方式，律師雜誌，民國 89 年 7 月號，第 250 期，頁 41-2。

[71] 國防部自民國 83 年 7 月 9 日起，即邀集三軍各單位及聘請專家學者，以及司法院與法務部代表成立「軍事審判法研究修正委員會」，就「軍事審判法」作全面之檢討，其後司法院大法官會議於民國 86 年 10 月 3 日做成釋字第 436 號解釋，認為軍法機關所行使者為國家刑罰權之一種，並宣告舊有之「軍事審判法」部分條文與憲法意旨不符，國防部依此解釋，乃再作必要之修正，使軍事審判符合時代潮流，兼顧保障軍人權益之雙重目的。未來國防部仍將秉持嚴肅軍中紀律，鞏固領導統御，增強部隊戰力之原則，持續推動軍法法令之修正，並加強國軍官兵權益保障委員會之各項功能，以落實照顧國軍官兵之政策。「軍事審判法」於民國 88 年 10 月 2 日作全盤修正，及民國 91 年 1 月 30 日、92 年 6 月 11 日二次部分修正後，施行以來，雖無重大窒礙，惟為配合組織精進，軍事院檢之組織架構採三級二審，並以階級區分其管轄範圍，有進一步調整之需要。又「軍事審判法」係以職權進行主義為主要立法基礎，並採簡約立法之原則，大量準用「刑事訴訟法」之規定，然「刑事訴訟法」為採行改良式當事人進行主義，自民國 92 年 9 月 1 日修正施行後，於審判程序等方面作大幅度之修正，兩者之訴訟主義已有差異，相關配套程序亦有扞格，致「軍事審判法」產生能否準用及如何準用之爭議；為解決上開問題，杜絕爭議，實有再次修正之必要，國防部將秉持「保障人權，兼顧軍事特性」等基本原則，就前開問題再行檢討，使軍事審判發揮其肅正法紀及保障人權之功能。參閱國防部編，中華民國 93 年國防報告白皮書第七章，available at: http://report.mnd.gov.tw/chinese/7-22.htm (last visted, Sep. 29th, 2007)。

事效率」之功能目的[72]，人民一但喪失現役軍人身分後，不但已無續服軍事勤務之考量，亦無續受統帥權制約之必要，其於憲法第 8 條與第 16 條之基本權利亦再無因為維護軍譽[73]而膺受限制之理由，蓋如德國名將包狄辛所言，軍人為穿著軍服的國民[74]，其於憲法所應享有的權利義務，原則上除受法律限制外，其人身自由、生存權、工作權、財產權、訴願權、訴訟權、參政權等基本人權，理應與一般人民同受憲法之保障[75]；今憲法既已保障未著軍服之國民並無接受軍事審判之義務，則是否於訴訟上進行軍事審判程序，原即應以被告是否仍具現役軍人之身分為決定其受憲法第 16 條保障之訴訟權是否受侵害之

---

[72] 參閱常璇、田靜，法國軍事審判制度：軍事司法權?—于國家司法權，available at: http://www.people.com.cn/GB/junshi/1077/2442766.html (last visted, Sep. 29th, 2007)。我國一向認為，軍人負有保衛國家的神聖使命，軍隊以克敵致勝為首要，故軍人須服從軍令，而軍事審判具有貫徹軍令、嚴肅軍紀之特殊目的，自應與司法審判有所差異，參閱《法律案專輯第二百七十六輯—軍事審判法及軍事審判法施行法修正案》，頁 3，立法院公報處，民國 90 年 2 月。

[73] 有認為軍事審判機關立場洵以維護軍譽為首要目的。參閱薛欽峰，不要讓軍事審判淪為政策工具，available at: http://www.tahr.org.tw/site/data/comm/no2/page7.html (last visted, Sep. 29th, 2007)。

[74] 包狄辛將軍認為軍人是穿著軍服的公民，並強調軍人是基於公法的勤務關係而為國家的公務員之一，享有公務員的權利與義務，參閱陳新民，軍事憲法論，頁 163（揚智文化，2000.4 台北市）。

[75] 參閱呂啟元，軍事審判權之研究，財團法人國家政策研究基金會論文，available at: http://www.npf.org.tw/PUBLICATION/CL/091/CL-R-091-039.htm (last visted, Sep. 29th, 2007)。

前提[76]。不論停役、退伍或除役，只要是合法的離職離役，均足致其喪失現役軍人之身分；依釋字第 430 號解釋之說明，本質上軍人與國家間係存在公法上之職務關係，故現役軍人身分，除義務役外，實應為憲法所保障服公職權利所涵蓋，自權利之角度觀之，自得由當事人選擇放棄。既然現行兵役法及陸海空軍軍官士官服役條例之規定已將現役軍人本身可控制之事由明定為合法的離職離役事由，則於其範圍內，或已承認現役軍人享有決定是否接受軍事審判之權能。而於非志願性喪失現役軍人身分之情形中，既認其已不適於繼續服行軍人勤務，在被告喪失現役軍人身分後將該案件移送普通法院，亦難謂造成軍隊管理運作之障礙[77]。就憲法所建構之訴訟秩序而言，縱不對其繼續進行軍事審判程序，應無害於軍紀維護，亦不致對國

---

[76] 憲法第 16 條規定人民有訴訟之權，此即人民訴訟權之憲法保障。所謂訴訟權，係指人民權利遭受不法侵害時，得請求法院審判排除侵害或賠償，以維其權利之基本人權，其屬「司法人權」（Justizgrundrecht）或「受裁判之權利」。由於憲法上保障人民的各種實體性基本權，必須仰賴訴訟權方能確保，故凡憲法所保障之權利，遭受公權力或第三人之不法侵害，國家均應提供訴訟救濟之途徑，並由司法機關作終局之裁判，亦即國家應建構完整的司法體系。從而近代司法制度建立的主要目的，即在於保障基本人權，並透過權力分立原理，確保司法獨立，以具體審判權的達踐履，實現公平正義。因此，人民訴訟權的伸張，端賴法院代表國家適正行使審判權。參閱何子倫，軍事審判上訴制度之研究，財團法人國家政策研究基金會論文，available at: http://www.npf.org.tw/PUBLICATION/CL/091/CL-R-091-040.htm (last visted, Sep. 29th, 2007)。

[77] 就同為軍購弊案之聯勤採購案與海軍採購案而言，前者係依軍事審判，後者由普通法院審判；雖後者之運作無案件移送之關係，尚難謂海軍之軍紀管理因此出現重大之窒礙。

軍戰力有相當影響。

此外，關於普通法院法官對於軍事案件無法做出適當之判斷，而堅持軍事案件應交由軍法機關審判之論點。在德國基本法第 96 條修定時，德國學者 Lambertus Metzner 教授即曾自實證之觀點指出：純軍事性犯罪僅佔軍人犯罪態樣的一小部分，若為處斷純軍事犯罪，即於平時設立軍事刑事法院，殊不經濟，實際上軍人所犯之罪，亦以一般性及肇致交通事故之可罰行為佔多數，再就其中之軍事性犯罪而言，多數之犯行為恣意缺職及逃亡罪，普通法院審理這些案件並無困難，實無惟此設置特種法院之必要，上述軍人犯行種類與數目之概況，似乎也說明了所謂只有當法官與部隊共同生活，並熟悉部隊戰力等特性，方足以勝任處罰軍人之職務要求的見解，有待商榷[78]。因此將案件移送於普通法院，尚不致出現普通法院法官對於軍事案件無法做出適當判斷之現象。況且依軍事審判法第 5 條第 3 項之意旨，該等軍事犯罪亦由普通法院管轄，而移送普通法院後，在該條依行為時之身分適用實體法律（軍刑法）規範下，被告未必因此能獲判較輕的刑罰。

---

[78] 參閱蔡新毅，解構關於軍事審判之迷思，律師雜誌，第 250 期，頁 55，2000 年 7 月。

陸、以憲法第 9 條做為刑事審判權劃分之應然——代結論

關於刑事審判權歸屬在被告喪失現役軍人身分後應如何劃分之問題，本文在理解軍事審判程序，較之司法審判程序，在某些方面將對被告基本權利造成更為強烈地限制後，肯認即便在目前已修正後的軍事審判法制架構下，刑事審判權應如何歸屬仍屬一值得重視之重要議題。由於在實然面上，目前軍司法審判實務關於刑事審判權應如何歸屬係以司法院院字第 1078 號解釋為判斷標準，從而本文乃針對該號解釋之沿革及基礎，進行考證與探討。透過憲法最高性原則之法理，本文認為：在應然面上，既然憲法第 9 條規定：「人民除現役軍人外，不受軍事審判。」，一但被告於軍事審判程序繫屬中喪失現役軍人之身分，即無繼續接受軍事審判之義務。換言之，現役軍人於服役中犯軍刑法或其特別法之罪，亦於服役中被發覺，但於偵查、起訴或審理時已不具現役軍人身分者，應回歸憲法第 9 條之明文，立即終止軍事審判程序，並將該案件移送普通法院依刑事訴訟法規定進行。司法院院字第 1078 號解釋將因違反現行憲法第 9 條規定，而不再適用。至於因該號解釋停止適用後，關於軍事法院繫屬中案件於被告喪失現役軍人身分後應如何移送之法律漏洞，則可類推適用軍事審判法第 5 條第 1 項但書：「案件在追訴審判中離職離役者，初審案件應移送該管第一審之法院，上訴案件應移送該管第二審之法院審判。」之規定辦

理。從而,在這樣的觀點下,不少繫屬在軍事法院的案件,於
案件進行中將因被告喪失現役軍人身分而必須移送普通法院。
被告也得因移送普通法院後,避免源自前述「軍事審判程序應
否實行交互詰問之爭執」之不利益。

　　基於前述說明,本文認為,在憲法第 9 條之規範下,軍事
審判程序進行與否將繫屬於被告是否仍具有現役軍人身分之
上。從而軍事審判之範圍亦將限縮至「本質上易於速審速結之
案件」,蓋若非屬本質上易於速審速結之案件,案件之偵查或
審理難免會因繁雜而導致被告在案件推移過程中喪失現役軍人
之身分。軍事審判雖因此而無法對複雜之案件作出「本案判
決」,惟於訴訟前階段之偵查、審理程序中,證據之調查與保
全實係本案判決能否妥適、正確的重要基礎,因此在複雜案件
之處理上,軍法機關即應將偵審之重心置於證據保全部分,以
求充分發揮軍法機關之司法功能。果如此,則不但如前述劉岳
龍案所引發軍司法機關間之爭執將因該案件必須移送普通法院
而不存在,將複雜難解之案件於被告喪失現役軍人身分後移送
普通法院管轄(通常為涉及採購等貪瀆案件或其他社會矚目之
重大案件),亦符權力分立結構下,司法監督之憲政目的。而
採本文將重大軍事案件交司法機關審理之主張,除具可防止當
權者透過人事調動任免等權力[79],不當地影響軍法機關之司法

---

[79] 按目前軍法官仍由現役軍人擔任,其任職調動須受階級、停年等拘束。若未
占高缺,尚有年限退伍之壓力。在此結構下,上級長官似有可能透過年限退
伍之壓力,影響軍法人員之職務行為。

職能（例如：指示軍法單位盡量不進行偵查中或審理中之案件，或是遲遲不起訴或不判決）之優點外，在軍事案件終審已回歸普通法院審理的法制下，尚不致對現行司法審判實務造成負面影響，則以捍衛憲法為宗旨之大法官們或最高法院諸先進等，似可考慮正式宣告司法院院字第 1078 號解釋不再適用，而將軍司法審判權歸屬之劃分，真正地交由憲法第 9 條來處理。（本文前身「憲法第 9 條刑事審判權歸屬劃分之實然與應然」曾發表於 96.03 台灣法學會 2007 刑事法學新銳講座系列研討會）

12 非常上訴制度中「審判違背法令」意義之初探

一兼論最高法院 79 年台非字第 246 號判決之商榷

壹、前　言

　　刑事訴訟是確定國家對於人民刑罰權有無之制度，基於法律安定性之要求，凡刑事案件一經判決確定，即應受到一事不再理原則之支配，任何人均不能再循通常之刑事訴訟程序予以爭執，以維法的安定性。惟判決者，乃出於法官之判斷，法官亦為人也，難免因七情六慾，愛恨向背，影響其專業素養而使判斷發生錯誤。此時若堅持「法的安定性」而對所發生之錯誤均不加以救濟，亦與刑事訴訟所要求之具體正義有違。刑事案件當事人被告之利益若因此違法、錯誤之判斷而致其侵害無法回復時，難免憤恨不平，進而不信賴司法，使司法威信受到嚴重損害。故刑事訴訟制度在一定之條件下，允許於判決發生錯誤時，賦予救濟程序，此即非常上訴程序所由設之原因。

　　按判決確定後，發現該案件之審判係違背法令者，最高法

院之檢察長（現為檢察總長）得向最高法院提起非常上訴，刑事訴訟法第 441 條定有明文。是故，必以「該案件之審判係違背法令」為由，方得准許非常上訴之提起。惟「審判違背法令」應為如何解釋，實影響非常上訴之得否提起及其提起有無理由。通常言之，咸認非常上訴制度專為糾正原確定判決適用法令之錯誤，藉以統一法令之適用為主旨；實務上更常見以：「非常上訴審應以原確定之事實為基礎，僅就原判決所認定之事實，審核其適用法令有無違誤」[1] 來說明非常上訴審對原審所確定之事實得加以審酌之權限。然而對於原確定判決關於事實認定有錯誤時，可否認係「該案件之審判係違背法令」，並藉提起非常上訴之方式來對該「事實認定之錯誤」加以制度上之救濟？法無明文可據；實務上雖常以上述觀點為據，學者間並進而更謂：「……，如因認定事實之錯誤或不明時，至適用法令有無違背發生疑義時，此項事實並非非常上訴審所得糾正」[2]。惟觀乎歷年來有關之解釋[3]，實難求得一有體系、符邏輯之說明。本文之作，導源於最高法院 79 年台非字第 246 號案件之基本事實及對其所作判決理由說明之質疑，並祈自公平正義之觀點出發，對上述問題加以分析探討，冀求於非常上訴中「審判係違背法令」一詞定義之釐清。

---

[1]　如本文所引之最高法院 79 年台非字第 246 號判決即一適例。
[2]　參閱陳樸生氏著，刑事訴訟法實務第 557 頁。
[3]　如釋字第 146 號、第 181 號解釋。

貳、案例事實摘要

　　被告 A 因妨害公務案件，經臺灣新竹地方法院於 76 年 10 月 23 日以 76 年度易字第 1506 號判處有期徒刑六月，緩刑三年，同年 11 月 23 日確定在案，詎案外人 B 於 77 年 12 月底某日，在台北市中山北路二段台北市政府警察局中山分局前地下道出入口，拾獲 A 所有之駕駛執照乙枚，乃意圖為自己不法之所有，將該駕駛執照據為己有，並加以變造，換貼其本人照片，並基於概括之犯意，連續假冒 A 名義使用。嗣 B 於 78 年 2 月 23 日，另在台北縣新莊市行竊，為警查獲，仍持變造之 A 駕駛執照假冒身分應訊，同日台北縣警察局新莊分局將 B 以 A 名義移送台灣板橋地方法院檢察署以 78 年度偵字第 1955 號提起公訴，經台灣板橋地方法院以 78 年度易字第 921 號判處有期徒刑六月確定，嗣聲請人誤以為 A 在緩刑期內更犯罪，受有期徒刑以上刑之宣告，爰聲請撤銷緩刑，並經臺灣新竹地方法院於 78 年 6 月 5 日以 78 年度撤緩字第 36 號裁定撤銷緩刑，並於 82 年 10 月 19 日確定。而上開 B 偽造署押部分亦經台灣台北地方法院以 78 年度易字第 3803 號判處有期徒刑八月確定，台灣板橋地方法院始根據台灣台北地方法院 78 年度易字第 3803 號判決，以 79 年度聲字第 430 號裁定更正該院 78 年度易字第 921 號判決原本及正本所載之「A」為「B」。復查台灣台北地

方法院曾以 78 年度訴字第 245 號判處 A 竊盜無罪[4]在案。因之
臺灣新竹地方法院 78 年度撤緩字第 36 號撤銷緩刑宣告之裁定
所憑之台灣板橋地方法院 78 年度易字第 921 號判決，已為其後
之裁定所更正。是則臺灣新竹地方法院 78 年度撤緩字第 36 號
撤銷緩刑宣告之裁定，其憑以裁判之基礎事實與原審加以援以
裁判之法文間，即難謂適當無訛。嗣臺灣新竹地方法院檢察署
於 78 年度執減更字第 127 號執行案件中發現上述誤判事實，為
求救濟因法院審判作業之疏失所可能造成之人權侵害（令 A 服
其原毋需服之刑），遂以 79 年度聲非字第 24 號聲請書，聲請
最高法院檢察署提起非常上訴[5]。案經最高法院檢察署於 79 年
10 月 19 日（七九）台正字第 10377 號函送最高法院提起非常
上訴；同年 11 月 23 日，最高法院 79 年台非字第 246 號判決駁
回非常上訴。

---

[4]　同於台灣板橋地方法院檢察署 78 年度偵字第 1955 號起訴案件之犯罪事實。

[5]　理由略以：A 未緩刑期內更犯罪，而係受 B 冒名應訊之累，是 A 非於緩刑期
間更受有期徒刑以上刑之宣告。原臺灣新竹地方法院 78 年度撤緩字第 36 號
撤銷緩刑宣告之裁定，與刑法第 75 條第 1 項第 1 款撤銷緩刑之規定不符，參
照最高法院 44 年台非字第 41 號判例之要旨，茲依刑事訴訟法第 442 條之規
定請求對臺灣新竹地方法院 78 年度撤緩字第 36 號撤銷緩刑宣告之裁定提起
非常上訴。

參、最高法院 79 年台非字第 246 號判決要旨

第查最高法院 79 年台非字第 246 號判決旨以:「按非常上訴審應以原判決確認之事實為基礎,以裁判其適用法律有無違誤。至非常上訴審所得調查之事實,僅以關於訴訟程序、法院管轄、免訴事由及訴訟之受理者為限。本件被告 A 前因妨害公務案,經臺灣新竹地方法院於 76 年 10 月 23 日以 76 年度易字第 1506 號判處有期徒刑六月,緩刑三年,同年 11 月 23 日確定。案外人 B 因竊盜案被獲,變造 A 遺失之駕駛執照,冒名應訊,經台灣板橋地方法院以 A 名義對 B 判處六月確定。檢察官固誤以 A 於緩刑期內更犯罪,受有期徒刑以上刑之宣告,向法院聲請撤銷前判決關於緩刑之宣告。然原法院係依檢察官提出之 A 妨害公務案及 A 竊盜案之確定判決,二人之性別、出生年月日、身分證統一編號、住居所完全相同,因認定 A 於緩刑期內更犯竊盜案且經判處六月徒刑確定之事實,而裁定前案之緩刑宣告予以撤銷,經核其認事用法,並無違背法令之可言。至嗣後原審判 A 竊盜案之法院,雖發現係 B 盜用 A 之姓名年籍應訊,致誤認犯罪者為 A,乃以裁定將被告乙欄之記載更正,並告確定。然此項錯誤既發生在原裁定後,且非原裁定法院依據原案資料適用法則錯誤,非常上訴審無從進行調查未經原確定裁判認定之事實,本件非常上訴難認有理。」為由,駁回非常上訴。

檢視最高法院 79 年台非字第 246 號判決駁回非常上訴之理由，實可歸納為二點：

（一）、原裁定法院係依檢察官提出之 A 妨害公務案及 A 竊盜案之確定判決而作成，茲因二人之性別、出生年月日、身分證統一編號、住居所完全相同，因認定 A 於緩刑期內更犯竊盜案且經判處六月徒刑確定之事實，爰裁定前案之緩刑宣告予以撤銷，經核其認事用法，並無違背法令之可言；

（二）、嗣後原審判 A 竊盜案之法院，雖發現係 B 盜用 A 之姓名年籍應訊，致誤認犯罪者為 A，乃以裁定將被告乙欄之記載更正，並告確定。然此項錯誤既發生在原裁定後，且非原裁定法院依據原案資料適用法則錯誤，非常上訴審無從進行調查未經原確定裁判認定之事實。

然而，非常上訴審是否必須完全依據原審所確認之事實加以裁判？或者必須完全依據原審卷證內已存之資料而為裁判？觀之法無明文規定。惟如欲求得上述二命題之解決，即應自刑事訴訟法中對於非常上訴所為規定及非常上訴制度旨以建立所憑之「統一法令解釋與適用之目的」為出發，來探尋所謂「案件審判違背法令」之意義、範圍，進而探討上述二命題是否為其所指之內容及範圍。

肆、非常上訴制度之源起、意義、目的及功能

　　查法律適用之正確與否，究數法官之職責，除案件當事人可對未確定之判決依審級制度請求救濟外，對於已確定之判決，法院亦建立一自我審查內部救濟程序，此則「非常上訴制度」所由設也。非常上訴制度，源於法國之「為公益上訴」及「為法律上訴」二者；而我國之非常上訴制度，即仿自日本所設之非常上告制度[6]。非常上訴乃係判決確定後，以審判違背法令為理由，而行之非常救濟程序；因其以違背法令為理由，專以統一法令之解釋與適用為主要目的；對案件為具體性救濟乃成為附隨性目的。詳言之，於在判決之具體性方面之法的安定性，與在法秩序之抽象性方面之法之安定性發生矛盾之情形，寧顧後者而捨前者，即屬非常上訴制度之意義所在。是則透過非常上訴制度所欲救濟者，乃是於具體個案中受違法判決所扭曲的法之公平正義，以求裁判本身之適法性、妥當性及公平性。從而，非常上訴審之判決，原則上，效力不及於被告，新判決只具有形式上或理論上之效力；故非常上訴制度，以一般言之，並不危害在判決之具體性方面之法的安定性；只有在原

---

[6]　惟現行刑事訴訟法除第 447 條第 2 項為我國所獨有之規定外，餘均為承襲日本舊刑事訴訟法非常上告制度有關之規定。

判決不利於被告之例外情形中[7]，為公平起見，非常上訴審之判決[8] 始具有實體上或現實上之效力。

伍、「案件之審判係違背法令」之意義及範圍

刑事訴訟法第 441 條規定：「判決確定後，發現該案件之審判係違背法令者，最高法院之檢察總長得向最高法院提起非常上訴。」是知非常上訴之有理由者，必以「該案件之審判違背法令」。案件經由法院所得審判者，無非「實體事實」及「訴訟程序事實」二者。而所謂之「審判」，乃審理與裁判之意。亦即，不僅判決本身違背法令時，得成為非常上訴之理由；同時，於判決前之訴訟程序違背法令時，亦得成為非常上訴之理由。蓋非常上訴既以統一法令之解釋與適用為主要目的，則刑事訴訟法第 441 條中所謂之審判違背法令，其範圍自應涵蓋判決與整個審判程序。是則，得為非常上訴之客體者有「判決」、「裁定[9]」及「訴訟程序」三者；而最高法院得依非常上訴程序對原判決加以糾正者，必以「原審判決本身之違背

7　刑事訴訟法第 448 條。

8　即撤銷原判後之另行判決。

9　依最高法院 44 年台非字第 41 號判例要旨認其包含實體裁定。

法令」或「原審訴訟程序之違背法令」爲由。

　　非常上訴審，應就非常上訴理由所指謫之事項，調查裁判之，此觀刑事訴訟法第 445 條第 1 項之規定自明。從而非常上訴理由所指謫之事項，即便非訴訟程序之違背法令亦當屬判決本身之違背法令。然而，何謂「判決違背法令」？何謂「訴訟程序違背法令」？按「判決違背法令」者，自設置非常上訴制度之主要目的在於統一法令之解釋適用而言，係指其判決對於確定事實之援用法令，與當時應適用之法令有違背者而言[10]。按刑事訴訟法第 378 條明定判決違背法令爲：「判決不適用法則或適用不當者」；此外，刑事訴訟法第 379 條更列舉 14 款當然違背法令之事由。則依刑事訴訟法第 445 條第 2 項準用同法第 394 條第 1 項之規定可知，「判決違背法令」一詞自應包含刑事訴訟法第 378 條所定「判決不適用法則或適用不當者」及刑事訴訟法第 379 條列舉之 14 款當然違背法令之事由。

　　而所謂訴訟程序，乃指對於具體之犯罪，對被告應爲如何追訴，如何處罰所設之程序，故訴訟程序違背法令所違背者應僅限於程序法，不及於實體法；通常言之，應包含二種情形。其一爲，單純之訴訟程序違背法令；亦即，對訴訟上之事實雖無誤認，但因對訴訟法本身之適用有錯誤，而產生訴訟程序違背法令之情形。其二爲，因對訴訟上之事實有誤認，以致產生訴訟程序違背法令之情形。於前者之情形，當然，須指摘其錯

10　最高法院 25 年非字第 139 號判例參照。

誤，並撤銷違背法令之部分，以警惕將來再犯相同之錯誤。而
於後者之情形，因嗣後如不再誤認事實，則未必再有違背法令
之情事發生；按對訴訟程序違背法令所為之撤銷，既不具有救
濟該具體案件之效果，而僅於為將來之警惕，則於後者之情
形，似無必要撤銷違背法令部分之訴訟程序。然而，關於訴訟
法上之事實認定，並不明示於判決，故究竟有無訴訟法上事實
之誤認，實難加以辨別；因之，對於後者之情形，亦不得不對
該違背法令之部分為撤銷處分。同時，即使於後者之情形，明
白宣示違背法令係因誤認訴訟法上之事實所致，並對違背之部
分加以撤銷，仍將對將來之訴訟發生警惕之作用。刑事訴訟法
第 445 條第 2 項所以明定準用刑事訴訟法第 394 條第 1 項所規
定者，乃在於承認對訴訟法上之事實，非常上訴審得於調查
事實後，自行認定之[11]。惟學者間亦有認：「原訴訟程序違
法，不影響判決者，不得提起非常上訴[12]。」、「訴訟程序
的違法，應視其違法是否影響判決的結果，來決定可否提起
非常上訴，並非不問情由，一概都可提起[13]。」。而司法院
大法官會議所作釋字第 238 號解釋所認：「……其非上述情形
之證據，未於調查者，本不屬上開第 10 款之範圍（依本法應於

---

[11]　參閱黃東熊氏著，刑事訴訟法論第 679 頁。

[12]　參閱陳樸生氏著，刑事訴訟法實務第 556 頁、林山田氏著，刑事訴訟法第 458
頁、褚劍鴻氏著，刑事訴訟法論第 634 頁。

[13]　參閱陳涵氏著，四十年來之非常上訴；收載於當代法學名家論文集第 345 頁
以下。

審判期日調查之證據），縱其訴訟程序違背法令，惟如應受同法第 380 條之限制者，既不得據以提起第三審上訴，自不得為非常上訴之理由。……」亦同此見解。然因非常上訴制度非如通常上訴制度係以對個案之救濟為主要目的。因此，就訴訟程序違背法令言之，第三審上訴理由與非常上訴理由，即應有所不同。按刑事訴訟法第 394 條第 1 項但書所規定者雖僅係「得調查事實」而非「應調查事實」，然此僅應解為於具刑事訴訟法第 380 條訴訟程序違背法令而顯然於判決無影響者之情形時，為免第三審法院於審級救濟程序中踐履已顯無必要之調查事實程序所設之便宜規定，不宜以此做為第三審法院得任意為事實調查之法律依據[14]。惟因非常上訴制度本身並無審級救濟之使命與功能，且其目的係在糾正法令適用之違誤，以統一法令之解釋及適用。故實不應據刑事訴訟法第 380 條即謂於原訴訟程序違法，不影響判決者，不得提起非常上訴。亦即，刑事訴訟法第 380 條之規定，並不適用於非常上訴審；只要原審審判對法令之適用或解釋有錯，即構成非常上訴之理由，而不問原審之結果是否有錯。易言之，以非常上訴之性質觀之，只要原審之訴訟程序有違背法令，即得成為非常上訴之理由，而不問其是否對判決有影響[15]。

　　然而因審判違背法令之情形多端，有必須予以救濟者，亦

---

[14]　即其仍須於判決理由中說明如何顯無影響於判決。

[15]　參閱黃東熊氏著，刑事訴訟法論第 681 頁。

有不須予以救濟者[16]。就刑事政策而言，若均對之提起非常上訴，有時反致司法資源之浪費。是故刑事訴訟法第 441 條之規定，係檢察總長「得」向最高法院提起非常上訴（而非「應」向最高法院提起非常上訴），即法律將此審酌之權限，賦予檢察總長，由其多方考量後，決定是否提起，以收法律救濟之實效[17]。惟檢察總長所審酌考量應否提起非常上訴者，應以提起非常上訴之提起是否具「救濟實效」為斷，而非以該審判違背法令是否對該判決有影響為其決定因素；只是就結果面而言，往往於訴訟程序違背法令不影響判決者，檢察總長即本於其職權，否決掉提起非常上訴之聲請而已。然則此點實乃因非常上訴之提起係採便宜主義所致，並不表示非常上訴之提起端賴訴訟程序之違法不影響於判決也。或謂：「……縱未予說明，致其訴訟程序有所違背，惟既於判決顯無影響，，自仍應受刑事訴訟法第 380 條之限制，不得據為非常上訴之理由[18]。」，惟刑事訴訟法第 380 條既不適用於非常上訴審之程序，則其見解實有倒果為因，忽略非常上訴與第三審上訴間差異之弊，自不足採。

　　此外，於非常上訴審中所謂「判決違背法令」者，其範圍實應異於第三審上訴審中所謂之「判決違背法令」。蓋「判

16　如在某些案件，雖對之提起非常上訴，但判決結果毫無實益。

17　參閱陳涵氏著，四十年來之非常上訴；收載於當代法學名家論文集第 345 頁以下。

18　參閱最高法院 82 年台非字第 156 號判決。

決」屬訴訟程序中之一環，通常言之，爲終結訴訟所不可或缺之程序，職故判決違背法令實難解免於訴訟程序違背法令之一種類型。此觀於刑事訴訟法第 379 條所列舉 14 款「判決當然違背法令」之上訴第三審事由中，亦含訴訟程序之違背法令[19]可知。又自非常上訴旨以統一法令之解釋及適用之本旨觀之，其不具審級制度中審級救濟之色彩，不言可諭。因之，於非常上訴審中，不應完全依據第三審程序所應行之訴訟程序而爲非常上訴程序之進行，此觀刑事訴訟法第 445 條第 2 項之規定係「準用」而非「適用」刑事訴訟法第 394 條之規定亦明。從而，只要不屬前所述「單純之訴訟程序違背法令」或「因對訴訟法上之事實有誤認，以致產生訴訟程序違背法令之情形」，皆應認非常上訴理由中所指謫之事項係屬判決違背法令事項。蓋依刑事訴訟法第 448 條之規定，惟有在該案件屬「判決違背法令」之情形，非常上訴審所爲之判決，其效力方及於被告。爲避免被告因法院認事用法違誤而致本身利害受到侵害時無法適時獲得救濟，自當採此見解，方爲洽當。

　　另一方面，關於非常上訴理由中所指謫之事項，究屬「判決違背法令」？抑或「訴訟程序違背法令」？法雖無明文規定，惟觀乎司法院大法官會議所作釋字第 181 號解釋：「……。依法應於審判期日調查之證據，未於調查，致適用法

---

19 諸如第 4 款：法院所認管轄之有係不當、第 5 款：法院受理訴訟或不受理訴訟係不當……等。

令違誤，而顯然於判決有影響者，該項確定判決，即屬判決違背法令，應有刑事訴訟法第 447 條第 1 項第 1 款規定之適用。」及依據最高法院於民國 29 年 2 月 22 日所作成之總決議：「……訴訟程序違背法令，雖影響於判決；但並非足認原審應為其他判決者，僅為訴訟程序違背法令……」，實可知其應以「是否應為其他判決而不為其他判決」為判斷是否違背法令之依據。按原審於「應為其他判決而不為其他判決」時所為之判決，自難解免於法令之違背。於實務上最高法院 68 年台非字第 50 號判例亦曾指出：「對於已判決確定之各罪，已經裁定定其應執行刑者，如又重覆定其應執行之刑，自係違反一事不再理之原則，即屬違背法令，對於後裁定，得提起非常上訴。」。第查本案例中原審之所以重覆定其應執行之刑，無非對於原應調查之證據[20]漏未調查審認，否則法院當不致為此重覆裁定之錯誤；其所以認為對於後裁定，得提起非常上訴者，莫不因其程序上漏未調查已構成訴訟程序之違法；而其後重覆裁定之效力，之所以不及於原案之被告，似應解為原審訴訟程序已足致「應為其他裁定（駁回原聲請）而不為其他裁定」也，否則若只認其屬程序上之違背法令，依刑事訴訟法第 448 條之規定，判決效力當不致及於原案之被告。而於作上述解釋時，不論自「透過非常上訴制度所欲救濟者係於具體個案中受

---

[20] 例如：對於已判決確定之各罪，已經裁定定其應執行刑之事實。

違法判決所扭曲的法之公平正義」之觀點出發，抑或自「避免
被告因法院認事用法違誤而致本身利害受到不當侵害」之角度
檢視，不僅符合非常上訴制度之立法精神，於原審應為其他判
決而不為其他判決時，為免原案被告被不當侵害之權益無法回
復，認其屬「判決違背法令」，亦不失為一妥適之方法。從
而，以非常上訴理由中所指謫之事項是否足認原審「應為其他
判決而不為其他判決」來判斷究屬「判決違背法令」或「訴訟
程序違背法令」，於法於理，實無悖離。

陸、最高法院 79 年台非字第 246 號判決之商榷

　　綜上所述，最高法院 79 年台非字第 246 號判決所持以駁回
非常上訴之理由，實值斟酌。查其認：「原裁定係基於臺灣新
竹地方法院 76 年易字第 1506 號判決及臺灣板橋地方法院 78 年
易字第 921 號判決而作成，是以認定 A 於緩刑期內更犯它罪而
裁定撤銷前案之緩刑宣告之部分，其認事用法，並無違
誤。」。然則此點只不過足認原「裁定」本身之適用法令無違
誤爾 [21]。惟 A 是否於緩刑期內更犯它罪係刑法第 75 條第 1 項第
1 款明定所憑據以撤銷緩刑宣告之基礎事實；亦即屬得否適用

---

[21] 即不構成刑事訴訟法第 378 條、379 條所定之判決違背法令。

刑法第 75 條第 1 項之基礎事實。依釋字第 238 號所爲之解釋：
「……，指該證據在客觀上爲法院認定事實及適用法律之基礎
者而言。……」。亦即只要是法院認定事實所應據之證據[22]，
應認具備「調查之必要性」而屬刑事訴訟法第 379 條第 10 款所
指證據之範圍。蓋法院於裁判前應盡調查之能事；依同法第 2
條第 1 項之規定，亦應於被告有利或不利之情形，一律注意
也。惟學者間有認：「既曰案件之審判係違背法令，其專在糾
正法律錯誤，至爲明顯……，關於事實之認定，如因認定事實
之錯誤或不明時，至適用法令有無違背發生疑義時，此項事實
並非非常上訴審所得糾正」[23]。按非常上訴審亦屬法律審，關
於實體法上之事實，因其係決定刑事責任之存否及刑罰權應予
如何實現之問題，須經嚴格的證明，非常上訴審自無從爲必要
之調查，而應受確定判決所認定之事實之拘束。從而非常上訴
意旨爲證明其主張之實體法之適用所提出之有關證據，非常上
訴審自不得逕就該證據爲原確定判決實體法適用當否之判斷而
予以調查。此點觀乎最高法院 25 年非字第 29 號判例：「因之
以調查實體法上事實爲前題之非常上訴，自難認有理由。」亦
明。惟自司法院大法官會議所作釋字第 146 號解釋：「刑事判
決確定後，發現認定犯罪事實與所採用證據顯屬不符，自屬審
判違背法令，得提起非常上訴，……」可知：雖非常上訴審無

---

[22] 即該事實之存否對判決之結果顯有重大影響者。
[23] 參閱陳樸生氏著，刑事訴訟法實務第 557 頁。

法逕就所指證據為原確定判決實體法適用當否之判斷,但只要發現認定犯罪事實與所採用證據顯屬不符,即可認定其屬「審判違背法令」,而得允對其提起非常上訴。亦即關於訴訟程序部分,並非可謂非常上訴審法院不得對原審所應踐行之程序事項為調查審認:蓋原審之審判違背法令多出於不自知之情形,其間或有於原案卷證內可發現者,惟大多數之情形,均難見於原案卷內,從而,於非常上訴審法院對原審所應踐行之程序事項為調查時,其得加以審酌之範圍,應不限於已存於原案卷證內者;蓋判決違背法令者,參照刑事訴訟法第 393 條但書第 2 款、第 4 款、第 5 款前段所為規定,有時乃因誤認事實所引起;於此情形下,非常上訴法院如不就實體法上之事實為調查證據,便無從得知判決有無違背法令[24]。其既屬得依職權調查之事項,則原「應行訴訟程序」究否踐行,自得依刑事訴訟法第 393 條、第 394 條第 1 項但書之規定而依職權主動為事實之調查;是故,非常上訴審法院即便應以原審所認定之事實為基礎,惟對原判決所以認定事實之訴訟程序,並非毫無審酌之餘地。觀乎最高法院 82 年台非字第 156 號判決:「依法應於審判期日調查之證據未予調查,致適用法令違誤而顯然於判決有所影響者,固屬判決違背法令,但此所稱應調查之證據,係指與待證事實有重要之關係,在客觀上有其調查之必要性者而言。若非此所稱之證據而未與調查,本不屬上開所稱應調查證據之

---

24 參閱黃東熊氏著,刑事訴訟法論第 633 頁。

範圍，當亦不生訴訟程序違背法令之問題。……」，亦當明瞭。；從而原最高法院 79 年台非字第 246 號判決所云：「然此項錯誤[25]既發生在原裁定後，且非原裁定法院依據原案資料適用法則錯誤，非常上訴審無從進行調查未經原確定裁判認定之事實。」，即屬可議。按 B 盜用 A 之姓名年籍所應訊之竊盜案件，其審判權仍係對 B 行使，不因 B 冒用 A 之姓名年籍應訊而謂對 B 不發生訴訟繫屬之關係[26]。職故，A 未於緩刑期內更受有期徒刑以上刑之宣告者，實可確定。依法應於審判期日調查之證據[27]而未予調查者，無論其發現之時點為何，莫非導源於原審法院為訴訟程序之疏漏所致；或謂：「原臺灣新竹地方法院 78 年度撤緩字第 36 號裁定基於臺灣新竹地方法院 76 年度易字第 1506 號、臺灣板橋地方法院 78 年度易字第 921 號二判決而認定 A 於緩刑期內更受有期徒刑以上刑之宣告部分，其認事用法並無違誤。」，然原臺灣板橋地方法院 78 年度易字第 921 號判決本身誤 B 為 A 之錯誤，並不能阻卻於原判決（裁定）程序中對應調查事項為調查之義務，蓋錯誤之判決本身不過有形式之確定力爾。其既屬原審法院訴訟程序上之疏漏，自難解免於訴訟程序之違背法令。否則，待其錯誤之判決已為其後臺灣板橋地方法院 78 年度易字第 921 號裁定所更正時，原撤

---

[25] 即嗣後原審判 A 竊盜案之法院，發現係 B 盜用 A 之姓名年籍應訊，致誤認犯罪者為 A，乃以裁定將被告乙欄之記載更正。

[26] 參閱蔡墩銘氏朱石炎氏合著，刑事訴訟法第 36 頁

[27] 關於 A 是否於緩刑期內更受有期徒刑以上刑之宣告。

銷緩刑之臺灣新竹地方法院 78 年度撤緩字第 36 裁定不惟失其所據，其因之所造成之違誤狀態[28]，亦無從加以救。果惟如此，不啻將法律所追求之公平正義，淪為文字邏輯論戰之犧牲品矣。

　　於刑事訴訟制度採行職權進行主義之國家，訴訟程序上之疏漏實不應歸責於為被告之當事人，而應由為審判之「司法」負起補正該疏漏之責任；倘若因此而使為被告之當事人受有若何之不利益，甚或因此侵害人權，實不足以保障人民憲法上基本權益，亦不足以贏得人民對於司法之信賴。法院對於應調查之事項（該事項顯有重大影響於判決之結果）漏未調查，應屬法院本身義務之違反，而於錯誤發生後，竟不急思其補救管道，卻因此反謂：「既發生在原裁定後非原裁定法院依據原案資料適用法則錯誤，非常上訴審無從進行調查未經原確定裁判認定之事實。」，而將造成此疏漏之責任諉由為被告之當事人加以承受，洵非正當。再者，關於應調查之證據，不論是否存於原審訴訟案卷內，參照前開說明[29]，原審對其未加以調查斟酌適足以構成應踐行程序之違反而屬訴訟程序之違背法令；基於最高法院民國 29 年 2 月 22 日所作成之總決議：「……訴訟程序違背法令，雖影響於判決；但並非足認原審應為其他判決

---

[28]　亦即 A 不應被撤銷緩刑卻遭撤銷緩刑。

[29]　調查於裁判所據以成立之基礎事實應踐履之程序——即於法條構成要件成立與否有重大影響事實之調查程序——自應屬得依職權調查之事項。

者，僅爲訴訟程序違背法令……」以原審「是否應爲其他判決而不爲其他判決」爲判斷是否屬「判決違背法令」依據之見解，當可認原審疏漏於原案卷證外「應調查之證據」時，足以該當非常上訴審中所謂「判決違背法令」。是則臺灣新竹地方法院 78 年度撤緩字第 36 號撤銷緩刑宣告之裁定，自爲非常上訴所應加以糾正之對象。非常上訴審忽略於此，其見解實難贊同。

從而，臺灣新竹地方法院檢察署於 79 年度聲非字第 24 號聲請書，聲請最高法院檢察署提起非常上訴所持理由[30]，應值贊同。非常上訴審法院應撤銷臺灣新竹地方法院 78 年度撤緩字第 36 號撤銷緩刑宣告之裁定，並另行爲駁回聲請人撤銷緩刑宣告之聲請，方爲妥當適法。

柒、檢討與建議（代結論）

對於確定判決之救濟，於現行法體制中，只有再審及非常上訴二管道可資援引；按再審乃對於確定判決有事實認定上之重大錯誤時，所設之救濟方法；然非常上訴則係針對判決違背法令所設置之救濟制度。依司法院大法官會議所作釋字第 146

---

[30] A 未於緩刑期內更犯罪，而係受 B 冒名應訊之累，是則 A 非於緩刑期間更受有期徒刑以上刑之宣告。原臺灣新竹地方法院 78 年度撤緩字第 36 號撤銷緩刑宣告之裁定，與刑法第 75 條第 1 項第 1 款撤銷緩刑之規定不符，……。

號解釋：「得提起非常上訴之審判違背法令，如其具再審原因者，仍可依再審程序聲請再審……。」可知，二種「非常救濟程序」間應各自依其是否成立而運行，彼此間並不具互相排斥之關係。蓋依刑事訴訟法第 420 條、第 421 條、第 422 條之規定，法律乃以列舉之方式對再審之提起加以限制。而於非常上訴，只以概括之「審判違背法令」為其條件。從而，即便對確定判決有事實認定之錯誤發生時，再審所得加以救濟者，實有其限界所在。雖非常上訴制度之本旨非於救濟認定事實違誤；然則，於原審認定事實之程序有違誤時，並非不得認其為「審判違背法令」而藉由非常上訴之提起加以救濟。是以，並不能以非常上訴之本意非在為救濟認定事實違誤為理由，而主張於原確定判決認定事實有錯誤時，不得依非常上訴制度之手段作為救濟原確定判決認定事實有錯誤之管道；只要其情形符合非常上訴之要件（案件審判違背法令），即應允其所請。法院之設置不惟在維護法規範正確之運作，抑有進者，乃在於人民訴訟權之保障，藉以避免人民之基本權利受到不當之侵害。是以法律制度之運作，亦應以「法規範之正確運作」、「人民訴訟權之保障」為目的，以求不違法律制定之本意。法院對於法律制度之運作，基於公平、正義、合目的性及合憲性之考量，應盡可能求於該制度內解決實際上所面對的問題；方符司法制度人權保障之要求。尤其當該問題係肇因於法院本身之疏失時，更應汲汲於違誤本身之補救，自解決問題之角度出發，本於法之公平正義，在現行法律體制中尋求合法、合理、合國民法律

感情之法律適用；祈求解決已發生錯誤之遺憾；而不應一味自盡速結案之角度，因循於所謂的「通說」、「判例」而不顧程序正義與實體正義的基本要求。惟有如此，方可求法院於所為法律適用之過程中，贏得人民對司法之尊重與信賴；爾等所追求「法治國」之目標，方有來臨之一日。

　　本文之作，以法條文義為經，以實務見解為緯，祈能對非常上訴制度中「審判違背法令」之內涵，作一體系化之概念釐清。惟著者學植為深，為文論述，諸多不當；尚請先進賢達，不吝指正。（本文為 85.12 第一屆務實法學論文獎得獎作品）

附錄：驚見司法「秘密」改革？

　　據悉司法院透過立法委員提案擬增訂法院組織法第 17 條之 2 第 2 項規定，授權司法事務官得承法官之命，辦理民事訴訟爭點整理、刑事訴訟勘察證物以及彙整當事人於準備程序所表示的意見以及其他經司法院所指定之事務。查其修正理由主要係以前述事項較不具訟爭性，適合由司法事務官擔任為主要說明基礎。乍看之下，前述修正理由並未違憲法上「由獨立且中立司法機關處理訟爭事項」之權力分立原理。惟若仔細分析修正條文內涵，卻不免產生憲法上法官保留原則是否已遭受立法實質侵害之違憲疑慮，實有進一步釐清之必要。

　　按法官保留原指刑事訴訟之強制處分（例如羈押）須由法官審理並同意後，檢察官或是司法警察才能執行之意；廣義而言，亦包含所有訟爭性事項應由獨立中立司法機關（包含仲裁）決定之意。因此，只要涉及訟爭性事項，原則上均應由法官解決爭議，不具法官身分之行政官（含檢察官），因其身分之中立性與獨立性不足，本不應行使紛爭解決之司法權。雖然司法院大法官釋字第 639 號解釋允許法院合議庭授權個別法官獨任行使羈押權，亦因被授權者具有法官身分，而未違法官保

留原則。因此，只要所涉事件具有訟爭性，憲法秩序只允許具有法官身分（非僅是法官資格）者行使裁判權，以維程序公平，並保障人權。一旦偏離了前揭法理，憲法上權力分立之精神與原理，即有遭受不當侵奪並有違憲之虞。

今查司法院所提之修正法案，雖表示僅授權司法事務官辦理較不具訟爭性之事項，惟查其條文授權內容，卻包含許多本質上具有訟爭性之事項，恐有名實不符之譏。蓋民刑事案件之爭點整理雖規定於準備程序，不過其內涵卻與審理之核心部分息息相關。設若司法事務官所整理之爭點與實際審判之法官對於爭點出現不同的認識，由於心證須由法官形成，因此法官對於未能形成心證之部分，勢必另行整理爭點，並另開審理程序，如此一來即與合理分配並節省司法資源之立法目的相互矛盾，更無謂地增加人民勞力、時間與費用的不必要支出。再者，修正草案創造了嶄新的「勘察」制度，既然修正理由明文事務官勘察異於法官勘驗，在未承認其為法定證據方法之前，即使由司法事務官完成了勘察程序，其是否能通過傳聞法則的檢驗，又將造成新的法理論戰，鑑於勘驗程序旨在避免法官因未實際直接接觸證據不易形成心證，在法官保留原則之要求下，此種實際上屬於證據調查勘驗部分之勘察，因其具有確定事實（紛爭）之功能，實不應由具有行政官地位之司法事務官越俎代庖地行使。而第3款允許事務官通知檢察官並徵詢當事人之規定，除可以預見地將造成檢察部門被不當矮化的批評外，假設將來檢察官亦類推適用該規定依樣畫葫蘆地指派檢察

事務官參與此款徵詢彙整程序，此種由院檢雙方代理人出席的程序，更因對法官與檢察官無實質拘束力，徒浪費被告之勞力、時間與費用，實無任何必要可言。又在授權明確性之要求下，其第 5 款僅泛言「其他經司法院指定之事務」，亦恐將授權不明確而使得將來司法院之指定事項，出現違憲之爭議。

過去司法改革花了相當長的時間，經由檢、辯、審、學的參與，確立與落實了實質審理的原則，今司法院所提出的修正草案，本質上限縮了法官實際參與的必要，恐有導致審判程序又回復到司法改革前書面審理之疑慮，果真有必要做如此龐大的修法，本亦應再由司法各界形成共識，如此倉促企圖藉由法院組織法之修正以達調整行為法（民事訴訟法與刑事訴訟法）目的之作法，除規避了修法過程應先形成共識的程序外，由於事涉法制重大改變，此種修法模式亦不當地阻絕了人民參與的正當程序。有鑑與此，立委諸公實應站在人民的立場，要求司法院提出一套完整的修法理論，並形成修法共識，面對以前述名實不符的理由提出法院組織法第 17 條之 2 第 2 項修正案，企圖暗渡陳倉秘密地進行司法改革，立法院本應予以否決。

國家圖書館出版品預行編目資料

改良式的證據法則與刑事訴訟／張明
偉 著.--初版.--臺北市：五南，2008.05
面； 公分
ISBN 978-957-11-5179-3（平裝）
1.證據 2.刑事訴訟法 3.論述分析
586.6　　　　　　　　97005290

1T12

改良式的證據法則與刑事訴訟

作　　　者－張明偉(203.3)

發 行 人－楊榮川

總 編 輯－龐君豪

主　　編－劉靜芬　林振煌

責任編輯－李奇蓁

封面設計－童安安

出 版 者－五南圖書出版股份有限公司

地　　址：106台北市大安區和平東路二段339號

電　　話：(02)2705-5066　傳　真：(02)2706-6

網　　址：http://www.wunan.com.tw

電子郵件：wunan@wunan.com.tw

劃撥帳號：01068953

戶　　名：五南圖書出版股份有限公司

台中市駐區辦公室/台中市中區中山路6號

電　　話：(04)2223-0891　傳　真：(04)2223-3

高雄市駐區辦公室/高雄市新興區中山一路290號

電　　話：(07)2358-702　傳　真：(07)2350-2

法律顧問　元貞聯合法律事務所　張澤平律師

出版日期　2008年 5月初版一刷
　　　　　2010年10月初版二刷

定　　價　新臺幣650元